On the Art of the Kabbalah

JOHANN REUCHLIN • On the Art of the
                              Kabbalah

                              De Arte Cabalistica

===

TRANSLATION BY MARTIN AND SARAH GOODMAN
INTRODUCTION BY G. LLOYD JONES

Introduction to the Bison Book Edition by Moshe Idel

UNIVERSITY OF NEBRASKA PRESS
LINCOLN AND LONDON

Copyright © 1983 by Abaris Books, Inc.
Introduction to the Bison Book Edition copyright © 1993 by the
University of Nebraska Press
All rights reserved
Manufactured in the United States of America

First Bison Book printing: 1993
Most recent printing indicated by the last digit below:
10   9   8   7   6   5   4   3   2   1

Library of Congress Cataloging-in-Publication Data
Reuchlin, Johann, 1455–1522.
[De arte cabalistica. English & Latin]
On the art of the Kabbalah=De arte cabalistica / Johann Reuchlin; translated by
Martin and Sarah Goodman; introduction by G. Lloyd Jones.
p.   cm.
English and Latin.
"Bison book edition."
Includes bibliographical references.
ISBN 0-8032-8946-4
1. Cabala—History—Early works to 1800.   I. Title.
BM526.R4613   1994
296.1'6—dc20
93–13872
CIP

Reprinted by arrangement with Abaris Books, Inc.

∞

Introduction to the Bison Book Edition
by
Moshe Idel

I. The Beginnings of the Christian Kabbalah?

Johannes Reuchlin is one of the major exponents of the Christian Kabbalah; he may even be conceived, as we shall attempt to show it below, as one of the earliest founders of this type of Christian theology. However, to describe an author writing at the end of the fifteenth and the beginning of the sixteenth centuries as an early founder of Christian Kabbalah—that needs both elaboration and clarification.

The historical beginning of the Christian Kabbalah is a matter of debate, as it is in regard to the beginnings of the Jewish Kabbalah. Precisely when a certain phenomenon is conceived as existent depends on the minimum that is required to define this phenomenon; thus the modern scholarly tendency today to describe the Jewish Kabbalah as emerging, on the historical plane, in the last decades of the twelfth century in Languedoc pushes the identification of the Christian parallels or similar phenomena to the thirteenth century. If we accept the ten divine powers, the ten *sefirot,* as a vital component of Kabbalah, it will be difficult to find Christian discussions of this topic before the end of the thirteenth century. However, if we accept other ways of defining Kabbalah, found already in the eleventh century, as an esoteric tradition concerning the divine names, the situation may be much more complex.[1] Indeed, some passages dealing with divine names recur in Christian texts early in the thirteenth century, as the discussions of Joachim de Fiore demonstrate.[2] At the end of this century, Arnauld of Vilanova had completed a whole treatise dealing with the divine name.[3]

However, it is possible to approach the question from another angle: it is not so much the passage of some traditions from one type of religion to another that is the defining moment of the emergence of a certain new phenomenon, but the absorption, especially the creative one, of the techniques that are characteristic of one type of lore, by a religious thinker belonging to another religion. In our case, the ques-

Introduction to the Bison Book Edition

tion would be not when a Christian has adopted some forms of Jewish esoteric traditions, but when a Christian thinker has adopted a Kabbalistic type of thinking. Thus, the occurrence of a certain combinatory technique of interpretation of the first word of the Bible by separating its letters, as practiced by Alexander of Neckham,[4] or of the peculiar combination of letters by means of concentric circles, apparently under the influence of Jewish sources, as evident in the work of Ramon Null,[5] may fit this second approach.

What lacks in all these examples is the explicit awareness that, when dealing with divine names or with combinatory techniques, the Christian author operates in a speculative realm that, at least from the point of view of the primary sources, is a characteristically esoteric type of Jewish lore. However, already in the last third of the thirteenth century, such an awareness was apparently existent. Alfonso Sabio's nephew, Juan Manuel,[6] testified as to the concerns of his famous uncle:

> "Ostrosi fizo traslador toda le ley de los judios et aun el su Talmud et otra scientia que han los judious muy escondida, a que llaman Cabala."

> "Furthermore he ordered translated the whole law of the Jews, and even their Talmud, and other knowledge which is called qabbalah and which the Jews keep closely secret. And he did this so it might be manifest through their own Law that it is a [mere] presentation of that Law which we Christians have; and that they, like the Moors, are in grave error and in peril of losing their souls."

If this passage is reliable, and I see no reason to doubt it, then a significant segment of Kabbalistic literature had been translated as soon as the seventies of the thirteenth century. However, even this testimony, as well as some other dated from the fourteenth century up to the middle-fifteenth century, interesting as it may be, did not relate to texts that become part of a larger cultural phenomenon. At the court of Alfonso Sabio no Christian sort of Kabbalah was cultivated, while the uses of Kabbalah in the writings of converts like Alfonso de Validolid or Paulus de Heredia did not incite the imagination of their contemporaries, and they did not produce significant repercussions.

Whatever the evidence regarding the penetration of Jewish esoterism before the end of the fifteenth century is, or may turn out to be, it

Introduction to the Bison Book Edition

seems that before the writings of Pico della Mirandola (1463–1494) those Jewish elements did not become a considerable part of any defined Christian circle, neither were they cultivated by a movement that consciously continued the steps of some founding figures. In other words, while we can easily accumulate interesting pieces of evidence dealing with the acquaintance of various Christian authors with Jewish esoteric topics, they are scanty, disparate, and incontinuous.

II. The Emergence of Christian Kabbalah in the Florentine Renaissance

The much greater dissemination of Kabbalistic ideas, evident since the end of the fifteenth century, is to be understood in the general contexts of the Italian intellectual ambiance in Florence and the dissemination of printing. The latter factor contributed substantially to cultural developments that took place in Northern Italy, helping them to transcend the small circle around the Medicis; printing ensured also continuity. However, the more interesting question still remains: how and why did the early Christian intellectuals adopt Jewish esoterics as a domain of interest and even creativity? An answer to such a question is never simple, and we should better allow a coalescence of more than one type of answer.

First and foremost, Kabbalah was studied, translated and amalgamated into Christian speculation in a very specific intellectual circle, which started a similar process two decades before the concern with Kabbalah. Marsilio Ficino (1433–1499), the translator who was instrumental in rendering into Latin the huge Platonic, Neoplatonic and Hermetic corpora, at the same time offered a synthesis between the various forms of thought he translated and Christian theology.[7] The openness of his circle to the ancient pagan patrimony is a crucial fact that stands at the background of the next stage of translation: that from Hebrew. Without their acceptance of the relevance of the pagan corpus, I wonder whether the Hebrew mystical writings would have been embraced so warmly by them. In any case, the circle that produced the Florentine Renaissance, under the aegis of the Medici family, is very relevant for Reuchlin's Kabbalistic project. Reuchlin was incited by a conversation with Pico to embark on the study of Kabbalah, and he was also inspired by Pico's Christian and magical un-

Introduction to the Bison Book Edition

derstanding of Kabbalah. In fact, *De Arte Cabalistica* has been dedicated to Leo X, a pope stemming from the Medici family. Reuchlin indeed continued, consciously, a cultural Florentine phenomenon.

This substantial acquaintance with Kabbalistic material on one hand, and cultural continuity on the other, seems to ensure the status of the late-fifteenth-century Florentine interest in Jewish mysticism as the founding moment of Christian Kabbalah. Such a definition is based upon cultural intellectual assumptions more than the conceptual ones. Certain Kabbalistic concepts that were known or absorbed by a Christian thinker cannot, in my opinion, help in describing a significant intellectual phenomenon that played a certain role on the cultural scene of Europe. By these two criteria—acquaintance with Kabbalistic material and cultural continuity—Reuchlin is to be conceived as one of the founders of this branch of Christian thought.

III. A Fiction of the Open-Minded Spanish Kabbalist?

The main exponent of the Jewish Kabbalah in *De Arte Cabalistica* is the Kabbalist Simon ben Elazar of the Yohaidic family, who was an inhabitant of Frankfurt and takes part in the friendly debates with the Pythagorean Philolaus and the Muslim Marranus. The name of the Kabbalist Simon is fictitious though relevant; there can be no doubt that the name of the fictitious author of the book of the *Zohar,* Rabbi Shimeon bar Yohai, inspired Reuchlin. Nevertheless, despite the fact that the *Zohar* has been mentioned in Reuchlin's book, actual quotes from this classic of Kabbalah cannot be detected in it. Therefore, the Kabbalist Simon represents a cultural image, whose more precise identity is not elaborated. Unlike the two other participants, the Pythagorean Philolaus, a Phoenician, and Marranus, who came to Frankfurt from Constantinopole, the Kabbalist seems to be an indigenous person. However, this fact is not explicit, and the way Philolaus tells us about his acquaintance with the fame of the Kabbalist may indicate something about Simon. As pointed out in the introduction, Philolaus learned about the greatness of the Jew from expellees from Spain, who came to "Scythia and Thrace" twenty-three years ago. Those Jews told him about Simon's vast knowledge. At least implicitly, this means that the greatness of Simon was described through the eyes of Spanish exiles, their view being the only source, and criterion, for acknowledging the fame of the Kabbalist. I take this way of

Introduction to the Bison Book Edition

introducing Simon as an indication of his possible Spanish origin which, I would like to emphasize, is not stated explicitly. However, Philolaus's mentioning that after the Expulsion from Spain the Jews scattered in all directions may be an additional hint at the origin of the Frankfurtian figure.

In any case, the nexus between Simon and the book of the *Zohar*, implicit in his name, also strengthens the possibility that Reuchlin had in mind a Spanish Kabbalist. The influence of the *Zohar* was, before the expulsion from Spain, marginal outside the Iberian Peninsula. Also most of the geographical names occurring in the quotes from Kabbalistic books in Reuchlin's text are Spanish, like Gerona and Castile. On the other hand, Germany was not conceived to be a center of Kabbalah, and it would be bizarre to assume that Reuchlin, a German, did not know this fact as late as 1517. For these reasons I assume that the Christian Kabbalist presupposed a Spanish extraction for his invented Kabbalist Simon. For historical reasons, the encounter between the various types of lore could not take place in Spain, so Germany became the host for the imaginary trialogue.

With this hypothesis in mind, let me address its possible implications. The possible Spanish extraction of the Jewish protagonist of Reuchlin's book may not be a matter of chance; it may reflect the historical fact that most of the Jewish Kabbalistic literature, up to the composition of *De Arte Cabalistica,* was composed by an overwhelming majority of Spanish figures, most of it in Spain. Thus, Reuchlin apparently adopts a cultural image that was both correct and well-known. However, the nature of Kabbalah as attributed to the Jew hardly does justice to the understanding of this mystical lore among the Spanish Kabbalists, whose Kabbalah was much more particularistic than the Italian one.[8] We may assume that there are two main sources for Reuchlin's knowledge of Kabbalah: whatever he learned in Italy, from either Christian or Jewish thinkers, and what he studied by himself from Kabbalistic manuscripts. We may assume that both sources did not prevent him from ascribing to the Jewish Kabbalist a very great openness to philosophical knowledge. In Italy, both the Jewish and Christian Kabbalists embraced an exoteric vision of this kind of Jewish lore, which was interpreted in light of different forms of philosophical thought. This is evident from the writings of Yohanan Alemanno or Abraham de Balmes on one hand, or Pico della Mirandola on the other. Basically oriented toward Neoplatonic

Introduction to the Bison Book Edition

and Aristotelian sources, these thinkers paid only marginal attention to the concordance between Kabbalah and the numerology of the Pythagorean thought, though, as we shall see below, they did not ignore the Greek thinker in their discussions on Kabbalah. Unlike the Kabbalists in Italy, the late fifteenth-century Kabbalists in Spain expressed sharp anti-philosophical views, which were combined with anti-Christian and anti-scientific statements.[9] Therefore, while the Spanish Kabbalists were indeed the great experts in matters of Kabbalah in Reuchlin's generation, none of them would indulge in attempts to introduce a Greek philosopher as expressing views consonant with Kabbalah. The only exception I am acquainted with, that of the Kabbalist Rabbi Abraham ben Eliezer ha-Levi, who presented Aristotle in a positive light, did it only because he assumed that Aristotle had recanted his previous philosophical stands and accepted a type of theology closer to Kabbalah.[10] Neither, I think, would a Spanish Kabbalist—unlike some of his Italian contemporaries—engage in an intellectual conversation on matters of Kabbalah, as Reuchlin would like us to believe it happened in Frankfurt. However, I assume that the content of the Spanish particularistic Kabbalah was not so obvious in 1490, when Reuchlin learned about this lore from Pico. Therefore, the possible cultural image of the learned Spanish Kabbalist, who would converse with non-Jewish persons on the most esoteric Jewish topics, is characteristically Italian. Reuchlin has projected his own acquaintance with more open-minded Italian Jewish intellectuals, some of them knowledgeable in matters of Kabbalah, onto a more particularistic Sephardi expert in Kabbalah.

On the other hand, as we shall see below, the types of Kabbalah that Reuchlin was acquainted with from a Kabbalistic manuscript he studied would not prevent him from creating the hybrid notion of a Spanish open-minded Kabbalist. Most of the thirteenth-century Kabbalistic treatises found in that manuscript reflect either the relatively more philosophically oriented Geronese Kabbalah or short tracts belonging to the ecstatical Kabbalah, both representing much more universalistic stands that the Spanish Kabbalah in general, and the fifteenth-century Spanish Kabbalah in particular. Though there are also Kabbalistic texts that do not belong to any of the above corpora, even in these writings the general tendency is not anti-philosophical. Thus, both his personal experience, and whatever he read in Kabbalistic texts, had encouraged Reuchlin to offer a picture that, in spite of the

Introduction to the Bison Book Edition

fact that it was based on some firsthand correct observations, ultimately turned to be an historical fiction. Reuchlin presented Kabbalah as the source of Pythagoreanism,[11] and therefore as fully consonant with this type of philosophy, a view that had some few, and partial, predecessors in some Jewish texts written at the end of the fifteenth and early sixteenth century in Italy.

IV. On the Status of Pythagoras in Jewish and Christian Renaissance

The Pythagorean aspect of ancient philosophy has been neglected by the Middle Age Jewish and Christian sources; it seems that one Pythagorean topic has generally been conceived as reminiscent of an important Kabbalistic issue: the notion of metempsychosis. It was referred to several times by medieval and Renaissance Jewish thinkers in different contexts,[12] though rarely in a positive manner. Maimonides, for example, grouped Pythagoras together with the obsolete ancient philosophers,[13] and the negative attitude of Aristotle to Pythagoreanism has been indubitably decisive in his marginalization.[14] Even the Kabbalists, who were only marginally affected by the negative evaluations of the Aristotelian-biased philosophers, do not mention this figure but very rarely. Their interest in numerology, metempsychosis, or magic seems to be independent from a direct and significant influence of genuine or spuriously attributed writings of "the head of the philosophers."

Thus, the more numerous references to Pythagoras in the Renaissance period by Jewish authors cannot be understood, not even partially, as the result of the scanty medieval mentions of Pythagoras. They constitute a new approach, which reveals mainly the impact of the ancient Greek and Hellenistic sources that were translated by the Christians and quoted by the Renaissance writers.[15] Especially important in this case is the contribution of Eusebius' *Preparatio Evangelica,* which was printed in 1470, and became immediately influential in both the Jewish and Christian milieux.[16]

However, what is even more important for our discussion than Eusebius' text is the fact that Pythagoras has been a constant figure in Ficino's lists of the *prisci theologi;* as in the other cases, in his commentaries on Plato's dialogues, Pythagoras is portrayed without mentioning a Hebrew source for his philosophy.[17] It is only in his *De reli-*

Introduction to the Bison Book Edition

gione Christiana that he quotes Ambrosius, to the effect that Pythagoras was a Jew.[18] However, in an earlier discussion[19] and what is more significant even later on,[20] Ficino ignores the whole variety of ancient and medieval sources that explicitly linked, in one way or another, the Greek philosopher with the Hebrews,[21] and presents again the multilinear theory, namely the view that religions and philosophical truths were revealed to both Jewish and pagan figures.[22] Pico's view of this figure is, however, more complex; in an important discussion, he proposes a multilinear theory as regards Pythagoras's thought:

> "Both Luke and Philo . . . are very authoritative testimonies that Moses was very learned in all Egyptian doctrines. And all the Greeks who have been considered superior—Pythagoras, Plato, Empedocles, Democritus—used the Egyptians as masters . . . Also the Pythagorean Hermippus attests that Pythagoras transferred many things from the Mosaic law into his own philosophy[23] . . . Taught by them [the Egyptians], Pythagoras became a master of silence."[24]

It is difficult to explain what exactly was the precise theory of traditions informing Pythagoras that Pico adopted in this passage; a possible interpretation would be that Moses studied the Egyptian lore, as the Greek philosopher had done and hence the basic similarity between Mosaic law and that of the Greeks. Moreover, according to the testimony of a Pythagorean, the master was instructed in both Egyptian and Mosaic lore, so that ultimately there were two distinct sources for his philosophy, though, at least partially, the two sources were intertwined. It is conspicuous that, although the historical affinity between Pythagoras and Mosaic sources is secured by mentioning Hermippus's tradition, the Egyptian alternative is as strong as the Hebrew one, even Moses being portrayed as a student of the Egyptian lore. Pico's teacher in matters of Kabbalah, Flavius Mithridates, has mentioned also the two sources of Pythagoras' thought: In concordance with Eusebius' *Preparatio Evangelica,* he pronounced the following statement: "Ut Numenius Pythagoricus in volumine de bono scribit, Plato atque Pythagoras quaea Abrahmanes et Iudaei invenerunt ea ipsi graece exposuerunt."[25]

Though one of greatest experts in matters of Kabbalah in the fifteenth century, Mithridates did not present Pythagoras as extracting

Introduction to the Bison Book Edition

his knowledge from Kabbalah, but from Jews, among others, in general. It is only at the beginning of the sixteenth century that a more explicit approach to the Greek philosopher as a student of the Kabbalists emerged in a writing of a Christian author; Reuchlin, who was considered a *Pythagoras redivivus,* described his enterprise to the Pope, Leo X, as follows:

> "For Italy's part, Marsilio Ficino has published Plato, Jacob Faber of Estaples has brought out Aristotle for France. I shall complete the pattern for Germany. I, Capnion, shall bring out the reborn Pythagoras with your name at its head. His philosophy, however, I have only been able to glean from the Hebrew Kabbalah, since it derives in origin from the teachers of Kabbalah, and then was lost to our ancestors, disappearing from Southern Italy into the Kabbalistic writings. For this reason, it was almost all destined for destruction and I have therefore written of the symbolic philosophy of the art of Kabbalah so as to make Pythagorean doctrine better known to scholars."[26]

It is highly interesting that Reuchlin ignores here the whole series of *prisci theologi* and selects only the classical figures, Plato and Aristotle, as paragons of learning, to whom Pythagoras is to be compared. The other pagan philosophers or magicians, like Zoroaster, Orpheus, or Hermes, though sometimes mentioned, did not play any decisive role in Reuchlin's writings. However, what is new with Reuchlin is the fact that for the first time in the work of a Christian thinker, Kabbalah was presented as the source of a major type of philosophy to be revived for the benefit of Europe; Reuchlin indicates that the affinity between Kabbalah and Pythagoreanism is not a matter of different *corpora* which share similar theological views but that the Pythagorean philosophy has been extracted from the Hebrew sources. By doing so, he did not propose something that was totally new; the Jewish source for Pythagoras's philosophy, and even, according to some sources, his Jewish extraction were already somehow "documented" long before Reuchlin. It is the introduction of the Kabbalah as the source for Pythagoras that represents a decisive turn in the status of Kabbalah, after Pico's eulogies to the address of this lore.

A stand that was exposed by Rabbi Eliahu Hayyim ben Benjamin

Introduction to the Bison Book Edition

of Genazzano, a late fifteenth-century Italian Kabbalist, apparently reflects a view similar to that expressed later on by Reuchlin,[27] and he seems to be one of the first who related, explicitly, Pythagoreanism and Kabbalah. In the context of a discussion on the metempsychosis and Zoroaster he wrote:

> "I have also found that similar views were held by Numenius the Pythagorean[28] and by Ornaldus.[29] Numenius, out of his love of Moses' Torah, thought that Moses' soul had been reincarnated in his own body[30] . . . And as regards this statement [31] according to which the Kabbalists maintained that human souls are reincarnated in animal bodies, I answer that this view is to be found only in the works of later Kabbalists,[32] and I did not find any support for this view in our Sages' statements. However, I have found that this is the opinion of a certain ancient philosopher, i.e., Pythagoras and his sect."[33]

From the manner Genazzano has previously presented Zoroaster, and from the way Numenius was described, we may assume that the theory of metempsychosis was considered by this Kabbalist as an authentic Kabbalistic view, which subsequently reached Pythagoras in one way or another. However, as to the specific aspect of reincarnation into animal bodies, it seems that the Kabbalist was much more reticent; being unable to corroborate the existence of this peculiar type of metempsychosis from earlier Jewish sources, he mentions Pythagoras. What the implications are of such a reliance is quite difficult to say: does it mean that Pythagoras preserved ancient Jewish traditions which do not occur in the "ancient" Kabbalistic texts, but only in the later layers of Kabbalah? Or, alternatively, does this Kabbalist criticize the later Kabbalists for inventing a new speculation regarding metempsychosis, on the ground of alien material extant in Pythagoreanism? Whatever will be the answer, it is obvious that the affinity between Pythagoras and a Kabbalistic principle is well established by this Kabbalist.

A contemporary of Genazzano, who has also been sharply criticized by him in another context, was Isaac Abravanel. He attributes the belief in the metempsychosis not only to the Kabbalists but also to "the divine Socrates" as he was portrayed by Plato in his *Phaedon*, and also to Pythagoras and other ancient authors whose views were

Introduction to the Bison Book Edition

similar to those of the two thinkers. Then he added: "Perhaps they did receive this [view] from the generations of the old and from the time of the prophets. But Aristotle and the interpreters of his books refused to accept this view assuming that the metempsychosis is an absurd thing."[34]

The hesitation of allowing to the ancient theologians, including Pythagoras, an independent status, is obvious. Here again, the assumption of the Jewish author is that Pythagoras and the Jewish tradition correspond on an issue that is characteristic of the Kabbalistic thought. A contemporary of the two Jewish authors mentioned above, Yohanan Alemanno, has contributed another detail to Pythagoras' "relation" to the Hebrews. In the introduction to his *Commentary on the Song of Songs,* he describes the philosopher's involvement with geomancy, and then he points out that Pythagoras "studied with the Hebrews."[35] Whether Alemanno implies that geomancy was taken over from the Jews is not clear; nevertheless, such an opinion is reasonable.

Despite the dependence of Reuchlin's view of Pythagoras on Ficino and Pico, in my opinion he differs from them on one crucial point, which brings him closer to his Jewish predecessors: Pythagoras was conceived by the Christian thinkers as one of the many *prisci theologi,* who belong to a tradition that is independent of the Mosaic one, a tendency that can be described as multilinear; Reuchlin, unlike his Florentine predecessors, adhered to the main line of the Jewish thinkers whose propensity was, definitely, toward the view that true philosophy depends upon a reception of ideas from the Mosaic tradition, a view that can be described as unilinear.[36]

Let us turn to an interesting reverberation of Reuchlin's vision of Pythagoreanism as stemming from ancient Kabbalah. His description of the latter as "a symbolic philosophy of the art of Kabbalah" is a simplification of the much richer spectrum of Kabbalistic phenomena, like the mythological, Aristotelian or magical elements. However, this reduction of the content of Kabbalah to Pythagoreanism can be easily understood as part of his rhetoric, intended to create for Reuchlin a special field of contribution, different from that of Ficino's and D'Etaples's. This vision of Kabbalah as a kind of philosophy, namely a symbolic one,[37] is reminiscent of the more modern visions of Kabbalah as a certain type of "narrative philosophy," in Schelling and Scholem.[38] The Renaissance philosophizations of Kabbalah, both among the Jewish and Christian thinkers, have been reverberated by the moderns.[39] Is Scholem's own remark that would he believe in metempsychosis, he would perhaps see Reuchlin's soul as having transmigrated in himself a mere metaphor? Or does Scholem disclose something more profound: that the line of research in modern Jewish studies does not only start with Reuchlin but also still follows his conceptual vision, at least insofar Kabbalah is concerned?[40] Reuchlin's influence is conspicuous in Scholem's, and his followers', overemphasis on the paramount importance of the symbolic language and thought as representative of and essential to the Kabbalah.[41]

It should be mentioned in this context that for Reuchlin, the classical Maimonidean identification of the account of Creation, *Ma'aseh Bereshit,* with the science of nature, namely Aristotelian physics, and of the account of the Chariot, *Ma'aseh Merkavah,* with the science of the divinity, understood as Aristotelian metaphysics, is a Kabbalistic view.[42] Thus, in the vein of the more philosophically oriented Kabbalah, even Maimonides' views became in Reuchlin's book representative of Kabbalistic thought[43] and were understood as referring to the Talmudists and Kabbalists, respectively.

V. On Reuchlin's Kabbalistic Manuscript

In his lecture on Reuchlin as the founder of the modern research of Kabbalah, Gershom Scholem has made a very important remark as to Reuchlin's main source of Kabbalah: codex Halberstamm 444, now in the Jewish Theological Seminary, Mic. 1887. According to Scholem, this codex informed Reuchlin's knowledge of Kabbalah.[44] There can be no doubt as to the importance of Scholem's remarks; indeed, as he indicated, most of the Hebrew quotes found in *De Arte Cabalistica*[45] can be traced to Kabbalistic treatises found in this codex. Scholem's pathbreaking observation was not exploited by the modern scholarship of Reuchlin. However, a careful examination of the manuscript may open the possibility that this particular codex could not be the precise manuscript quoted by Reuchlin, though it indubitably mirrors another codex, which was similar from many points of view to the New York codex. Let me give some examples for my proposal to somehow qualify Scholem's latter statement, and attempt to bring some evidence to his earlier view, to the effect that though Reuchlin has indeed studied a codex that reflects the structure

Introduction to the Bison Book Edition

of the Halberstamm manuscript, it is plausible that he possessed another codex:

(1) Scholem's claim that Reuchlin used the name Tedacus Levi, which represents a distortion of the name Todros ha-Levi, is, in my opinion, correct.[46] However, this misreading cannot be explained as a misreading of the acronym found on the first folio of the Halberstamm manuscript, where the letters compounding the name Todros are clear, and I see no paleographic explanation for the mistaken reading: the letter *reish,* which according to Scholem was misread as *Kaf,* is clear-cut. I accept in principle Scholem's explanation, but I assume, as Scholem himself has hinted also in some instances, that in another, for the time being unidentified, codex, such a misreading could have induced the creation of the name Tedacus.[47] In this context, it should be mentioned that the verses, whose first letters form the name Todros, are indeed the concluding poem to Todros Abulafia's *Sha'ar ha-Razim,* a commentary on Psalm XIX, which is found later on in the Halberstamm codex, fols. 44a–63a; however, in *De Arte Cabalistica,* Reuchlin attributes this work to a certain Rabbi Ama,[48] while the text attributed by the Christian Kabbalist to Rabbi Tedacus was not written by him. So, for example, he quotes a certain text which, as I have attempted to show elsewhere, is part of the Zoharic literature, as if it is entitled *Liber de decem numerationibus*. In the Halberstamm codex, the text quoted under the above name is not designated as an interpretation of ten *sefirot*.[49]

(2) When Reuchlin cites from treatises found in Ms. Halberstamm, he sometimes offers a version of the quoted passage that differs from that found in this manuscript. So, for example, he quotes a Hebrew passage from a writing of Rabbi Jacob ben Jacob ha-Kohen,[50] under the name of Rabbi Azriel, which is found in the Halberstamm codex, fol. 4b.[51] However, the varia between the manuscript and Reuchlin's Hebrew version are of a nature that do not allow an explanation of misreading as the reason for the divergences.

(3) Reuchlin quotes, twice, a certain book named *Yahid,* authored by an otherwise unknown Rabbi Asse.[52] The two quotes can be identified in an anonymous *Sefer Yihud* preserved in many manuscripts,[53] inter alia in codex Halberstamm 444, fols. 23b–25a. I see no way, on the basis of the examination of this codex, to explain the authorship of the text or its distorted title. The name Asse occurs a third time in Reuchlin's book[54] where his collection, *collectura,* is mentioned. In

Introduction to the Bison Book Edition

fact, this is a quote found in the Halberstamm codex, fol. 26a, and again I cannot account for the attribution of this small text to Asse.

(4) A final observation, which in itself is not conclusive, but rather intriguing: from my reading of Hebrew manuscripts used and quoted by Christian authors, a pattern becomes evident. When a certain passage is quoted by the Christian author, the corresponding text in the original manuscript is marked in one way or another. However, in the Halberstamm codex there is no special sign beside the dozens of quotes, and no sign at all that a Christian has inspected or studied the manuscript in general.

It should be emphasized that notwithstanding these discrepancies, which may indicate that another codex had informed Reuchlin's studies of Kabbalah, the content of the Halberstamm codex is very helpful in identifying sources for important segments of Reuchlin's book. So, for example, the very lengthy description of the meaning of the letters of the Hebrew alphabet, offered by Simon[55], is found in an anonymous commentary on the alphabet—apparently extant only in this manuscript. This commentary combines Kabbalah with strong philosophical, namely medieval Aristotelian, terminology, and is preserved in the Halberstamm codex, fols. 39b–43b; Reuchlin summarizes the content of fols. 40b–43b. Here is not the place to enter in a detailed comparison between the Hebrew original and the way Reuchlin presented it; it should only be mentioned that this is, perhaps, Reuchlin's lengthiest quote from any Kabbalistic text, and its content shows the artificial and highly eclectic nature of many of Reuchlin's discussions: he simply put together Kabbalistic unrelated material found, randomly, in a certain codex. The editor, or the copyist of the codex that Reuchlin studied, had collected material from various Kabbalistic schools which had very little in common. Reuchlin attempted to offer a rather unified concept of Kabbalah, as the singular in the title of his book indicates, and by doing so he attempted to do the impossible. Aristotelian Kabbalah, ecstatic treatises, linguistic Kabbalistic tracts like Gikatilla's *Garden of the Nut,* Geronese theosophical Kabbalah, the writings from a thirteenth-century Kabbalistic school named by the scholars the circle of the *Book of Speculation,* late thirteenth-century Castilian Kabbalah like *Sha'ar ha-Razim*—all were put together by Reuchlin from manuscripts and from the Latin translations of Paulus Riccius. This implicit harmonistic vision of the whole field of Kabbalistic writings as belonging to

Introduction to the Bison Book Edition

one type of thought, is a very interesting effort, which had some affinities to more modern attempts to offer a monolithic vision of Kabbalah as a whole as a symbolic mode of thought.

VI. The Completion of the Divine Name

The main subject of Reuchlin's first book on Kabbalah, *De Verbo Mirifico*, was to expose the miraculous powers of the hidden divine name, the Pentagrammaton, formed from the insertion of the letter *Sh*, the Hebrew *Shin*, in the middle of the Tetragrammaton; this name formed, according to Reuchlin and his source Pico della Mirandola, the secret name of Jesus.[56] Secret names are part and parcel of the Kabbalistic lore; from this point of view, the Christian Kabbalists did not invent anything in principle. In the Jewish Kabbalah we can find formations of "divine" names that cannot be detected in classical Jewish texts, which are as bizarre as the form YHSVH. Here I would like to deal with the idea, found in a text quoted by Reuchlin, that the divine name will be completed in the Messianic era, which was formulated in a conspicuous anti-Christian context, and the way Reuchlin dealt with this passage. The analysis of this quote will show that either Reuchlin misunderstood his sources, or at least he read them superficially. He quotes from an anonymous text, which belongs to the ecstatic Kabbalah, named *Haqdamah*,[57] meaning *introduction*, as follows: "and this is the secret of the king Messiah, who will come swiftly, in our days. All his action [its] beginning [is] with *VH*, and also *YH*, which is the secret of the seventh day,[58] and this is the name, the complete name, and the whole work will be completed by its means."[59]

The Hebrew version translated here is not corroborated by any of the four manuscripts of this writing that I am acquainted with.[60] However, I wonder whether another, apparently corrupted manuscript was the source of this obscure text. By comparing Reuchlin's Hebrew quote to the Hebrew manuscript we can easily see how some of the words here are misunderstandings: so, for example, the clumsy phrase "[its] beginning [is] with" translates the Hebrew form *tehilah*. Any reader of Hebrew will notice the absence of the verb. Indeed by inspecting the Hebrew manuscript, we find *titalleh*, which means "it will depend upon," a reading that makes complete sense, and differs from *tehilah* only by one letter: the original Hebrew *tav*

Introduction to the Bison Book Edition

was read as *het,* a mistake easily understandable for any person acquainted with medieval Hebrew paleography. The meaning of the text is now clear: the Messiah, who will advent in the seventh day, will complete the divine name, since he will act by the dint of the two last letters of the Tetragramaton, *VH*. This completion is hinted, as we learn from the context, by these two letters, because they are the acronym of the two words *Va-yakhulu Ha-shamayim,* "and the heaven will be completed." Also the Hebrew phrase translated by "and this is the name, the complete name" is meaningless, the correct Hebrew version, which has also been misread, meaning, "the name will be complete in His days." Namely, only in the time of the Messiah, the Tetragrammaton will be completed.

I have dwelled upon those misreadings of the Hebrew texts not in order to discredit Reuchlin's knowledge of Hebrew, and implicitly his understanding of Kabbalah, by pointing out how he changed a *tav* for a *het*. It seems to me that much more may stand beyond the way he managed the above quote; according to the Hebrew statement that immediately precedes the above quote "the secret of the sixth day is, by the way of *gematriah, Shu henriytz,*[61] and he acted by means of the half of the Tetragrammaton, which is *YH.*"[62]

There can be no doubt that the mysterious *Shu henriytz* is but a permutation of the consonants of the Hebrew *Yeshu ha-Notzriy,* namely Jesus of Nazareth. He was described as acting only by means of the first half of the Tetragrammaton, while the Jewish Messiah, who will come in the future, will complete the Tetragrammaton. In fact, this is a veiled anti-Christian statement, which emphasizes the inferiority of the Christian savior, in comparison to the Jewish one. The potential danger involved in this view was obvious to the writer, who states that "would the nation of Edom[63] will be told about this topic, a great danger will be involved in it."[64] Thus, any reader of the text, for sure a Christian one, would be aware of the actual meaning of the quote brought by Reuchlin. However, it seems that either Reuchlin did not understand the anti-Christian stand involved in the view that the Messiah complete the Tetragrammaton, especially because of the anagrammed writing of the name of Jesus, or he preferred to ignore this subtle insinuation, perhaps as part of the controversy on the confiscation of the Hebrew books he was involved in a few years before composing his introduction to Kabbalah. It seems that a third answer is more plausible; in Ms. Halberstamm 444, fol. 12a, the anagrammed

Introduction to the Bison Book Edition

words *Shu henriytz* as well as "the nation of Edom" do not appear at all. However, even if we assume such a censored version, an intelligent reading of the context would lead someone to the conclusion that the future Messiah of the seventh day is transcending a former, lower type of similar phenomenon. These considerations show that not only were the Hebrew Kabbalistic texts sometimes misquoted but also the general intention of the whole text was not, in some cases, entirely realized by Reuchlin. Strangely enough, the Christian Kabbalist who emphasized more than any other the secret of the miraculous name of the Christ, as the Pentagrammaton, misunderstood the most elaborate Kabbalistic attempt to show that the Christian Messiah is connected to an incompleted form of the Tetragrammaton. In both cases, however, the idea of the completion of the divine name is connected to the Messianic age, a notion that is found in many pre-Kabbalistic and Kabbalistic sources.[65]

VII. Kabbalists versus Talmudists

Most of the Jewish Kabbalists exposed mystical theories that were consonant with the Rabbinic texts. Indeed, some of the important legalistic figures in Judaism since the Middle Ages were at the same time also mystics. This rule has some exceptions, one of the most important of them being Abraham Abulafia's critique of some Rabbis, a critique which is, in some instances in his later writings, indeed very sharp.[66] It may well be that details of those critiques were known by Reuchlin, who actually mentions books of Abulafia, without specifying their titles.[67] However, it seems that the stark dichotomy between the Talmudists and the Kabbalists as proposed by Reuchlin in several instances,[68] reflects a distinctly Christian attitude to Judaism. The view of the Talmudists as worshiping God out of fear, while the Kabbalists do it out of love, is mirroring the famous Christian distinction between Jews and Christians. In fact, Kabbalah is conceived of in Reuchlin in terms which are very close to the way the Christians understood Christianity. This attitude, already found in Pico, become much more elaborate in Reuchlin. He has even exploited distinctions that are indeed found in the Jewish tradition between topics like the account of creation and that of the chariot, or the perfection of the body and that of the soul, already mentioned above,[69] as if they reflect the dichotomy of Talmudists versus Kabbalists. In this case we see

Introduction to the Bison Book Edition

how the cultural hermeneutical *grille* of a Christian Kabbalist changed dramatically the sense of some distinctions found in the Jewish tradition. This Christian orientation is particularly evident in the two attitudes toward the Messiah in the Talmudic, versus the Kabbalistic camp.[70] While the first emphasizes the corporeal salvation, the latter stresses the spiritual one, which means also the world's redemption from sins by the Messiah, in a clear Christian manner. A similar claim is made also in the context of the presentation of a passage of Rabbi Azriel of Gerone; while the Jewish Kabbalist, as he has been quoted, conditions the advent of the Messiah by the prior disappearance of sin,[71] Reuchlin himself claims the very opposite, namely that the knowledge of the Messiah will put an end to sin.[72] Strangely enough, the above mentioned ecstatic tract entitled *Introduction* made a very similar distinction, according to which it is the Christ who stands for the past, corporeal Messianism, while the Jewish Messiah stands for the future spiritual redemption.[73] More were the Kabbalists portrayed as spirituals, more were the Talmudists conceived of as immersed in a corporeal kind of life. His attraction to the esoteric lore of the Jews has provoked, dialectically, a negative reaction to their exoteric law.

To a certain extent, Reuchlin, the most learned Christian author in matters of Judaica of his generation, continued the much older religious polemics between Christianity and Judaism, using classical clichés. What is new in the Renaissance transformations of the older confrontation is that in addition to the usage of Midrashic and Talmudic material in order to combat Judaism, as in the Middle Ages, some Renaissance Christian authors resorted also to Kabbalistic material which was, likewise, put in the service of the new polemics. Curious and willing to learn about the Jewish mysteries as they were, from the theological point of view there are not great differences in the relationship to Judaism between the Renaissance and medieval Christian theologians.[74] When writing *De Arte Cabalistica*, immediately after his fierce controversy over the Jewish books, Reuchlin is defending a type of Kabbalah that, in many cases, is not only far away from the content of the original texts he quotes but, in some instances, eventually contradicts their main messages. Nevertheless, Reuchlin's direct appeal to Baruchias earlier in *De Verbo Mirifico*: "Turn away from the Talmud"[75] does not reverberate, conceptually or literally, in the later *De Arte Cabalistica*. This call would be indeed

Introduction to the Bison Book Edition

bizarre for a scholar who became meanwhile better acquainted with the nature of Kabbalah in general, but it would be especially surprising if coming from the pen of a student of a codex that mirrors the content of the Halberstamm one; long folios of these manuscripts deal with Kabbalistic interpretations of Rabbinic legends, as found in Rabbi Ezra of Gerona's *Commentary on the Talmudic Aggadot*.[76] In general, the latter book, with its emphasis on contemplation and symbols, is less inclined to the overemphasis on magic that characterizes, under the influence of Pico, his earlier *De Verbo Mirifico*. Since this book culminates with a typically Christian topic, the hidden name and the occult power of the Christ, it is less perceptive toward the claims of the Jewish Kabbalah. In the *De Arte Cabalistica*, the Christological interpretation notwithstanding, the attitude toward the Jews is much more liberal, even sympathetic.

The cultural and theological hermeneutics of the Renaissance thinkers was, nevertheless, much stronger than the philological and historical inclinations of their humanist contemporaries. Philology was good enough to fathom the original sense of the ancient classical, mainly pagan culture, but it failed, rather systematically, when confronting the contents of the Hebrew theological texts. It seems that only by studying the full context of the original Hebrew Kabbalistic texts, which were perused and quoted by Reuchlin, that we can become aware of the depth of the metamorphosis those texts underwent when exposed by Reuchlin. However, a full account of this process still waits a detailed analysis of many of Reuchlin's quotes on the basis of manuscript material. Only then we may become more aware of the great impact that Reuchlin's religious beliefs had on his presentations of the Hebrew material. Far from being the founder of the studies of Judaism in Europe, as he was once described[77], he was an asiduous student of Jewish texts who was a deeply Christian theologian, and also informed by the Florentine Renaissance. But he had gone much further than any of the born Christians who had preceded him, in his knowledge of Kabbalah.

NOTES

1. See Moshe Idel, "Defining Kabbalah: The Kabbalah of the Divine Names" in *Mystics of the Book: Themes, Topics & Typologies*, ed. Robert A. Herrera (Peter Lang, New York, 1993), pp. 97–122.

Introduction to the Bison Book Edition

2. See Beatrice Hirsch-Reich, "Joachim von Fiore und das Judentum" in *Miscellania Medievalia*, IV *(Judentum im Mittelalter)*, ed. P. Wilpert (Berlin, 1966), pp. 228–63.

3. Joaquin Carreras Artau, "La 'Allocutio super Tetragrammaton' de Arnaldo de Vilanova," *Sefarad*, vol. IX (1949) pp. 75–105; Jose M. Millas-Vallicrosa, "Nota Bibliografica acerca de las relationes entre Arnaldo de Vilanova y la cultura judaica," *Sefarad*, vol. 12 (1956), pp. 149–53.

4. See Yehuda Liebes, *Studies in the Zohar* (SUNY, Albany, 1993), pp. 151–52.

5. See Moshe Idel, "Ramon Lull and Ecstatic Kabbalah: A Preliminary Observation" *Journal of the Warburg and Courtauld Institutes* vol. 51 (1988), pp. 170–74.

6. *Libro de la caza*, ed. J. Gutierrez de la Vega, *Biblioteca venatoria*, 5 volumes (Madrid, M. Tello, 1877–99) vol. III, p. 4, and also *Libro de la caza*, ed. J. M. Castroy Calvo (Barcelona, Consejo Superior de Investigationes Cientificas 1947) II, quoted from Norman Roth, "Jewish Collaborators in Alfonso's Scientific Work," ed. Robert I. Burns S. J., *Alfonso X the Learned of Castile and His Thirteenth-Century Renaissance* (University of Pennsylvania Press, Philadelphia, 1991), pp. 60, 225 note 7.

7. See the monumental contributions of Chaim Wirszubski, *Flavius Mithridates, Sermo de Pasione Domini* (The Israel Academy of Sciences and Humanities, Jerusalem, 1963); *Pico della Mirandola's Encounter with Jewish Mysticism* (Harvard University Press, Cambridge, Mass., 1987).

8. See Moshe Idel, "Particularism and Universalism in Kabbalah: 1480–1650" in *Essential Papers on Jewish Culture in Renaissance and Baroque Italy*, ed. David B. Ruderman (New York University Press, New York & London, 1992), pp. 324–44.

9. *Ibidem*, pp. 332–34.

10. See M. Idel, "Jewish Kabbalah and Platonism in the Middle Ages and Renaissance" in *Neoplatonism and Jewish Thought*, ed. Lenn E. Goodman (SUNY, Albany, 1993), p. 344.

11. Below, pp. 39, 328.

12. See, for example, Israel Adler, *Hebrew Writings Concerning Music* (G. Henle Verlag, Muenchen, 1975), general index, p. 379; R. Shem Tov Falaquera, *Sefer Moreh ha-Moreh* (Presburg, 1837) p. 148; Moses of Narbonne, *Ma'amar bi-Shelemut ha-Nefesh (Treatise on the Perfection of the Soul)*, ed. Alfred L. Ivry (The Israel Academy of Sciences and Humanities, Jerusalem, 1977), pp. 12, 25.

13. See Alexander Marx, "Texts of and about Maimonides," *Jewish Quarterly Review* (NS) vol. 25 (1934/35): 380; see also the *Guide of the Perplexed*, II, 8.

14. Though Aristotle never mentioned Pythagoras himself, he is rather negatively disposed toward Pythagoreanism. See, for example, *De caelo* II, 9.

15. See, for example, the conception that Pythagoras has discovered music in Yehudah Moscato's *Nefotzot Yehudah*, Sermon I (cf. Adler, *Hebrew Writings Concerning Music*, p. 224) and Samuel Archevolti's *Arugat ha-Bosem*, fol. 118a (cf. Adler, *ibidem*, p. 97), Abraham Portaleone, *Shiltei Gibborim* (cf. Adler, *ibidem*, p. 256), Joseph Solomon del Medigo, *Sefer Elim* (cf. Adler, *ibidem*, pp. 119–20). See also R. Shelomo ibn Verga, *Sefer Shevet Yehudah*, ed. I. Baer (Jerusalem, 1957) p. 158. Leone Ebreo was also acquainted with Pythagorean theories which were quoted sometimes in the *Dialoghi d'amore*. For the later use of Pythagoras and his views in

Introduction to the Bison Book Edition

Abraham Yagel, see David B. Ruderman, *Kabbalah, Magic, and Science: The Cultural Universe of a Sixteenth-Century Jewish Physician* (Cambridge, Mass.: Harvard University Press, 1988), index, p. 230 *sub voce* Pythagoras.

16. This patristic source has explicitly been quoted in connection with Pythagoras by several Jewish authors: see Flavius Mithridates, in his *Sermo* (to be quoted here below); Gedaliah ben Yehiya, *Shalshelet ha-Qabbalah*, p. 237; Yehudah Muscato's commentary on Rabbi Yehudah ha-Levi's *Kuzari*, named *Qol Yehudah*, part II fol. 76a; Isaac Cardoso, *Philosophia Libera*, cf. Yosef Hayim Yerushalmi, *From Spanish Court to Italian Getto, Isaac Cardoso* (Seattle: University of Washington Press, 1981), pp. 221–22.

17. See Daniel R. Walker, *The Ancient Theology: Studies in Christian Platonism from the Fifteenth to the Eighteenth Century* (London: Duckworth, 1972).

18. *Opera*, p. 30. See Ambrosius's *Epistle 58, Patrologia Latina*, vol. XVI, c. 1051.

19. See Ficino's introduction to his translation of the *Corpus Hermeticum*, dated 1463.

20. For example, the lists of ancient authorities adduced in the *Commentary on Philebus*.

21. See Nemesius of Emessa, John of Damascus and Shahrastani, referred to by H. A. Wolfson, *Studies in the History of Philosophy and Religion*, eds. I. Twersky, G. H. Williams (Cambridge, Mass.: Harvard University Press, 1973) vol. I, p. 357, and Sa'id al-Andalusi, *Tabaqat al-umam*, tr. G. Blachere (Paris: 1935), pp. 57–62, and Franz Rosenthal, *The Classical Heritage in Islam* (London: 1975) p. 40. See also Isidore Levy, *La legende de Pythagore de Grece en Palestine* (Paris: 1927).

22. See David B. Ruderman, "The Italian Renaissance and Jewish Thought" in *Renaissance Humanism*, ed. A. Rabil Jr. (Philadelphia: University of Pennsylvania Press, 1988), vol. I, pp. 411–12, 431–32, note 152 and note 37 below.

23. Eusebius, *Preparatio Evangelica*, X, 1, 4; Clement, *Stromata*, I, 15, 66.

24. *Heptaplus*, tr. J. Brewer McGaw (Philosophical Library, New York, 1977) p. 16. Compare *ibidem*, pp. 51–52: ". . . Hebrew dogmas . . . showing how much these ideas agree with the Egyptian wisdom, how much with the Platonic philosophy, and how much with the Catholic truth." See also Reuchlin, below, p. 212. On Pythagoras as *magister silentii*, see Edgar Wind, *Pagan Mysteries in the Renaissance* (Harmondworth: Penguin Books, 1960), pp. 12, note 40, 53–54.

25. See Wirszubski, *Sermo De Passione Domini*, p. 101. Mithridates has also translated from Greek a writing attributed to Pythagoras; see *ibidem*, p. 49.

26. See below, p. 39. This text should be compared to another, similar, discussion on p. 238. See also S. K. Heninger, Jr., *Touches of Sweet Harmony: Pythagorean Cosmology and Renaissance Poetics* (San Marino: 1974), p. 245.

27. On his Kabbalah, see Alexander Altmann, "Beyond the Realm of Philosophy: R. Elijah Hayyim ben Benjamin of Gennazano," eds. M. Idel, W. Z. Harvey, and E. Schweid, *Shlomo Pines Jubilee Volume* (Jerusalem: 1988), vol. I, pp. 61–102. [Hebrew].

28. Numenius was indeed one of the latest major Neopythagoreans. See also the quote above from Mithridates's *Sermo*, p. 101.

29. On Orlandus, see Moshe Idel, "Differing Conceptions of Kabbalah in the

Introduction to the Bison Book Edition

Early Seventeenth Century" in *Jewish Thought in the Seventeenth Century,* eds. I. Twersky and B. Septimus (Cambridge, Mass.: Harvard University Press, 1987), pp. 158–61.

30. On Numenius's belief in metempsychosis into animal bodies, see John Dillon, *The Middle Platonists* (New York: 1977), pp. 377–78. It is worthwhile to note that R. Elijah mentions later in the passage that Numenius allegedly stated that he was an reincarnation of Moses. Though Numenius was indeed an admirer of Moses, I could not trace the origin of this self-evaluation. See the discussion on Numenius and Moses in John G. Gager, *Moses in Greco-Roman Paganism* (New York: 1972), pp. 64–68. It is possible that R. Elijah's statement is a distortion of Numenius' well-known dictum: "What is Plato but Moses speaking Attic" (see Gager, *ibidem,* pp. 66–67), which occurs several times in Renaissance authors such as Ficino and Pico; see Charles Trinkaus, *"In Our Image and Likeness"* (University of Chicago Press, 1970), vol. II, pp. 741–42.

31. That is, R. Joseph Albo's *Sefer ha-'Iqqarim,* part IV, ch. 29. Albo attacked there the belief in reincarnation into animal bodies.

32. The concept of transmigration of the soul in animal bodies apparently occurs only in the works of the Kabbalists who wrote since the late thirteenth century. They are mentioned and quoted by Rabbi Menahem Recanati as "the later Kabbalists." See Alexander Altmann, *"Sefer Ta'amei ha-Mitzwot,* Attributed to R. Isaac ibn Farhi and its Author," *Qiriat Sefer,* vol. 40 (1965), pp. 256–57 [Hebrew]; Efraim Gottlieb, *Studies in the Kabbalah Literature,* ed. J. Hacker (Tel Aviv: 1976), p. 380. [Hebrew].

33. See *'Iggeret Hamudot,* ed. A. Greenup (London: 1912), p. 13. On this passage see some more details in Idel, "Differing Conceptions of Kabbalah," pp. 158–61.

34. See Isaac Abravanel's *Commentary on Deuteronomy,* on Ch. 25, verse 5. Compare another mention of Pythagoras in Abravanel's *Mifa'lot 'Elohim* (Lemberg, 1863), fol. 59a.

35. *Sha'ar ha-Heshek* (Halberstadt, 1860), fol. 10a. On Pythagoras and geomancy, see Heninger, *Touches of Sweet Harmony,* pp. 240–42. Alemanno mentions Pythagoras also in other contexts; in his *Collectanaea,* see Ms. Oxford 2234, fols. 10a, 17a, where he deals with matters of psychology.

36. On this distinction between the Jewish unilinear versus the Christian multilinear views, I hope to devote a separate study.

37. See also below, p. 354. Reuchlin is very fond of the term *symbola.* See, for example, pp. 98, 186, 208, 222, 224, 226, 232, 236, 238, 334, 350. Reuchlin adopted this concept found, *inter alia,* in Pythagoreanism in order to describe Kabbalah. This transposition of Pythagorean concepts for the description of Kabbalah, very conspicuous on p. 238 for example, is worthwhile of a separate study, and I hope to deal with it elsewhere. For the concept of *symbolon* in Pythagoreanism, see Walter Burkert, *Lore and Science in Ancient Pythagoreanism* (Cambridge, Mass.: Harvard University Press, 1972), pp. 166–92.

38. See Gershom Scholem, *On the Kabbalah and Its Symbolism* (New York: Schocken Books, 1969), p. 87.

39. On this phenomenon in general, see Moshe Idel, *Kabbalah: New Perspectives*

Introduction to the Bison Book Edition

(New Haven, Conn.: Yale University Press, 1988), pp. 5–6.

40. *Die Erforschung der Kabbala von Reuchlin bis zur Gegenwart* (Pforzheim, 1969), p. 7.

41. See *ibidem*, pp. 23–24; idem, "The Name of God and the Linguistic Theory of the Kabbala," *Diogenes*, vol. 79 (1972): 60–61; idem, *Major Trends in Jewish Mysticism* (New York: Schocken Books, 1967), p. 26; Nathan Rotenstreich, "Symbolism and Transcendence: On Some Philosophical Aspects of Gershom Scholem's Opus," *Review of Metaphysics*, vol. 31 (1977/78): 605. Compare Idel, *Kabbalah: New Perspectives*, pp. 200–210.

42. See below, p. 94. The English translation on p. 95 does not do justice to the Hebrew text as quoted by Reuchlin. See D. Ruderman, *Renaissance Quarterly*, vol. XXXVII (1984), p. 433.

43. A similar phenomenon is obvious on p. 98, where Maimonides's description of the two goals of the Torah—the perfection of the body and that of the soul—is interpreted as pointing to Talmudists and Kabbalists, respectively. See *Guide of the Perplexed*, III, 27. On the perceptions of Maimonides as a Kabbalist, most of them in Italy, see Gershom Scholem, "Maimonide dans l'oeuvre des Kabbalistes," *Cahiers juifs*, vol. 3 (1935), pp. 103–12; Wirszubski, *Pico della Mirandola*, pp. 84–99; Moshe Idel, "Maimonides and Kabbalah" in *Studies in Maimonides*, ed. Isadore Twersky (Cambridge, Mass.: Harvard University Press, 1990), pp. 54–76.

44. See *Die Erforschung*, pp. 12–13; however, in his *On the Kabbalah and Its Symbolism*, p. 180, note 1, and his "New Remnants from Rabbi Azriel of Gerona's Writings," *A. Klein and S. Gulak Memory Volume* (Jerusalem: 1942), pp. 204–5, he is more cautious, mentioning also the possibility that a copy of this manuscript might also be Reuchlin's source. Scholem indicated there that he intended to write a separate article on this issue, but as far as I know he did not publish such a study. In any case, it seems that it would be better to assume that the codex, which indubitably was similar to the Halberstamm manuscript, served as Reuchlin's source, but stems from another branch.

45. It seems that, despite the importance of the material reflected by the Halberstamm codex for the understanding of *De Arte Cabalistica*, in his earlier *De Verbo Mirifico*, the role of the Kabbalistic material found in that codex is marginal, its main subject being the powerful, the magic name. On the context and content of this book, see the important study of Charles Zika, "Reuchlin's *De Verbo Mirifico* and the Magic Debate of the Late Fifteenth Century," *Journal of the Warburg and Courtauld Institutes*, vol. 39 (1976): 104–38.

46. *Die Erforschung*, p. 13.

47. The only other codex, which is very similar in its content to the Halberstamm codex, is found also in the library of the Jewish Theological Seminary in New York (Ms. Acc. 78467, Mic. 2194), but this is a later manuscript which was copied after Reuchlin's death. There are also other manuscripts, which reflect partial identity to the content of the Halberstamm codex, but they cannot solve the questions mentioned here.

48. See, for example, below, p. 92, and p. 238, quoting from *Sha'ar ha-Razim*, Ms. Halberstamm 444, fol. 48a. Francoise Secret, *La Kabbale (de arte cabalistica)* (Paris: Aubier, Montaigne, 1973), p. 208, note 17, mentions here a certain Ms. Heb.

Introduction to the Bison Book Edition

844, fol. 10. I don't know the precise meaning of this reference.

49. See fols. 1a–2a; I have printed this text, referring to Reuchlin's quote from it "An Unknown Text from *Midrash ha-Ne'elam*," in *The Age of the Zohar*, ed. J. Dan (Jerusalem: 1989), pp. 73–87. [Hebrew].

50. See Scholem, "New Remnants," p. 206.

51. See below, p. 120.

52. Below, pp. 340, 348. This book is identified by Reuchlin on p. 92, with a certain book *Yahid* quoted by Abraham ibn Ezra. Indeed, this author quotes a certain *Sefer ha-Yihud*, which however has nothing to do with the Kabbalistic text quoted under the name of Rabbi Asse.

53. See, for example, Ms. New York, JTS 2194, fol. 59a; Ms. Oxford 1945, fols. 1a–4a. On this book, see Gershom Scholem, *Origins of the Kabbalah*, tr. A. Arkush and ed. R. J. Zwi Werblowsky (Princeton University Press, 1987), pp. 323–24 and note 257.

54. Below, p. 344.

55. Below, pp. 314–22.

56. See Wirszubski, *Pico della Mirandola*, pp. 165–67.

57. On this text, see Moshe Idel, *Abraham Abulafia's Works and Doctrines*, Ph.D. diss., Hebrew University, Jerusalem, 1976, pp. 78–79. [Hebrew]. En passant, Reuchlin offers a faulted vocalization of the title: *Hacadma* in lieu of *Haqdamah*. Another quote from this text, this time without mentioning the source, is found in *De Arte Cabalistica*, below p. 284, to be compared to Ms. Halberstamm 444, fol. 10a. There is a discrepancy between the Hebrew version in this manuscript and the way it was transmitted by Reuchlin. Here, it seems that indeed Reuchlin had before his eyes a version in which the ancient Jewish poet Kalir was mentioned, while this detail, which is very appropriate in the specific context, does not occur in the abovementioned codex.

58. *Melekh ha-Meshiah*, the king Messiah, is numerically equivalent to *Yom ha-Shevi'i*, the seventh day, 453.

59. P. 110. This translation of the Hebrew text quoted by Reuchlin differs in some details from that offered by the Goodmans. Compare *ibidem*, p. 111. For more on the view found in this passage and his sources in Abraham Abulafia's writings, see Moshe Idel, *Studies in Ecstatic Kabbalah* (Albany: SUNY, 1988), pp. 52–55. See also Yehuda Liebes, *Studies in the Zohar* (Albany: SUNY, 1993), pp. 49–50.

60. Ms. Halberstamm 444; Paris, Biblitheque Nationale 776, Mussaioff 11; and Jerusalem, NUL 476.

61. *Yom Shishi*, the sixth day, is numerically equivalent to *Shu henritz;* namely both are equivalent to 671 or 670.

62. Ms. Paris, Bibliotheque Nationale 776, fol. 184b.

63. This is a reference to Christianity, called Edom in many Jewish medieval sources.

64. *Ibidem*.

65. See discussions on the theurgical-eschatological significance of the change in the status of the divine name, especially in the early Kabbalah, in Haviva Pedaya, "'Flaw' and 'Correction' in the Concept of the Godhead in the Teachings of Rabbi Isaac the Blind," ed. J. Dan, *The Beginnings of the Jewish Mysticism in Medieval Europe* (Jerusalem: 1987), pp. 157–286. [Hebrew].

Introduction to the Bison Book Edition

66. This aspect of Abulafia's thought still waits a separate analysis.

67. Below, p. 92.

68. See, for example, below, p. 96.

69. See above, end of paragraph IV.

70. Below, p. 106.

71. Below, p. 108. The text is found in Ms. Halberstamm 444, fol. 66a, and was printed by Scholem, "New Remnants" p. 211 and see also Scholem's discussion of Reuchlin's use of the text, *ibidem*, pp. 204–5. I cannot enter in here the interesting details of Reuchlin's treatment of this passage, but it is a fine example for the Christian turn he gives to the cited text.

72. Below, *ibidem*.

73. See Idel, *Studies in Ecstatic Kabbalah*, pp. 52–54.

74. See also Heiko A. Oberman, *The Roots of Anti-Semitism in the Age of Renaissance and Reformation*, tr. J. I. Porter (Philadelphia: Fortress Press, Philadelphia, 1984), pp. 24–31.

75. See Oberman, *ibidem*, p. 27.

76. See Isaiah Tishby's description of the relevant material found in the Halberstamm manuscript, especially fols. 25a–39b, in his introduction to *Commentarius in Aggadot Auctores R. Azriel Geronensi* (Jerusalem: 1945), p. 15. [Hebrew].

77. I see no reason for Scholem's description in Reuchlin as the founder of the studies of Judaism in Europe. See *Die Erforschung*, p. 7: "der erster Erforscher des Judentums." However, his Pythagorean vision of Kabbalah, part of his Renaissance approach, has indeed affected modern scholarship, as we have attempted to indicate above, in our discussion of Kabbalah as a symbolic lore.

Contents

Introduction to the Bison Book Edition	v
Introduction	7
Notes for the Introduction	28
Book One	34
Book Two	126
Book Three	234
Proper Names Appearing in the Translation	361
Notes	371

On the Art of the Kabbalah

"The Triumph of Reuchlin" *(CAPNION)* Woodcut. 150 x 415 mm. Berlin-Dahlem (D354-10)

Introduction
by
G. Lloyd Jones

In his "Apotheosis of that Incomparable Worthy, John Reuchlin," Erasmus of Rotterdam depicts the object of his admiration being escorted to heaven by Jerome, the great exemplar of Christian scholars. The dialogue ends with the following collect which could be used to honor the memory of this leading Renaissance linguist:

> O God, thou lover of mankind, who through thy chosen servant John Reuchlin has renewed to the world the gift of tongues, by which thou didst once from heaven, through thy Holy Spirit, instruct the apostles for the preaching of the gospel, grant that all men everywhere may preach in every tongue the glory of thy son Jesus. Confound the tongues of false apostles who band themselves to build an impious tower to Babel, attempting to obscure thy glory whilst minded to exalt their own; since to thee alone, with Jesus thy Son our Lord, and the Holy Spirit, belongs all glory, for ever and ever. Amen.[1]

Although Reuchlin's many enemies must have scoffed at such a memorial, Erasmus was determined that the contribution of this erudite German to biblical scholarship should be appreciated. Thus Reuchlin's hope, expressed to Pope Leo X on the final page of the *De arte cabalistica,* that "the Church in years to come would not be ungrateful" for his labors, was at least partially realized. It remained only a partial realization, since Erasmus, in his prayer, chose to concentrate on Reuchlin's competence in the languages of the Bible and excluded the two other aspects of his career which Reuchlin would have wished to emphasize: his patronage of Jewish literature and his extensive study of the Kabbalah. For present purposes, these three areas, the linguistic, the literary and the Kabbalistic, provide a suitable framework for a brief review of Reuchlin's contribution to Hebrew learning. In conclusion, notice will be taken of the attitude adopted by some of his contemporaries to the ideas expressed by this illustrious Christian humanist.

Introduction

The trilingual miracle

When Giovanni Pico, a count of Mirandola and a prominent figure in fifteenth-century Italy, began taking a scholarly and cultural interest in Hebrew, he was entering a field of study not at all well known in Christian Europe. Several factors contributed to this ignorance of the language among gentiles. In the first place, a marked mistrust of the Jews had developed among Christian scholars during the later Middle Ages. It was claimed that the rabbis had purposely falsified the text of the Old Testament and given erroneous explanations of passages which were capable of a christological interpretation. The text of the Vulgate might well stand in need of correction, but there was no guarantee that the Hebrew original was any less corrupt. A solid phalanx of Christian teachers rejected Jewish tradition out of hand and could see no value whatever in it. Secondly, the cause of Hebrew scholarship was weakened by being left to a few interested individuals and not placed on an official footing. An attempt had been made by Pope Clement V in 1311 at the Council of Vienne to establish chairs of Hebrew, Arabic, Syriac and Greek in the four "studia generalia" of Christendom, namely Oxford, Paris, Bologna and Salamanca. It was recommended that each university should have two teachers for each language who were to provide instruction and produce Latin translations of important works. The decree was prompted both by missionary ideals and by the desire to advance the cause of biblical exegesis. Yet, despite the fact that the Church thereby gave official approval to what the Franciscans and the Dominicans had already been doing, the injunction was a dead letter. It failed for lack of financial support and because the attitude of the hierarchy was, to say the least, lukewarm. Although the decree was reissued by the Council of Basle in 1434 it had no appreciable impact on Hebrew learning among Christians.[2] Finally, there was the difficulty encountered by non-Jews in their attempt to get private tuition. Gentiles found it almost impossible to persuade the Jews to teach them Hebrew. Admittedly, there was no dearth of educated Jews in fifteenth-century Italy. By 1492, after their expulsion from Spain and Sicily, Italy was in fact the only country in Christian Europe open to them. But the desire of Christians to learn Hebrew was not universally welcomed by Italian Jewry. The appropriateness of imparting the mysteries of the Law in its original language to gentiles was the subject of fierce debate among the Jews themselves.[3]

Introduction

But in spite of every obstacle, a few prominent scholars and ecclesiastics were making considerable progress in Semitics by the beginning of the sixteenth century. Christians, ordained and lay, began to employ Jews and converts from Judaism as teachers of Hebrew on a private basis.[4] Two Renaissance popes, Nicholas V and Sixtus IV, made valuable collections of Hebrew manuscripts and commissioned Latin translations of Jewish works. The concern of prominent churchmen with Hebrew lore, however, was motivated by conversionist considerations rather than by a genuine academic interest. This was especially true of Spain where converts from Judaism attacked their former faith and sought to rationalize their own apostasy by quoting from Jewish works.[5] Although the polemical motif was less apparent in Italy, the controversial writings of Giannozo Manetti, the Florentine scholar and statesman, do offer evidence of a determination to read Jewish authors for apologetic purposes. Manetti reiterates the principle laid down by the missionary orders when he stresses that Christians must know Hebrew and be familiar with rabbinic literature if they are to succeed in converting the Jews.[6]

Gradually the emphasis shifted from polemics to scholarship. Men of letters, especially those associated with the Platonist Academy in Florence, were anxious that Hebrew should be acknowledged as one of the three historic languages of the West and studied alongside Latin and Greek. Knowledge of the language would give the student access not only to the Old Testament in the original but also to postbiblical Jewish literature. The usefulness of the latter, especially the great medieval commentaries, would soon become apparent to the Christian exegete. Hence we find Marsilio Ficino, leader of the Academy, making use of rabbinic writings in his *De Christiana religione* (1474).[7] Though his quotations from Saadia, Rashi and Gersonides may have been obtained through translations or secondary sources, such as Nicholas of Lyra's *Postillae*, thus necessitating hardly any knowledge of Hebrew, it is clear that Ficino utilized the Hebraic tradition and wished to promote the study of it among his colleagues. Pico, a Christian layman, stood in the forefront of this movement. He wanted to be able to read rabbinic literature, and to this end he applied himself to the study of Hebrew and Aramaic. But despite the assistance of Jews and Jewish converts to Christianity, there is no clear evidence that Pico made much headway as a Hebraist. The extent of his knowledge of the language is still an open

Introduction

question.[8] Of the study of Jewish literature, however, he was a powerful advocate.

Reuchlin was a disciple of Pico. They met for the first time at Florence in 1490 while Reuchlin was on a diplomatic visit to Italy. There Pico communicated to him his enthusiasm for all things Hebraic, urging him to master the Hebrew language without delay. Reuchlin needed no further persuasion, and returned to Germany determined to take Pico's advice. Not that Hebrew was entirely new to him. If the reminiscences of his nephew, Melanchthon, are correct, he was taught the rudiments by John Wessel of Gansfort while he was a student at the University of Paris in 1473.[9] Ten years later Rudolph Agricola alludes in a letter to their mutual interest in the language.[10] In 1488 Reuchlin himself writes that, under the influence of Jerome, he has been studying Hebrew and Greek so that he can read the Bible in the original.[11] We may assume that, until 1490, Reuchlin had no more than an elementary knowledge of Hebrew. Convinced by Pico that he should take the study of the language more seriously, Reuchlin hired the Jew Jacob Loans, private physician to Emperor Frederick III, as his tutor. Clearly the pupil held his master in high regard for he refers to him as "humanissimus praeceptor meus ille Jacobus Jehiel Loans doctor excellens."[12] It was with pride that he wrote a Hebrew letter to Loans in 1500 to demonstrate the progress he had made in the language.[13] Although he never forgot his debt to this learned physician, Reuchlin also employed the services of Obadiah ben Jacob Sforno to further his knowledge of Hebrew. Sforno, who was renowned for his exegetical and philosophical writings, founded a talmudic school at Bologna. He taught Reuchlin while the latter was in Rome from 1498 to 1500. Thanks to his teachers, Reuchlin's passion for Hebrew and the Hebraic tradition remained undiminished until the end of his life. He never tired of stressing the importance of Hebrew for a proper understandng of the Bible. "I assure you," he wrote in 1508, "that not one of the Latins can expound the Old Testament unless he first becomes proficient in the language in which it was written. For the mediator between God and man was language, as we read in the Pentateuch; but not any language, only Hebrew, through which God wished his secrets to be made known to man."[14] To his existing expertise in Latin and Greek Reuchlin added Hebrew; in the words of an admirer he became a "miraculum trilingue."

Introduction

Since he considered a working knowledge of Hebrew essential for a true appreciation of the Bible and rabbinic literature, Reuchlin devoted much of his time to providing students with the necessary apparatus for attaining it. In 1506 he published a Hebrew grammar and dictionary, the *De rudimentis hebraicis*. As its title suggests, this was intended "not for the learned but for those with elementary knowledge and those who are to become erudite."[15] He admits that it has meant much hard labor and cost him a small fortune, but the need of students for a manual, coupled with the great importance of the Scriptures, persuaded him to persevere.[16] Evidently, he was proud of his accomplishment, for on the last page he quotes Horace: "I have erected a monument more lasting than bronze."[17] The work is divided into three sections: a description of the alphabet with directions for reading it, a Hebrew-Latin dictionary and a brief survey of Hebrew syntax. In the lexicographical section, which is the longest and most important part of the book, Reuchlin has frequent recourse to medieval Jewish commentators and grammarians. He quotes freely from Rashi and from David Kimchi's *Book of Roots*. He stresses that anyone wishing to make a proper philological investigation of the Hebrew Scriptures should regard such authors as indispensable. The *De rudimentis* was followed in 1512 by an edition of the Hebrew text of the seven penitential psalms *(In septem psalmos poenitentiales)* with a translation and commentary. This again was intended for beginners and has the distinction of being the first Hebrew text to be printed in Germany. Finally, six years later, he published the *De accentibus et orthographia linguae hebraicae,* a treatise on accents, pronunciation and synagogue music. In the dedication, addressed to Cardinal Adrian, we catch another glimpse of Reuchlin's perennial concern for the dissemination of Hebrew learning among Christians. His intention is, and always will be,

> to give the youth, bent upon studying languages, a leader under whose banner they would be able to fight, if need be, with those ferocious and rabid dogs who hated all good arts; against the disease and pestilence of everything old; against the burners of books who thirsted for the destruction and extermination of the most ancient monuments. As an old man he might cease to teach elements of grammar, fit only for children and young people, but his zeal for the spread of the study of Hebrew makes him forget all objections.[18]

Introduction

Though the *De accentibus* was his last major work, completed four years before his death in 1522, Reuchlin never stopped propagating Hebrew studies.

Reuchlin's importance in the field of biblical scholarship is that he established philology as a recognized and independent discipline entitled to discuss the meaning of words in the Bible.[19] While he was an accomplished philologist, on his own admission he was no expert in theology. "I do not discuss the meaning, like a theologian, but rather the actual words, like a grammarian," he wrote under one of the entries in his dictionary.[20] This philological approach led him to criticize the Vulgate's rendering of the "Hebraica veritas" and to correct it at several points. In the *De rudimentis* alone there are over two hundred such corrections.[21] Reuchlin justified his action by claiming that where the theologian may err in his interpretation, the philologist will arrive at the truth. His studies were motivated at all times by an earnest desire to discover this truth. "He pined after truth," writes S.A. Hirsch, "the mainspring and fountain-head of which he wished to reach. He refused to acquiesce in the evidence of others who declared a truth to emanate from a certain source."[22] It was in his search for truth that Reuchlin discovered for his fellow Christians not only the treasures of the Hebrew Bible but also a rabbinic literature which eventually became an important branch of study at every seat of higher learning.

The protector of Jewish literature

In spite of Reuchlin's admiration for his teachers and his enthusiasm for Judaica, the fact remained that early in the sixteenth century it was considered unwise for a Christian to display excessive interest in Hebrew. Those Christian scholars who ventured to swim against the tide by seeking help from Jewish tradition to elucidate Old Testament passages were promptly branded as Judaizers. Ignorant friars, alarmed by the progress of the new learning, thundered from the pulpit that a new language had been discovered called Greek, of which people should beware, for it was this which produced all the heresies. Ridiculously, they referred to a book called the New Testament, written in this language, asserting that it was now in everyone's hands, and that it was "full of thorns and briars." There was also another language called Hebrew which should be avoided at all costs, since those who learned it became Jews.[23] Reuchlin was well aware of

Introduction

the trouble that lay ahead if he persisted in advocating the study of Hebrew. In his *De rudimentis* he wrote:

> I believe that enemies will oppose our dictionary, in which the interpretations of many are frequently criticized. "What a crime!" they will exclaim. "Nothing is more unworthy of the memory of the fathers, no crime more cruel, than the attempt made by that most audacious man to overthrow so many and such saintly men who were imbued with the holy spirit. The Bible of the most blessed Jerome was accepted in the Church, as Pope Gelasius testifies. The venerable father Nicholas of Lura, the common expositor of the Bible, is considered by all who are faithful to Christ to be the soundest of men. Now a certain puff of smoke has appeared who claims that these have translated erroneously in a great many places." To such threatening shouts I reply with these few words: allow me what was allowed to those famous luminaries.[24]

Just as Jerome had criticized the Septuagint and Nicholas of Lyra had criticized Jerome, so Reuchlin felt that he had the right to make a judgement on the work of his predecessors, and in so doing promote Hebraic studies.

In view of the prevailing attitude of the Church towards Judaism it is not surprising that Reuchlin's promotion of Jewish literature encountered fierce opposition. Early in 1510 a converted Jewish butcher, one Johann Pfefferkorn, came to him with a strange request. The Jews of Cologne and Frankfurt had appealed against an order made by Emperor Maximilian, at the instigation of the Dominicans, that all Hebrew books considered to be inimical to Christianity should be burned. Pfefferkorn, in his capacity as spokesman for the ecclesiastical authorities, asked Reuchlin to assist in the case, and from his vast knowledge of Hebraica decide which books should be condemned. Predictably, Reuchlin sprang to the defence of the Jews and their literature. Although he regarded them as mistaken in their religious convictions, and traced their endless misery to their own unbelief rather than to the uncharitable attitude of the Church, he insisted that they should have the same rights as any other human beings. As a graduate in law from the University of Orléans, and as a practical statesman, he was aware that whatever deprivations they had suffered during the Middle Ages, they had always been treated with fairness and equality in legal matters. He knew of the charters

Introduction

granted by popes and emperors which guaranteed their religious liberty and permitted them to keep their prayerbooks and doctrinal works.[25] Neither the Dominicans nor anyone else had the right to confiscate their property. Pfefferkorn's malicious campaign offended Reuchlin's sense of justice and made him all the more eager to protect the Jews on humanitarian grounds.

With regard to specific books, Reuchlin published a short memorandum in which he divided Jewish literature into several classes, only one of which ought to be destroyed.[26] The Old Testament, naturally, must be kept. The Talmud might well contain some anti-Christian remarks, but how many Christians in Germany could read it, much less be offended by what it said; he admitted that he had not read it himself. If, as his opponents maintained, it deserved to be banned, surely Christians in previous centuries would have dealt with it. As for the Kabbalah, even popes had recognized that it could be of use to Christians, and had gone so far as to commission Latin translations of Kabbalistic works. Furthermore, had not the learned Pico shown convincingly that it contained the principal doctrines of Christianity? Exegetical works, such as the commentaries of Rashi, Kimchi, Ibn Ezra and other notable rabbis were of great value to the Christian expositor. They should be considered by every serious student as valuable aids to the understanding of the Old Testament. Little would remain of Nicholas of Lyra's *Postillae* if they were shorn of their rabbinic quotations. Liturgical works, which provided directions in matters of worship and ceremonial, could in no way be regarded as a threat to Christianity. Only writings which were insulting to Christ, such as *Toledoth Yeshu* (the Jewish *Life of Jesus*) and *HaNiṣṣachon* (*The Victory*) were to be burned. To add weight to his recommendation Reuchlin pointed out that what is forbidden usually attracts people; confiscation would only lead to greater interest. He urged Christians to direct their efforts to the conversion of the Jews, not to persecution and the willful destruction of their literary heritage. Those who rejected Christ must be brought to see the error of their ways by discussion and debate. But if Christians were to enter into a useful dialogue with Jews, they must first have a thorough knowledge of the writings of Jewish exegetes and philosophers. In order to achieve this purpose he proposed the foundation of two chairs of Hebrew in every German university with provision for the teaching of biblical and rabbinic Hebrew. The Jews should be asked to supply the students with books. This, however,

Introduction

was not what Pfefferkorn wanted, and the result of their disagreement was a bitter controversy which quickly went beyond the original quarrel and lasted for almost a decade. The "battle of the books," as the dispute was later known, was to prove decisive for Jews and Christian humanists alike.[27]

For all his love of Jewish literature and his respect for Jacob Loans, Reuchlin was no friend of the Jews. His opposition to Pfefferkorn and the Dominicans sprang from humanitarian and educational motives, not from any philo-Semitic feelings. While he deplored the expulsion of the Jews from Spain and their constant harassment in Germany, he did so because he feared that the resultant loss of the Hebrew language would be detrimental to Christian biblical scholarship.[28] He saw himself, primarily, as a defender of Christianity, not as a crusader for the rights of Jews. Although he criticized the ignorance and corruption of the clergy, he remained loyal to the Church of Rome. "Pledged to Christ," he wrote in 1518, "I devoted everything to the Christian Church. . . . I am led by genius and the love of piety."[29] His interest in the Old Testament sprang from the belief that it was basically Christocentric. "The whole of sacred Scripture is about Christ." Everything that is written in both the Old and the New Testaments concerns him and his work.[30] While the Hebrew Bible must therefore be preserved, Reuchlin admitted to the Dominican Konrad Kollin that he too opposed Jewish writings hostile to the Christian faith.[31] In company with almost every other Christian theologian of the Renaissance period, he considered the Jews to have brought their sufferings upon themselves by blaspheming the name of Christ and rejecting the Gospel. Their punishment would end whenever they acknowledged Jesus to be the Messiah. Meanwhile, it was the duty of all Christians to pray that they would be "freed from the devil's captivity," as the Good Friday collect put it.[32] With regard to his own missionary endeavors, he complained that he had experienced nothing but bitter persecution at the hands of his fellow Christians:

> I have suffered innocently for many years because of my very great wish to strengthen the orthodox faith and my most ardent desire to enlarge the Catholic Church, because I felt that those who were outside the faith, the Jews, Greeks and Saracens would not be attracted to us by insults. For I considered it unbecoming of the Church to drive them to holy baptism by tyranny or severity.[33]

Introduction

The preservation of Jewish literature was a significant by-product of this fervent zeal for the Christian faith and for the conversion of the Jews.

The Christian Kabbalist

At their meeting in Florence, Pico shared with Reuchlin his consuming interest in Jewish mystical writings, writings to which he himself had been introduced by his Jewish teachers. Though not the first gentile to study this esoteric literature, Pico may be described justly as the "father" of Christian Kabbalah inasmuch as it was he who persuaded other humanists to take it seriously.[34] He sought to convince his contemporaries that Kabbalistic teachings could be used to confirm the truth of the Gospel. He justified his standpoint by claiming that the Kabbalah contained an ancient divine revelation which had been lost. Since it came from God, such a revelation should not be despised; it could do nothing but strengthen the Christian faith. According to Pico, the main doctrines of Christianity were to be found in the works of Jewish mystics. On reading the Kabbalah he found in it

> not so much the Mosaic as the Christian religion. There is the mystery of the Trinity, there the Incarnation of the Word, there the divinity of the Messiah; there I have read about original sin, its expiation through Christ, the heavenly Jerusalem, the fall of the devils, the orders of the angels, purgatory and the punishments of hell, the same things we read daily in Paul and Dionysius, in Jerome and Augustine.[35]

Because of its usefulness to Christians, Pico incorporated the Kabbalah into his theological system. This he eventually published in nine hundred theses, seventy-two of which were derived from Kabbalistic sources. He offered to defend his views publicly in Rome. The debate, though promised, was never held. Instead, the Pope launched an inquiry, with the result that Pico was charged with heresy. Not surprisingly, the Vatican was disturbed by the thesis which stated that "there is no knowledge which makes us more certain of the divinity of Christ than magic and Kabbalah."[36] This claim, though modified later in the face of fierce opposition, strikes the keynote of Pico's contribution to Hebraic studies: the creation of a

Introduction

Christian Kabbalah. By pinpointing the specifically Christian elements which, according to him, were embedded in the secret lore of the Jews, he gave the Kabbalah a new interpretation. This should appeal to his co-religionists, for Jewish mysticism could now be used to reinforce Christian religious convictions. Although he does not sound so blatantly polemical as some of his predecessors, Pico too believed in the value of the Kabbalah for controverting Jewish teachings. "Taken altogether," he writes, "there is absolutely no controversy between ourselves and the Hebrews on any matter, with regard to which they cannot be refuted and gainsaid out of the cabalistic books, so that there will not be even a corner left in which they may hide themselves."[37] By means of their own literature the Jews could be made to see the error of their ways.

When Pico was prevented by an early death from taking the study of Christian Kabbalism any further, his mantle fell upon Reuchlin. Writing to the latter in 1503 Konrad Muth, a leading German humanist, expressed the hope that he would "soon accomplish precisely what Pico promised."[38] In fact, Reuchlin had turned his attention to the Kabbalah soon after meeting Pico, and in 1494 produced his first Kabbalistic work, the *De verbo mirifico*. In this book, presented as a dialogue between an Epicurean, a Jew and a Christian, he tries to make the morphology of Jewish mystical works intelligible, and to give prominence to the Kabbalah in the current debate about magic and the occult.[39] The "wonder-working word" of the title is not the Tetragrammaton (*YHVH*) but the Pentagrammaton (*YHSVH*: the letters of the Hebrew form of the name "Jesus") whose power and significance are discussed in the second and third parts of the book respectively. By demonstrating how the practice of Jewish mystical techniques could lead men to Christ, and that the essential Christian doctrines were to be found in the Kabbalah, Reuchlin was attempting to vindicate Pico's claims and defend him against attack. But the *De verbo mirifico* was the work of a beginner. By 1517, the year in which he published his *De arte cabalistica,* Reuchlin had become a proficient Hebraist and was regarded as the leading Christian authority on postbiblical Jewish writings. During the twenty-three years which separated the two works many more kabbalistic texts had become known to him, some of them, such as Joseph Gikatilla's *Gates of Light,* in a Latin translation.

Introduction

This second treatise, intended as an apologia for the Christian study of the Kabbalah, was written when the battle of the books was at its height. The dedication to Pope Leo X indicates how anxious Reuchlin was to enlist the support of Rome in his fight against obscurantists and anti-Semites. Such support, if it were forthcoming, would not be misplaced. It would help to promote knowledge of the Kabbalah which was essential for a full contemplation of the divine:

> God has given to men who walk upon the earth nothing they could more desire than this contemplative art. . . . Nothing admits more of the search for salvation in this world and everlasting life in the next. It is by this means that the mind of man, so far as nature allows, achieves that Godlike state which is the "peak" of blessedness. . . . In that state man's life lacks nothing.[40]

Kabbalah is of the greatest importance to man, for "without it none can achieve something as elusive, as difficult, as the apprehension of the divine."[41] He seeks to persuade the Pope that this is reason enough for protecting Jewish books from the hatred and envy of stupid fools who seek to burn them.[42]

Like its predecessor, the *De arte cabalistica* is divided into three books and presented in the form of a dialogue. The participants are Simon the Jew; Philolaus, a young Pythagorean philosopher; and Marranus, a Moslem. As with any work in dialogue, it is not always easy to extrapolate the author's own thoughts from this treatise. But on reading through it, three main areas of interest emerge. The first is messianism, to which half of the first book is devoted. Simon introduces the subject. In answer to his companion's question about the nature of Kabbalistic revelation, he states that the Kabbalah contains "none other than the universal revelation, after the primordial Fall of the human race, which is called salvation."[43] This holiest and highest revelation was made originally to Adam by an angel immediately after the Fall:

> Don't lie there shuddering, burdened with grief, thinking of your responsibility for bringing the race of man to perdition. The primal sin will be purged in this way: from your seed will be born a just man, a man of peace, a hero whose name will in pity contain these four letters— *YHVH* —and through his upright trustfulness and peaceable sacrifice will put out his hand, and take from the tree of life, and

Introduction

the fruit of that tree will be salvation to all who hope for it.[44]

Every one of God's revelations can be reduced to this announcement of the birth of a savior who will grant an amnesty to prisoners; it encapsulates all the principles of the Kabbalah and the traditions concerning the divine. But the promised Messiah did not come from the family of Adam, and was not to be identified with Isaac the son of Abraham. He would be a member of the tribe of Judah, as foretold by Jacob in Genesis 49:10, where the word "Shiloh" is interpreted as "the anointed one." The true Messiah would have the same characteristics as the servant in Isaiah 52:13-53:12, thus bringing reconciliation, not in the arrogant manner of kings, but through his humility, tolerance and mercy, and especially through his willing acceptance of death at the hands of his enemies. His name is the holy Tetragrammaton *YHVH* with an *S* inserted between the second and third letters, thus identifying him with Jesus. It is to him that all the scriptural prophecies of salvation point; it is in him that every true Kabbalist puts his trust.

Equally prominent in the *De arte cabalistica* is Reuchlin's interest in Pythagoreanism.[45] In the dedicatory epistle he informs the Pope that by means of his book he hopes to make the works of Pythagoras better known in the scholarly world. Through him the ancient Greek philosopher will be reborn. He seeks to achieve his goal by equating certain elements in the Pythagorean system with the Kabbalah. "I am quite certain," says Philolaus after listening to his friend's definition of Kabbalah, "and I see clearly that everything Simon showed us squares exactly with the Italian philosophy, that is, with Pythagoreanism. If I declare that Kabbalah and Pythagoreanism are of the same stuff, I will not be departing from the facts."[46] Reuchlin was not the first to make this equation. It had already been made by Pico in his attempt to convince the ecclesiastical authorities of the significance of Jewish mysticism for Christians. Pico wrote, with reference to the Kabbalah, "In those parts which concern philosophy you really seem to hear Pythagoras and Plato."[47] Pico, like Reuchlin and most Renaissance scholars, made no distinction between Neoplatonic and the Pythagorean writers of antiquity.

The "Italian philosophy" lent itself to such parallelism for several reasons. The first, and most obvious, was its interest in the theory of numbers. In the Pythagorean scheme everything had a corresponding number. For example, justice was symbolized by the number four since four points on a page could be arranged to form a square with equal sides. Five was the symbol of marriage because it was the sum of two and three, the male and female numbers respectively. Both Philo and Augustine had employed Pythagorean numerology to expound biblical texts. "We should not belittle the theory of numbers," wrote Augustine, "for its great value is eminently clear to the attentive student in many passages of the holy Scriptures. The praises of God do not for nothing include this statement: "Thou hast ordered all things by measure and number and weight."[48] Their preoccupation with number symbolism led the Christian Kabbalists of the Renaissance to ally themselves to the Pythagoreans and to find references to the Tetragrammaton within the Pythagorean philosophy.[49] Another aspect of Pythagoras's teaching which promoted its fusion with the Kabbalah was mysticism. This element had been emphasized by the Neo-Pythagoreans of the first century B.C. as a method of approaching the truth alternative to, but not necessarily in conflict with, philosophical thinking. On the eve of the Renaissance it had come to the fore again in the debate between rationalists and mystics. Influenced by Nicholas of Cusa's teaching on "learned ignorance," Reuchlin declares that rationality and intellect fail us when we try to penetrate the mystery of the divine.[50] He condemns the "sordid sophistic reasoning" of the Schoolmen and turns instead to the mysticism of the Kabbalah, for truth will not be captured by syllogisms.[51] His aversion for scholasticism is supported by the Kabbalah. The Kabbalist begins where the philosopher ends.[52]

> The mind of the Kabbalist, in a state of unutterable delight, rejoicing in spirit, in the depths of inner silence, driving away from itself humdrum earthly matters, is carried away to the heavenly and the invisible that lie beyond all human sense. Then, though yet a guest of the body, he becomes a fellow of the angels, a sojourner in the home above the heavens: his frequent intercourse may be recognized as being in heaven. When he travels to the higher regions, he does so in the company of angels, he often sees the soul of the Messiah.[53]

Throughout the book Reuchlin contrasts Kabbalistic-Pythagorean mysticism with the rational thought of the Schoolmen, even inventing, quite incorrectly, a parallel conflict between Kabbalists and Talmudists. One further reason for the appeal of Pythagoras's

Introduction

philosophy was its great age. Renaissance scholars witnessed the rebirth of antiquity. In their search for truth they went "ad fontes," turning for guidance to the primary sources of whatever subject interested them. Their love of the antique led them to regard the wisdom of the ancients as being pure and holy. Reuchlin linked Kabbalah and Pythagoreanism by tracing both of them to Moses. Pythagoras mediated the secrets of the Kabbalah to the Greeks.[54]

The third and final feature of the *De arte cabalistica* which commands attention is the author's interest in the "practical Kabbalah." Like other Kabbalists of his own day, Reuchlin demonstrates how Christians can make profitable use of Jewish mystical writings, and therefore shares with the reader his understanding of the *art* of the Kabbalah. This involves him in a detailed discussion of the principles and techniques of "angel magic," in which the Kabbalah is used to penetrate the mystery of the divinity. To overcome the problems posed by the doctrine of God's transcendence, the early Jewish mystics had developed an emanation theory in which the alphabet played an important part. They taught that the universe was divided into ten angelic spheres, each one governed by an intermediary or emanation of the divine. There were seventy-two inferior angels through whom the intermediaries could be approached. Contact with this celestial world was achieved by manipulating the sacred letters of the Hebrew alphabet.[55] By means of the power invested in Hebrew letters, the help of angelic beings could be obtained and a way opened to God. "Thus arises the Kabbalist's initmate friendship with the angels, through which he comes to know, in the proper manner, something of the divine names and does wonderful things (commonly known as miracles)."[56] This invocatory technique may be traced through the works of Jospeh Gikatilla to the famous thirteenth-century Kabbalist Abraham Abulafia.[57] Furthermore, the practical Kabbalah could be used as a means of protection. There were good and bad spirits in the universe. In the practice of his art the mystic might unwittingly summon the powers of evil and do harm to himself. But if he employed the Kabbalah he would be protected against such a mishap, for Kabbalistic techniques ensured that only good and beneficial spirits responded to the invocations of men.[58]

The *De arte cabalistica* represents the climax of Reuchlin's Kabalistic studies. This keen interest in the Jewish mystical tradition, exhibited here and in the *De verbo mirifico,* was a driving force

Introduction

behind his determination to master Hebrew and safeguard the existence of Hebraic literature.[59]

Reactions to Reuchlin

The publication of the *De arte cabalistica* was, then, an important element in Reuchlin's fight against his enemies. But the true significance of the famous literary battle continues to be a matter of debate. Many historians regard the controversy as a clash between humanism and scholasticism, scholarship and ignorance, light and darkness. Behind Pfefferkorn were the mendicant orders; behind Reuchlin were the literati of Europe, who regarded his cause as their own. According to this view, the Dominicans were not merely criticizing Reuchlin for defending the Jews, they were attacking the humanist movement as a whole. The conflict was between two intellectual traditions.[60] Others, however, take a different view of the affair. They see it primarily as a struggle, not between humanists and obscurantists, but between anti-Semites and those Christians who were anxious to uphold the right of the Jews to preserve their writings and practice their religion. While Reuchlin advocated toleration and respect towards the Jews, the Dominicans were consumed with hatred and prejudice.[61] There is truth in both points of view, for Reuchlin's supporters are found among more than one group of his contemporaries and not all such supporters gave him the wholehearted approval for which he hoped.

Ready sympathy for Reuchlin's ideals emerged from his native Germany.[62] Ulrich von Hutten, a younger contemporary of Reuchlin, was an outspoken critic of all who opposed the revival of letters. The corruption with which he considered the Church to be rife, he blamed on illiterate priests. Since these same clerics opposed Reuchlin, they could be attacked in the name of the new learning. Hutten, and others of a similar persuasion, formed a closely knit group under the leadership of Konrad Muth, a vigorous opponent of scholasticism. In advocating the study of the Bible and the works of the early Fathers, Muth made plain his admiration for Pico and quoted him as an excellent example of this type of scholarship.[63] Yet, he did not support Reuchlin without reservation. He was never convinced that the mysteries of the Kabbalah should have been popularized and made truly available to all. However, though not an

Introduction

activist himself, Muth certainly stirred others to action. So great was the respect in which he was held that the group of friends which surrounded him at Gotha and the neighboring University of Erfurt called itself the Mutianic Circle. Cortus Rubeanus, one of its more influential members, wrote to Reuchlin: "You do not lack supporters: you have on your side the illustrious Mutianic order which is comprised of philosophers, poets, orators, and theologians, all ready to fight for you if you so desire."[64] It was this circle which produced the famous *Epistolae obscurorum virorum* in 1515. The title suggests satire, for in the previous year Reuchlin had published *Clarorum virorum epistolae,* a collection of letters sent to him by prominent scholars in support of the new learning. The "obscure men," however, wrote letters complaining of the current state of affairs to Ortwin Gratius, professor at the University of Cologne, who, though an enthusiastic humanist, shared Pfefferkorn's anti-Semitic views. The letters, fictitious creations of Reuchlin's admirers, are all written in a similar vein, and are designed to exhibit the foolishness and pedantry of the opposing party. They bear eloquent testimony to "the slaying power of satire."

Martin Luther, though still an Augustinian friar when the Dominicans brought their case against the Jews, sided with the Reuchlinists. The voluminous correspondence which he had with George Spalatin demonstrates the love and respect which he had for the "innocent and learned Reuchlin." "You know," he wrote in February 1514, "that I greatly esteem and like the man, and perhaps my judgment will therefore be suspected, but my opinion is that in all his writings there is absolutely nothing dangerous."[65] In Luther's view, the Cologne censors had far worse things to worry about than Reuchlin's opinions. They might start with the corruption and idolatry within their own ranks. So far as the Jews were concerned, Luther argued that since they were of the lineage of Christ, they were within their rights in resisting conversion to Roman Catholicism. In any case, who would want to become a Christian once he had discovered the true state of the Church. "If I had been a Jew," he wrote, "and had seen such dolts and blockheads govern and teach the Christian faith, I would sooner have become a hog than a Christian."[66] He deplored the methods of conversion adopted by the friars and appealed for greater kindness towards the Jews. Slandering them and treating them like dogs would do no good at all. This eirenic attitude of the

Introduction

young Luther sprang from the expectation that he would succeed where Rome had failed. In the 1520s he was confident of being able to persuade the Jews of their errors and of witnessing a mass conversion to Christianity. In his old age, however, he held very different opinions. Shortly before his death he published a trilogy of tracts which evince a totally different attitude.[67] The Jews had proved far more stiff-necked than he had anticipated; they deserved persecution. During the final years of his life Luther would have had little sympathy for Reuchlin's promotion of Jewish literature and his cultivation of a Christian Kabbalah.

In view of the support given by many prominent scholars, whatever their motives, to all that Reuchlin stood for, the equivocal attitude of Erasmus is somewhat surprising. As the prayer quoted above demonstrates, he admired Reuchlin's erudition and was not unmindful of his immense contribution to learning. From at least one of his letters it appears that he sympathized with him in his battle with the friars. He realized that this was no isolated case and that humanist scholarship in general was being attacked by the obscurantists. In 1515 he wrote on Reuchlin's behalf to Cardinal Riario, one of the most powerful men in Rome. He ends his letter thus:

> One thing I had almost forgotten. I beg and beseech you earnestly, in the name of those humane studies of which your Eminence has always been an outstanding patron, that that excellent man Doctor Johann Reuchlin should find you fair-minded and friendly in his business. At one stroke you will render a great service to literature and all literary men, for the greater their learning the greater their enthusiasm for him. He has all Germany in his debt, where he was the first to awake the study of Greek and Hebrew. He is a man with an exceptional knowledge of the languages, accomplished in many subjects, eminent and well-known throughout Christendom for his published works.... The time had come when for his part he deserved to enjoy at his time of life a pleasant harvest from his honourable exertions, and we on our part looked to see him bring out the results of so many years' work for the common good. And so it seems outrageous to all men of good feeling, not Germans only but English and French as well, to whom he is well-known through his letters, that a man of such distinction and such outstanding gifts should

Introduction

be persecuted with such unpleasant litigation. . . . Believe me, whoever restores Johann Reuchlin to the arts and letters will win countless men's grateful devotion.[68]

Although this paragraph, admittedly, comes at the end of a letter which discusses other matters, and seems to have been added as an afterthought, it does testify to Erasmus's concern for the aging Reuchlin and to the high regard in which he held him as a scholar.

Yet, while Erasmus defended Reuchlin sincerely and eloquently on occasion, he did not associate himself too closely with his cause, especially during Reuchlin's own lifetime. His attitude has been explained in various ways. One contributing factor was his dislike of the Jews. There is no doubt that in his heart of hearts Erasmus was anti-Jewish. Just as he feared that the revival of Greek literature would lead to a resurgence of paganism, so he feared that the study of Hebrew would lead men to Judaism, a religion which he found totally meaningless. In February 1517 he wrote to Wolfgang Capito whom he greets as "a true expert in the three tongues," expressing his fear that the rebirth of Hebrew studies might "give Judaism its cue to plan a revival, the most pernicious plague and bitterest enemy that one can find to the teaching of Christ."[69] While he may have valued the humanist ideal of "Hebraica veritas," his interest in it was overshadowed by a fear of the erroneous creed of the Jews.[70] His attitude to the Talmud and the Kabbalah was entirely negative. In another letter to Capito he writes: "Talmud, Cabala, Tetragrammaton, Gates of Light, these are but empty names. I would rather see Christ infected by Scotus than by that rubbish. Italy has very many Jews; Spain has hardly any Christians."[71] He persistently refused to accept that the writings of medieval Jewish mystics could have any value whatsoever for a Christian.

But apart from his negative attitude towards the Jews, Erasmus had other reasons for not giving Reuchlin his unqualified support. It is certain that he wanted peace at all costs. For this reason he disapproved of the satirical *Epistolae obscurorum virorum,* and saw no point in crossing swords with Pfefferkorn, who "though a fool with a forehead of brass," was a dangerous man. He felt that party labels were of no advantage, and was anxious to keep clear of conflict, not out of timidity or the desire to please his patrons, but out of prudence. Furthermore, he opposed the excessive emphasis on ceremonial and ritual which found expression in Reuchlin's Kabbalistic works. Such ceremonies as were advocated in the *De arte*

Introduction

cabalistica, though they conformed to orthodox Christian practice, would not, in Erasmus's estimation, help to bring about the reform of the Church he so passionately desired. Salvation would come, not by adopting the esoteric practices advocated by Jewish mystics, but by leading a blameless life. Not only did the study of the Kabbalah open the door to the pernicious influence of Judaism, it also encouraged a form of piety which was the complete antithesis of all that Erasmus stood for.[72]

Reuchlin's philological expertise in biblical studies thus found an influential body of admirers; this included even English scholars and divines. In a letter written from Antwerp in 1516 Erasmus reminds Reuchlin of the esteem in which he is held by the whole scholarly world, and especially by two prominent Englishmen:

> You have been the acquaintance and friend of so many of our greatest men; you are even now so dearly beloved by all our noblest men and our best scholars that, were you their father, you could not be more intimately beloved by all of them. The bishop of Rochester [John Fisher] has an almost religious veneration for you. To John Colet your name is sacred. Had not his servant lost your letter, he would keep it, he told me, among his holy relics.[73]

The previous year Fisher had written to Erasmus with reference to Reuchlin:

> If he has published any book which is not yet in our hands, pray see that it is brought to us. For I am very pleased with his erudition: I do not think there is another man alive that comes so near to Giovanni Pico. . . . Commend me warmly to Reuchlin, whom I should certainly visit myself were it not for these my sacred garments.[74]

Though Reuchlin's books were awaited eagerly in England his Kabbalistic teachings did not find ready acceptance, and when the *De arte cabbalistica* arrived in 1517 it was given a cool reception. Colet, the Dean of St. Paul's, wrote thus to Erasmus after reading it:

> It is a book about which I dare not pronounce an opinion. I am aware how ignorant I am and how dimsighted in matters so transcendental, and in the works of so great a man. And yet, as I read, it seemed to me at times that the wonders were more verbal than real; for according to this system, Hebrew words have something mysterious in their

Introduction

> very characters and combinations. Erasmus! Of books and knowledge there is no end. But for this short life there is nothing better than that we should live in purity and holiness, and daily endeavour to be purified and enlightened and fulfil what is promised in those Pythagorean and Cabbalistic treatises of Reuchlin. This result, in my judgement we shall attain by no other way, than by ardent love and imitation of Jesus Christ. Wherefore, leaving detours, let us take a short road to attain it quickly.[75]

With characteristic humility Colet bows to Reuchlin's immense learning, but feels nevertheless that he must draw the line at the Kabbalah. The pursuit of Hebrew studies for a better understanding of Scripture was one thing, but the search for Christ in the works of the Kabbalists was another.[76]

Reuchlin's friends and acquaintances chose to remember their learned contemporary primarily as a linguist who taught them to appreciate the Hebrew Scriptures in the original. They were justified in doing so, for within a few years of his death Hebrew was recognized by Christians as being necessary for the sutdy of divinity, and therefore regarded as the "third language" of scholarship alongside Latin and Greek. They found his interest in Jewish mysticism, however, more difficult to appreciate. His efforts to promote the Kabbalah as a substitute for barren scholasticism were greeted with little enthusiasm by theologians and divines. Neither Rome nor the Reformers could see any abiding value in ransacking the works of medieval Jewish mystics for the truths of Christianity. It was to Renaissance Neoplatonists and to those who, in later generations, professed an interest in magic that Reuchlin's Kabbalistic studies really appealed.[77] The Venetian friar Francesco Giorgi, whose books became important channels for the transmission of the Christian Kabbalah, made frequent use of Reuchlin's ideas in his *De harmonia mundi* (1525). John Dee, the renowned Elizabethan Magus, was enlightened by Reuchlin's explanation of the angelic hierarchies as he wrote his *Philosophia Moysaica* (1638) in which he combined the Hermeticism of Ficino with the teachings of the Jewish Kabbalists. Examples of such influence extending into the eighteenth century could be multiplied. But perhaps enough has been said to demonstrate the relevance of Reuchlin's *De arte cabalistica* to anyone concerned with occult philosophy during the age of Renaissance and after.

Notes for the Introduction

1. *The Colloquies of Erasmus,* Eng. trans. by C.R. Thompson, Chicago 1965, p. 86.

2. See R. Weiss, "England and the Decree of the Council of Vienne on the teaching of Greek, Arabic, Hebrew and Syriac," *Bibliothèque d'Humanisme et Renaissance,* Tome 14, 1952, pp. 1 ff.

3. See C. Roth, *The History of the Jews of Italy,* Philadelphia 1946, pp. 153 ff; M. Shulvass, *The Jews of the World of the Renaissance,* Leiden 1973, pp. 148 ff.

4. For evidence of what little cooperation there was between Jews and Christians see G.E. Weil, *Elie Lévita: Humaniste et Massorète (1469-1549),* Leiden 1963, pp. 53 ff; J.W. O'Malley, *Giles of Viterbo on Church and Reform,* Leiden 1968, p. 70; E. Zimmer, "Jewish and Christian Hebraist collaboration in sixteenth-century Germany," *Jewish Quarterly Review,* vol. 71, No. 2, 1980, pp. 71 ff.

5. See F. Secret, "Les débuts du kabbalisme chrétien en Espagne et son histoire à la Renaissance," *Sefarad,* vol. 17, 1957, pp. 36 ff.

6. See his *Contra Judaeos et Gentes.* This work was not available for consultation, but the following description of it appears in Vespasiano da Bisticci's *Life* of Manetti, *The Vespasiano Memoirs: Lives of Illustrious Men of the XVth Century,* Eng. trans. by W.G. and E. Waters, London 1926, pp. 372 and 395: "With his knowledge of Hebrew he was able to write a treatise in ten books for the confusion of the Jews." The books "ought to be remembered for the high character of the subject. In all these he showed his virtuous mind and his devotion to the religion in which he had been born; he loved and rated it so highly that he spoke of it not as faith but certainty. No modern scholars have written against the Jews save a certain Geonese Porchetto, and Piero d'Alfonso, a Spaniard, but neither wrote with the elegance and style of Giannozzo." Vespasiano was a younger contemporary of Manetti.

7. *Marsilio Ficino: Opera Omnia,* ed., P.O. Kristeller, Turin 1962, vol. 1, pp. 31-105. See especially the section of "Testimonia phrophetarum de Christo," pp. 60-76.

8. See Ch. Wirszubski, "Giovanni Pico's Book of Job," *Journal of the Warburg and Courtauld Institutes,* vol. 32, 1969, p. 173.

9. *Corpus Reformatorum,* vol. 11, Halle 1943, "Oratio continens historiam Ioannis Capnionis," col. 1002.

10. *Johann Reuchlins Briefwechsel,* ed., L. Geiger, Stuttgart 1875, Letter 5, p. 7.

Introduction Notes

11. Ibid., Letter 15, p. 16. See also M. Brod, *Johannes Reuchlin und sein Kampf,* Stuttgart 1965, p. 80 for a reference to an otherwise unknown Jew named Calman who taught Reuchlin Hebrew in 1486.

12. J. Reuchlin, *De rudimentis hebraicis,* Pforzheim 1506 (reprinted 1974), p. 619.

13. *Briefwechsel,* Letter 72, p. 67. According to Reuchlin himself, Loans was his first Hebrew teacher: "Is me . . . fideliter literas hebraicas primus edocuit," *De rud. heb.,* p. 3.

14. *Briefwechsel,* Letter 102, p. 105.

15. *De rud. heb.,* p. 3.

16. *Briefwechsel,* Letter 130, p. 138. See also J. Reuchlin, *In septem psalmos poenitentiales,* Tübingen 1512, preface: "Feci rudimenta hebraicae linguae, quae multo sudore et algu prece premio et precio per longa tempora corraseram, haud sine incredibili diligentia et aere non parvo publicitius imprimi."

17. *De rud. heb.,* p. 621.

18. Quoted in translation by S.A. Hirsch, *A Book of Essays,* London 1905, p. 143.

19. For Reuchlin's contribution to philology see W. Schwarz, *The Principles and Problems of Biblical Translation,* Cambridge 1955, pp. 61 ff. For a complete list of his works see J. Benzing, *Bilbliographie der Schriften Johannes Reuchlins im 15. und 16. Jahrhundert,* Vienna 1955.

20. *De rud. heb.,* p. 123.

21. See. L. Geiger, *Johann Reuchlin sein Leben und seine Werke,* Leipzig 1871, (reprinted 1964), pp. 122 f. This influential book continues to be indispensable for any serious study of Reuchlin.

22. Op. cit., p. 124.

23. See J.I. Mombert, *English Versions of the Bible: A Handbook,* New York 1883, p. 77, quoting Hody, *De textibus bibliorum,* p. 456.

24. P. 548.

25. G. Kisch, *Zasius und Reuchlin,* Constance 1961, pp. 23-36, argues that legal training rather than literary interests inspired Reuchlin to defend the Jews. For papal protection of the Jews see S. Grayzel, *The Church and the Jews in the XIIIth Century,* Philadelphia 1933, pp. 76 ff. For favorable legal treatment of the Jews by the state up to c. 1350 see G. Kisch, "The Jews in Mediaeval Law," *Essays on Antisemitism,* ed., K.S. Pinson, 2nd ed. rev., New York 1946, pp. 103 ff.

26. See F. Barham, *The Life and Times of John Reuchlin or Capnion: The Father of the German Reformation,* London 1843, pp. 121 ff; L. Geiger, *Johann Reuchlin,* pp. 227 ff.

Introduction Notes

27. For an account of the dispute see H. Graetz, *History of the Jews,* London 1892, vol. 4, pp. 451 ff; W.S. Lilly, *Renaissance Types,* London 1901, pp. 175 ff; S.T. Hirsch, op. cit. pp. 73 ff; A.W. Ward, *Collected Papers,* Cambridge 1921, vol. 3 (i), pp. 79 ff; M. Brod, *Johannes Reuchlin und sein Kampf,* pp. 178 ff.

28. *De rud. heb.,* p. 3.

29. J. Reuchlin, *De accentibus,* preface.

30. J. Reuchlin, *In septem psalmos,* preface.

31. *Briefwechsel,* Letter 131, p. 140.

32. J. Reuchlin, *Tütsch missive: warumb die Juden so land in ellend sind,* Pforzheim 1505. This "German missive" was written in reply to a nobleman who wished to know the cause of the misery of the Jews. Reuchlin's attitude toward them ameliorated somewhat in later years.

33. *Briefwechsel,* Letter 215, p. 245.

34. See *De arte cabalistica,* Eng. trans. p. 137 where Reuchlin describes Pico as "the one who introduced 'Kabbalah' into Latin." Cf. J.L. Blau, *The Christian Interpretation of the Cabala in the Renaissance,* New York 1944, p. 19.

35. *The Renaissance Philosophy of Man,* eds., E. Cassirier, P.O. Kristeller, J.H. Randall Jr., Chicago 1948, "Oration on the dignity of man," p. 252.

36. *Johannes Picus Mirandulanus: Opera Omnia,* ed., E. Garin, Turin 1971, p. 105.

37. *The Renaissance Philosophy of Man,* pp. 252 ff. Many Jews saw the threat which Christian involvement in the Kabbalah posed to their own religion. Abraman Farissol (d. c. 1525) forbade his students to discuss Kabbalistic teachings with gentiles. See D.B. Ruderman, *The World of a Renaissance Jew,* Cincinnati 1981, p. 50.

38. *Briefwechsel,* Letter 87, p. 83. For Reuchlin's Kabbalistic studies see F. Secret, *Les kabbalistes chrétiens de la Renaissance,* Paris 1964, ch. 4.

39. For an analysis of the *De verb. mir.* see C. Zika, "Reuchlin's *De Verbo Mirifico* and the magic debate of the late fifteenth century," *Journal of the Warburg and Courtauld Institutes,* vol. 39, 1976, pp. 104 ff.

40. *De art. cab.,* p. 45.

41. Ibid., p. 61.

42. Ibid., pp. 91 ff. for a list of important Kabbalistic works.

43. Ibid., p. 65. For a description of the work see J.L. Blau, op. cit., pp. 49 ff. A French translation with introduction and notes has been made by F. Secret, *La Kabbale (de arte cabbalistica),* Paris 1973.

Introduction Notes

44. Ibid., p. 73.

45. For the Renaissance interest in Pythagorean philosophy see L.W. Spitz, "Reuchlin's philosophy: Pythagoras and Cabala for Christ," *Archiv für Reformationsgeschichte*, vol. 47, 1956, pp. 1 ff. S.K. Heninger Jr., *Touches of Sweet Harmony: Pythagorean Cosmology and Renaissance Poetics*, San Marino 1974.

46. *De art. cab.*, p. 147. Cf. also ibid., pp. 127, 233, 239 for the equation of the Kabbalah with Pythagoreanism.

47. *The Renaissance Philosophy of Man*, p. 252. For the connection between Pythagoreanism and Platonism see P. Merlan, *From Platonism to Neoplatonism*, The Hague 1953.

48. *City of God*, Loeb ed., vol. III, bk. 11:30. See V.F. Hopper, *Mediaeval Number Symbolism: Its Sources, Meaning and Influence on Thought and Expression*, New York, 1938, ch. 5 for the interest shown by early Christian writers in numerology.

49. *De art. cab.*, pp. 155 ff.

50. Ibid., p. 123. For Nicholas's teaching on "learned ignorance," see P.E. Sigmund, *Nicholas of Cusa and Medieval Political Thought*, Cambridge, Mass. 1963, ch. 10. See also W.J. Bouwsma, "Postel and the significance of Renaissance Cabalism," *Journal of the History of Ideas*, vol. 15., 1954, p. 223.

51. *De art. cab.*, p. 57.

52. The antiphilosophic stance of the Kabbalists is noted by G.G. Scholem, *Major Trends in Jewish Mysticism*, Jerusalem 1941, pp. 24 ff.

53. *De art. cab.*, p. 123. The "soul of the Messiah" was the highest level of mediation before the godhead.

54. Ibid., p. 145.

55. On the mystical value of the Hebrew language see G.G. Scholem op. cit., pp. 17 ff.

56. *De art. cab.*, p. 123.

57. Gikatilla's works were a major source of the *De art. cab.* See p. 95 below for Reuchlin's estimate of Gikatilla as a Kabbalist.

58. *De art. cab.* p. 347.

59. See *De rud. heb.*, p. 4.

60. See H. Holborn, *Ulrich von Hutten and the German Reformation*, Eng. trans. by R.H. Bainton, Yale 1937, p. 54.

61. See H. Graetz, *History of the Jews*, vol. 4, pp. 473 ff; S.W. Baron, *A Social and*

Introduction Notes

Religious History of the Jews, vol. 13, New York 1969, p. 188, quoting Reuchlin's *Der Augenspiegel,* Tübingen 1511; J.H. Overfield, "A new look at the Reuchlin affair," in *Studies in Mediaeval and Renaissance History,* vol. 8, ed., H.L. Adelson, Lincoln, Nebraska 1971, p. 191.

62. For a list of Reuchlin's supporters see F. Barham, op. cit., pp. 187 ff; *Ulrich Hutteni Opera,* ed., E. Böking, Leipzig 1859 (reprinted 1963), vol. 1, pp. 130 ff.

63. C. Kraus, *Der Briefwechsel des Mutianus Rufus,* Kassel 1885, Letter 137, p. 174.

64. *Ulrich Hutteni Opera,* vol. 1, Letter 14, p. 29.

65. P. Smith, *The Life and Letters of Martin Luther,* London 1911, p 29.

66. *Luther's Works,* American ed., vol. 45, Philadelphia 1962, p. 200.

67. *On the Jews and their Lies, Of the Shem Hamphoras and the Race of Christ,* and *The Last Words of David,* 1543.

68. *Collected Works of Erasmus,* vol. 3, Toronto 1976, Letter 333, pp. 90 ff.

69. Ibid., vol. 4, Toronto 1977, Letter 541, p. 267.

70. See W.L. Gundersheimer, "Erasmus, Humanism and the Christian Cabala," *Journal of the Warburg and Courtauld Institutes,* vol. 26, 1963, p. 43.

71. *Opus Epistolarum Des. Erasmi Roterodami,* ed., P.S. Allen, Oxford 1910, vol. 3, Letter 798, p. 253. For Erasmus's negative attitude to Judaism see also M. Krebs, "Reuchlins Beziehungen zu Erasmus von Rotterdam," *Johannes Reuchlin 1455-1522,* ed., M. Krebs, Pforzheim 1955, pp. 139 ff.

72. See C. Zika, "Reuchlin and Erasmus: Humanism and Occult Philosophy," *Journal of Religious History,* vol. 9, 1977, pp. 230 ff.

73. *Collected Works of Erasmus,* vol. 4, Letter 471, p. 85. Cf. ibid., vol. 5, Toronto 1979, Letter 713, p. 204.

74. J. Rouschausse, *Erasmus and Fisher: Their Correspondence 1511-1524,* Paris 1968, Letter 3, p. 45. See also *Collected Works of Erasmus,* vol. 3, Letter 324, pp. 62 ff.

75. J.H. Lupton, *The Life of John Colet D.D.,* 2nd ed., London 1909, p. 225. See also *Collected Works of Erasmus,* vol. 4, letter 593, p. 398.

76. For the reaction of early sixteenth-century English scholars to Reuchlin see further G. Lloyd Jones, *The Discovery of Hebrew in Tudor England: A Third Language,* Manchester 1982, ch. 4.

77. See Frances A. Yates, *Giordano Bruno and the Hermetic Tradition,* London 1964; *The Occult Philosophy in the Elizabethan Age,* London 1979.

ON THE ART OF KABBALAH

by Johann Reuchlin of Pforzheim

MAXIMILIANVS diuina fauente clementia El. Romano
rum Imperator semper Augustus &c. Recognoscimus per præsen
tes. Cum THOMAS ANSHELMVS pro comuni studio
sorum commodo & utilitate libros Hebræos, Græcos & Latinos,
raros & ante hac non editos magna solertia, & nō sine graui impen
sa ubicȝ perquirat, ingeniosocȝ charactere excudere, & in lucem
edere intendat. Nos indemnitati suæ consulere cupientes, ne ab aliis
huiuscemodi libri imprimātur, & ipse laboribus & commodo debi
to priuetur, præsentium tenore Statuimus & ordinamus, ne aliquis
cuiuscuncȝ status aut conditionis existat per sacrum Romanum Im
perium, huiusmodi libros per Quinquēnium proxime futurum im
primere, aut alibi impressos adducere & uēdere audeat. Quod si qs
contrafecerit, pœnam amissionis librorum, & quincȝ Marcarum
auri puri Fisco nostro applicandarum se nouerit incursurum. Man
damus iccirco omnibus & singulis principibus ecclesiasticis & secu
laribus, Comitibus, Baronibus, Capitaneis, Vicedomis, Præfectis,
Locūtenentibus, Gubernatoribus, Ancianis, Iudicibus, Consulibus
Comunitatibus, & cæteris quibuscuncȝ nostris & Imperii sacri offi
cialibus, & subditis fidelibus dilectis, cuiuscuncȝ gradus, cōditionis,
seu præeminentiæ fuerint, ut prefatum Anshelmum huiuscemodi
priuilegio nostro uti & gaudere permittāt, in eo manuteneant & de
fendant, & contrafacientes pœnis supradictis mulctent, nostræ pa
rituri uolūtati. Harum testimonio literarum sigilli nostri a tergo im
pressione munitarum. Dat. in Terzolas die XXI. Mensis Aprilis.
Anno M.D.XVI. Regni nostri Romani tricesimo primo.

Per Cæsarem.   Ad Mandatum Cæsareæ
                                Maiestatis in consilio.

                                Serntiner subscripsit.

On the Art of Kabbalah

MAXIMILIAN, by the grace and mercy of God, Emperor of the Romans, eternal Augustus, etc.:

By this letter we acknowledge Thomas Anshelm for his careful seeking out of rare and hitherto unpublished books in Hebrew, Greek, and Latin for the general convenience and utility of scholars, and for the not inconsiderable expense he has thereby incurred, and for his intention to print these books in fine type, and bring them to light. We, desirous of protecting his copyright, so that he be not deprived of his labors and the benefits owed him, hereby officially forbid anyone of any rank or station throughout the Holy Roman Empire to print copies of this book for the next five years or to transport or sell unauthorized copies. Contravention of this order will be punished by the loss of the books and a fine of 5 marks of pure gold payable to our Treasury. We therefore require every prince of church and state and every count, baron, captain, deputy, general, lieutenant, governor, sheriff, judge, mayor, and corporation with all the other inhabitants of our Holy Empire and our loyal subjects of all ranks, to allow the aforementioned Anshelm to enjoy the privilege herein granted and to protect him in it, and to punish offenders as specified above in accordance with our will. The authority of this letter is guaranteed by the stamp of our seal on the reverse. Signed in Terzolae on 21 April 1516, in the thirty-first year of our rule in Rome.

The Emperor's command

His Majesty's command in Council

Checked and signed.

SANCTISSIMO LEONI DECIMO PON TIFICI MAXIMO IOHANNES
Reuchlin se supplex commendat.

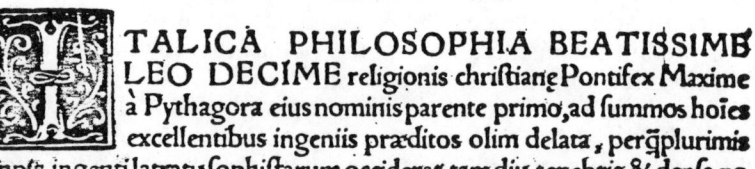

ITALICA PHILOSOPHIA BEATISSIME LEO DECIME religionis christianę Pontifex Maxime à Pythagora eius nominis parente primo, ad summos hoīes excellentibus ingeniis præditos olim delata, perq̃ plurimis annīs ingenti latratu sophistarum occiderat, tam diu tenebris & densa nocte sepulta, q̃usq̃ deū fauore Sol oīs generis optimorū studiorum clarissimus Laurentius Medices pater tuus, Magni Cosmi propago Florentinæ ciuitatis princeps exoriret. Quē &si nouimus animo & scientia gubernādi Rempub. & domi belliq̃ oīa consilio ac prudentia gerendi, tam fuisse cōpotem ut nemo ætate sua in ciuili exercitatione uideret magis laudādus, tñ ad hoc nobis eū fateri oportet commodius natū esse pinde atq̃ coelitus demissum, ut post eloquentię disciplinas & bndicendi artes a Petrarchis, Philelphis, Aretinisq̃ rhetoribus ante iuuētuti Floretinę traditas q̃ esse absq̃ cōtrouersia possent ciues cunctis nationibus exteris nitidiore scribendi ca lamo & puritate lingue ornatiores, ipse tandē patrię inserret q̃q̃ illā expultrice uitiorū sapientia & arcanorū inuestigandi rationē q̃ in libris & monumentis priscorū ad sua usq̃ tempora latuissent. Ad id prouinciæ diligēter acciuit undequaq̃ doctissimos & ueterū autorū peritissimos uiros qbus cū rerū sciētia etiā satis esset eloquētiæ, Demetriū Chalcondylen, Marsiliū Ficinū, Georgiū Vespuciū, Christophorū Landinū, Valorē, Angelū Politianum, Ioannē Picum Mirandulę comitē, cæterosq̃ orbis eruditissimos qbus antiqrum solertia & arcana uetustas malignitate casuū obliterata in luce rediret. Hoc egere summi uiri certatim. Nā docuit hic, cōmentabat alter, legerat iste, interpretatus est ille, ac linguas uertit in linguas. Marsilius Græciā duxit in Latium, Romanos in Gręciā Politianus reduxit. Instabant omnes operi, nemo non summas Medicibus laudes afferens. Hos in heroas Beatīs. LEO tuus natalis uirgula, ut aiunt, diuina fœliciter cecidit, Diīs gratia, certe ut non restaret ullum elegantioris doctrinæ genus in q̃ tu non euaseris peritior, adeo quidem puer amplexus politissimi suauitatē Politiani. Quid multis? Florentia illo æuo nihil erat floridius. In qua renascerentur optimarum artium quæ ante cecidere omnia, nihil remansit intactum de linguis & literis quo non exercerentur nobilissimi Florentini. Ea fama ego tum quidem uehementer mouebar tactus eius loci cupiditate, ac non solum magnificentissimi & insueti nobis Hercyniis ædificii auitæ domus tuæ, quam Magni Cosmi nominarunt, uerum etiam parentis tui desyderio uisendi, unde nostro seculo tanta commoda prodiissent.

On the Art of Kabbalah

This book is dedicated to His Holiness Pope Leo X, by his humble friend Johann Reuchlin

Holy Father, philosophy in Italy was once upon a time handed down to men of great intellect and renown by Pythagoras, the father of that school. But over the years it had been done to death by the Sophists' wholesale vandalism, and lay long buried in obscurity's dark night, when, by God's grace, that sun that shone on every field of liberal study, your father Lorenzo de' Medici, son of the great Cosimo, rose up the chief citizen of Florence. We knew that his natural ability for affairs of state, his knowledge of such matters, and his wise handling of war and domestic policy, were such that no man in politics was more worthy of praise than he. But it must be said that when, in addition to this, his scholarly activities are taken into account, his birth seems heaven-sent. Petrarch, Philelph, and Aretino brought the arts of oratory and fine speech to "the youth of Florence," so that there could be no disputing that her people wrote more lucidly and spoke more accurately than any other nation. But it was your father who added to Florence's store of learning—wisdom that probes into the past, wisdom that lay hidden until his day in books and memorials of past times. Zealously he brought to his country learned men from every land, men familiar with the ancient authors, whose fluency equaled their scholarship: Demetrius Chalcondyles, Marsilio Ficino, Giorgio Vespuccio, Christoforo Landino, Valla, Angelo Poliziano, Giovanni Pico della Mirandola, and others. Through them was the wisdom of the ancients, by misfortune lost or hidden, restored to the light of day. They were hard workers: one would teach, another write commentaries, one read, another interpret and translate. Marsilio put Greek into Latin; Poliziano put Latin into Greek. They were all eager, and all were greatly praised by the Medicis. And then, there among these heroes, you were born, most blessed Leo, as if some heavenly wand had been waved at the God-sent moment that would ensure your acquisition of the accomplishments of every field of the humanities—particularly since, as a boy, you were influenced by the urbane Poliziano's polished style. Say no more. Nothing flourished as did Florence then: all those dead arts were there reborn; no aspect of language or literature was left untouched by those celebrated men. The fame of such learning led me to visit Florence, not just for its magnificent palace, built by your grandfather Cosimo the Great, and quite unlike any other, but because I also wanted to see your father, the man who had given our generation so many advantages.

DE ARTE CABALISTICA

Igitur in Italiã profectus cũ illustri Eberhardo Probo Sueuorũ nostra ęta te primo Duce, cui a Secretis fiebã, intraui Florẽtiã circiter xii.Kal.Apriles Anno Christi M.cccc.lxxxii. Cũcg insignẽ Medicę gentis nobilitatẽ ei duci cõmendassem ut pro rei ueritate profecto debui, optabat cum eo sibi ui ro colloquiũ habere. Quod ubi aniaduertisset nescio q̃ reuelãte Laurẽti⁹, apphendit peregrini dexterã perqhumaniter, oẽscg nos domũ suã duxit, singula uisu digna ostendens. Primo, faberrima eqrũ stabula, deinde arma mẽtariũ oĩ apparatu bellico refertũ, post itẽ singulos thalamos ptiosissi mis auleis ornatos pulchroscg tapetas, & ĩ excelso culminis tecto arborib⁹ cõsitũ nemus, hesperidũ hortos ac aurea mala, cuius bibliothecã cũ in cœ los uscg uerbis extollerẽ, phumaniter ut solebat uirsuauissim⁹ respõdit ma iorẽ sibi thesaurũ in liberis esse q̃ in libris. Queso te Papa sanctissime, sinas me loq tecũ aliq̃to liberius infimatẽ de media plebe hoiem, Q̃ ita putas me tũ captũ admiratione cũ q̃dã insigni gaudio qñ uniuersis applaudẽtibus au diuissem ad summa te rerũ fastigia cõscẽdisse optimũ optimi sapiẽtissimicg principis diui Laurẽtii Medicis filiũ, recordabar subito tanq̃ hierophãtes aliqs paternũ illud uaticiniũ uerae prophetiae par. Quid hac ex Laurentio laurea fruticari queat, nõ modo lauretib⁹ populis sed etiã toti orbi pciosi⁹, qs maior excogitari thesaur⁹ possit q̃ sit illud tuũ ieffabile regnũ, vñ nobis oẽs diuitię tãq̃ ex Pactoli abysso fluut, oẽs gratię, oẽs optimarũ literarũ or natus, & oĩe q̃d est in humanis bonũ. Semina iecit pater uniuersę ueteris philosophię, q̃ nũc te filio in culmos surgũt, ut te regnãte nobis spicas illius metere liceat in oĩb⁹ linguis, greca, latina, hebręa, arabica, chaldaica & chal diaca, qb⁹ hoc tpe libri tuę Maiestati offerũt, & uberius oĩa pficiũt sub tua ditione q̃ sũt a parẽte tuo prudẽtissime ĩchoata. Quare cogitãs sola studiosis Pythagorica defuisse, q̃ tñ sparsim ĩ academia laurẽtiana delitescũt, credidi haud ĩgratũ tibi futurũ si & ea foro afferrẽ q̃ Pythagoras nobilescg Pytha gorei sensisse dicũt, ut tuo sœlici numie legerẽt latinis hactẽ⁹ ignota. Italię Marsili⁹ Platonẽ edidit, Galliis Aristotelẽ Ia.Faber Stapulẽsis restaurauit, Implebo numerũ & Capnion ego germanis p me renascẽte Pythagorã tuo noi dicatũ exhibebo. Id tñ abscg hebręorũ Cabala fieri nõ potuit, eo cp Py thagorę philosophia de Cabalęorũ pceptis initia duxit, q̃ patrũ memoria discedens e magna Grecia rursus in Cabalistarũ uolumia incubuit. Eruẽda igit ide fuerãt fere oĩa. Quare de arte Cabalisticã cg symbolica philosophia est scripsi, ut Pythagoreorũ dogmata studiosis fierent notiora. In qbus oĩ bus nihil affirmo, Tm ut ut opinãt infideles recito, q̃ Simonẽ Iudęũ Cabalę peritũ audituri Francofordię in unã cauponam e diuerso itinere conueni unt Philolaus iunior Pythagoreus, & Marranus Mahometista. Iam uero reiectis ĩ diuersorio sarcinulis pegrini famẽ pellere cupiẽtes horrẽt cõuiua rũ tumultuantę gregẽ, at illis post symposia tabernã deserẽtibus ita cœpit

On the Art of Kabbalah

So I set our for Italy with Eberhard Probus, first Duke of Swabia, whose private Secretary I was. I entered Florence on or about 20 March 1482. I spoke enthusiastically to my Duke about the nobility of the Medicis—in truth, I was bound to do so—and he expressed a desire to speak with Lorenzo himself. When this was brought to Lorenzo's attention—by whom, I don't know—he shook hands with us strangers in the most gentlemanly way and led the way to his palace, pointing out the sights en route. There was good stabling for the horses, a well-stocked armory, then rooms hung with precious tapestries and fine carpets, and on the highest point of the roof gable a forest of trees, like the garden of Hesperides and its golden apples. I praised his library to the skies. He replied that his treasure lay more in his children than in his books.

Holy Father, I beg leave to talk to you one day, with less restraint despite my low birth, of the admiration and joy I experienced when I heard that, unanimously approved, you had achieved the highest position—you, the best among the sons of that best and most wise prince, the saintly Cosimo de' Medici. I remembered suddenly the insight into the future your father had, prophetic vision. Fruit borne of the Laurentian laurel is most precious not just for Lorenzo's people, but for the whole world. No treasure could be richer than your reign, of which no tongue can speak. From it flow riches as water from the Pactolian depths, and the charm and graces of belles-lettres, all that is good in man. Your father sowed the seeds of ancient philosophy in his children. With his son they will grow to reach the roof tops; in your reign we shall reap the harvest in every language—Greek, Latin, Hebrew, Arabic, Chaldaic, and Chaldaean.

Your majesty is now offered books treating of all these languages, and under your direction the work your father began flourishes yet more lavishly. Having found that, except for some desultory and obscure work in the Laurentian Academy, the work of Pythagoras alone has not been touched by scholars, I thought it might give you pleasure if I brought to light the beliefs of Pythagoras and his followers, that you might enjoy unknown authors in the Latin. For Italy's part, Marsilio Ficino has published Plato, Jacob Faber of Étaples has brought out Aristotle: I shall complete the pattern and for Germany I, Capnion, shall bring out the reborn Pythagoras, with your name at its head. His philosophy, however, I have only been able to glean from the Hebrew Kabbalah, since it derives in origin from the teachers of Kabbalah, and then was lost to our ancestors, disappearing from Southern Italy into the Kabbalistic writings.

For this reason, it was almost all destined for destruction, and I have therefore written of the symbolic philosophy of the art of Kabbalah so as to make Pythagorean doctrine better known to scholars. I take no sides in all this. I tell my story as an outsider.

In my tale, two men come separately to Frankfurt in order to visit one Simon, a Jew with knowledge of Kabbalah. They meet at an inn. They are Philolaus, a young follower of Pythagoreanism, and Mar-

LIBER PRIMVS

MARRANVS. Temperaui à multis mihi uerbis in tanto murmure coepulonum indigenarum, qui nimium poti à prandio nunc abeunt, ueritus ne male audissem si quouis sermone aduena ego fremitus intercalassem eorum quos exitiosa temulentia onustos nouerim. Post uero q̃ hinc illis profectis, soli nos in isto pridem diuersorio conuenimus, ambo, ut est uidere, peregrini, & haud parum ab itinere fessi, iubeas oro cauponi, si tua mecum stat sententia, ut secundæ mensæ ferantur & bellaria minimè Sybaritica, quãdo liberiore gestu cõuiuere licet & colloqui. At ecce structores accedunt nescio quæ promentes tragemata, cum nucibus & caseo utinam bithynio & cratere incertum zythico an uinario, quanquã nobis omnium nihil monentibus. Tum PHILOLAVS haud mediocri dexteritate ait, cauponariam agit hic institor, ut qui nummis ubicq locet pedicas, etiam hospitibus addat aurita ministeria, quo plus uini obliguri re gestientibus uendat, mox enim atcq de bellariis sermo excidit, fercula præsto sunt. Nunc sane inter honesta pocula opto nobis laxiora sodalitia fore. Nam utricq me consule uultus, mi cõuiua, capiendus est nouus & lassatis membris curanda requies. Potissimum uero mihi post longam nimis & scabram uiam, durosq calles, quos hucusq sum emensus. Quid tibi sit integrum ignoro, cum de tua peregrinatione nondum factus sim certior, q̃ longinque, aut quis tu, aut undenam ueneris? E Byzantio, inq̃t ille, Constantini urbe, quam multi Nouam Romam appellant, sum enim patria Byzantianus, studio uarius, siue græce uelis, aut hebraice, seu magis latine, Arabum tamen doctrinam plus calens, & nisi molestum est, tu uicissim indicare ne recuses qui uir ipse sis. Philolaü me nominant, inq̃t iste, Alanũ natione, disciplina Pythagoreum, & fortasse haud absimilem tui linguacem, sed quod tibi erit uocabulum quæso? Cõstantinupolitani Marranum me uocat, ait ille, nomen à Cherintho & Ebione, scholasticis notum, cp̃ & aqua tinctus & recutitus apella, utrincq alioqui tam Moysi legibus q̃ Christianorum doctrina sum initiatus, scholasticos memoras audio. Philolaus ad hęc. Id rogo aũt sunt ne humanitatis scholæ Constantinopoli modo, inter istos maxime omnium crudeles & truculentissimos Thurcos? Plurimæ, inquit ille, quibus se excellentissimis ingeniis homines dediderunt. Est enim plus illic discipulorum q̃ decem millium, è Persia Græcia Latio, & Iudaismo in unis moeniis, inter q̃s cũ iam annis duo de uiginti multarum artium auditor fuerim, libuit tãdem expaciari alio, si forte uel trans alpes inuenirem studio sapientiæ præditos, qui de maximis quæstionibus copiose queant probabiliterq̃ dissertare. Tum cuiatis philosophiæ? petebat Philolaus, & Marranus, Cuiusuis retulit, cum sim nullis ipse unius disciplinę legibus astrictus, quo minus ne secta quidem fidei libere quicq̃d sensero defendere prohibeor. Certe par habes mecũ

B

Book One

ranus, a Moslem. Depositing their luggage at the inn, the travelers want a meal, but shudder at the riotous jollity of the crowd there and leave the taproom once they have dined. They begin a conversation.

MARRANUS: I refrained from saying very much with all those boisterous locals around us. Now they are leaving after lunch, but they have had too much to drink, and I was afraid of rough treatment if a stranger like me were to break in when they were so befuddled. But they have gone now; we have been the only people here for some time. If you wish, do call the landlord and have the tables laid nicely, and some not too extravagant dessert brought. Then we can relax and talk. But look! The waiters are bringing sweets and nuts and cheese — I hope it's Bithynian — and a jug with beer or wine in it, I'm not sure which. And we haven't ordered anything at all.

PHILOLAUS: This landlord knows his business. If there's any money about he'll trap it; that's why we're getting this attentive service. If we want to splash out more money on wine, he'll provide it. You mentioned dessert — right away here it is. Now I'd like to drink and settle down. I think we both need to wash and change and rest our weary limbs. I do at any rate. It's been a long hard journey. But perhaps you are feeling fresher — I have no idea. Tell me about your journey. How long was it? Who are you and where do you come from?

MARRANUS: I come from Byzantium, the city of Constantine, which a lot of people call New Rome. That's my home town, I have studied Greek, Hebrew, and Latin, but my strong point is Arabic studies. But, if you don't mind, who, may I ask, are you?

PHILOLAUS: My name is Philolaus. By nationality I am an Alan,[1] by persuasion a Pythagorean. I think I am just about able to match your linguistic abilities. What is your name?

MARRANUS: In Constantinople I am known as Marranus; the name comes from Cherinth and Ebion, and is well known among the scholastics. I have been both baptized and circumcized, and am equally schooled in the Law of Moses and in Christian teachings.

PHILOLAUS: I note that you mention the scholastics. Tell me, are there schools of the Humanities in Constantinople — among all those grim and bloodthirsty Turks?

MARRANUS: Plenty, and they have produced some excellent scholars. There are more than ten thousand students there, from Persia, Greece, Latium, and Jewry, all in the one university. Over eighteen years I have studied many subjects there, and have finally decided to travel elsewhere to see if I can find north of the Alps famous men of learning with whom to discuss my many subjects of investigation.

PHILOLAUS: What, then, is your philosophy?

MARRANUS: None in particular. I am not bound by the rules of any school of thought. I do not want to be prevented by the constraints of any sectarianism from freely defending what my conscience allows.

DE ARTE CABALISTICA

Philolaus inquit ut uideo explorandi desyderium. Nam ad Germanorū nobile hoc emporium Francofordiense migrantibus è Thracia mercatoribus comitem me iunxi, ϙ acceperim hic esse Iudæum magnæ in opera Cabalistica famæ, ac ingentis existimationis, quæ una facultas (ut sepe audiui doctissimos homines suaui ocio & consiliis uberrimis affluentes me præsente arbitrari) præ cæteris esse queat philosophiæ Pythagoricæ cognatior tanquam nihil similius. Nam esse Pythagoram omnia ferme dogmata istinc expiscatum aiunt. Iudæo illi Simon esse nomen perhibēt Eleazari filio ex antiqua Iochaicorum prosapia, quem nunc remotis mensis adoriri stat sententia. Ego uero, inquit Marranus, si per te licet tecum ipse uirum accedam, tametsi Pythagorica parum edoctus, semp eru mihi Arabes magis uenerationi fuere Algazel Alpharabius, Abucaten, Hali, Abumaron, Abensina, quem latini Auicennam & Abenrust quem Auerroem uocant, & reliqui consimiles peripatetici. Quanquam nemini unquam mea ætate negatum fuit Constantinopoli qualemcunq singularum prope linguarum atq sectarum philosophiam cōsequi maxime dissimilium gentium præceptoribus in dies publice docentibus, Tum Philolaus, Confide, nam facile, inquit, Pythagoreus sit qui & libenter uerbo credit, & pro tēpore tacere potest, & omnia præcepta intellectualiter intelligit, At ille, astabo saltem ubi patieris tanquam Pythagoreus aliqs & audiam quâ de re sermo inter uos fiat. Itaq inenarrabili gaudio delibutum me reddes cum per magni æstimauero in conuersatione sapientū fuisse. Et Alanus, Veniam⁹ ait, nam in pomario domi eius in qua habitat deambulare nūc solus dicitur, ac certe hic loci est, & ostium patet. Cernis ne istum ex horto nos uersus incedentem, Age maturius ingrediamur, Salue magister. Cui Simon de more gentis, Dominus uobiscū. Tu ne Simon ille Iudæus? rogat aduenæ, Tum is, Vtruq, nam & Iudæus sum & Simon. Quæ aūt noīa uestri amborum accipiā? quo rectius uos alloquar. Vterq ad id, Ego Philolaus, & ego Marranus responderūt, ac diuersis itineribus alter alterius nesciens, post longā peregrinationē huc tandē cō uenimus, qs non hoc emporiū tam late iminens tanto cōmeatu prope toti Europæ decantatū, ac tot & tam pciosis mercibus illustres nundinæ, tam diuersarū gentiū confluxu speciosę ad sui contemplationem traxerūt, sed unius tui fama pduxit ea cupiditate, ut nobis de omni Cabalistica ratione magnoq ut doctis uisum est & colenda & expetenda, nobiles illas & tam in Scythia q̄ in Thracia cōmendatas ingenti laude cogitationes tuas breuiter & cōmode aperires. Ad hęc. Est ne Simon, inqt, memoria nostri etiā apud Scythas & Thracas gentē tam longinquā. Est profecto, ait, uterq multo maxima, Nam abhinc ante triennium circiter quatuor lustra qñ tpe illo supputabant uestri a mundi exordio post quintum millenariū annos ducentos octo & triginta pulsi ex Hispania Iudæorum centena quatuor

On the Art of Kabbalah

PHILOLAUS: Then your thirst for new fields of enquiry equals mine. I came to Frankfurt, this great German entrepôt, in the company of some merchants from Thrace because I had heard that here there was a Jew known for his work in Kabbalah and highly thought of on that account. This kind of knowledge most nearly approaches Pythagorean teaching, or so I am given to understand by scholars when they have the time for discussion and are in an expansive mood. They say that Pythagoras derived most of his ideas from this source. This Jew's name is Simon ben Eleazar, of the old Jochaicean[2] family. When we have finished eating, I would like to pay him a visit.

MARRANUS: I too would like to see him, if that's all right with you, though I hardly know anything about Pythagorean teachings. The Arab philosophers were more my special interest — Algazel, Alpharabi, Abucaten, Hali, Abumaron, Abensina (you will know him as Avicenna), Abenrust (that is, Averroes), and other peripatetics like them. I am ignorant in spite of the intellectual tolerance and opportunities available at Constantinople.

PHILOLAUS: Don't worry. It's easy enough. The Pythagorean is he who gives credence to what is said, remains silent to begin with, and understands all the precepts.

MARRANUS: If you will allow me, I shall stand around as if I were one of the converted, within earshot of the discussion. You have no idea how much pleasure this would give me. I very much appreciate being present when men of learning converse.

PHILOLAUS: Let's go. They say that at this time of day he walks in the orchard at his house. Here we are; the gate is open. Isn't that him, coming towards us from the garden? Come on, in we go. Good day, sir.

SIMON: The Lord be with you. (This is the customary greeting among Simon's people.)

PHILOLAUS: Are you Simon the Jew?

SIMON: I am both. I am a Jew and I am Simon. What am I to call you two? I wish to address you correctly.

PHILOLAUS AND MARRANUS: I am Philolaus. I am Marranus. We have just arrived here after long journeys, separate ones. We didn't know each other before. We didn't come here because this city is a great trading center, though Frankfurt is known throughout Europe, nor for the fine market in precious goods, nor because of the huge influx of population here. No, it is just news of you that brings us, for we should like you to explain to us the philosophical method of Kabbalah. Scholars speak of it as something to be sought after and cultivated. Lay your thoughts open to us, briefly and simply; they are praised in Scythia and Thrace.

SIMON: Do people really know of me as far away as that?

PHILOLAUS: They are well aware of you in both places. About twenty-three years ago (in 5238 according to your way of calculating from the Creation[3]), 420,000 Jews were expelled from Spain. They

LIBER PRIMVS

& uigīti millia, indeq̃ discriminatim illorum maxima pars ad loca nostra exules profecti, multam in te homine sibi ut affirmant perq̃ notissimo artium disciplinam, multas literas, incredibile ingenii acumē, & philosophici sermonis expeditam integritatē, p̃sertim quocq̃ Cabalisticæ speculationis diuinam peritia, & uniuersis auditoribus admirabilē inesse p̃dicant, ita ut in oīm oculis discendi cupidorum ultra Sauromatas & glaciales fulgeas Oceanum. Sup̃ quo suscepit ille. Tanta de me uestra existimatio uiri Pythagorei, non mediocrem rubore mihi affert, qui uereor ne si iudiciū hoc uestrū ex populari rumusculo conceptū frustrer aut fallam, q̃ tumuis id contingat fragilitate mea, ipse uidear in tam diuinū Cabalẹ studiū prope mea ignauia dolenda iniuria cōmisisse, quo plane quicqd in me langui dum, fractum & impfectum dep̃henderitis, id in huius sapientiẹ qua desy deratis quandā uergat ignominia, quasi opificis defectus tendere debeat in artis indignitatem, id q̃d minime omnium uelim. Nam ego ipse q̃ tuluscunq̃ sim qui scio q̃ sim exiguus aut mecū cæteri Cabalistẹ oēs quicqd uero esse putentur, laudati si uultis an despecti mitto dicere, tn̄ hac cōtemplandi arte nihil est hoīm generi usq̃ua qui humi degūt, & præ aliis egregie pollent ingenio ac mente florent, a deo collatum expetibilius, nihil ad salutē animorū cōmodius, nihil ad immortalitatē cōsequenda aptius, quo congruēter naturẹ mens humana propinquus ad deificationē ascēdat, hoc est ad beatitudinis summū, q̃d telos græci dicūt, siue id uobis extremū aut ultimū uocare placuerit seu finẹ, unde cōtingat, nihilo indigētes, absolute, semp absq̃ impedimēto fortunate, tranq̃lle, fœliciter uiuere, cū artificiose admodū p̃ q̃uedā symbola terrenis oībus reiectis, semotacq̃ rerū materia, formā e forma decerpserimus, q̃uscq̃ ad prima oīformē & informem ascēderim⁹ formā. De q̃ intelligūt Cabalistẹ diuinū geneseos hūc iussum, producat terra aīam uiuentē ad speciē suā, scilicet ad diuina Idea, q̃ & ipsa est terra uiuētiū in uirtute dei uiui ea uita influetis p nomē Adonai, ut cognoscatis, autore Iosue, cp̃ deus uiuus intra uos est, & disperdet in cōspectu uestro cōtrarias fortitudines. Hẹc in libri שַׁעַר אוֹרָה i. Porta lucis inscripti cap. ii. legūt. Quo fit ut oīa uitẹ habētia suo instinctu sursum tendāt, & oīa uita influētia uergāt deorsum. Cū n. in isto mūdo sensibili q̃cqd elemētis quatuor cōstat מוּרְכָּב i. mistū, id oē aut aīa careat diuersi et uagi mot⁹ effectrice, ceu iacēs imobiliter & q̃scēs, ut lapis & ferrū, aut uegetet & crescat ut plāta & herba, aut multifaria dimoueat, progrediat̃ & tn̄ uiuat ut aīantia bruta & cōchæ, aut etiā rōnaliter loquat̃ ut hō, q̃ solet adulescētes nr̃i de libro רוּחַ חַן i. sp̃us grẹ sic hebraice notanda discere הָרוּמָם הַצּוֹמֵחַ הַחַי וְהַמְדַבֵּר i. Iacens, pullulans, uiuens, & loquens, nihil p̃fecto eorum est q̃d intentum cœlo se nō modo q̃da arrigat q̃si eo cōspectu q̃uedam sibi uirtutis suẹ usuq̃ gliscens, & mores fingēs, ut altissimos terrẹ motes cœlū uers⁹, ab imis uallibus exurgere

B ii

Book One

scattered in all directions, but some of these exiles came to us. They assured us that there was much one could learn from you in the arts. Your wide knowledge of letters, your keen mind, and useful clarity of expression, and not least your ability in the field of Kabbalistic speculation, excite universal admiration. In the eyes of those who long for learning you are a guiding light.

SIMON: Dear Pythagoreans, you think so highly of me and credit me with such powers that I fear I may not live up to this popular reputation, and if through inadequacy I fail, I may do grave harm to the divine discipline that I wish to further. The last thing I could want is that my uninspired imperfections should discredit, in your minds, the wisdom you seek — as if the artist's fault should strip art of its value. However good I may be (and I know I am not very good), or however good are my colleagues in Kabbalah (meriting praise or contempt, as you will), this I know — that God has given to men who walk upon the earth nothing they could more desire than this contemplative art, and that Kabbalists more than others possess robust intellects and fertile minds; and that nothing admits more of the search for salvation in this world, and everlasting life in the next. It is by these means that the mind of man, so far as nature allows, achieves that Godlike state which is the zenith of Blessedness. (The Greeks call it *telos* — you could use the words "far point," "the ultimate" or "end.") In that state man's life lacks nothing; it is a life of absolute, unimpeded blessedness: by means of symbolism, all earthly things are thrown away, and the stuff of matter is cast off; we strip Form from Form, until we reach the primal Form, that is both the Form of all things and yet without Form. In this way, so the Kabbalists believe, did God conceive his command at the Creation, when he said: "Let the earth bring forth living creatures after their kind" — that is, "in accordance with the divine Idea." Thus the very world of living things exists by virtue of the living God, who in his name, *Adonai,* flows through all life, and so we understand Joshua's phrase: "The living God is among you, and will scatter in your sight the forces massed against you." And in the second chapter of *The Gate of Light* is written: "Hence it is that all that has life tends upwards by instinct, and all that influences life falls from on high." In our world of the senses, the things in which the four elements are mixed are either quite lifeless and unable to cause motion, and so lie still (as iron and stone), or they are alive and grow (plants, for example), or their movements are many and various and they develop, and actually live, as do brute beasts and shellfish. They may even be able to talk rationally. Our young men learn the names of these groupings, derived from the book, *Spirit of Grace.* These are "Lying," "Sprouting," "Living," and "Speaking." There is not one member of these classes that, being set toward heaven, does not thereby stimulate itself in some way by that sight, longing for some use to be made of its own particular characteristics and developing new patterns of behavior, as we see happening to the highest hills of the earth. From the deepest valleys they rise, turned toward heaven. As the Psalmist says: "The mountains are risen up and the plains sink low."

DE ARTE CABALISTICA

cernimus, iuxta Psaltę carmē. Ascēdūt mōtes & descēdūt cāpi, ut expimur in altum procellas maris erigi, ut ascendit mare fluctuans in Ezechiele, ut flatus aeris è cauernis exuperare sentimus. Nam & naturæ dominus in illo eodem propheta erumpere facit spiritum tempestatum, ut deniq̃ oīa ignea leuari uidemus. Ascendit enim ignis de petra in Iudiciū uolumine. Ita uiri præstantes quæ uestra ingenii uis est, intelligitis quadam necessitate coactos fateri nos quanto quæq̃ res nobiliore natura extat, tanto eam adeptione sublimiori gaudere, ceu granum frumenti iactatum in terram q̃d non quiescit donec glebæ uiscera fragat, & extra telluris meatus suspiciat & cœlesti aura fruatur. Eadem est ratio in metallicis quoq̃ cum id q̃d generosius est in altiores spiritus ebullit ab alkimia sublimatum, ut puriora semper ea uideantur quę sunt sublimiora. Sic quæ apud inferos esse dicuntur lurida & squalentia, sordibusq̃ depressa iudicamus, quæ apud superos cādida & illustria incredibiliq̃ decore ornata miramur, & p̄conio laudum prosequimur. Quanto magis oīm opinione cum solers natura rebus iacentibus, uegetantibus, spirantibus ingenia talia ingignat ut altiora petant, profecto non uidetur ea hoīem neglexisse omnium animantiū dominatorem, animal decorum & uenerandum, animal nobilissimum, cæteris præfectum, non modo prudens & sapiens, uerum & contemplatiuū & religionis capax, quin melioribus & sanctioribus ipsum dotibus ornauerit, & p̄sertim id generis donauerit conditione, ut ex insito sibi naturæ desyderio quibuscunq̃ possit uiribus ad summa & optima tendat. Hominem enim melior natura deus ut extat sacratissima historia ex duobus composuit limo terræ & spiraculo uitæ, ut limo indutus corporea prudēter curet, & spiraculo uitæ p̄ditus, sapienter amet diuina, producatq̃ terra animam uiuentem ad speciem suam atq̃ propriam, uidelicet illam peculiarem Ideam, non brutorum, non plantarum, non lapidum aut lignorum, sed ab ore dei natam, & in faciem eius diuino spiritu afflatam mentis

H suæ ipsam illuminationem. Hęc illa est quę paulo ante a nobis uocabatur deificatio, cum ab obiecto præsente per medium suum exterior sensus transit in sensionem interiorem, & illa in imaginationem, & imaginatio in existimationem, & existimatio in rationem, & ratio in intellectum, & intellectus in mentem, & mens in lucem, quæ illuminat hominem, & illumi-

I natum in se corripit. Hinc recte acceptum esse apparet cp̃ Cabalistæ in arbore decem numerationum Thiphereth μικρόκοσμον in medio Sephiroth ponendum censuerūt, magnum illum Adam quasi lignum uitæ in medio Idealis paradisi, aut quasi lineam rectam, ut aiunt, mediam. Fecit enim deus hominem rectum Ecclesiasti regio tam ad supera q̃ad infera flexibilem, ut per Empedoclis litem & amicitiam in numerationibus illis subter notatam quæ designantur per צחצח והוד humana se cogitatione agnoscat elementorum & mundani huius regni esse participem. Timo-

On the Art of Kabbalah

Similarly we may witness the rising up of storms out at sea, the heavy sea in Ezekiel, and feel blasts of wind funneling up words from caves. According to the same prophet, the Lord of Nature caused the spirit of the storm to break forth. Then too we see that all flames rise. In the book of Judges fire rises from rock. Men as obviously intelligent as you will understand that we have to acknowledge that the more noble the subject matter the more it benefits from higher attainment. Like a grain of corn sown in the ground, it does not rest until it has broken through the topsoil, stretching above ground and enjoying the fresh air. Similarly with metals; for the finer metals bubble up to form superior vapors, when drawn out by the art of alchemy. So whatever is higher is seen as being purer.

In this way everything in the world below is said to be yellowed, stiff with filth, weighed down with dirt, while in the world above we can only marvel at the gleaming whiteness, the shine, and the unbelievable appearance of things, and join in its praise by telling it abroad. How much more are we driven to this belief when we see how careful nature has planted in things that lie, grow and breathe, the instinct to reach upward. Clearly she has not neglected man, the master of all living things, a handsome animal, worthy of respect, the noblest animal, leading all the others, not just wise and knowledgeable, but capable of contemplation and religious feeling. Surely man has been endowed well and holily, and above all given the condition of his race, in which he reaches out for the highest and best with all the strength of which he is able. In making man, God went one better than nature, as is told in the holy story, and fashioned him out of the dust of the earth and the breath of life. And so in his garment of mud, man takes care of his bodily needs, and with the breath of life he wisely loves divine things. Out of dust God forms a living soul in his very own image (that is, in accordance with the idea peculiar to himself), born not of brute beasts, nor of plants, nor of stones or trees, but from the mouth of God, whose spirit breathed into his face his mind's enlightenment.

This is what used to be called "deification," when exterior sense passes from the immediate object to the inner sense, and that passes to the imagination, imagination to thought, thought to reason, reason to understanding, understanding to reflection, and reflection to the light which enlightens man and clasps to itself that enlightenment. This seems to have been correctly observed by the Kabbalists, who thought that the Beauty of the physical world should be placed in the middle of the tree by which the ten sephiroth are numbered, being that great Adam[4] who is like the tree of life in the midst of an ideal paradise, or as they say, like the straight line, the median.

For God made man upright according to royal Ecclesiastes, to enable him to attend both to the world above and to the world below. He intended man to realize by native wit that he is part both of the elements and of this worldly kingdom, as is shown by the strife and friendship of which Empedocles spoke—the same qualities are denoted in the Sephirot by the words *Netzah* and *Hor*.

LIBER PRIMVS

re autem dei & sanctificatione per פחד וחסר quæ supra eum expandūtur, trium simplicissimæ deitatis notionum כתר חכמה בינה pro suo captu apprehēsiuum. Igitur ad id natus est homo, & ad hoc eum natura finxit atq; formauit, ut & pedibus cum bestiis ambulet in terra, & solus ex omnibus animantibus erecto capite cum angelis in coelo couersetur. Manus autem utrasq; inter pedes & caput locatas, tum ad uictum necessarium laborādo figat in tellurem, tum ad uitam æthernam contemplādo leuet in coelum, ad quarum tutelam oculorum orbes soli ex omnium sensuum instrumentis homini motabiles inditi sunt, ut in terram pro corporis, & in coelum pro animi conspiciāt salute. Talis est aptitudo atq; uis hominis, hæc facultas, hæc potentia, quam non implantauerit utiq; siue deus seu natura, nisi facultas in usum, & potentia quandoq; redigeretur in actum, præsertim in homine industrio & ad id se præparante. Si enim captus ille diuinitatis non esset homini possibilis, frustra de syderiū eius natura ingenuisset, homo nanq; agilis & idoneus haud unq; corporeorum sensu & rudi coemetorum tactu satiatur, quin & omni cogitatione ad separatorum puritatem & altissimarum rerum cognitionem prouehatur. Ea est plane cunctorum studiosorum irrequietudo, quibus & uehemēs animi applicatio per morales, naturales & mathematicas ueritates, ad supernaturalium dispositionem agnascitur, & tandem ad primam entitatem fidelis ascensus indulgetur. Verbi causa. Luculentissimū procul igne exardescere uidetis, intenditur forma eius per illustre mediū quod græci appellant diaphanon, usq; ad oculum corporeum. Expectat intra spiritualis uisio & obiectæ rei propriæ formā suā esse percipit, qua re ipsam ceu affinem ac propinquam libenter hospitio suscipit, & per medium apparentiæ quæ a uobis dicitur græce phantasia, spiritualiter iudicio sensitiuo ac brutali offert, quam quidem effigiem rursus ad iudicium humanum superne producit, & paulo superius totum illud ad ipsam rationem promouet, tum ea tandem post agilem discursum, ita sublimatam & cribratam corporalis ignis abstractionem transfert ad intellectum. In isto igitur ascensu tres inueniuntur regiones, & in singulis unus abstractionis status. In prima regione obiectum, diaphanon, sensus exterior, & ibi statur. In secunda interior sensus, phantasia, iudicium brutum, & secundo statur. In tertia, iudicium humanum, ratio, intellectus, & tertio statur. Horum oīm domina mēs, recepto lumine supiori, hois intellectū illustrat & perficit. Ec quid aliud opinabimur Cabalistas, de Sechel, Sandalphon, & Mettattron docuisse; Status aūt quilibet duplice habet differētiam. In primo eī cessat corpus, & incipit aīa, vn noīatur aīal. In secundo, cessat aīa, & incipit ratio, unde nominatur homo. In tertio, cessat intellectiua potentia, & incipit mens, q̄ sola sine controuersia deforis aduenit, unde noīatur

B iii

Book One

But through the fear of God, and the hallowing of him, by the fear and loving-kindness spread out over him, man can apprehend God in His simplicity through these three methods: Crown, Wisdom, and Understanding.[5]

This then is the end of man, to which nature formed and made him: to walk like the animals with his feet on the ground, but alone of all the creatures to hold discourse, head held high, with the angels in heaven. His hands are positioned between his feet and his head to enable him both to work the land for his essential food, and to lift them in contemplation to heaven, towards eternal life. To protect his hands, his eyes have been made mobile, unlike the other sense organs, to enable him to survey the earth, to help in looking after the needs of his body, and to survey the heavens for the needs of his soul. This is the ability Man has been given, his strength, the power he wields, and neither God nor nature would have given it to him if the ability were not to be used nor the power translated into action, particularly in a man who works hard and prepares himself for it. If man were incapable of achieving godliness, then in vain would nature have given him the yearning for it, for any man with a lively mind will never be satisfied with physical sensations or the feel of raw syncretic matter. All his thinking will bear him away to the purity of a separate world and the cognition of the highest things. Hence the restlessness of all scholars. For when they apply themselves to morality, and the truths of mathematics and natural sciences, then they realize their longing for the supernatural and allow themselves to give their assent to the Primal Entity.

To take an example: you see a bright fire some distance away: you view its shape through a lucent shimmer, called *diaphane* by the Greeks; and the shape finally reaches your physical eye. You receive it with your spiritual visual sense and perceive the shape to be that of the original object itself — you welcome it gladly as a near relation. By means of its "appearance" — *phantasia,* as you say in Greek — it is submitted by the spirit to the judgment of the brute senses; then the image is led to judgment again, human judgment, higher on the scale; then it moves a little higher to reason itself, and now finally, after this swift process, a refined and sifted abstraction of the actual fire is brought before the intellect.

These then are the three regions to be found on this ascent, with some state of abstraction belonging to each. In the first region are the object, the "shimmer," and the outward sense. In the second are the inner sense, the appearance, and the brute judgment. In the third are human judgment, reason, and intellect. The mind is mistress of all of these, since with light from above it illumines and makes complete man's intellect. This is what the Kabbalists taught on Sechel, Sandalphon, and Mettattron.[6] The states, however, differ in two ways here. In the first state the body stops and the soul *(anima)* takes over; this is called "animal." In the second, the soul stops and reason takes over; this is called "man." In the third, reason stops and mind takes over; mind alone, unrestricted, can leave man behind; this is called

DE ARTE CABALISTICA

Deus, iuxta oraculum, Ego dixi dii estis. Statuũ itaq̃ nomina sunt sensus,
N iudicium & intellectus. Interuallorum aũt media, ipsas species deferentia
sunt diaphanon, phantasia & ratio, cui rei haud absimile proferũt in Mer
caua Cabalistæ tres patres, qui sunt Abraham superior, Ishac inferior, Ia
cob medius. Cum igitur trium regionum duo interualla sensus & iudiciũ
duplicantur secundum inferius & superius, & utraq̃ ad binos reducũtur
terminos, restãt decem scalæ gradus per quos ad cognitionem omnium
O quæ sunt uere aut sensu, aut scientia, aut fide ab imo ad summum ascẽde
re possumus. De quo Abraham Cabalista in libro mirabili letzira sic ait

עשר ספירות בלימה ׃ לא טי ׃ ולא יא הבן
בחכמה וחכם, בבינה בחון בהם וחקור מהם
והעמד דבר על בוריו והשב יוצר מבוצו

Id est. Decem numerationes præter quid, decem & non nouem, decẽ &
non undecim. Intellige in sapientia & sape in intellectu, inuestiga in eis, &
proba ex eis, & statue rem sup puritates suas, & repone creatorẽ in thro
num suum, hactenus ita. Intellectus enim humanus quæ supra sunt intel
ligit in sapientia, & quæ infra sunt sapit in intelligentia. Et sensus exterior
statuit rem ab obiecto per species oblatam, & sensus interior statuit rem
super puritates, id est abstractiones specierum, quæ ante fuerant diapha
no ac demum phantasiæ sunt peculiares. Deinde iudicium inter phanta
siam & rationem, inuestigat ex eisdem apparẽtiis, & ratio discursu uario
conclusioneq̃ probat in eis. Tunc redeo ad initium & dico, q̃ intellectus
creatorẽ ut causam, omnium causarum primam reponit in thronũ suũ
quæ est ipsa mens שבל הפועל Habetis itaq̃ uiri solertissimi de
cem numerationes quibus homini contingit rerum apprehensio, q̃ sunt
obiectum, diaphanon, sensus exterior, sensus interior, phantasia, iudicium
inferius, iudiciũ superius, ratio & intellectus, & hæc omnia non tam sunt
P quid, q̃ quo. Suprema uero mens in homine aliud quid est. Quapropter
sicut deus in mũdo, ita mens in homine inter decem Sephiroth regni ge
rit diadema, & recte cognoĩatur כתר id est corona, quæ ut Aristote
les asserit in secundo de generatione animalium libro. Sola diuina est &
sola extrinsecus homini accedit, à cuius lumine recepto, uirtutes infe
riores diriguntur & gubernantur עד השבל והמשכיל
והמושבל אחד Id est, quousq̃ intellectus intelligens & intelle
ctum sint unum et idem, ut scribit Cõmentator arboris decem Sephiroth
q̃d magistri sup uerbis Prophete, In lumine tuo uidebimus lumen ita
diiudicarunt, כי בשפע השבל אשר שפע ממך
נשביל ונתישר Hoc est, q̃ in influentia mentis quæ influit ex te
intelligimus & rectificamur. Puto iam esse patefactum omnibus qui natu
ræ hu

"God," in accordance with the prophecy: "I have said that ye are Gods."

The names of these states then are sense, judgment, and intellect. The states are identified by the intervening media: *diaphane*, appearance, and reason. These are not altogether dissimilar to the three fathers of Kabbalah in Merkavah[7]: Abraham above, Isaac below, and Jacob between. The two intervals between the three regions, sense and judgment, are doubled accordingly as they are higher or lower, and each can be reduced to two end points. There remain to be found the ten rungs of the ladder on which we climb to know all truth, be it of the senses or of knowledge, or of faith; from bottom to top we climb.

Abraham writes on this matter in his marvellous book on the Creation: "There are ten sephiroth, without which nothing—ten, not nine; ten, not eleven. Understand them in wisdom, be wise as to them in understanding; search among them, prove from them; order things according to their purity and reinstate the Creator on his throne." So, the human intellect understands in its wisdom the things that are above, and is wise in its understanding about what is below. The outer sense orders what is brought to it from the object by means of what is seen, and the inner sense orders things with respect to their purity (i.e., the abstractions of what is seen), which formerly were particular to the *diaphane* and *phantasia*. Judgment, coming between the *phantasia* and reason, investigates these same manifestations, and reason examines them using various arguments and conclusions. Now I shall go back to the beginning and assert that intellect reinstates the Creator, the prime cause of all causes, on his throne, which is mind itself (active understanding). So, my friends, there you have ten sephiroth by which man apprehends things: the object, the *diaphane,* outer sense, inner sense, *phantasia,* lower judgment, higher judgment, reason, and intellect. These are not the "what" so much as the "how" of acting. The highest thing in man—mind—is something else again. Just as God wears the Crown in the kingdom of the world, so is the mind of man chief among the ten sephiroth, and so it is rightly called "The Crown," as Aristotle says in book 2 in his *Growth of Animals.* It alone is divine and it alone can rise beyond man. The lower powers are directed and governed by it.

"The intellect, the intelligent, and the object of the intellect are one and the same," as the commentator on the tree of the ten sephiroth writes, where he states that the rabbis interpreted the words of the prophet: "In your light we shall see light" as meaning: "In the flood of understanding that flows from You, we have understanding and are put right."

I think it is now clear to anyone who has studied human nature, firstly that by natural yearnings we are led, or more accurately, drag-

LIBER PRIMVS   IIII.

ræ humanæ conditionem diligenter scrutati sunt, primo ⫷ desyderio na
turali ducimur, uel si rectius libet dicere trahimur ad apprehendendū res
summas & diuinas. Secūdo,⫷ eas quantum ad nostram beatitudinē satis
est, data opera pro modo & captu nostro apprehendere possumus, ad al
terum nos inclinat natura, ad alterum diuinitas, utrū⫷ per ignis figuram
sursum tendentis, & omnia quodam modo comphendentis & lambētis
artificiose a Cabalistis demonstratum. De quo Rabi Ioseph Castilien.
in horto nucis lib. secūdo iter cętera, his uerbis ait.
נפש השכלית הנאצלת באדם ומציירת בו
צורת עליונה Id est. Scias, quia anima intellectiua infusa in ho
minem, & repsentans in eo formam supmam, ipsa uocatur ignis. Cui ap
plicat Salomonis illud. Lucerna dei spiritus hominis. Vt plane tn satear
id quod uerum esse tum ratio probat, tum exercitationis confirmat expe
rimentum, non paucis oportet artibus, non ualde minutis humanorū stu
diorum scientiis, non leui doctrina eum prius instructum esse, cuius indu
stria promptitudo & ingenium ad formarum separatarum ac simpliciū
mundi superioris & intelligibilis substantiarum contemplatione ita man
suescat, ut in ipsa ferme dei penetralia irrepat. Ante omnia nan⫷ pruden
tium uirorum ethicis & bonis moribus eruditos esse nos conuenit, ut tur
pia uitemus sequamur honesta. Quod Ecclesiastes admonuit. Custodi pe
dem tuum cum iueris ad domum dei, quia Ethan Ezraita in eruditiōe sic
psallit. Iusticia & iudicium præparatio sedis eius. Quo carmine non tantū
opera hoium quæ ipsa debent iusticia perfici, uerum etiam & cogitatio
nes cordis & oris uerba complectitur, ⫷ recto iudicio constare oportet.
Quare una uoce ac consimili sensu tradunt Cabalistæ. כי במשך
אחר התאוה לבד כמו הסכלים יבטלו
התשוקות העיוניות Id est. Q: indulgendo concupiscentiæ
at⫷ libidini tm ut faciunt stulti corrumpuntur desyderia speculationum
Post mores ita⫷ compositos & animum purgatum (taceo quidem nūc
pene infinitas siue recte seu uere aut bene loquendi regulas, quæ solum
uestibula & fores scientiarum sunt, non aūt sciētiæ) tum opus erit mathe
maticis & physicis quæ innumerabilia complectuntur, Arabum & Græ
corum & Latinorum ubi⫷ uoluminibus comphensa, uel de uniuerso nu
mero pondere & mensura. Vel de omni motu & quiete rebus essentiali
ter inhærente quam dicunt naturam. Est enim natura ut Rabi Iuda Ben
Leui scribit in libro Alcozer. התחלה והסבה אשר בה
ינוח רצוע הדבר אשר הוא בו בעצם ולא
במקרה Id est, Principium & causa qua quiescit & mouetur res
in qua est per se, & non per accidens. In hac terminatione uidetis quantꝰ

                                                          B iiii

ged, towards the understanding of the highest things of the divine; and secondly, that with help, we are able to understand these things enough to achieve our own state of blessedness, to the extent of our ability. That nature turns us one way and the divine the other has been cleverly shown by the Kabbalists with their image of fire reaching upwards and licking and devouring everything in some way. On this, Rabbi Joseph of Castile mentions in his book, *The Nut Garden:* "You should know that because the understanding spirit is infused in men and represents the perfect form within him, it is itself called fire." Solomon's words can be applied here: "The torch of God is the spirit of man."

I must make clear one thing, the truth of which is shown by reason and confirmed by experience. It requires a good deal of skill, a minute knowledge of the humanities, and much hard learning for eagerness and intelligence to accustom a man to the contemplation of the separate Forms and the simple substances of the intelligible world above sufficiently for him to creep into God's own sanctuary. First we need to know the ethics and morality of sensible people, so that we avoid base behavior, aiming for integrity. As Ecclesiastes warned: "Guard your steps when you enter God's house"; and Ethan the Ezraite wrote the song "Justice and Judgment are before his seat."[8] This hymn refers not only to the justice of a man's actions, but also to the thoughts in his heart and the words of his mouth. Hence the concurring opinion of the Kabbalists, that: "Indulging your lust, your evil inclinations, as do the stupid, destroys the desire for speculation." Once one's morals have been put in order, and the mind cleansed (here I say nothing on the regulation of correct, truthful, or good speech, which is only the gateway to knowledge, its entrance hall, not knowledge itself), then one must study mathematics and physics in all their many branches, in Arabic, Greek, and Latin texts, taking in all numbers, weights and measures, and all there is on the subject of motion and rest—the essential states, as they say, of nature. On nature, Rabbi Judah Halevi writes in his book, *Alcozer:* "The principal cause of motion and rest is in things themselves; it does not come about by accident."

In this mapping-out of the subject, you see its extent, the nature of the task, how huge, how unbounded it is. In our investigation of

DE ARTE CABALISTICA

& quales quot & q̃ interminatæ res congerutur, ut ferè sint omnia nobis
T   suscipienda naturam inuestigantibus, q̃ a supremo cœlo ad infimum ter
    ræ centrum continentur, siue suo nitantur robore ac substent, seu q̃ quo
    modo se habentia innitant & accidant, ut non tota ętate hominis uel ipsa
    nomina singularũ inueniri taceo proprietates, conditiones, uires, mores
    & operationes queant, propter eorum q̃ scire cupimus prope infinitatẽ
    & uirtutis nostræ rationalis capacitatem, & rerum inuestigandarũ diffi
    cultatem, & humanæ potentię fragilitatem, & desyderii nostri multiplicẽ
    distractionem. Quid enim? nonne Abrahæ dictum fuit, Suspice cœlum
    & numera stellas si potes, nec potuit ipse, quanq̃ suo tempore secun du
    Rambam insignis astrologus erat. Vnde tradũt Cabalistę q̃ כל מה
    שבשמים לא ידע האדם דבר ממנו אלא בזה
    השעור הלמודי המעט .i. Omne id quod in cœlis est non
V   scit homo aliq̃d ex eo, nisi ad ipsum modum Matheseon seu disciplinarũ
    usq̃ adeo modicum. Quorũ hoc dicto admoneor, multa errasse ueteres
    in Mathematicis, etiam in quibus illi totam penè uitam, ut mos est studio
    sorum, contriuere. Quod in suis recordatur scriptis Abubacher posteris
    nobis attestatus antiq̃s eo sæculo etiã usq̃ Ari stotelis post tempora
    nõ plene Mathe matica sciuisse, Ait em sic כי הלמודים לא
X   נשלמו בזמנו .i. q̃ Mathematicæ scientiæ non erant tempore
    Aristotelis perfectæ, cum igitur, ut Salomon inquit, cunctæ res sint diffi
    ciles, & in ipsis naturalibus quorum saltem principia nobis nota sunt, aut
    esse possunt, החומר הצורה ההעדר Materia, forma, pri
    uatio, tanta in hoĩbus sedeat apprehensionis tarditas, quid futurum de no
    bis cogitabimus supremas illas spiritualium causarum species intueri que
    rentibus? Ad q̃d omnium inferiorum abstractionibus, discursu, ratione ac
Y   logicis speculationibus opus erit, quæ facile possent totam hoĩs uitam oc
    cupare, ut est nõ nullius põderis discere המאמרות q̃ appellamus
    p̃dicamenta, & ut ad illorum consuetudinẽ loquar genera generalissima,
    uidelicet quæ sunt עצם כמה איכות הצטרפות מתי
    אנה מצב לו יפעל יתפעל .i. Substantia, quantitas, qua
    litas, relatio, quando, ubi, situs, habitus, agens, patiens, istis enim & consta
    re putant & intelligi, quæcunq̃ in hoc conditoris orbiculari globo conti
    nentur. Inueniri aut nihilominus & q̃ de his ipsis ac eorum comprehẽsis
    diuulgent atq̃ dicant ob idq̃ prædicabilia nominari סוג מין
Z   הבדל סגולה מקרה .i. Genus, speciem, differentiã, propriũ,
    accidens. Horum omniũ dies atq̃ noctes aucupia, plagas & indagines in
    stitu ũt p̃ singu las cuiuslibet rei cãs, q̃ sunt החומר הצורה
    הפועל והתכלית .i. Materia, forma efficiens & finis. Ex quibus
    ut nobis

On the Art of Kabbalah

nature we will have to look into almost all that subsists in the universe, whether it is founded in its own strength or it relies on support from outside in some way. Not even names for these things can be found in the man's lifetime, let alone their properties, conditions, strengths, modes of action, and functions. There is no end to the number of things we want to know. Our rational capacity is too small, the questions too difficult, human powers too frail, and the distractions multifarious. Was it not to Abraham that it was said, "Look toward heaven, and number the stars, if you are able to number them," but he could not, although he was in his time, according to Maimonides, a celebrated astrologer. From this Kabbalists hand down the saying: "A man knows nothing of what is in heaven, save what little he learns from studying this." I take this saying to heart, when I remember all the mistakes the ancients made in mathematics, though they devoted their whole lives to the work, as scholars do. Abubacher noted in his work that even in the generation that followed Aristotle the ancients did not fully understand mathematics. He says: "Mathematical knowledge was still not perfect at the time of Aristotle."

As Solomon says, all things are difficult, and men have been so slow to grasp the facts of nature, whose principles—matter, form, negation—we are, or at least could be aware of, that what is to become of us when we attempt the investigation of the highest spiritual causes? To this end we will need abstractions of lower things, argument, reasoning, and logical speculation. These can easily take up one's whole life, for it is no easy task to learn a thing's properties—in the normal terminology, predicates, the most general logical genera: substance, quantity, quality, relation, time and place, arrangement, appearance, active, and passive; it is believed that everything on this globe exists and is understood in these ways. Nonetheless, we shall have to discover the facts themselves and what is understood by them: why it is thought worthwhile to give them predicates—their genus, species, and difference, and whether they are inherent or dependent qualities. Day and night men set nets and traps to catch one by one the causes of each thing: the material, formal, efficient, and final causes.

LIBER PRIMVS V.

ut nobis ipsi molliter blandimur omnis negocii ueritatem uenari quea/
mus quadam euidenti, ut aiunt, demostratione quam מופת appellāt, A
scilicet de altero ad extremum alterum, tanq̄ è carceribus ad meta discur
rentes in modum cuiusdam artificii cui nomen הקש indiderunt. At ue
ro qua solertia & quibus ambagibus illorum hoīm qui hæc plus ostenta
re soleant quàm præstare sophismata præstruantur, nostri sic docuere

יתחבך כל הקש ומופת משתי הקדמות
הגדולה והקטנה בשלשה חלקים והם
הנקראים גבולים אחד מהם נושא המבוקש
והוא הנקרא הקצה הקטן והשני החלק
המשתותה והוא הנקרא גבול אמצעי
והשלישי נשוא המבוקש והוא הנקרא קצה
הגדול ומאלו תולדה :

i. Componitur omnis syllogismus B
& demonstratio ex duabus propositionibus siue præmissis maiore & mi
nore, secundum tres particulas, qui uocantur termini, una ex eis est subie
ctum quæsiti, & dicit extremitas minor. Et secūda pars est participans, uo
catur q̄ terminus medius. Et tertia est p̄dicatum quæsiti, quæ nominatur
extremitas maior, & ex illis conclusio. Hoc est illud rete, hic ille hamus,
uiscum & illex, hoc uinculum quo illorū opinione libera capitur ueritas,
& quo uel circa naturæ subiectas res ut sunt physica, uel naturam comita
tes ut mathematica, uel naturam q̄dam modo excetes ut meta ta physica
indistincte ac q̄nq̄ frustra utuntur. Quę aūt à natura prorsus & ab omni C
materia & motu sunt essentialiter absoluta & separata, dicimus theologi
ca, quippe istis linguacitationibus & syllogisticis susurris non subiecta, ut q̄
rum tanq̄ immediatorum non sit proprie loquendo scientia, sed firmior
ac ualidior notitia. Quo absolutius Aristoteles in librorum illustriū q̄s
post naturalia scripsit uolumine primo nobis insinuat, q̄ illius quidem no
titiæ possessio est non humana, tum ut conspicimus quia raro & uix è mil
libus uni contingit, quasi uideatur magis diuinitus illabi q̄ humanitus ac
quiri, tum q̄ in summa constituit difficultate propter tenuem (arbitro r)
& exilem intellectus nostri ab initio instinctum. Quod figura quadam in
nuit Zophar in libro Iob. Pullus onagri homo nascitur. Deinde ob na/
turalis aptitudinis commoda eruditione adiutæ inopiam & defectum.
Eo q̄ longo iam tempore à malis p̄ceptoribus delusi nondū prudetes pu
eri tenera in ætate relictis optimarum literarum studiis, ad sordida sophis
mata compellunt, illorum suasu, q̄rum aures p̄ter utrum hoc & utrum il/
lud cum suis propositiōibus & corrolariis aliud nihil admittunt. Accedit
in causa, celeris promotio discipulorum ad gradus superiores, quibus

Book One

With all this activity we cheerfully flatter ourselves that we can hunt down truth with some self-evident (as they call it) demonstration, which goes from one extreme to the other (like running from starting line to winning post) using that device known as a syllogism. The cunning and evasion on which these sophistries (where men prefer showing off to actually proving anything) are based is shown in the following:

> Every syllogism and demonstration is made up of two premises, major and minor, and each has three particulars called terms, one being the subject term, called the lesser extremity, the second being the shared term, called the middle term, and the third being the predicate term, called the major extremity; from these is drawn the conclusion.

This is the trap, the snare, the bait, the noose in which, in their opinion, free truth is to be captured. This is what they employ in studying things like physics, dependent on the natural world, or mathematics, adjunct to it, or those that in some way escape nature, like metaphysics.

Those subjects that are separate from the natural world, essentially distinct from matter and motion, we call theology. This is not susceptible of treatment by those gossips and talebearers, syllogisms, for it is not, properly speaking, a science of the immediate world. It is a more reliable, more robust form of knowledge. Aristotle elaborates on this saying (in the first volume of the fine works that follow his natural history), that the possession of such knowledge is not something human; because it is rarely achieved — scarcely one man in a thousand has it — it seems to sink in by divine agency more than be acquired by human means; and the greatest difficulty was in the paucity (I think) and weak nature of the intellectual endowments we start with. Thus, figuratively, Zophar in the book of Job: "Man is born of the foal of an ass." And, furthermore, the pathetic inadequacy of our natural ability is reinforced by education. For a long time now it has been the case that boys who have not yet reached the age of discretion are, when still of tender age, led astray by bad teachers. Abandoning the study of literature, they are forced on to sordid sophistic reasoning, beguiled by men who will hear of nothing but "on the one hand this and on the other hand that" — with all the premises and corollaries that go with it. Swift promotion to higher grades is the incentive they give their pupils, who cannot believe that

DE ARTE CABALISTICA

nondum credenda erant tam excelsa qñ in literis humanioribus parum adhuc olei cosumpserunt, quare in tot & tantis sentibus & dumetis labore molesto frustra defatigati resiliunt anteq̃ ad uenerandæ senectutis annos peruenerint, nempe adhuc ætate uirili florescẽtes. Audite aũt uos obsecro uerba Iob. In antiquis est sapientia & in multo tempore prudentia. Ideo motus quondã Rab Eleazar dicenti sibi benigne magistro suo Iohanan. Veni docebo te opus , de Mercaua. i. de sublimiorib⁹ contẽplationibus, respondit לא קשאי. i. non incanui, quasi nondũ consenui. Nouerat em discipulus ille sagax & præcocis adulescens ingenii ad tam sublimẽ & altam sapientiam nõ esse aptos nec idoneos, nisi eos qui iam sedatis & extinctis cupiditatum ardoribus & calore iuuenili refrigerato, annis prouecti, cum quadam tñ naturali probitate senescunt. Nam quid huc afferret senium commodi? nisi probitatem & constantem uitæ integritatẽ adderet. Iccirco uelim credat omniũ nemo q̃ ii sint uere theologi q̃tumcũq̃ senes, quacunq̃ præditi contentiosa loquacitate, qui uitiorum q̃libet genere foedati, suꝑbia, hypocrisi, auaricia, odio, inuidia, & sæpe tecta religione luxuria, neglecto mentis lumine affectiones sequuntur animales. Assilit huic meæ opinioni Salomon qui ait. Abominatio dei est ipse peruersus, hic est ille qui ab altitudine auersus uergit ad decliua, q̃tumuis cum natura erexerit in alta. Non ignorauit Algazel Marrane tuus, ille Mahumetista hos sibi cõtrarios in anima motus sursum & deorsum homini docto q̃ infoelicissimos fore, cum in libro de scientia diuina demonstrat q̃ ex cõtrarietate huiuscemodi attrahentium impꝑssionum sit cruciatus in anima fortissimus & maxime formidolosus. Sic præter uitia etiam peruertũt & auertunt secularia negocia, dum forte parentes, uxor, liberi, res familiaris, amici, inimici, casus, euenta, & quælibet propinq̃rum necessitudines, haud sinunt uires hoĩm summos intelligentiæ gradus ascendere. Sed fac quisq̃s uestrum erit, nihil in nobis situm esse q̃d impediat, finge captum ingenii nostri foelicem & faustum, nulla sit dementiæ aut desipientiæ ne species quidem. Iam parata succurrant omnia q̃ ad suscipiendum res altissimas ꝑtineant, ut de nostra fragilitate recte queri nemo possit, tñ a speculando nonne plurimos deterrebit excelsior cœlo, profundior tartaro, diuinorũ obscuritas illa nec sensu nec rõne peruestigabilis, quæ a studiis nostris nõ ut cæteræ scientiæ lucẽ recipit, sed secum affert & quasi de suo ipsa promptuario in uiros non indignos radiat atq̃ lucet, quanq̃ nec sua sponte ut uilem sese passim prostituit, nec non inuitata se offert, sed a nostra uoluntate humanis ante scientiis perornate instituta non ualde repugnãs attrahitur, quemadmodum si retusum ferrum, ut ait Salomon, & nõ prius politum fuerit, exacuetur multo labore, & post industriam sequẽt sapientia. Etenim quæ a sensu prouehuntur ad intellectum, diligentia quadã studiorum

D

such heights could be reached when their education in the arts is still incomplete. "Why wear yourself out in all those thorny thickets for nothing?" they ask themselves, and before they even reach a venerable old age, while still in the prime of youth, they find real thought rebarbative.

Now listen, please, to the words of Job: "In age there is wisdom and prudence in the fullness of time." With similar feelings Rabbi Eleazar, when his master Jochanan kindly said: "Come, I will teach you something of Merkavah" (works of sublime contemplation), replied: "No, I am not yet a gray-head," meaning, "I am not yet old." This pupil, so discreet, so preciously clever, knew that a man is not suited to such lofty sublime wisdom till the heat of desire is dead, a young man's ardor cooled, till he is far advanced in years and has grown into natural goodness — and that is the only appropriate quality brought by old age — goodness, steady integrity in life. I do not want it to be thought that all old men, no matter who they are, are theologians; "old men" include in their number the loquacious and the argumentative, those tainted by all kinds of vice, from pride, hypocrisy, and avarice to hate and jealousy, and often lust, under cover of religion; all of them following their animal bent, neglecting the light of the mind. In this Solomon confirms my thinking, when he says: "The perverse man is an abomination unto the Lord" (meaning, the man who, even though nature has raised him on high, turns his back on the heights and turns to the depths). Your Moslem Alcazel, Marranus, notices this as well; he realizes that the opposing mental strains tugging him up and down are most unfortunate for a scholar. In his book on divine knowledge he shows that the mind is severely and unpleasantly tortured by such conflict.

But secular business apart from actual vice can also sidetrack and distract one. Parents, wife, children, family, friends, enemies, chance events, all kinds of domestic ties and immediate needs inhibit a man's concentration of the upward path to understanding. But let us assume that nothing gets in the way of our studies, and that we are lucky enough to have the mental capacity, with no trace of the mad or the silly. We are geared up to the high task. Still the obscurity of these divine matters, obscurity penetrable by neither sense nor rational thinking, illuminated not from without, as are the other sciences, but from within itself, from its own storehouse irradiating those who are worthy (though it does not offer itself at its own prompting, as a common prostitute, but comes only when invited), still this obscurity, higher than the heavens, deeper than the pit, will turn many away.

When organized by us, who are forearmed with the sciences, it gives up without much of a fight. As Solomon says: "Iron sharpens iron — blunt metal gives way to polishing — and when the work is done, wisdom follows."

LIBER PRIMVS   VI

diorum & artificiali ratione colligunt, ultra uero quæ ab intellectu ad mentem & ad eius lumen pertingunt quasi diuinam induūt personam, & idolio carent humano, ut iis queat nihil a nobis cogitari profundius. Sup ea igitur re ingemuisse uisus est idem Salomō cum ait, Alta profunditas seu profunda profunda, ita eñ hebraice legit, quis inueniet eam? Non dixit quis habebit eam, nonnulli enim habuerunt. Sed quis inueniet, tanq̄ difficile, non aūt quoq̄ modo impossibile, quia dñs dat sapientiam, & beati q̄ inueniunt eam, ut est in sacris oraculis, Paucorum est igitur inuenire illam & eorum q̄dem beatorum, super q̄s nō suis meritis sed dono dei coruscat tam uenerandi luminis splēdor. Sane arbitror neminem fore qui nesciat, nō esse multitudinis audire dei sermones, quapropter clamabat ad Moysen, Loquere tu nobis & audiemus, non loquatur nobis deus. Te inq̄unt te audiemus, quod Onkelus interp̄tatur Nekabel. Quare in capitulis patrum ita legitur, Mose kibel. i. Moyses audiuit & accepit legem de Sinai. Vnde Kabala dicit ab auditu acceptio. Quod animaduertendum & memori puto mente reponendum, ex tanta fuisse hoīm multitudine tot etiā sanctorum, Moysen ipsum qui ad ueri & æqui agnitionem ab ore dei recipiendam unus & præter eū nec alter aliquis esset destinatus, Sic eñ Cabalista ille Azariel Bar Salomo Garonensis scribit,

לא כל הנביאים היו יכולים לשמוע הדבור השכינה כי אם משה

.i. Non quidem prophetæ oēs fuerunt potentes audire sermonem ab ore dei, nisi Moyses. Vos igitur optimi uiri quorum aīos meo erga uos amori comunia studia mirifice deuinciunt, ex his facile p̄spicitis q̄ mihi obiter exciderunt, rem ualde necessariam humano generi cœlitus indultam esse Cabalam, sine qua nemo tam raram tam difficilem adipisci queat app̄hensionem diuinorum, quę certe non sunt mortalium rationum probationibus, non senticosis inanium uerborum contentionibus, non humanis syllogismis propter eorum diuinitatem subiecta, quin immo tam magna, tam grandia, tam infinita, ut una hois ætate uel si libeat deniq̄ pluribus omni q̄tūcunq̄ indefesso labore supari non possint, etiā si uitæ nostræ anni tēdant in multa sæcula, nobis plane in hoc luto, in hac argilla & densi corporis cœmento spirantibus, & corporeo sensu cūcta p̄lumentibus. Aiunt eñ sapientes Hebræorū magistri.

בי להגיר כח משה בראשית לבשר ודם אי איפשרי

.i. q̄ ad explicandum uirtutem operis de Bresith carni & sanguini, Impossibile. Quanto magis de Mercaua. Quare faciamus oportet ut singulares technographi & artifices docēdo solēt. Credamus unicuiq̄ in arte sua perito. Nā logicus de parte orationis a grāmatico recepta credit, Rhetor a logico argumētationum assumit locos, Poeta & orator à musico, Geometra proportiones ab arithmetico mutuatur, Astronomia numeris, figuris

Book One

Information transmitted from the senses to the intellect is acquired by persistent study and careful reasoning, but what is transferred from the intellect to the mind, to the light of the mind, takes on the character of the divine; there is no human form with which to clothe it. No thoughts are more profound than these. This it seems is what moved Solomon to cry "Profound depths. . . " (or "Deep, deep," as in the Hebrew) ". . .who will find them?" Not "who has them?" for some have had them. But "who will find," since it is difficult, but not impossible; for it is the Lord who gives and the blessed who find wisdom — as in the prophecy: "Few will find it, and they shall be blessed." Above them glitters — not by reason of their own worth, but by God's gift — the wonder of that shining light. I think that no one is unaware of the fact that God's utterances are not for the crowd to hear. It was for this that they shouted: "Speak to us, we will hear you, don't let God speak to us," to Moses. "Speak," they said, "we will hear." This Onkelos interpreted as *Nekabbel* — "we will receive it." Thus, in the ancient writings: "Moshe kibbel" — "Moses heard," and received the law at Sinai. So Kabbalah gets its name: receiving what is heard. I think it is worth remarking, and committing to memory, the fact that it was Moses, alone of numerous holy men, who was chosen to receive, by himself, the true and just commandments uttered by God. The Kabbalist Azariel Bar Salomon of Garonne writes this: "None of the prophets was strong enough to hear the words proceeding from the mouth of God, save Moses."

My friends, in my regard for you, I have, through our studies together, imposed on you an awe-inspiring obligation. From remarks I made in passing you will see that Kabbalah is a study heaven-bestowed and of the utmost importance to man. Without it none can achieve something as elusive, as difficult, as the apprehension of the divine. For it is certainly not material given to the proofs of mere mortal reasoning, empty-worded thorny arguments, man's syllogisms: the subject matter is divine; so big, so great, so infinite is it that in one generation even the tireless work of man could not master it — even if our life-span stretched to many generations — since we are obviously living in this mud and clay of the thick lump that is a living body, and we use the bodily senses in all we take on. The Hebrew sages say: "explain the power behind the work of Creation — impossible." How much more so with Merkavah. So we must do as specialist writers do: trust individuals in their own fields. The logician depends on a grammarian for his prose; the speechwriter takes some of his arguments from the logician; the poet and orator need help from the musician, geometers borrow proportion from arithmeticians, astronomy relies

DE ARTE CABALISTICA

ac dimensionibus mathematicis fidem habet. Transnaturalia utuntur cō iectura naturalium. Et omnis scientia superior recte præsumit de statutis inferiorum, nihil eorum conata probare quæ ab arte ulla priori audiuerit esse firmata, sed liberaliter dictis credit, ne ante tota hoies uita deficiat q̃ uniꝰ possit disciplinæ uel minima ratio perfecte inuestigari. Q̃ si hoc in humanis fit & quasi uilioribus ac sellulariis opificiis ut ab auditu recipiant atq̃ credant eis uiris q̃s præ aliis doctrina esse singulari p̃ditos arbitrantur, an in summarum & diuinarū rerum sciẽtia quam nostris uiribus ne unus itẽ et alter attingere uix possumus traditionem sanctorum hoim

G & receptionem fore contemnendam putabimus? quæ Cabala hebraice dicitur. Est enim Cabala diuinæ reuelationis, ad salutiferam dei & formarꝰ separatarum contemplationẽ traditæ, symbolica receptio, quam qui cœlesti sortiuntur afflatu, recto noīe Cabalici dicuntur, eorum uero discipulos cognomento Cabalæos appellabimus, & qui alioquin eos imitari conantur Cabalistæ nominandi sunt. Perinde atq̃ circa editos illorum sermones quotidiano labore desudantes. Eqdem Philolae, Marranus inqt, si per te licet opinor hunc Iudæum uno fasce quicquid de Cabala dici potuit Nestorea eloquentia complexū esse, ut pnoscamus quid nomen ipm designet, ac unde oriatur, sit ne in natura uel in hoim usu aliquid eiuscemodi quod Cabalam uocant, deniq̃ cuius causa uel propter quid ita sit, quatenus & ad quid utilis, & diuinæ contẽplationi q̃ uideatur esse necessaria, q̃umq̃ homini possibilis idoneo & ad eam se præparanti. Quis dici Cabalicus, quis Cabalæus debeat, & quis Cabalista, quid opus est uerbis? totū a capite ad calcem, in hoc laudandus, q̃ nullas oculis tenebras offundit. Tum Philolaus. Soluisti funem Marrane ingressus mare magnum & uix sulcabile, nondum in portu nauigas, & quæ Simon iste tanq̃ in breuem tā bellam depinxit, uideris per caliginem uidere, ac per mediam nebulam in tueri, Adhuc enim ne ad fores qdem eius artis adducti sumus, quare mi Simon hebręorū contemplatissime, amabimus te, pergas ultra, nobis enim hactenus non plus profueris q̃ ut ansam præberes de arte Cabalistica latius cogitandi, quid illud sit quod reuelatum est, quis reuelauerit, quis receperit, quid commodi afferat ea receptio, quis modus artis huius, p̃ quā (ut rumor est) miracula fiãt, nam id ultimum de longinq̃ me huc appulit. Expostulabo, inquit Simon, illud oīum primum de Nestorea eloquentia cuiꝰ a Marrano insimulor. Ea enim & philosopho mihi & Iudæo esset me

H iudice opprobrio futura tanq̃ adulationes amanti cum nequeat tanta breuitate sermonis contineri eloquentia q̃ & uerborum & rerum copiam de

I syderat, & Iudęis nobis in more nõ sit, ut fucos dicendi sequamur: Nã loq proprie non eloqui sub ferula didicimus, & causę ueritatem magis q̃ locutionis ornatum quærimus. Sed absoluam paucis, q̃d uehementer optatis

ne tot

On the Art of Kabbalah

for numbers, figures, and dimension on mathematics. Metaphysics makes use of the conjectures of the natural sciences. Every higher science rightly takes for granted the conclusions of the more basic forms of knowledge and makes no attempt to demonstrate what is already proved. Assertions are unreservedly trusted, otherwise no man could in one lifetime fully investigate the smallest chain of reasoning in any one discpline. If this is what happens in human sciences, where men accept cheap, mechanical tradesman's stuff by word of mouth, and trust those they think are good on one subject alone, then are we to despise the tradition (handing down — hence "Kabbalah" in the Hebrew) of these holy men, in accepting this knowledge of the divine, where none of us is really able even to approach the subject?

Kabbalah is a matter of divine revelation handed down to further the contemplation of the distinct Forms and of God, contemplation bringing salvation; Kabbalah is the receiving of this through symobls. Those who are given this by the breath of heaven are known as Kabbalics; their pupils we will call Kabbalaeans; and those who attempt the imitation of these are properly called Kabbalists.[9] Exactly this, day by day they sweat over their published works.

MARRANUS: Well Philolaus, I think this Jew has, with the eloquence of a Nestor, in one go dealt with all that can be said on Kabbalah. Now we know the meaning and origin of the word, whether anything in the world of nature, or in man's usage, corresponds to what they call Kabbalah, and finally, what it is for, how useful, how essential it seems to be for the contemplation of the divine, and how feasible it is for one suited for it and prepared for it. Why do we need the distinction between Kabbalics, Kabbalaeans, and Kabbalists? He certainly deserves praise for not having clouded us with dark mysteries.

PHILOLAUS: Marranus, you have cast off onto a great sea that is hard to cross, and you are not yet into port. So far Simon has only sketched an outline which you seem to be looking at through a thick fog. We haven't even reached the gateway yet. Simon, most thoughtful Israelite, do go on. We shall be most grateful. So far you have just given us a handle for further thought on Kabbalah. Now tell us what it is that has been revealed, who it is that revealed it, by whom it has been received, what good has been derived from it, and how this skill gives rise to miracles — rumor has it that way — for in the end it is this that has dragged me here all this way.

SIMON: First I must protest at the Nestorean eloquence Marranus attributes to me. Both as a philosopher and a Jew I find such "eloquence" distasteful — like lovers' simperings. Eloquence cannot be contained in short speeches; it hankers after masses of words and things, and we Jews are unaccustomed to the joys of public speaking. Accuracy, not eloquence, is what the schoolteachers have taught us. We look at the truth of an argument rather than its decorative verbal presentation.

LIBER PRIMVS

ue tot & tam discriminosis itineribus defatigatos, uel neruarum ambagi
bus quasi oscitantes uos animo pendere sinam, post enim q̄ sine ullo ut ap
paret tedio audiuistis, ego quibus uestigiis & indiciis q̄t & quibus ueluti
canibus diffinitionem Cabalæ uenatus deprehēderim, ne uos in ipso nō
mine contingat errare, sicut sophistarum quidam irrisione digni propria
temeritate uel si malueritis negligentia discendi falso asseruerunt Caba
lam fuisse hominem diabolicum & hæreticum, unde Cabalistas hæreti
cos esse omneis (abstinete obsecro si potestis a risu, quanquam est ridicu
lum ingens, at definite uelim hęc hominum monstra & portenta ridere)
commodum ea proferam de quorum certitudine dubitantes me roga
stis, si pri⁹ commonuero Cabalam nec sensuum rudi tactu, nec imperiosis
logici artificii argumentis esse quærendam, cuius fundamentum in tertia
cognitionum regione constituitur, ubi non iudicium urgens, non proba
tio euidens, non syllogismus demonstrans, quinimmo ubi nec ipsa homī
nis ratio dominatur. Sed nobilior quædam notitia ubi lumen mentis ca
dens super intellectum mouet liberam credendi uoluntatem. Quæ enim
sensu percipiuntur infra scientiam sunt & ratione certiora, que autē mens
influit, supra scientiam ponimus, perinde atq̣ rationali discursu solidiora
Constiti paulisper & commoratus sum ne res tam diuinas, fragilitatis hu
manæ inuētionibus & regulis, ut aiunt, logicalibus subiectas putetis, igno
scite amici non affero meditata, sed utut causæ intercidunt alia ex aliis tra
ho, Iam enim ad id quod uultis propero, quid illud sit, quod reuelatum
est, nemo a me impetrabit ut existimare queā de omni uos id reuelatiōe
proposuisse cunctorum creditorum, que prope uidentur esse infinita, qu
potius quid illud sit primarium uniuersale atq̣ præcipuum diuinitatis re
uelatum, in quod singulæ reuelationes diuinorum feruntur & reducunt.
Certe id quidem ipsum, Philolaus inquit. Tum Simon. Recte uero, & est
profecto aliud nihil q̄ post ruinā primordialem generis humani uniuer
salis restauratio, quæ a nobis יְשׁוּעָה & a latinis salus nominatur. Eius
ipsius extat oīm prima nr̄æ speciei facta reuelatio, si examussim uniuersā
mundani exordii pondero qua nulla fuit prior, non enim insomnio corre
ptus quasi diuinaret Adam per afflatum propheticum de uxore post so
porem locutus est. Hoc nunc os ex ossibus meis, & caro de carne mea, sed
minus se costarum alterius lateris experrectus habere sentiens, postquā
ad cuncta singulatim animantia terræ maris ac aeris facto circuitu peru
e
nisset, de subito intuitus Heuam, uir robustus & iuuenis adulescentulam
succi plenam, facie uenusta, uultu blando, & humana energia præditam
mutua prurigine cœpit exardescere, ac geniali cupidine oppleri, que tum
se non erga ullum animal aliud tetigisset, Sic em̄ Eleazar ait ille Magister
noster & Salomon commentator sacrarum scripturarum ordinarius.

C

Book One

In a few words I will tell you what you so much want to know. I shan't wear you out with lots of digressions in order to make distinctions between this and that, nor weight your mind, leaving you open-mouthed, with long rambling speeches. You have listened to me hunting out a definition of Kabbalah, with hints as my hounds, without signs of flagging. I do not want you to credit the falsehood asserted by some ridiculous sophists — either they haven't thought about it or they are just ignorant — when they say that "Kabbalah" was a man whose heretical ideas came from the devil and that all Kabbalists are heretics. (Please, I beg you, don't smile. I know it's silliness, but such horrible monstrosity is no laughing matter.)

This is a good opportunity to discuss the matters that were worrying you that you wanted to talk about, now that I have warned you that Kabbalah cannot be discovered by the senses, nor by the domineering of clever logical arguments, that its basis in fact lies in the third region of understanding, a place where cogent judgment, the burden of evidence, and syllogistic exposition hold no sway — not even reason rules there. This knowledge is nobler; where the light of the mind falls upon the intellect, and moves our free will to believe. What is perceived by means of the senses is science, and is determined by reasoning, but what the mind influences we put higher than science: such things are more real than rational discourse.

I have persevered with this a little to stop you from thinking that divine matters are subject to the finding of weak humanity and to the so-called rules of logic.

Do excuse me for taking one instance after another quite at random. I am speaking without having thought out first what to say. Now I will come to your question. What is it that has been revealed?

No one would have me believe that you are asking me to tell you all the revelations that have ever been put forward, for they are countless. Rather, you want the primal, all-embracing, special revelation of the divine, to which all individual revelations can be brought back
PHILOLAUS: Yes, it is that.
SIMON: Well, it is none other than the universal restoration, after the primordial Fall of the human race, which is called salvation. It was concerning this that the first revelation of all things appeared to us, if you have an accurate picture of the beginnings of the world, when before there was none. Was not Adam dreaming, and after sleeping did he not speak to his wife as a seer, inspired: "Bone of my bones and flesh of my flesh." On waking he felt a rib missing on one side, and he went on a round trip to all creatures of earth, sea and air, one by one, till suddenly he caught sight of Eve. Now he was a lusty young man, and she a spirited young woman, beautiful to look at, pleasing of face, full of energy. He felt the pull of sexual attraction and so did she. He was suffused with delightful desire, quite unlike those that had come to him when confronted by any other living thing. Hence our Rabbi Eleazar and Rashi, the usual commentator on the sacred Scriptures:

שבא אדם על כל בהמה וחיה ולא נתקררה דעתו בהם עד שבא על האשה

i.Q: uenit Adam ad omne iumentum & animal & non commouebatur sensus eius in illis usq; dum ueniisset ad uxorem. Quibus é uerbis proh hominum fidem ob tortum scelus malignitate peruersorum hominum contigit, si modo sint homines, ac non magis diaboli incarnati, & laruę furiales existimandi, qui seditionem Christianitatis aduersum nos, quamuis secundum leges imperatorum innocenter & pacifice uiuentes, tamen quolibet genere iniuriarum excitare parati, cum saepe alias tum nuper in ista urbe dicta Magistrorum nostrorum falso interpretati sic exposuerunt, Q: Adam tunc cum omnibus bestiis & animalibus foede coiuerit, Deus bone, quanta turpissimorum nebulonum audacia, infantium sophistarum assensu & fauore adiuta. Nunquam enim בוא iuxta linguae hebraicę proprietatem luxuriae coitum significat, tametsi quandoq; pro necessario materiae subiectae complexu per quandam illud metaphoram de coitu seminali exuerecundiae modestia intelligatur, ut Genesis sextodecimo capite. Ingredere ad ancillam meam si forte saltem ex illa suscipiam filios, quo in loco בא id est. Ingredere ad ancillam, non autem dixit, coeas cū ancilla. Quod etiam hic par non est, usq; adeo, ut ab hominibus quantumcunque nequam nequeat accipi consimiliter, propter negocii eius de quo sermo fit impossibilitatem. Nam certe qui fieri posset? ut tantus uir & tam magnus Adā cum cimice, pulice, musca, & cicada seminaliter coiuisse intelligatur. Haec eam ob causam recensui, ut his & huiuscemdi falsariis, maledicis & male dictis ac leuissimis transfugis, neque in hac neq; alia ulla in parte fidem habentibus nihil contra nos de sacra quam non nouerunt scriptura credatur. Redeo ad id unde digressus sum, Naturae itaque instigatione soli cum uterque in mundo essent, uir sentiebat uxorem ad se pertinere, non dum igitur Cabala haec fuit. Caeterum & hoc ingenii erat uidelicet singularis & acerrimi ut cuiq; rei protoplastus ipse iam orbis dominus spontaneo positu nomen adderet, quo cognoscamus uoluntatis id fuisse, non naturae. Nec illud non rationis extiterit, post legis transgressionem q; poenam mortis in monitorio comminatam formidauerit, quam ductu rationis iudicabat fore non corporalem, eo q; se mox atque de ligno comederat mori non sensit. Ergo iuxta Ramban, moriendum in peccato intellexit, sicut & nos Cabalistae intelligimus. Iam quid in omnibus his oro diuinae reuelatiōis fuisse putādū est? certe nihil hucusq; comperimus q̄d non totum aut consilio ratiōis aut motui sensus paruisse dubitauerit oim prorsus nemo, at illa tam perniciosa legis transgressio, tanta in deum opti

On the Art of Kabbalah

"Adam came to every beast and living thing but was not sensually aroused until he came to Woman." This saying has been twisted by men with warped minds, or rather by the devil incarnate or deadly evil spirits — though how people can believe such a malicious lie, I do not know. These perverts try to incite all good Christians to turn against us, though we live blamelessly and peaceably observing the laws of the state. But they are ready to occasion us all kinds of harm — often in other places and just lately here in this town.[10] They put false constructions on the words of our rabbis: this passage they interpret as: "Adam then copulated foully with all beasts and living creatures" — good God, the audacity of these wretches, and all the more so when egged on by the approval of infantile sophists! The Hebrew word *bo* never means copulate, though, where the subject matter requires, it may be understood metaphorically as a euphemism for copulation, as in Genesis 16, where "Go in to my maid; it may be that I may have children by her," uses the word *bo*. But it says clearly "go in to" my maid, not "copulate."

But this is not quite the same thing. There is another reason everyone would reject this equation and that is, that in the business we are discussing, this interpretation is quite impossible. How could it be like that? That a man like Adam is meant to have mingled in sexual manner with bugs, fleas, flies, and grasshoppers? I am going into all this detail to warn you of forgeries like this, and the wicked, petty slanderers, rats leaving the sinking ship, with no sense of responsibility in this or any other matter. Do not grant them anything that discredits our holy writings — they don't know them at all.

To get back to where I left off. When these two were alone in the world, natural instinct made man realize that woman was for him — and this was before there was Kabbalah. But this too shows singularly acute intelligence: the first man, now lord of the world, spontaneously gave a name to everything, which teaches us that this resulted from voluntary powers, not instinct. And his fear of the warning threat of the death penalty after he had broken the law also shows powers of reasoning, for deductive reasoning judged that the punishment would not be inflicted on the body, since just after eating of the Tree of Life he did not feel himself dying. So, according to Maimonides, he understood that he was to die in sin. We Kabbalists understand it this way too. In all this, what is to be considered divine revelation? Without doubt, nothing we have looked at could be judged to be directly independent of either rational or instinctive motives, except for that baleful breaking of the law — oh, that insulting assault on

mum maximum contumelia, tam infesta temeritas, tam contagiosa libido
tam tetra, tam uenenosa pestis toxica & foeda lues, generis humani corru
ptrix, in uenarum cuniculis insides & cum ipso profluuio seminis in poste
ritatem continuo meatu serpens, an qua possit uia quo ue modo expiari
& auerti nulla ualuit humanæ fragilitatis cogitatio præsumpta concipere. P
Hic inquam hic ad imminetis desperationis quo morbo nihil pnicionisus,
efficax subsidium diuina reuelatione opus erat, ac ne tunc figmentū suum
fictor deus omnino deseruerat, sed spem quandā iniecit, fore no impossi
bile hoc ipsum quis imane crimen & contra infinitā maiestatē admissum
tn tractu temporis finito, aboleri tolli & extingui. Dixit igitur ad angelos
audiente Adam, Et nunc ne mittat manum suam & sumat de ligno uitæ,
& comedat, & uiuat in æthernum, & emisit eum dñs deus de paradiso uo
luptatis. Vox ultima hæc erat quam ab ore dei miser audiebat cum iā ex
horto pelleret, qua tñ inter tot mœrores atq luctus firmam erga creato
rem suum recepit spem illā q tam horribilis sententia successu temporū
fieret ex dei misericordia reuocabilis, istudq sibi uerba indicabant oracu
li, ait em. Nunc siue iam ne mittat manū suā & sumat de ligno uitæ. Nepe Q
haud frustra dictione nunc uel iam addidit deus, q præsens tempus designa
tur, insinuando sententiam non fore perpetuā, sed posse contra eam futu
ro post tpe abolitionem impetrari, siqñ ueniret homo ad uescendum de
ligno uitæ destinatus, q uis tum semetipsum suspicaret dum spiritus suos
regeret artus irreuocabiliter pendere pœnas, quia non fuisset secu peren
die deus ut solebat facie ad faciem locutus, qd palam indignationis erat si
gnum, & alienati ab Adam animi, ut qui ante cum singulis qbusq animā
tibus atq bestiis loqbatur oim creator deus, iam cum homine peccatore
loqui ore ad os dedignaret. Ne tamen illum prorsus omni consolatione
destitueret dementissimus pater, continuo misit angelum quo plenius tā
tæ ruinæ futuram disceret reparationem. Sic enim Cabalistæ in commen
tariis circa librum Ietzira scribunt. שהאבות הבותיהם היו
מלאכים ידועים רבו של אדם רזיאל .i. Q patrū
præceptores fuerūt angeli noti, uidelicet præceptor ipsius Adam Raziel
Hic aut summi dei nutu expiationis ei uiam ostendit, & diuinum sermone
per allegoriam recipiendum, more Cabalistico exposuit, cuius no modo
uerbum ullum sed ne litera qtumcunq minuta & exilis ac ne apex qdem
frustra ponitur. Te autem appello Philolae, & te Marrane omnium ex do
ctis doctissimi uiri accomodate hāc uenia q forte religio me prohibitu
ra fuerit alienis a secta nostra & ritu Iudaico non initiatis tam recōdita &
tam arcana prodere, quorum cognitio, ita me deus amet, discipulis etiam
propriis sæpe multumq denegatur, ut uix raris in libris eadem liceat sal

C ii

Book One

the great and good God, such outrageous impudence; such polluting wantonness, poisonous, pestilential, stinking filth, as has corrupted the race of man, poison sinking deep into our veins, spreading slowly — by the flow of semen — through the generations. And our frail human thought processes cannot picture how it is to be purged, in what way the stream diverted. Now, I say, now at the point of near despair of this destructive disease, was there need of divine revelation's powerful assistance, and God the Creator did not abandon his creatures. He hinted at hope, still possible despite the monstrous offence against his infinite majesty. He allowed that after a certain passage of time the charge should be wiped out, cancelled, annulled. In Adam's hearing he said to the angels: "And now, lest he put forth his hand and take also of the Tree of Life, and eat, and live forever. . ." And he sent him forth from the garden of delight. These were the last words, as he was driven from the garden, the poor man heard from the mouth of God. But in it he found hope in his Creator, hope, in the midst of torments and grief, that with the passing of time his fearful sentence would, through the mercy of God, be remitted. The very words showed him that, when he said: "Now, lest he put forth his hand and take also of the Tree of Life." Now God, then as now, never employs a word without a purpose, and his use of the present tense suggests that the sentence would not be in perpetuity. At some time in the future it would be possible to obtain remission; there would come a man chosen to eat of the Tree of Life, though for his own part Adam suspected that his punishment was irrevocable while there was breath left in his body. God no longer talked with him face to face as he had done, a clear sign of his anger and his estrangement. God the Creator of all had once held conversation with all living things, both man and beast; now he disdained to talk face to face with the sinner man.

The Father is of great forbearance. Not to leave Adam bereft of consolation he straightaway sent an angel to teach him how the ruins could one day be rebuilt. In the commentary on the *Book of the Creation,* the Kabbalists write:

"Our fathers' teachers were famous angels. Raziel was Adam's." By the will of God this angel showed him the path to atonement. He gave Adam divine words, to be interpreted allegorically, in the way of Kabbalah. No word, no letter, however trifling, not even the punctuation, was without significance. I ask you Philolaus, and you Marranus, learned as you are, to understand that my religious obligations prevent me from exposing hidden, sacred mysteries to outsiders with no initiation into Jewish rites. As God loves me, we often have to withhold such matters even from our own pupils. They are to be found only in a few

DE ARTE CABALISTICA

tem tegumētis ac ænigmatis obuoluta inueniri. Sic ēm in Thalmud legit
אֵין מוֹסְרִים סִתְרֵי תּוֹרָה אֶלָּא לְיוֹעֵץ וְחָכָם
חֲרָשִׁים וּנְבוֹן לָחַשׁ .i. Non traduntur abscondita legis nisi cōsi
liario & sapienti magistro iuuenum, & intelligenti mago. Quare dicam
ne amplius an taceam? non parum dubitare me faciūt, tum magistrorum
interdicta, tum ad scrutandas res altissimas ardor ingens utriusq; uestrū
(ut arbitror) diuino igne inflammatorum. At audacter tamen indulgē
tior mihi ipsi, temperabo asperitati præceptorum qui uideo solis lumen
absq; discrimine super omnes dispergi quotquot obicem remouerint, di
camq;, tametsi pro more gentis nostrę perquam ineleganter, tamen utut
potero, quæ homines doctissimos sapientissimosq; dixisse, & scripta diui
nitus reliquisse acceperim. Et explicabo nihilomin⁹ orationem sane ocul
tissimam a creatore mundi cum beatis angelis in suæ diuinitatis penetra
libus habitam. Dixit nanq; deus. Ecce Adam sicut unus ex nobis, nō ex uo
bis inquit, sed unus ex nobis. Nā in uobis angelis, numerus est & alteritas.
in nobis, id est deo, unitas infinita, æthena, simplicissima & absolutissima.
Nec ipsum unum in angelis si quid sit, esse potest sicut in deo. Non igitur
connumerauit sibi angelos deus, cum de unitate loqueretur, quoniam re
pugnat idem aliquid esse unu in natura cum deo & angelis, tāta est creato
R ris & creaturæ distantia. Quid igitur est quod ait, Ecce Adam sicut unus
ex nobis? Hinc sane coniicimus alterum quendā esse Adam cœlestem, an
gelis in cœlo demonstratum, unum ex deo, quem uerbo fecerat, & alterū
esse Adam terrenum, repulsum a deo quem ex luto manibus suis finxerat
& horto exegerat. Iste, unus est cum deo, hic non modo alter est uerum
etiam alius & aliud a deo. Post miserabilem itaq; generis humani casum
docuit angelos suos deus de restitutione aliquando futura salutis, per quē
nam uentura esset, & quidem docuit non quātum ipē docere, sed quantū
capere angelica conditio poterat, in præsentia demonstrans quis esset hu
manum genus redempturus, tunc enim prædestinata plane fuerat salus
hominum, quapropter, Ecce inquit hic est ille Adam qui non tātum post
orbis & uestri ortum essentialiter est, sed etiam ante omnem creationem
i: æthernitate fuit unus ex nobis antequam tempus fieret. Quod Onke
lus chaldaice sic interpretatur. הָא אָדָם הֲוָה יְחִידִי
בְּעַלְמָא מִנֵּיהּ .i. Ecce Adā fuit unigenit⁹ me⁹ siue unicus meus in
æthernitate ex me ipso, quo uocabulo utitur deus ad Abraham dicens,
Tolle filium tuum unigenitum. Cunq; futuri personam redemptoris iam
angelis indicasset, ne forte putarent eundem ipsum mox perfunctorie
subita quadam intercessiōe hoc odium tam scelerosi criminis auersurum,
remouit illico dubitationem & negocium in tempus distulit, subiungēs,

scattered books, cloaked in obscurity and disguised in riddles. As it is written in the Talmud: "The secrets of the Law are given only to men of good counsel, to the sages, who teach the young, and to wise men of learning and intellect."

Shall I go on? I hesitate. I cannot help it when I weigh first the rabbis' warnings, and then your burning desire to examine the highest matters, an ardor kindled, I think, by divine fire! So I will be bold, but making my own reservations: I shall restrain myself in the most difficult of the precepts, for I see that the sun's light is shed on all without distinction when the barriers have been taken down. My phrasing may be rather clumsy, as it is with our people, but as best I can I shall tell you, as I understand things, what the wise and learned have said and what is in the writings that have providentially remained. Now I shall reveal the most secret conversation, no less, that the Creator of all held with the angels in his hidden sanctuary.

God said: "Behold, the man is become as one of us." Not "one of you," but "one of us." Among the "You," the angels, there are distinctions of rank, but in the "us," that is, God, there is unity—infinite, eternal, without qualification or conditions. There could not be a "one" like this, like God, among the angels. God, then, did not include the angels with himself when he spoke, for an undivided being spoke. There is an inconsistency that one thing should have the same nature as God and as the angels: the separation between Creator and created is too great. So what is said in "Behold, Adam is . . . as one of us"? We may infer from this that there is one heavenly Adam, the one shown to the angels in heaven, an Adam from God, made by his word, and another, earthly Adam, fashioned from clay by the hand of God, and driven out of the garden. One is one with God; the second is not only "the other one," but "different," quite "other" from God.

After this unhappy fall of the race of man, God taught his angels the reinstatement that would one day come, and what he taught them was limited in its scope not by his didactic abilities, but by the angels' powers of comprehension. He showed them who would redeem the human race—for man's salvation was already provided for—and on this he said:

"Behold, here is that Adam who has existed in essence since the dawn of the world and of you, but who also was one with us in eternity, before the Creation, before time began." Onkelos interprets this, in the Chaldaic, as "Behold, Adam was my only son," that is, the only one begotten by me in eternity. (This is the word God uses in addressing Abraham: "Take now thy only son.") After showing the person of the redeemer to the angels, he removed all doubts by fixing a time for the task, in case they should think this redeemer would remove all the offence of such a beastly crime by some hasty and perfunctory act in the near future. He added:

LIBER PRIMVS IX.

Et nunc præsenti hoc tempore ne iste meus in æthernitate unicus qui subsistit ex me ipso, manum suam mittat & sumat etiam de ligno uitæ, innuendo scilicet ut q̃d solum nunc fieri prohiberet id olim concessurus sit. Quo prudenter intellexerant cp̃ tametsi non nunc attñ post, temporis successu per istum Adam cœlestẽ deo coæthernum ruina hæc ueniret de fructu ligni reparanda. Domino itacp̃ uniuersorũ sedenti super thronum suum, oẽs cœli exercitus assistẽtes ei, ut inquit Michaea dextris & a sinistris, pro tanta erga mortalium imbecillitatem clementia gratias egerunt. Missus est igitur angelus Raziel ad Adam collapsum & mœrore plenum, ut consolaretur eum, cui sic dixit. Ne supra modum conficiaris gemitu & molestia cp̃ te duce genus humanum in summã corruit perditionẽ. Qm̃ originale peccatum hoc expiabitur. Nam ex tua propagatiõe nascetur homo iustus & pacificus, uir heros, cui nomen continebit in miserationibus, etiã has quatuor literas i.h.u.h. & ille p̃ rectam fidem & placidam oblationẽ mittet manum suam, & sumet de ligno uitæ, & eius ligni fructus erit oĩm sperantium salus. Quo sermone finito, ille damnatus & erumnosus Adã inter miserias oẽs quas incidit, inter dolorem, inter luctum, quo in tanta calamitate fuerat affectus confidens in deum mutandi delicti spem concepit, & iccirco incredibili erga factorẽ suum amore tactus, diuinæ clemen tiæ gratiam habuit. Hæc fuit omnium prima Cabala, primordialis salutis nuncia, O rem gratam, o causam desyderabilem. Quid commodius? qd acceptius? quid potuit magis opportunum p̃ditæ conditioni mortalium a superis afferri? quid opis p̃stari conuenientius q̃ ut salutem publicã captiuis nunciarent. Hęc est illa reuelatio sanctissima & summa, in quam oẽs diuinæ reuelationes reducunt, hæc optatissima traditio, hęc saluberrima receptio, in qua oẽs Cabalisticæ receptiones recapitulant, oẽs diuinorum traditiones, oẽs cœlestium eruditioẽs & uatum uisiones & beatorum meditationes uniuntur & cõicantur. Quam ob rem cum singula hæc Adam uxori suæ palam renunciasset cœpit ea p̃sente ad posteritatis commemorationem & gratiarũ actionẽ erecto altari deo sacrificare. Ita.n. Magistri nostri tradiderũt. שגם אדם הראשון הקריב שור פר
.i. cp̃ tum Adam primus obtulit iuuencum. At Heua iam futura uiuentiũ mater summota desperatione, tandem a uiro suo cognita concepit, & peperit primogenitũ. Vnde ingẽti & incredibili gaudio p̃fusa, cp̃ putaret eĩ mox saluatorẽ esse natũ sic exclamauit קניתי איש את יהוה
.i. Acquisiui uirum illum quatuor literarũ, quas literas ab angelo iam pridẽ n receperant, & acquisitum noĩauit Cain. Quem ubi parẽtes agnoscerent, præter spem prauis moribus q̃uersum, alteram inchoarunt natiuitatem & genuerunt Abel. Adulescentibuscp̃ tunc utriscp̃ filiis, tradiderunt hanc Cabalã .i. ab auditu de salute restituenda receptionem, tum ab Abel

C iii

Book One

"And now at the present moment we must not allow my only-begotten in eternity, who subsists by me myself, to stretch out his hand and take also from the Tree of Life"; which suggests surely that the one thing now banned would one day be permitted. From this it has been reasonably deduced that though it will not happen now, later, in the fullness of time, it will come about that the ruin deriving from the eating of the fruit of the Tree will be repaired, through that heavenly Adam coeternal with God. The whole host of heaven that stood about the Lord of All as he sat upon his throne, to right and left (according to Micha), gave thanks for such compassion for the weakness of men.

So the angel Raziel was sent to Adam as he lay grief-stricken, to console him, and the angel said:

> Don't lie shuddering, burdened with grief, thinking of your responsibility for bringing the race of man to perdition. The primal sin will be purged in this way: from your seed will be born a just man, a man of peace, a hero whose name will in pity contain these four letters— *YHWH* —and through his upright trustfulness and peaceable sacrifice will put out his hand, and take from the Tree of Life, and the fruit of that Tree will be salvation to all who hope for it.

After this speech, Adam, while abandoned, condemned to all the unhappiness, the pain, the grief he met, still in such adversity, trusted in God and hoped for forgiveness of his transgression, and moved by a love for his Maker that is beyond belief, was thankful for divine mercy.

This was the first Kabbalah of all—the announcement of primordial salvation. How praiseworthy, how much to be desired! What could be more apt, what more fitting a gift that those on high should bestow on men in their hopeless situation; no succor could be more timely, as with the announcement of an amnesty to prisoners.

This is the highest and most holy revelation of all. All God's revelations can be reduced to it. This is the most beloved of "handings down." It encapsulates all the principles of Kabbalah, all the traditions concerning the divine, knowledge of heaven, visions of the prophets, and meditations of the blessed.

Adam told all of this openly to his wife, and, so that posterity should remember and give thanks, he built an altar and began sacrifice. The rabbis tell us: "Adam was the first to offer up a bullock." And Eve was now to be the mother of living men, her despair ceased, and in time she lay with her husband, conceived and bore her first child. Flushed with immense, unbelievable joy, she thought she had given birth to her Savior. "I have the man of the four letters," she cried aloud, meaning the letters the angel had mentioned. She called her new son Cain. When his parents realized that, contrary to their hopes, he was vicious and bad, they again set about the process of giving birth and produced Abel. To the two young men they handed down the Kabbalah they had themselves received, concerning the restoration to well-being.

DE ARTE CABALISTICA

ardenter amatam, tum à Cain uiliter despectam. Opinione uero ductus Abel, q̃d ipse foret idem ille de quo reuelatam expectarent restauratione cum se deo gratum, fide recta et oblatione accepta sentiret, eo q̃ ad ipsum
V respexerat dn̄s & ad munera eius, ad Cain aūt & ad munera illius non respexit, toto coepit pectore mentisq̃ affectu ligni fructum desyderare, quẽ in oblatione uitæ constitutum esse iudicabat, eaq̃ rōne lignum uitę dictũ & ita cognoiatum, q̃ esset per lignum uita creatori offerenda, qui dedit illam, quare manum suam eo conat⁹ est mittere, q̃ de ligno acciperet, abs sumeret ac aboleret, hoc em̄ אבל designat. Vnde fratris cōtra se odiũ patienter tulit & quærenti occasionem rixæ, uehementer etiam irato, nō se blandis uerbis expostulauit, ut mitigaret illum, sed prorsus tacuit. Cũq̃ uideret sibi mortem rapto de arbore ramo uel lignea claua Cain minantem, q̃ maxime lætatus est, sperans ligno interfici, non enim tum erat ferri usus ante ortum Thubalcain, qui primus fuit malleator & faber in cūcta opera æris & ferri. Claua itaq̃ lignea & prægrãdi munitus dixit Cain ad Abel fratrem suum. Et fuit cum essent in cāpo & insurgebat Cain in Abel fratrem suum & occidit eum. Romani addunt legendo dixit Cain, Egredi amur foras, q̃d non est in sacræ scripturæ contextu. Abel aūt inermis armato non restitit, sed uolens & libens se morti obtulit. Cum non tm̄ satis dare pro nobis creditori deo, uerum etiam & originale debitum omnino soluere si fieri posset, & acceptabilis deuota constitutaq̃ hostia in solutũ præstari paratus esset. Post uero q̃ iste decesserat sine liberis, sustinuit Adam multo tempore, si forte q̃d in filiis non inuenisset, id contingeret in nepotibus. Sed quid iam speraret in reproba Cain gn̄atione de qua pridem omnis fiducia euanuit, uidebat eam omnem sellulariis artibus & opificiis incumbere, studio seruili nauare opam, tenuiora cōmoda & officia corpori necessaria sequi, nihil diuinum cogitare, nihil liberale, nihil heroico uiro dignum, quare aliam prolem & aliud semen à deo petiit & impetrauit, quo plane supra q̃ dici queat exhilaratus est pientissimus pater sic
X dicens, Posuit mihi deus semen aliud pro Abel quem occidit Cain. Ideoq̃ uocauit nomen eius Seth, quem genuit ad imaginem & similitudinẽ suã, non q̃ cęteri eius liberi non habuissent formam & imaginem humanam qui & hoīes quoq̃ erant. Sed quia reliq̃rum hactenus pter Abel, potius dæmoniorum gn̄atio q̃ hoīm dicenda fuerat, propter illorum execrabilẽ maliciam & uitia detestanda. Non igitur q̃ dæmones & diabolos substantiuos genuisset, id ita nunc additur, q̃d impii & prophani quidam mentiũtur. Sed q̃ uoluntate malos. Nihil aūt est malum nisi uitium & dæmoniũ Pergam itaq̃ si uultis ut qua ianua sint ingressus ultra proficiscar. Et illi p ge diligenter obsecramus inquiunt. Denuo Simon ait, pater noster Adã, rursus ex Seth nepotem suscepit, memor eius Cabalæ quã sibi Raziel tra
                                                        diderat

On the Art of Kabbalah

Abel took all this to heart; Cain paid no attention. Abel thought that it was from him that the restoration could be expected. He felt himself in God's favor, his faith was unswerving, his offerings were accepted. God looked kindly on him and his gifts, not on Cain and his. Abel began to long for the fruit of the Tree with all his heart and his mind, for he judged that in his offerings there was life, so that they could reasonably be said to be "the Tree of Life," because it was through this Tree that life was to be offered up to the Creator who gave it. He tried to reach it with his hand, so that what he got from the Tree he might consume and destroy—hence the name "Abel." For this reason he bore patiently his brother's anger with him, and when he tried vehemently to pick a quarrel with him, made no attempt to mollify him. He just said nothing. He was happy when he saw Cain brandishing the branch of a tree or a wooden club, threatening to kill him, for he hoped that it would be by wood that he was to die. (There were no iron weapons before Tubulcain, the first smith, who forged bronze and iron for all purposes.) Cain, then, ready with a wooden club, spoke with his brother Abel. And so it was that when they were in the fields Cain rose up against Abel his brother and killed him. (The Romans add this reading: "Cain said, let us go outside," but this is not in the text of the Holy Scripture.)

Abel, unarmed, made no resistance to his armed adversary. He offered himself to death freely and willingly. But this gift was not enough to redeem our debt to God. Even so, one day the original debt will be altogether absolved, and an acceptable offering, an appointed victim will come forward ready to absolve us.

Abel died childless. For a long time Adam waited to see whether he would find in his grandchildren what he had not found in his children. But no hope was to be had in the rejected offspring of Cain. All his confidence in them had vanished long since. They were all busy with trade, manufacture, servile occupations, chasing after their trivial creature comforts, concerned for the needs of the body. They had no thought for the divine, nor for noble matters, or the things worthy of Godlike men. So Adam begged another child from God and his request was granted, at which this pious father was beside himself with happiness: "God has given me another child, in place of Abel whom Cain slew."

This new child he called Seth. He looked just like his father—not that the other children were not in human form, they were men too, but except for Abel, all the rest seemed more like a crop of devils than men, such was their malice and wickedness. I must add that he did not actually produce demons and changelings as some of the vulgar and irreverent have falsely claimed. Simply, they were men with evil dispositions, though nothing is bad except through vices and evil spirits.

Shall I go on? That is, if you would like me to; now that we have crossed the threshold, I may as well proceed.

The others attentively begged him to go on.

SIMON: At last our father Adam was presented with a grandson by Seth. Adam still held in mind the Kabbalah he had received from Raziel: that from his seed would be born a savior. So the child was

LIBER PRIMVS

diderat cp ex sua propagatiõe nasceretur homo futurus saluator. Quare uocatus est Enos.i.homo, tunc putabatur & quidem ualde speratum fuit eum appellandum fore iuxta Cabalam angelicã per nomen quatuor literarum i.h.u.h. uel saltem magis Cabalistice in miserationibus per Sin literã de medio quatuor litera̱rũ, i.h.u.h. Sic enim in sacra historia scribit אָז הוּחַל לִקְרֹא בְּשֵׁם יְהוָה qd latini non admodũ docte legunt. Iste coepit inuocare nomen dñi, sed rari quidam & contemplantissimi Cabalistarum, rectius quo ad linguę proprietatem interptant ita de גִימַטְרִיָא tunc expectatus est uocari per Sin literã, quę in arte Cabalistica idem quod בְּרַחֲמִים i. in miserationibus, & Mem lřa per Notariacon designat מִתּוֹךְ i. de medio scilicet quatuor istarum literarum i.h.u.h. Perinde atcp hoc modo intelligi deberet אָז הוּחַל לִקְרֹא בְּשִׁין מִתּוֹךְ יְהוָה i. tunc expectatus est uocari per Sin de medio i.h.u.h. quasi pro angeli enunciato Enos sumeret de ligno uitæ mundumcp redimeret, heros ipse nominatus i.h.in miserationibus u.h. notate arcanum & animaduertite mysterium. Cũ uero iam nullius angeli destinatiõe hoc modo appellaretur, tum isto relicto in aliũ spem suam locarunt. Angelorum nancp.i.dei nunciorum monitu nomĩa patribus indita sunt pro quibuslibet euentis, siue præteritis ut quia posse di uocatus est Cain. Seu p̄sentibus ut quia uir, uocatus est Enos, aut futuris ut quia parentibus luctum p̄biturus, uocabatur Abel. Expectatio hæc in quartam trahitur Enos progeniem, & de Iared natus est Henoch, qui ambulauit cum deo, sed disparuit, qm̄ abstulit eum deus. Tertio abhinc tractu uenit Noe in consolationem omnium publicam illam auditu receptam salutem recta fide sperantiũ, quorum ex uniuersa plebe tm̄ octo inuenti sunt qui placeret deo. Fuit etenim Noe uir iustus & perfectus in generationibus suis, & ambulauit cum deo, qui recepit in mandatis ut faceret arca de lignis in qua saluaret mun̄dum. Cabalice igitur sperauit in lignum, sic enim Iob ait כִּי יֵשׁ לָעֵץ תִּקְוָה i. quia est ad lignum spes, de hoc fato certior fact̄ cp in ligno uita homini suisset promissa. Sed post ebrietatem sequuta est confusio. Vnde & Babel cognōiatur, q̄ nunc Babylon a Balbel.i.chaldaice confusio. Hęc sub familia & liberis Noe fuit orta. Erant aũt filii eı̄9 Sem Ham & Iapheth. Futu̱ro itacp dei seruo Sem in quo salutẽ præ cæteris sperabat, ita bñdixit בָּרוּךְ יְהוָה אֱלֹהֵי שֵׁם qd Cabalistice tra̱ducit̄. Benedictus quatuor literis dei Sem, per hoc inq̄t Cabaliste הוֹדִיעַ כִּי יִהְיֶה שֵׁם עוֹבֵד הָאֱלֹהִים .i. Notum fecit cp futurus erat Sem seruus dei, ut scribit Rabi Moyses Gerundensis. Quo intelligimus desyderium pii patris fuisse cp Sem benediceretur appellatione quatuor literarum i.h.u.h. ut fieret originalis peccati redemptor. At ne tunc quidem illud uenisse tempus a deo statutũ, quo

C iiii

named Enos, that is, "man." It was thought, indeed strongly hoped, that his name would accord with the kabbalah of the angel, the four-letter name, *YHWH,* or be at the least, "in mercy" or, more Kabbalistically, that he would have the letter *S* between the four letters.[11] In the sacred account is written, though the translation here is not too well phrased: "They began to invoke the name of the Lord." The translation is accurate, but some more thoughtful Kabbalists have made a more correct interpretation than is rendered by the literal translation. According to Gematria,[12] "He wanted to be called by the letter *S*." In the art of Kabbalah this is equivalent to "in mercy." Now according to Notaricon,[13] the letter *M* stands for "in the middle of" (understood, the four letters *YHWH*). Thus the phrase is altered to read: "He wanted to be called by the letter *S* in the middle of the four letters *YHWH*." Enos would take from the Tree of Life in accordance with the angel's message, and redeem the world, as a Godlike man bearing the name *YH-in mercy-WH*. Note this well. It is a sacred mystery.[14]

But he had been named without guidance from the angels, and they turned away from him and placed their hopes elsewhere, being God's messengers. The patriarchs were named on the angels' advice. Their names all signify events: whether in the past, like Cain, indicating that he was possessed; or present, like Enos, indicating a man, or future, as Abel, indicating that he would bring grief to his parents.

Something was expected of Enos' descendents. Enoch was born, the son of Jored, and he walked with God, but he disappeared. God had stolen him away. Three generations later came Noah, to the comfort of the righteous faithful who lived in hope of the salvation of which they had heard — in all the world there were found only eight such men who pleased God. Noah in his generation was just, and righteous, and walked with God. He was instructed in how to build a wooden ark to rescue the world. A Kabbalistic touch: he put his trust in wood[15] (as Job says, "There is hope in wood"), and by doing so he was made certain that through wood life was promised to man. After the flood, chaos came, known as Babel (in the same way, Babylon, from Babel), from the Chaldaic word for chaos. This came about under Noah's family. His sons were Shem, Ham, and Japheth. Hoping that Shem rather than the others was to be the servant of God, he uttered the benediction "Blessed be the Lord God of Shem." In Kabbalist tradition this is "He makes it known that Shem will be God's servant," as Nachmanides wrote. From this we understand that the devout father's longing was for Shem to be blessed with the four-letter name, to become the redeemer of the original sin.

DE ARTE CABALISTICA

tanti casus reparatio cõtingeret angelus Iophiel ipsi Sem adnũciauit, Ita enim scribunt Cabalistæ רבו של שם יופיאל .i. præceptor ipsius Sem fuit Iophiel. Suspendebant igitur ea secula super eiuscemodi re cogitationes suas, usq; in annos Abrahæ filii Tharhæ qui primo nomine fuit Abram, Ei uiro erat angelus quidam familiaris Zadkiel, sic n.

A scribunt Cabalistæ: רבו של אברהם צדקיאל .i. Præceptor Abrahæ fuit Zadkiel, qui eandem ei Cabalam tradidit recipienti, quam Adę protoplasmati Raziel. Deniq;, ut arbitror, reliqua sunt haud ignota q̃ quanto ille tpę uocatus fuerat Abram & uxor eius Sarai tam diu nũq̃ sibi hæredem genuerant. Post uero q̃ nomen uiri mutabatur Abrahã & uxoris nomen Sara, mox Ishac susceperunt filium; de quo cum ei iussisset deus ut unigenitum tolleret quem diligebat Ishac, & eum in excelso Morię quodam monte super ligno imolaret, incredibile uidetur quo gaudio & quanta lętitia exultauerit, diuinæ promissionis memor, qua pollicebat̃ ei deus his uerbis. Statuam, inquit, pactum meum inter me & te & inter semen tuum post te in gñationibus suis fœdere sempiterno, ut sim deus tuus & seminis tui post te, atq; in te benedicentur uniuersæ cognationes terræ. Quapropter quã diximus humanæ uniuersitatis salutem in filio se confidebat allaturum, quem subito ad uocem dei assumpsit, & oblationis omē lignum suis ipse manibus excidit. Nempe lapsum originalem per lignum reparari posse, oraculũ docuit. Vnde scriptura dicit, q̃ tulit Abraham ligna oblationis, imposuitq̃ super Ishac filium suum, & posuit eũ in altare sup struem lignorum, extẽditq̃ manum & arripuit gladium ut imolaret filium suum. Nisi n. recepisset Ishac a patre suo traditã humanæ salutis Cabalam p lignũ uitæ atq; hois cuiusdã iusti oblationem futuræ, ut est cunctis uiuentibus horribile mori, non utiq; fuisset tanta beneuolentia & tam alacri uultu animiq; hilaritate uisam impendere præ oculis mortem sponte amplexus, sed uelut est mortalium cõditio aut strictũ mucronē declinasset, aut uerbis saltem quibusdam lenioribus patris sęuiciam uel mitigasset tñ, uel fugisset. Atqui suspicatus sese fore illum quo futura esset primordialis ruinæ restauratio, nihil sibi ea imolatione duxit iucundius, nihil dulcius ea morte, cuius gratia totum opinione sua redimeret̃ genus humanum. Prębuit sane illi hanc ipsam spem eo firmiorem q̃ eundem locum de-

B ab orbe condito sacrificiis destinauerat. Terra nãq; Moria est digito dei Abrahæ demonstrata, in qua primus Adam struxit altare, obtulitq̃ deo munera, ubi & Cain & Abel, ubi & Nohe filiiq̃ sui sacrificarunt. Sicut Magistri nostri disputãt in capitulis Rabi Eliezer, astipulante Ramban et Rabi Ioseph filio Carnitolis in libro portaȩ iustitiæ, & in loco eodē urbs sancta Ierusalem cõstructa est Salomone Gallo teste. Re aũt infecta cum è Moria discederet pater atq; filius, audita est uox Zadkielis ad Abrahã prolata

On the Art of Kabbalah

But that even then God's appointed time for repairing such a fall had not come was told to Shem by the angel Jophiel. (Thus the Kabbalists write: "Jophiel was Shem's instructor.")

Succeeding generations clung onto thoughts like this, till the time of Abraham the son of Terah; he who was first called Abram. Zadkiel was his familiar angel — the Kabbalists write: "The teacher of Abraham was Zadkiel." From him he received the same Kabbalah as Adam, the first man, had had from Raziel. The rest, I think, is well known: how as long as he was called Abram and his wife Sarai they produced no heir, and how later, having changed their names to Abraham and Sarah, they had a son, Isaac. God ordered Abraham to take this only son whom he loved and bring him to the summit of Mount Moriah, and there sacrifice him, on a heap of wood. It is hard to believe how happy, even light-hearted, he was, when he bore in mind God's promise to him that "I will establish my covenant between you and your seed after you in their generations forever, that I shall be your God, and the God of your seed, and that in you shall all the nations of the earth be blessed." But on this account he believed that by his son he would bring about the very salvation of man we have been discussing.

At God's word he seized his son without warning, and with his own hands stacked the wood for his offering. According to the prophecy, after all, the original fault could only have wood for its remedy. And so it is written that Abraham brought all the wood for his offering, and Isaac his son as well, and placed him on the altar on top of the stack of wood, and reached out, and grasped the sword with which to sacrifice his son. Now had Isaac not received from his father the Kabbalah that human salvation would derive from the wood of life, and the offering of a just man, he would not have reached out willingly and so receptively to the death he saw hanging before his eyes — all living things find it hard to die — but, as is only human, he would have cringed at the drawn sword, or at the least pleaded with his father to calm him, or escaped. But he felt that it might be through him that the rebuilding of man's ruin was to be effected, and so nothing could be more agreeable than this sacrifice, nothing sweeter than this death through which the whole race of man would, he believed, be saved. The ground of Moriah had been marked out by the finger of God to Abraham. There had Adam first built an altar and brought gifts to God, there had Cain and Abel, Noah and his sons made sacrifice. Our rabbis worked out, in the writings of Rabbi Eliezer, with the agreement of Maimonides and Rabbi Joseph Gikatilla in his book *Gates of Justice,* that the holy city of Jerusalem was built there on the same spot. The business was left unfinished: father and son came down from Mount Moriah. Then was heard Zadkiel's voice saying to Abraham: "In your seed shall all the na-

prolata benedicentur in semine tuo omnes gentes terræ. Quo salus uni/
uersa in futuram generationem cognoscebatur esse protelata. Et uox ipa
dei per angelum Raphaelē super Ishac quocg cœlitus delapsa. Benedicen
tur in semine tuo oēs gētes terrę, ne forte seipsum fore salua, torem illum
cre deret. Nā hoc quocg Cabalistarum est qui scribunt sic רבו של
יצחק רפאל .i.p̄ceptor ipsius Ishac fuit Raphael. Ei uiro de filio
rum altero spes nō erat, qui iam benedictionem paternam exercitatiōe ue
nandi amiserat. Esau nomen fuit. de altero magna sibi pollicitus pater p̄di
xit his uerbis rei uenturæ uaticinium p̄tendentibus. Seruient tibi populi
& adorabunt te gentes. Non acciderat igitur sine causa de Iacob (sic em̄
appellabatur iste filius) tam ingens maioribus nostris uniuersę salutis ex
pectatio, sed quia omnium mortalium primus ip̄e uidit portam cœli aper
tam, & scalam a terra in cœlum porrectam, & in ea consistentes quatuor
literas i.h.u.h. quas apprehendere gerebat in uotis. Cōsonantem q̄cg Sin
per Notariacō שמך .i. unctionem designantē, operi adiecit, q̄ delibutū
lapidem in templum q̄ddam noīe Bethel exædificauit. Augebat suspicio
nem, cp angelus Peliel Iacob erat familiaris. qui multa constanti & opini/
one & sermone p̄monuit, tum cp Iacob elegit sibi deus, tum cp beatus erit
ille cui deus Iacob in adiutorio eius. Scribunt autem Cabalistæ sic רבו
של יעקב פליאל .i. Præceptor Iacob fuit Peliel, Sed edoctus ab
angelo suo Iacob, se non illum fore saluatorem quē hactenus cœlestis Ca
bala prætulerit, negocium in aliud seculum diuina reuelatione reiecit, sic
dicens, Congregamini & adnunciabo uobis q̄d continget in postremo di
erum. Non auferet sceptrum de Iuda, & legislator de femore eius, donec
ueniat Silo, & eidem congregatio gētium. Quo uaticinio innotuit aliquē
q̄ncg fore saluatorem humani generis qui & ex Iuda & in postremis die
rum nasceret, & esset Silo, & sceptrum regni gereret, & ad ipsum gentes
confluerent. Quare post hos patriarchas magnus ille Moyses nō sua spō
te morti se obtulit, sicut quōdam Abel, sicut olim Ishac, sed renuit & a cu
ra populi subtrahere se uoluit, quanq̄ loquebat̄ cum deo ut amicus cū ami
co, facie ad faciem, & baculo utebat̄ pro sceptro, & tota Iudæorum gēs ad
se confluebat. Nouerat tn̄ se non de familia Iudæ, sed de domo Leui ortū
esse, nec natum in postremis dierum, nec esse Silo, q̄d secundum Syriacā
translationem Onkeli Chaldęi significat unctum, quem nos appellamus
Messiha. De omni tn̄ ratione atcg modo restaurandi originalis casus satis
sup̄cg institutus fuit ab angelo suo Metattron. Ita em̄ Cabalistę scribūt,
רבו של משה מטטרון qui est nūcius Sadai. Hanc itacg san
ctissimi Iacob reuelationem uniuersitas prophetarū recepit, q̄d in postre
mis dierum nascat̄ is ex semine Iuda qui peccatum originale sit aboliturꝰ,
Messiha rex pacificus, desinēte tum sceptro ac p̄fectura Iudæ, couocatiscg

tions of the earth be blessed." And so he realized that the salvation of all had been postponed to a future generation. The word of God fell on Isaac too, brought from heaven by the angel Raphael: "In your seed shall all nations of the earth be blessed," emphasizing that he was not the Savior. (Some Kabbalists write that Isaac's teacher was Raphael.)

Of Isaac's sons, there was no hope in one because he had lost the blessing of his father while out hunting; to the other, much was promised by Isaac, whose prophetic words stretched into the future: "Let the people serve thee, and nations bow down to thee." There was good reason for our ancestors to anticipate universal salvation through Jacob (such was the name of the son in question). He was the first man to see the gate of heaven opened, and a ladder reaching from earth to heaven, and on it he saw, while praying, the four letters *YHWH*. There he set up the stone he had anointed as a shrine, known as Bethel, and by his labor added in an *S*, which by the Notariacon method signifies *shemen*, or "anointing oil."[16] Added to this was Peliel his personal angel, who by consistent thought and advice taught that Jacob had been chosen of God, and that he who was helped by the God of Jacob would be blessed. (The Kabbalists write: "Peliel was Jacob's instructor.") But Jacob was told by his angel that he was not able to be the Savior proffered by the heavenly Kabbalah, and by divine revelation he found out that the event was to be brought forward to another generation—as when he said: "Gather yourselves together and I shall tell you what shall befall you in the last days. The scepter shall not depart from Judah, nor a lawgiver from between his feet, until Shiloh come, and unto him shall the gathering of the people be." By this he prophesied clearly that a savior of the human race would be born from Judah in the last days, that there would be Shiloh, that he would wield a king's scepter, and that all nations would flow to him.

After those patriarchs came great Moses. Because of this prophecy he did not volunteer for death as had Abel and Isaac. He shied away, wanted to give up the care of his people, even though he talked with God face to face, as one friend to another, even though he used his staff as a scepter, and all the Jewish people gathered around him. He knew that he was not of the tribe of Judah, but of the house of Levi, nor was his birth in the last days, nor was there Shiloh. *Shiloh,* according to Onkelos's Syriac rendering, means "the anointed" in Chaldaic; him we call the Messiah. He was told everything concerning the root of the original Fall and the manner of the restoration by his angel Metattron. (Thus the Kabbalists write: "Moses' teacher was Metattron," the messenger of the Almighty.)

All the prophets took in this most holy revelation of Jacob, that in the last days would be born of the seed of Judah the Messiah, a

DE ARTE CABALISTICA

simul undiquaq; gētibus. Haec usq; huc receptio a patribus ad collegium prophetarum per successionem transmigrauit, qui singulatim cuncti tra

G ctatione q̃tidiana inter se conferebant de aureo Messihae seculo, in illa beata spiritus sancti schola exultantes p̄ summa laetitia & imo de pectore gaudia sua promentes, uno q̃dam societatis uinculo in ipso Messiha saluatore cōnexi, quanq; diuersis a se temporibus de illo eodem uenturo rege multipharia multisq; modis differentes singuli tn̄ quicq; parem & plane haud absimilem sententiam absoluerunt. Hic quidem his uerbis, Obsecro dn̄e mitte שלחני quem missur⁹ es, alter in persona Messihe inquit, Mitte me hoc est qd in Arithmetica progressiōe p artificiosum Cabalę mo

H dum, tum quatriliteram excellentię dignitate, tum ipsum quoq; iuxta Razielis traditionem supius commemoratā rectum nomen illius Messihae per aequalitatem numeri trecentorum nonaginta octo significat. Et iterū Vtinam dirumperes coelos & descenderes. Alius sic. Excita potentiā tuā & ueni ad saluandum nos, deus reuerte nos, & ostende faciem tuam & salui erimus. Alius, Expg̃ctabo deum saluatorē meum. Alius, Ecce dn̄s egredietur de loco suo & descendet. Alius, Deponet iniquitates nostras & proiiciet in profundum maris oīa peccata nostra. Alius, Veniēs ueniet & nō tardabit, egressus es in salutem populi tui, in salutem cū Messiha tuo. Ali⁹ qui consolabat̄ gentem nostram dicens. Abstulit dn̄s iudicium tuum. Rex Israel quatuor literis in medio tui erit, non timebis malum ultra. Domin⁹ deus tuus in medio tui erit fortis, ip̄e saluabit. Alius q in persona Messihę pollicebat̄. Et erit sicut eratis maledictio in gentibus domus Iuda & dom⁹ Israel, sic saluabo uos & eritis benedictio, & erunt sicut fuerunt qn̄ non proieceram eos. Et alius ita. Orietur uobis timentibus nomē meum sol iusticię. Quid multis moror? omnes uno corde gaudere, uno ore omnes oīa bona dicere & laudare huius saluatoris illum diem, & optare illud tēpus de q̃ Dauid coram deo exclamauit, Mitte lucem tuam & ueritatem tuam, illa quietabunt me, & reducent me in montem sanctum tuum & in habitacula tua. Super isto aūt lucis uocabulo dixit Rabi Salomō Gallus. Lucem

I tuam, id est regem Messiham, secundum q̃ scriptum est, Paraui candelabrum Messihae meo. Vnde certiores facti sumus nulla de se ductum esse opinione Dauid q̃ ipse idem ille foret rex Messiha, qui genus humanum deo conciliaret, tametsi diuinum emanauerit oraculum. Inueni Dauid seruum meū, oleo sancto meo unxi eum (quia unctus dicit̄ Messiha) & ego primogenitum dabo illum, supiorem regibus terrae. In aethernū custodiā illi misericordiam meam, & pactum meum fidele illi, & ponam in seculū seculi semen eius & sedem eius sicut dies coelorum. Contulit ergo Dauid spem oēm in semen suum, ob idq; filiū ex Bathsaba natum appellauit Salomonem, q̃ auditu receperat, crediderat q; Messiham, quo salus mūdo ueniret

peaceable king, who would wipe out the original sin, and that then would end the ruling kingship of Judah, and the nations would be gathered in.

This message has passed down from the patriarchs through the fellowship of prophets. One by one all talked among themselves as they went about their daily business of the golden age of the Messiah, rejoicing in that schoolroom of the Holy Spirit, exuding deep happiness. They were joined, as it were, to the Messiah, the Savior himself, by this chain of comradeship. Though they lived in times far removed from the kingdom to come, and were in many ways very different individuals, they felt that everyone was serving what was plainly much the same sentence. One prophet says, "I beseech you O God: send whom you will." Another, in the person of the Messiah, says, "Send me" (*Shalachni* in Hebrew. By the arithmetic system worked out by Kabbalah, this signifies both the supreme four letters and the correct name of the Messiah in the tradition of Raziel by their numerical equality to three hundred and ninety-eight[17]). Elsewhere we have "Oh break open the heavens, come down." "Thy power be roused, O God, turn again to us, show us thy face, and we shall be saved." "I will wait for God my savior." "See, God will leave his holy place, he will come down." "He will take away our iniquities and cast our sins into the depths of the sea." "He who comes will not be slow, you have come out to save your people, to save them with your Messiah." Elsewhere we find one comforting our people with "God has quashed your sentence. The King of Israel, he of the four letters, will be in the midst of you, you shall fear no ill. The Lord God will be strong in the midst of you, he himself will save." Another in the person of the Messiah: "As once you were a curse among the nations, house of Judah and house of Israel, so you will be a blessing, and they will be just as they were before I threw them out." Another: "The Sun of Justice will dawn on those who fear my name."

Why go on? All were like-mindedly joyful. All praised, all blessed that day of salvation, all lived in hope of that time of which David cried out to God: "Send your light and your truth. They will bring me rest, they will lead me back to your holy hill and your dwelling place." Commenting on this word "light," Rashi said: "Your light is the Kingdom of the Messiah, as in the writing 'I have prepared a lamp for my Messiah.'" So by this we know that David did not think of himself as the Messiah to reconcile man to God, despite God's word: "I have found my servant David. I have anointed him with my holy oil (note: the Messiah is "the anointed") and I will give him that firstborn child to be over earthly kings. I will keep mercy with him to everlasting, and faithfully keep my covenant with him. I will establish his seed from generation to generation, and his rule as the days of heaven." Thus David placed all his hope in his offspring, and accordingly names the son Bathsheba bore him "Solomon," because he had heard and believed that the

LIBER PRIMVS XII.

hiret utiçp principem pacis fore,iuxta Cabalam sibi reuelatã.In diebus ei9
erit abundantia pacis donec auferat luna. De alio igitur semine suo intel
ligendum fuit q̃ de filio Bathsabę,is em̃ Salomon adamauit mulieres,per
quas cor eius deprauatum est ut sequeretur deos alienos,nec erat cor ei9
pfectum cum dño deo suo sicut cor Dauid patris eius. Quapropter susci
tauit deus Satan contra Salomonem, ut ei non esset pax integra qui pacis
solum nomen haberet.Quotquot igitur Cabalistarum sunt qui uniuer
sam salutem in Salomonem retorserunt,alium quendam Salomohem in
tendunt q̃ filium Bathsabæ,& aliud quoq̃ templum q̃ eius Salomonis q
templum a se constructũ diruptionis iuri subiecit,cui prædixit deus. Tẽ
plum quod sanctificaui nomini meo proiiciam a conspectu meo.Qua de
re peccatum originale non ualuerũt abolere,necq̃ Salomon hic,necq̃ tem
plum hoc, quantumuis in Porta lucis à Cabalista sic scriptum extat.

K

בתחלת בריאתו של עולם שכינה הית שרויה
בתחתונים ובהיות השכינה למטה נמצאו
שמים וארץ אחרים והיו המקונות והצינורות
פועלים בשלימות ונמשכים מלמעלה למטה
ונמצא השם ית ממלא מעלה ומטה בא אדם
הראשון וחטא ונתקלקלו השורות ונשתברו
הצינורות ופסקה הברכה ונסתלקה השכינה
ונתפרדה החבילה אחב בא שלמה ובנה את
הבית ואז חזרו הצינורות והחמשבות:

i. Ini
tio creationis mundi diuina cohabitatio erat descendens in inferiora,&
cum esset diuina cohabitatio inferius, reperti sunt cœli, & terra uniti,&
erant fontes & cannales actiui in pfectione,& trahebant a superiore ad in
ferius,& inueniebatur deus complens superne & inferne.Venit Adã pri
mus & peccauit & diruti sunt descensus, & confractæ cannales, & desiit
aquæductus,& cessauit diuina cohabitatio,& diuisa est societas. Postea
uenit Salomon & exædificauit domum,& tunc reuersæ sunt cannales ac
deriuationes seu ductus, atq̃ reliqua.Vbi de Salomone loquentes Caba
listæ rei potius uident q̃ uocabulo alludere,cum illud intelligant de uen
turo q̃dam rege pacifico iuxta Isaiæ uerba, quę noĩa bit ipe miraculos9
operator,cõsiliarius,deus fortis,pater futuri seculi שר שלום .i.prĩ
cipem pacis Sane putauerũt aliqui Ezechiam regem hic fuisse designatũ
sed alii uerba legentes sequentia, Multiplicabit eius impium,& pacis nõ
erit finis super solium Dauid & sup regnum eius,intelligunt de rege Mes
siha qui ablaturus sit uniuersorum peccata, in animis hoĩm q̃tidiana bella

Book One

Messiah, through whom would come salvation to the world, would be a prince of peace, as the Kabbalah revealed to him: "In those days peace will abound, till the moon is swept away." He understood that the Messiah must come from other of his offspring when he realized that Solomon, Bathsheba's son, loved women too well. They corrupted his judgment, he ran after strange gods; unlike David his father he was ill at ease with the Lord God. And so God raised up Satan against Solomon. Only his name retained any trace of peace. Those Kabbalists who credited universal salvation to Solomon had in mind another Solomon, not Bathsheba's son, and another temple, not this Solomon's temple built by him and fated for destruction. As God predicted, "The temple I have made holy by my Name I will throw down in my sight." So neither this Solomon nor this temple had the power to wipe out the original sin, despite what is written by the Kabbalist in *Gate of Light*.

> To begin with, at the creation of the world, God came down to dwell on earth. And while he dwelt here below, the heavens were open and were one with the earth. There were springs and water channels in perfect order which led from the world above to the world below, and there was God filling out the world above and the world below. Then came Adam, the first to sin, and the link snapped, the water channels were broken, the flow of water ceased. God no longer dwelt on the earth. he cut himself off. Afterwards came Solomon who built the temple, and then the water channels were replaced and the flow of water began again.

When Kabbalists talk of Solomon, they seem to allude to a state of affairs rather than the word. They understand a peaceful king to come, who in Isaiah's words "shall be called Wonderful, Counsellor, the mighty God, the everlasting Father, the Prince of Peace." Some have taken this to mean King Hezekiah here, but others, taking the words that follow : "Of the increase of his government and peace, upon the throne of David, and upon his Kingdom," conclude that this is the Messiah who will take away the sins of all.

DE ARTE CABALISTICA

& pugnas mouentia, quæ parentes nostri peccauerunt, ut scripsit Ieremi
as in libro Threnorum. Patres nostri peccauerunt, & non sunt, & nos ini
quitates eorum portauimus. Ita uideri qdem poterat Ionathæ Chaldæo,
qui pro Sar Salom, id est principe pacis traduxit superiore in loco.

L משיחא דשלמא .i. Messiha pacis. De quo iterum Isaias. Disci
plina pacis nostrę super eum, & in cicatrice ac liuore eius sanati sumus.
Hic erit ille Salomon qui templum multo sublimius eriget plane sempi
ternū & indissolubile. Sic. n. Cabalistæ scribūt. כי בית המקדש
של מטה מכוון כנגד בית המקדש של מעלה
.i. cp domus sanctuarii quæ est inferius disponitur iuxta domum sanctua
rii quæ est superius. A Salomone igitur illius terrestris templi conditore

M usce ad regem Iehoachin eundem qui & Iechoniah (habent nāce ambo
noia eaſdē literas tametsi transmutatas) expectatio salutis uniuersę apud
oēm cœtum prophetarum in ueturo Messiha collocata fuit, ab Isaia uscę
ad Malachiam qui aiebat. Statim ueniet ad templum suum dñator quem
uos quæritis. Sup quo Rabi Dauid Kimhi scribit cp dñator hic sit Messi
ha, qui & ipse nuncius erit testamenti, quem Ionathan Chaldęus Rabona
interpftatur. Post prophetas aūt, expectatio salutiferi aduentus Messihæ
totace Cabalistica exercitatio qualiscūce extat, quam recte in eiuſdē Meſ
sihæ sempiternam liberationē inglomerant, implicant atce reducūt, oñis
ea plane ad scribas legis & seniores quos appellarunt capita patrum qui

N præ multitudine haud numerantur, & ad magni concilii uiros descendit,
successiue recepta scholasticorum more, ab Ezra qui Cabalā tradidit Si

O meoni iusto sacerdoti magno synagogę pfecto, rursus ab illo recepit eius
auditor Antigonus cum sociis suis, de qbus fuerunt Zadok & Bethus, ra
dix hæreticorū, unde dicti sunt Zadokai & Bethusai, ut scribit Iudas leui
ta in libri Alcosder sermōe tertio. Deinde Ioseph filius Ioetzer, & Ioseph
filius Iohanan Hierosolymitanus, ab iis Iosua filius Parahiah, cuius fuit di
scipulus qdā Iesus Nazarenus Machabeorū ętate, non ille christianoꝶ. Et
Nithai Arbelensis, a qbus & Iuda filius Tabai, & Simeon filius Sota, de q
bus Semeia & Abtalion, ab his Hillel & Samai q habuerūt multa millia
discipulorū, ab istis Rabban Iohanan Ben Sdachai, & ille discipulos qnce
fouit, qui fuerunt Eliesder quem scribunt Eliezer filius Hircani, Iosue fili
us Hananię, Ioseph Cohen, & Simeon filius Nathanael, & Eleasdar filius
Arach. De Rabban Iohanan qui centum & uiginti uixit annos sortitus est
Cabalam suam Rabban Gamaliel, a q̃ Simeon filius, a quo ex liberis eius
Iuda Nagid qui magister noster sanctus dicit, eum filius Gamaliel recipi
endo imitatus est. Hucusce Cabalæi q̃rum dicta & reliquas sacræ scriptu
ræ allegoricas expositiones sequuti sunt Cabalistarum cœtus, Hanania fi
lius Acasiæ, Abba Saul. Rabi Tarphon. Acabia filius Mahalalleelis. Ha
nania

On the Art of Kabbalah

Those sins, those our parents commmitted, bring on the daily wars, the struggles in man's mind. As Jeremiah wrote in Lamentations, "Our fathers have sinned, not we ourselves, and we have borne their iniquities." Jonathan ben Uzziah has a similar interpretation, for he renders "Prince of Peace" in the phrase above as "Messiah of Peace" in Chaldaean.

Again Isaiah on the same theme: "The chastisement of our peace was upon him, and with his stripes we are healed." This will be the "Solomon" who builds a loftier temple, eternal, unshakeable. So the Kabbalists write: "The Temple below is laid out in accordance with the Temple above."

Thus from Solomon, founder of the earthly temple, down to King Jehoiachin (or Jechoniah — the names are the same, though the letters have been put in different orders), the prophets were all waiting for the universal salvation brought by the Messiah-to-come, from Isaiah down to Malachi, who said "The Lord whom you seek shall suddenly come to his temple." Rabbi David Kimchi writes that this Lord is the Messiah, who will proclaim a new covenant. Jonathan ben Uzziel translates this as *Rabona*.

After the prophets, this expectation of the coming of the Messiah bringing salvation, and all the practice of Kabbalah which is centered directly on the enduring deliverance of the Messiah, circles round it and leads back to it — all this was handed down to the scribes and elders (who are called "heads of the fathers," and are too many to count), to men of the Great Council. One man handing on to another[18] — in the same way as the scholastics did — Ezra to Simeon the Just, High Priest and head of the synagogue, he to Antigonus and his companions, who included Zadok and Bethus, originators of the heresies known as Zadokian and Bethusian,[19] (as Judah Halevi writes in his third lecture in *Alcosder*). Next Yose ben Joetzer and Yose ben Jochanan of Jerusalem; then Joshua ben Perachya (who taught a certain Jesus of Nazareth, though we are in the Macabite period, not the Christian). Next Nittai of Arbela, whose pupils were Judah ben Tabbai and Simeon ben Shetah, who in turn taught Shemaiah and Avtalyon; from them it was passed down to Hillel and Shammai, who themselves had several thousand followers, and then Rabbi Johanan ben Zakkai, who had five pupils — Eliesder (spelled "Eliezer") ben Hyrcanus, Joshua ben Hananiah, Yose Na Cohen, Simeon ben Bethanel, and Eleazar ben Arakh. From Rabbi Johanan, Rabbi Gamaliel also received the Kabbalah (Johanan lived to be a hundred and twenty); Simeon ben Gamaliel was taught by his father and in his turn taught one of his own sons Judah ha Nasi, called Rabbi, who taught his son Gamaliel in the same way. Such are the masters of Kabbalah: all Kabbalists have followed their pronouncements and what remains of their allegorical explanations of Holy Scripture. Their names: Hanania ben Acasia, Abba Saul, Rabbi Tarphon, Akavyah ben Mahalel, Hanania Segan

LIBER PRIMVS XIII.

tania princeps sacerdotum, Hanina filius Thradionis, Hanania filius Hachinæi, Nehonia filius Hacona, Halaphtha, Duschai filius Iannai, Hanina filius Dusa, Dosa filius Harchinas, Rabi Akiba, Eleazar filius Azariç, Eleazar Hasma. Rab Leuitam, Rabi Iohanan filius Baroca, post eum Simeon ex liberis. Deinde Tzadok, tum Iosi, huc sequitur Ismael, & de alio genere Rabi Meir, a quo recepit Eleazar filius Iacob, & Iohanan Sadlar, & Eleazar filius Samua. Deinde Neorai, pòst quem Ianai & Mathathia & Samuel minor, & Elissa filius Abuiah, & Eleazar de Kaphar, & Iuda filius Thema, & Iosua filius Leui, & præter illos alii multi qui aliquando propter disputationes Thalmudicas appellantur Thanaim ceu dictatores, & propter summarum rerum meditationes ab inferioribus singulis ad excelsiora quæcg reductas, a maioribusque receptas, & posteris traditas, quibus toto studio innituntur Mekablim hebraice, ac nostra ætate à latinis, autore Ioanne Pico Mirandulano Comite, ante quem nomen eorum Romanæ linguæ incognitum erat Cabalistæ aut Cabalici dicuntur. Tum MARRANVS. Nosti ne inquit eum uirum peritissime Simõ qui primus latinis Cabalæ uocabulu prodidit. Et SIMON. Noui nempe (ut opinor) ipsum ait olim domo exulantem apud Gallos & Allobrogas pulsumcg patria & fugatum acerrime ab inuidis quadam detestabili persecutione propter eximia philosophiæ studia sua & nobile ingenium. Est adeo genus hominum, ut ait Terentius, qui esse primos se omnium rerum uolunt, nec tamen sunt, ex coruo forte nati, quæ auis usque ad Coronei annos, ut est in fabulis, uestita prius albis plumis, posterius nigris, colorem indumenti eis præbet candidi & atri, unde fratres atrati dicuntur, quippe uolucris ea ob impiam delationem semper odiosa phœbo. Sed utrique uestrum nota est hęc poesis, hi tunc fuerunt œstrum, hi mastiges hi canes tam generosi & tam eruditi christiani, nostro seculo multa Hebræorum arcana dogmata Romanis auribus perquam docte impertiti. Ad hæc PHILOLAVS. Relictis ait rebus gestis ad artem Cabalisticam si mihi creditis reuertendum nobis esse consulo, quoniam aliquanto post aduesperascet, & uota nostra uix dici queat quam alio tendant. Percucurri equidem singula, inquit Simon, nihil salsius de me ultra expectabitis. Et Marranus, Si sic inqt, ego certe fregerim sermonem tuum ualde incommode. Nam orationis filum texebas tum maxime aptum ei rei quã desyderamus, & nihil erat quod magis placuit quàm post rectam Cabalię definitionẽ nosse quid illud sit quod pter cętera mortaliũ generi egregius reuelatum fuerit, tum quis quid reuelauerit, & quis receperit, quo in puncto mea interpellatione abductus es, id quod subdoleo. Quare mi tu oramus ut redeas. Ego uero hilare quidem obsequar, SIMON inquit.

D

Book One

ha Kohanim, Hanina ben Teradyon, Hanania ben Hakhinai, Nehunya ben Ha Kanah, Halafta, Duschai ben Iannai, Hanina ben Dosa, Dosa ben Harkinas, Rabbi Akiva, Eleazar ben Azariah, Eleazar Hasma, Rabbi Levitam, Rabbi Johanan ben Beroka, and after him his son Simeon. Then Zadok, and Yose and Ishmael followed, and in another line of descent, Rabbi Meir, from whom Eleazar ben Jacob, Johanan Ha Sandelar, and Eleazar ben Shammua received the tradition. Then Nehorai, Yannai, Mathathia, Samuel, Elisha ben Avuyiah, Eleazar Ha Kappar, Judah ben Tema, Joshua ben Levi, and many others besides, sometimes called *Tannaim* or "rulegivers" on account of their Talmudic responsa, and *Mekablim,* "receivers," for their meditations on the sublime, in which they move from lower things to higher; this tradition they received from their elders and passed on to their followers. The use of the term "Kabbalists," or "Kabbalics," was first introduced to the Latin by Pico della Mirandola. Before him it was unknown.

PHILOLAUS: Did you know this scholar, the one who introduced "Kabbalah" into Latin?

SIMON: Yes, I did, I think. I knew him when he was in exile in France and Savoy. He was forced to fly the country, persecuted by people who were envious of his fine work in philosophy and his superior ability.

As Terence said, there are some men who want to be first in everything, but aren't. Such men are perhaps children of the crow, the bird which, so the story goes, was clothed in white feathers till the Coronis affair. It subsequently turned black—thus the black and white color of the plumage and hence the name "Brothers in black." The bird's ungodly sneaking information stinks to high heaven—but you know the poem, both of you.[20] These then were what goaded, whipped and hounded such a noble-spirited, learned Christian, who imparted the mysteries of Hebrew doctrine to Latin-speakers.

PHILOLAUS: Let us leave the past. I think we should get back to the art of Kabbalah. Evening has been drawing in some while now and it hardly needs saying that we wanted something other than past history.

SIMON: I have in fact gone through your requests one by one. But you won't see me digress again.

MARRANUS: In that case, it's my fault for interupting your discourse with such irrelevance. The thread of your argument fitted just what we wanted—nothing could have been more welcome than to have known the correct definition of "Kabbalah," and then what that all-important revelation to mankind was, who revealed what, and to whom—at which point you were sidetracked by my interruption, for which I apologize. So please do go back there.

DE ARTE CABALISTICA

& tandem ad modum artis quem optare uos animaduerti properabo, nisi iam uespera imminet, quando & uos audiendo forte cum fastidio, & ego ipse loquendo defessi sumus. Satis enim multa nobis tam breuibus horis exciderunt, & quæ mea fuit uel temeritas si uultis, uel quod uerius est singularis erga uos dilectio, quod in tanta re fieri non debuit, omnia imparatus dixi ex tempore. Tum PHILOLAVS, At obsecramus uterque, compleas abacum calculo autorum qui Cabalam & tenuerunt & tradiderunt, ne hoc sermonis membro nondum perfecto ad diuersorium nostrum ut oportet coenaturi abeamus. Quo dicto rursus Simon Extant sane, inquit, meo arbitratu Cabalistæ innumerabiles (nec enim numero comprendere refert) eorum partim qui audiere tantum, alii uero qui & auditores & scriptores fuere, tamen quando ita urgetis recensebo perfunctorie nonnullos quorum libri de Cabalisticis contemplationibus quotidiano ueniunt usu, quantum mihi suppetit memoria, quanquam non in omni parte omnes integri, aliquorum enim sola fragmenta enatarunt, reliqui proh dolor ita extincti sunt ut uix nominum recordatione doctissimorū hoīm monumētis innotescāt. Nā ut prisca patres uolumina iniquitate temporum & longo tractu annorum perdiderunt, cum haud mediocri posteritatis damno quorum nostri tamen meminerunt, ita nos iam in ipso mundi sexto millenario uiuentes, maiorum nostrorum libros uel uetustate quæ omnia consumit, uel bellorum malignitate, uel inundatione ac uastitate, uel improuiso ignis casu, uel quandoque odio & inuidia turpi & detestanda, quæ incendiarios librorum inertes & stultos etiam æuo nostro sollicitauit amisimus. Citantur ab hominibus fide dignis Henoch libri & Abrahę patris nostri, quin & Moyses allegat libros bellorum domini. Iosue librum iustorum, & uniuersitatem librorum Kiriath sepharim quam Athniel duce Caleb expugnauit. Asuerus libros memorabilium. Ionathas in Machabæis libros sanctos de Spartiatis. Paralipomena commemorant libros lamentationum. Libros Samuel uidentis, & Nathan prophetæ, & Gad uidentis, & Semeiæ prophetæ, & Haddo uidentis, & Ahię Silonitis, & libros Iehu filii Hannani, qui omnes nusquam sunt. Querimur & bibliothecam Darii, ut est in Ezra, fuit ea in Ecbatanis pretiosa. Pari exemplo innumeri nostro seculo autores periere, tametsi non dubitamus superesse plurima quæ ipsi nec dum uidimus, nec istam de me gloriam cum Mirandulano iactare possum ϙ quæ ille quondam Ezra, de Cabalisticis secretis septuaginta conscribere uolumina iussit, ea mihi summa impensa conquisierim, cui ne tantidem prope auri & argenti sit quo eos libros si superarent ac offerrētur licitari queam. Vtimur autem non adeo libro si attamen pro nostra uirili Abrahæ libro patris no

On the Art of Kabbalah

SIMON: I would happily obey, and move on quickly to the method, which I see is what you want, but it is evening already and perhaps you find listening as tiring as I find speaking. We have got through a good deal in a short time, and through my want of judgment, if you like, or perhaps it's due more to my liking for you, I have done what one should never do in matters of importance, namely speak extempore and without preparation.

PHILOLAUS: But we beg you, both of us, to finish the tally of authors who had and handed on the Kabbalah. Otherwise we shall go off to our lodgings for dinner, as we should, leaving this section of your talk incomplete.

SIMON: There are, I believe, countless Kabbalists. Nor is there much point in counting them up. Some of them just listened; others listened and wrote. But since you insist I shall go over, somewhat perfunctorily, some of those whose books on Kabbalistic contemplation are in everyday use—as many as I can remember. Not all these are complete, there are some of which only fragments are left, and the rest are sadly so destroyed that only the record of names remains as a memorial of these learned men. Our fathers lost many ancient volumes through the ravages of time and in the course of long years; a considerable loss for succeeding generations, though we still remember them. Even now, in the sixteenth century, in our lifetimes, we have lost books—through age, which consumes everything, through the mischief of warfare, through floods and devastation, sudden catastrophe, like fire, sometimes through hatred and the low, disgusting envy that makes stupid fools burn books, even in our day.[21]

Cited on good authority are the Books of Enoch and our father Abraham. Moses mentions the books of the Wars of the Lord, Joshua a Book of the Just and Kiriath-Sepharim which was the collection of the books of Kiriath-Sepharim, which was captured by Athniel under Caleb's leadership. Ahasuerus cites books of Remembrance; Jonathan, in the Maccabees, holy books on the Spartans. Books of Lamentations are mentioned in Chronicles. Then there are the books of Samuel the seer, of Nathan the prophet and Gad the seer, of the prophet Semeia, of the seer Haddo, of Ahijah the Shilonite, and of Jehu the son of Hanani. None of these is extant.[22] Then we have the loss of the priceless library of Darius, noted in Ezra, which was in Ecbatana. In similar fashion many authors have been lost in our days, though doubtless many survive that I have not seen. Nor can I boast with Mirandola of having, like Ezra who once ordered the seventy to write out volumes on the secrets of Kabbalah, spent vast sums collecting books. I have hardly enough money to acquire books, even if they were to survive and be put on the market.

The less learned among us for our part, however, use the book of Abraham our father, entitled *On the Creation*. Some quite well-read

LIBER PRIMVS

stri, cui est inscriptio יצירה de creatione, quem non parum literati quidam assignant Magistro Akiba profecto nobilibus scholiis ornatum, ut qui alioquin existat reconditus & obscurus. Et libro הזוהר de splendore, quem composuit Simeon filius Iohai cum in qdam uasto & tenebricoso specu quatuor & uiginti annos delituit. Et libro הבהיר de Candore qui a uestris Lucidarius dicitur. Sunt & qs edidit in Cabala ille Abraham Alaphia, & insignes commentarii Ramban, nam ita collectiue notatur Rabi Moyses filius Nehmani sup arcana legis que appellatis Gerundensem, & Commentarii oium doctissimi receptoris Rabi Mnahem Racanat super arcana Ramban. Et liber pplexorum Rambam, in fine per Mem, id est Rabi Moysi filii Maimoni que uocant Moysen egyptiu. Et liber שערי צדק i. porte insticie que coscripsit Rabi Ioseph filius Carnitolis. Et liber שער אורה i. porta lucis Magistri Ioseph (ut ferut) Castiliensis in Hispania. Et liber האמונות i. de credulitatibus, cuius autor fuit in Asia Rabi Saadia. Et liber סוד התורה de mysterio legis quem sapiens ille Abraham Aben Ezra confecit. Et liber Rabi hamai filii Hanina qui dicitur eloquentissimorum caput in Cabala, & eiusdem autoris liber העיון id est speculationis. Alius denicq liber פירוש קדושה i. commentariu sanctitatis, quem scripsit Rabi Azariel. Et liber שמות i. de noibus. Et liber explanationum alphabeti, cuius est inscriptio סדר פירוש האלפאביתא ex rabi Akiba. Et liber Rabi Ama שער הרזים de reconditis psalmi undeuigesimi. Et liber היחיד i. singularis de unione seu collectione, cuius meminit Rabi Abraham Aben Ezra de mysterio legis capite primo. Et liber סודות i. mysterioru. Et liber questionum abstrusarum. Et libellus Cabalae que edidit Azariel, aliis Oriel Garonensis. Et liber qui praenotatur דרך האמונה ודרך הכפירה de fide & expiatione. Et liber radicum Rabi Ioseph Albo cui pariter Cabalae titulum praefixerunt, quamuis ille magis ethica commentetur q anagogica. Extat demum liber elegantissimus in Cabala aduersum philosophastros nomine Alkozer more arabico, quem composuit Rabi Iuda Leui, cuius haec sunt uerba כי אין קבלה טובה אלא עם חלב הטוב i. Qz non sit Cabala bona nisi cum corde bono. Vbi plurimum mihi uisus est sapienter a tam sancta contemplatione malignos sophistas repulisse, qui tanquam muscae

D ii

Book One

men ascribe this to Rabbi Akiva. It is indeed very well annotated, though in some places obscure and rather hard. Then there is the *Zohar,* translated "Splendor," written over twenty-four years in a dingy cave by Simeon bar-Yohai.[23] There is the book *Ha Bahir,* which you call "The Torch."[24] There are also Abraham Abulafia's books on Kabbalah; Ramban's distinguished commentaries (Ramban is Rabbi Moses ben Nachman, sometimes known as "Gerundensis" in Latin. He He collected and noted the more recondite parts of the Law.); and the commentaries of his very learned pupil, Rabbi Menahem ben Benjamin Recanati. There is Rambam's *Guide to the Perplexed* (note the spelling with an "m" at the end; this is Rabbi Moses ben Maimon, the "Egyptian Moses"). There is *The Gates of Righteousness,* by Rabbi Joseph ben Abraham Gikatilla, and *The Gate of Light,* supposed to have been written by the same Joseph in Spain; the book on articles of belief written by Rabbi Saadia Gaon, in Asia; the book *The Mystery of the Law,* by the sage Abraham Ibn Ezra; a book of Rabbi Hamai bar Hanina, who is said to be the best stylist in Kabbalah, and another of the same author called *Speculations.* There is *Explanation of Holiness* by Rabbi Azariel of Gerona; *Names,* and *An Explanation of the Alphabet* by Rabbi Akiva; *The Gate of Mysteries* by Rabbi Ama, on the hidden meaning of Psalm 19; *The Unity,* in which Rabbi Abraham Ibn Ezra discusses the mysteries of the first chapter of the Law; *On Mysteries; Of Abstruse Questions,* the pamphlet Azariel of Gerona wrote on Kabbalah (some call him "Oriel"); *On Faith and Atonement;* and *The Roots,* by Rabbi Joseph Albo, which they call a Kabbalist work, though his commentary is more ethical than allegoric. Finally the very gracefully written book on Kabbalah called *Alkusari,* written in Arabic by Rabbi Judah Halevi to discredit bad philosophers. "Good Kabbalah is not possible without a good heart" is a quote from this. It was wise of him, it seems to me, to have driven malevolent sophists away from such sacred contemplation. These people are like dying flies in the precious ointment, putting to waste all its sweetness,

DE ARTE CABALISTICA

morientes, omnis ungenti quantumuis preciosi suauitatem perdunt. Vti
mur denicʒ commētariis in librū יצירה Magistri Iacob Cohen & in
eūdem librum compositiōe Rabi Ishac quem inscripsit explanatiōe no
minis sancti. Est liber etiam quem edidit Rabi Tedacus Leui de decē nu
meratiōibus Cabalisticis. Nolo addere librum, Salomoni sub nomine Ra
zielis inscriptum, quia est fictio magica, hactenus quidem rei meæ fami
liaris penuriam chartaceam quam cæteris non solebam certe uobis pere
grinis planissime aperui, at mea tamen sententia nemo unquā de ista scri
psit arte uscʒ dudum artificiosius, nemo distinctius, nemo lucidius q̄ Rabi
Ioseph Bar Abraham Castiliensis ciuis Salemitanus, tria huius facultatis
uolumina studiose molitus, quibus omnem Cabalistarum institutionem
fecit clariorem, primum de dictionibus, secūdum de literis, & tertium uo
lumen de punctis. Eius libri titulus extat גנת אגוז id est Hortus nu
cis, iuxta Salomonis cātica, In hortum nucis descendi, ut uiderem amœna

V uirgulta. Apparet nucem hanc esse ut pomum aureum argenteo retiacu
lo inclusum, ut legitur in prouerbiis. Mala aurea in lecticis argenteis uer
bum prolatum iuxta modos suos. Ita est Cabala pomum illud aureū atcʒ
diuinum argenteis filis, uidelicet ingeniosis institutionibus & humanis ar
tibus circumligatum, quale fieri consueuit aurificum opificio qui subtili
bus cælaturis aureum boni odoris pomum non omnino tegunt aut ope
riunt argento, ut nihil eius uideri queat, sed cauatis quibusdam foramini
bus & argēteis cācellis tum pomi colorē eminere tum ambrę odorem ef
flare sinunt. Aspicientibus tamen longinque totum id quod reticulatum
est uidetur argentum esse integrum, propius autem intuentes si studiose
rimentur simul aurum quocʒ reperient, & quo magis aurū ab argento di

X stat, eo longe plus ab arte Cabalistica probatur differre Cabala, quamuis
ambas species unum genus spiritualis instinctus complectatur. Sed altera

Y præcedit alteram ut oraculum Hierophantas, utcʒ unius generis aurum
id quidem bonum est, illud autem optimum, ad quem modum in Penta
teucho de Heuila narratur, cp̄ aurum terræ illius bonum est, non enim il
lic scribitur optimum ut quidam legunt, sed bonum. Et in Isaia de Ophir.

Z Dignabor hominem plusquam aurum optimum & aurum de Ophir. Ita
quicquid de sacra scriptura homines optimarum artium amatores scien
tia naturali addiscunt, auro bono par est, & appellatur opus de Bresith.
Quod uero scientia spirituali recipimus opus de Mercaua dicitur, & au
ro æquatur optimo atque purissimo. Scribunt enim Cabalistæ ita.

A שמעשה בראשית חכמת הטבע ומעשה
מרכבה הוא חכמת האלהות׃ i. Q̄ opus de Bresith
est sapientia naturæ & opus de Mercaua est sapiētia diuinitatis. Et quoniā
utracʒ sapientiạ utcuncʒ circa mundum & ea q̄ cōsistūt in mundo uersat̄,

On the Art of Kabbalah

however strong that may be. Finally, we use the commentaries on the book of the Creation by Rabbi Jacob ben Jacob ha Kohen, and the piece on a similar subject by Rabbi Isaac ben Samuel, written to explain the name of God. There is also Rabbi Todros ben Joseph ha Levi Abulafia's book on the Kabbalistic enumerations. I will not include the book inscribed "to Solomon" under Raziel's name. It is occult nonsense.

I have revealed to strangers what I usually keep to myself, namely my family's poverty of books. In my opinion there is no one writing on Kabbalah as clever, clear, or lucid as Rabbi Joseph ben Abraham Gikatilla, who comes from Salemita. He has produced three scholarly works of this kind, which shed light on the whole setup of Kabbalah; one on words, one on letters, one on punctuation. The whole book is called *The Nut Garden*: as in the song of Solomon: "I went down into the garden of nuts to see the fruits of the valley."

Picture this nut as a golden apple in a net of silver thread. It says in proverbs, "A word fitly spoken is like apples of gold in filigree work of silver." Kabbalah is that golden heavenly apple, wrapped in silver thread, bound up in complicated rules and human skills—as is the case with goldsmiths' work, when they skillfully ornament a sweet-smelling golden apple yet do not mask it completely in silver. They leave holes in the silver latticework which let the color of the apple shine through and the scent of amber drift out. If you look at the apple from a distance you see the covering and think it is all silver, but on closer inspection you discover the gold. And as gold differs from silver, so Kabbalah from Kabbalistic art, though both are facets of the same kind of spiritual insight. One precedes the other as prophets precede priests. There is gold of one kind, some of which is good, some the best: in the Pentateuch in the story on Hevila, it is said that the gold out of the ground is good—but good, not "the best," as some read it. And in Isaiah: "I think man is worth more than the best gold, even gold from Ophir." All that lovers of choice knowledge learn about Holy Scripture is like good gold. This kind of labor is called *Bereshith*.[25] But the work of which knowledge is gained spiritually is known as *Merkavah*. This is like the best and finest gold. The Kabbalists write: "Work on *Bereshith* brings wisdom in nature. Work on the *Merkavah* brings wisdom in divine things."

Each of these wisdoms is of this world, for their subject matter is the world, and they are founded in it.

LIBER PRIMVS   XV.

Estq̢ Thalmudistarū & Cabalistarū ea in re unanimis arbitrat̃, q̧ duo
sunt mundi, Primus intellectualis, qui uocat̃ עוֹלָם הַבָּא .i. mū dus il
le uenturus scilicet q̃ ad nos. Et secundus sensibilis, qui dr̃ עוֹלָם הָזֶה
.i. mundus iste præsens, q̃d ex uerbis sapientum nostrorum recepimus, de
nominis diuini quadraginta duarū literarum studioso cultore sic dicentiū
q̧ talis dubio ,p̃cul existat אָהוּב לְמַעְלָה וְנֶחְמָד לְמַטָּה
וְנוֹחֵל שְׁנֵי עוֹלָמִים הָעוֹלָם הַזֶה וְהָעוֹלָם הַבָּא׃
.i. Dilectus sursum & desyderatus deorsum & hæreditans duos mundos,
mundum p̃sentem & mundum futurum. Iccirco diuidunt Thalmudici &
Cabalistæ secedentes in duas facultates, tametsi ex creditis receptionibus
ambæ similiter oriantur & emanent. Nam utriq̧ maiorum suorum tradi
tionibus fidem habent, etiam nulla ratione reddita. Sed hac distinguūtur
deputationis ordinatione, q̧ omne studium, oẽm operam, omne consiliū
laborem & diligentiā, uniuersam quoq̧ mentis suæ intentionẽ Cabalista
fœlix ille atq̧ beatus a mundo sensibili finaliter ad mundum intellectualẽ
transfert & traducit. Thalmudista uero in mundo sensibili permanet ac
aĩam uniuersi huius mundi non transcendit, q̧ si q̃nq̧ liceter ad deum &
beatos spiritus pergat, non tñ deum ipsum ut immanentẽ & absolutū ac
cedit, sed ut opificem causamq̧ rerum & circa sua creata occupatū, Ange
los aũt ad ministeria quotidiana, diuinæq̧ uoluntatis effectus exequẽdos
mancipat, altissimarum rerũ contemplationes ad hunc inferiorẽ mũdum
semper referens. Earum tñ facultatum altera sæpe alterius sensa mutuat̃,
& ad suũ desyderiũ trahit. Emuero q̃nq̧ studia ultro citro iter se cõicant
Thalmudici & Cabalæi, ut actiua uita & cõtemplatiua, licet unũ eũdẽq̧
sacræ scripturæ contextum plærunq̧ alter ad timorem seruilem, alter ad
amorem filialem suo more lepida suasione inuitet. Apparebit eñ acri stu
dio Thalmudista ille circa legis p̃cepta & mandata residere, illa exponere
illa dirigere, illa uenerari & exosculari, ut nihil aliud recte definiam' thal
mud esse q̃ legis explanationem ad intentionẽ autoris. Vnde Thalmudici
מְפוֹרְשִׁים dicti sunt, & פָּרְשֵׁי .i. expositores & pharesai, qui de
suggestu & cathedra Moysi semp̃ instant operi, p̃dicant, & plebem hor
tantur cum propheta regio dicentes. Seruite dño in timore, ac cum Iosue.
Timete dñm & seruite ei. Quin & hoc ita facite ac illud sic obmittite cum
tali & tali moderamine, unde sescenta & tredecim præcepta uno uerbo
תַּרְיַ״ג comp̃hensa in duo capita redegerunt עֲשֵׂה לֹא תַעֲשֶׂה
.i. fac ne facias, quæ uos affirmatiua & negatiua cõsueuistis appellare, mul
tum scitu commoda & usu perq̧ necessaria. Cabalistæ aũt q̃uis teste ueri
tate uiri sint legem pie obseruan tes, tñ conteplationi plus incumbunt,
Ideoq̧ appellantur אַנְשֵׁי עִיּוּן מִבַּעֲלֵי הַתּוֹרָה .i. uiri spe

D iii

Book One

On this the Talmudists and Kabbalists agree: that there are two worlds. The one is intellectual, called "the world to come" (to us, that is). The other is physical, being the present world. We derive this from what our sages said when speaking of the assiduous student of the divine name of forty-two letters. Such a man, they say, feels no doubt; he is "beloved above, longed-for below. He is the heir of two worlds," of this world and of the world to come. But here Talmudists and Kabbalists divide in two camps, though both derive equally from received tradition. They both rely uncritically on the traditions of their forefathers. But they are distinguished by how they order their thinking.

The Kabbalist, blessed with happiness, directs all his studies, all his efforts, all his judgment, all his diligent application away from the physical world, concentrating on bringing it into the world of the intellect. The Talmudist, on the other hand, remains in the world of the senses. He does not transcend the spirit of this all-pervading world, and if he does progress toward God and the blessed ones, he realizes not God himself, immanent and absolute, but God the Creator, the First Cause, a God whose business is his creatures. He entrusts day-to-day tasks to his angels, together with the carrying out of his divine will. A Talmudist, then, always relates contemplation of the highest things to the world below.

Each of these approaches derives some of its notions, somewhat altered, from the other, taking what it wants for itself. Whenever Talmudists and Kabbalists juggle their studies between them, now this side, now that, it is a safe generalization that, as befits the contrasting lives of action and contemplation, using the same passage of Holy Scripture the Talmudists will extract the message of a slave's fear, while the Kabbalist will extract one of a son's love. It seems that the Talmudist devotes his great effort to the teachings and instructions of the Law, to exegesis, to giving directions, veneration and instruction. We can define the Talmudist as a man who interprets the Law in accordance with the author's intentions. Thus the Talmudists are called *pharisees,* or "the explainers." They sit on a dais, beside the throne of Moses, wholly engaged in preaching, exhorting the people, saying "Serve the Lord in fear," as did the royal prophet, and "Fear the Lord and serve him," as did Joshua. They pronounce on what to do, what is allowed with what, and to what degree. They have reduced the six hundred and thirteen precepts[26] contained in the word *tharig* to two categories, headed "Thou shalt" and "Thou shalt not," positive and negative commandments, and as such, much easier to become familiar with and put to use.

Kabbalists, on the other hand, while they keep the Law devoutly (there is ample evidence of this), are more inclined towards contemplation, and so are called "men who speculate on the matters of the Law."

DE ARTE CABALISTICA

culatiõis ex magistris legis. Hi curam reipublicę ac priuatorum domi bel
F licę ritus & cõsuetudines in iudicialibꝰ & moralibus cū sua historia penes
Thalmudistas relinquentes ea sibi tm̄ quæ ad animi quietem & tranquil
litatem pertinent,& ad amorem dei reseruarunt. Sic enim aiunt בְּוָנַת
כָּל הַתּוֹרָה שְׁנֵי דְּבָרִים וְהֵם תִּקּוּן הַנֶּפֶשׁ
וְתִקּוּן הַגּוּף. i. Intētio uniuersę legis duę sunt res, bona dispositio aię
et bona dispositio corpis. Tota nanqꝫ lex p̄cipue ad p̄fectionē hois tēdit,
& secūdum eam duas cõsequimur perfectiones, mentis alteram & alterā
corporis, longe uero dignior ea est & p̄eminentiæ altioris q̄ animā iuuat
& uitam perpetuat, quanq̄ idonea corporis habitudo & debita cõpositio
est tempore naturaqꝫ prior. Igitur altiore loco & digniore gradu habēdi
G sunt Cabalistæ illā legis expositionē sequentes, q̄ per quædā symbola mē
tis eleuationem ad superos & ad rem diuinā q̄ maxime propellit, hanc ap
pellant græci uestri anagogicam institutionē quæ nõ modo philosophia
sit sed & sophia ipsa, hoc est sapiētia. Vnde merito sapientes denotant
לָהֲלוֹךְ נֶגֶד הַחַיִּים ut concionator inquit Salomon, qm̄ per-
gunt illuc ubi est uita, & pro mortalium captu adhuc in corpusculis habi
H tantes a tp̄e ad æthernitatem, & ab infimis ascēdunt ad summa. Facite pe
riculum si uultis honorandi aduenæ. In principio creauit deus cœlum &
terram. Sane cœlum Thalmudicis uocātur omnia uisibilis mundi quæ su
pra lunam sunt, & quæ subter eam appellant terram. Deinde cœlum qꝫ
interp̄tantur formam, & terram esse uolunt materiā, quare in principio
aiunt creauit deus formam & materiam, quarum denuo compositionem
in singulis quibusqꝫ opifice oraculo fabrefecit, & omnia non tam manu
tornauit q̄ nouies uerbo dolauit. Legitur enim וַיֹּאמֶר אֱלֹהִים
.i.& dixit deus, Fiat lux, & dixit deus, Fiat firmamentum, & dixit deus, Cō
gregentur aquę, & dixit deus, Germinet terra, & dixit deus, Fiant lumina
ria, & dixit deus, Producant aquæ reptile, & dixit deus, Producat terra, &
dixit deus, Faciamus hoiem, & dixit deus, Ecce dedi uobis omnem herbā.
Igitur perfecti sunt cœli & terra cum omni attinentia & tota supellectili
eorum, ut sunt quatuor elementa quæ dicunt tenebræ primo nominatæ,
spiritus dn̄i, aquæ sub firmamento, & arida. Sequunt pariter & cętera mi
sta q̄ uulgo elemētata uocāt, ut aues & uolatilia, bestię ac reptilia, pisces &
cete grandia, & eorum oīm dn̄ator homo cui ex uniuersis corporeis uni
concessum est liberum arbitrium, quo ne male uteret̄ figitur ei leges, pro
mulgantur constitutiones, comminant̄ transgressionis pœnæ. Cūm item
ignis instliens nuncupet̄ cœlum, id est שָׁמַיִם quasi אֵשׁ וּמַיִם id est
ignis & aqua, & nihil ex se producat, sed producta solum cœlesti, hoc est
humido calore foueat, tum recto q̄dem ordine recitant̄ in illo constituta
fortissime influētia sol & luna, q̄bus duabus omnes reliqui notant̄ exerci
tus, lu

On the Art of Kabbalah

They leave public affairs and domestic problems, the conduct of war, and legal usage and morality to the care of the Talmudists, and then achieving stillness and tranquility of the spirit, lay their minds open to the love of God. They say: "Taken as a whole the Law intends two things: that the soul be well ordered, and the body well ordered." All the Law tends principally towards the perfection of men, and following it we pursue two kinds of perfection, the one of the mind, the other of the body. By far the most important and preeminent is the perfection that supports the soul and preserves life, although naturally the first concern is to have the body in a fit state.

In this way the Kabbalists must be held to be on a higher, worthier level in their exposition of the Law, which through certain symbols lifts the mind to higher things, raises it toward the divine. Your Greeks call it "teaching by analogy," and this is not just a philosophical system, but *sophia,* wisdom itself. They deserve to be known as "wise men," for "they go," says Solomon the preacher, "to the place where there is life." Given the limits of human ability, they go, still in mortal form, from time into eternity, and ascend from the depths to the highest.

Take this risk if you like, noble strangers."

"In the beginning God created the heaven and the earth." According to the Talmudists, by "heaven" is meant all the visible world above the moon, and everything below it is earth. Then they also interpret "heaven" as "form," and "earth" as "matter"; thus: in the beginning God created form and matter. In turn he puts these together. A craftsman in speech, he constructs each thing, for he works not with his hands, but with words, and that nine times. Thus we see: it is written: "And God said, Let there be light . . . ," and "God said, Let there be a firmament . . . ," and "God said, Let the waters . . . be gathered together . . . ," and "God said, Let the earth bring forth seed . . . ," and "God said, Let there be lights . . . ," and "God said, Let the waters bring forth . . . creeping things . . . ," and "God said, Let the earth bring forth . . . ," and "God said, Let us make man . . . ," and "God said, Behold I have given you every herb. . . ." So the heavens and the earth were finished, and everything belonging to them, which are the four elements that are said to have been first called darkness, the spirit of the Lord, the waters under the firmament, and the dry land. There follow in the same way the rest of the species—known in common speech as "categories"—the birds and insects, beasts and creeping things, fish and great whales, and the master of them all, man. He alone of all creatures was granted free will, and to prevent its abuse, laws were made for him, constitutions published, and punishment threatened for wrongdoing.

Another reading of "heaven" is "an inflow of fire," from *esh vemayim,* meaning "fire and water," instead of *shemayim,* "heaven." It produces nothing from itself, but it alone preserves the products in life through its heavenly nature, that is, its humid heat. Next, its constituent parts can be recited in order, starting with the most important, the sun and the moon, under whose leadership the rest of the host can

LIBER PRIMVS   XVI

tus, luminaria & stellæ, nox & dies, splendor & tenebræ, signa & tempora
dies & anni. Hæc itacʒ de globo corporeo & reclusis in eo mistis. Duo ue
ro mundi a Cabalistis sunt recepti, corporeus & incorporeus, uisibilis &
inuisibilis, sensibilis & mentalis, materialis & idealis. Inferior mundus &
superior, cum legunt In principio creauit deus cœlum & terrā, & ita sym
bolice cœlū summa, terrā, ifima designare putāt, hoc modo interptātes
בהתחלה ברא השם העליונים והתחתונים .i. Ini
tio creauit deus summa & infima. quo nimirum arbitrant simplice & im
materialem mundum summa cōtinere, compactum uero & cementariū
hūc, infima, unde & lege diuinā Bresith de creatiōe promulgatā cœpisse
ab ipsa litera beth q̄ in arte arithmetica inter numeros duo significat, pe
inde atcʒ sic notatorie insinuaret, duo principaliter creauit deus, totum
mundum supremum cum omnibus in eo degentibus, & totum mundum
infimum, omniacʒ ad illū ptinentia. Nam Sin aliter, fuisset uticʒ satis.
Moysen ita scripsisse ראשית ברא אלהים שמים וארץ
quod haud secus ac eodem illo more a latinis legeret. Initio creauit deus
cœlum & terram. Potuit enim summariū illud creationis non incipere a
beth litera. Sicut Salomon in prouerbiis. Dominꝰ possedit me principio
uiarum suarū, ubi sine beth & abscʒ ulla alia ppositione ponit principii di
ctio. Cęterum p̄ter consuetudinem duobus istis creatis adiunxit bis binos
articulos את & ה. Vnum excellentis demonstrationis qui dicīt ha, &
alterum omnimodę comp̄hensionis qui constituit ex aleph primo alpha
beti elemento & ultimo thau, & est id q̄d græci aiunt alpha & o, & Roma
ni prora & puppis, ubi uisus est per cœlū, oīa excellenter simplicia spiritu
alia complecti, ab aleph ad thau, id est a primo ad ultimū, & per terram si
militer a capite ad calcem oīa excellenter corporalia & iis cōtenta, nihilo
tn̄ minus singula in ipso uno principio tāq̄ unicū creatum. Sicut Ezechie
lis rota in rota, cum suis q̄buscuncʒ inuolutis uisa est una esse similitudo
gloriæ dn̄i, & ut ipsius Rabi Saadiæ in libro Amunoth .i. credulitatū
propriis uerbis utar כחלמון בתוך ביצה .i. Sicut uitellus in
medio oui, seu ut ego ipse dicere soleo, instar alboris oui unius, testaceo
firmamento contenti, uitellū ipsum inglomerantis, ita primus mundus ille
intelligibilis secundū implicat, ut tota uirtus eius inde gubernet, quo sit ut
constringāt utricʒ uinculis concordiæ, adeo ut sæpe tam suas q̄ comp̄he
sorum naturas & appellationes mutua sibi liberalitate condonent. In se
cundo nancʒ hoc est sensibili mundo sphæræ nouē mouent ab empyreo
immobili cui Metattron assiduo p̄est, at in primo nouem angelorū chori
mouentur ab immobili deo, Sicut in immobili silentio, cūctorū creator
primo simul omnia creauit, postea nouenario sermone ad proprias singu
la quæcʒ distinctiones loquēdo commouit. Noīantur & uicissim ignis se

D iiii

be delegated; the heavenly bodies; the stars; night and day; brightness and darkness, constellations and seasons, days and years. This is what they teach on the physical world and the kinds of things revealed within it.

But the Kabbalists posit two worlds, one physical and the other not — the visible and the invisible; one of the senses, the other of the mind; one of matter, the other of ideas — the lower world and the higher. Reading "In the beginning God created the heaven and the earth," they understand "heaven" as symbolizing the highest and "earth" the lowest, in this way interpreting it as "In the beginning God created the highest and the lowest." As to this they think it beyond doubt that the "highest" consists of the simple, immaterial world, and that the world of syncrete, raw matter is the "lowest." For which reason, the book of the Law concerning God's creation begins with the letter beth, which is also the arithmetical figure 2;[27] and therefore by Notaricon, the notion is introduced that principally God created "two," the whole higher world and everything within it, and the whole lower world and all that belongs to it. If Moses had written *reshit* instead of *b'reshit,* the passage would still be translated no differently from the existing "In the beginning God created the heaven and the earth." There was no need for the history of the Creation to begin with the letter beth. Solomon says in Proverbs, "The Lord possessed me in the beginning of his way," in which God's words are reported with neither a "b" nor any other preposition. Furthermore he twice employs, contrary to normal usage, the two particles *et* and *ha-,* prefixing the two things that were created.[28] The *ha-* designates; the other can be understood in many ways. It is composed of the first letter of the alphabet, aleph, and the last, tau (in Greek, alpha and omega: the Roman "bow" and "stern"). So, in "heaven" everything spiritual is seen to be included, everything from aleph to tau, from beginning to end, and in the same way, in "earth" is contained everything physical from top to toe; and nonetheless, each individual thing was created in that beginning as if it were the only one. Just as Ezekiel has a wheel within a wheel, rolled into each other, in which the glory of God is seen undivided, so Rabbi Saadia writes inn his book *Items of Faith* that it is "like the yolk in the middle of an egg," to quote his words. I myself would say "Like the white of an egg," the white being inside the shell, which is the firmament, while itself it surrounds the yolk. In this way the first, the intelligible world is bound round the second, in such a way that all its strength is governed from there; and thus it is that they are bound together in union to such an extent that often each gives to the other with equal generosity both its own nature and title and those of the things they both embrace. In the second, sensible world, there are nine spheres moved by unmoving fires, of which Metattron keeps continuing control. But in the first of the nine, bands of angels are moved by an unmoving God — just as in unmoving silence the Creator of all things first created everything, and then, by his ninefold utterances, moved individual things into their proper divisions.

raph,aer cherub,aqua tharsis,ariel terra,& q̃ in mundo sunt inferiori ea non parum multo meliore nota sunt in superioribus.quapropter hæc inferiora congruenter appellari queãt uerorum exemplaria,& adumbratę supnorum imagines,signa, notæ ac symbola quibus mouemur ad cogitã dum de supcœlestibus & angelicis substantiis uirtutibus & operatiõibus quodam tramite abstractionis uel assimilationis uia uel alia quadam ratione ac modo nobis carne indutis possibili. Vnde statuũt duos quoq̃ paradisos,alterum cœlestem & alterũ terrestrem,in quibus prœmia uirtutũ consequantur utriq̃s tam homo terrenus q̃ homo cœlestis,ut in huius orbis terra q̃ diu in corpore fuerit hospitatus tanq̃ in aliq̃ corruptibili horto uoluptatis,gloriam & honorẽ gaudium & lętitiam,omneq̃ desyderium delectationis suæ ob alicuius heroicæ ac p̃eminentis & a filiis huius seculi laudatæ uirtutis causam lucretur,q̃ tñ umbræ sunt & res caducæ fumo similes.In cœlesti uero terra & uerius uiuentium supcœlesti ubi extat amœnitatis æthernæ immarcessibilis paradisus,aĩae hoĩs in uita mortali olim secundum uirtutem recte operati,nunc exutæ clementissimus ille maximus & optimus deus ostendit omne bonum,q̃d nę uidere quidem antea potuisset tam graui & tam deso cadauere obscuri corporis,onerata,illud noĩatur & in Cabala & in Thalmud אִסְפַּקְלַרְיָא הַמְּאִירָה .i.Speculatio illuminans,hoc est uisificans, quã uos cognitionẽ intuitiuã dei appellatis,ut q̃ contingat animæ separatæ per lumen gloriæ,ac a maturissime p̃esitãtibus,sola esse beatifica probet. Nã alia sit p̃ spẽs conatu rales q̃ nõ est beatifica & אִסְפַּקְלַרְיָא שֶׁאֵינָהּ הַמְּאִירָה .i.Contemplatio quæ non sit illuminans uocatur.Nunc uero qñ clara dei uisio & perpetua summæ diuinitatis fruitio,pro supma hoĩs parte,intellectu & uoluntate beatis donantur,iccirco iure optimo ea nisi in supmo mũdo, contingunt nemini,Sic aiunt Cabalistæ כִּי טֶרֶם שֶׁיָּשִׂיג רְאִיָּה תִפָּרֵד נַפְשׁוֹ מֵעָלָיו: .i.q̃ anteq̃ apprehendit hanc intuitionẽ separatur aĩa eius ab eo.Quare mor, tali homini siqñ deus uideri dicit̃,id per angelum fieri putatur בְּמַרְאוֹת הַמַּלְאָכִים ut scribit Ramban Gerundensis in Exodo.Quamobrem pro duplici homĩs conditione spirituali & corporali,ac pro duplicis mercedis retributione, duplicem, ut audiuistis, paradisum asserunt ita dicentes כִּי גַן עֵדֶן וְנַהֲרוֹתָיו עִם הָעֵצִים שֶׁתִּרְאֶה בְּמַעֲשֵׂה בְרֵאשִׁית כֻּלָּן כְּנֶגֶד צוּרוֹת הַשִּׂכְלִיּוֹת עֶלְיוֹנוֹת הֵן מְכֻוָּנִים: .i. Q̃ paradisus & flumia cum singulis rebus quas cernis in opere Bresith,oĩa iuxta formas intellectuales & supnas sunt dispositã,id ita sentio etiam cum auro de Heuila bdellio ac onychino, cęterisq̃ infiniti pretii gemmis.Eodem modo & eadem forma duplicẽ gehenam scilicet duos tartaros esse deputatos iidem Cabalistę asseuerant,superioris & inferioris

On the Art of Kabbalah

The elements are named in turn: fire is *seraph,* air is *cherub,* water *tharsis,* land *ariel,* and whatever is in the lower world is very much better named in the upper. Things in the lower world can be grouped together and called copies of truths, shadows of things above, pictures, signs, marks or symbols, by which we are moved to consider heavenly angelic essences, virtues and works, by using a process of abstraction or some other method, so far as we can while still embodied.

Going on from this it was decided that there are also two paradises, one in heaven, one on earth, where heavenly man and earthly man pursue the prize of virtue.

While man is the guest of body in this world he is in a corruptible garden of delight. He gains glory and honor, joy and happiness, all the desirables that he delights in, because of some piece of heroism or some outstanding qualities, the things applauded by this generation now. All these are illusory and fleeting things, like so much hot air. But in the heavenly land, where men live closer to the truth, there stands an unfading paradise of eternal bliss. There the soul of the man who followed virtue and light in all he did in mortal life, now stripped naked, receives all things good from the most merciful, the great, the all-good God, whom previously no soul could see, when hampered so by the dead weight of the solid body. The process, both in Kabbalah and in Talmud, is known as the "speculation that enlightens," or that enables one to see — what you call the intuitive cognition of God. Through the light of glory it touches disembodied souls, and it has been proved by the deepest thinkers to be the only path to blessedness. (There is another process of the same kind that does not bring blessedness, called "unenlightening speculation.") Clear vision of God, and unending enjoyment of the divinity, to the limits of human ability, understanding and desire — these are the gifts granted to the blessed. Thus it is well judged that none attains these but in the highest world. The Kabbalists say: "Before a man grasps this intuition, his soul is separated from him." So when it is said that God has been seen by a mortal man, it is thought that this comes about by means of an angel, as Ramban of Gerona writes in his *Exodus.*

As you have heard, they posit two paradises for man's dual nature, physical and spiritual, and in accord with his double reward, saying "The Garden of Eden, the rivers and all the different things you see in Genesis are ordered according to the intellectual Forms above." I think it is the same with the gold from Hevila,[29] gum, onyx, and priceless gems. The Kabbalists similarly assert that we must think of a double Gehenna — two hells, if you like — of the upper and lower world, for

inferioris mundi ad tor quēdum nociua corpora in tpe, ac animas prauas in æthernitate. Nomen eis comune inditum est אַרְקָא .i. Arka, hic est tartareæ pœnæ locus, qui pter cætera, septem immaniora durissimarum pœnarum receptacula, criminum reis iusto dei iudicio destinata comprehendit. Sicut Cabalista ille in Horto nucis uolumine secundo de septē habitaculis inferorum, tractat his uer bis.

שְׁנֵי מִינֵי גֵיהִנָּם חֶן
עֶלְיוֹן וְהַתַּחְתּוֹן · אֶחָד לְגוּף בָּעוֹלָם הַזֶּה אֶחָד
לְנֶפֶשׁ בָּעוֹלָם הַבָּא אַחַר זֶה · וְהַמָּקוֹם הַכּוֹלֵל
כָּל אֵלּוּ הוּא הַבִּקְרָא אַרְקָא כִּי בּוֹ הֵם גֵּיהִנָּם
וְשַׁעֲרֵי מָוֶת וְצַלְמָוֶת וּבְאֵר שַׁחַת וְטִיט הַיָּוֵן
וַאֲבַדּוֹן וּשְׁאוֹל .i. Duę species Gehenā sunt, supior & iferior, una ad corpus in mundo isto, una ad aīam in mūdo uenturo post istū, & locus cōphendens omnia hæc, est uocatus Arka, qm in eo sunt, Gehenam, & portæ mortis, & umbra mortis, & puteus interitus, & lutum fęcis, & perditio, & fouea, hucusc̄g Ioseph Castiliensis. Iam hæc uincula, hic carcer, hę compedes, hæc seruitus, hæc captiuitas peccata noxiorum manent, tā cōrporum in mundo p̄sentic̄g animarum in mundo futuro, ut iustos equa comitentur uirtutum prẹmia, & iniq̄s debita sequantur uitiorum tormēta. Quid nam aliud debetur rectis q̄ uita & honor? quid aliud prauis q̄ mors & horror? Nec id usc̄g adeo temporaliter intelligē, dum est. Sed ut Cabalistę uolunt, etiam intellectualiter, sic.h. scribunt צַדִּיקִים אֲפִילוּ
בְּמִיתָתָן קְרוּאִים חַיִּים · וּרְשָׁעִים אֲפִילוּ בְּחַיֵּיהֶם
קְרוּאִים מֵתִים .i. Iusti etiam in morte sua dicunt uiuentes, & maligni etiam in uita sua dicunt mortui. Quo peritis in Cabala non erit obscura dei sententia. In die qua comederis ex eo morte morieris, uidelicet non corporali sed spirituali. Nam uixit Adam post esum uetitum ultra nongēs annos, in momento tn ipo mox atc̄g legē transgressus erat morte moriebatur. In peccato, inq̄, suo, toti humano generi & prolis futuræ propagationi æthernis inferorū habitaculis destinatę sontico nimis & contagio so. Quousc̄g dei placito ueniret Messiha ille redemptor, qui hoiem in p̄radisum reduceret non terrestrem sed cœlestem, & uita liberis redderet, quam parens amiserat, æthernā non temporalem, animæ non corporis, illam ipsam dei familiaritatē & iucundissimum diuinitatis aspectum, omi uoluptate plenissimum. In hunc oēs ueri Cabalistæ non sophistici totā suā fiduciam figunt atc̄g locant. In hunc omnia sanctarum scripturarum salutaria uaticinia retorquent. De terra promissionis, de Ierusalem ciuitate cū ius participatio est in idipsum, de monte dei, & loco sancto eius, & uia sancta, & sanctuario, & atriis domini, & templo domini, & domo domini, & porta domini, & cæteris similibus multis, quæ Rabi Moyses ægyptius

Book One

the torture of evil-doing bodies in time, and perverse spirits in eternity. The name common to both Genennas is *Arka*. Here are the pains of hell. Here, among other things,, are the seven dreadful dens of the most terrible punishments, reserved for the wicked by the judgment of God. Here are the Kabbalist's comments on the seven dwelling places below, in the second volume of *The Nut Garden*.

> There are two kinds of Gehenna, the upper and the lower. One is for the body in this world. the other for the soul in the world to come after this one. The place in which all these are contained is called Arka. In it are: Gehenna, "the gates of death," "the shadow of death," "the well of decay," dregs and dirt, destruction and the pit.

Thus Joseph of Castile. These chains, this jail, these shackles, slavery and captivity lie in wait for the sins of the vicious both in the present world of bodies and in the future world of souls, the rewards of virtue for the just accompanied equally by the torments of vice for the wicked. What else but life and honor do the just deserve; what else but death and horror the wicked? Nor should this be understood to apply only in time. The Kabbalists apply it on the intellectual level. They write: "The just, even in death, are called living, and the wicked, even in their lifetimes, are called dead."

In Kabbalah, God's judgment on these dead will not be hidden. On the day you are consumed, the death you die will come from him, and not in the body, but in the spirit. Adam lived for nine hundred years after eating the forbidden thing, but he died the death at the very moment in which he broke the Law. For his critical and disease-ridden sin, then, the whole race of men, and all its future generations, were ordained to live in the lower world unendingly, until it should please God that the Messiah, the redeemer, should come to lead men back to a paradise not on earth, but in heaven, to restore to the children the life that their father had lost, eternal life, not temporal, life of the soul and not of the body, and to restore intimacy with God himself, the delightful face of the divinity, brim-full of everything pleasurable.

All true, non-sophistic Kabbalists put their trust in the Messiah. Onto him they turn all the salvationist prophecies of the Holy Scripture — of the Promised Land, of the city-state of Jerusalem which forms part of it, of God's mount and his holy place, the sacred road, the sanctuary, the halls of the Lord and his Holy Temple, the gate of the Lord, and many other like things, which Maimonides, in his

DE ARTE CABALISTICA

P
in suo Misne id est deuteronomio, sic etiam intelligi de coelesti beatitudine uoluit. Qua de causa multum & sepe cum Thalmudistis certamus, & plurimum utriq; in duas imus sententias. Illi oēm liberationem regis Messihæ de corporali captiuitate seu uerius dispersione nostra conant ad tu multum, ad strepitus armorū, ad expeditiones bellicas, ad expugnationes regionum & deuastationes terrarum, & Israelitici exercitus uictoriam referre, ut q̃ndam saluatore Moyse legimus aduersum Chananæos & Palestinos nostris maioribus contigisse, aut saltem ad exq̃situm euasiõis ingeniũ quo sunt in aliis liberationibus ut multi uafre ut ego puto sancte usi, quando tot seculis sub tot regnis dispersi exularunt, ut sub Babylonico annos septuaginta, sub Persico quinquaginta quatuor, sub Græco centum & triginta, nunc sub Romano mille quatringentos nec dum finis. Nos cõtra, meo arbitratu, rectius Cabalistice Messiham esse uenturum putamus ad liberandũ miseros humani generis mortales, de uinculis iniusticiq; originalis, ad dimittendum peccata, & ad saluandũ pie deo seruientium aĩas

Q
in Adam patre nostro a uita æthierna exclusas, usq; ad satisfactionẽ Messihæ, qui ut consumme͠t iusticia misericordis & clementis dei manum suã mittat & sumat de ligno uitæ & comedat de eo, ut per illum uiuamus in æthernum. Ea satisfactio non in fastu regio, nec iactantia honoris ac gloriæ fieri debuit, eo q̃ originale peccatum a Messiha expiandũ de supbia & elatione pullulauit. Quin potius in humilitate ac tolerantia, non in curribus & in equis, sed in noĩe dñi dei nostri, & nõ in uictoria, nec humano triumpho, sed in labore, ieiunio, uigiliis, fortitudine animi, contemptu cenodoxiæ, misericordia compassibili, amore dei p̃cipuo, dilectione hoĩum recta, & in ipsa tandem heroica liberali ac spontanea morte, qm contra uitium sola uirtute pugnat, & imperia, principatus, stemmata, coronas, huiꝰ

R
seculi nemo sapiens unq̃ magni duxit. Quin hoc est sapere, gloriam huius mundi contemnere, qm̃ cum interierit gloriosus diues, non sumet omnia (ut inquit Psaltes) neq; descendet cum eo gloria eius. Quicquid igĩt de trophæis & de subiectione populorum scribit in literis consecratis, id oẽ post creditam nihilominus historiam si q̃ facta enarrant, de mundo tñ intellectuali & supernis potestatibus a Cabalistis ĩtelligitur, ita ut Messiha rex futurus optimo iure leuia & abiecta hæc istius seculi deliramenta magistratus honores & regna tanq̃ uana & stulta non modo neglecturus sit, uerum etiam contempturus, qui ad abolendum humanæ speciei reatum, & ad aperiendum uirtuti uiam adueniat. Vnde uerus ipse Messiha si recta ducimur ratione de solo Isaiæ nobili capite clariꝰ cognoscet, quod sic incipit הִנֵּה יַשְׂכִּיל עַבְדִּי .i. Ecce intelliget seruus meus, & sic de

S
sinit וְלַפֹּשְׁעִים יַפְגִּיעַ & pro trãsgressoribus orabit, quo supra q̃ dici queat miror non absq; singulari apud cæteros exterarum nationũ
homines

On the Art of Kabbalah

Mishnah on Deuteronomy, suggests should be seen as sharing the bliss of heaven.

On this matter we frequently clash with the Talmudists, and opinion is often divided on such matters. The Talmudists attempt to make the liberation of the royal Messiah relate to our physical captivity—our dispersion—and hence refer to upheaval, the noise of fighting, to military expeditions, border attacks, scorched-earth policies, and the victory of an Israelite army, like Moses' actions against the Canaanites and Philistines that we read about. Or at least they want to relate it to the cunning escapes effected so ingeniously, and too, I think, holily during the long dispersion under so many governments—70 years under Babylonian jurisdiction, 54 under Persia, 130 under Greece, now 1,400 under Rome and yet no end in sight. We Kabbalists, on the other hand, I think more correctly, believe that the Messiah will come to free the wretched men of the human race from the chains of the original breach of justice, to let their sins fall, to save the souls of those who loyally serve God, souls our father Adam shut out of eternal life until the Messiah makes amends. For the Messiah, in order to bring about the justice of the merciful and forebearing God, will stretch out his hand and take from the Tree of Life, and eat from it, that we through him may live forever.

This making of amends is not to come about through the arrogance of kingship, or bragging of honor and glory, since the original sin to be expiated by the Messiah was born of pride and arrogance. It should come about rather in humility and tolerance, not with horses and chariots, but in the name of the Lord our God; not in victories nor in human triumphs, but in work, in simplicity, vigilance, strength of mind, a contempt for heresy, compassionate mercy, and especially in love of God, in men choosing the right, and, at the last, in a heroic, free, and willing death. For against vice can only virtue fight, and in this generation no wise man takes much account of power, high office, or the trappings of power. To be wise is rather to despise this world's glory, for when the vainglorious rich man dies, he will not take all his things with him (as the Psalmist says), nor will all his "glory" go down with him. Whatever is written in Holy Scripture about the prizes of victory, and the suppression of peoples, while nonetheless accepting it as history, while it treats of events, the Kabbalists understand it to refer to the intellectual world, and to higher powers. Thus the Messiah, the king to come in perfect law, will not only ignore the silly and mean absurdities of the time—public office, honor, government—as being empty and stupid, he will actually hold them in contempt, for he comes to wipe out the guilt of the human race, and to open up the road to virtue.

The true Messiah, if we have worked this out properly, is most clearly seen in one single noble chapter in Isaiah, the one that begins: "Behold, my servant shall understand . . . ," and which finishes, "and he shall pray for sinners."

I admit to some singular hesitancy which I find hard to put into words when speaking to men of other nations about this—and I am

LIBER PRIMVS XVIII

homines uerecundia (uobis ego solis confidenter loqr) Rabi Salomoné & Dauidem Kimhi aliosq́ de nostra secta non parū doctos uiros nescio qua pusillanimitate uel si forte coram gentibus pudore, totum illic cōtextum Isaiæ de solo populo Israel nunc passim disperso torue interp̄tari, cū planissime sit de illo ipso Messiha prophetatū, q̇d Chaldai ca Ionathæ traductio noiatim exprimit dicens הָא יִצְלַח עַבְדִּי מְשִׁיחָא .i.Ecce prosperabitur seruus meus Messiha. Hic est ille ab Isaia in spiritu prophetico uere uisus eo loci, homo dolorum & infirmitatis exp̄tus, uultu abscōdito, nullius honestæ reputationis uir, diuina percussione tactus, despectus & uitatus, tonsus ut agnus, occisus ut ouis, a terra uiuentium abscisus, & cum sceleratis reputatus & inter filios hoium inglorius. At uero quid inter filios dei? plane multum exaltatus & eleuatus & sublimis ualde. Nam gn̄ationem eius quis enarrabit, et d̄ni dei uoluntas per manū ei dirigitur, & d̄ns aboleuit in eo iniquitatem omnium nostrum, quia de scelere populi percussit eum. Ip̄e.n. uulneratus est propter crimina nostra & attritus est propter iniqtates nostras, qui certe iniqtatem non fecit unquā & nō fuit dolus in ore eius. Sed d̄ns uoluit contusionem eiusdem uulnerati. Quapropter cum sit ipse iustus dei seruus, multos iustificabit per agnitionem sui, & iniqtatem illorum ipse portabit, & peccata multorū tollit, & pro peccatoribus intercedet. De uero Messiha hæc oīa uidit Isaias & profecto non est mentitus. Ista firmiter est illa congregatio Israel iuxta Cabalistarum opinionem, & illud salutare dei nostri tam sæpe promissum ut iustificemur בְּרַעְתֶּךָ .i. in cognitione eius, non ut saluemur in tumultu nec in fuga, sed sub uno rege ac in uno fidei consistentes exercitu, libere T mur in morte atq̇ cognitione Messihæ qua finitur peccatum, & remouet obstaculum claræ uisionis dei, hoc est humani generis originalis ac contagiosus reatus. De quo sic in libro Cabalæ de fide & expiatione legitur.

דֶּרֶךְ מוֹרֶה כֹּחַ הַנֶּאֱצָל שֶׁהוּא כֹּחַ הַנִּבְרָא
הַמִּתְנַהֵג בְּשֶׁבַע תְּמוּרוֹת שֶׁהֵם י״ג סְדָרֵי
סְלִיחָה שֶׁהָעוֹלָם מִתְנַהֵג בָּהֶם עַד שֶׁיִּכְלֶה
הַחֵטְא וִיבֹא הַמָּשִׁיחַ שֶׁהוּא כֹּחַ אֱלֹהֵי
וּבְכֹחַ הָאֲצִילוּת שֶׁהוּא כֹּחַ הַמַּלְאָכוּת וּבְכֹחַ
הַנֶּאֱצָל מִמֶּנּוּ שֶׁהוּא כֹּחַ הַנָּבִיא תָּנוּחַ עָלָיו
רוּחַ הַשֵּׁם רוּחַ חָכְמָה וּבִינָה רוּחַ עֵצָה
וּגְבוּרָה רוּחַ דַּעַת וְיִרְאַת יְהֹוָה הֲרֵי שֶׁבַע
תְּמוּרוֹת שֶׁהַמָּשִׁיחַ מִתְנַהֵג בָּהֶן לְהֵיטִיב
לְטוֹבִים וְלַחֲרֹב אֶת הָרְשָׁעִים כְּרָכְתִי בְּרוּחַ
שְׂפָתָיו יָמִית רָשָׁע i. Via demonstrans uirtutem gratificatam

Book One

telling this to you alone, in confidence—namely that Rabbi Solomon and David Kimhi, two coreligionists who were quite knowledgeable men, made, whether through a lapse in concentration or through embarrassment—"not in front of the Gentiles"—and I don't know which it was, this severe interpretation of the whole passage, which is that it refers only to the people of Israel in the Dispersion—even though the prophecy quite clearly concerns the Messiah himself, as is explained in pseudo-Johnathan's translation. He reads: "Behold, the Messiah, my servant, will be made happy."

It is he who is seen by Isaiah in this prophetically inspired passage: the man of sorrows and acquainted with grief, his face hidden away, a man well regarded, smitten by God's touch, despised and rejected, shorn as a sheep, slaughtered like a lamb, cut off from the land of the living, reckoned with the wicked and inglorious among the sons of men. But among the sons of God he is openly exalted, raised on high. For none will tell of his begetting, and the will of the Lord shall prosper in his hand, and God has absolved all our sins in him, by striking him for our wickedness. He was wounded for our transgressions and bruised for our iniquities, for certainly he never did evil, and there was no guile in his face. But the Lord willed his bruising and his wounds. And since he is a just servant of God, he will make many just by their acceptance of him; he himself will bear their iniquities, remove the sins of many, and intercede for sinners.

Isaiah saw all these things concerning the true Messiah, and assuredly he did not lie. This, Kabbalists believe, is that ingathering of Israel, and this is the often promised salvation of God, when we will be pardoned, in his cognizance of us; we will be saved not in conflict, nor in flight, but under one king, and assembled in one army of faith; in death we shall be set free, and in the knowledge of the Messiah shall we be freed, who will put an end to sin and take away that block before our clear vision of God that is man's original sin, his sick guilt. In the Kabbalist book *On Faith and Atonement,* we read:

> There is a way showing the strength of grace that has been bestowed, which is a created strength. The way follows a route of seven exchanges, which are thirteen orders of forgiveness by which the world is to be guided until there be an end to sin and the Messiah come who is the strength of God. And in the strength of grace (which is the strength of angels), and in the strength on which grace has been bestowed (which is the strength of the prophet), there will rest upon him the spirit of the Name of God, the spirit of wisdom, the spirit of understanding, the spirit of counsel and of strength, the spirit of knowledge and the fear of the Lord.[36]

DE ARTE CABALISTICA

V seu infusam quæ est uirtus creata ducitur septem uariationibus, quę sunt tredecim ordines expiationis, quibus mundus dirigit, quousq̧ finitū fuerit peccatū, & uenerit Messiha qui est uirtus dei. Et in uirtute gratiæ quę est uirtus angelica, & in uirtute gratificata & infusa ab ea q̃ est uirtus prophetæ, requiescet sup eū spiritus dn̄i tetragrāmati, spiritus sapientię & intellectus, spiritus consilii & fortitudinis, spiritus scientiæ & timoris dn̄i. Ecce septē uarietates qbus Messiha utit ad benefaciendū bonis, & ad de-

X struēdū malignos, secundū q̧ scriptū est. Et spiritu labiorum suorū interficiet impium. Hæc sunt commemorati uoluminis Cabalistici uerba, quibꝰ monemur regem Messihā non manu sed ore, non armis sed spiritu, uincere populi dei aduersarios, donare aut̃ dei gratia septemplici pios, interficereq̧ impios, & hæc oia spiritu oris id est doctrina sua spirituali quam p uiros iustos & electos iusti discipulos, sparget ac seminabit in oēs gentes, per q̧d Isaię illud ad tēpꝰ Messihæ relatū oraculū Hauritetis aquas de fontibꝰ saluatoris Ionathā filiꝰ Uzielis chaldaice inter p̃tatus est, iis uerbis.

ותקבלון אולפן חרת בחרוה מבחירי צידקא

Y .i. Et recipietis doctrinam nouam in gaudio ab electis iusti. Ea uero est doctrina illa noua, q̧ uerū lumen luceat, & qui odit in tenebris est, & qui diligit uersatur in luce. Finis igitur p̃ceptorū hic est, ut diligamꝰ inuicem in doctrina Messihę.

שירה העמים ללכת ברכי יהוה

.i. Qui docebit populos ambulare in uiis tetragrammati, ut scribit Rabi Dauid Kimhi super eunde prophetā capite LI in uersu, quia lex a me exibit, quā scilicet q̧ fecerit salua bitur, q̧ contēpserit peribit. Vetera em̃

Z timoris sunt, noua charitatis של אהבה ישרה מלב שלם quæ est dilectionis rectæ ex corde integro secundum magistros nostros. Erit igitur Messiha exemplum uitæ omnium liberandorum, a q̧ uniuersa dependet mundi salus, q̧ dicitur salus æterna, & exponitur a nostris p oēs dies seculorū, ubi legitur Israel saluatus est in Ihuh, salute æterna. De q̧ nonnihil scribitur in libro Cabalæ Hacadma והוא סוד מלך

המשיח שיבא במהרה בימינו שבכל פעולתו
תהלה על וה וגם יה שהוא סוד יום השביעי
והוא השם שמו שלם ותשלם כל המלאכה
ידו׃

.i. Et hoc est arcanū regis Messihę q ueniet cito in diebus nostris, cuius omnis opatio incipiet in .v.h. & etiam .i.h. q̧d est mysteriū diei septimæ, & hoc nomen, est nomen suum integrale, p̃ficietq̧ omne opus in manu eius. Ecce definitum est a sapientibus Cabalistis oia p Messiham fore perficienda, & totam eius opationem fieri sacratissimis quatuor literis .i.h.u.h. in mysterio diei septimæ, non a numero uidelicet dierum sic apellatæ, sed a trāsitu de uita actiua ad uitam contemplatiuā, id est in ipsa quietudine animi & pacata tranq̧llitate, secedendo ab huius mūdi nimia

sollicitu

On the Art of Kabbalah

Behold the seven methods employed by the Messiah to bring well-being to good men and to destroy the evil, as it is written: "And with the breath of his lips he will slay the wicked."

These words come from the Kabbalistic book mentioned above which warns us that the kingly Messiah conquers the enemies of God's people not with his hands, but with his words; not with weaponry, but with his spirit; that he grants the grace of God sevenfold to the faithful, but slays the faithless; and this by the breath of his mouth, that is, his spiritual teaching, which through just men and his chosen followers, he will scatter and sow among all the nations. Here Isaiah's words are applied to that age of the Messiah: "You will draw water from the spring of salvation." Pseudo-Jonathan interpreted it as: "In joy will you learn a new teaching, from the chosen of the just." This in truth is that new teaching, which the true light shall fill with light; he who hates it is in darkness, he that loves it is in light.

This, then, is the purpose of these words of instruction, that we in turn may love the Messianic teaching. "Whoever will teach the people to walk in the ways of the holy name," writes David Kimhi commenting of the fifty-first chapter of Isaiah ('because the law shall go forth from me'), "whoever does so will surely be saved; whoever despises it shall perish."

The old things are those of fear, the new those of love (according to our rabbis, of "a righteous love proceeding from the whole heart"). The Messiah will be a model for the lives of all those to be set free. The world's well-being depends on him, and this, it is said, is its eternal well-being. Our writers explain it as being for all ages, and one reads "Israel has been saved in the eternal salvation of *YHVH*." There is a piece on this in the Kabbalistic book *Hacadma:* "And this is the secret of the king Messiah who will come swiftly, in our days. All his work will begin with the *VH* and the *YH,* which is the mystery of the seventh day and this name is his whole name, and everything is accomplished by his hand."

You see, the wise Kabbalists state that everything is to be accomplished through the Messiah, and that all his works are done through the Tetragrammaton *YHVH,* in the mystery of the seventh day. Not that the number of days leads to its being called a mystery; it is rather the passage from a life of action to a life of contemplation, consisting in peace of mind, quietness and calm, and setting ourselves apart from the trouble and material cares of this world. It is written:

LIBER PRIMVS   XIX

sollicitudine & a cementariis operibus patratis. Scriptum est em̄. Et requi
euit die septimo ab uniuerso opere quod patrarat. Quis aūt thalmudistæ
multa regi huic attribuant noīa, ut intelligere licet ex plurimorum docto
rum allegationibus in libro Sanhedrin uolumine Helek, citatis a capite
ubi scribit. Et Rabi Iohanan dixit, Messihæ q̄d est nomen? usq̃ ad locum
Suscepitq̃ Rabi Eliezer dicens, Dies Messihæ. Et post in multis eorū scri
pturis sicut cōmentariis in canticū synagogæ הוא מקרא ראש
וראשון: Exponunt noīa Messihæ Silo, iinon, Dauid, Hanina, ger
men, iustus, consolator, ea tn̄ singula putatur agnomina uelut imaginaria
instar septem exemplorum illic recēsitorum, q̄ sunt, arca, propiciatoriū,
tabulæ, uirga Aaron, urna mannæ, & spiritus dei. Sed iuxta Cabalistas
unum hoc nomen ineffabile יהוה audiuistis q̄ sit propriū Messihę, q̄d
integrabit & perficiet nomen eius substantiuum, docent em̄ credi oporte
re hoc esse nomē suū integrale, q̄d pie sanctęq̃ integrat in miseratiōibus
cui nemo Thalmudista inficiator subrepit, cum dixerit magnus ille Magi
ster in Thalmud cōmemorato in loco, q̃ nomen Messihæ ueniet appellā
dum consimiliter Hannina id est misericordia, citādo uersum Ieremię xvi.
quem tn̄ licenter ac improprie Romani sic legunt, qui non dabunt uobis
requiem. Sed ea nō est etymologica interpṅtatio. Ita em̄ rectius me iudice
legatur, q̃ non dabo ad uos misericordiā. Hoc Ionathan Chaldęus tradi
xit רחמין .i. miserationes, ut qui secundū Thalmudistas dicere uellet
q̃ uobis ambulantibus in prauitate cordis ut deum non audiatis non erit
Messiha qui noīatur miserationes, quo dare innotescit ברחמים .i. in
miserationibus de medio .i. h. u. h. nomen fore propriū saluatoris Messihę
cuius & dignitas & officiū tametsi rigore ac seueritate constet iuxta regis
Dauid uaticiniū absq̃ ullius cōtrouersia de ipso Messiha expr̄ssum. Iudica
bit populum tuū, inq̄t, in iusticia & paupes tuos in iudicio, tn̄ qm̄ iudiciū
.i. משפט secundum omnes Cabalistas cum iusticia etiam admittit de
mentiā. Sic. n. legit in Portæ lucis capite iiii. כי המשפט תציר
דין והציץ חסד .i. Q̃ iudiciū est partim rigor & partim, demē
tia, qbus modis primi lapsus recōciliatio p iteratā unione, & noua quandā
populi cū deo desponsatione futura est, ut Hosea p̄dixit. Spōsabo te mihi
in iusticia & iudicio. In misericordia & in miserationibus, ubi ponitur
ברחמים Ne quis igit putet illū ipsum Messihæ aduentū ex aliqua
iuris necessitate ac nō poti⁹ de gratia mera & dono dei liberalissimo esse
destinatū recte imponet huic saluatori nomen dementię indytū, q̄d ex oib⁹
literis tā uocalibus q̃ consonante sola misericordia & pterea nihil aliud si
gnificatib⁹ erit cōpositū. Idq̃ fore cōiicimus p sanctas quatuor literas qb⁹
tanq̃ notis & symbolis ineffabile depingit, & p Sin cōsonante q̃ nomen
ineffabile noīatur. Tritum. n. in Cabala est q̃ hęc nota Sin exponit שדי
per Notariacon שם יהוה מקרא .i. Nomen tetragrāmaton uo

112

Book One

"And he rested on the seventh day from all his work which he had made."

The Talmudists attribute many names to this king, as can be seen from the proofs adduced by a good many learned men in chapter "Helek" in the tractate *Sanhedrin,* quoted in the passage running from "Rabbi Johanan said, 'What is the Messiah's name?'" down to "Rabbi Eliezer took up the question, saying, 'The day of the Messiah.'" The question is also mentioned in their later writings, for instance in the commentaries on the synagogue hymn, "He is called the Head and the Beginning." Names given to the Messiah are: Shiloh, iinon, David, Hanina, the embryo, the just, the one who consoles. These are all held to be epithets, like the seven metaphorical kinds of image examined there, which are the Ark, the mercy seat, Aaron's rod, the measure of manna, and the breath of God.

According to the Kabbalists, the Messiah has only one name, the unpronounceable *YHWH.* This will fulfill and perfect his ordinary name. Their teaching is that one should believe this to be his full name, devoutly and holily kept so through mercy. No meddling Talmudist will crawl around this teaching, for the great Rav himself, in a well-known passage in the Talmud, said that the name of the Messiah will come to be called something like "Hanina," that is, mercy; and he quotes a verse of Jeremiah. This verse has been willfully mistranslated in the Latin as "who will not give you rest." But this is no etymological reading. In my opinion it is better read as "I will not give you mercy." Pseudo-Jonathan uses "mercy." According to the Talmudists he means here that if you walk in such wickedness of heart that you do not listen to God, there will be no Messiah whose name is mercy. Plainly it becomes clear here that "in mercy" comes in the middle of the Messiah's proper name, *YHWH,* together with "merit" and "service" and "with rigor and harshness." However it is agreed that this last phrase must be interpreted in the light of the prophecy connected with King David, (that beyond all doubt spoke of the Messiah himself), that: "He will judge your people in justice, and your poor in judgment." According to all Kabbalists, judgment with justice requires clemency — "Judgment is part rigor and part clemency," as we read in *Gate of Light,* chapter 3. Thus, atonement for the initial Fall will come about through reunion, through the people's new betrothal with God. As in Hosea: "I shall betroth thee unto me, in justice and judgment, in loving kindness and in mercies" (hence "in mercy"). Lest it should be thought that the Messiah's coming is ordained by some exigency of Law, rather than by unmixed grace and God's most generous gift, the name of the Savior includes the word "clemency."

This name will be made up of all the letters (vowels and consonants) that stand for "mercy," and no others. We contend that these will be the four holy letters by which, as with marks and symbols, the ineffable is represented, together with the consonant *S,* the way the ineffable is named. (In Kabbalah it is common to explain *S* by Notaricon as standing for *shem YHWH Nikra,* that is, "The ineffable name is

DE ARTE CABALISTICA

catum,hoc eſt,prolatū.Nullæ aūt ſunt literę alię q̃bus ſola nūde miſericor
dia deſignatur,niſi hæ quinq; i.h. u.h. & conſona Sin .i.s. De uocalibus
quatuor in libro Portarū iuſticię ſic legit וזהו סוד שאמ״רזל
בי הנה יהוה יוצא ממקומו ממדת
רחמים .i.Et hoc eſt myſteriū q̃d dixerunt Magiſtri noſtri quorum
memoria ſit in pace, q̃ ecce quatriliterū (inq̃t Micha) i.h.u.h. egredietur
de loco ſuo,egredietur per proprietatē miſerationū, De conſonante aūt
Sin,uniuerſi Cabaliſtæ qui non ſunt neſcii in Cabaliſtica גימטריא
Sin literam totius in ſe complexus quatriliteri ex arithmetica proportiōe
rationem continere, haud inficias ibunt, eandem q̃q; ab ea poſſideri pro
F   prietatem clementię ac miſericordiæ.Oīum igitur hominum ſalus de ſola
dei miſericordia expectanda eſt,q̃d palam expſſit Habacuk deum ſic allo
qués.Cū iratus fueris miſericordię recordaberis. Vbi Dauid Camhi quē
noſtri appellāt Kimhi (ſicut alii pronūciāt Rabi, & Alemania dicit Ribi p̃
facilē uocis a ĩ i cōuerſionē,ut & de grecis ac latinis extāt par iudiciū,illi.n.
grāmatiki & logiki, nos grāmatica & logica, illi mitir nos mater, ita Sāſon
Simſon,& Cāhi Kimhi,& alia plura) Ille inquā Dauid Iudęus Hiſpanięſis
p̃ nomē רחם .i.miſericordię illic poſitū ſecundū arithmeticā proportio
nē cabaliſtice hoc eſt ſymbolice intelligendū eſſe docet Abraham, quaſi
Habacuk ſic diceret.O deus cū tu ira peccati nr̃i tāgeris, memēto ſeminis
Abrahę cui p̃miſiſti q̃ in eo bñdicēt uniuerſę cognatiōes terrę. Et ruſſū.
O deº tu illū affatus es,bñdicent in ſemine tuo oēs gētes terrę, Vt aūt indi
caret Habacuk ipſe,q̃d nā futurū eſſet illud ſemē ſubiūxit. Egreſſus es ĩ ſa
lute populi tui, in ſalute cū Meſſiha tuo, ubi idem Dauid Kimhi ſic ſcribit
הוא משיח בן דוד .i.hic eſt Meſſiha filiº Dauid. Aio igit cū ſa
pietibus Cabaliſtis oīm nr̃i uerā ſalutē in Meſſiah pēdere q̃tq̃t attingim9
illū. Quo ſit ut ab oib9 nos rebus creatis q̃ad poſſum9 abſoluētes p̃oēs gra
G   dus aſcēdere ac migrare in eū conemur, ut ipm ſi min9 cōſequamur, at uł
aſſequamur certe, pro ſingulorū q̃ruq; uirili. Nā hic eſt nr̃i ipſe ,in cuius
aduētū oīs lex a nobis ętiā itellectualiter refert, & nō Moyſi tm ſcriptura
ſed & p̃phetarū & q̃cq̃d in Hagiographis cōtinet. Totū nāq; id cōtextū
H   q̃d Eſſrim Varba.i.uiginti quatuor nos dicim9, & uos Biblia noīatis, totū
inq̃ התורה .i.legis appellatiōe nūcupam9.Vt in Danielis cap.ix. Am
bulādo in lege dñi dei nr̃i quā tradidit corā nobis p̃ manū ſeruorū ſuorū
p̃phetaꝶ.Hāc ſolā ſcripturā decreuim9 tā ſtabilē & adeo eſſe firmā ut ſup
eā cogitatº oīs nr̃os tuto fundare queam9, & ſublimes ſpeculatiū hoīm cō
teplatiōes haud p̃plexim locare, tū qa ſummi dei uoce p̃mulgata ſit, tū qa
tātis energię uirib9 in hoīm cōteplātiſſimorū mētibus ſolet opari, ut p̃ eā
de q̃buſcuq; libet miſtis ad ſimplicia, de ſimplicib9 ad ſimpliciſſima, de cau
ſatis ad cauſas, & a mūdo deniq; īferiori ad ſupiorē, a ſupiore ad Meſſihā
q̃ mētis nr̃ę obiectū ſupmū & in ultio gradu cōceptibile ſit tāq̃ ad regē ſe

On the Art of Kabbalah

called *YHWH*.") There are no other letters by which "mercy" by itself can be denoted — only the five: *Y, H, W, H,* and *S.* Of the first four, it is written in *The Gate of Justice* that: "This is the mystery of which our rabbis of blessed memory spoke: behold, the Tetragrammaton *YHWH* will come forth from its place," (quoting from Micah); "It will come forth through its property of mercy."

On the letter *S,* any Kabbalist who knows anything about Kabbalistic Gematria will agree that the numerical value of the letter *S* comprises the other four letters, and that it also possesses the same properties of clemency and mercy.[31]

Therefore the awaited salvation of all men rests on God's mercy alone — Habbakuk openly expressed this when he addressed God, saying "In wrath remember mercy." On this, David Kamhi — or Kimhi, in our pronunciation (like the way some say *rabbi,* and the Germans say *ribbi* because it's easier; and like the divergence of opinion of Greek and Latin on *grammatiki* and *grammatica,* and *logiki* and *logica, mitir* and *mater,* and so to *Samson* and *Simson, Kamhi* and *Kimhi,* and so on) — anyway, this Jew, David, a Spaniard, teaches that in this passage we ought to understand by the name "mercy," "Abraham" (symbolically through the Kabbalistic numerical values).[32] Thus Habbakuk would say "O God, when you are moved to anger for our sins, remember the seed of Abraham, he whom you promised that in him all the nations of the earth would be blessed"; and, "O God, you declared unto him: 'in your seed will all the nations of the earth be blessed.'" Habbakuk himself indicated what that seed would be, adding, "You have gone forth for the salvation of your people, for salvation with your Messiah." Here this David Kimhi comments, "This is the Messiah, the son of David." So I am with all the wise Kabbalists in saying that true salvation in the Messiah depends on the degree of nearness to him that we attain. To this end we release ourselves, so far as we are able, from all created matter, trying to climb the ladder and reach him. And if we cannot get there, yet we must approach, each according to his ability. This is our man; all our law refers to his coming, not just Moses' writings, but all the Prophets and all the other books of Holy Scripture (the whole text that we call *'Esrim v'arba,* "The Twenty-Four," and you call "the Bible"; that is, what we call "Torah," "the Law"). As it is written in Daniel, chapter 9: "walking in the Law of the Lord our God, which he set before us through the hands of his servants the prophets." Only these writings have we ordained stable and firm enough to enable us to use them as a foundation for all our reasoning, and without complication place on them the sublime meditations of the contemplatives; in these the voice of the great God is proclaimed, here the mental force and energy of contemplative men is deployed. Through them we have the strength to climb from muddled confusion to the straightforward, from the straightforward to the plainest things, from effects to causes, and, at length, from the lower world to the higher, and from the higher world to the Messiah, who is the supreme object of our thinking, and who can be comprehended only on the last rung. The whole is as if we had the strength to ascend to the King of Ages.

LIBER PRIMVS　　XX

zulorũ afcẽdere ualeam⁹, p̃ quẽ plane tandẽ in deũ trãfeamus incomphẽ
fibilẽ, tum etiam qm̃ per has facras literas quafi per fcalam Iacob, cacumi
ne tangentem coelos cui deus ipfe innitatur noftri afcendunt angeli & de
fcendunt, uectores hinc precum inde donorum, qui ultro citroq̃ portant
hinc petitiones inde fuppetias, ut ex ueftris quidã ait. Et profecto nihil fen
tio aliud etiam quod uel fingi poffet animum noftrum arctius deo pinde
atq̃ aliquod ftamen introtexere q̃ illam ipfam cuius mentio fit facram
fcripturam, quæ nos primo in diuinorum admirationem ducit, tum in eo
rum pro humano captu agnitionem, deinde in illum ardentiffimum qua
litercunq̃ cognitæ diuinitatis amorem, præ fe ferentem certiffimum fpei
effectum. Per hanc cum Ezechielis animalibus et rotis de terra eleuamur,
ut cum euntibus eamus, & cum ftantibus ftemus. Hic eft folus ueræ contẽ
plationis campus, cuius fingula uerba, fingula funt facramenta, & finguli
fermones, fyllabæ, apices, punctaq̃ eius plena funt arcanis fetifibus, nõ tm̃
nobis autoribus, uerum etiam chriftianis atteftantibus. Hæc eft Cabala
quæ nos humi degere non finit, fed mentem noftram extollit ad altiffimã
comprehenfionis metam, quæ tamen nequeat animam Meffihæ rationa
biliter tranfcendere, nifi quodam incomprehenfibili intuitu quafi uia mo
mentanei raptus, quo putamus haud impoffibile Cabaliftis nobis in fpiri
tu prope tertium mundum corripi, ubi eft Meffiha omnibus inferioribus
influens. Mundi enim generaliffimi numero tres funt. Primus materialis,
fecundus formalis, & tertius informis. Seu quando fic uultis primus inq̃
infimus qui & fenfibilis, fecundus fupremus & mentalis qui & intelligibi
lis, & tertius ὑπέρτατος i. fuperfupremus, uel fi dicere liceret fupremiffi
mus, incomparabilis & diuinus. Mundum autem cenferi primum quo ad
nos uolui hunc corporeum, cæteris fubfiftentem, ordine forte peruerfo,
qui iufta ratione in genere caufarũ fuiffe debebat ultimus, quafi recepta
culum omnium fuperiorum. Ifte conftituitur primo ex coelis & coeleftibꝰ,
fecundo ex elementis & elemẽtatis, tertio ex na tura humana & fingula
riis hominibus, qui dicunt hebraice עולם הקטן græce μικρόκοσμος
& latine paruus mũdus. Vniuerfum hoc corpus, ut Ariftoteli ueftro pla
cet in libro de Mundo eft globus ex coelo & terra & iis contentis naturis
conftitutus, quippe cum feptem habitaculis coeleftibus, & feptem habita
culis terreftribus, quæ quidem enumerat Rabi Mnahem Racanat in ca
pite xxv. Leuitici nominibus, iftis primo ad coelum pertinentibus.
שמים רקיע שחקים זבול מעון מכון ערבות
Secundo ad terram ארץ אדמה גיא יבשה חרבה
תבל חלד Septem quoq̃ habitacula inferorum Iofeph Salemita
nus in Horto nucis (ut paulo fuperius audiuiftis) nominatim recitauit.
De Microcofmo autem id quoq̃ haud clam eft omnibus nobis, ad homi

B ii

Book One

Through the Messiah we come to the unknowable God; we come thither through these holy letters, as if on Jacob's ladder, the ladder that touches the roof of heaven and while God rests upon it the angels ascend and descend, carrying prayers up and gifts down, bearers of petitions and assistance, as some of your people say. I am of the opinion that there is nothing else that could bind us closer to God — as close as warp and weft — than the Holy Scriptures of which I have been speaking. They first bring us to wonder at the divine, then to understand (given man's limitations) and at last to love the divinity, limitedly understood, a love that brings about the most assured fulfillment of our hope.

By these Scriptures let us be lifted from the earth with the beasts and wheels of Ezekiel's vision. Let us go when they go, let us stop when they stop. This only is the area of real contemplation, where individual words, individual mysteries, syllables, diacritic and punctuation marks are full of secret meaning. This is attested to not only by our authors but also by Christians. This is the Kabbalah which will not allow us to stop at ground level, it lifts our minds to the highest stage of understanding. Our minds cannot, however, by rational means, climb to the soul of the Messiah, except by some incomprehensible intuition that comes in a flash.

By such means, we believe, it is not beyond possibility that Kabbalists can in spirit be snatched up to where the Messiah flows into all lesser things, near to the third world.

There are three kinds of world. The first is material, the second formal, the third formless. Or, if you prefer, the first is the lowest world, that of the senses; the second is the highest, that of the mind and the understanding; the third is above the highest, or, if you want, the very highest — indescribable, divine. I want the first kind of world to be considered this physical world, depending on the other two — the order is misplaced, perhaps, because properly this world is the last in the chain of causes, a repository for everything from higher up.

The world then is constructed thus: first from heaven and heavenly things, second from elements and categories, third of human nature and individual men; this last is called, in Hebrew, Greek, and Latin "the small world," *olam ha-qatan, mikrokosmos.* This whole "body" (as you and Aristotle chose to call it in his book, *On the World*) is a sphere made up from heaven and earth and their contents — the seven heavenly dwellings and seven earthly dwellings listed by Rabbi Menahem Recanat in his commentary on Leviticus XXV. The names associated with heaven are: heaven, firmament, dust, habitation, house, dwelling, deserted place. Secondly, those associated with earth: earth, *arka,* valley, dry land, desert, inhabited earth, world of life. Joseph of Salem also gives the names of the seven lower dwellings in the book *The Nut Garden* which I have already mentioned.

Turning first to this "small world" (the microcosm), it is clearly

DE ARTE CABALISTICA

his conditionem, quamlibet in partem respexeritis septem attinere, quæ sunt corpus, anima, & ex iis compositū, quod נפש appellamus, ut est illud regis Sodomorum תן לי נפש Id est. Da mihi hominem, ex quatuor scilicet potentiis animæ compositum, & quatuor qualitatibus mundi maioris, qui sane mundus cum sit animatus illustratur mente propria quæ dicitur Metattron. Secundus est mundus supremus intelligentiarum separatarū que a Cabalistis appellantur שבלים נפרדים a philosophis autem Hebræorum דעות נפררות Eum quidem mundum & speciebus plenum, & formis, & mentibus solutis, & angelis, complectitur, ambit & regit ipsa Messihæ anima, quæ apud Cabalistas est idea Idea omnium uitarum, ad quam refertur omnis uitalitas indiuidualis, specifica, & generifica. Inde quasi ex uiuario depromit uita, ois & nominatur, a Cabalistis terra uiuentium. למיכך דרשו בפסוק תוצא הארץ נפש חיה למינה זו נפש של משיח Id est. Ideoq₃ commentantur in uersiculo producat terra animam uiuentem ad speciem suam, hæc est anima Messihæ. Quæ uerba leguntur ita in Portæ Lucis capite secundo. Et sicut in mundo humano qui dicitur Microcosmus, animæ hominis dominatur mens, ita mundo cœlesti dominatur Metattron, & mundo angelico dominatur anima Messihæ, & mundo incomparabili dominatur Adonai, Quin etiam sicut lux mentis est intellectus agens, ita lux Metattron est Sadai, & lux animæ Messihæ est Elhai, id est deus uiuus, & lux Adonai est Ensoph. Cunq₃ consultissimis rerum naturalium scrutatoribus facile uideatur superioris naturæ infimum, cum inferioris naturæ supremo communicare, in tantum quidem ut sepius de proxime connexis dubitari possit, contigua sint an continua, & cuius nam existat naturæ illud quo continua uniuntur, haud secus atq₃ id quo equi pes & eius ungula conueniunt, corneum ne sit an carneum, propter immediatam existentium connexionem, Iccirco etiam nunc magis sine iniuria dici arbitror q₃ homo Microcosmus & mundus sensibilis ille magnus, communicant in mente. Mundus item corporeus & mundus intellectualis, communicāt in Metattron, qui est intellectus agens primi mobilis, unus cum natura cœlesti tanquam inferiori, & cum natura angelica tanquam superiori, mundus autem supremus cum mundo tertio incōparabili ac supsupmo cōicant in aīa Messihę quasi essentia quadā utrinq₃ & angelico & diuino mūdo cōtinua, nec em iterstitio ullo aīa. Messihę, & Elhai distāt. Sed est El-hai fons aquarū uiuentium, & anima Messihæ riuus uitæ. Tertius mundus est deitatis, qui constituitur ex eo quod Seraphim uocauerunt Sanctus Sanctus Sanctus tetragramatus. Dicitq₃ in Deuteronomio, Magnus potens & terribilis, seu potius reuerēdꝰ. Magnus ante creationē, potēs in creatiōe, & reuerēdꝰ

On the Art of Kabbalah

known to us all that seven things affect the human condition (however you look at it). These are: body, spirit, and what is made up from them, which we call *nefesh* (as the king of Sodom said, "Give me a *nefesh*," a "man"), and is made up of four powers of the spirit and the four qualities of the greater world, which is itself endowed with spirit, and enlightened by its own mind, called Metattron.

The second world, the highest world of distinct intelligences, Kabbalists call the world of separate *sechelim,* and the Hebrew philosophers call the world of *de'ot.* This world contains types, forms, disembodied minds, and angels, and is enclosed, circumscribed, and ruled by the soul of the Messiah, which, according to the Kabbalists, is the idealized Idea of all living things, and applies to all life, individual, specific, and general. From it — as from a farm of livestock — all life is drawn; and the Kabbalists call it the "Land of the Living." "The comment made on the verse, 'Let the earth bring forth living things after their kind,' is 'This is the soul of the Messiah.'" Thus we read in chapter 2 of *Gate of Light.*

In the human world (microcosm), the mind is ruler of the human soul; in the heavenly world Metattron is in control, and in the angelic world the soul of the Messiah governs, while in the world that is beyond description the Lord holds sway. Further, just as active intellect is the light of the mind, so Shaddai is Metattron's light, *El Hai* ("the living God") is the light of the soul of the Messiah, and *En Sof* is the light of the Lord.

On a very careful inspection of nature it is easily seen that the lower end of the higher world touches on the higher end of the lower to such an extent that at the border it is more often than not a matter for doubt whether these worlds are contiguous or continuous. All the continuous connection is like the join between a horse's foot and its hoof: too close for one to say whether it is horn or flesh. On the same lines, I think I can say this without damaging the case: the "man-microcosm" and that great world of the senses touch on each other in the mind. The physical world and the intellectual meet in Metattron, the prime mover in active intellect. The heavenly nature is slightly lower than he, and the angelic nature is slightly higher. The highest world touches on the third, indescribable "super-supreme" world in the soul of the Messiah, which is like a continuum of both the angelic and divine worlds, there being no point of divide between the soul of the Messiah and the living god. *El Hai,* the living God, is the wellspring of living waters, and the soul of the Messiah is the stream of life.

The third world is that of the Deity, consisting in him whom the seraphim call "Holy, Holy, Holy *YHWH,*" him whom Deuteronomy calls "the great, powerful and terrible" or rather "awe-inspiring" — great before creation, powerful in creation, terrible after creation. This is

LIBER PRIMVS

post creationē. Et hic est אחד .i. un9, imo magis proprie, principiū uni
tatis, qa Aleph designat principiū & had.unum. quasi principiū unius, oia
in sua simpli, citate unitatis complicās. Cuius talis est emanatio secūdum
Cabalistas רוח דבר קול .i. Spiritus uerbum uox. Sic enim Rab
Azariel in cōmētario san ctita tis, post etiā ea q̄ nūc recitaui scripsit his
uerbis מרוח יוצא הדבר והקול בלא פתוחת
שפתים ובלא דבור לשון ולא נשמת אדם
.i. Ex spiritu producitur uerbum atq; uox, non per apertionem labiorum
& non per sermonem linguae, nec anhelitu hominis. Et hi tres unus est spi
ritus qa unus est deus, ut in libro Ietzira de creati, one Iegim9 his uerbis.
אחת רוח אלהים חיים ברוך הוא ומבורך
שמו של חי העולמים קול ורוח ודבר וזו
היא רוח הקדש שתים רוח מרוח .i. Vnus spiritus
deus uiuens, benedictus ipse & benedictum nomen eius qui uiuit in secu
la, uox & spiritus & uerbum, & hoc est spirit9 sanctus, duo spiritus ex spi
ritu. Hęc Abrahā pater noster. Et iuxta id q̊d Rab hamai in libro היחוד
de speculatione scripsit. Hi tres qui sunt unum, inter se proportionē habēt
ut אחד מיוחד יחיד .i. Vnus, uniens, unitum. Quin & paulo
superius idē ait והם ראש ואמצע וסוף .i. Et sunt principi
um et mediū & finis, & hęc sunt unus punctus, & est אדון הכל .i.
Dominus uniuersi. Sic in uolumine citato. Mundus itaq; ille tertius incō
parabiliter summus ex istis tribus quae sunt unum cōstitutus, quasi ex sum
ma essentia potentia & operatione, in aethernum & ultra extenditur, nec
concauus, nec cōuexus, nec carinatus, nec sup, ficiē hūs. Nam ut scribit
Aza, riel in li, bro pridē allegato sanctitatis. הוא ראשון בלי
תחלה והוא אחרון בלי תכלה .i. Hic est prim9 absq;
initio, & hic est ultimus absq; termino, sane quo ne cogitatus quidē nostri
pertingere possunt, & noiatur Ensoph, id est infinitudo, quae est summa
quaedam res secundum se incomprehensibilis & ineffabilis, in remotissi
mo suae diuinitatis retrocessu & in fontani luminis inaccessibili abysso se
retrahens & contegens, ut sic nihil intelligatur ex ea procedere, quasi ab
solutissima deitas per ociū oimoda sui in se ipsa clausione immanēs nuda
sine ueste ac absq; ullo circūstātiarū amictu, nec sui profusa, nec spledoris
sui dilatata bonitate indiscriminati ens & nō ens, & oia q̄ rationi nsę uide
tur inter se contraria & cōtradictoria, ut segregata & libera unitas simpli
cissime implicās, sic.n. legit in lib. de fide & expiatiōe. בכח אמרתי
לך כי המצא יש מאין איננו חסר וכי
יש הוא באין בעניין איז והאין הוא באין
יש ללמוד שהאין הוא היש והיש הוא האין

B iii

Book One

ehad, the "one," or better, the beginning of oneness, for the letter aleph ("e") in *ehad* stands for "beginning," and *-had* is "one," hence "the beginning of one." In his absolute oneness he embraces all things. From this emanate (according to Kabbalists) spirit, word, and voice. Rabbi Azariel, in his commentary on holiness (it follows the note I mentioned earlier), writes: "From the spirit comes the word and voice — not from parting of the lips, nor from the speech of the tongue, nor from the breathing of a man." These three are one spirit, for God is one, as we read in the book *Yetzira* ("On the Creation"): "The Living God (blessed be he, and blessed be his Name, who lives for ever) is one spirit: voice and spirit and word. And this is the holy spirit: two spirits from the spirit." (These are the words of our father Abraham.) Connect with this what Rabbi Hamai wrote in *On Contemplation:* "These three are one, and bear these relations to each other: the one, the unifying, the unified." A little before this he writes: "And they are the beginning and the middle and the end, and they are one point: the Lord of the universe." So the third, indescribably higher world is made up of these three which are one, as of the highest being, power and activity; it extends to eternity and beyond, of no shape — concave, convex, hemispherical — and with no surface. For as Azariel writes in the aforementioned book on holiness: "He is the first-without-beginning, the last-without-end."

Not even our thought can grasp him, he who is called *En Sof* — "Infinity," a concept according with him who is unknowable and unutterable, hidden away in the furthest recesses of his divinity, into the unreachable abyss of the fountain of light, so thus nothing is understood to come from him — as if at ease the absolute Deity held all kinds of things in his compass, himself remaining naked and unclothed, without the cloak of attributes. He is not extravagant of himself, or of his splendor, yet indiscriminately spreads goodness about him. He is being and non-being — all that to our rational minds seems contrary and self-contradictory. He is like a being apart, untrammelled oneness, uncomplicatedly binding all together.

So we read in *On Faith and Atonement:* "Now I have told you that Being issuing from non-Being has need of nothing, and that Being is in non-Being insofar as it partakes of non-Being, and that non-Being is in Being insofar as it partakes in non-Being. From which we learn that non-Being is Being, and that Being is non-Being."

DE ARTE CABALISTICA

Q .i. Iā dixi tibi q̇ producēs ens de nō ente nulli9 eget,& q̇ ens est in nō ente q̇ ad rē nō entis,& nō ens est in ente q̇ ad rē entis.Et infra. Quo discas q̇d nō ens est ens & ens est nō ens,ita illic scriptum legitur.Istud aūt oēm nō strum intellectum transcendit qui nequit contradictoria in suo principio combinare uia rationis,qm̄ per ea q̇ nobis ab ipsa natura manifesta fiunt ambulamus,quæ longe ab hac infinita uirtute cadens, ipsa contradictoria per infinitum distantia connectere simul nequit,ut quidam Germanorū philosophissimus archiflamen dialis annos paulo ante quinquaginta & duos posteritati acceptum reliquit.Temporaliū igit̄ curarum grauamine

R semoto & aniliū disputationū sophismatibus contēptis, fœlix Cabalista p̄ Cabalam.i.recepti & crediti semitam tenebras erumpit & prosilit in splen dorem quo attingit lumen,& sic a lumine migrat in lucem & per lucē q̇tū humana potest capere natura illud uerum luminare comprehendit sub modo entis,non autem non entis,nisi fiat hoc per omnium abstractionē quæcunq̇ non sunt principium absolute primum. Cunq̇ frequenter hac uia per ineffabile gaudium & alacritatem spiritus ipsa mens Cabalistę in tra profundę taciturnitatis secretum humilia deserens atq̇ terrena,ad su percœlestia & inuisibilia transfertur omnem transcendentia humanū sen sum,tunc &si adhuc mortali in cute hospitatus,tamen socius fit angelorū perinde atq̇ domicilii supercœlestis quidam inquilinus cuius tam crebra conuersatio in cœlis esse cognoscatur, & tum quandoq̇ cum illis tanq̇ uiarum suarum comitibus ad altiora spaciatur,animāq̇ Messihæ uisitat, quandoq̇ autē ad inferiores tam cœlestes q̇ cæteras naturæ uirtutes an/ gelico ductu nec tn̄ sine propria q̇q̇ ratione descendit,& earum dignita tes operationesq̇ intelligere ac singulari honore uenerari studet. Vnde

S oritur intima Cabalistę cum angelis amicitia, per quam aliquando noīa diuina rite cognoscens,res admirandas conficit,quæ uulgus miracula no minat,ut Rabi Meir per nomen diuinum uel ab ethnico prolatum ipsam uxoris suæ sororem a corruptione diuersorii lupanaris præseruauit, quā ui prostitutam nullus ganeonum uerbo dicto etiam quātumuis robustus uiolare ac stuprare ualuerat.Hæc in Portæ lucis exordio & alia id genus plurima cum suis autoribus recitantur.Tamq̇ facilis eiuscemodi erat pa trum memoria Cabalistis miraculorum operatio,ut ii ab inuidis & pro/ phanis sæpius ignominiose uersuti magici cognominarentur, quasi non illa opera perfecisset Michael sed multo maxime Samael,uidelicet per in cantationes ægyptiacas & arcana quædam, tametsi uirga Cabalistarum semper deuorat uirgas præstygiatorum,& salubrius agit quodcunq̇ dī uinum q̇ ullum dæmoniacum.Semper enim ad hominum salutem tendit Cabalæ artificium, cōtra uero semper ad perditionem uergit magicæ ua nitatis ueneficium, hoc per nomina tenebrarum & cacodæmonum, illud

per noīa

On the Art of Kabbalah

This goes beyond the intellectual faculties of all of us: we are unable by rational methods to entertain things that are by definition contradictory. We are used to things that are by their very nature obvious. Rationality falls far short of the infinite power we have been talking about, it cannot simultaneously connect these contradictories that are separated by infinity. (A German philosopher-archbishop handed down this dictum some fifty-two years ago.[33])

The burden of temporal cares is flung off then, and old-womanish sophistries held in contempt: the happy Kabbalist, following the path of received truth that is Kabbalah, breaks out of the shadows, leaps into the circle of lamplight, from here moves on to daylight, and from the clear light of day comes understanding to illumine (within the limits of human ability) that truth of being — but not non-being, except by the abstraction of all things which are not absolute first principles. Often like this the mind of the Kabbalist, in a state of unutterable delight, rejoicing in spirit, in the depths of inner silence, driving away from itself humdrum earthly matters, is carried away to the heavenly and the invisible that lie beyond all human sense. Then, though yet a guest of the body, he becomes a fellow of the angels, a sojourner in the home above the heavens: his frequent intercourse may be recognized as being in heaven. When he travels to the higher regions, he does so in the company of angels, he often sees the soul of the Messiah. When he goes down to the lower powers of nature, which are as heavenly as the others, then with angelic guidance, and with proper reasoning, he applies himself to understanding their value and service, and honors them with special respect. Thus arises the Kabbalist's intimate friendship with the angels, through which he comes to know, in the proper manner, something of the divine names and does wonderful things (commonly known as miracles). Rabbi Meir, for instance, through the name of God (or one made up by the heathen), saved his wife's sister from the brothel — she had been forced into prostitution, but none of those fornicators (and that is the word for them) had succeeded in violating or deflowering her. (This is related in *Gate of Light*, along with many like it, and those who performed them.) According to our forbears' records, the working of miracles of this kind was so easy for Kabbalists that many spiteful cynics called them sly magicians — all as if it were not Michael who worked these deeds, but Samuel, through the medium of Egyptian spells and secret signs, and this despite the fact that the Kabbalists' wand always stays the conjurors', and that godliness works far more effectively than any devilry.

The skills of Kabbalah tend to work for the good of man, while the poison of false magic leads to their downfall. The one employs the

LIBER PRIMVS

per nomina lucis & beatorum angelorum, de quibus nisi more nostro Sabbathi feriatus dies iam uesperi hac ipsa hora ingrueret, quoniam huc attinet, tanquam huius artis fructus quem adeo desyderatis ego sane tum quicquid sentirem magis ample tractarem. At parum abest quin nox ru at optimi uiri, secedendumcȝ nobis est, non modo ne præcepti negligens multa uapulem, uerum ne etiam professioni Cabalicæ desiam, si hoc sab batho ultra Sabbathai qui est Saturnus suprema arcana & recondita la bore operoso effodiam, ac non potius silentio remorer, & ocio perfruar tantisper dum sequens dies pretereat. Cętera hic perendie uel quotoqȝ loco utut elegeritis de arte Cabalistica explanabimus. Tum Philolaus, Es inquit difficillimas dicendi partes sortitus nostri causa, qui post meridi em adortis nobis tot res tam admirandas & tanto numero perpetua ora tione protulisti, quanquam nulla plane moueri uisus molestia. Et ille tum, Amor inquit erga uos meus ut spero mutuus omnem molestiam abstulit Qȝ nisi adesset feriæ, non putarem mea interesse uos tales ac tantos dis cendi gratia huc profectos ita Cabalæ doctrina ieiunos & inexpletos di mittere, sed parendum est legi. Ad hæc Marranus, Ego uero Simon re cte fateor nunquam me a cuiusquam conspectu magis doctum abiisse, mi hicȝ uel si malis ambobus ut pro hoc quocȝ recipiã abs te quidem cumu late quantum id temporis pati creditum est sat esse factum. Mox Philola us. Tu solius inquit tui causam Marrane agas uelim, ego nondum istis quanquam maximis & ad doctrinam Pythagoricam familiarissime acce dentibus tamen auidiori mihi copiosius hauriendis, fore satisfactum puta uero, si non comperendinata dies finem artis afferat. Qua de re post Sab bathum istud tuum Simon, quando singulari tua comitate nos ita fers, re dibimȝ. Et ille redite dum ait intrepide ac interea, ualete bona ualetudine.

Finis Libri Primi.

Book One

names of ghosts and evil spirits, the other uses the names of light and the blessed angels, of whom I would tell you more were it not now dusk and our Sabbath, the holy day, drawing in, and almost here. As it is I feel quite strongly that, given the force of your longing for this rewarding art, I must develop the subject in greater depth. But very shortly night will fall, and, gentlemen, we must part. I shall not only get into trouble for being careless about the rules, but will also betray my Kabbalistic creed, if on this Sabbath I sweat at unearthing that farther Sabbath (Saturn), the highest secret mystery. I would rather be silent now, and take a rest until the end of tomorrow. We shall discover the rest of the art of Kabbalah here then — or in any place you choose.

PHILOLAUS: You chose the most difficult job, that of speaking on our behalf. You have talked nonstop since noon, bringing so many remarkable matters to our attention, although you clearly don't seem to have been affected by it.

SIMON: My affection for you (which I hope is not one-sided) has outweighed all the difficulties. If it weren't that the day of rest is upon us, I don't think any of my own affairs would hinder my teaching you who have come here to learn of Kabbalah, leaving me to send you away hungry, without explanation. But the law must be obeyed.

MARRANUS: Truly, Simon, I must admit that I have never met anyone whom I left as well informed as I do you. I — or rather, we, for I think I speak for both of us — think that enough has been accomplished in the time allowed.

PHILOLAUS (quickly): Speak for yourself, Marranus; I don't think I have heard enough of these important matters which are so very close to Pythagorean doctrine. I could absorb a good deal more, and what has gone so far would not suffice, were it not that the rest will come the day after tommorow. On this matter, Simon, we shall return after this Sabbath of yours when we may again enjoy your remarkable company.

SIMON: Do not hesitate to do so. Meanwhile, goodbye, and keep well.

END OF BOOK I

DE ARTE CABALISTICA
IOANNIS REVCHLIN PHORCENSIS
Legum Doctoris, Liber Secundus.

ABEVNTIBVS INDE VTRISQVE PHILO
lao iuniore Marranocʒ domum,uarius inter eūdum erat fermo, &
non ineptus, quippe doctis fupra modum philofophis de hoc ipfo He
bræo, cuius cum fumma doctrina fingularem etiam commendabāt erga
peregrinos humanitatem, & in oībus atcʒ prę oībus morum dignitatem:
Placuerunt cuncta eius hōis, pter unum iftud Sabbathum futuro, ut iudi
carunt, tædio plenum, quo a tanti magiftri gratiffimo colloquio diuelle
rētur, & in diem reiicerent ufcʒ adeo tertium, non abfcʒ tpis molefto dif
pendio, cum quid acturi effent luce craftina, ignorarent. Tum ambulādo
ita ruminati acceptæ fuccum doctrinę, breues dictorum epilogos mutuo
percenfebant. Ardentibus autē illis difcendi feruore uenit in mentem &
rediit fubito in memoriam admirabilis uiri Iudæi oratio, difputandi acri
monia, inftitutio grauis & erudita quæ fine fatietate delectet, non fucata,
non colorata, fed quæ ubi maxime careat floribᵍ ibi plurimum pariat fru
ctus. Cuncʒ fe iam ab itinere in diuerforium corripuiffent, mox in ipfo cō
feffu antecʒ refpiraffent cœpit ita MARRANVS. Omnium fapien
tum qs equidem à teneris audiuerim annis haud fcio an ullus fuerit uncʒ
qui argutior in dicendo & fublimior in fentiendo uifus mihi fit hoc uno
Simone, quem uel reminifcens iam memoria teneā, ita fermone fuo tǣetfi
plano, fimplici non affectato, nō domi quæfito, minimecʒ Demofthenis
oleū olente, fed magis extēporali & ǭtidiano meū animum ad ardua con
templanda excitauit, ut nihil conceperim gratius. Dii boni, homo Iudæus
ex Iudæis ortus, alitus, educatus, & edoctus, q̄ natio ubicʒ gentium barba
ra fuperftitiofa uilis abiecta, & a fplendore oīum bonarum artium aliena
eft habita, perpetuā crede mihi hanc noctem prodiui defyderio meo uiri
huius uidiffem uultus, audiffem uerba loquentis, fi non miferum hoc ue
fperi Sabbathum interueniffet. Tum Philolaus. Ne græci quidem omēs
inquit quibus oīm confenfu tribuitur multarum artium difciplina, ingeni
A   orum acumen, dicendi copia, tam afcendere potuiffent in alta rerum arca
narum faftigia, nifi forte unus Pythagoras ille meus, philofophiæ pater,
tamen qui non a græcis eam doctrinæ pſtantiam quin potius ab illis ipis
Iudæis receperit, Itacʒ receptor optimo iure ipfe q̄cʒ id eft Cabalifta no
minādus erat, q̄uis ut poft diuturnam peregrinationem è longinq̄ aliqd
admiratione dignum referret in patriam, q̄d facilius uulgo crederet, ipfe
nomen illūd Cabalæ fuis incognitum primus in nomen philofophiæ grę
cum mutauerit. Quod eo argumento recte coniicimus, q̄a nullam difcipu
lis fuis reliquit aliqua ratione perquirendi facultatem, quin id primum fui
dogmatis

ON THE ART OF THE KABBALAH
By Johann Reuchlin of Pforzheim
BOOK II

Young Philolaus and Marranus set off from home, discussing with some intelligence, for they were more than usually learned philosophers, a number of the points raised by the Jew. They were full of admiration for the quality of his teaching, his extraordinary kindness to strangers, and above all for his dignified manner. They were in all respects delighted with the man except for his Sabbath, which, they thought, they would find rather tedious, having torn themselves away from such rewarding discussion with so great a teacher, and being put off until the day after next. It was a nuisance to waste so much time, and they did not know what to do with themselves meanwhile. While walking, they went over the train of thought of the discourse, and briefly summarized what had been said.

Fired with passion for learning, they called to mind the Jew's extraordinary speaking style: incisive in argument, serious and erudite in instruction, its delight never palled. It was plain and straightforward without artifices or high coloring, but by its very lack of floweriness it yielded fruit. Reaching the inn now, they sat down and Marranus began, hardly drawing breath.

MARRANUS: Of all the wise men I have heard since my youth up, I am not sure if any has seemed to reason so acutely or make such lofty observations as this Simon. And he talks plainly and without affectation, which is so rare where I come from, with little oratorical grease, tending rather to the informal or everyday. As a result I find I can remember it all clearly. And his words have inspired me to meditate on these difficult matters, to the point where I can conceive of nothing I would rather do. Good God! A Jew—born, brought up, educated and put to study among Jews. And people consider Jews an uncivilized, superstitious, base, low people, unenlightened strangers to fine learning. Believe me, I wanted to hear more so much that I would have stayed up all night to watch that man's face and listen to him talking. If only this wretched Sabbath had not intervened this evening.

PHILOLAUS: Not even the Greeks could have risen to the heights of these mysteries, and by common consent they are the masters in most fields, with their penetrating minds and facility of expression. Perhaps I must make an exception for my mentor Pythagoras, the father of philosophy. Nevertheless his preeminence was derived not from the Greeks, but again from the Jews. As "one who received," he can quite justly be termed a Kabbalist. After much traveling he brought back to his hometown something worth admiring and he first renamed Kabbalah *philosophy*, a Greek word hitherto unknown, to facilitate general understanding. We can see clearly on this evidence that he left his followers no means of making rational inquiry, since he

dogmatis principium esse uoluit, ut quærentibus causam responderent
αὐτὸς ἔφα .i. Ipse dixit, more Cabalistarum q̃ ferme haud aliter rerū cognoscendarum rationes citant q̃ cp aiunt אמרו חכמים .i. Dixerunt
sapiētes. Sic noster ille αὐτὸς ἔφα .i. Ipse dixit. Ipse aūt idem est Pythagoras
qui hoc modo philosophiæ nomen indidisse perhibetur, qm̄ summi Hebræorum autores Hachamim & Græcorum ante se olim Sophi cognoīarentur, ita ueterem disciplinam noui conatus est nois ornamēto uestire.
Non aūt eo tibi debent minori p̃conio digna uideri quæ Simon Iudæus
protulit cp sint ab ignobili hebrææ gentis doctore tanq̃ ex barbaris autoribus desumpta, & ab homine barbaro allata, q̃n idem omnium maximꝰ
noster Pythagoras simul cum barbaro q̃dam nois Zora scientiarum prima studia iniit, adeocp id extra Græciam, quo tpe apud ægyptios secum
philosophati sunt, qui tum dicebātur prophetæ, & Assyriorum Chaldęi
& Gallorum Druidæ, & ex Bactris Samanæi, & Celtarum non pauci, &
apud Persas Magi, & apud Indos Gymnosophistæ, & ille Anacharsis
apud Scythas, & in Thracia Zamolxis ante ipsius Pythagoræ seruus, q̃d
omē Alexāder ille cognomēto polyhistor in libro περὶ Πυθαγορείων συμβόλων
.i. de Pythagoricis notis scriptum reliqt, & apud Indos denicp Iudei q̃s ap
pellarunt Brachmanas, ut Aristobulus peripateticus meminit. Sane licet
uera dicere, non est certe uscp repertus Pythagoras quicq̃ rerum aut diuinarum aut humanarum uel a græcis didicisse uel a Romanis. Sed ut Antiphon edidit in libro περὶ τ̃ βίου τῶν ἐν ἀρετῇ πρωτευσάντων .i. de uita eorum qui
uirtute p̃stiterunt. Accessit discēdi gratia Pythagoras ad ægyptios & Arrabas, & ad Chaldæos postq̃ e Syria q̃ & est & noīatur Iudæa Pherecidē
sibi magistrum & p̃ceptorem nactus fuisset. Vnde Syrius uulgo ipse q̃cp
tum appellabatur, quem alii Tyrium dixere, alii Tyrenum ὥστε βάρβαρον
ἀλλ' οὐχ Ἕλληνα γεγενέαι πρὶν ὁμολογεῖν ἐν πρώτην φιλοσόφων .i. ut barbarum &
non græcum fuisse p̃dicarent hunc oīum philosophorum primum. Hæc
Marrane cōuiua mi doctissime penes Eusebium Pamphili scripta legisti
certo scio, in uolumine, si rite recordor, de p̃paratione euangelica undecimo, qui & hoc addidit. μόνον ὅτι πρὸ δὲ τῶν σοφῶν Ἑλλήνων ἔχον αὐλὸς, πᾶσα σοφίας
καὶ ἀπορείας ὑσοικουώντων .i. Tm̄ cp a sapientibus græcis habuit nihil, penuria sa
pientiæ ac indigentia cohabitantiū. De qbus, ut est in Timæo Platonis,
barbarus q̃ndam ægyptius, iscp ua! 'le senex, uere admodum uisus est Soloni dixisse. O Solon Solon græci semper pueri estis, nullam habentes antiquam opinionem nullam disciplinā tpe canam. Nec illud non erit maxime laudandum in Pythagora p̃stanti sapientia & nobilitāte uiro cp in alieno & longinquo solo, quæ a barbaris hoibus labore ingenti algu & sudore multa commētatione atcp meditatione, nō paucis etiam annis corrasit, ea non dicam meliora sed tamen splendidiora in patriā ac uscp adeo
in Italiam quæ tunc magna Græcia dicebatur, ceu humeris ipse suis repor

Book Two

wanted the basic principle of his doctrine to be that the reply to those who asked "Why?" should be, "The Master said so," which is just like the Kabbalistic habit of never giving any reason beyond "The sages said so." It is said that Pythagoras chose the name *philosophy* on account of this attitude. The greatest Hebrew writers were known as *hachamim,* and the Greeks before him *Sophi.* So he attempted to embellish an old discipline with a new name.

What Simon the Jew told us should not be held less praiseworthy because it comes from an unknown Jewish scholar, or because its origins are, as one might say, outlandish, coming as they do from a man untouched by civilization as we know it. The greatest of all our masters, Pythagoras, began his study of knowledge outside Greece, with a man called Zora. At that time in Egypt the people then known as prophets practiced philosophy with him as did the Chaldees of Assyria, the Druids in Gaul, the Shamans of Bactria, a number of Celts, the Magi in Persia, the Gymnosophists; then he studied with Anacharsis of Scythia, and with Zamolxis, who had been Pythagoras' slave, in Thrace.[34] (All this can be found in Alexander Polyhistor's book *On Pythagorean Symbols.*)

Lastly, he also studied philosophy with the Jews in India called Brahmans. This fact is recorded by Aristobulus the peripatetic. In fact, Pythagoras cannot rightly be said to have learnt anything from the Greeks and Romans in either theology or the humanities. Rather the case is as presented by Antiphon in his book *Lives of Outstanding Men:* "Pythagoras went to Arabia and Chaldaea to be taught. Later, in the part of Syria known as Judaea he found a master and teacher in Pherecides."

As a result Pythagoras was often nicknamed "The Syrian," sometimes "The Tyrian," or "The Tyrenian," and it is often said that this, the first of all philosophers, was not a Greek but a barbarian. Marranus, my learned friend, I am sure you have read Eusebius Pamphili. If I remember rightly, in chapter eleven of his book *Praeparatio Evangelica,* he adds the comment: "So he got nothing from the wise Greeks, such was the poverty and want of wisdom among his countrymen." On the same lines, in Plato's *Timaeus,* it appears that an old Egyptian native once said to Solon: "O Solon, Solon, you Greeks are still boys. You have no ancient beliefs, none of your learning has gone grey with age." Even without this, would Pythagoras, an outstanding man of supreme intelligence, not be worthy of praise that alone over so many years in faraway lands, he scraped together what had been arduously worked out and put together by men of other civilizations in the cold sweat of the brow? This wisdom—not so much "better," rather "more distinguished"—he brought home to Italy (known at the time as Magna Graecia)—in his luggage as it were.

DE ARTE CABALISTICA

tauit cum incredibili cunctorum de se atcʒ suis sectatoribus admiratione, ita ut ois qui sapiētia & doctrina excelleret Pythagoræ auditor fuisse crederetur. Vnde philosophia Italica potissimum ab illo nomē accepit. Astipulatur huic laudi Numenius Pythagoricus in primo uolumine de bono cum ait, cp̄ Plato atcʒ Pythagoras quæcūcʒ Brachmanes Magi, ægyptii, Iudæicʒ inuenerunt, ea græce ipsi exposuerunt. Quo uehementissime suspicamur uerum esse q̄d asserunt uiri doctissimi, & uariarum linguarum periti, Iudæorum quæcʒ tam recepta q̄ inuenta exponi alienis furtis hinc græcorum inde latinorū, nihilcʒ nostrum esse in philosophia q̄d non ante Iudæorum fuerit, q̄ tumuis hoc seculo adimat eis merita gloria, & nūc uniuersa eorum contemnant, qm̄ præsens ætas oīm studiorum explicationem magis illustrem perpolitamcʒ desyderat. Tum uera optime Philolae refers inquit Marranus quo magis assentiar Euripidis Hecubæ. λόγες ἐκ τ᾿ ἀδοξούντων ἰὼν κ᾿ ἐκ τῶν δοκούντων αὐτὸς οὐ ταυτὸν σθένει. i. Sermo nancʒ ex ingloriis progrediens atcʒ gloriosis, idem non idem ualet. Nam si Aristoteles aliqs aut Theophrastus quispiam ea protulisset quę nos Simon hodie docuit, nihil oīm sententia esset dignius auditu, nihil grauius, nihil memorabilius, addidisset tm̄modo dicendi genus magis æquabile & aliquē eloquentiæ fucum. Nunc qm̄ Iudæus est q̄ suo more agrestius paulo & p̄ssius rem omnem tractauit, haud dubium quin sordida sint futura in auribus illorum nostro æuo sophistarum ut ipsi sibi uidenʒ plane p̄ subtiliū si qui audiant aut sint audituri uel potius uniuersis nūc aut praue aut stulte philosophantibus appareant implicata obstrepera hiulca, ieiuna, horrida, rusticam asperitatē & peregrinam insolentiam sonantia, tametsi etiam ut mos eorū fert prius non q̄tum oportet examinata q̄dem, quasi aurū, nō sit aurum q̄d in luto quærimus. Post uero q̄ ab hoc iam hoie in diuersorium ecce nostrum recta uia nullo monstrante rediuimus qn̄ cœna forte nobis p̄stinata nondum est, consulo ut quiscʒ sua recitemus inter nos, pręsertim digniora q̄ audiuimus, & figamus memorię ne labant dum recens oīa tenemus. Et Philolaus q̄ prudenter ait illa p̄cogitasti Marrane, sic em̄ ad audiēdum paratiores uirum accedemus perendie post hoc Sabbathi monstrum cultacʒ Iudęo, ut ait Ouidius, septima sacra uiro. Interea tu sellam hanc arripias, ego alteram, & cōsidentes dicamus celeriter de oībus donec apparent quæ ad cœnam congruant. Cęterum ne detur frustra cōtentioni locus cum solisimus, id em̄ aliud nihil esset q̄ tempus perdere, tu prior quicquid in buccam uenerit uel p̄teritorum aut p̄sentium recordandi uel commentandi gratia q̄cuncʒ accidat modo, eloquere. Sic igit̄ Marranus exorsa texuit. Et quanq̄ negocium omne, inquit, circa q̄d postmeridiano hoc tp̄e conuersati sumus mihi singula examussim perpendenti uideatur esse altius q̄ ut id nos humi strati suspicere possimus, tn̄ sępe numero quæ hoībus prima specie apparent ardua & impossibilia tandem co-

On the Art of Kabbalah

Everyone was astonished, and full of admiration for him and his followers, to the extent that anyone of outstanding knowledge or intelligence was said to have studied under Pythagoras. Thus the principal school of Italian philosophy got its name. The Pythagorean Numenius agrees with this favorable account. In volume I of his book *On Good,* he says that Plato and Pythagoras expounded in Greek what had been discovered by the Brahmans, the Magi, the Egyptians and the Jews. We very much believe that what these learned masters of several languages assert is correct: all the Jewish traditions and discoveries have been popularized by non-Jewish plagiarists, first in Greek and then in Latin; there is nothing in our philosophy that was not first developed by the Jews, although by this time they do not get the recognition they deserve and everyone now despises Jews and anything associated with them. The present generation prefers its scholarly works clear and well polished.

MARRANUS: You allude to Euripides' Hecuba, my dear Philolaus: "The words spoken by the famous and the infamous are the same, yet in impact they are not the same," and I entirely agree with you on that. If an Aristotle or a Theophrastus had produced Simon's lecture today, all would agree that nothing was more worth listening to, important, or historic. Their additions would merely have been a less uneven style, and more grace in expression. But since it is a Jew handling the subject, a little jerkily and oversimply perhaps, but such is his manner, without doubt what he says would seem rubbish to the sophists of our time if they heard him now or later, for all that they think themselves so clever. Or rather, to all the bad or stupid philosophers his argument would appear involved, confusing, gaping with holes, barren, blunt, a harangue of primitive ferocity and outlandish affectation. As usual, they would not stop to examine it as they should — as if gold were not gold when found in a bog.

But, look, we have got back to our inn without getting lost and without having to ask the way. We ordered dinner but it's probably not ready yet, so I suggest that between us we go over what we have heard, the more important parts in particular, and fix it all in our minds while it is still fresh, in case we forget bits.

PHILOLAUS: That's a good idea, Marranus. In this way we shall be all the better prepared to listen when we next go to Simon, the day after tomorrow — after this dreadful Sabbath. "The seventh-day festival is holy to the Jew," says Ovid. You grab that chair, and I'll fetch another. Let us quickly go over all in our minds before the table is laid for dinner. Set speeches would be out of place here, we are by ourselves, and there's no time to waste, so do you start by recalling or commenting on whatever springs to mind of past or present remarks.

MARRANUS: Although the whole subject we have been discussing since midday today seems to me, as I ponder each point carefully, too elevated for us who are at ground level to reach in thought, yet perhaps there are many things that to men seem at first impossibly high, which

LIBER SECVNDVS

tinuis & indefessis exercitationibus duroq; labore fiunt & plana & facilia iuxta Maronis illud. Labor omnia uincit. Iccirco libenter in medium conferam quæ ab isto me audiuisse meminero, addamq; illis q̃d ipse sentiam Hebrę́us sane p̃ceptor noster de Cabala nobis petentibus tractaturus cõmodum ostendebat, eo noīe q̃d sit intelligendum. Nam Cabala receptionem designat, simul & hoc attulit q̃ ea nostris animis esset insita semp̃ ad summa conditione naturali tendentibus, quapropter eius desyderium nobis constaret ingenerari, & q̃ summæ res ac diuinę sublimiores haberēt atq; digniores q̃ q̃ ratione humana comp̃hendi ac discerni queāt. Id aūt triuiale idoneis peripateticis est dogma, ut eī in principio meos Arabas cū q̃bus mihi extat solita familiaritas citare liceat, Alpharabius in libro quẽ de scientiis p̃scripsit, hac utitur sententia, q̃d res diuinæ ac pia fide credibiles, sunt altioris ordinis, cum sint assumptæ ab inspiratione diuina, q̃m in eis sunt secreta diuina, a q̃rum comp̃hensione debilitant ratiões humanę, necq; consequunt ea, hæc Arabs ille, quod & Simon noster affirmauit, q̃ eos ordines appellat regiones, & in animæ nostræ tertiam regionem cõstituit res incorporeas ac substantias ab omni materię pensione liberas et immunes, non q̃ Antisthenes cogitauit phantastica illa & logica uniuersalia, Sed ipsas inq̃ reales formas, species, ideas, essentias, q̃ sunt res altissimę circa quas uersant Cabalistæ, ut audio, contemplationibus suis prope inenarrabilibus, & ea singula q̃ nos sentire aut scire arbitramur, huc conferunt, ac demum uniuersa in unũ q̃d est ipsum bonum atq; primum p̃ media reducunt tanq̃ ad nostræ mētis saluberrimum finem. Quod Aristoteles ī xiiii. libro eorũ q̃ post naturalia scripsit, id q̃d est αὐτάρκες ϗ̀ ἰ σωτηρία .i. Sibi sufficiens & salus esse dixit, & Simon hebraice יְשׁוּעָה noīauit, Sicut & regius Psaltes ait. Dn̄i est salus, & sup̃ hanc generis humani salutem, oīm Simon Cabalistarum fundamenta iecit, q̃ nec sint a ratione inuestiganda, nec per rationem inuestigata, ut q̃bus nec sensus præbuit hypostasim, nec ītellectus disciplinam, summa eī sunt, & q̃rum causa nequeat adæquata reperiri, a q̃rum cognitione disertissimus sectæ peripateticæ Theophrastus scīētiæ abstulit facultatē, sic.n. in suis sup̃naturalib̃ scripsit. Μέχρι μὲν οὖν τινος δυνάμεθα διαιρίων θεωρεῖν, ἀρχὰς ἀπὸ τῶν αἰσθήσεων λαμβάνοντϋς, ὅπου δὲ ἐπ᾽ αὐτὰ τὰ ἄκρα καὶ πρῶτα μεταβαίνομῑν, οὐκ ἔτι δυνάμεθα. εἴτε δὲ ᾗ μὴ ἔχῃν αἰτίαν, εἴτε ζ̃ τὴν ἡμετέραν ἀσθένιαν. i. Vsq; ad aliq̃d q̃dẽ possumus p̃ causa speculari, principia à sensibus sumentes, q̃n autẽ ad ipsa extrema & prīma transierimus, non amplius possumus, siue propterea q̃ nõ habemus causam, seu propter nostram infirmitatem. De supernis eī & diuinis q̃bus nihil est prius, undenam queso posset demōstrationis aliq̃d mediũ sumi? Quare Plato ait in Timæo, q̃ illa explicare plus est q̃ nostræ uires sufficiant, credi aūt iis iubet qui ante dixerunt quanq̃ nulla demōstrationis nēcessitate loquant. Hæc ipsa Platonis uerba & ueri sapientię mandata ego

Book Two

still with continual, unflagging effort and hard work eventually become quite clear and simple. As Virgil said, "Work conquers all." For this reason then, I shall gladly set out what I remember of Simon's discourse, and add to this what I feel is the most useful thing our Hebrew instructor explained to us about Kabbalah, namely, what should be understood by that word. Kabbalah means "a receiving." He also implied that it is innate in us and that we naturally reach out towards the highest things, thereby proving that the desire for Kabbalah is implanted in us and that matters touching the high and the divine must be considered too high and too important to be understood or determined by human reason. This doctrine is commonplace among the respectable Peripatetics. I shall start with the Arabs, with whom I am most familiar. In his book on knowledge Alpharabius puts forward the view that divine things, those that are the subject of righteous and faithful belief, are of a higher order, since they are adopted by divine inspiration. They hold the secrets of the divine, they defy the comprehension of human rationality. This is according to the Arab—and on this Simon agreed with him, calling these orders "regions," and postulating an incorporeal substance, free of all matter, in the third region of our minds. This substance is not, as Antisthenes thought, made up of shadowy logical universals, but of real forms, species, ideas, essences. These are the lofty matters that preoccupy Kabbalists in their meditations, and are so difficult to put into words—or so I understand things. All the particular things that we feel or know are collected in this area, and everything leads back through various steps to the One that is itself good and the first thing, to the good that is most beneficial to our minds. What Aristotle called in Book 13 of the *Metaphysics* "self-sufficient salvation," Simon called *yeshu'a* in Hebrew. "Salvation is of the Lord," says the royal psalmist. Simon has based all Kabbalah on this kind of human salvation. These bases are not susceptible to rational investigation, nor have they been rationally investigated; the senses furnish no substance for them, nor the intellect any knowledge of them. They are the highest things, where no sufficient cause can be found. Theophrastus, an important Peripatetic, declared that the faculty of knowing was inadequate in their understanding. In the *Metaphysics* he wrote: "Up to a certain point we can explore by means of causality, taking the senses as our starting point; but when we reach the most distant first principle, we can go no further, either because we have no cause to go on, or because we are inadequate." Concerning the heavenly and the divine, nothing is prior to them; thus there is no way of proving them. On this, Plato, in the *Timaeus,* says that to explain these things is beyond our powers, but he bids us believe previous philosophers, despite their lack of vigorous proof.

DE ARTE CABALISTICA

tanti existimo, ut ea oraculi mecum loco duxerim habenda. Et si ulla Cabalæ rata & stata fundamenta sunt, hæc sunt. Quapropter acerrimum diuinæ cognitionis mera & nuda fide constantis, hostem & insidiatorem arbitror logicum esse syllogismū, qui Theosophistarum ausu atq̃ usu, deū & angelos mentesq̃ beatas & simplicissimas ultra mundani seculi uirtutes & omne simul æthernitatis agmen, & quicquid est usquā historiarum de rebus supnaturalibus, id totum humanæ mortalitati subiiciat rationis discursu inueniendū, probandum, dirigendū. Perinde atq̃ illas tam illustres substantias in Tullianum aliq̃d includere conetur. Hoc nimirum est Iouē uincire uelle ac salice uiminea, aut resti nautica ligare. Quod ne Thetis q̃dem autore Homero p̃mitteret, aut Cētimanus Briareus ille ægeon. Quo magis contentiosos theologistas & nugiuendos sophistas iudicabo cœlitum & supcœlestium expugnatores non minus esse q̃ Aloidas geminos immania corpa, ut ait Virgilius, qui manibus magnum rescindere cœlū aggressi. Haud secus atq̃ Sinaaritas ac Babylonios olim filios Adam hoc est ex humana imbecillitate quā in se non agnouerunt prognatos, turrim altissi¯mā exædificantes, cuius culmē pertingeret usq̃ ad cœlū, primores בלבל .i. confusionis autores. Vnde Babel, quam uos Babylona dicitis, nec alterum alterius linguā intelligentes. Per hos. n. garrulos syllogistas in rebus credendis pietas erga diuinorum uniuersitatem o̅is amittit̄, atq̃ uincendi studio fraternum odium concitat̄, uenaticos canes ad seditionem paratissimos, summæ contēplationis uenenum orbe toto expellendum. Triumphent hæc si phas est syllogismorū artificia, in natura & humanis inuentionibus atq̃ figmentis. Sed in sacris oraculis locū sibi ne sperent illum. Hoc em̄ Parmenides apud Platonem de substantiis separatis Socrati dogma tradidit ita dicens. ἀλλὰ ὁμοίως ἡμεῖς ἐκείνων οὐκ ἄρχομεν τῇ παρ᾽ ἡμῖν ἀρχῇ, οὐδὲ γινώσκομεν τὰ θεῖα οὐδὲν τῇ ἡμετέρα ἐπιστήμῃ. i. At similiter nos illis non imperamus nostro imperio, neq̃ cognoscimus diuini quicq̄ n̄ra scientia. Ei sermoni & peripatetici astipulant̄ & Aristoteles ipse tum artifex tum organū, ut ait....sciendi, cum in resolutiuorum posteriorū uolumine primo, immediatorum scientiā esse indemonstrabilē affirmat. Post paulo ingt̄. Et non solum scientiam, sed & principium scientię esse aliq̃d dicimus q̃ terminos cognoscimus. Principiū sciētię Themistius ibi appellat nostram mentem, terminos uero ex qbus uidelicet componuntur dignitates maxime subiectum & p̃dicatum. Sed Philoponus q uulgo noiat̄ Ioannes grāmaticus explanauit hæc nō parū sublimi & uerius ita scribēs. ὁ μὲν φιλόσοφος τὴν ῥῆσιν τοῦ προσκειμένου ῥητοῦ οὕτως ἀπέδωκα. ἀρχὴν μὲν πιστήμης τὸν νοῦν. ἄλλ᾽ φῶς οὐ τὸν ἡμέτερον ἀλλὰ τὸν θεῖον καὶ ὑπὲρ ἡμᾶς. ὅρους δὲ τὰ νοητὰ καὶ θεῖα εἴδη. ὅρους δὲ αὐτὰ καλεῖσθαι διὰ τὸ πέρατα εἶν πάντων. i. Philosophus hic quidem enarrationem p̃iacentis dicti sic tradidit. Principium q̃dem scientię. Mentem accipiens, nō nostram, sed diuinam & supra nos. Terminos

autem

134

On the Art of Kabbalah

I think so highly of these words of Plato, as the instructions of a man who was truly wise, that I have considered it worthwhile to keep them with me as a kind of oracle. And if there are any fundamental beliefs, any fixed points in Kabbalah, then these are they.

I think that the bitterest factor militating against an understanding of the divine through faith pure and simple is syllogistic logic. By brazenly applying this to God, sophistic theologians have subjected him, together with the angels, all bliss and virtue untainted by this present world, the whole range of eternity, everything contained in the accounts of the heavenly, to human mortality, for they are to be discovered, tested, and directed by rational processes. It's like an attempt to throw these glorious beings into the Tullian dungeon, or trying to tie up Zeus with withies and anchor cable — and according to Homer, Thetis and the hundred-handed giant Briareus would not allow that. These argumentative theologians and petty sophists are mounting an attack on heaven and higher heaven equal to that of the giant twin sons of Aloeus, who, in Virgil, attempted to tear the sky apart with their bare hands.* They are like the Shinarites and Babylonians, descendents of Adam who, unaware of their inherent human weakness, built a huge tower whose top was to touch the sky, who thus became the first *Balbel,* "authors of confusion." (Hence Babel, or Babylon, so-called because no one spoke anyone else's language.) Through these babbling syllogists has come about the loss of all reverent belief in the divine. The rat race leads to hatred of one's fellow man, a pack of hounds all ready to turn on each other — and thus the delights of higher contemplation are driven from the world. Let this logic-chopping have its triumph, where fit, in the domain of nature and in human discovery and invention. But it should expect no place in sacred matters.

The Socratic teaching given by Parmenides in Plato is: "Similarly our powers hold no sway; we do not come to know God by our kind of knowledge;" the Peripatetics say the same, as does Aristotle himself (first the designer, then the tool, as they say, of knowledge). In volume 1 of the *Posterior Analytics,* he states that knowledge of immediate things cannot be proved, and later, that "we will call 'the beginning of knowledge' and not just 'knowledge,' that by which we recognize 'terms'." Themistius, in his paraphrase, identifies as the "beginning of knowledge," our minds, and says that "subject" and "predicate" are the terms from which the highest order of knowledge is drawn. However, Philoponus (John the Grammarian) has explained the matter in these truly inspired words: "The present philosopher has made explanation of the quoted phrase in the following way: by 'the beginning of knowledge' we understand 'mind'; not our own mind, but the divine mind above us. Moreover, the terms themselves are intellectual

LIBER SECVNDVS

autem ipsas intellectuales & diuinas formas. Terminos quippe illas uocari, propterea cp fines sint omnium. Cognitio itaque supernaturaliū cre
ditorum a mente pendet, non a ratione, quæ ratiocinando potest errare
Sic enim idem scribit Aristoteles ἐπιδέχεται τὸ ψεῦδος οἷον δόξα, καὶ λογισμός.
Id est. Suscipit falsum, ut opinio, ita etiam logismus, quod est ratiocina-
tio. Vnde syllogismus nuncupatur. Idem denique concludit posteriora
sic. Scientia, inquit, omnis cum logo, id est cum ratione est. Principiorum,
scientia quidem non utique erit. Quoniam autem nihil uerius contingit
esse scientia quàm mentem, mens utique erit principiorum. Principia ue
ro dicuntur res primæ, & Hesiodus priscicp omnes Theologi deos fece-
runt esse principia, igitur hæc cognitio proprie nominatur diuina. Et ut
in postnaturaliū primo ille idē stagirita scripsit, eius est possessio ἀκριβῶς
ἂν οὐκ᾽ ἀνθρωπίνη. Id est. Iuste uticp non humana, cp uel solus uel omnium
maxime illam deus habeat, & indignus sit homo quærere circa eum
ullam scientiam. Deus enim solus hunc habet honorem iuxta Simoni-
dem. Sed cum nobis nihil magis conducat ad beatitudinē quàm summarum & diuinarum rerum cognitio, qua (te rogo) uia Philolae alia homini ad eas pergendum est, si non scientia? quibusue modis comprehenden
da tanta summitas? Tum PHILOLAVS. Per ecastor ipse tu, iter
ostendisti planum atque patens. Cum enim quinque sint cognitionum
opifices, Ammonio teste, post Aristotelem, qui eorum quatuor tantum
in primo de anima libro meminit. Sunt autem νοῦς. διάνοια. δόξα φαντασία.
αἴσθησις. Id est. Mens, discursus, opinio, imaginatio, sensus. Mens quidem
& sensus non syllogissant, alterum longe superius, alterum multo inferius ratione. Sed nec imaginatio quoque cum sit statio sensus & apparitio-
num inde migrantium reseruatio. Sensibus autem nequaquam ratioci-
nantibus, ne putandum quidem est apparentia sensuū ratiocinari posse.
Restabunt igitur opinio & discursus, at opinio est ipsius discursus conclu
sio, quapropter ea ipsa non syllogissat, soli ergo discursui que dianœa no
minatur relicta est syllogissandi facultas, hucuscp Ammonii sententia est
in cōmētariis quæ edidit ad Aristotelis prima resolutiua. Et qm attigi enu
meratione cōmprhensiones & cōmprhensa breuiter, ne uaget oratio mea
longius, opinor diuina esse supra syllogismum, nec rōne humana intelligi
posse q non ducant originē cognoscendi a sensu, sed ex mera dependent
fide, tm ob amorem reuelantis recepta & hoim beatitudinē credita. Sunt
tn plurima sane q sic diuinę sę speculationi sæpe immiscent, ut unius fami
liæ solent qñcp liberti & inquilini comune sibi nomen usurpare, atcp illa
crebro (ita em fateor) se a theologica facultate tractari patiuntur, qa uel
aliqualem ordinē obtinuerunt ad deū, aut per se aut per reductionē, uel
alia forte ratione ut creationis, conseruationis, perfectionis, iustificatiōis

F

Book Two

and divine forms. They are called 'terms' because they form the limits of everything." The understanding of beliefs concerning what is beyond nature is dependent on mind, not on reason, for reasoning can go astray. Aristotle wrote: "Logic (the rational process) admits of error, as does belief." (The word "syllogism" is allied to "logic.") Later he finishes the *Posterior Analytics* thus: "All knowledge is acquired using logic" (that is, by reasoning).

Certainly knowledge is not one of the prime elements, but knowledge is rightly most associated with mind, and mind itself is certainly one of the prime elements. "Prime elements" is better termed "first principles." Hesiod and all the earliest religious thinkers had the gods as primal elements, so this kind of understanding can rightly be called "divine." And Aristotle wrote in Book 1 of the *Metaphysics* that its possession "is not really within the power of man," for God has it all to himself, or most of it at least, and it is inappropriate to man to search for any knowledge concerning him. According to Simonides, God alone has this honor. But when an understanding of the high and divine is most conducive to man's happiness, I ask you, Philolaus, how is man to proceed, if knowledge is no use? By what means is man to attain these heights?

PHILOLAUS: But goodness, you have yourself pointed out the easy and obvious way. As Ammonius says, paraphrasing Aristotle, there are five routes to knowledge (Aristotle in fact mentions four in Book 1 of *De anima*). These are: mind, argument, belief, imagination, and the senses. Neither mind nor the senses operate syllogistically; mind is far superior to reason, and the senses work on a much lower level. Neither does imagination, an extension of the senses which harbors all the images that stray from them. Since the senses never employ rational processes, one should not think that manifestations of the senses can conclude any matter by reason.

Argument and belief, then, are left. Argument is the product of thought, and so cannot operate syllogistically; therefore thought alone (termed *dianoea*) remains as having the ability to form syllogisms. This is Ammonius' opinion in his commentary on Aristotle's *Prior Analytics*.

I have now touched briefly on the different kinds of comprehension and things comprehended. I will cut the discussion short by saying that I believe divine things to lie beyond syllogistic reasoning, and that what does not derive from the senses cannot be understood by human reason, but must be taken simply on trust, accepted and credited for love of the One who reveals, and for the happiness of man. Many things become involved with the search for the divine in this way, like family retainers assuming the family name. I admit that many such things bear theological treatment, thus aquiring a status near God's, either by their own nature, or by a process of reduction, or else, perhaps, by some other kind of reasoning; things having to do with creation, preservation, perfection, justification, blessedness, salvation, and the like.

beatitudinis, salutis, & similiū. De illis eqdē nō cogito in p̄sentia q̄ sciā ea naturaliter nobis cognita fieri, q̄rū aut in postnaturalibus afferī ostēsio q̄ sint, aut in theologicis, propter qd sint. Permitto nimirū illis rōnem qp pe a sensu q̄ndā ortis & discursui humano deditis, sed q̄rum ueritas a sola pēdet autoritate reuelātis, eorū haud arbitror esse sciētiā, nec in illis dn̄ari syllogismū uelim. Sed id tm̄ q̄d oīb⁹ erit p̄stātius fides, quā q̄ hēt, is ab Aristotele in prioribus resolutiuis appellat̄ ἔλπον ἀκέμφος ἠ ἐπίτυχεται ἐλὼς .i. melius disposit⁹ q̄ si esset sciēs, q̄d explanauit ita Philoponus, id esse, melius cognoscere q̄ p demōstrationē. Ad hæc Marran⁹, Assentior tibi Philolae, inq̄t, & tecū q̄q̄ illa ip̄a q̄ merę sunt fidei & pure credibilia ueto subiecta esse logicis tediculis, q̄ plane magis sunt cōtēplātibus detrimēto q̄ lucro, idq̄ nr̄i pariter asseuerāt tā græci q̄ latini. Hieronym⁹ ille Dalmata in psalmū cētesimū quartū scribēs, syllogissandi arte theologię applicatā cōparat plagis egypti, et sic ait, Cyniphes dialecticę artis stimul⁹ intelligit̄ q̄ licet paruū uideat̄ re ipsa hēre seductiōis aculeū, grauissime tn̄ sauciat mentes humanas. Quapropter doctissimus iste uir hāc technā quā & uanitatē sens⁹ & obscuritatē mētis agnoīat, oīno ab hebraicis dimouit studiis atq̄ reiecit, cū sępe alias tū aptissime ad Damasum de q̄stiōib⁹ sibi p̄positis qn in secūda iis uerbis utit̄. De hebraicis disputātē, nō decet Aristotelis argumēta cōgrere. Et in psalmo Cxliii. de theosophistis ita scribit. Qn tecū coeperint disputare sic uerba eorū breuia sunt, sic artificī sermone cōdusa, ut euadere tibi difficile sit, cū. n. te ligauerint syllogismis suis, & te clauserint, & quasi maceriā syllogismū tibi texuerint ac ędificauerit, nō potest corruere, nō potes trāsire, teneris idus⁹, nō est ruina maceriæ necq̄ trāsit⁹. Cūq̄ ibi tenuerint te quasi q̄dā giro indusum, tūc nō eris in angusta uia q̄ ducit ad uitā, sed in lata q̄ ducit ad morte. ἐπὶ κ̄ ἐ τ ἁπλότηρς πίσπο, ἐη τ̄ων ὃς τ ἐκ σοφιοχρασίας πιθανολογίας. i. Qn̄ & simplicitatis fides melior est q̄ curiositatis p̄suasiua rō, ut dixit Athanasius in lib. iii. aduersus Arianos, cōfirmat hoc idē in ope cōtra grecos, q̄d sic icipit. ἠ μὴν περὶ τ̄ θεοσεβείας κ̄ τ̄ των ὅλων ἀληθείας γνῶσις, οὐ τοσοῦτον τ̄ ἀπὸ τῶν αἰρέτων διδασκαλίας δέη, ἔσιν ἀφ' ἑαυτῆς ἐκ θ' ἐν δείμη) .i. Ipsa qdē de cultu diuino & de uniuersorū ueritate cognitio, nō tā instituta ab hoīb⁹ doctrina eget q̄ ex se ipsa hēt notoriū suū. Sic Athanasius. Hoc nihil esse uerius quisq̄ sibi constituat. Quo enim dicendi studio aut q̄ p̄suadēdi conatu opus erit ei⁹ q̄d mea spōte parat⁹ sum credere, q̄dq̄ iā solo erga reuelātē amore meo ac singulari ueneratiōe libēter recepi, ne minimę q̄dē rōnis ui coact⁹ aut iduct⁹, quā saltē tenebricosa in hoc corp· demersi ac uincti aī obtusitas posset excogitare, Multo uberius hæc tractat Iustinus ille phūs christian· ī lib. de recta cōfessiōe iābū priscū istuc citās. οὐδὲν ἡ ἀνθρώποισι τῶν θεῶν ρ̄φες.i. Nihil. n. hoīb⁹ diuinorū manifestū, q̄ & Socratis fluxit ab ore Fert ita Xenophōtis Socratici ad æschīnē ep̄la, ubi oīb⁹

On the Art of Kabbalah

For the moment I am not concerned with things that I know we become aware of by natural means, whether demonstrated by metaphysics or explained in theology. I concede the rationality, certainly, of what is drawn from sense-perception and passed on to human discourse; but where "truth" rests wholly on the authority of revelation, I do not allow that to be knowledge, and I would prefer that the syllogism not be used in such cases. What will be most helpful to us here is to take it on trust: Aristotle said, in the *Prior Analytics,* that the man who can do this "is better off than if he just knew." Philoponus enlarges on this by saying that here a man "knows better than any proof."

MARRANUS: I agree with you, Philolaus, and go along with you in saying that matters of simple belief, to be taken simply on trust, should not be allowed to get within reach of the clutches of logic. Plainly, that stranglehold does the contemplative more harm than good, as both Greek and Latin authors have asserted. In his commentary of Psalm 104, Jerome, a native of Dalmatia, compares the use of syllogisms in theology to the plagues of Egypt: "By *lice* we are to understand the sting of the practice of dialectic, for though it be but a pinprick, it is seductive, and does grave harm to men's minds." So this scholar called this form of argument sense-deception and mental obfuscation, and threw it out of Hebrew studies altogether; and elsewhere, talking to Damasus about the questions put to him, he said (and this has some point) that "in problems of Hebrew, one ought not to look to Aristotelian argument." On the theologians, he writes in connection with Psalm 143 that "when they start to argue with you their speech is so terse, and so neatly rounded off, that you find it hard to escape; they will have you tied up and shut in with their syllogisms, they'll have built a wall with the syllogism and hidden you behind it: you can't break through and you can't climb over. You are caught, for there is no way to break down that wall or climb over it. There they have you, caught in a spiral: this is not the narrow path that leads to life, but the broad one that leads to death." As Athanasius says in Book 3 of *Against the Arians:* "Even the faith of the simple-minded is better than the persuasive reasoning of the curious," and he reiterates this in his *Against the Greeks,* for he begins: "Understanding of the worship of God and of the truth of the universe has no need of doctrines set up by men: it is self-evident."

Nothing could be more true, as all will agree. What is the use of studied argument or attempts at persuasion in a matter that I am already voluntarily prepared to believe? In my love, in my reverence for the One who reveals it, I have gladly accepted it, not in the least led on or influenced by any set of reasons that some dim and stupid mind, drowned or bound in this flesh, could think up. Justin, the Christian thinker, wrote this as the first sentence of his *De recta confessione:* "Nothing that concerns the divine is clear to man." Socrates also said this. An epistle of Xenophon the socratic to Aeschines is also recorded,

LIBER SECVNDVS XXVI.

inqt patet diuinas res cognitiõe humana cõphẽdi nõ poſſe, quare ſufficit pie ipſos deos ex aĩo colere, quales autem ſunt, nec inuenire nobis poſſibile eſt, nec phas quærere, nec enim ſeruis conducit, nec eis laudabile dixerim ſi dominorum ſuorum cõſilia niſi q̃um ad miniſterium ſuum ptinet ſcrutari uoluerint. Et ut de Socrate aliorumq̃ philoſophorũ ſectatoribꝰ ſcripſit idem in Memorabilibus, ἐθαύμαζε δ' εἰ μὴ φανερὸν αὐτοῖς εἴη, ὅτι ταῦτα οὐ δυνατὸν εἴη ἀνθρώποις εὑρεῖν. i. Mirabaſ aũt uidelicet Socrates, ſi non manifeſtum ipſis ſit, cp ea nõ eſt poſſibile hoĩbus inuenire. Talis ſempꝫ fuit oĩm ætatum & oĩm ferme religionũ ſententia, ut humano intellectu non capiantur q̃ prius in hois ſenſu non fuerãt, & q̃ intellectus non capit, ea nec ratio diſcutit, q̃ autẽ rõ non diſcutit ea necꝫ ratiocinationis diſcurſus quam διάνοιαν uocant iudicabit, q̃d tum maxime diuinitus reuelatæ ueritati congruit, etiam ſi de earum aliqua imaginarios nobis animi cõceptus formemus, ut quicquid religioſe pieq̃ receperimus id argumentationis uiolentiæ non ſubdamus uel ullo nobis phantaſmate propoſito. Maiores itaq̃ imitatus ille Naziãzenus Gregorius, q̃ eminet inter oẽs noſtrates in omi theologicæ facultatis genere, omni uerborum & ſententiarum uenuſtate ſimul & grauitate, huic doctrinę haud abſimiliter adſtipulat in libro theologiæ ſecundo affirmans, τὸ, μὴ ληπτὸν εἶν ἀνθρωπίνῃ διανοίᾳ τὸ θεῖον, μὴ δὲ ἄλω ὅσον ᾖ φαντάζεσθαι. i. Non comphẽſibile fore humano diſcurſu diuinũ necꝫ totum quicq̃d contingit imaginari. Ne mi tu Marrane Chriſtianorũ me prorſus expertem aut negligentem ſuſpiceris. Philolaus reſpõdit, memini Athenagoram philoſophũ Athenienſem ad imperatores M. Aurelium Antoninum & L. Aur. Commodum pro Chriſtianis legatum ſic dixiſſe. ἐπὶ καὶ διάντων τῶν δογμάτων, οἷς προσέχομεν, οὐκ ἀνθρωπικοῖς οὖσιν, ἀλλὰ θεοφάτοις καὶ θεοδιδάκτοις πείσαι ὑμᾶς μὴ ὡς περὶ ἀθέων ἔχειν δυνάμεθα. i. Atqui & per ipſa dogmata qbus innitimur nõ humanis certe ſed diuinitus miſſis & deo doctis, perſuadere uos (non ſicut de prophanis tenentes) poſſumus. Vbi aliter de prophanis perſuaderi, aliter de diuinis inſinuat. Tametſi aliquã multos ex uobis nouerim, qui omnia logicis adinuentionibus confundũt & ſuſcꝫ deocꝫ naturalia mathematicis principiis, ac rurſus theologica naturalibus ſtatuunt confirmantcꝫ. Sed haud quaq̃ cauſæ diuinæ ſunt naturalibus pares, nec ualent naturalia dirigere diuina, longeq̃ minus illa q̃ ſola fide conſtant ulla ratione poſſunt demonſtrare humanitus ſcibilia, Sicut nec ea quæ ſunt pure credita neceſſario inferunt naturaliter ſcita, pſtantiſ ſimus enim ille ueſter Dionyſius Areopagita quem ego aut reliquias aut imaginem Pythagoreorum (ut arbitror) haud inſipiẽter exiſtimauerim, ſnp theologicis iſtis cognitionibus in libro ſuo de diuinis noĩbꝰ ıta loqtur οὐδὲ ῇ inquit ἀκριβῶς ἐμφερεῖα τοῖς αἰτιαθεῖσι καὶ τοῖς αἰτίοις. ἀλλ' χὶ μὲν τὰ αἰτιατὰ τὰς τῶν αἰτίων δεχομένας εἰκόνας, αὐτὰ δὲ αἰτιατῶν αἰτιατῶν ἐξῄρηται. καὶ ὑπερίδρυνται κατὰ τὸν τῆς οἰκείας ἀρχῆς λόγον. i. Necꝫ em conſequens illatio cauſatis & cau

F ii

Book Two

in which he states, "It is evident that divine matters cannot be comprehended by man's understanding. It is enough to worship from the heart the gods themselves. It is not possible to find out — nor is it even right to try to find out — what they are like. It is not the place of slaves to want to scrutinize their masters' intentions, except insofar as these impinge on their duties, nor would I say that there was any merit in it should they do so." In the *Memorabilia* he also comments on a conversation between Socrates and some student of another philosopher that "it was a source of wonder to Socrates that they did not find it obvious that it was not within the scope of human ability to discover such things."

In every period almost every religion has held that the human intellect does not comprehend what has not passed through the senses, and that what the intellect does not comprehend, the reason cannot handle, and that what is not matter for reason cannot be the object of the reasoning process known as "thought"; and so, whatever accords with the truth of revealed divinity — even though we form imaginary "concepts" of related matters — that we should reverently and dutifully believe. We should not give such matters over to the force of argument or to any unreal hypothesis.

One follower of the ancients is Gregory of Nazianzus; he is outstanding in all branches of theology on account of the charm of expression of his opinions, without any diminishment of their value. His teaching is not dissimilar to that outlined above: the divine cannot be an object of human thought; a man cannot even form the relevant concepts.

PHILOLAUS: Do not suppose I am unaware of Chistian teaching, Marranus. I remember what the Athenian apologist Athenagoras said when emissary of the Christians to the emperors Marcus Aurelius and Commodus: "By the very beliefs we hold which are the communications, not of man, but of God, are we able to sway you. We hold no earthly beliefs." Sometimes he used secular arguments, sometimes religious ones. Although I know that many of you plunge all nature into utter confusion with logical devices and mathematical principles, and then set matters of theology on a par with natural science and judge them by these standards, yet divine causes do not run parallel with those of nature, nor can a science of nature rule the divine, still less can it demonstrate that knowledge of what rests solely on trust can be acquired by human reasoning. One does not infer that what is just "believed" is "known" in the ordinary course of things. That friend of yours, Dionysius the Areopagite (who has, I think, learned something from the Pythagoreans, or is at least strongly reminiscent of them), says in his book *On Divine Names,* in the passages dealing with theology: "There is no logically necessary relationship between causes and what is caused. What is caused holds the image of its causes. The causes themselves are abstracted from what they cause, and are enthroned above as their inherent nature requires."

DE ARTE CABALISTICA

fis, sed habent quidem causata illas causarū receptas imagines. Ipsę autem causae causatis abstractae sunt, & superne resident iuxta cuiuscę principatꝰ rationem. Quo captiosius aliqrum ex uestris retiaculū & fallacius dogma est, in rebus sola fide reuelata cōstantibus, syllogismorum proprietate ne dum utendum, uerum etiā pari dignitate credendum esse quicqd ex sacris oraculis per syllogisticum artificiū seqtur, ac bona formali necessaria logicacę cōsequētia infertur. Nihil enim tam distat ꝗ esse diuinitus reuelatum & humanitus inuentum. Vnde in mera fide pure credibiliū, credere & scire sunt maxime disparata, ubi nuncę conclusio syllogismi fore potest euidentior ex p̄missis, etiam si p̄missis euidentia certa misceatur, tn̄ semp̄ conclusio, partem sequitnr infirmiorem. Recte igitur uel hoc affirmamus cę in eodem subiecto & respectu eiusdem ueritatis, non potest simul stare habitus fidei acquisitae & habitus scientiae per demonstrationem genitę. Qui ergo contradicit sacris oraculis, is execrabiliter contradicit fidei. At uero qui alicui conclusioni humano ingenio, subtilibus inuētiunculis, Aristotelicis technis, Eleaticacę disciplina, cuius autor fuit Zenon τῆς ἐλεϊκῆς φιλοσοφίας ἀρχηγός. ut Galenus ait, siue Chrysippi tendiculis aut sophistarum syllogismis ex sacrorum oraculorum reuelatis collectae atcę illatae contradicit, is iam non fidei contradicit, sed scientiae humanae repugnat, non diuinam illuminationem, sed mortalem industriam abnuens haud execrabiliter, sed erranter forte, aut quandocę perspicaciter, non aūt turpiter. Quonam modo igitur affirmare quis ausit; diuinitus reuelato & humanitus inuento pari dignitate credendum esse, nisi qui totus pascatur syllogismo sicut bos foeno. Sane quae (amabo te) intercedit dignitatis paritas istius & illius? Fidele illud, at istud scibile. Mens illius sedes est, istius ratio, illud defluit a lumine superno, istud ex sensu ducit originem. In mentis regione aliqua sunt necessaria, quę in ratione sunt impossibilia. In mente datur coincidere contraria & contradictoria, quae in ratione lōgissime separantur. Non est igitur omnino uerum, si praemissae sint de fide conclusionē iccirco fore de fide. Nam execrabilis est propositio haec, nullum adorandum est creator, Multo etiam execrabilior ista, Omne sculptile est adorandum. In eis nanque ambabus blasphematur fides, attamen & sacra & fidelis non est hęc, inde consequens, nullum sculptile est creator, quam naturali ratione demonstrare possumus, ergo ueritas eius non pendet ab autoritate reuelantis. Sed eius euidentia longe credita fide minor est. Pari suasu fallimur assentiendo, quia conclusio sit de fide, iccirco aliquā praemissarum necessario esse de fide. Quis enim ignorat Hebraeis, Christianis & Agarenis esse summa fide creditum cp sculptile non sit adorādum, ad cuius tamen assertionem inferendam naturalibus utar praemissis, nullum lapidem esse adorandum, sculptile autem uidemus lapidem esse.

On the Art of Kabbalah

And even more insidious is the belief held by some of you (a snare and delusion) that while one should not employ the syllogism in matters that rely solely on revealed faith, one may, however, believe what follows from Holy Scripture when using the device of syllogism, and what is inferred from them by good, formal, necessary, and logical succession. Divine revelation and human discovery are poles apart. In matters of pure undiluted faith in worthy objects, believing and knowing are states that could not be more different. The conclusion of a syllogism can never be clearer than the premises from which it is derived, and even when the premises contain clear certainties, the conclusion always follows from the weaker premise. So we are justified in asserting, given the same subject and the same degree of faith, that the states of "acquired faith" and "knowledge derived by proof" cannot coexist. A man who denies Holy Scripture denies faith, and stands accursed. But a man who denies some conclusion or other derived by mortal men from sacred writings, whether by means of some invention of slender value, or by Aristotelian logic, by the Eleatic method[35] (first taught by Zeno, who was, in the words of Galen, "the father of dialectic"), or by the snares of Chrysippus or the syllogisms of sophists, he is going against not faith, but man's knowledge, not the light of God, but only human activity. He is not accursed, just wrong. Or he might be right — but never is he to be seen as immoral. How dare anyone have it that divine revelation and human discovery are to be held of equal value? Only the cow whose fodder is syllogism alone would believe such rubbish.

How can they be of equal value, I ask you. One is a matter of faith, the other of knowledge. One belongs to the mind and the other to reason; the source of one is divine light, the other derives from the senses. In the field of mind there are some things that are necessary which in reason are impossible. In the mind contraries and contradictories may coincide, in reason they are always distinctly different.

It is not altogether true that if the premises are derived from "faith," the conclusions will therefore be matters of "faith." Here is a deplorable proposition: "No creator is to be worshipped," and even worse: "All idols are to be worshipped." In both there is blasphemy against faith but their consequent, that "no idol is a creator," has nothing to do with either holiness or faith, and we can prove it by ordinary reasoning. Its truth does not depend on the authority of revelation. It is very much less certain than the belief of faith. We are duped into agreeing that because the conclusion is one held in faith, one of the premises must also be thus held. It is well known that among Jews, Christians, and Moslems, it is an axiom of faith that idols are not to be worshipped. I could use "natural" premises, namely these: "No stone is to be worshipped," and "A statue is a stone."

LIBER SECVNDVS   XXVII.

Tum Marranus, Commodū mihi Philolae reducis inquit in memoriam noſtrorum q̃rundam elenchos ſophiſticos, cum dicunt, conduſio eſt hæretica, ergo aliqua p̄miſſarum. Qua in cauſa miror ſupra q̃ dici poteſt, q̃ iſti aliquos uel hoies qñcʒ inueniant, qui eis talia credant. Sed quid ego æthiopem lauare conor, qui nulla opa candeſcit. Sunt p̄terea q̃ tametſi re uelantur, tñ etiam ſequuntur de reuelatis, q̃ ſi accepentur a credēte, fides potius erunt cp̃ reuelata q̃ ſcientia cp̃ illata. Sicut quæ p̄cipit eccleſia mea eſſe credenda etiam q̃cunqʒ ingenio compoſita, præſumuntur potius a ſpiritu ſancto eſſe reuelata, q̃ humana ratione inuenta, q̃tumuis quadam ſyllogiſtica ſubtilitate inducant. Sic ille ad eccleſiam Alexandrinā ſcripſit Impator Conſtantinus de concilio Nicęno dicens. ὁ γὰρ τοῖς ϝιακοσίοις ὁμοῦ ἥρεσιν ἐπισκόποις, οὐδὲν ἐσιν ἕτερον ἢ ἡ τοῦ γνώμη, μάλιςα ὁπου τε τὸ ἅγιον πνεῦμα τοιούτων καὶ τηλικούτων ἀνδρῶν ταῖς διανοίαις ἐγκείμενον, τὴν θείαν ϐούλησιν ἐξεφώτισε .i. Quod enim trecētis ſimul placuit epiſcopis, nihil eſt aliud q̃ dei ſentētia maxime ubi ſanctus ſpiritus talium tot & tantorū uirorum mentibus incumbens diuinam uoluntatem declarauit. De epiſcopis loq̃tur hic, eccleſiā uniuerſalē ſpiritu diuino agitatam repſentantibus, non de q̃rumlibet q̃rū cunqʒ polyphemorum heteroclitis ſine cerebro capitibus. Abeant igitur in officinam ſuam miſtiones ſyllogiſmorū de eſſe, de neceſſario, & de con tingenti, aut ſi qua ſint alia logicæ curioſitatis poſſibilia ſeu impoſſibilia. Nulla eī̃ eſt orōnis fideliter creditæ ad neceſſariā propoſitionem æqua compatio, cum neceſſaria poſſit eſſe dubitabilis, reuelata uero nihil ſit eui dentius. Ne igitur occupēt eiuſcemodi miſtiones adyta ſacrorū, ne moleſtent hierophātas, q̃nimo ſecedant (ſi aliqd poſſe uelint) ad artes ſellularias aut naturas cemētarias aut ſupputatiōes mathematicas, ne trāſeant limites, ne attingant τὴν ἀδίδακτον ϰ κρυφίαν τῶν μυσηρίων κỳ συμϐόλων πρᾶδωσιν Recta, inquit Philolaus, incedis amice ad Pythagoræ profecto uiri diuiniore doctrina imbuti obſcuras latebras, nullis humani ingenii argutiolis pueſtigandas, q̃ nobis ambigendi formidinem magis incutiunt q̃ generēt adhærendi firmitatem. Non eī̃ poterit diuinorū tantus ſplendor p̃ tam tenues et aniles ſophiſmatum rimulas tam ſtrictim a noſtris noctuinis oculis cerni. Sed opus erit ampliſſimis cogitandi & credēdi uiribus, maxieqʒ (ut ait Terentius) fide & taciturnitate. Quo motus Pythagoras, oībus diſciplinis toto orbe hauſtis primus philoſophiæ creditor, nihil prius, ut ſcripſit Apuleius, diſcipulos ſuos docuit q̃ tacere. Nam hoc erat primum contemplatiuæ ſapientiæ rudimentum, meditari condiſcere, loquitari de diſcere. Perinde atqʒ tam auguſtę maieſtatis Pythagorica ſublimitas mul to eſſet dignior q̃ cp̃ pueriliter iactatis gerris loquitando & garriendo cō prehendi poſſet. Satis uero nobis patet ex iis q̃ e Simone accepimus, etiā Pythagoram ſicut cætera Cabaliſtarū ita hoc q̃qʒ genus doctrinæ in græ ciam attuliſſe, ſcilicet q̃ de quæſtione altiſſima diſcipulus interrogaturus   G

F iii

Book Two

MARRANUS: You have given me a useful reminder, Philolaus, of the over-complicated proofs used by some of our academics, when they state that if the conclusion is heresy then one of the premises must be. I am dumbfounded when they find people who believe such things. But why scrub a black man — you'll never get him white. There are some revealed truths that follow logically from revealed truth. If accepted by a believer, they will be revealed faith rather than a known inference. The articles of belief that my religion lays down are, no matter how carefully formulated, or however much formal argument is deployed, assumed to be the revelation of the Holy Spirit rather than the discovery of human reason. As Emperor Constantine wrote to the Alexandrian church on the subject of the Council of Nicaea: "What is unanimously agreed by three hundred church leaders is God's decree, no more, no less. For the Holy Spirit, resting on such a multitude of such great men, has declared the will of God."[36] Here he is talking about these leaders of the church in their capacity as representatives of the universal church, guided by the Holy Spirit, and not about a crowd of unpredictable, brainless, one-eyed monsters. So away with these muddles of syllogisms on being, necessity, contingency, or whatever else, possible or impossible, that logic bothers its head with. Let them go away and mind their own business. There can be no comparison between the dictates of faith and necessary propositions. Something that is "necessary" can be open to doubt, but nothing is clearer than revealed truth. Let us not allow aberrations of this kind to bar the gate to the sanctuary or molest the priests. If they want something to do, let them go away and ply their trades and skills, let them busy themselves on the firm ground of natural science or with mathematical problems. Let them not cross the threshold, lest they "touch the untouchable, the arcane symbols and mysteries."

PHILOLAUS: You are on the right track, my friend. You are getting nearer to the dark alleys of Pythagoras — certainly he was imbued with sacred learning — alleys the incisive human mind should not explore. They strike terror of misunderstanding into us more than they yield any certainty in holding them. Sitting in the dark, our eyes could not make out the shining aura of the divine through the thin, narrow chinks of sophistry. We need great powers of reflection and belief. Especially we need, as Terence said, faith and silence.

Thus, according to Apuleius, when Pythagoras had drained the world of learning, or had become the first to believe in philosophy, he taught his disciples to keep silent. The first element of contemplative wisdom is that meditation is learning; in speaking, one forgets. Pythagorean heights of such venerable majesty are of far more worth than what can be understood in talk and chatter and nonsense childishly tossed out. From what Simon said it is clear enough that Pythagoras brought to Greece, along with the rest of Kabbalah, this teaching that a disciple about to ask the deepest questions should keep

taceat.Interrogatus uero solum respondeat αὐτὸς ἔφα. Ipse dixit. Sic Cabaꝶ
listæ respondent אָמְרוּ חֲכָמִים .i. Dixerunt sapientes. Et Christia
ni quoq̃ suis dicunt πίστευσον .i. Crede. Tum Marranus, Fortasse nos taxas
Philolae quibus id & Imperator Iulianus improperauit dicens, ὑμῶν ἡ ἀλοꝶ
γία καὶ ἀγροικία, καὶ οὐδὲν ὑπὲρ δ᾽, πίστευσον, τῆς ὑμετέρας ἐστι σοφίας.i. Vestrum ir
rationalitas & rusticitas,& nihil ultra ipsum crede,uestræ est sapiētię. Cui
conuitio Nazianzenus in prima inuectiua prudenter occurrit, q̃ pariter
hoc Pythagoreis sit primum & maximum disciplinæ fundamentu, tacere,
deinde nullam dictis exhibere rōnem nisi αὐτὸς ἔφα,quapropter is inique
nos redarguat,quippe εἰς ταυτὸν ἥκοντος τοῦ, αὐτὸς ἔφα; τῷ, ᾗ ἡμῖν πίστευσον, ἐν
ἁπλαῖς συλλαβαῖς τε καὶ ῥήμασι.i.In idē cedente isto,ipse dixit,& apud nos cre
de,licet aliis syllabis & uerbis,ita Nazianzenus. Habemus nunc memori
ter eorum q̃ præ q̃buscq̃ ceteris sacra diligentius tractauerunt unanimem
discendi morem uidelicet, Cabalistarum אָמְרוּ, Pythagoreorum ἔφα,
Christianorum πίστευσον. Cæterum quicq̃d aliorum est diuinum non est.

H Equidem ante multo cogitaui tm̄,Philolaus ait,ea oīa ex Hebrẹorum flu
xisse Cabala, iam certo certius scio,dare nanc̃q̃ uideo, quæcunq̃ Simon
nobis ōnderit philosophiæ Italicæ,hoc est Pythagoricis adamussim qua
drare,ut haud ab re iudicauero Cabalistarum & Pythagoristarū inter se
cuncta eiusdem esse farinæ. Oīa nanc̃q̃ studia nostra utrīcq̃ reducūt ad hu
mani generis salutem,& omnia entia quę subsistunt,aut substant cōtinuo
ad Ideas referunt q̃ uere sunt,& idearum ideam. Vnde utricq̃ ternos esse
mundos asseuerant,& tertium infinitum,uel potius non finitum,tribusc̃q̃
constare oīa. καθάπερ γάρ φασιν οἱ πυθαγόρειοι δ᾽ πάντα καὶ τὰ πάντα τοῖς τρισιν ὥρισται
.i. Quemadmodum em̄ dicunt Pythagorei,omne & omnia tribus termiꝶ
nantur,ut in libris de cœlo scripsit Aristoteles. Nam alia qdem,inqt̃,sunt
corpora & magnitudines,alia uero habitant & obseruant corpa & magni
tudines,alia denic̃q̃ habitantium & custodū principatus sunt & origines.
Quod ita intelligo. Q̃m̄ mundus inferior complectit̃ corpora & magniꝶ
tudines singula cum suis uirtutibus & intelligentiis sphærarum motorib̃
appropriatis & generabiliū corruptibiliūc̃q̃ curatoribus ac custodibus q̃
obseruare dicunt corpora prouide,ut est cuic̃q̃ tributa prouincia q̃s anti
quitas qñc̃q̃ uirtutes,qñc̃q̃ angelos,tum aliq̃n & deos,item & dæmonas,
uel pro rerum anxiarum sollicitudine q̃bus allegant crebro dẹmonia q̃c̃q̃
noīauit. De quibus canit Homer9. θεοὶ ὀλύμπια δώματ᾽ ἔχοντες.i. Dii olympi
ca tecta inhabitantes, scilicet q rebus naturalibus p̃fecti sæpe querula tur
bantur affectione ac a summis ad ima relegati laborū suorū causas dicūt
πολλοὶ γῆς τλῶμεν ὀλύμπια δώματ᾽ ἔχοντες, ἐξ αὐθρῶν, χαλεπ᾽ ἄλγε᾽ ἐπ᾽ ἀκήλοισι τι
θέντες.i. Multi em̄ patimur olympica tecta inhabitātes a uiris,graues dolo
res inter eos uicissim reponentes,ut est in Iliados quinto. Nam olympū
intelligunt pristi quintam essentiam siue naturam hoc est cœlum, quare
tecta

On the Art of Kabbalah

silent. When asked a question a man should only reply, "He has spoken." Similarly, the Kabbalists reply, "The sages have spoken," and the Christians too say to their disciples, "Believe."

MARRANUS: Perhaps Philolaus, you reproach us in the same terms as the Emperor Julian when he said: "All your wisdom is but the irrationality of a peasant — nothing more than this 'Believe.'" Gregory of Nazianzus was careful to meet this charge in his first invective. There he compares it to the first and fundamental tenet of Pythagorean teaching, that of keeping silence and giving no reason for one's answer, saying only "He has spoken." Thus Julian is unfair in reproaching us, for to quote Gregory: "Though the words may be different, Pythagoras, in falling back on 'He has spoken,' is doing the same thing as us when we say "Believe.'" We can now call to mind how all those who have taken religion seriously have in their teaching methods been of one mind about this, whether they are Kabbalists saying, "They said so," or the Pythagoreans saying, "He has spoken," or Christians saying, "Believe." What others say is not to do with the divine.

PHILOLAUS: I myself have up to now given much consideration to the question of whether all this came from the Hebrew Kabbalah, but now I am quite certain and I see clearly that everything Simon showed us squares exactly Italian philosophy, that is, Pythagoreanism. If I declare that Kabbalah and Pythagoreanism are of the same stuff, I will not be departing from the facts. Both disciplines lead to the salvation of the human race. All subsisting entities, whether subsisting for a long period or for an instant, take us back to Ideas which exist in reality, and to the Ideas of the Ideas.

Both assert that there are three worlds, and that the third is infinite, or rather "non-finite," and that all things persist in these three. "The Pythagoreans say that all and everything is bounded by the three," writes Aristotle in *De coelo*. Mass and dimension are among these, others are the things that have possession of and keep watch over mass and dimension; and still others are the beginnings or origins of the second group.

This is how I understand matters: the lower world contains bodies with mass and dimension, with their particular qualities, and intelligences that move the spheres and are set on one side, with the job of watching over and guarding the things that can be created and destroyed. These are said to keep careful watch over material bodies. Each has an area allotted to it. In antiquity they were called virtues, or angels, sometimes gods as well, and likewise spirits, or frequently, because of their alleged interest in the troublesome, devils. In his poetry Homer calls them "the gods who dwell in the halls of Olympus." These rulers of nature are often plunged into a state of agitation with their tendency to complain and put their cases when sent off to the lowest of their tasks from the highest. As it says in Book 5 of the *Iliad*: "We inhabitants of the Olympian halls suffer greatly at the hands of men, when we inflict great pain on each other."

The ancients thought Olympus was the fifth essence or quality, that

LIBER SECVNDVS XXVIII

tecta olympica sunt sphęrę cœlestes seu cœli dicti a celando sicut tecta à tegendo. Deniq̃ uirtutes cœlestes & uires elementares ac rerum naturaliũ proprietates Hesiodus deos ex cœlo & terra dicit genitos in sua theogonia, & Orpheus græcorum primus theologus ad Musæũ scribens eosdem appellat dæmonas his uersibus. δαίμονας οὐρανίοις καὶ κορίοις καὶ ἐνύδρους καὶ χθονίους καὶ ὑποχθονίους ἢ διὰ πυριφοίτους .i. Dæmones cœlestes & aereos & aquaticos & terrestres & subterraneos & ignisequos seu igni assistentes In operũ q̃q̃ ac dierum libro Hesiodus, Dæmones inquit boni sunt terrestres custodes mortalium hoĩm. Ipse quidem Apollo se suiq̃ similes dæmonas roganti q̃ndam Theophilo respõdit angelos esse pro incumbẽte sibi administrationis officio ut est in oraculis. Sic enim cecinit ut ferme solet omnia heroice. εὔνομα μηδὲ λόγῳ χωρούμενον ἐν πυρὶ ναίων, τοῦτο θεὸς μικρὰ δὲ θεοῦ μερὶς ἄγγελοι ἡμεῖς .i. Nomen ne ratione capiendum in igne habitãs, hoc deus, Parua aũt dei portio angeli nos. Erigamus si libet ad altiora ingeniũ nostrum, q̃ppe ad uniuersi huius globi uitales influxus. Nam mundus superior cõplectit̃ superos, essentias incorporeas, diuina exemplaria & orbis huius sigilla, q̃rum instar, oĩm rerum inferiorum facies sunt factæ, quẽ Pythagoras appellauit ἀθανάτους πρῶτα θεοὺς .i. Immortales prima deos, uelut principia rerũ ex mẽte diuina productas ideas ut sint essentiales ἀρχαὶ principatus & origines habitãtium corp̃a, id est specierum, compositas huius mundi res informantiũ. Quo plane intelligit alios etiam illic esse imortales secunda deos, prima em secunda referunt, entia incorporea singularia & indiuidua nõ materiali numero sed formaliter formali inter se differentia, puta spiritus ab oĩ materia liberos, simplices & impermistos, sua pte natura extra cœlum sensibile commorantes, & ut ait Aristoteles, nec tempori nec loco astrictos unde nec senescant nec transmutent̃, multomagis nulla uariatione nec alteratione, nulla deniq̃ passione affecti sufficientissimam sibi & optimam ducant uitam, habitentq̃ æthernitatẽ, q̃d nuncupatur æuum, & grece αἰὼν quasi ἀεὶ ὢν .i. semper ens, qm̃ idem illud seculũ semper fuit, est, erit, intemporaliter, in mente diuina, ex energia tñ dei soras creatum, & extra cœli nostri conuexa constitutũ, pro domicilio splendidissimo spirituũ beatorum, q̃s Pythagorei ueros deos existimant in sublimi ætheris uertice locatos cum prorsus obiectu, tum retro partu æuiter nos, scilicet æuo immortali & diuino p̃ditos. Ab ipso aũt eodem æuo etiã aliis dispẽsatum est & tributum esse & uiuere, his q̃dem clarius, his uero obscurius ut idem dixit Aristoteles. Quid aũt id sit per q̃d dispensẽ & tribuaẽ, ab hoc æuo diuino & immortali rebus aliis, hoc est inferioribus esse ipsum, non fortuitum obiter, aut perfunctorie illapsum, sed cuius libet speciei consimiliter substãtiuũ, certe primi oĩm Pythagorei Socrates & Plato sequentes p̃ceptorem suum, discipulos illius familiæ docuerunt, cũ aũ

F iiii

Book Two

is, heaven. Thus the Olympian halls are the heavenly spheres, or "heavens" (*coeli*) as they "hide" things (from the Latin *celare*) — just as "halls" (*tecta*) come from "to cover" (*tegere*).

Hesiod, in the *Theogony*, says that the powers of heaven, the forces of the elements, and the characteristic qualities of nature are gods born of heaven and earth. Orpheus, the first Greek theologian, writing to Musaeus, calls them spirits: "The spirits of the heavens, the air, the waters, the ground, underground and of fire." In *Works and Days*, Hesiod says: "The good spirits are the earthly guardians of mortal men." Apollo himself said, in reply to a question once put by Theophilus, that he and the spirits like him were angels with a duty laid upon them to help others, and that his duty lay with the oracles. In heroic verse, as usual, he says: "The name of God, inhabiting the fire, is incomprehensible to reason. We angels are but a small part of God."

Now let us direct our thoughts upwards, towards the higher things, to what influences life on the whole of this earth. The upper world contains the celestial beings, incorporeal essences, divine patterns, and the seal from which this world is pressed.

All the externals of everything in the lower world are made in their likeness. Pythagoras called them "the first principles, the immortal gods," as though things began with ideas from the mind of God. Thus they are the essentials — sources, beginnings — of things possessing bodies, that is, outward appearances; they are what gives form to the regular in this world. From this, plainly, other immortal gods are to be understood to be there, too, in second rank, since "first" implies the existence of a "second." These are separate and individual incorporeal beings. They differ from one another not by the reckoning appropriate to matter, but that appropriate to form, namely spirits, free of all matter, absolute, unalloyed. By their very nature they remain outside the heavens that the senses perceive. As Aristotle says, they are bounded neither by time nor by space, and thus they do not change or grow old. They suffer no variation or change, they feel no emotion. They are self-sufficient; they lead the best of lives. They inhabit eternity. This is called *aevum* in Latin, and *aeon* in Greek, from *aeon* — "always existing." This same "time" has always been, is, and will be, outside time, in the mind of God. It was created from the energy of God, and established outside our own overarching sky, to stand before the shining home of the blessed spirits whom the Pythagoreans think are true gods, to be found on the highest point of the highest part of the upper air, eternal as they look forward to the future, eternal as they look back to the past, enjoying the "time" of the undying and godlike. Out of that same "time" have others too been granted the privilege of living and being — some in positions of prominence, others in obscurity, as Aristotle says. The question now is how this grant, this allotment made out of divine time, was made to other things, namely those in the lower world. The grant did not come about by chance, in an unguarded moment, nor as an afterthought. In all respects it resembles the underlying substance of any specific thing you see.

DE ARTE CABALISTICA

diuissent Pythagoram semper de diuinis obscure loquentem, dicere solitum, cp tetractys traderet animæ nostræ fontem perennis naturæ, tunc plane intellexerunt Tetractyn esse Ideam in mente diuina tradentem, & fontem esse Ideam exemplarem traditam, & perēnē naturam esse Ideam rerum essentialem receptam. Quare Alcinoo teste dixerunt hoc modo. ἔστιν ἰδέα ὡς μὲν πρὸς θεὸν, νόησις αὐτοῦ, ὡς δὲ πρὸς τὸν αἰσθητὸν κόσμον, παράδειγμα. ὡς δὲ πρὸς αὑτὴν ἐξεταζομένη, οὐσία. i. Est idea quoad deum qdem cognitio sua, q ad sensibilem autē mundum exemplar, quoad se ipsam uero consyderata, essentia, ceu loquentis uox (uti est apud Areopagitam) una cum sit atcp eadem, a multis auribus ut una percipitur. Est em uox primo in uociferatore, secūdo in uocalitate, & tertio in qlibet auditore. Quō aūt in mūdo sensibili semper sphæra prior in oēs eam sequentes influit, ita in mundo itellectuali non tm singulos choros superiores influere arbitramur in omēs choros inferiores, uerumetiā totum mūdum supiorem influere in totum mūdum inferiorem, ut oīa pro suo captu qtum fieri potest momentanea ad ætherna & infima reducanť ad summa. Nihil tñ mere creaturarum ad tertium mundum reduci potest, nihil enim tantæ sublimitatis suapte natura capax est, nisi deus. atqui tertius inquā mundus ille super supmus omēs alios mundos continens solius deitatis est, unacp diuina constat essentia, ut plane mihi uidetur recte cognoīata παντοκρατορική ἕδρα. i. oīpotens sedes locata immo existens super omne æuum & sup omne seculum (est em seculum seculorum) ὑπάρξεως, ὑποστάσεως, οὐσίας, φύσεως, ὀντότης καὶ ἑνότης προοῦσα. i. Existētiæ, substātiæ, essentiæ, naturæ, entitas 8! unitas prexistens. Quod Pythagoras noster ἓν appellauit, & Parmenides Pythagoreus ὄν, utercp haud absimili ratiōe ὅτι ὑπεφούσιον, ἓν, καὶ ὃ ὄν, ἓν. i. cp supessentiale unum, & ens, unum. Sed nemo antiquitatis tam perosus aut tantus contemptor maiorum esse optauerit, ut tm & tam sapientē Pythagorā existimet tam anili amentia correptum fuisse cp putaret abaci numeros aut pueriles talos q bus iactarent uultorios quatuor, aut mercatorum calculos cęteracp id genus esse rerum oīm principia, que non solum rebus non pssint, uerū etiam secundum res accidant. Quin potius intelligi uoluit ipsum essentialiter & simpliciter unum, a quo, & ex quo, & per qd, & in quo, & ad qd oīa sunt, & ordinanť, & pmanent, & continentur, & implenť, & cōuertuntur; ideq esse primum unum & primum ens, qd in secundo postnaturalia testatur Aristoteles his uerbis. Πλάτων μὲν γὰρ καὶ πυθαγόρειοι οὐχ ἕτερόν τι τὸ ὄν, οὐδὲ δʼ ἓν, ἀλλὰ τοῦτ' αὐτῶν τὴν φύσιν εἶν, ὡς οὔσης τῆς οὐσίας ταυτὸ, δ' ἐν εἶν καὶ ὄν. i. Plato nancp & Pythagorei nō aliud aliqd ipsum ens, necp ipsum unum, sed hoc eorum nąturā esse, ceu existentis essentię idem unum esse, & ens aliquod. Sane Xenophanes ille Parmenidis přceptor & idem Pythagorę coæuus, quanq oīa celare mos illorum fuit, tñ uisus est clarissime nobis explanare quid ipsum unum esse intellexerūt, de q in rerū principiis uerba fecerint.

Dixit

On the Art of Kabbalah

Socrates and Plato, the first Pythagoreans of all, were, in teaching the disciples of their school, clearly following their master Pythagoras on this, for they had heard Pythagoras speaking on matters divine, something he always did in obscure terms. He used to say that the Tetractys would transmit to our souls the source of everlastingness. They understood by "tetractys" the Idea in the mind of God that was "transmitting,"[37] and by "source" the model of the Idea that was transmitted. "Everlastingness" they understood to be the essential Idea of things that were received. Thus they said, as Alcinous records, "There is an idea which, with regard to God, is knowledge of him; moreover, with regard to the world perceptible to the senses is a model, and with regard to itself is a subject of examination, an essence." This is like the voice of a speaker (this is Dionysius the Areopagite's example) which is one and the same, and is heard as such by many. A "voice" exists first in the shouting out, second in the sound made, third in hearing it. In the same way as in the world of the senses the first sphere always influences everything that comes after it, so, in the world of intellect we do not only think of individual higher formations influencing all lower formations but further, of the whole higher world influencing the whole lower world. Thus, so far as can be understood, all things of brief duration are brought to the eternal, and the lowest to the highest.

However, no created thing can be drawn into the third world, for there is nothing inherently capable of such sublimity except God. This thrid world is the very highest of all; it contains the other worlds, and belongs to the Deity alone. It is one with the divine essence, and is thus, it seems to me, rightly named "the seat of all power." This seat is sited in — more, it rises above — all ages and generations (for it is an age of ages), it is "a single being, having existence, substance, essence, quality;" Pythagoras called it *hen,* "one," and his follower Parmenides *on,* "being." Both agree "that it is one that is above essence, and as a being, it is one."

No one in antiquity so detested and despised his elders as to hold that Pythagoras had gone soft in the head, and thought that abacus beads, or boys' persistently unlucky dice, traders' tallies, or anything of that kind could be the basis of all things. Far from being more important than matter, numbers are in fact secondary to it. Rather, he wanted it to be understood as "one" in essence, quite uncomplicated; by which and from which, through which and in which, and in accordance with which all things are, and are ordered, persist, cohere, are fulfilled, and change. It is the same primal "One" and primal "Being" which Aristotle mentions in Book 2 of the *Metaphysics.* "For Plato and the Pythagoreans did not say that Being and One differ in any way; they reckoned the nature of One and Being was roughly that there is an essence of Existence that is both One and Being."

Xenophanes, who taught Parmenides, and was a contemporary of Pythagoras, seems to me, notwithstanding the obfuscatory habits of these people, the one who explains most clearly what they thought the

LIBER SECVNDVS   XXIX.

Dixit aūt illud unum, esse deum, quò liquidius Pythagoræ arcana nobis patefiunt cum statuit infinitū & unum & numerum esse prima rerū principia. Per infinitum nihil aliud significans q̄ ipsum posse, nihil em q̄s unq̄ ne cogitauerit quidem, prius ipso posse, q̄d maxime infinitum in deo est, immo ipsum, infinitus deus est, in q̄ non separantur esse & posse, q̄d oīum producibilium & singulorum q̄rumq̄ continet essentias uirtutes & opationes cum oībus proprietatum & accidentium connexibus differentiis & unionibus. Cæterū Pythagoræ assentīt etiā ea in re Anaxagoras ante q̄s uiros nullam græcos oēs dei habuisse cognitionem Eusebius Paphili autor est. Dixit em Anaxagoras, qm̄ erant oīa simul. Et Democritus, erāt inqt omnia simul potentia, uidelicet δυνάμ. i. in ipso posse. Hæc est illa q̄q̄ mistura siue rerum cōmistio Empedoclis & Anaximandri, nequaq̄ tn̄ in aliq̄ Hesiodi aut Aristophanis chao nocte & erebo confusa, sed in deitatis pleno lumine discreta, & in ipso infiniti luminis intimo penetrali ordinata, quāq̄ si haud inique intelligatur Hesiodus, certe chaos noctem & tenebras nō esse rerum principiā, sed ex principiis orta statuit. Id. n. in Theogonia protulit. ἦ ἀρχῆς κ̄ ἐπσὶ ὅτι πρώτα γίνετ' αὐτῶν. ἴτοι μὲν πρώτισα χάος γίνεο Deinde sequit ἐκ χάεος δ' ἔρεβός τε μέλαν τε νὺξ ἐγένετο. i. Ex principio & si qn̄ aliquid primo factum eorum est, certe primum chaos factū est. De chao aūt erebus nigraq̄ nox nata sunt. Aristophanes uero aliter in auibus scripsit χάος ἦν καὶ νὺξ ἔρεβός τε μέλαν πρῶτον. i. Chaos erat & nox erebusq̄ nigrum primo. Sed ita fingit poetice musarum more alludēs suis auibus ut ex ouo posset amorem excubare, ac simul Orphei supparasitat in Argonauticis, non absimiliter sentienti quapropter hoc idem repetendo rursus iterūq̄ meminerim, oīa & singula in illo ipso posse, non confuse, non in chao, nō in erebo, nec obscura nocte, sed discrete ac ordinate in pleno lumine scilicet in ipsa luminosa & oīm fulgentissimorū radiorum splendidissima claritate ac illustris & illustrantis essentiæ diuinæ intuitu notitia cognitione uersari, quæ optimo iure ab antiq̄ssimis philosophorum Idea nominatur ἐκ τ̄ ἰδῶ, δ̄ γινώσκω cuius qdem posse esse, cum oīa complectatur mentalia, rationalia, intelligibilia, sensibilia, uitalia, substātialia, adhæsibilia, & adhæsiua, non tm̄ eorum q̄ sunt, uerumetiam quę non sunt, tum uere illud poterat infinitum appellare Pythagoras, quod & a sapientissimis dictum erat ἀπιροδύνασθαι. i. Infinite posse, qm̄ & ipsum est infinitum, & una eadēq̄ infinita & essentiali Idea complectit̄ res infinitas. Nihil em̄ uel fuit, uel est, uel erit in supcœlestibus, cœlestibus, terrenis, corporeis aut incorporeis, in angelis, in hoībus, in brutis, in plantis, in tota uniuersi natura q̄d non possēt uel ut grammatice loquamur potis est. Ex hoc omīa prodeunt, & hæc est ἐπιροδύναμος κ̄ πατροδύναμος δυναμπιός ὄνταμε. i. Infinitepotens & oīpotens potentifica potentia, q̄ nihil aliud est q̄ diuina essentia, intra quam ante oīa

Book Two

"One itself" was when these word-mongers were discussing the question of how all things began. He said that the One was God. The mysteries of Pythagoras were made much clearer to us when he said that infinity, the One, and number were the ultimate bases of things. Infinity simply designates God's potency, for no one could ever consider that anything preceded that, which is what is most infinite in God, or rather, is itself the infinite God, in whom are existence and potency, undivided because he unites the essence, the inherent characteristics and workings of every generative and distinct thing, with all the connectives, differences, and unities of their properties and accidents. On this matter Anaxagoras agreed with Pythagoras — before them none of the Greeks knew anything of God, says Eusebius Pamphili. Anaxagoras says: "Everything existed at the same time." Democritus: "Everything existed together by power, or rather, for 'by power,' 'in potency itself.'" This then is the mingling or intermingling of things that Empedocles and Anaximander refer to — not muddled together in chaos and dark night as Hesiod and Aristophanes have it, but as distinct parts in an ordered whole, existing in the full light of the Deity, and at the innermost center of infinite light. However, to be fair on Hesiod, he did not say that chaos, night, and darkness were how things began, but that they came into being from the beginnings. He says in the *Theogony:* "From the beginning: if anything was made at the very first it is certain that chaos was the first thing made." "From chaos were darkness and black night born."[38] Aristophanes has it otherwise in *The Birds,* and writes, "In the beginning was chaos, darkness and black night." But here he has the benefit of poetic license, joking about his birds and how love is on the watch right from the egg, and is at the same time parodying Orpheus' *Argonautica*.

Because our opinions on the matter are much the same, I shall go over this once more and start again. All and everything dwells in that very potency, not in confusion, nor in chaos, nor in darkness, nor in dark night, but in distinct and orderly fashion in the full light — and understand by "full light" the light-filled and gleaming brilliance of all those glittering streams of light — and abides in the sight of and by a conception and apprehension of the luminous and illuminating divine essence. This essence was well named by the ancient philosophers, the "Idea" (from the Greek "seeing," meaning "understanding") since it includes everything pertaining to the mind, reason, intellect and the senses, everything living, all substance, and everything to which things appertain; and not only those things which are, but also those which are not. Pythagoras could well call that "infinite" which other sages called "infinite potency," when it was both infinity itself, and by one and the same infinite and essential Idea encompassed infinite things.

For there is nothing which either has been, or is, or will be, beyond or within the heavens or on earth, corporeal or incorporeal, among the angels or among men, in beasts or plants, or in the whole ordered world which does not "have the power," or, to be grammatical, "is possible." Everything stems from this. This is the "infinitely powerful, all-powerful, empowering power," and is none other than the divine

DE ARTE CABALISTICA

unū producit duo. Hic tenes Marrane totū meum Pythagoram. Duo primus numerus est, unum uero pricipium numeri. Q; si credis Xenophani ut ante audisti, unum illud deus est, & cum intra essentiā diuinā productio duorum manserit (numerus em se ipso constituit, Boetio peripatetico autore, iuxtaq; unum solus binari⁹ naturaliter est) tum necessario, duo q; illa, deus sunt, q̄niam intra deum nihil nisi deus est. Tres igit̄ hæ res principium & primum cum sint, & unam dei essentiā non exeant, tum deus plane unus sunt, non em essentia eó scinditur, q; ex uno duo producta numerāturfi̇cut in rebus q;q; corpeis sæpe sit ut unitas mota in duitatem (sit uenia comparationi) usq; ad terna progrediat̄ manente rerum substantia ut stipitis & surculorum, uel æquius ut hois corpus brachium & digitus. Ex uno itaq; in diuinis producente, duobusq; productis, trinitas oritur, q̄b⁹ rebus si addatur essentia ab eis formaliter distincta, erit formalis quaternitas q̄ est infinitum, unum, & numerus duorum Omnis numeri substantia, perfectio, & finis. Nam unum duo tria quatuor collectiuo progressu decem conficiūr, & extra decem nihil est. Quare hoc ipso intellexit Pythagoras oīm q̄ddam rerum principium esse, q̄d Tetractyn noīauit. Nam tetras græce, quaternitas est, & actis, formale solis, siue radius, ex quali formalitate licet iam supsubstātiali, meus ipse, unū illustre nomen constituit quaternitatis, ueluti quatuor inter se formaliter distinctorum. Vtq; sacræ a prophano segregaret, optima ratione nomen sanctū p y psilon scripsit, cum ἀκτίς uulgo per iota scribi consueuerit. Adhuc aūt & ipse q̄q; Tetractyn ut deum aliquē hoc loco excellenter in genere masculino protulit, q̄ more latini ueteres Cupidinem aut Venerē masculine pronunciarunt, cū alias instrumētalem quaternitudinis numerum ipsam Tetractyn genere foeminino eloquant. Deum autem se illū ostendere uoluit p quem ipse iurauit μὰ τὸν πέρακτὺν quo nihil haberi debeat ueneratiōe dignius. Nam ut Aristoteles ait ὅρκος τὸ τιμιώτατόν ἐςιν. i. Iuramentum est honorabilissimum. Ego sane hocin loco Hierodi non astipulabor qui aurea carmina Pythagoram ipsum conscripsisse opiṇor. Atq; pariter optarem propter mirificę sanctitatis reuerentiā, q; Tetractys romana lingua non quaternarius nec quaternitas, sed uoce mutata quaternio aut quaternitudo noīaretur, quale apud uos christianos obseruatis, sacrum a prophani uulgi usu secernentes, cum em a ter ternus & ternitas populariter legi debeat uos sacrosanctam hypostasin alterato uocabulo trinitatem appellatis, quasi triū unitatem, s̄licet. n. literam ab ipso uno propter unitām singulorū naturam mutuantes. Sed ut receptui canam, oīum rerum, inq̄, una quędam summa res est Tetractys, Pythagoricum principium. Tum Marranus, bellissimū recardor ab hoc exemplo Philolae illud quatuor literarum charagma, in quo uniuersa generis humani salus p̄to sit. Quod nobis Simon tanta scripturarum

essence, within which, above all, the One produces two. Hang onto this, Marranus. This is Pythagoras in a nutshell. Two is the first number; one is the basis of number. If you accept the piece of Xenophanes already quoted, that the One is God, then since the production of two remains within the divine essence (a number stands alone, according to Boethius the Peripatetic, and in like manner "one" by itself inherently contains "two"), necessarily these two are also God, since within God there is only God. Since these three things are the source and beginning, and do not depart from the one essence of God, they are obviously the one God, for his essence cannot be split up. Two things are counted as derived from the one — compare how in physical matters a unity becomes duality (do excuse this comparison), or even a tri-ality, while the substance remains the same. It is like a tree trunk and its branches, or, just as good, a man's arm and his fingers. So, from the one, which produces two, three appear. If the essence, strictly separate from these, is added to them, there will be a conceptual "quaternity" which is an infinitude, and one, and two, and the substance, completion, and end of all Number. One, two, three, and four, added together, make ten, and nothing more than ten. It was from this that Pythagoras understood that there was a particular starting point for everything, and he called it the Tetractys. *Tetras* is Greek for "quaternity," and *actis* is Greek for "beam" — strictly a sunbeam, but it can also be "my own beam or ray," also admissible in this instance, as something necessary to life. This goes to make up the one illustrious word "quaternity:" four things formally distinct from one another. To separate sacred from profane, he, very sensibly, spelled the holy name with a "y," instead of the "i" that is commonly used in *actis*. He also put Tetractys in the masculine gender, treating it here as if some kind of god, and acted most admirably in so doing: in the same fashion, the old Latin authors treated Cupid and Venus as masculine. In other cases Tetractys, denoting a group of four things, is used in the feminine. Further, he wanted to show that it was a god, and would swear by it — *ma ton Tetracton* — indicating thus that nothing else deserved such reverence. For in Aristotle's words: "an oath is much the most honorable thing."

Here I am not in agreement with Hierocles since I am of the opinion that Pythagoras himself wrote the Golden Verses. Equally, I should like Tetractys to be translated, with due respect for its extraordinary holiness, not as "quaternary" or "quaternity," but in some different way, as "quaterny" or "quaternitude," like the custom you Christians have of separating the sacred from ordinary profane use by changing *ternus* or *ternitas,* the normal words for something threefold, into "trinity" when calling on the sacred person; "tri-nity," a unity of three. You take the letter "n" from "one" to represent the unity of its individual constituents.

But, sounding my retreat, I will say this: there is one great thing above all things and that is the Tetractys, the first principle of the Pythagorean system.
MARRANUS: I am reminded by your example, Philolaus, of that marvelous four-letter device through which the salvation of the whole human race is at hand. Simon backed this up with an abundance of quotations from

LIBER SECVNDVS XXX.

pturarum ubertate cōfirmauit,ubi profecto mihi Iudæorum Tetragram
maton ac potius ipsas quatuor literas ex qbus nomen Saluatoris compo
natur non male uisus est Pythagoras in Tetractyn græcum symbolū cō
mutasse. Mox tum.Ego uero,inqt Philolaus, illo Tetragrammato & illa
salute ad quam totum pene genus humanū reduxit Simon plane nondū
satiatus discessi,quare cum ad eum rediero de istis rebus si uolet amplio
ra quæram,præsertim de illo hoie q salutem singulis quibusq3 nobis al
laturus sit tanq uniuersorum rex unctus,ideoq3 Messiha dictus. At uide
modo uelim num sit Esculapius denuo uel p transaĥimationē,ut aiunt, in
hunc mundū uenturus, de q Iuliani9 Imp.in lib.ii.cōtra Galilęos ita scribit. K
ὁ δὲ ζεὺς ἐν μὲν ταῖς γοκρῖς ἐξ ἑαυτοῦ τὸν ἀσκληπιὸν ἐγέννησεν, εἰς δὲ τὴν γῆν διὰ τῆς
ἡλίου γονίμου ζωῆς ἐξέφηνεν. οὗτος ἀπὸ γῆς ἐξ οὐρανοῦ πεποιημένος πρόοδον, ἑνοειδῶς μὲν ἐν ἀν
θρώπου μορφῇ περὶ τὴν Ἐπίδαυρον ἐφάνη. πληθυνόμενος δὲ ἐντεῦθεν ταῖς προόδοις ὑπ
πᾶσαν ὥριξε τὴν γῆν τὴν σωτήριον ἑαυτοῦ δεξιὰν ὅπως ἐπανορθοῦνται τὰς ψυχὰς πλημ
μελῶς διακειμένας καὶ τὰ σώματα ἀσθενῶς ἔχοντα,.i. Iupiter em in suis intelligi
bilibus ex se ipso Esculapium genuit,& in terram p solis genitalis uitam
destinauit,hic in terra ex cœlo faciens progressum uniformiter qdem in
hois specie circa Epidaurū apparuit,auctus itaq3 illic successibus sup uni
uersam porrexit terram,salutarē eius dexteram, ut restauraret aias male
dispositas & corpa inualide habentia.Qui si compositū ex illis quatuor li
teris q̃uis etiam alio legendi charactere addito nomen habuisset, prorsus
Saluator ipse putandus esset, Aut certe q̃tusquantus ille fuerat Hercules
Alcmenæ filius a Ioue prognatus diuinum semen quem Thassii Saluato
rem noiarunt,& monetæ publicæ inscripserūt sic ἡρακλέους σωτῆρος Θασίων
.i.Herculis saluatoris Thassiorum.Eiuscemodi nummum argenteū prisce
pcussum ego nup,ut soleo,erga res antiqssimas incredibili uoluptate his
meis digitis uerti legens & reuerti.Quo non ab re coniectabam,oium uo
ce ac consensu Herculem inter deos relatū & saluatorē esse promulgatū.
Prǫter eos fuisse alioquin aliqmultos qui mortalibus opem tulcrint salua
tores,haud dubium qdem est,q̃rum e numero meminimus Ptolemæum
regem ægypti cui nomen Soter.i.Saluator extitit.Romanis q̃q3 Curtius
ipse sua morte terram reddidit saluam,& sua capita duo Decii pro patria
seruanda fortiter deuouere,comunis salutis mirifici autores. Tum Mar
ranus,Libenter, inquit,te interpellando monerem ut q̃ nobis a Simone L
tradita sunt pspicacius animaduerteres & paulo ęqus intelligeres.Post n.
q̃ multa de Cabala ille uir oisariam sectę suę peritus disseruisset qd modo
esset,& ad qd utilis,ostendissetq3 & q̃ esset recepta reuelatio,& q̃ facile
nobis iter aperiret ad beatitudinis fastigium & summā fœlicitatem, tum
rogatus a nobis quidnam illud esset quod præcipuum diuinitatis reuela
tum fuisse putaret,ad quod generatim omnes diuinorum reuelationes re
ducerentur,aiebat id esse qd dicitur,post ruinam primordialem generis

Book Two

the Scriptures. It seems to me that Pythagoras took the Jews' Tetragrammaton, or rather the four letters which go to make up the name of the Savior, and changed it into the Greek Tetractys symbol.

PHILOLAUS: Certainly I have by no means yet learned all I want to on the subject of the Tetragrammaton and the salvation to which Simon was bringing almost the whole human race. When I go back to him I shall question him in greater detail on this if he is willing, particularly on the man who is to bring salvation to every one of us, the one who is the anointed king of all creation, called "Messiah" because anointed. I wonder if Aesculapius will be the one who comes into the world for the second time by that they call transmigration.

The Emperor Julian mentions this in *Against the Galileans*. "Jupiter himself engendered Aesculapius from himself among the intelligible gods, and through the life of the generative sun, sent him into the world. He came down to earth from heaven like this, and unaccompanied and in the form of a man made appearances in the Epidauros area, but afterwards he multiplied himself, and by his visitations he stretched out his saving right hand over the whole earth, that he might heal sick souls and infirm bodies." If his name were composed of those four letters, with perhaps some other letter added, he might be thought the Savior.

Or Hercules now—how very great he was—the son of Alcmene and Jupiter, and thus of divine stock. The Thassians called him Savior, and the state mint struck coins inscribed "Of Hercules, Savior of the Thassians." Lately I have taken to reading old silver coins, turning them over and over in my fingers as I do so, loving things belonging to antiquity. From this I made the pertinent conjecture that Hercules was placed among the gods and proclaimed a savior by unanimous and wide-ranging agreement.

There have been others besides them who have as saviors brought help to men. Among their number we should certainly call to mind Ptolemy, king of Egypt, who was named "Soter," meaning Savior. And among the Romans there is Curtius, who by his own death rendered the land safe again, and the two Decii, who bravely laid down their lives to save their country, quite exceptional men, who brought safety to the state.

MARRANUS: I should like to interrupt and advise you to pay closer attention to what Simon told us and to take a slightly more accurate view of it. He is an all-round expert in his school. First he discussed Kabbalah at length, telling us what it was like and what use it was, that it was revealed, and how easily it opens up for us a road that leads to the height of blessedness and the greatest happiness. Then he was asked by us what it was that might be thought to be the particular revelation of the divinity to which all revelations of the divine might in general be reduced.

DE ARTE CABALISTICA

humani uniuersalis restauratio q̄ salus noīatur,& quam daturus foret hō iustus & pacificus,uir heros,cuius nomen quatuor contineret in miseratrionibus literas,ad quem nos ipsos cunctis negociis secularibus absoluentes libere conari debeamus p̱ oēs gradus idoneos ascēdere ac migrare in ipsum,pro sua quisq̆ uirili,q̄q̆ sint huc oēs actus nostri formandi,huc oīs contemplatio dirigenda,huc tendat oīs sacra Iudęorum scriptura quę nobis quasi scala Iacob fore queat sup̱ terram sita & cacumine tangēs coelos,per eam transcendere nos mundum hunc posse corporeū usq̆ in alterum mundum angelicū,etiam ad ipsam Messihę illius Saluatoris aīam, q̄ sit oīum aīarum saluandarum reqes & satietas,extremusq̆ finis,ultra quē progredi nusquā ualeamus,qm̄ terminet summum habitaculū mundi supremi,& comunicet cum mundo sup̱sup̱mo,siue dum p̱ grammaticos dicere liceat sup̱missimo,quin potius incompabili,ad summum, hanc esse oīum hoīum p̱petuam salutem cunctorum bonorū aggregatione cōpletam.Que si memineris a Simōe sic esse proposita,quanq̄ p̱ ambages,mea q̄dem sententia non dubitabis,nec illos tuos saluatores,nec etiā iudęorū q̄sdam de q̄bus uigintiquatuor biblia sæpe honorificam fecere mentionē in tanta unq̆s fuisse dignitate constitutos,ut generi humano salutem uniuersalem afferre potuissent,p̱ quam hoīes in omni orbis terrarum spacio q̄tq̄t essent,sempiterno æuo læte frui,& cum deo post lapsum redire ualerent in gratiam.Quid enim de tuo Esculapio complures senserint alii,tu uideris,qui asserūt illum meretricio incestu natum ex Coronide uenusta muliercula,de qua canitur.Pulchrior in tota q̄ Larissæa Coronis nō fuit. æmonia,& eam sæpe in templo Apollinis subegerint atq̆ comp̱sserint sacerdotes,q̆ adulterinis complexibus a se genitum Esculapiū,finxerunt dei filium esse isto loco culti.Apis aūt ægyptius q̆ arte medicinæ primus gręciæ intulit tam insignis eo seculo tēplarius,ut etiā mortuus in templis pro deo coleret̄,singulari erga sacerdotes Apollinis fauore ductus infantem suscepit alendum & instituendū,quem discipulo q̄ndam suo Chironi Cētauro deinde commendauit medico pitissimo,ut artem curandi tuendiq̆ corpis in Esculapium transfunderet.Quo facto,in uirum euasit Esculapi⁹ & fama & opib⁹ magnum.Auaricia uero tum instigatus,& cupiditate honoris diuersas mundi regiones ad pecunias arte medica corradendas pa grauit.Iamq̆ diuitiis plurimū abundans,& fama ingenti p̄ditus stulte se deum noīauit,promittens non solum ægrotis sanitatem,uer̄uetiam mortuis denuo uitam,sup̱ quo Ioui sup̱biæ sup̱ poenas dedit,nam fulmine ict⁹ periit.Sic em̄ Pythagoreus ille Pindarus Pythionicarum tertio sup̱ Esculapio cecinit. χρσοὶ δ'ἄρα χροσίων ρί̄τας διάμφοῖν , ἀμπνοὰν s̄ερνων καθ̄λον ὀκί ως. ἄσων δὲ κεραυνὸς ἐνσκι̅τε μόρομ.i.Manibus ergo Iupiter proiiciens ambabus,respirationem p̄cordiorū desumpsit subito.ardēs aūt fulmen inflixit

mortem

On the Art of Kabbalah

He said that it was the one called "salvation"—the restoration of the human race after the first fall—and that it would be brought about by a just man, a man of peace, a heroic figure whose name would, in mercy, contain four letters. We ourselves should try by all suitable steps to climb up to him, first ridding ourselves of all our secular business ties to be free to do so. Each man should do all this to the limits of his ability. All our acts should be shaped to this end, thither should tend our meditations. All the Holy Scripture of the Jews points to this. It can be our Jacob's ladder, which, placed on earth, touches heaven at its other end. On it we can cross from this world to the other world of the angels, and even to the soul of the Messiah who is that Savior. That soul is rest for and fulfillment of all souls which are in need of salvation. It is the final point. Beyond it we can never progress. It is at the limit of the highest region of the highest world, and joins it to the super-supreme world. (While language purists would have this as "most supreme," it is rather the world "beyond compare," at the very top.) It is everlasting salvation for all men, and is brimful of everything good.

Now, if you remember, what Simon put forward—though its expression was somewhat obscure—was what in my opinion you will not doubt, namely that neither these saviors of yours nor the Jews often mentioned with great respect in the twenty-four books[39] were worthy enough to be able to bring universal salvation to the human race. Through that salvation men throughout the wise world, however many they be, shall in gladness enjoy eternal life, and will be able to return to be with God once more after the Fall.

You shall see what a good many other people have thought of your Aesculapius. They say he was born of a prostitute, Coronis, a pretty little thing, or so the songs have it. There was no girl in Thessaly more beautiful than Coronis of Larissa. The priests in the temple of Apollo would often lie with her and have sex, and it was in these illicit couplings that Aesculapius was conceived. They made him out to be the son of the god worshipped there. Apis the Egyptian, who was the first to introduce medicine to Greece, and who was at that time so distinguished a member of the temple staff that after his death he was worshipped as a god, held the priests of Apollo in such high regard that he took over the child's care and upbringing. He entrusted the baby to Chiron the centaur, one of his pupils, who was a very experienced doctor, and who would pass on to Aesculapius the skills of caring for the body and keeping it in good order. This was done, and in manhood Aesculapius acquired both fame and riches. But driven by greed and wanting to be honored he toured the world raking in the cash for his medical skills. And then, dripping with riches, outstandingly well known, he was foolish enough to call himself a god. He promised not just health to the sick but life to the dead. For this piece of arrogance he was punished by Jupiter and died, struck by a thunderbolt. The Pythagorean, Pindar, wrote this on Aesculapius in this third Pythian ode: "So Jupiter, throwing with both hands, took suddenly the breath from his chest. The flowing thunderbolt dealt death."

LIBER SECVNDVS XXXI.

mortem. In hanc sententiam Apollo querulus super Esculapii filii morte Euripidi fingit. Ζεὺς ἡ κατεκτὰς παῖδα ὃν ἐμὸν αὐ πιος ἀσκληπιὸν ςἐγνοιση ἐμ ζὰ πι εωρ φλόγα. Quare nisi plane in diuinis plumbei sumus hoīem tam alienū a dignitate, saluatorem esse humani generis non putabimus, et ne in uniuerso qdem sanatorem, qui opem non alibi q̃ in Pergamum, & Ioniam, & Taranta, & Romam, & Con. et ægas, ac in eas circa regiones contulit. Nimio tu uictus amore tuorum Marrane, Philolaus inquit, plus q̃ ueritate, omis hoies minoris æstimas immo q̃ minimi censes, qui non Galilæi sunt. Peruersus hic mos est mea sententia (sit uenia uerbo) non modo laudem alienis nõ admittere sed & uituperare, nec tibi ut uideo satis fuerit tuiq; similibus, optimos uiros suo seculo uirtute claros q̃s antiq̃tas ob egregia facta in deos retulit non esse deos contendere, nisi & se diabolos tartareos feceris. Ita Lactantium tuum hoc in loco imitatus, q̃ decimo capite libri primi ad Constantinũ Imperatorem sic scripsit. Esculapius & ipse nõ sine flagicio Apollinis natus, quid fecit aliud diuinis honorib9 dignum, nisi q̃ sanauit Hippolytum, mortem sane habuit clariorem q̃ a deo merunt fulminari, hæc ille. At lingua ois quæ selle inficitur uero gustu caret, fatetur is tñ rem esse diuinis honoribus dignam, largiri sanitatem, q̃d & secum pēs fatentur ægroti. Sed q̃d aliud fecerit Esculapius si nesciat Lactantius, Socratem sapientissimũ interroget, q̃ gallum ei offerendũ uouit, ut est in Platonis Phædone, non ut sibi corpus sanaret, qui iam morti adiudicatus uenenum biberat, sed ut parenti Apollini hoc est primo & incorporeo Soli æthernæ uitæ dispensatori, animum tranquille morientis cum lætitiæ iubilo & pæane redderet. Nam gallus Apollini Phœbo q̃ Sol nominatur sacer est, horarum & diei lætus nuncius. Esculapius aūt dictus est a ueterib9 Iubilatio Apollinis uictoria & triũphus q̃ pæan appellat̄, eo q̃ paua cessationem & quietē post liberationem noiarint. Ea eñ ætate consueuerunt inituri pugnam prius Marti, & post pugnã uictores Apollini pæana referre. Q̃ apte igit̄ Socrates in Esculapio q̃ est pæan solem uitæ datorē ueneratus sit iam iãq; moriturus, doctissimorũ hoīm recta iudicia uiderint, dignum sane ratus & optimo cuiq; officiosum, huius mundi Pythone maximo serpente uicto & pedibus calcato, qñ p mortem celeriter ad ueram uitam iter capessitur Esculapio qdem offerre id est pæana celebrare. Sic Orpheus uetustissimus uatum & coetaneus istorũ deorũ, nam cum Tyndaridis & Hercule nauigasse perhibetur, in hymnis cecinit. ἰητὴρ πάντων ἀσκληπιὲ δέσποτα παιάν, ἐλθὲ μάκαρ σωτὴρ βιοτῆς τέλος ἐσθλὸν ὀπάζων. i. Sanator oīm Esculapie domine Pæan. Veni beate saluator, uitæ finem bonum præbens. Multos se Iulianus Impator nouisse asserit in maximis periculis Esculapio adiutos, & se ipsum egre laborātem sæpe medelis eius salutē euasisse fatetur, ad hoc testem citans Iouem. Sed q̃d hæc ad uniuersum mun

G

Book Two

Euripides had Apollo complain of the death of his son in these words: "Zeus has struck down my son, flinging his fire at his breast. Alas for Aesculapius."

Unless we are complete dunces when it comes to questions of the divine, we shall not think a man of this type the savior of the human race. It is not even that he healed the whole world: he confined his activities to Pergamum, Ionia, Tarentum, Rome, Constantinople, the Aegean and their environs.

PHILOLAUS: You are more in love with your own kind, Marranus, than with truth. For you, no one counts unless he's a Christian. In my opinion, this habit of yours of not hearing a word of praise for others, and in fact, running them down instead, is corrupt, if you don't mind me saying so. It is not enough for you, and people like you, I see, to contend that the foremost men of their time, famous for their virtue and elevated to godly status in antiquity for their outstanding achievements were not gods; you have to go beyond this and make them out to be devils from hell. You are copying your man Lactantius, he who wrote in chapter 10 of his first book addressed to Emperor Constantine: "Aesculapius' affiliation to Apollo was not altogether free from disgrace. He did nothing meriting divine honors except to cure Hippolytus; and to be struck by lightning at the hand of a god was a rather more distinguished death than he deserved."

So he says. But a tongue tipped with poison loses its sense of taste. He does admit that giving out good health in abundance is worthy of honor as a god, as all sick men would agree.

But what else did Aesculapius do? If Lactantius doesn't know, he had better ask Socrates, the wisest of them all. Acording to Plato's *Phaedo,* Socrates vowed him a cock as an offering, not in return for a doctor's cure—for he had already been condemned to death and drunk the poison—but to give to Apollo, the father of Aesculapius, who is the primal, incorporeal sun and the treasurer of eternal life, the mind of a man who dies peacefully, in joy and happiness. The cock is sacred to Phoebus Apollo who is called the sun, because it joyfully cries the hours and the days. Aesculapius was called "the joyful shout for Apollo's victory" and "Triumph" or "Paean," referring to the inactivity, the rest that comes after freedom is granted. At that time, on entering battle, a paean was first sung to Mars, and on winning, to Apollo. The most learned of men have seen fit to judge how apt it was that Socrates should worship the sun, the giver of life, in the form of Aesculapius-Paean, when on the point of death. As a good man, Socrates thought it right that since Pytho, the Great Serpent of this world, had been conquered, trampled underfoot, he should make an offering to Aesculapius—that is, sing a paean—so that he might more swiftly make the journey through death to true life.

Similarly, Orpheus, the oldest of the seers, coeval with the gods (for he is said to have sailed with Hercules and the sons of Tyndarus) sang, in the words of his hymn: "Healer of all, Aesculapius, Lord, Paean! Come, blessed savior, grant a good end to life."

The Emperor Julian says that he knew of many who had been helped by Aesculapius in their greatest danger, and confesses that when on the sickbed himself, he had often escaped safe and sound because of his remedies, and he calls Jove as his witness.

DE ARTE CABALISTICA

dum, respōdit Marranus, cuius Messiha p̄dicatur Saluator, nec corporū modo sed animorum. Et Philolaus ad id. Tu uero Marrane quid de Her cule? nonne morum formator & ois ingenuæ disciplinæ in cunctis orbis terrarū locis p̄ceptor fuit. Inde illa imago Herculis apud Celtas puetusta q̄dem & uero similis, ubi senex ipse hoīes innumerabiles singulos cathe nulis aureis colla rēuinctos a lingua pendentibus trahit q̄ uult cunq̄. Cel tæ uernaculo sermone Ogmion noīant. A Luciano sit eius memoria in al loquio de Hercule Celtico, sup̄ q̄ illi dicunt. ἡμεῖς τὸν ἡρακλέα λόγῳ τὰ πάντα ἡγούμεθα ἐξεργάζεσθαι, σοφὸν γνώριμον .i. Nos Herculē uerbo & ratione omnia opinamur effecisse cum sapiēs fuerit. Nam uirtute domare uitia, & igno rantiam auferre doctrina, nihil aliud est q̄ calcare monstra, & angues neca re, leōnem Nemeæū claua percutere, hydrā lernæam interimere, aprum erymanthium occidere, ceruā in Menalio nemore aurea cornua gerentē capere, stymphalidas aues in nube sagittis cōfodere, Antæum intra ulnas strangulare, columnas in Oceano figere, Geryonem tricipitem uincere, boues abigere, taurū perimere, Acheloum Monomachia superare, omit to & Diomedis equos, & cerberum & aurea hesperidum mala, idq̄ gen⁹ facinorum cætera quamplurima, totum uirtutis fuit, totum rectæ instituti onis officium & bene uiuendi exemplum. Tum Marranus, Dicerem, in quit, aliorum de illo existimationem, nisi tu prius eiuscemodi tulisses ægre, breuiq̄ ostenderem fuisse hominem, ut nos sumus, uel paulo indigniorē, licet Prœti Agenorisq̄ prosapia nobilem. Siquidem ex Agenore Prœ tus erat, Agenoris autem Belus frater, quo natus est ægyptus, quo Lyn ceus, quo Abas, quo Danae, cuius fuit Perseus, cuius Alcæus, cuius Am phytrio, cui⁹ ut putabat Hercules, quē tn̄ reuera Iouis aiūt id est adulteri cuiusdā fuisse filiū. Nā ex Alcmena Iphidus Amphytroni & Hercules Io ui uno partu, si famæ creditr, editi sunt in lucē. Hercules uero incensus igni sacro periit, qm̄ Deianirę uxoris attētatā pudicitiā in Nessum Cētaurv̄ iā culo uindicauit, quā ipse in Iole captiua puella nō exhibuit, perq̄ inique su spicionē adulterii sola ult⁹, q̄ ex adulterio cōcept⁹ adulteriū pariter ipse cō misit, in ęteros nescio q̄iust⁹, in se ipm̄ certe iiustissim⁹. Tu ne talē mudi sal uatorē fore credas Philolae, q̄lis fuit Hercules aut q̄lis Esculapi⁹ si nō alia ob rē uel ob id saltē q̄ uterq̄ turpi nota decesserit, nā ut de ambob⁹ apud Lucianū in ecclesia deorū Momus ait ἐπὶ τὰ ὁμοία ἰχνεῖ τῇ πυρὸς. iadhuc si gn̄a tenēt ignis, q̄ exusti ambo sūt. Curtiū & Decios magnanimitatis lau dāt alij, ego imprudētię accuso. Quid q̄ aliq̄ bladitiis & adulatiōib⁹ ducti, aut ui a tyrannis coacti eū saluatoris nomine ornarunt, qui non modo iI los non sanauit, nec seruauit, sed prorsus deuastauit ac perdidit, ut Siculi Veirē publica statua in Syracusis inscripserunt σωτῆρα id est qui salutem dedit. Ciceronis testimonio in accusatione quarta Verrinarum. Sed nī

On the Art of Kabbalah

MARRANUS: But what bearing has this on the world as a whole — for it is the whole world that the Messiah is to save; not just its bodies but its minds too.

PHILOLAUS: Well then Marranus, what about Hercules? He set the pattern of morality and taught the liberal arts across the entire world. Hence that Celtic statue of Hercules — a very old one that is indeed a good likeness — where he is represented as an old man dragging about wherever he wills countless individuals with their necks in irons and dangling by gold chains from his tongue. In Celtic he is called Ogmion. Lucian mentions this in his dialogue on the Celtic Hercules. There is a saying: "We think that Hercules achieved everything by speech and reason; he was a wise man." Overcoming vice by virtue and instructing ignorance was just what Hercules was doing when he trod monsters underfoot, killed the snakes, clubbed the Nemean lion, slew the Lernaean hydra, cut down the Erymanthian boar, captured the golden-horned stag in the grove of Menalius, shot through with arrows the Stymphalian birds in flight, strangled Antaeus barehanded, set up the pillars on the edge of the Atlantic, conquered the three-headed Geryon, drove off the cattle, killed the bull, defeated Archelous in single combat — and I'll skip Diomede's horses, Cerberus, the golden apples of the Hesperides, and many more deeds of this kind. All were manly deeds, the deeds a proper upbringing requires, and an example of right living.

MARRANUS: I would tell you what others think of Hercules had you not been so upset before by what I said about Aesculapius. I would show you that he was man; just as we are, or even a little less worthy of respect, though he was nobly born of the stock of Proteus and Agenor. Proteus was the son of Agenor, whose brother was Belus. Belus' son was Aegyptus, and his son was Lynceus, and his Abas, then Danae, then Perseus, then Alcaeus, then Amphytrion, whose son Hercules was thought to be, though it is said that he was in fact the son of Jupiter, by adultery. Alcmena, so the story goes, was delivered in the same birth of Iphiclus who was Amphytrion's son, and Hercules, who was Jupiter's. Indeed, Hercules died from the burn of the sacred fire. In spearing the centaur, Nessus, he avenged the attack on the chastity of his wife Deianira, although he himself did not show much restraint with the girl captive, Iole. He avenged adultery on the merest suspicion, though he had been conceived in adultery, and was equally ready to commit it. I do not know how justly he dealt with others: towards himself he was indeed very just.

You are not to think that the savior of the world is a man like this, Philolaus. Reject Hercules and Aesculapius — if for no other reason — because of the way each is marked out by a dishonorable death. Momus says of each in Lucian's *Meeting of the Gods*: "They retain the marks of the fire." Both were burned.

Some people admire Curtius and the Decii as stout-hearted men, but I would accuse them of recklessness. Sometimes people are led on by fawning and flattery — or they are forced to it by tyrants — to call a man "Savior" when he has not only failed to heal or save them, but has killed and destroyed them; like the Sicilians, who put up a public statue to Verres, with the word "Savior" inscribed on it, as if he had saved them. (Cicero says this in the fourth Verrine Oration.)

LIBER SECVNDVS XXXII.

hil ad hunc locum, ubi de uera hominum salute agitur, quam illi non pstiterunt, uera nanq; salus est, sempiterna permanentia q̃ in deo est, & a deo tribuitur, ut in libro de mundo ad Alexãdrum scripsit Aristoteles. Ex deo inquit & per deum nobis oĩa consistunt, nullaq; natura per se sufficiẽs est carens illa quæ ex eo est salute. Dein adiungit, τῆ γ οὐσία, σωτὴρ μὲν ἡ ὄντως ἁπάντων ἕξιν.i. Ipsa quidẽ essentia, saluator etem̃ enter seu essentialiter uniuersorũ est deus. Vnde in libro xiiii.post naturalia rursum sic ait Aristot. θαυμαστὸν δ' εἰ τῷ πρώτῳ καὶ ἀιδίῳ καὶ αὐτάρκεστάτῳ τοῦτ' αὐτὸ τὸ πρῶτον οὐχ ὡς ἀγαθὸν ὑπάρχει τὸ αὔταρκες καὶ ἡ σωτηρία.i. Mirum si primo & sempiterno & sibisufficientissimo hoc idem primum non ut bonum inest, ipsum sufficiens & ipsa salus, per qd monemur, ueram nobis salutem in primo sempiterno & sufficientissimo bono q̃ est deus optimus maximus constare, nec aliunde quærendam, Solus em̃ ille summus mũdi opifex & rector de sup eminentis liberalitatis clementissima uoluntate corruptibilibus dare pōt incorruptionẽ, & tẽpori subiectis eternitatẽ, & insolubilẽ transitoriis pma nẽtiam, q̃rũ tñ propria natura est ut orta occidant & aucta senescant, Sic em̃ in Timæo Platõis loq̃ deus. Quæ a me facta, indissolubilia sunt, me uolente, alioqui ligatũ qdẽ omne, dissolubile est, Ecce nõ tm̃ peripateticis sed etiam Platone ipso & Platonicis testatũ recipimus sola dei uoluntate pmanentiam concedi rebus quibuslibet pro captu suo, & hęc est uera sal°, Nam saluari dicimus, a læsione seruari ut res tranquille pmaneant. Quod unanimi consensu Græcorũ q̃ndam magnifici & ornatissimi legati anno a natiuitate IESV, M. CCCC. XXXVIII. uniuersali concilio Basiliensi illustri quadam & disertissima oratione exposuerunt his uerbis dicentes. Τὸ δ' σώζεσθαι καὶ σώζεσθαι καὶ ἡ σωτηρία ἁπλῶς οὐδὲν ἄλλο παρὰ τοῖς Ἕλλησι κ̃ τῇ ἡμετέρᾳ βούλεται πλάτϯα, ἢ τὸ διαμένειν κ̃ εἶν.i. Ipsum aũt saluare & saluari & ipsa salus simpliciter nihil aliud apud Græcos & in nostra uult lingua q̃ pmanere & esse. Homines igitur q de sui natura morti sunt obnoxii ut cessent esse, cum ita se dei conformant uoluntati, ut futuri sint immortales, & beato æuo fruantur, recte dicuntur salutem consequuti, & qui eis illã largitur immortalitatis beatitudinem, is recte dicitur saluator, quod uocabulum usu cepit Ciceronis posteritas antea inauditum ut nũc Saluator latine dici queat. Sane omnis alia improprie ac imaginarie nominatur salus, qd enim, q̃ animanti bruto medicus hodie confert sanitatem, & illud peren die relabitur in pestem, moriturq; nunquam rediturum, num ea uocabit salus? Quid illud q̃ flori marcescẽti hortulanus opitulatur, q̃ flos postri die casurus sit, & in puluerem conterendus num hæc tridua conseruatio rei prorsus inconstantis salus nominanda est? Sic Hercules Thassios semel adiuuit, quo salutẽ illis dedisse dicitur, qui post sępe interierũt, & ho enihil eorum nisi nomen extat. Sic Ptolemæus ægyptum seruauit, tot

G ii

Book Two

But all this is out of place and has nothing to do with man's true salvation. What they offered was not the true salvation; true salvation is eternal life in God, granted by God. Aristotle, in his book *On the Cosmos,* wrote this to Alexander: "From God and through God, all that is ours exists. No substance is sufficient to itself, for it lacks the salvation that is from him." Then he adds: "It is indeed his essence, for God is, by his being or by his essence, the universal Savior." In Book 13 of the *Metaphysics,* he says:

> "It would be astonishing if the being which is first, eternal and perfectly self-sufficient did not have as its first good quality the fact of being itself self-sufficient and salvation."

From this we learn that our true salvation lies in the first, eternal, supremely sufficient good, which is God that is most good. It is not to be sought elsewhere. The most high creator of the world and ruler from on high is alone able, by his compassion and generosity, to give incorruptibility to the corruptible, eternity to those subject to time, and everlasting life that cannot be destroyed to the transitory, to things whose nature it is to fall dying once risen, to grow old once grown. As God says in Plato's *Timaeus,* "That which I have made cannot be dissolved, but everything that is bound in any other way can, if I wish it, be dissolved." So we have evidence not just from the Peripatetics, but from Plato and the Platonists as well, that continuity is granted by the will of God alone to everything proportionately. This is true salvation.

We say that to be saved is to be protected from harm and to preserve a state of calm. This view, held without exception by the Greeks, was put forward most ably by the most eminent and distinguished delegates at the Council of Basle[40] in the year of Our Lord 1438: "To save, to be saved, and salvation itself means nothing else, in Greek or in our tongue, than simply to continue and to be." Frail men by their nature die and cease to be; but when they so conform to the will of God they become immortal, and enjoy blessed, never-ending time, they are rightly said to have achieved salvation. And he who grants them the blessing of immortality is rightly called the Savior — a word Cicero was the first to employ in general use in Latin.

What about all the improper and fanciful applications of the word "salvation"? If a doctor today cures a dumb animal, and the day after it suffers a relapse, and dies irrevocably, will this be called salvation? It is like a gardener watering a wilting flower. Tomorrow it will fall, to be trodden in the dust. Is this three-day preservation of something impermanent to be called salvation? Once Hercules helped the Thassians and for this he is said to have brought them salvation. But they have all since died, and today nothing remains but the name. It was in this sort of way that Ptolemy delivered Egypt; the country has since been laid

DE ARTE CABALISTICA

postea bellis & incursionibus hostium deuastatam. Sic Decii Romam liberauerunt, attamen sequenti subuersione atq3 incendio dirutam. Imperfecta (crede mihi) salus est omnis quae tempore frangitur, perfecta est q̃ caducum aeternat, ut de Helena morte sublata in Euripidis Oreste Apollo docuit cum sic ait. ἣ δ᾽ ἔστιν, ἣν ὁρᾶτ᾽ἐν αἰθέρος πτυχαῖς σισωσμένη τε, κ᾽ οὐθανοῦσα πρὸς σέθεν. ἐγώνιν ἐξέσωσα. Id est. Ista est quam cernitis in aetheris conuexitatibus. saluata quidem. & non mortua iuxta te. ego eam saluaui. Vtq3 non simus ignari salutem illam non ab Apolline, nec a diis aliis nisi tanquam mediatoribus prodiisse, quin uerius a summo deo cui propriam ipsa se in signi uirtute dicauit, tum ita subiungit, ζηνὸς γὰρ οὔσην, ζῆν νιν ἄφθιτον χρεών. Id est, Iouis enim existentem, uiuere eam incorruptibilem decebat. Per Castorem Helenae fratrem, Marrane uera praedicas, inquit Philolaus, & sapienter uideris de uera salute locutus, assentiorq3 Saluatorem de quo tam magnifice ac tam perpetuo sacra uaticinãtur eloquia, eum fore oportere, qui non tam huius grandis mundi, non regionum & urbium, non in fimorum elementorum & syderum, non lignorum & lapidum, non plantarum & arborum, non piscium, non uolucrum, non pecorum, quae oĩa naturam ducem & suae conditionis instinctum inerranter & probe sequuntur, & ad constitutum sibi finem manent quod sunt, q̃ istius minoris mundi seruator & restaurator sit, hoc est hominis, qui ab aequitatis sibi tradita norma & rectę rationis sententia saepe decidens generositatem suam coaceruatione uitiorum in stagna profunda malorum & sempiternae corruptionis barathrum uoluntarie praecipitat, unde reuocare gradum propriis uiribus & sua ope nequeat. Hic Marrane hic inquam salute nobis hic saluatore opus est. Hoc genus creaturarũ appellat Pythagoras

M ἀνθρώπους αὐθαίρετα πήματ᾽ἔχοντας. Id est. Homines spontanea electione detrimenta habentes. De quibus ita scripsit in aureis carminibus. τλήμονες οἴ τ᾽ἀγαθῶν πέλας ὄντων οὐκ ἐσορῶσιν, οὔτε κλύουσι, λύσιν δὲ κακῶν ταύροι ζωῆς ῥίψ τοῖς μοῖρα βροτῶν βλάπτει φρένας, οἱ δὲ κυλίνδοις, ἄλλοτ᾽ἐπ᾽ἄλλα φέροντ᾽ ἀπείρονα πήματ᾽ἔχοντες. Id est. Miseri, hi quidem bona prope existentia non aspiciunt neque audiunt, solutionemq3 malorum, pauci intellligunt, talis sors mortalium laedit mentes, hi autem rotis ex aliis in alia feruntur infinita damna hñtes. Sane noster ipse philosophorum princeps hoc nimirum a Cabalistis Hebraeis sumptum ut é Simone accipere possumus, sensit rationalem esse hominem rebus aliis nobiliorem utputa diuiniorem, non tantum una operatione nec uniformi effectu contentum ut caetera quae sola natura trahuntur semper eodem modo agente, sed uariis dotibus instar pandorae praeditum, quibus sponte utatur in omnem euentum pro libera uoluntate, ob quam libertatem ait. θείου γένος ἐστὶ βροτοῖσιν οἷς ἱερὰ προφέρουσα φύσις δείκνυσιν ἕκαστα. Id est. Diuinum genus est hominibus quibus sacra

On the Art of Kabbalah

waste by numerous wars and enemy invasions. Similarly with the Decii when they freed Rome: Rome was subsequently overthrown in fire and destruction.

All salvation that is weakened by the passage of time is imperfect, believe me. Perfect salvation is what makes the transitory live forever, as Apollo told us in Euripides' *Orestes,* when he spoke of the death of Helen: "There she is. You can see her in the vaulting of the sky. She is saved. She is not mortal as you are. I have saved her."

We should not be unmindful of the fact that salvation does not come from Apollo or other gods except in their intermediary role. It comes, rather, from the highest God to whom Helen virtuously dedicated herself, for Apollo adds: "She exists through Zeus, and lives for ever."

PHILOLAUS: By Castor (Helen's brother!), Marranus, you are right, and I think you have spoken with some wisdom on the matter of true salvation. I agree with you that the Savior of whom so much is foretold in high-minded and oft-repeated holy utterance ought not to be one who saves and restores this wide world — its kingdoms and cities, or physical elements — stars, stocks and stones, plants and trees, fish, birds, cattle. All these are slaves to their natures, faithfully and unerringly they follow their natural instincts. They remain what they are until their preordained ends. The Savior ought to be he who saves and restores the lesser world of men. Man has often fallen off from well-reasoned judgments, the precepts of justice handed down to him. Often has he taken his whole nature, loaded it with vice and flung it into the pool of evil, the pit of eternal corruption, when no one can, aided or by his own efforts, retrace his steps.

It is man, Marranus, man, I say, who needs salvation, and man who needs a savior. It is this species of creation that Pythagoras termed "Men suffering by their own choice." In the *Golden Verses* he wrote of them: "Unhappy men, those who do not notice, do not hear, the good that is so close to them. Few — such is the fate afflicting the mind of man — understand the way to end their evils. They are carried from one torment to another, suffering endless hurt." Without doubt our prince of philosophers got this from the Hebrew Kabbalists, as we have it from Simon. He felt that man, being rational, was nobler than other beings, was more like God. Unlike other creatures which are total slaves to instinct, man always does things the same way, never content with one kind of activity or with uniform purpose. Like Pandora he has been endowed with all manner of gifts, which he uses independently to every effect and with free will. Hence Pythagoras says that freedom is "the divine streak in men to whom the holy nature shows each thing." The holy nature is an intellectual soul.

Through intellect man comes close to God, as that which is without alteration to that which is without admixture, but when he uses his lower senses, man is drawn apart from God, as the impure from the pure. Thus whenever reason, which, as Pythagoras said, makes the distinctions for us, turns to mental activity, we are made happy. But whenever it runs off after whatever the senses fancy, we are most unhappy. In this way man seems poised between virtue and vice. This brings to mind the Pythagorean letter "Y" with its upright split into two branches. This was the choice that Hercules, when still a young man, sat down to think over in Prodicus' story.

LIBER SECVNDVS   XXXIII.

promouens natura ostendit singula, quippe illa sacra natura est anima intellectiua, secundum igitur intellectum deo accedit homo ut mero syn cerum, atq3 secundum sensus inferiores a deo recedit tanquam impurum a puro, quo fit ut ratio quæ nobis, ut inquit ipse, ostendit singula, dum se ad mentis fruitionem conuertit beatos nos faciat. contra uero dum ad sensuum discurrit libidinem, miseros, ut inter uirtutem & uitium medius homo positus uideatur, uelut substitutus apex in litera Pythagoræ discri mine secta bicorni, ad quem Hercules ille Prodicius tenera tum ætate cogitabundus resedit. Quemadmodum uero ut Solon apud Herodo tum Crœso affirmauit, ante obitum nemo supremacq3 funera debet di ci beatus, ita nemo certe miser putandus est dum hanc uitam uiuit. Sed sci licet ultima semp expectanda dies homini est, q̃ si abiecto corpe tũc uitiis permanserit oneratus, incipiat esse uere miser, & eam miseriam ut supio re oratione accepisti Pythagoras in duo genera diuidebat. Nã post mor tem miseri, aut bona prope habẽt quæ sunt beatitudinis dona, q̃uis ea nec aspiciant nec audiant, quia dei uisione nondum fruantur, hi de saluandoꝶ numero sunt, non extrema miseria grauati, ut tandem aliq̃n pœnas eua dant constitutas, aut deniq3 ab eis bona longissime distant, ut mala nunq3 ullum habitura sint fine, & ii appellant infinita damna habentes. Duo igĩt inferorum habitacula hic describunt, Elysius campus.i.transitorius, illoru q̃bus bona prope sunt, supera ut contexa reuisant. Et tartarus ab horribi li sono tartar quasi tortor teter terror uocatus, illoru q̃bus sua damna sunt infinita, qui kylindris radiisq3 rotarum districti pẽdent, ubi sedet æther nũq3 sedebit infœlix Theseus, & ei similes. ὅθεν ὅυ ποτὲ ἐκβαίνουσιν ut est a Pla tone Pythagoram imitate scriptum.i. Vnde nunq̃ egrediunt. Hic mihi ac cedant obiurgatores q̃ blacterare in eundẽ Pythagorã non desinũt tantũ & tam p̃cipuum uirum, cuius dictamini ceu oraculo deorum creditũ est. Quare dictator ueritatis uelut alter Apollo illi seculo noiabatur, q̃d ip̃m uocabulum Pythagoras designat. Rumorem aũt de illo passim diuulgãt, hanc eius fuisse opinionem ꝗ aĩa humana ẽrudam post mortem corpa brutorum informet, q̃d uiris rõne utẽtibus incredibile uideri debet, de tã excellenti philosophiæ autore & abundantissimo scientiarum fonte unde ad nos emanauit diuinarum & humanaru rerum cognitio. Quin poti9 ea suspicio trãsanimationis ex hoibus Pythagoricorum mysterioru partim ignaris partim ob inuidiã perosis orta est. Nõ em caruit æmuloru liuore p̃stantissima eius uiri uirtus, innocẽtissima uita, egregia doctrina, celebris fama, utq3 sit, nihil non pollutum reliqueru̅t inuidi carptores, Tymon, Xe nophanes, Cratinus, Aristophon, Hermippus, & alii q̃rum nõ exigua mul titudo est, q de Pythagora suis in libris mendacia plurima scripserunt, ac ea prodiderunt q̃ nusq̃ ab illo uel dicta uel scripta fuere, aut eiuscemodi

                                                                 G iii

Book Two

In this vein, while indeed Solon (according to Herodotus) did remark to Croesus that no one should be called happy till dead and buried, still no one is with any certainty to be thought unhappy while he still lives this life. Man must await his last day. If then, when he has shaken off the body, he is still weighed down with evildoing, he will indeed be wretched. And as you have already been told, Pythagoras divided this unhappiness into two kinds. Some of those who are unhappy after death are within reach of the gifts of happiness, but can neither see nor hear them because they do not yet have the benefit of sight from God. These are among those who are to be saved. They are not burdened with extreme misery, and may yet escape their allotted punishment. Others are so far away from goodness that there will never be an end to their ills. It is these who are said to receive external punishment.

Thus, two abodes of the dead are described here. One is the Elysian field, which lasts but for a short while, where those who are close to goodness are found: they can see the higher things as if in a dome above them. The other is Tartarus, so named for the spine-chilling sound "tartar," like torturer, terror, taint. This is for those whose suffering is unending: those who dangle spread-eagled on the axles and wheel-spokes. Here sits Theseus, wretched; he will sit here always with those like him. "They will never leave this place," wrote Plato, quoting Pythagoras.

And as far as I am concerned, all the croakers who never cease slighting the great Pythagoras—a man of such pre-eminence—can end up here. His slightest dictum was treated as the word of God. Hence he was called "dictator of the truth"—as if he were the Apollo of his age—and this is what "Pythagoras" means.

There is a widespread rumor abroad that Pythagoras believed that after death the human soul enters and influences animals' bodies. To rational men this should appear incredible, attributed as it is to the founder of such an outstanding school of thought and a man who is the source of so much of our knowledge, and by whom we have achieved an understanding of things human and divine. The notion of transmigration of souls surely arose among men partly ignorant of Pythagorean mysteries, and partly motivated by spite and ill will. The man's outstanding reputation, blameless life, distinguished teaching and celebrated fame are not without their enemies, as tends to happen. These malicious carvers leave none unsmeared—Timon, Xenophanes, Cratinus, Aristophon, Hermippus—and there is no mean crowd of others. They wrote a good many lies in their books about Pythagoras, and put in things he never said or wrote, or else they twisted the sense of something he had written so that it could easily be thought such a great man had suffered a mental lapse and wandered off course, whether in his teaching on the origins of things, or on numbers, or on not eating beans or meat, on the lower world, and on the matter we are now discussing, the transmigration of souls.

DE ARTE CABALISTICA

si qua dixisset, tñ ita in peiorem ea sensum peruerterunt, ut facile crederet talis ac tantus uir inconsyderate docendo aberrasse, de rerū principiis, de numeris, de faba nō gustāda, de abstinēdo ab aīatorū esu, de inseris, deçz metēpsychosi & transitu aīarum, de q̄ nūc tractamus. Qui ēm exemplaria & species rerum ita distinxit, ut mutuo transmutari confundi ue neçzant, q̄ nam modo humanā essentiam q̄ sua est forma comunicaret brutoç̄ cū & autore se ipso ne unitas q̄dem substantiua certi numeri secundum naturam est unitas alterius numeri. Quare ait αἱ δὲ μονάδες ἐν τῇ δυάδι αὐτῇ, πρὸς τὰς ἐν τριάδι αὐτῇ ἀσύμβλητοι. i. Vnitates in duitate ipsa, ad eas q̄ sunt in ternitate ipsa, sunt inconiectibiles. Ita in physicis constat quanq̄ longe secus agitur in Mathematicis, de qbus nihil in psentia nobis est negocii. Vnum autem cuiusçz rei est essentia participata, q̄ alterius rei essentiam non occupabit, ἑκάστη μὲν οὐσία ἑνὸς εἴδους μετέχει. i. quęlibet ēm substātia una specie participat. Ideo in disparis animantis uita transire nō pōt, uel ulla qualiscuçz bestia, quin potius manet in suę lege naturę suum tenēs munus, ὥστε τὸ εἶδος δεῖ τοῦ ζῷου ἔχεται. i. Itaçz species speciei non coincedit. Tametsi nanq̄ unū sigillū multis impressum plures ceras effigiat, nō tñ plurium sigillorum formas diuersas eadem cera ferre poterit. Haud igitur sigillum formæ humanę q̄ est imago dei, naturam inferiorem sigillare pmittitur, q̄d ut oīa sua Pythagoras ęnigmatice proposuit, sic & huius opinionis certam sententiam nota propria designauit, cū iter alia symbola istud sibi gratissimū celebraret ἐν δακτυλίῳ θεοῦ ἐικόνα μὴ περιφέρειν. i. In sigillo, dei imaginem non circūferre, q̄d meo arbitratu recte intelligit ad hūc ferme modum. Imaginē dei q̄ est anima hois naturas alias circum circa non sigillare nec̄z formare posse. Sic ēm Hermes Trismegistus ægyptiorū doctor in libro ad Asclepiū. Hois inquit una pars simplex est quā uocamus diuinæ similitudinis formam, & paulo inferius ita, duæ sunt imagines dei, mundus scilicet & homo. Qz ini quę igit explanauerint eum uel inuidi uel ignari, de transitu aīarum post mortem, simul etiam de illarum descensu ante hois gñationem, profecto nullus modo extat q̄ non id mecū sentiat uel ulla mente p̄ditus. Qñ nanq̄z multi aīam hois de potentia materiæ putabant educi, statuit noster ipse magis credendum esse, infundi eam corpori ab ipso deo, & ob id eam asseruit ante corpus esse, q̄d non tpe intelligendum est, sed puritate & naturę dignitate. Hanc itaq̄z infusionem appellauit aīæ descensum, quem postea multis ambagibus uarie sectatores tractauerunt sua quisçz uia, non semp pro autoris uoluntate, q̄ descēsum aīæ humanæ in corpus non secundum situm accipi p̄cepit, nec iuxta motum a mundo intellectuali per singulas sphæras ad mundū elementarem ut Proclus & astipulatores alii, sed pro naturaliū formarum serie in qua corpis humani ultima p̄fectio est aīa rationalis, q̄ ita totum perficit ut homo aīal diuinum optimo iure appelletur.

Voluit

On the Art of Kabbalah

Pythagoras distinguished the "forms" and the outward appearances of things, to prevent their being exchanged or confused with one another. How could he associate the human essence, his own form, with animals? He says himself that not even the substantive oneness of a definite number is, in the physical world, the oneness of another number. Thus he says: "The unities in a twofold entity cannot be linked to the unities in a threefold entity." This is the position in physics, although it is rather different in mathematics, but we are not dealing with that at the moment. The "one" of each thing is an essence which is shared, but which does not possess the essence of another thing: "Any substance shares in the one outward appearance." Thus it is not possible to cross into the life of other living things of a different kind, whatever they may be. A man must remain bound by the rules of his own constitution, keeping his own endowments, so that "species be not confused with species." One seal may impress its image many times onto a good many pieces of wax, but that same wax image cannot bear the different impress of several seals. The seal of the human form, the image of God, does not allow an impression to be made on a lower nature. Pythagoras put this in riddles, as he did all his teaching, but he gives appropriate indications of the definitive statement of his thoughts on the matter. Among all the precepts, this one, he declares, is most dear to him: "not to publish God's image on a seal." In my opinion this is correctly understood in this sense, that the image of God, which is man's soul, cannot impress its shape, as a seal does, on any other natures round about. Here is what Hermes Trismegistus, the Egyptian scholar, says in his book addressed to Aesculapius: "One part of man is simple and we call it the form of God's likeness," and a little later: "There are two images of God, namely, the world and man."

It was either the envious or the ignorant therefore who made such unjust pronouncements on the subject of the transmigration of the soul after death, and it is the same with the doctrine of the descent of souls before man's birth. In no way will anyone with any claims to intellectual ability disagree with me on this.

Many have thought that the soul of man was drawn out of the power of matter. Our master decided that it was more plausible that it was poured into the body by God himself. Thus he asserted that the soul is in existence before the body; "in time" is not to be understood here, but that it is prior in purity and intrinsic worth. This inpouring he called "the descent of the soul." Later disciples treated this idea with many and various subtleties, each in his own way, and not always as its author would have wished. For Pythagoras saw the descent of the human soul into the body not as a matter of spatial arrangements, nor as a matter of movement from the intellectual world through each sphere to the elemental world, as Proclus and his followers would have it, but as a series of natural forms in which the ultimate perfection of the human body consists in the rational soul, by which it is that man can best be called a divine animal.

LIBER SECVNDVS   XXXIIII.

Voluit igitur Pythagoras animātia sola q̄rum sacra natura id est ratio de monstrat singula, diuinum esse genus, scilicet a deo propagatum, ut aureis edidit carminibus, cuius species nec mutet nec conuertat, sic generum singulorum formas esse pmanentes, licet in eadem sua forma dissimiles. Post hois uero mortem si iustus decesserit aīam eius transcēdere purum æthera, & æuum degere cum beatis, tanquam deum cum diis. Ita enim ait, ἰδίοχου πνώμω εἴσας καθ᾽ὕπερθυ ἀείσιν, ἢν λα᾽ ππμέϊτας σῶμα, ἐς ἀθιρελεύθερον ἐλθνσ, ἔσεαι ἀθάνατοσ θεὸς ἄμβροτος οὐκέτι νυτὸς. i. Aurigam iudicium statuens supne optimum, cum relinquens corpus in ætherem liberum uenies, cris imortalis deus, incorruptibilis, nec ultra mortalis. Sin aūt iniustus & scelerosus in peccatis insanabilibus & mortalibus decesserit hō, tunc aīa meius oēm suū reatū uariis diluere pœnis docuit, easq̃ pœnas pro magnitudīe ac multitudine criminū magis atq̃ minus fore duras & durabiles, qbº delegata sint loca hæc nature inferiora, & corpa tū imaginaria seu figuralia; tū qñcq̃ uera, non q̃ informet ut essentialis portio, sed q̃ inquilini more, pœnarum sustinendarū causa inhabitet, aut qbus per indistantiam localē assistat, uelut motrix intrinseca mobili, uel circa quæ cruciatibus subiecta torqueat, ut Tityus circa uultures, & Ixion ad serpentum rotas, & Tantalº in flumine, & Sisyphus apud saxū, & Prometheus cum aqlis. Qñqdē dæmon tartareus potest corripe ac obsidere corpus, cur nō aīa turpis ad inferorum pœnas damnata, uel uerum cuiuscunq̃ speciei corpus ingrederetur dei dispensatione, uel aerem induta, ostentaret quamlibet aspectib² nostris formam, ut Dido moritura æneam alloqtur. Sequar atris ignibus ardens. Et Plinius iunior rem scribit creditam, de domo quā Athenodorº Tarsensis philosophus coemerat, eam fuisse importuno strepitu infamē, q̃ ibi simulacrū horridi senis aspiciebat, & q̃tidie nostra q̃q̃ etate similia occurrunt terriculamenta, modo tenuioribus, modo crassioribus exuuiis. Tum uariæ illudunt species atq̃ ora ferarum, fiet em subito sus horridus atraq̃ tigris, squamosusq̃ draco & fulua ceruice leæna, aut acrem flammæ sonitum dabit, oīa transformat sese in miracula rerum, igneq̃ horribileq̃ seram, fluuiūq̃ liquentem. Hæc sane corpa uocamus phantastica, hoc est, apparitiua, q̃ assumere possint tam animæ hoīm solutæ q̃ dæmones, ut de Lamia nouimus Menippi Licii philosophi procace proca in pulchrā mulierem apud Corinthum cōuersa, quā Apollonius Tyanneus publice deprehendit lemurem esse, ut deniq̃ senex ille pannosus & mendicus Ephesiis q̃ndam causa pestilitatis, hoc genere metamorphoseωs notatur, quem lapidibus obrutū aiūt uisum esse canem quasi Molossum. De utrisq̃ scripsit Philostratus secundus, in libro de uita Apollonii quarto. Eius aūt q̃d Pythagoras dixisse fert, se q̃ndam Euphorbum fuisse alia ratio est, nō em talem dicendi morem ipse primus instituit, sed longe prius in populari cō

G iiii

Book Two

Pythagoras wanted only those living things whose sacred nature—that is, whose reason—distinguishes differences in things, to be the divine genus—generated by God, as he says in the *Golden Verses*. Their appearance does not alter or suffer change. He wanted the form of an individual genus to remain the same, though there might be different forms in their common form.

When a just man died, his soul climbed to the pure upper air and spent eternity with the blessed ones, as a god among gods. Pythagoras says: "Taking the best of heavenly judgments as your guide, when you set the body aside and come to the free upper air, you will be an immortal, incorruptible god, and no longer mortal."

But as for the unjust and wicked man who died in mortal and irremediable sin, Pythagoras taught that his soul paid for all his offences with various punishments. These were on a scale of harshness according to how great the crime was or how many had been committed. The places appointed for this were in the underworld; the bodies were imaginary and figurative, but nevertheless real. The guilty soul does not mould this body as if it were really part of it, but is more like a temporary resident, there just for the purpose of being punished. Either it stands by the body—not, that is, in a different physical location, but in the same internal relation as the impulse that moves the body has to the body that is moved; or it stands physically close to what is subjected to torture, and is thus tortured, as with Tityus with his vultures, Ixion on the wheel of serpents, Tantalus in the river, Sisyphus on the rock, Prometheus with his eagles.

Since a devil from Tartarus can seize a body and occupy it, why should an evil soul which is being condemned to hellish punishment not either enter the real body of some species or other with God's dispensation, or, cloaked in air, present some kind of outward appearance to our view. The dying Dido says to Aeneas: "Burning with black fire shall I follow," and Pliny the Younger committed to writing the widely held belief that the house bought by Athenodorus, the philosopher from Tarsus, was known for distressing wails, and that the spectre of a wild old man could be seen there. In our own time similar horrors are an everyday occurrence; evidence for them may be weak, or sometimes more solidly based. They play about with shapes and faces of wild animals of all kinds: suddenly they become a savage boar and a coal-black tigress, scaly snake, a tawny-maned lion; or they emit the fierce noise of flames. They transform themselves into amazing things: a fire, a terrifying wild beast, a running river. These bodies we call phantasms or apparitions; men's unfettered souls can take them on, as well as devils. We learn this from the story of Lamia, who at Corinth changed into a beautiful woman and was the shameless suitor of Menippus Licius, the philosopher. There she was publicly exposed as a ghost by Apollonius of Tyana. We learn too from that old and tattered beggar who once caused an outbreak of plague at Ephesus, who was known for metamorphoses of this kind: when stoned, they say, he was seen to be a dog, like Molossus. Both these stories are from Philostratus the Younger, in Book 4 of his *Life of Apollonius*.

However, what Pythagoras is said to have declared—that he was once Euphorbus—has another explanation. He was not the first to speak in this

suetudine apud uetustissimos usurpatum fuit, qƷ qua esset quisqƷ uirtute aut uitio præditus, alteri assimilaret, q eminenter eadem conditione olim fuisset, uirum em que libuisset robore p̄stātissimū dixerunt esse Herculē. Ita M. Varro. Rusticellus, inqt Hercules appellat⁹ mulū suum tollebat. Et Numenius Pythagoricus apte scribit nihil aliud esse Platonē q̃ Moysen attica lingua loquentē. Sæpe q̃qƷ Cicero dictus est latinus Demosthenes esse, o͞es a uirtutum & opum paritate ac similitudine morum, non aūt ob unius substantiæ comunionē, ita Litanus Plauti seruus Argyrippū dixit esse Solonē q pariter leges conscribat, de illo in Asinaria sic ait. Nūc etem est negociosus interdius, uidelicet Solon est, leges ut cōscribat. Ista Plauti uerba inolitam priscorū loquendi consuetudinē indicāt, ut hunc hoi͞em, dixerint illum esse quendam, qui fuerit natura, ingenio, moribus, amore, affectione, & opere similior. Vnde Romani solebant huic adagio particu lam, alter, adiungere, ut tu es alter ego, & ego sum alter tu, licet scientes & uidentes qƷ reuera nec ego sū tu, nec tu es ego. Sed in utrisqƷ nobis sen tietes esse idē ingeniū, par studiū, eandem uolutatem, eundē conatum, spi ritum, animum οὐ τῆς οὐσίας αὐτῶν μεταδιδομένης. Nam a͞ios antiq dixerunt motus hoi͞m & uoluntates, quare unius moris curæ ac diligentiæ, cōsimi lis propositi, æqualis motiuū ac paris motus & sensus eiusdem hoies usita te appellāt unanimes. Est aūt a priscis philosophis haud quaq̃ alienum ut dicat a͞ia esse motiuū & sensitiuū in hoi͞e τὸ ἔμψυχον ἢ τ̃ ἄψυχs inqt Aristot. δυοῖν μάλιϛα διαφέρειν δοκεῖ, κινήσει τε καὶ τῷ αἰσθάνεσθαι. i. Animatum em ab ina nimato duobus maxime differre uidetur, motu & sensu. QuicunqƷ igitur erga rem eandem afficiunt & mouent, idemqƷ sæpe ac sentire uident, uni⁹ esse ψυχῆς i. animæ uulgo dicunt. Vnde illa famosa μεταψύχωσις. i. transani matio nihil aliud reuera est uiris recte doctis q̃ æqualis cura similis mo tus & par studium alicuius hois mortui, post aliq̃ tpe, in altero uel eodem reptum hoi͞e uiuo. Tali æmulatione triti & usitati sermonis, Pythagoras q̃ndam rediens a Persarum Magis (ita em sapietes illi suos noiant) forte inter amicos exhilarādi conuiuii gratia more Magorum uti poterat, & di cere se Euphorbi olim militis Troiani, Calliclis, Hermotimi, Pyrrhi, Py randri, Calidonæ, Alces, & demum suā Pythagoræ a͞iam in se ipso conti nere, qƷ inclinatam ad quædam p̄clara in singulis illorum p̄cipue sita ge reret affectionem, studium & uoluntatē, ad q̃ illi ipsi propensius in uita eo rum fuerunt moti. O͞im aūt maxime cū in Euphorbo Troiano claruisset bellica uirtus, ipse Euphorbi a͞iam nactus esset quasi iam cor Euphorbi ha bēret. Dēq̃ nimirum se iactare potuit, cum laudarent eum pugiles studii bellici, cernentes laterum & brachiorum totiusqƷ corpis sui robur & in credibilem erga fortissimos Athletas amorem pensantes, quem illis tum & p̄cioso apparatu & magnifico sumptu ostēdebat, ante em caricis siccis
                  & molli

On the Art of Kabbalah

idiom; it was in popular use among the ancients long before him. It is used to liken someone displaying some virtue or vice to someone else who has been similarly outstanding. Any extraordinarily strong man was called a Hercules. Marcus Varro talks of "a bit of a bumpkin called Hercules who could carry his own mule." Numenius the Pythagorean aptly described Plato as none other than Moses speaking Attic Greek. Cicero is often called a Latin Demosthenes. All these are so called because of the parity of and the similarities between their deeds and abilities and behavior, not because they shared the one substance. So Litanus, the slave of Plautus, said that Argyrippus was Solon because he too made laws, and in the *Asinaria* he says: "For he is busy all day now, a veritable Solon writing the law." These words of Plautus exemplify a firmly-rooted custom among the ancients of saying that one man "is" this other man who was very like him in disposition, character, habits, loves, feelings and work. The Romans would add to this idiom the little word "another." Hence "You are another I" and "I am another you" although we both know and see that I am not in fact you, nor are you me. However, we feel there is the same character in each of us; equal diligence, the same will, the same endeavor, spirit, mind, but without "changing the essence."

Minds, the ancients said, were men's motives and will. Thus those who were equally painstaking and accurate, with similar aims, with the same impulses, the same feelings and emotions, were said to be "of one mind." Nor is it at all unlike philosophers to call the soul the motive and sensitive force in man. "The animate differs from the inanimate in two particular ways," says Aristotle, "in motion and in feeling." So those who are affected and moved by the same things, and seem to think and feel the same things, are commonly said to be "of the same mind." And here we get this famous "transmigration of souls." To the well educated it is in fact nothing but the phenomenon of the concerns, the motives and the inclinations of one who is long since dead, being found identical with those of another man or the same man while he is alive.

Pythagoras told this well-worn tale. On one occasion, returning from the Magi of Persia (this was the name they gave their sages), he chanced on some friends, and, thinking to cheer up the company, he spoke in the way the Magi did. He told them that he had in him the soul of Euphorbus, the Trojan soldier, and of Callicles, Hermotimus, Pyrrhus, Pyrandrus, Calidona, Alces, and lastly his own, Pythagoras. The soul would engender a powerful inclination toward all the particular things to which they had themselves in their own lives been particularly drawn. Courage in war had most distinguished, among all these, Euphorbus of Troy, and Pythagoras himself had obtained the soul of Euphorbus. It was as if he now had the heart of Euphorbus. He could well boast of this, for boxers devoted to fighting would exclaim in praise when they saw the strength of his arms, his legs, his whole body, and one should bear in mind his unusual devotion to the strongest athletes which he demonstrated in the costly equipment and the extraordinary expense lavished on them.

LIBER SECVNDVS

& molli caseo triticoq; nutriebant athletæ, ipse uero noster eos carnibus tunc primus nutriisse comptus est. Admirantibus igitur illis ɋ in philosopho literarum studioso esse posset tantus amor pugnæ, qd mirum si responderit Euphorbi aiam in se uigere, hoc est, ingenium, studium, motū, & uolūtatem Euphorbi apud se residere, q tametsi esset pacis p̄ceptor & quietæ contemplationis autor, tn̄ in se ipso sentiret belli tanq̃ Troiani desyderium. Quo audito, mox rumor inter temere credulos ortus erat & fama percrebruit, uel ignorantia mysteriorum Pythagoricorū, uel malignitate inuidorum q̃ semper optima quęq; puertunt & recitant audita secus multo q̃ sint dicta, cp̃ Euphorbi aia in bello Troiano perempti trāsmigra uerit in Pythagorā. Quæ opinio postea fuit adiuta scriptoribus atq; poetis. Inde Ouidius in Transfigurationis lib. xv. hæc inter alias nugas a græcis Cretizin asuetis more suo mutuatus sic de Pythagora cecinit. Morte carent animæ semp̃q; priore relicta sede, nouis domibus uiuunt habitātq; receptæ. Ipse ego (nam memini) Troiani tp̃e belli Panthoides Euphorbus eram, cui pectore q̃ndam hæsit in aduerso grauis hasta minoris Atridæ. Cognoui clypeum læuę gestamina nostræ nup̃ Abanteis templo Iunonis in Argis. At noli obstupescere p̃stans Marrane, nihil horum in Pythagoræ libris scriptum inuenies. Nam tria ipse solum edidit uolumina, primum πωλιτικὸν secundum πολιτικὸν tertium φυσικὸν quem Lysidi qdam ascribunt, sit igitur tertium nobis aurea carmina. Percurre singula quæq; & nusq̃ reperies in eo uiro de transanimatione quicq̃, q̃ credas facilius rumore falso seminatum esse p̃ inuidos quicqd de illa μετεμψυχώσει fingitur, qd diuersitas narratiōis plane indicat, cū alii clypeum hunc esse in tēplum Iunonis relatum apud Argos. Alii dicatum Palladi Athenis affirment, & cp̃ eius clypei hæc ipsa fuerat inscriptio. μέχαλα εἰντα, μενέλεως ἀπ Εὐφόρβου .i. Palladi Mineruæ Menelaus ab Euphorbo, autor est Tyrius Maximus disputatione xvi. Quantam nūc eiuscemodi testimonio habere fidē oporteat Iurisconsulti uiderint. Eqdem adduci non possum ut credam Ouidii de transitu aiarum fabulam, tam excellentem in omni scientia & grauē uirum docuisse, atq; eo minus credendum putauerim quo magis p̃stantes autores aliter tradidere. Nam cp̃ asserunt multi, apud græcos Pythagorā inuenisse primum aias esse immortales, manifeste falsum dicunt. Homerem græcorum fere antiq̃ssimus lōge prior hoc dogma prodidit, cui apud inferos aiæ defunctorum de multis rebus disserunt, & uaticinant multa, ecqd aliud (oro te) uiri eius tā admirabile carmē insinuat ΑΙ δλης τ τυχας q̃ animas nostras post mortem p̃manere. Deinde in sociis Vlyssis palam ostendit, imprudentes hoīm aias a corpore separatas, non quidem bestiarum naturas, sed tm̄ habitus brutorum induere, atq; cū tali horrore pœnas luere, quas Circe iusserit. Quicūq; aūt radicē & florem tenent Moly

Book Two

Previously athletes had lived on a diet of dried figs, soft cheese and wheat. Our teacher was the first to give them meat to eat. It was a source of wonder to them that a studious intellectual should love the fights so much. To this wonder he would reply that the soul of Euphorbus flourished within him, that is, that the character, enthusiasms, impulses and desires of Euphorbus lived in him, so that although a teacher of peace and the originator of quiet meditation, he felt inside himself a longing for a war like the one against Troy.

When people heard this, whether through ignorance of the Pythagorean mysteries, or through the spite of evil wishers who often twist the good and repeat something quite different from what was said, the rumor soon sprang up among the foolish and incredulous, spreading far and wide, that the soul of the Euphorbus who had perished in the Trojan War had migrated to Pythagoras.

The belief was later useful to poets and writers. Ovid, in Book 15 of *Metamorphoses*, writes about Pythagoras among other things. He tends to borrow from the unreliable parts of Greek writing, and in his words it becomes:

> "Souls do not die, but when they leave their former seat, they find new homes, there living and dwelling. I was myself (for I remember) Euphorbus son of Panthous at the time of the Trojan War, he whose breast was once pierced in battle by the heavy spear of Atreus' younger son. I have seen the shield, my left arm's armor in the temple of Juno in Abantian Argos lately."

But do not boggle at this Marranus. You will not find any of this in Pythagoras' own books. He published only three volumes: *Education* was the first, *Politics* the second, and *Physics* the third. Some ascribe the last to Lysis, so perhaps the *Golden Verses*[41] should be our third. Run through each of these. Nowhere will you find in them anything about transmigration of souls. For this reason you may be more convinced that the stuff about "metempsychosis" was an invention, a piece of hearsay put about by the spiteful. Inconsistencies in the narrative show this clearly. Some say that the shield was taken to the temple of Juno in Argos. Others assert that it was dedicated to Pallas Athene in Athens, and that there had been written on the shield: "To Pallas Athene, Menelaus from Euphorbus." (Maximus of Tyre, Disputation 16, is the authority for this.) Lawyers will know the extent to which one should rely on evidence of this kind. I cannot bring myself to believe Ovid's tale about souls transmigrating, or that such a serious and scholarly man should have taught this, and I think it all the less plausible given the differing accounts of other authors.

Many hold that Pythagoras was the first Greek to discover the immortality of the soul. Clearly they are wrong; Homer, perhaps the earliest of the Greeks, had given birth to this doctrine. In Homer, the souls of the dead below engage in discussion on many topics, and prophesy much. That our souls live after death is a theme (don't you agree) running through the whole of that marvellous section of the epic *On the Whole World of the Dead*. Then, coming to the companions of Ulysses, he shows clearly how foolish men's souls, separated from their bodies, take on no intrinsic bestiality but certainly the condition of beasts, and in this appalling state suffering the punishments Circe ordered. But, according to Book 10 of the *Odyssey*, the souls of those who hold the root and flower of the Moly plant will be safe and under Mercury's protection.

DE ARTE CABALISTICA

eorum animas, autore Mercurio, fore securas, ut est in Odysseæ decimo libro. Sed ad illā de Euphorbo ironiam reuertamus, de q̃ idonei q̃tiẽs scribunt oīa Pythagoræ diuina dogmata fatentur αἰνίττεσθαι hoc est allegoria obscuriore tradi. Quod Apollonius Tyanēsis ille Pythagoreus tractatu cum Thespesione archiphilosopho gymnosophistarum habito in Philostrati uolumine sexto confirmat ita loquens. εἰ δ' αἰνιγμάτων ἅπτομαι, σοφία τοῦ Θαγόρου ξυγχωρεῖ ταῦτα, ηλίσκε δὲ καὶ τὸ αἰνίττεσθαι. i. Si ænigmata tango, sapiẽtia Pythagoræ cōcedit hęc, tradidit eṁ & ænigmatizare. Qñ aũt cũ Indorū Brachmanibus in libro eiusdem tertio disputabat, querens de aīa quō sentirent. Iarchas, inquit, sicut Pythagoras qdem uobis, nos aũt ægyptiis tradidimus. Suscepit Apollonius. Num igit te aliquem Troianorū fuisse dices: ut se Pythagoras Euphorbum. Audi iam Marrane q̃ Thespesion cate responderit prius interrogās, quemnam ex græcorū ducto Troiam exercitu, admiratiōe digniorem existimaret. Cui Apollonius, q̃ Achilles primas Homero nactus esset. Tum Iarchas. πρὸς ὃν τὴν ἔφη ἀπολλώνιε καὶ τοῦ προήγουν θεωρεῖ τὸν ἐμὸν μᾶλλον δὲ, τὸ προήγονον σῶμα· τουτὶ ἦ ᾖ πυθαγόρας, εὔφορβος ἐξήτο. i. Ad istum, inquit, Apolloni etiam progenitorē ęstima meū, magis aũt progignens corpus, hoc eṁ & Pythagoras Euphorbum putauit. Deinde recitat Gangen Indorum olim regem Gangis fluuii filiū multis uirtutibus Achillem supasse, illumq̃ ipsum fuisse illud progignens corpus, q̃d ipse iam esset. Verba hæc non aīarum transmigrationem, sed corporum transmutatiōe indicant, instar cuiuslibet materiæ q̃ sit apta istius uel illiꝰ formam recipe. Perinde atqꝫ comœdia diceret ego prius tragœdia fui, qa ex eisdem tragœdia nascit̃ & comœdia literis ac elementis, ut Aristoteles ait in libro de gñatione primo. Aut canis quidam si diceret, ego ante diu equus fui, propter cuiusdā equi corpus q̃d depastus est canis, q̃ alimento in substantiam rei alitę̃ conuerso, equus ille plebeio sermone dicatur ipsius canis πρόγονον σῶμα. i. progignens corpus fuisse, uidelicet unde prognatus sit. Non aũt equi aīam in canem transīisse, quispiam ex hoc sermone arbitrabitur. Qua igitur re Pythagoram docuisse crederem aīas trāsire in alia corpa, eo solum, q̃ se Euphorbum prius fuisse dixerit, cum hic manifeste constet atqꝫ cōueniat non qdem aīam, sed ipsum corpus iudicatum fuisse Euphorbum, & nihilominus hoc ipsius dictum non fuisse planū, sed merū ęnigma, q̃ arcanum q̃ddam illi seculo incognitum uoluerit innuere, scilicet materiam primam oīm formarum non solum capacẽ, sed auaram etiā esse ac semper desyderio motam nulla forma satiari. Quod M. Antonino Impatori philosophissimo ęque uisū fuit, cū in libro ad se ipm tertio scripsit. ὅτι οὐδὲν οὕτως φιλεῖ ἡ τῶν ὅλων φύσις, ὡς τὸ τὰ πάντα μεταβάλλειν καὶ ποιεῖν νέα ὅμοια. σπέρμα δὲ ῥότερ τινὰ πᾶν τὸ ὂν τοῦ ἐξ αὐτοῦ ἐσομένου. i. q̃ nihil ita cupit uniuersi natura ut entia transmutare & facere noua similia. Semen enim

modo

On the Art of Kabbalah

However, let us go back to that play on words relating to Euphorbus. Several good writers say on this that all the divine Pythagorean teachings indicate their allegorical transmission. The Pythagorean Apollonius of Tyana confirms this in the discussion he holds with the leading gymnosophist, Thespesion. In Book 6 of *Philostratus* he says: "If I verge on riddles, the wisdom of Pythagoras goes well with them. For to speak thus is what he handed down."

In his disputation with the Brahmans of India (in Book 3), he asks where they stand on the question of the soul. "Iarchas, like Pythagoras, taught you. So we taught the Egyptians: Apollonius took this up." Are you saying that you were one of the Trojans, as Pythagoras says he was Euphorbus?" Now mark, Marranus, how cannily Thespesion, who had been asking the questions, answered. He said that of all the Greek army that went to Troy, he thought him worthy of fuller admiration. To this, Apollonius said that for Homer, Achilles had taken first place. "Think of him as my ancestor, Apollonius," said Iarchas, "Or rather, as my begetting body, for this is what Pythagoras thought Euphorbus." Then he tells how Ganges, a former king of India and son of the river Ganges, had far surpassed Achilles in heroism, had himself been a "begetting body," which he himself now was.

The language here points to a transmigration of bodies rather than of souls. It is rather like some substance that can take this shape or that. Or it is like a comedy saying "I was tragedy before," because both tragedy and comedy were born of the same letters, the same alphabet, as Aristotle puts it in Book 1 of the *Generation of Animals*. If a dog were to say "I was a horse for a long time," because the dog had been feeding on the flesh of that horse, and because that food had subsequently been turned into the substance of the thing fed, that horse could in common speech be said to be that dog's begetting body; that is to say that the dog had been engendered by it. But let no one think from this turn of phrase that the soul of the horse has crossed to the dog.

Thus, I would think that Pythagoras' teaching, that souls migrate to other bodies, rests solely on his saying that he had been Euphorbus before. And from this it clearly appears, indeed it can only be appropriate, that he thought that it was not his soul but his body that had been Euphorbus. Nonetheless, what he said was not at all obvious, it was unalloyed allegory. He wanted by it to hint at a mystery unknown in his time, that basic matter is not only capable of taking all forms, but is filled with the desire, always impelled by the longing, not to be impregnated with any form at all.

The philosopher-emperor Marcus Aurelius had a similar view, for he wrote in Book 3 of *Meditations*: "The nature of the universe desires nothing so much as to change all beings, and to make new things like the old. For the seed is, in a way, everything, since it is itself the being of what will come out of itself."

modo quodam omine, ipsum est ens ex se futuri. Et idem in libro septimo, ἡ τῶν ὅλων φύσις, ἐκ τῆς ὅλης οὐσίας ὡς κηροῦ νῦν μὲν ἱππάρειον ἔπλασε, συγχέασα ἆῤ εἰς ἄνθρωπον φύσιν, ἐπεχρήσατο τῇ ὕλῃ αὐτοῦ ἐπὶ εἰς ἀνθρωπάκιον εἶτα εἰς ἄλλο τι. Vniuersi natura ex uniuersa essentia tanq cerae, nunc qdem equuleum sinxit. Confundens aūt id in arboris naturam, simul usa est materia eius. Deinde in homunculū tum in aliud quippiam. Vnde noīatur ab Orpheo natura istis epithetis πολυμήχανος μήτηρ .i. multū machinatrix mater. Et ἀλοξία μορφοδίαπις .i. alienarum figurarū decretrix. Quicquid fuerit, eqdem longe poti⁹ opinabor Pythagorā si Euphorbū, aut aliū quēpiā se fuisse dixerit, exēpli causa id aenigma introduxisse. Sin aūt credat historiā texuisse, profecto non aliam ob rem fecisse putandus est q̄ ut ostenderet posse aīam, separatam a corpore rursus eandē ipsam, autore deo, in idem ipsum corpⁱ redire q̄d penitus iam reliquit & deseruit, atq̄ nō in aliud ullum, unū nāq̄ & idem fuisse corpus q̄tumcunq̄ diuersis noībus appellatum, in q̄ toties reuixerit Pythagoras ab Iarcha Indorū sapientissimo iam pridem discere potuimus, non in magnitudine & quantitate, sed in substantia & entitate, ut mare quanq̄ est homogenes atq̄ unum, tn̄ hoc esse dicimus aegeum, illud Ionium, istud Myrtoum, aliud Crisaeum. Ita & unū hoīem sepius renatum primo noīarunt aethaliden, deinde Euphorbū, post Hermotimum, tum Pyrrhum, demū Pythagoram illum nostrum q tot regenerationes tanq̄ philosophus maxime speculatiuus & diuinus non attribuit naturę uiribus, sed soli deo, quem, ut refert Heraclides Ponticus in hac Palingenesia, Mercuriū nuncupauit, ut ostenderet neminē reuiuiscere nisi uirtute diuina. Nam ut Iustinus recitat ille philosophus & martyr christianus in paraenetico ad graecos, hoc deus cognomēto a Pythagora est honoratus p̄cipue, ut dicatur ἥχωσις τῶν ὅλων .i. Animatio uniuersorum, eo q̄ animā infundat hoībus uniuersis & insusam auferat & ablatam restituat q̄ties & qn̄ uoluerit, quale sepius etiam in aliis hoībus uisum & expientia certa cō pertum est, referentibus nobilissimis scriptoribus. Nam Aristeas q̄ndam Proconessi mortuus fuit in officina cuiusdam fullonis. Deinde septimo post anno, eius urbis ciuibus idem uiuus apparuit, & ipe tunc carmina de hyperboreis Arimaspis composuit, cuius in quarto historiarū Herodot⁹ egregie meminit. Caeterū uixit & in Armenia Er, genere Pamphylⁱ, q cū occubuisset in p̄lio, sublatis aliis decimo die cadauerib⁹ iam corruptis, integer qdem incorrupto corpore repertus fuit, domumq̄ delatⁱ pro officio sepulturae, ubi duodecimo a morte die dum pyrę esset impositus, resurrexit, & quae interim uiderat, retulit. Haec Plato scripsit de Repub. uolumine decimo. Huc etiā illud occurrit, q̄ legimus puellā Romae moī suā, cum sepulchro afferret a Tyanensi Apollonio uitae restitutam, in quarto Philostrati libro, & Alcestis q̄q̄ narrat ab Hercule resuscitata rursum diu uixisse. Tum Marran⁹ inquit. Q̄ prope accedis ad nostra Philolae, nam si

Book Two

And in Book 7 he writes: "The nature of the universe, from the essence of the universe, now makes, a foal, as if from wax. It melts it then into a tree, and the stuff of the tree is at the same time used up. Then into a little man. Then into anything at all." Hence the epithets Orpheus applied to nature—"Mother much-inventing," and "governor of many moulds."

Whatever else it may be, I prefer to think that when Pythagoras said he was Euphorbus—or indeed anyone else—he was introducing allegory for the sake of example. But if he is to be thought to have fabricated the story, he should be thought to have done so to no purpose other than to point out that a soul separated from the body may again, with God's help, return to that same body which it has totally abandoned and deserted—but not that it may go to any other body. That the body in which Pythagoras spent so many lives and was given so many different names was one and the same, we may learn from Iarchas the Indian sage. It is the same body not in size or extent, but in substance and entity. In the same way, although the sea is one homogeneous thing, we call this bit the Aegean, that bit the Ionian, this part the Myrtoan, another part the Crisan. So a single man several times reborn is first called Aethalides, then Euphorbus, later Hermotimus, next Pyrrhus, and at last, Pythagoras, our master.

As befits a speculative thinker on divine affairs, he did not attribute so many rebirths to the powers of nature, but to God alone, whom, as Herclides of Pontus mentions in Palingenesia, he called Mercury. So he showed that none might return to life without God. Justin Martyr, the Christian thinker, relates in *Encouragement to the Greeks* how Pythagoras honored God especially by calling him the "Lifeforce of the universe." He calls him this because he pours soul into all men, then takes it away, then returns it, when and how he wills it. Something of this kind is often seen in and ascertained by the actual experiences of other men, and the most celebrated writers refer to this. Aristeas of Proconnessus died once in a fuller's workshop. Then, seven years later, he appeared to his fellow townsfolk alive and composed the poems concerning the hyperboreal Arimaspi. Herodotus has recorded this outstandingly well in Book 4 of the *Histories*. Another case is that of Er, a Pamphylian living in Armenia. He was killed in battle, but when nine days later the bodies were cleared away, already in a state of decay, he was found untainted, his body quite fresh. He was carried home for the funeral, where twelve days after his death, as he was placed on the pyre, he came back to life, and gave an account of what he had seen in the intervening period. (This is in Book 10 of Plato's *Republic*.) We read in Book 4 of *Philostratus* of a similar occurrence when a girl who died in Rome was taken out of her tomb by Apollonius of Tyana and brought back to life by him. Alcestis too is said to have been resuscitated by Hercules and to have lived a long while thereafter.

MARRANUS: You are coming close to our ideas, Philolaus.

DE ARTE CABALISTICA

coram astaret Simon recenseret nobis de libris hebraicis q̃ deus olim abstulit de spiritu qui erat in Moyse & dedit septuaginta uiris. Post aliqua denuo tempora sublato ex hominibus Elia spiritus eiusdem iclinauit sup Eliseum, & item filium Sunamitidis ipse mortuũ reuiuiscere fecit. Addo nunc Samuelẽ mortuũ quem suscitauit quædam mulier in Endor, q̃ post resurrectionẽ suam cum Saule rege locutus est. Audi uero qd Ezechiel uiderit ille propheta, campum. s. plenum aridis ossibus mortuorũ, & accesserunt ossa ad ossa, unumq̃dq̃ ad iuncturã suam, & ecce sup ea nerui & carnes creuerunt, & extẽta est in eis cutis desup, & ingressus est in ea spiritus & reuixerunt, steteruntq̃ sup pedes suos. Hæc in sacris literis continẽtur hebræorum, multo plura uero in historiis Christianorũ descripta legunt. Eqdem pro me tibi hoc affirmare ausim, absq̃ parabola, sine ænigmate, & omni remota ironia, q̃ uere & plane Iesus Nazarenus fratrem Marthę suscitauit Lazarum noie quatriduo ante mortuũ. Adhuc cuiusdã etiam uiduæ filiũ extinctũ, uitæ reddidit. Et Iairi synagogæ principis filiã, aliosq̃ in sancta scriptura commemoratos. Huncipsum q̃q̃ Iesum resuscitauit deus, & in eius morte corpa multa eorum q uita defuncti erant surrexerunt, & exeuntes de monumentis uenerunt in sanctam ciuitatem & apparuerunt multis. Paulus deniq̃ Tarsensis Eutychum q casu e uita migrauerat, luci restituit uiuum. Martinus nondũ epũs, immo nõdum baptizatus, tres mortuos suscitauit. Possem catalogũ proferre hoim ab interitu ad uitam pristinam reuocatorũ, nisi tu nõ ignorares christianis nobis esse creditu facile, animos hoim redire in corpa, q generalem oim corporum humanorum resurrectionẽ rursus ad uiuendum futurã plane cõfitemur. De qua pulchre disertissimus Athenagoras atheniẽ. phũs p christianis librum integrum περὶ ἀναστάσεως certe doctis auribus dignum cõposuit. Et Turcis, Mauris, Agarenis, Mahometh in Alcoran sic loqtur. Illis dicentibus, cum eritis ossa, uel ad nihilũ redacti, qualiter efficiemini hoies noui? Responde. Licet lapidei uel ferrei uel si qd est durius essetis, q uos prima uice creauit, ad uitã denuo uos resuscitados reuocabit, hucusq̃ in Azoara xxvi. Et rursus in xlv. sic ait. Qui nos primo plasmauit, secundo uiuifica bit. Vnde Pythagorã tanto maiore uelim prosequamur ueneratione, q̃to is propius q̃ cæteri græcorum philosophi ferme in oibus aliis, non solu in hac causa, nostrę accessit fidei. Aristoteles eĩ uidemus q̃ nihil eorum credidit q̃ non uel manu tetigit, uel oculis cernere potuit, uel apprehẽdere syllogismo. Propterea in fine tractatus de gñatione & corruptione, reditum P mortui hois nullatenus admisit, debili admodũ argumẽto usus, & Alcmę oni magis q̃ suis pceptoribus assensus, contra tritum suo tpę prouerbium οὐκ ἄν εἶεν τὰ αἰθρίαντα. Quem sequuti sunt alii qppe cohors philosophãtium, in hoc rephendendi q̃ se oĩa scire, alios omnia ignorare psumentes

Pythagoram

On the Art of Kabbalah

If Simon was here with us he would give us the account in the Hebrew scriptures of how God once took some of the spirit which was in Moses and gave it to the seventy. Sometime after Elijah died, his spirit fell on Elisha and he brought the Shunamite's son back from death. Then there was the dead Samuel: he was brought to life by a woman of Endor and spoke to the king, Saul, after his resurrection. Indeed, take note of the vision of the prophet Ezekiel. He saw a plain filled with the dry bones of the dead, bones piled on bones, each attached to the appropriate joint, and then, sinews and flesh grew, and skin spread out over them, and the spirit went into them, and they lived again, and they stood on their own feet.

This is described in the Hebrew scriptures. The Christian stories contain much more. I will be so bold on my own account as to assert to you, without metaphor, allegory, or any shade of ambiguity, that Jesus of Nazareth did, in fact, raise Martha's brother Lazarus when he had been dead four days. He also brought a widow's dead son back to life. Then there was the daughter of Jairus, the synagogue head, and other incidents recorded in holy writ. This same Jesus was himself brought back to life by God, and at his death the bodies of many of those who had departed this life rose again, and walked out of their tombs and into the holy city, appearing to many. Lastly, Paul of Tarsus restored to this life Eutychus, who had died in an accident; and Martin, before he was ever a bishop, or even baptised, brought three men back from the dead.

I could give you a list of the men called back to life from death, if you were unaware of the fact that we Christians readily believe men's souls return to their bodies, and that it is firmly a matter of faith that there is to come a general resurrection of all the bodies of men.

The Athenian philosopher, Athenagoras, who puts things very clearly, put together on the Christians' behalf an entire book *On Resurrection*. It is well worth even the attention of scholars.

Besides this, in the Koran, Mohammed, addressing the Turks, the Moors, and the Saracens says: "To those who say 'when you are bones returned to nothing, what kind of new men will you be made into,' reply: 'Though you be made of stone or iron or something still harder, yet he who first created you will call you back to life to breathe again.'" (Surah 26) Then at 45 he says: "He who first fashioned us will again give us life."

I feel from this that we should afford greater respect to Pythagoras who came so much closer than any Greek thinker to our beliefs in everything, not just the present matter. We see Aristotle believing nothing he could not touch with his own hand, see with his own eyes, or discover by syllogism. Besides, at the end of the tractate *On Generation and Decay*, he allows men no return from death at all. He uses a weak argument, agreeing with Alcmeon rather than his own teachers, and denying the well-worn saying of his day that "the affairs of men move in a circle." The rest of the philosophical gang have followed him, feeling that they know everything there is to know on this and assuming that everyone else knows nothing.

LIBER SECVNDVS

Pythagorā post reliqs irrident, & illud Luciani exclamant. τίς ὠνήσεται, τίς ἀνὴρ ἄνθρωπον ἐθέλει βούλεται, τίς εἰδέναι τὴν † παντὸς ἁρμονίαν, καὶ ἀναβιῶναι πάλιν .i. Quis emet Pythagoram, qs sup hoiem esse uult, quis scire uniuersi harmoniam & reuiuiscere denuo? Ita eum ridicule sub hasta licitantur quasi contemnendā iumētorū mercem, aut uile mancipiū. Illis ego multa nosse libenter pmittam, dūmodo patiant & alios nōnihil didicisse. Id adeo nūc stomachū ego commotus aduersum eos q solent antiqssimis pceptorib⁹ & philosophiæ principibus facile detrahere, prolixius q̃ oportuit excandui, ut pnoscas, me Pythagorā q̃cp tuum nō secus amare q̃ par est, & calumniatores suos uehementer odisse, non hoies sed monstra hoium. Tum Philolaus. Quidam, inqt, sunt qbus ignoscendū est cp tam recondita & arcana mysteria nesciant, non em oia possumus oēs. Ideocp redeundū cum illis in gratiā erit si qua imprudentes infamauerint. Qui aūt in eo qncp silentio exercitati, Pythagoreorū togā candidā abiecerint, & cōtumelia cœperint eius doctrinæ maiestatē lædere ac tanti philosophi caput minuere, eos ego non solū arrogantes uerū etiam hoies impurissimos iudicauero, q̃rum e numero Xenophanes est q de illo in Elegia sua lusisse ita phibet, ut cū uidisset aliqn Pythagoras canē cædi, miseratus dixerit. Sine hunc, est em cari sodalis aīa quā eius ex uerbis agnoui. Sed ea qdem manifesta Diogeni Laertio extat sugillatio, cpcp item Plutoni apud inferos Pythagoræ discipuli conuiuant, q & ipse uiderit aīam Hesiodi æneæ columnæ alligatam gemētē & stridentē. Tum Homeri q̃cp aīam de ligno pēdentē, & serpentibus circundatā. Hæc & istis similia sycophantiarū crimina diffamationes & calumniæ sunt leuissimorū sophistarū, q contactu oīa fœdant, immundo & polluunt ore dapes & uestigia fœda relinquunt. Quod aūt de carniū & aīatorum oīm esu diuulgant, quē asserunt prohibuisse Pythagorā, fere nil me pturbat, qm sunt clarissimi autores q ea mēdacia refellant, ait em Aristoxenus ille insignis scriptor Pythagorā nō abstinuisse ab aīmatis sed carnes comedisse, q̃d Porphyri⁹ in lib. primo περὶ ἀρχῆς ἐμψύχων probat, eo cp athletas ab aliis caseo ab aliis ante ficub⁹ nutritos, ipse prior oibus cibo carniū aluerit, dixeritcp carnes habere uirtutē ad acqrendum robur incredibilē, ita Porphyrius. Et Apollodorus arithmeticus testatur illum boues centū imolasse cū repisset ὅτι τρίγωνον ὀρθογώνιον ἡ τὴν ὀρθὴν γωνίαν ὑποτείνουσα ἴσον δύα? ταῖς περιεχούσαις. i. q̃d trianguli orthogonii subiectū latus tantundē ualeret q̃tū quæ continerent. Fuit tn modestissimæ uitæ, medio cris nutrimēti, paucissimi potus, ut scripsit Lycō Iaseus de Pythagora. Vnde rarus fortasse carniū sibi usus erat, sepe em solo tenui melle pascebat, hæc oīa Athenæus de cœnis doctorū hoīm lib. x. Atcp ob id si studiosos literarū ea q̃ grauis cibi forēt diligēter uitare cōmonuisset, ne cerebrū ab incauto stomachi onere lederet, q̃ ualeret cōteplationi uehementius incūbere, qs hoc nō laudi daret tā fido pceptori? ut q̃ didicisset apud hebreos duri alimēti esse in eorū lege prohibita, q̃ itē apud Indos fugienda cognō

H

Book Two

They jeer at Pythagoras and a whole lot of others. They shout out Lucian's tag: "Who will buy Pythagoras? Who wants to be above man? Who wants to know the harmony of the universe and then return to life again?" So, as if he were sordid merchandise, or a broken-down slave, they put him up for auction and mockingly make their bids. I would admit that their knowledge is great, if they would only acknowledge that others have learned something too. I am now in such a rage against these people who make such an easy practice of condemning ancient teachers and eminent thinkers, that I have gone on fuming with rage for longer than I should. Forgive me for not loving your Pythagoras as is proper, but I hate his detractors. They are not men but monsters.

PHILOLAUS: There are some who are unaware of mysteries so hidden and arcane and they should be forgiven, for not all of us can know everything. We should pardon those who have quite unthinkingly uttered slander. As for those who once practiced that silence but now have tossed aside the white garment of Pythagoreanism, who have insolently begun to injure the majesty of this teaching, to insult so great a thinker—these men are not just arrogant in my reckoning, they are totally abandoned. Xenophanes is one of their number. It is said that he joked about him in his Elegy, saying that when Pythagoras saw a dog being hit he said wretchedly, "Leave him, it is the soul of a dear friend—I know him by the way he talks." Then there is the gross insult of Diogenes Laertes who said that the disciples of Pythagoras live in the underworld with Pluto, and that he himself had seen the soul of Hesiod tied to a bronze pillar, groaning and shrieking, and the soul of Homer hanging from a tree surrounded by snakes. These and others like them are the charges of sycophants, the smears and lies off flippant sophists. They foul everything with their noisome touch, their lips defile the feast, and they leave their filthy trails behind them.

As to the popular belief that Pythagoras forbade the eating of meat and all living things, I am unworried: distinguished authors have rebutted these lies. The well known writer Aristoxenus says that Pythagoras did not abstain from animals but ate meat, and Porphyry corroborates this in Book 1 of *The Beginnings of Living Things*. He says that Pythagoras was the first to give athletes a meat diet. Up till then they had eaten cheese or fig, but he said that meat had the power to develop strength. The arithmetician Apollodorus gives evidence that Pythagoras sacrificed one hundred oxen when he discovered that the hypotenuse of a right-angled triangle has the same value as the other two sides. He did, however, lead a life of great moderation. He ate reasonably and drank little, according to Lycon of Iassus. Perhaps, as Athenaeus says in Book 10 he ate meat but rarely and often had thin honey by itself. If his advice to those engaged in study was to take pains to avoid heavy food and not to let an incautiously overfilled stomach impede the brain, so as to drive them to apply themselves more earnestly to contemplation, who could but praise such a devoted instructor? He had learned from the Hebrews that tough food was forbidden by their Law, and in India had discovered that certain foods were to be shunned, such as saltwater fish, which is neither fit food for man nor fit offering to the gods (whoever heard of a fish sacrifice?). And then in Egypt he learned

DE ARTE CABALISTICA

uisset ueluti pisces marinos ne stomacho qdē utiles, nec deorū oblatiōibꝰ acceptos (nemo em̄ unq̄ in sacrificijs imolatū esse piscē audiuit) q̄ deniqꝫ apud ægyptios accepisset de faba, q̄ nō sit mūdum legumē, ut in Euterpe sua notauit Herodotus, ea plane in pabulū nō sumerēt, tranqllitatē mētis ꝑpetuo l̄rarum studio querentes, q̄q̄ eiuscemodi pia monita noluit tā exacte & ad unguē ueluti lege xii. tabularū obseruari. Nā & ipse porculis minusculis & hedis tenerioribus uictitasse a Xenophilo et Aristoxeno qbusdamqꝫ alijs natu maioribus, suis ꝓpe coetaneis proditus est, quē & nullo esse legumēto sæpiꝰ usū q̄ faba ut aluū sensim leuigaret, in quarto noctiū atticarū Aul. Gellii cōperies. At de fabis post iter cętera symbola explanabit, nūc de numeris ueniāt tibi priora in mente q̄ dixi & pōsteriora q̄ dicturus sum, ut agnoscas q̄ impie turpes qdā philosophię Sanniones primate philosophorū Pythagorā postica sanna subsannāt, q̄ numerū docuerit esse oībus rebus principiū, q̄ cū sit q̄titas discreta uerius sequaℓ res q̄ antecedat, quasi proiectiles fuisse calculos intellexerit ipse, a qbus oīa sint orta. Quos miror pariter nō sine risu, q̄ cū audierit crebro testātibꝰ sapientissimis hoībus oēm ferme philosophiā Pythagoricā, & eā maxie q̄ de rebus diuinioribus extet, mysticā esse, ac p̄ ænigmata proposita, nihilominꝰ tn̄ hanc sapiētię diuinissimā parte de numeris, imitādo Tyrrhenorū stultitia, plane ac citra oēm metaphora accipi iubeāt. Fuit aūt id priscis & uetustissimi æui sapiētibus in more p̄ arcanarū literarū allegorias & sensuū mysteria sapiētię profundā inq̄sitionē tradere. Sic oīa sunt antiq̄ssimorū tā philosophorū q̄ poetarū ænigmatibus plenissima, & propter rerū obscuritatē & propter leuē uulgi cōtemptū, πραγμάτων δὲ ἀνθρωπίνης ἀδηλίας οἰκαθορωμένων ὀψεῶς, ἀχρονίστερος ἑρμηνεὺς ὁ μῦθες. inqt Max. Tyrius in disputatione decima. i. Rerū em̄ ab humana infirmitate nō pspectarū manifeste, aptior interpres est fabula, ea uero philosophos recte decet q̄ sub pio figmētorū uelamine honestis & tecta rebus & uestita noībus enūciaℓ, Macrobio autore, quā ego curiosissime scholasticorū ingenia in rerū admirādarū notionē excitare ac introducere arbitror, minori em̄ diligentia queriℓ qd añ fores pstō est, q̄ qd lōge situ in abysso ꝓfūdi recōdit, ita facilitas apphēdēdi (expto crede) discipulis studiorū negligētiā parit, & frigide petiℓ qd facillie obtineℓ. Euenit et qn̄qꝫ nos ulla uerborū ꝓprietate res abstrusas effari nō posse, q̄s lōgis ambagibꝰ & uarie cōposito sermōe cogeremur enūciare, nisi fuisset cōmode reptū breui enigmate uti. Nemō ꝉ ludi ī rē est, nā assolet aduersis castris belli duces q̄dā syntagmata edicere q̄ tesseraℓ noiant, ut suos qsqꝫ dux īternoscere milites et se q̄qꝫ īter se q̄ant. queadmodū ī bello Cęsaris Venꝰ genitrix, & Syllæ Apollo Delphicꝰ, & Marii Lar deꝰ, & Iephthę Siboleth. Ita nō fuerit utiqꝫ idecorū symbola doctrinę peculiaria & arcana familiaribus tradere, ut qcūqꝫ discipulorū ea magis usurpassent, dilectiores fierēt magistro, iterqꝫ se plus cęteris diligeret. Vnde Pythagorei symbolis qbusdā arcanis sibi quādā indissolubilis

about the bean — which is not a vegetable for polite company, a fact noted by Herodotus in his *Euterpe*. Those seeking to achieve peace of mind in study should certainly not include these things in their diet. On the other hand he did not want his well-meant advice to be followed to the letter and in minute detail as if it were the Law of the Twelve Tables.[42] It is said by Xenophilus and Aristoxenes, slightly older contemporaries of his, that he himself ate small pigs and young goats, and you will find in Book 4 of Aulus Gellius' *Attic Nights* that of all vegetables, Pythagoras most used the bean to lighten his digestion.

Of beans, and other symbols, I will say more later. Now focus your attention on what I said before about numbers and on what I am about to say. I want you to realize how base and shabby are those who ape philosophy and mimic the leading man, Pythagoras, in the mocking terms I have already outlined. Pythagoras taught that everything begins with number, because when you take quantity and matter apart, you find that matter follows rather than leads. The way they have interpreted this, you'd think Pythagoras believed that the source of everything was a flying slide-rule. I am both amused and amazed that although they have plenty of good evidence that nearly all Pythagorean philosophy is mystical and allegorical, especially where it concerns the divine, yet they would have us think that its most profound part, that dealing with number, is absolutely straightforward and quite unmetaphorical, imitating Etruscans in their fatuity. It was the way of the ancient sages to pass on their deepest investigations by means of allegory in secret letters and mysterious senses. All the writings of the ancients are full of riddles, partly because of the obscurity of subject matter, partly from a faint contempt for the masses. Maximus of Tyre says, in *Disputation* 10, "in matters imperfectly understood because of human weakness, parable is the better interpreter." "A philosopher does well to declare what he knows under a fair veil of imagery, covered with appropriate facts and dressed up in names," says Macrobius. I myself think that the parable does arouse scholars' inquiring faculties and leads them to investigate mattters worthy of wonder: fewer pains are taken in the search for something to be found on the doorstep than for something hidden deep in the far abyss. Ease of comprehension leads to pupils neglecting their studies — believe me, I know — and the search for what is to be had with ease is a cold one. Then sometimes it happens that we do not have the right words to express abstruse ideas and would be compelled to handle them in very roundabout ways, with discussion from several angles, were it not that an easier method, using the brief riddle, has fortunately been discovered. This is quite in order. After all, in war, generals of both camps give out passwords by which officers and men can identify each other. In Caesar's war it was "Venus Genetrix," Sulla used "Apollo Delphicus," Marius used the god "Lar," Jephtha used "Shibboleth." There is nothing wrong with passing on private and secret symbols to one's intimates. The more the disciples take them over to their own use, the dearer they will be to the master, and the more will they love each other within the circle.

In this way the Pythagoreans have made for themselves by their secret symbols — or Precepts — a bond of indissoluble love and friendship.[43]

LIBER SECVNDVS   XXXVIII

amoris & amicitiæ cathenam fabrefecerunt. Erat em̄ Pythagoras conciliandæ amicitię in primis studiosissimus, ac si quē didicisset symbolis suis communicasse, eum continuo socium amicumq̃ conscicebat, subscriptore Laertio. Eoq̃ factū est ut ardētius cuperent oēs Pythagoricis symbolis, hoc est mysteriorum notis uti, tum q̃ futuri essent p̃ceptori gratiores, tum ut cunctis apparerent nobiles esse Pythagorei. Quo motus apud Plutarchū in octauo conuiualiū Philinus, ex oībus conuiuis Syllæ Carthaginēsis ip̃e solus inter epulas ab animatis abstinuit ut agnosceretur esse Pythagoreus Quare is a Leucio patria Tyrrheno Moderati Pythagorici discipulo rep̃hensus fuit plus illius dogmatis seq̃ scriptum q̃ sententiam, q̃d & in aliis Pythagoristis fuerat rep̃hēsiōe dignū, q̃ modeste affecti moribus sepatis & singularibus, uel in sociorum & amicorum cœnis panē non frangebāt ut cæteri, uel cerebella non edebant, uel surgentes ab epulis stragula conuoluebant, uel nudis pedibus sacrificabant, uel locuturi, a sole se auertebant, uel relicta populari uia, p̃ diuerticula discedebant, uel cum ridentibg̃ nunq̃ aut parum ridebāt, uel a fabarum esu prorsus abstinebant, similiaq̃ egregie usurpabant magis sup̃stitione q̃ recta ratione ducti. Sola imitantes ad corticem symbola, negligentes uoluntatē, ut talibus notis innotesce rent, & uulgo Pythagorici eiusdē ordinis uiderent. Sunt igit̃ eiuscemodi symbola unius collegii signa. Cæterū addamus etiā q̃ diuinarū & humanaru rerū ampissima spacia dimetiētibus nobis & innumera tractantibus memoriæ plurimum conferant ænigmatica symbola, hoc est notæ q̃ sigū tur animo, ut quotiens recordari libuerit, cito nostris obtutibus offerant, symbolum ergo de rerum principiis cōmodissimū erit, unum & duo, q̃d enim citius occurrit res singulas intuentibus q̃ unū & duo, cum causas & originem uniuersorum scrutari uolum̃? Nam primo aspectu cernit̃ ocu   S
lis id q̃d est idē ipsum, & non est alterum. Ex q̃ ante oīa mente concipimus q̃ idem & alterum sunt unū & duo, Alcmeon aūt Crotoniates qui Pythagoræ uixit ætate, duo appellauit multa, q̃ dixit esse cōtrarietates tanq̃ lite forte Empedoclis, uaga tñ posuit illa et sine fine diuersa ut album & nigrū dulce & amarū bonum & malum, paruum & magnum. Aristotele in p̃ mo post naturalia teste. Pythagorici aūt diuersa illa rerum inter se ultro citroq̃ contrariarū, quas Alcmæonii contrarietates appellarunt propter arithmeticę artis amorem in numerum coartarunt denariū, celebrē illum & oīa continentem, ut finitum & infinitum, impar & par, unum & multa, dextrum & sinistrū, masculinū & fœmininū, quiescens & motū, rectum et curuū, lucē & tenebras, bonū & malū, quadrū & oblongū. At hęcita sunt utralibet, q̃ duo sunt, icc̃irco diuersa sunt qm̄ duo sūt. Nam si unū essent, contraria non essent. In decē uero uniuersa redegerunt, q̃ iste numerus   T
oium est perfectissimus, quo cunctæ nationes & oēs populi p̃ter Thra

H ii

188

Book Two

Above all else, Pythagoras was anxious to bring about friendship, and he immediately considered as his friend and ally anyone who had been taught his Precepts and now participated in them (see Laertius). Thus it came about that everyone desired even more ardently to know the Pythagorean Precepts, the distinguishing marks of his mysteries, so that they might be dearer to their teacher and might be seen as noble Pythagoreans by the rest of the world. It was to this latter end, according to Plutarch, in Book 8 of *Table Talk*, that Philinus was the only diner at the feasts of the Carthaginian Sulla not to eat meat, in order that others should know him to be a Pythagorean. Philinus was reproached for this by Leucius, an Etruscan disciple of the Pythagorean Moderatus, who said that he had followed the letter of the teaching rather than the spirit. It was a blameworthy trait in other Pythagoreans too, who affected special and different modes of behavior to excess. At dinner with comrades and friends they would break bread in a way different from the rest, or they would refuse to eat brains, or they would get up from a banquet and wrap themselves in a shroud, or make their sacrifices in bare feet, or turn away from the sun when talking, or leave the highway and depart by the footpaths, or never laugh when others do, or give up beans altogether. They were led enthusiastically to adopt these practices and others like them by superstition rather than right reason. They imitated the Precepts' outer shell, overlooking their inner purpose, and did so to become known by this kind of sign and to be seen by ordinary people as belonging to Pythagoras' band.

Following the precepts in this way was the sign of one fellowship. But I must add that in our analysis of the vast areas of human and divine affairs, where we handle countless matters, those gnomic metaphors suit the memory more — they are like markers fixed in the mind. Whenever we want to remember something, they are quickly spotted.

The most useful Precept on the question of the basis of nature will be "One and Two," because when we want to examine the causes and origins of the universe, it is these that come most quickly to mind. Upon first sight one sees that something that is identical with itself is not something else, and so immediately we grasp mentally the fact that "same" and "other" are "one" and "two." Alcmaeon of Croton, a contemporary of Pythagoras, called "two" "many," which he said was made up of contraries — rather like the "strife" of Empedocles — but he proposed that they were unfixed and endlessly diverse. The contraries are things like white and black, sweet and bitter, good and bad, small and large — see Book 1 of Aristotle's *Metaphysics*. But the Pythagoreans went further and in their love of the science of arithmetic confined those diverse qualities of things, opposite in every way, (which Alcmaeon's school called contraries), to a denary number, that celebrated number that comprehends all things, so that it is finite and infinite, equal and unequal, one and many, right and left, male and female, still and moving, a straight line and a curve, light and darkness, good and bad, square and oblong. These things can be either of two, because they are "two," and it is because they are two that they are different. If they were "one," they would not be contraries.

They reduced the whole body of things to a ten. This number is the most perfect of all numbers, and, except for the Thracians, all nations and peoples,

DE ARTE CABALISTICA

cas cum græci tum barbari singulas res numerant non sistentes citra, nec progredietes ultra, tanq̃ naturalibus calculis decē digitorũ. Sane illius pfectione ostendit iste ornatissimus mundus quē cernimus decē tm sphæris iuxta Pythagoreos moueri, tanto etiā reliqs est pfectior q̃to plura numerandi genera continet, par, impar, quadratũ, cubum, longum, planũ, primum incompositũ, & primũ compositũ, q̃ nihil absolutius cp in decē proportionibus quatuor cubici numeri consumant q̃bus dicunt Pythagorici uniuersa cōstare. Archytas q̃cp nobilis Pythagoreus ille Tarantinus oē q̃d est, denario numero cōplectit, quē stagirita imitatus Aristoteles peripateticorũ gymnasiarcha, decē genera entis noīat decē categorias q̃ noīe sibi uolumen inscribere placuit ostēdenti philosophice, ut Eustathius uoluit decem πϱάματα .i.entia realia, ut Alexander Aphrodisieus decē φωνάς .i.uoces, ut Porphyrius decē νοήματα .i.intellectus siue cōceptus. Vel ut Iamblichus forte rectius decē uoces simplices, non ut uoces, sed ut significātes res ipsas simplices medio decē cōceptuũ simpliciũ. Assentiunt huic Alexāder ægeus, Ammonius Hermiæ, & Simplicius, insignes sapientiæ amatores q̃ etiā gnauiter arbitrati sunt in istis decē generalissimis entib⁹ duo q̃dā p̃cipua repiri posse in q̃ diuidant, tāetsi ab una essentia ortis, ueluti substātiam & accidēs, siue corporeũ & incorporeũ, seu materiale & immateriale, aut simplex & compositũ. Ita nancp duo amat denarius ut ab uno progressus nascat p duo, & per duo redeat in unũ. Primus eñ incompositus ternarius est ex uno & duobus nō q̃dē cōpositus sed cōstans, q̃a unũ non het positionē secũdũ Iāblichũ, nō facit ergo cōpositionē, q̃n uerborũ seq̃ uolum⁹ ppietatem. οὔτε γὰϱ ἡ μονὰς μεϱίζ⟨ε⟩ἐπὶ μονὰς θέσιν πϱοσλαμβάνει οὔτε ἡ στιγμὴ μεϱίζ⟨ε⟩ στιγμὴ τὴν θέσιν ἀποβάλλ⟨ει⟩. ut inq̃t Simplici⁹ in cōmētariis sup p̃dicamētũ q̃ti. i. Necp eñ unitas manēs adhuc unitas positionē assumit necp pũct⁹, manēs pũct⁹ positionē abiicit. Ex q̃ differētiā cognoscere possum⁹ q̃ distat unitas a pũcto. Cũcp nihil sit añ unũ, recte dicim⁹ unũ esse primũ. Binari⁹ aũt nō est cōposit⁹ ex numeris, eo cp ex sola unitate una & una coordinet, & ideo prim⁹ numer⁹ est, q̃a prima multitudo est, a nullocp pōt numero metiri, pterq̃ a sola unitate oīm numerorũ mēsura cōi, semel eñ duo, nihil aliud q̃ duo est, q̃obrē ea mltitudo q̃ appellat ternari⁹, uerissime ab arithmeticis numer⁹ prim⁹ icōpositⁱ nũcupat, binari⁹ eñ hũc p̃cedēs nō est icōposit⁹ numer⁹, sed magis pprie nō cōposit⁹. Cupiēs itacp ternari⁹ nō esse ociosⁱ, q̃n potiⁱ bonitatē suā ĩ oēs creaturas abscp iuidia mltiplicari, de uirtute pgrediēdo ad opationē, illud fœcũdũ q̃d est in eo multũ multitudis, p̃du ctiuũ taq̃ numeri de nuo, et illud eēntiale q̃d est ĩ eo unũ oīs, p̃ductiōis fōs et origo simul & oīs, pcessiōis initiũ, & oīs substātiæ imutabilis p̃manētia ppetua mēte intuet ac respicit, & ita sese in se ipm retorquet, p modũ unitatis & duitatis semetipsũ multiplicās atcp dices, semel bis duo sũt quatuor

whether Greek or barbarian count in tens, neither more nor less, as if by the natural measure of the fingers. This most beautifully ordered world demonstrates the number's perfection: we see it moving, according to the Pythagoreans, in ten spheres. The world is more perfect, the more it contains many modes of numbering: equality, inequality; squares, cubes; length and area; primes or compound numbers. It could not be more complete in that four cubic numbers are used in ten proportionate relationships and on them, say the Pythagoreans, all things stand. Archytas of Tarentum, a leading Pythagorean, included everything that exists in the decad, and following him, Aristotle of Stagira, head of the Peripatetics, listed ten modes of being, or ten categories, which is the name he gave to his book on philosophy. Eustathius wanted ten "real things," Alexander of Aphrodisia spoke of ten "voices," and Porphyry had ten "senses" or "concepts." Iamblichus was much more accurate with his ten "simple voices," rather than just "voices," meaning the actual simple things in the ten simple concepts. Alexander of the Aegean, Ammonius son of Hermias, and Simplicius, all distinguished seekers after truth, agree with this. They believed most strongly that in these ten very general things, two especially could be seen between which they were divided, though derived from the same essence. Such might be substance and accidents, or corporeal and incorporeal, or material and immaterial, or simple and compound.

Now the decad loves two for, starting from one, it is arrived at by two; and it is by two that it is reduced to one. The first prime number is a triad, for it is not made up of one and two, but fixed. "One," in the words of Iamblichus, has no position, and cannot therefore be ranged together with others in composition. Simplicius in his commentary, *Problems of Quantity*, says "Unity, while it remains unity, does not admit of position, whereas a point, while it remains a point, does not reject position. In this we see the difference between unity and a point. Since nothing comes before one, we are right to say that one is first. But duality is not made up of numbers, because it commences from unity only, one and one. Thus it is the first number, being the first plurality. No number is its measure, unless you count sole unity, which is the common measure of all numbers. At the same time, two can be nothing but two, so that it is the plurality that is called a triad that mathematicians rightly term the first prime number, for the duality that precedes it is not a prime, but better a non-compound number.

The ternary number has no desire to rest idle: quite without jealousy it wants its goodness to be multiplied in all creatures. Moving from capacity to action, it contemplates that fecundity that is in it, a huge multitude, producing numbers from number as it were, and looks upon that essential which is in it, the source and origin of all generation and at the same time of all progress, and the persistent quality of all immutable substance. So it turns itself on itself, by means of unity and duality multiplying itself, saying "twice two is four."

LIBER SECVNDVS   XXXIX.

Ecce tetractys illa quaternitudo de qua mihi tecũ ante sermo fuit, hęc est oĩm q̃ creata sunt Idea, qm̃, ut aiũt arithmetici, quaternario oĩs progressio pficit. Vnde oriŕ decas illa quã appellam˙ decẽ oĩm rerũ gña gñalissima. Nã unũ duo tria quatuor de oĩ potẽte potẽtia ad energiæ actum exeũtia producũt decẽ, q̃rũ dimidiũ est qnq̃, pone igitur in mediũ qnq̃ tanq̃ aliquem signiferũ in medio exercitus & in eius latere dextro numerũ proxime supiorem q est sex, & in latere sinistro numerũ, pxime inferiorẽ q est quatuor, hæc duo iuncta etiã constituunt decẽ, pone iterum in latere eius dextro numerum proxime supiorem q est septem, & in latere sinistro numerum proxime inferiorem q est tria, hæc duo iuncta similiter constituũt decem, pone rursus in latere dextro numerum proxime supiorem qui est octo, & in latere sinistro numerum proxime inferiorem qui est duo, hæc duo iuncta constituunt q̃q̃ decem. Pone demum in latere dextro reliqua nouem, & in latere sinistro unum. Iam q̃ reduc illa nouem ad unũ & resurgunt decem, q̃ rursus ad uiginti relata incipiunt denuo esse unitas, & deinceps ad oẽs numeros Cardinales usq̃ ad cẽtum, sicut eñ bis unũ faciũt duo, & ter unum tria, & quater unum quatuor & similiter ultra, ita bis decem faciũt uiginti, & ter decem triginta & quater decem quadraginta, & similiter ultra, non aliter de centum, non secus de mille, ac ultra. Hæc qdẽ ratio erit cur decem per iota quæ uirgula est erecta græce scribimus, aut per solum punctum hebraice notamus, quæ tñ signa tam barbaris q̃ latinis alioqui simplicem repræsentant unitatem, quippe a qua numerus denarius oritur, & in quam desinit, cuius Pythagoricũ extat symbolum uidelicet unum duo, quæ Zaratas Pythagoræ pceptor per noĩa propagatiõis pronunciare consueuit unũ appellando patrẽ, & duo matrem, testimonio Plutarchi Cheronensis in Timæi Psychogonia. Nã ut ante accepisti unũ & duo cum essentia diuina producunt quaternitudinẽ illam Tetractyn Ideam oĩm rerum denario numero cõsummatarũ. Eam Pythagoras affirmat esse πηγὰν ἀενάου φύσεως .i. Fontem perpetuæ naturę, q̃ nihil aliud est q̃ cognitio rerum in mente diuina rationabiliter operãte. Mentem uero ipsam dei Pythagoras numerũ allegorice nuncupauit, cum diceret numerum esse uniuersorũ principiũ. Ita eñ Plutarchus in libro de placitis philosophorum quarto scribit. τὸν δ᾽ ἀριθμὸν πυθαγόρας ἀντὶ τοῦ προσλαμβάν .i. Numerum aũt Pythagoras pro mente accipit. Signum plane haud iniquum, qa in incorporeis nihil diuinius mente, in se patis nihil simplicius numero. Nec pterea cogitari aliqd potest menti similius, & ab hoc ppetuæ naturæ fonte per riuos & cannales defluit numerus Pythagoricus unum & duo, id q̃d ab æterno in ipso fonte immẽsi Oceani, fuit, erit, ĩmo semp est, ubertim scatẽs, q̃ hoĩes prisco seculo noĩarit Zena ipsum illud unum (ut Aristoteles uoluit hoc Homeri citãs. ἐν κοίρανος ἔσω .i. un˙ princeps sit)

H iii

Book Two

Here we have the Tetractys, that quaternity of which I spoke before. It is the Idea of everything created, for, as the mathematicians say, all progression is derived from four. From it arises the decad that we call the ten general, generalizing groups of things. One, two, three and four proceed from all-powerful capacity to the act of energy, and produce ten, whose mean is five. Place five in the middle, like a standard bearer in the midst of the army. On its right-hand side place the next number up, six, and on its left-hand side the next number down, four. The sum of these two is ten. Then, on the right-hand side put the next number up, and on the left hand the next down, three. These two also make ten. Again, on the right put the next number up, eight, and on the left the next number down, two. The sum of these two is again ten. Lastly, put the remaining number, nine, on the right, and one on the left. Add nine and one and the answer is ten. In relation to twenty, ten starts again as unity, and so on for all cardinal numbers up to a hundred. Just as twice one is two, three ones are three and four ones are four, and so on; so twice ten is twenty, three tens are thirty, four tens are forty, and so on. Going further, one hundred and one thousand are no different, and so it goes on. This will explain why ten is written in Greek with an iota, an upright line, and in Hebrew with a simple point. These signs stand for simple unity, both to those who understand Latin and those who don't, for from it the decad arises and in it it ceases. It is to this that the Pythagorean precept "One, Two" relates. Zaratus, who taught Pythagoras, used to recite this, calling one "father," and two "mother," according to Plutarch of Chaeronea, in *On the Procreation of the Soul in the Timaeus*. For, as you have already heard, one and two, together with the divine essence, make that quaternitude, the Tetractys, the Idea of all things, which is to be brought to its highest perfection in the decad. This, said Pythagoras, was the source of everlastingness, nothing other than cognition of things in the divine mind operating in accordance with reason.

Indeed, Pythagoras said that the mind of God was number, metaphorically speaking, when he said that number was the basis of everything. So in Book 4 of *Beliefs of the Philosophers*, Plutarch wrote "Pythagoras takes number for mind." The metaphor is not a bad one. In the realm of the incorporeal, nothing is more divine than mind; and with particular things there is nothing more absolute than number. There is nothing that can be thought to resemble mind more, and from this source of everlastingness the Pythagorean "One and Two" has flowed in streams and channels, which from eternity has been, will be and always is in that boundless source, the enormous sea, welling up in abundance. In earlier ages men called it Zena (as Aristotle does, citing Homer's "Let there be one king"). They called him Zena rather than

DE ARTE CABALISTICA

dicentes Zena pro Zeua uidelicet a uiuendo, quem Romani Iouê quasi Zeua nuncuparunt,& Cornutus in libro de græca theologia illum asserit totius mundi esse aïam. Duo autê, noïata est Hera, illius Zenos hoc est Iouis & soror & coniunx, de quo sic Homerus in decimoquarto Iliados. Ἥρα δ' εἰσεῖδε χρυσόθρονος ὀφθαλμοῖσιν αὐτοκασιγνήτην καὶ εἴρα ζῆνα δ' ἐπ' ἀκροτάτης κορυφῆς πολυπιδάκου ἴδης ἥμενον .i. Hera hoc est Iuno aspiciebat aurithrona oculis eundem fratrê & Leuirum Zena, hoc est Iouê in summo cacumine plurifontanæ Idæ sedentem. Quo facilius sensa possumus sapientissimorᵹ poetarum de origine rerū cognoscere, cp̃ in multifontana Ida q̃ mons sic a prospectu nominatur, ἀπὸ τῆς ἰδεῖν a præcognitione ἐκ τοῦ ἰδῶ τὸ γινώσκω Iupiter & Iuno resident, tanq̃ unum & duo in quaterniõis. Idea illa riuosa, Vnde fluūt oĩm rerum principia quæ philosophi ætate posteriori formā & materiam noĩarūt. Idemcp̃ apud nos est forma & materia prima quod apud uetustissimos philosophos unum & duo, apud idoneos illustrescp̃ poetas Iouis & Iuno, q̃ coeunt in Gargari montis Ida & conueniunt in diuine mentis Idea, binis ambo bigis & quatuor ambo equis ducunt̃, sed descendendo Iupiter in olympo manet, Iuno ad inferiora tendit Homero teste sic dicens. ἔμη γὰρ ὁ τομείς πολυφόρβου πείρατα γαίης. νῦν δὲ σοῦ εἵνεκα δεῦρο κατ' οὔλυμπε τὸ δ' ἱκάνω .i. Vado uisura pabulosæ extrema terræ, nunc autê tui causa huc p̃ olympi istud uenio, Neuter tñ alterum oĩno deserit. Hoc igitur modo exit à mente diuina uniuersi exordium. Respiciens eñ Tetractys ad sui essentiam q̃ est prima unitas, oĩm productrix, & simul originê suam a primo producto reminiscês q̃m binarius est, sic ait semel unum bis duo, mox constat quaternarius habens in cacumine uerticis sui summam unitatem, fitcp̃ subito pyramis, cuius basis est quaternarius planus apud arithmeticos supficiem significans. Sũp quam diuinæ unitatis iam memoratæ lux radians formam & speciê facit ignis incorporei. Propter Iunonis hoc est materiæ discessum ad inferiora, unde confestim oritũ natura luminis essentialis, non ustiui, sed illuminantis. Et hæc est creatio mundi medii, quem Simon Iudæus appellauit sup̃mum, q̃a deitatis mūdus compatione non patitur, ideocp̃ se iudice supersup̃mus & incompabilis ille noĩatur. Recte uero medius hic dicitur olympus, quia totus lucidus & separatarū formarum plenissimus est ἵν' ἀθάνατον ἕδος Iliados octauo .i. ubi immortalium area supficies siue pauĩetū extat, cognoĩatur eñ habitaculum deorum, seu ut rectius Maro in æneidos decimo Deum domus alta, cuius q̃dem culmen est unitas, parietes trinitas & supficies quaternitas. Idcp̃ dari us cerniť cum iam numerus a diuinitate sua emanãdo paululū declinauerit & diuerterit ad creaturarū figuram, tunc eteñ ponamus simul & pro Tetracty tetragonū, & in q̃libet eius angulo punctũ instar unitatū, & pro unitate fastigii q̃ nunc cœpit habere positionem eleuemus q̃tum fieri pōt

summum

Zea because of the Greek "Zen" meaning living. The Romans said Jove, for Zea, and Cornutus says in his book on Greek theology that he is the soul of the whole world. Two is called Hera, both wife and sister of Zenos or Jove, of whom Homer wrote in Book 14 of the *Iliad*: "Hera (Juno) looked and saw on his golden throne Zea (Jove), her brother and brother-in-law, seated on the topmost peak of many-fountained Ida." We can thus very readily appreciate the wisest poets' notions of how things begin. On many-fountained Ida (so called for its view, *idein* being to see; or for foreknowledge, *ido to ginosk* — seeing is understanding), sit Jove and Juno, one and two in the tetrad, that flowing-stream Idea.[45] Thence flow the bases of all things, which later philosophers call form and matter.

What we call form and matter are the same as the "One and Two" of the ancient philosophers, and the Jove and Juno of the great poets, who meet on Ida, the Gargarean Mountain, and come together in the Idea of the divine mind. They ride in two chariots, drawn by four horses. Jupiter stays on Olympus once there, Juno looks after the lower world. Homer portrays her saying "I rush on to see the ends of the bountiful earth. But now, for your sake, I come here to Olympus." Neither completely deserts the other. It is in this way that the basis of the universe proceeds from the divine mind.

The Tetractys scrutinizes its essence, the first unity, from which everything is produced, and at the same time reflects on its own origin, derived from the first, and on its dual nature. So it says "once one, twice two;" now there stands a quaternity, having at its topmost point the highest unity, and suddenly it becomes a pyramid, whose base is the four-sided plane figure which mathematicians call a surface. Above it shines the beaming light of the divine unity now called to mind, this light has the form and appearance of incorporeal fire. This is because of the departure of "Juno-matter" to the lower world, from which arises instantly the essential nature of that light that does not burn, but illuminates. And this is the creation of the middle world which Simon the Jew called the highest of all, the world of the deity which admits of no comparison, which he termed "supersupreme and incomparable." Indeed Olympus is rightly called the middle world, all clear, filled with distinct form, "where is the court or pavement, of the immortals" (*Iliad*, Book 8). It is also called the "gods' dwelling-place," or, as Virgil puts it more accurately in Book 10 of the *Aeneid*, "the Gods' high house," whose summit is a unity, whose sides are trinity, whose floor is quaternity.

This is seen more clearly when number falls away a little from its emanating divinity and turns to the shape of created things. Now we may use a tetragon in place of the Tetractys; we put a point, as a unity, in any one of its angles, and in place of the unity at the point of the roof, which now starts to occupy space, we erect the apex at the greatest possible height.

summũ apicē. Eo pacto, quatuor latera in altũ erecta, quatuor erũt triãgu/
li sup latitudine sua quadrãgula cõstructi, & in unũ pũctũ excelsum ducti,
ecce pyramis ipsa, q̃ est forma ignis, testimonio Timei Locri Pythagorei
in lib. de aĩa mũdi dorice sic scribentis. ἡ δὲ πυραμὶς τέσσαρας βάσιας κỳ τὰς
ἴσας γωνίας ἔχοισα. ῥυτίθεται, εἶδος πυρὸς ἐυκινατότατον καὶ λεπτομερέστερον. i. ex q̃ py
ramis quatuor bases & æquales angulos habens cõponit, forma ignis p̃ q̃
mobilissima & tenuissima. Est ea sane absq̃ materia, lux essentialis separata
proxima deo & uita sempiterna, ut in duodecimo libro q̃ postnaturalia in
scriptus est, & in secundo de cœlo legit̃ sic. Mentis opificiũ est uita, dei aũt
operatio est immortalitas, istud aũt est uita æterna. Hæc a Pythagoreis
mutuatus est Aristoteles. Atqui deus ipse non est lux creata, sed luci/
bilis autor oĩs lucis, quare pyramidem absolutissimã & retractissimã a tri
angula basi in altitudinem sese erigentē q̃ similiter igneum uigorē signifi
cat Deus Opt. Max. in diuina secum trinitate incompabilis mundi conti/
net. Vnde & Chaldæi & Hebræi deum esse ignem phibent. Quam uero
pyramidem quaternio producit, ignea lux est in corporei & immaterialis
separatarum intelligentiarũ mũdi, extra cœlum uisibile, q a græcis uocat̃
αἰών a nobis seculum æthernitas & æther. Vnde & æthra fulgor ætherni
tatis dicitur, ubi non est corpus, necq̃ locus, necq̃ uacuũ, necq̃ tempus, necq̃
senectus, necq̃ transmutatio, sed ibi sunt entia inalterabilia & impassibilia
optimam habentia uitam qua toto æone id est æthernitate seu eyo fruũt
Hæc ferme sunt ipsa uerba stagiritę Aristotelis, q̃ tam ipse q̃ Platonici &
Socratici ex Pythagora suxerunt, q̃ sic in aureis carminibus scripsit. Si re/
licto corpe in ætherem liberum pueneris eris immortalis deus, & his sci
licet in hac uita supatis cognosces immortaliũ deorum & mortaliũ hoĩm
cohabitationem quam eleganter ipse appellat σύστασιν a simul stando. per q̃d
tres nobis proprietates medii ostendit mundi, quem liberum æthera no
minat, ut q̃ a materiæ potentia segregatus & p̃seruatus in libertate cale/
scat dei ardore, ac insensibili motu inferiora calefaciat, dicitur em̃ æther
ἀπὸ τ̃ ἀεὶ θέρειν ἤτοι θερμαίνειν hoc est a semp calefaciendo. Proprietates autem
illius sunt hæ, conditio, chorus, & ordo. Mundi eius conditio est cp̃ totus
quicq̃d est purissima forma est, cuius asserũt Iouialem esse naturam, q̃ im
mortalia & mortalia informet, & sotu specifico cuncta utriusq̃ mundi in
suo esse conseruet, de q̃ extat illud Maronis. O pater o hoĩum diuũcq̃ ęter
na potestas, propterea ob fomentariũ calorem spiritalis sol ueteribus Iu
piter dictus est. Vnde salii Martis gradiui sacerdotes eum appellarũt Lu
cecium & Cretenses Phosphorũ, ab eocq̃ denoiatus est olympi, ʃ cp̃ totus
fulgeat, in q̃ Iouis totus p̃sidet & pest, immo totum q̃d est ipse est. Hinc il
lud q̃cp in ix. ænei. Annuit & totum nutu tremefecit olympũ. Eius inq̃ cõ
ditio est receptare formas simplices immateriales separatas p se existētes. ta

H iiii

Book Two

Once done, four faces are raised on high, four triangles constructed on the four-sided base, reaching to the one point at the top. Here then is the pyramid which, according to the Pythagorean Timaeus of Locri is the form of fire.[46] He writes in his book *On the World Soul*: "Because the pyramid has four bases, with equal angles, it is the form of fire, being very mobile, and very fine."

That this distinct light of essence, closest to God and eternal life, is altogether absent in matter, is found in Book 12 of the *Metaphysics*, and Book 2 of *On the Heavens*, where Aristotle writes "The mind's work is life, but God's work is immortality, or eternal life," and he took this from the Pythagoreans. However, God himself is not created light, but the enlightening source of all light. Thus, Deus Optimus Maximus, God most great, most good, comprehends within himself a perfect and distinct pyramid which rises to its apex from a three-sided base and also signifies the power of fire. He holds it with him in the divine Trinity of the incomparable world. Hence Chaldeans and Hebrews hold that God is fire.

The pyramid produced by quaternity is the fiery light of the incorporeal and immaterial world of distinct intelligences. It can be seen beyond the heavens. The Greeks called it *aeon*; we call it "age," "eternity," where there is neither body, nor place, nor vacuum, nor time, nor age, nor change. There are immutable, impassible beings. They have the best life, and enjoy it to all the *aeon*, to all eternity. Almost all of this comes from Aristotle who, along with the Platonists and Socratics, imbibed it from Pythagoras, who wrote in the *Golden Verses*:

> When you cast aside the body you come to the free aether, you will be a god and immortal. When the things of this life are overcome you will know the dwelling together (which he elegantly termed *sustasis*, because they "stand together") of immortal gods and mortal men.

He pointed out three characteristics of the world which he calls "free aether;" a world set apart and kept free from the power of matter which glows with the heat of God, and by its movement, imperceptible to sense, heats the lower world; it is called aether from its continual heating (*therein*, in Greek). These are its characteristics: its constitution; its harmonious motion; and its order.

This world is constituted out of all the purest form. It is said that in nature it is like Jove, whose nature gives form to things, mortal and immortal, and particularly cherishes all things of either world, preserving them in him. Virgil writes of him "O Father, O eternal power over men and gods," and because of his lenitive spiritual heat Jove was called sun by the ancients. The Salii, priests of Mars Gradivus, called him Lucecius, and in Crete he was Phosphorus. From him was Olympus given its name, because it glittered all over when Jove sat and stayed there; all that is, he is. Hence that line in Book 9 of the *Aeneid* "He nodded, and all Olympus trembled."

Thus, the constitution of this world is to take in simple immaterial and

DE ARTE CABALISTICA

uniuersales q̃ idiuiduas. Continet em̃ oēs Ideas Ideatas generum & specie
rum ceu exempla ipsa contractioribus exemplariis imitanda, q̃rum exem
plar signatorium consistit in mente diuina. Sic enim nominari uolum⁹ q̃d
est in mundo deitatis exemplar absolutum. In mūdo intelligibili exēplum
abstractum, & in mundo sensibili non exemplum sed exemplariũ illud cō
tractum, quō sigillum, figura, & cera sigillata. Huc accedit secundo chorus
altera proprietas ἀπὸ τῆς χαρᾶς .i. a gaudio beatorum spirituũ infinito & uo
luptate immutabili deorũ dictus, quernæ illius habitaculi & ciues olym
pionicæ myrtea corona ouantes ambrosia & nectare diuini conuiuii ppe
tuo fruunt, ridentes risum inextinguibilem. De q̃ sapientissimus poetarũ
Homerus ἄσβεϛος λάρινθρο γέλως μακάρεσσι θεοῖσιν .i. Inextinguibilis certe exci
tabatur risus beatis diis, q̃d omnino lętitiã illorũ sempiternã ostendit, quã
iugi concentu citharis & cæteris musarum instrumētis, tripudio, choreis,
symposiis, quietis cubilibus, & interdũ dulci somno, pclarus ibidem Me
lesigenes eleganter in Iliados primo libro expressit. Quid ni Marrane?
Quænã pōt maior cogitari uoluptas q̃ deũ uolentē & post eum rerũ oĩm
Ideas atcq̃ formas aspicere purius & transparentius q̃ secundarũ creatu
rarum ulla, deinde uisiones q̃cq̃ suas inferioribus pādere, q̃d omne deorũ
est propriũ atcq̃ suum. Ideocq̃ dei qñcq̃ uocantur latine, qui & græce thei
ἀπὸ τῆς θέας .i. a speculatione ac uisione, unde θεᾶσθαι significat aspicere uide
recq̃, noĩantur & qñcq̃ angeli dũ uisa cæteris enunciant, ut Orpheus Mer
curiũ inuocans ait. κλῦθί μου ἑρμεία δὸς ἀγγελε μαιάδος υἱέ. ἑρμηνῶ πάντων .i. Au
di me Mercuri Iouis angele Mæadis fili, explanator oĩm. Nã ἀγγέλλειν nun
ciare ac explanare dicimus. Crebro aũt alterũ pro altero usurpam⁹, nō cō
syderatis officiis, ita ut promiscue diis et angelis in cōi sermōe utamur. Cũ
em̃ Porphyrius in Isagogis scripsisset cp̃ & nos simus rationales & angeli
Boethius latine uertens, sumus inquit & nos rationales & dii, hoc modo
reperĩt in libris aliorum q̃plurimis. Quare nemo putet cum deos noĩam⁹
ipsos æquari summo & ineffabili deo q̃nomen non habet, supm̃ã nancq̃
maiestatem eo appellamus deum, cp̃ entia cũcta infinite penetrat & singu
la percurrit ἀπὸ τ̃ θεῖν .i. currere. Vniucicq̃ nēpe rei multo iterior est de⁹ &
magis intimus q̃ ipsa sibimetipsi, ut qui cum nullibi est ubicq̃ sit. At nō sic
deos appellamus, q̃ terminatam sibi tm̃ exequunt prouinciã, & ad destina
tum mittunt opus. Dæmones aũt q̃tumcunqq̃ boni, tñ a Pythagora secta
toribuscq̃ suis in hunc medii mundi chorum non admittunt. Sic enim Plo
tinus q̃, testantibus Porphyrio & Longino, mysteria Pythagoreorũ pfe
ctissime dictari uisus est, in libro de amore Deorum, inq̃t, genus esse passi
onis expers dicimus & putamus. Dæmonibus aũt passiones adiungimus
dicentes etiam sempiternos esse, sequenti post deos gradu. Præstat sane,
nullum in mundo intelligibili dæmonē appellare, quinetiam si ibi ponat
ipse dæ

On the Art of Kabbalah

distinct forms, self-existing, universal, as well as individual forms. It contains all Ideas of idealized "genera"and species, models to be themselves copied in a more restricted way; the original from which these models were formed is in the divine mind. So we shall call what is in the world of the deity the absolute exemplar; in the intelligible world, the abstract example, and in the sensible world, not example but the copy from the example—like the seal, the design on the seal, and the sealed wax disc.

The next characteristic is harmonious motion, called "chorus" from the Greek *chara*, meaning the infinite joy of the blessed spirits and the immutable delight of the gods, natives and citizens of Olympus, triumphant in crowns of myrtle, feasting on the divine ambrosia and nectar, and laughing, laughter never to be extinguished. Homer, sagest of the poets, wrote "Inextinguishable laughter arose among the blessed gods," which shows how complete was their everlasting happiness, with the harmonious blend of harps and other instruments of the Muses, religious and formal dance, conversation, peaceful rests, sometimes sweet sleep, all put with such precision by noble Homer in Book 1 of the *Iliad*—don't you agree, Marranus? What greater pleasure can you imagine for a god than that when he wants to look on all Ideas and forms he may see them more purely, more clearly, than any lesser creature. And so they are called *dei* in Latin, or *thei* in Greek, meaning seeing or sight, hence *theasthai*, meaning "to see" or "look at." They are also, when they announce to others what has been seen, called angels. Orpheus, invoking Mercury, says "Hear me Mercury, angel of Zeus, son of the Maead, explainer of all." For the Greek *angellein* means to announce or explain.

Frequently, we use one name in another's place, forgetting their proper uses, and in ordinary speech we employ "gods" and "angels" quite without distinction. Porphyry wrote in the *Isagoge* that both we and the angels are rational, and Boethius, translating this into Latin, wrote "both we and the gods are rational." Instances of this can be found elsewhere too. Let no one think that when we call them gods we are putting them on a level with God, the highest, the ineffable, who has no name. We call the supreme majesty "God," because endlessly he penetrates and runs through all things—hence *thei* from *theein*, "to run." In everything, God is much deeper within it, much further inside than it is even to itself; so that he is both nowhere and everywhere. This is not at all true of the gods, whose scope for action is limited and who are sent to their appointed tasks. Spirits, however good, are not included in the harmony of this middle world by Pythagoras and his followers. Plotinus, who, according to Porphyry and Longinus was a full initiate in the Pythagorean mysteries, says in *On Love*. "We say and we believe that this race of gods feels none of the passions. But we attribute passions to spirits, and we say that they are eternal, on the next rank down after the gods. It is clear that nothing in the intelligible world should be called a spirit, but that if a spirit were found there, we must think it a god."

LIBER SECVNDVS XLI

ipse dæmon, esse deum existimare. Hactenus ita Plotinus certe in omni do
ctrina sua breuis, at animo attento ponderandus, p̄sertim hoc in loco tam
difficili quo poetarum ueterũ arcana de diis loquentium poterunt absq̃
molestia & sine plurimorũ exacerbatione legi. Tertia intelligibilis mũdi
proprietas ab eodẽ Pythagora demonstrata est cum ipse dixit. Si recta ra
tione uixeris, male acta dolendo, & bene acta gaudendo, deosq̃ oraueris,
ut opus tuum p̄ficiant, tum exuto corp̃e profectus in æthere, eris immor
talis deus. Ordo nobis hic consyderandus est, quem in consequenda ho̅is
beatitudine Pythagoras obseruat. Istud nanq̃ medii mundi cœlum incor.
poreum ac iste beatorũ inuisibilis olympus nihil impurũ admittit, fugien
da ergo uitia sunt, & amplexandæ uirtutes. Deinde salus hoi̅m, misericor
dia dei est, quare diuinitas colenda, & sup̃i sunt exorãdi, ut opus nostrum
p̄ficiant, tum demũ nihil istuc materi̅e, nihil corporis, nihil p̄mixti recipi̅t,
ante igi̅t moriendũ est & sancte corpus exuendũ q̃ in deos referaris, Hic
est ordo seculi seculorum ut uita functis hoi̅bus puris & electis, deorũ in
digenarum sup̃ cœlestis q̃q̃ aula cõcedatur, & comunis sit pariter huma
næ naturæ cum sacrosanctis angelicis spiritibus p̃petuæ uit̃e conuersatio
in inuisibili & tn̄ oi̅formi sup̃cœlesti cœlo & orbe regeto extra sensibile
mundũ, ubi uer̃e est olympus non imaginarius nec̃ poeticus, non q̃ uol
uatur, qui rotetur nun q̃ ue quiescat. Tum Marranus, q̃ proxime, inquit,
sectis nostrorũ temporum accedit unus maxime oi̅m Pythagoras. In lege
nanc̃ christianorũ similiter legit cp̃ ho̅ies mortui de numero resurgetiu̅
sunt sicut angeli dei in cœlis ubi tabernaculum dei cum hoi̅bus. No̅ intra
bit aliqd coinqnatum aut abominationem faciẽs & mendacium. Erit istic
uox citharœdorũ citharissantium citharis suis, cantusq̃ nouus, & mortui
q̃ sunt scripti in libro uitæ uident cœlum nouũ & terram nouã. Prius em̃
cœlũ ac prior terra eis abierunt. Ibi etiam ciuitas beatorũ habens clarita
tem dei, & illius muri ex iaspide constructi, fundametaq̃ eius omni lapide
p̃cioso ornata. Et dominus oi̅potẽs templum istius ciuitatis est, & de sede
eius producit̃ fluuius aquæ uiu̅e ceu splendidus crystallus. Ciuitatis uero
eius fundamentum & sup̃ficies est tetragonus, uerba em̃ Apocalypsis un
de illa sumuntur sunt hæc. καὶ ἡ πόλις τετράγωνος κεῖται .i. & ciuitas tetragonus
iacet, q̃d explanauit Hippolyt̃ papa sic esse ἰσχυρὸν καὶ μέγιστον .i. propter
solidum & firmum. Id tu mihi reducere uideris ad Pythagoræ tui nume
rum, & figuram pyramidis, a tetragona basi erectã, quam mathematici so
lent inter solida reputare, plane quẽ uirum iure optimo non modo tuum
sed ueri̅s nostrum Pythagorã appellarem, & appellabo qdem nostrũ, du
uiuam, cp̃ ipse solus ex omni ueterum philosophorũ turba magis apte ma
gis concinne proprieq̃ nostra sapuit, nec̃ ualde & a Persis q̃q̃ & a Pale
stinis ac nr̃a ætate Arabibus in doctrinæ suæ fundamento distat, ideṁ ipse

Book Two

This is as far as Plotinus' teaching on this goes. He does not say very much, but it is worth weighing with close attention, especially on this difficult topic where one may read the secrets of the older poets talking about the gods without difficulty and without being exasperated by sheer length.

The third characteristic of the intelligible world to which Pythagoras called our attention was that which he referred to when he said, "If you live by right reason, grieving for evil deeds, rejoicing in good ones, you will ask the gods in prayer to accomplish your work; then you will cast the body aside and be carried into the aether, where you will be an immortal god." It is this "order" which Pythagoras sees in the blessed state that man must pursue that we must now consider. That incorporeal heaven of the middle world, an invisible Olympus of the blessed ones, admits nothing that is defiled. Thus vices are to be avoided, and virtues embraced. The mercy of God is then man's salvation: for this reason the divinity must be worshipped, and in prayer we must beseech the highest beings to complete our work. Finally, nothing material, corporeal or mixed is admitted there, so you must die and cast the body aside before you are carried away to the gods. This is the order of the age of ages, in which life is granted to the undefiled and chosen of the dead in the gods' own home above the heavens, and in which human nature participates equally in external life, in common with the most holy angelic spirits in the invisible superheavenly heaven that yet contains all forms, a tranquil globe beyond the sensible world. There is the true Olympus, not an Olympus of the imagination or of poetry, nor one that turns and revolves and never rests.

MARRANUS: Among them all, only Pythagoras has come so close to the beliefs in our own day. Christian teaching is, we find, very similar, holding that those dead who are in the band of the resurrected are as the angels, gods in the heavens where the tabernacle of God is set with men. Nothing that does evil, abomination or falsehood will enter. There will be the sound of harpists plucking their harps, and of new songs. The dead who are inscribed in the book of life will see a new heaven and a new earth, for the former heaven and the former earth have passed away. There too is the city of the blessed which enjoys the light of God, the walls are made of jasper, the floor is adorned with every precious stone. And the Almighty Lord is the temple of this city, and from his throne there springs a stream of living water like gleaming crystal. The base and surface of this city is tetragonal, for in the words of Revelation, from which all this is taken, "the city lies foursquare." Pope Hippolytus explained this to mean "it is firm and solid." You seem to me to be linking this to your Pythagoras' number: a pyramidical figure with a four-sided base, which the mathematicians include among the regular solids. Plainly I should not call him your Pythagoras, but "our" Pythagoras, and I shall call him "ours" for so long as I live, for he alone of the whole great mass of ancient thinkers is the one who is really in tune with our own thought. He may be the founder of Italian philosophy, but in the fundamentals of his teaching he differs little from the Persians, the Jews of Palestine and, in our own day, the Arabs. We read in Moslem law, in the first Surah, that God will

DE ARTE CABALISTICA

Italicæ philosophiæ autor. Sic em in lege Mahometh Azoara prima legimus deum paradiso bonos inducturū, ubi dulcissimas aquas, pomacʒ multimoda fructus uarios & decentissimas ac mundissimas mulieres, omecʒ bonū in æthernū possidebunt. Et in Azoara quinquagesima prima. Credentes aūt (inquit) & benefacientes pulcherrima loca paradisi possessuri, omne suum uelle pficiēt, hoccʒ lucrum est maximū, huiusmodi qdem pollicitū illis summā lætitiā denūciat. Deinde in doctrina Mahometh ita scribitur. Si ullum oblectamenti genus istic deesset, beatitudo minime plena esset. Frustra ergo deliciæ adessent si uoluptas deesset. Et paulo superius. Incolis qdem eius (ait) quicqd desyderari potest statim aderit, q & pfecti erunt oēs in statura qdem Adæ, in forma uero Iesu Christi, nunq incremētum aut detrimentū aliqd patientes. Et in Alkoran capite lxiiii. Illic qdem credentes accubabunt tapetis sericis stramentiscʒ purpureis, oibuscʒ sibi dilectis ppetuo potient, ducētcʒ puellas formosissimas, ut sunt hyacinthi & margaritæ, ab hoibus atcʒ diabolis nunq deuirginatas nec menstruatas. Erunt & illic arbores colore inter uiridem croceūcʒ nitentes, fontescʒ fortiter emanantes & palmæ pomacʒ punica. Nonne hic sentis Philolae cʒ pars maxima horum symbolica est & instar Pythagoricorū allegorice narrātur q audisti ferme oīa, id qd palā fatetur Mahometh in libro de doctrina cum ait. Seculum aliud post mundū istum, cuius nulla similitudo exponi potest, nec em coloni eius mortales, nec dies eius sub numero. Quo se ipsum declarat, q scripserit de diuinis allegorice scripsisse, non autē oīa plane ac aperte, qn numerauit dies beatitudinis, dies mille annorū & annos. quadraginta millia annorum. Et paradisum habere docuit pauimētū aureum smaragdis & hyacinthis crebro interpositis distinctum, omi fructifera consitum arbore, decurrentibus per amoena arua fluentis, qrū alia qdem lac, alia mel album, alia uinū purissimū fundunt. Hæc in libro de doctrina Mahometh, ubi p sensibilem paradisum designat illū quē ratio nō capit intelligibilis mūdi hortum. Duos em paradisos Mahometh in Alkoran nobis proposuit cum in Azoara sexagesima quarta sic ait. Qui timuerit coram deo stans, duos paradisos rerum multipliciū omnimodicʒ boni fœcundos, hæreditatem accipiet. Ita duas qcʒ ostēdit ciuitates Ierusalem cum in libro de doctrina quærit Abdias. Quare Ierusalem dicatur dom⸗ benedicta. Respōdit Mahometh quia in directo cœlestis Ierusalem sita sit. Hæc ad nostri Simonis Cabalistica q audiuimus haud parum alludūt de duobus scilicet paradisis altero cœlesti & altero terrestri geminos mun⸗ dos signīficantibus uisibilem & inuisibilem, illum nobis psentem, hunc nobis futurum, eum qdem de q satis multa paucis exposuisti, quare oro Philolae ut de nostro quem incolimus reliqua prosequaris. Faciam sedulo Philolaus ait, si prius te cōmonuero ne cum rudibʹ philosophastris erres

qui ca

lead the good to paradise, where the sweetest water, apples and all kinds of fruit, and the most handsome and elegant women will be theirs. In Surah 51 he says: "Believers and those who do good shall possess the most beautiful parts of paradise, they will gratify every desire and this is the greatest gain." It was with promises of this kind that he declared to them the heights of happiness. Then it is written that Mohammed taught that: "If any kind of delight were lacking, their beatitude would be less full," and a few lines before: "The inhabitants of that place will straightway have everything that can be desired. They will all be of full height as Adam, in form as Jesus Christ. Nothing shall be added to them or taken away from them."

In Surah 63 of the *Koran* it says: "There will the believers lie on silk carpets and rugs of purple, all their wants will be always satisfied. They will take for themselves the most beautiful girls, girls who are sapphires and pearls, whose maidenhead has never been taken by man nor devil, who have never been menstruant. There will be found trees whose bright color is between green and saffron, fountains playing, palm trees and deep red apples." You realize, I am sure, Philolaus, that most of this is symbolic, and that almost all you have heard is metaphor, in the manner of Pythagorean teaching, something Mohammed openly admits in his Tradition, where he says "there is another age after this world; it has no likeness to this world by which it can be explained, for neither are its inhabitants mortal, nor its days numerable." So he himself declares that when writing about the divine he had written in metaphor and not openly or straightforwardly, for he numbered the days of the blessed state — days of a thousand years and years of forty thousand years. And he taught that in paradise the floor was close-studded with emeralds and sapphires, that every tree that bears fruit is there, that streams run down through pleasant fields, some of milk, some of white honey, some of the purest wine. This is all in Mohammed's book *Tradition*, where by means of a paradise of the senses he outlines the garden of the intelligible world which reason cannot grasp.

In the *Koran*, Mohammed suggests to us two paradises, when he says in Surah 64: "He who feels fear standing in the presence of God shall receive two paradises overflowing with all kinds of good things as his inheritance." So, in *Tradition* he talks of two cities of Jerusalem. Abdias asks "Why is Jerusalem called the blessed house?" Mohammed replies "Because it is sited directly beneath the heavenly Jerusalem."

This relates more than a little to Kabbalist doctrine. We heard from Simon about the two paradises, one in heaven, the other on earth, standing for twin worlds, visible and invisible, the one we have now, and the one that is to come, where you have explained a lot in a short space. So do please go on, Philolaus, about the man to whom we are now devoting ourselves.

PHILOLAUS: I shall do so most readily, but I must first warn you

LIBER SECVNDVS   XLII

qui ea tm̄ sapiunt quæ oculis cernūt, ut de Antisthene scripsit Ammoni9 Hermiæ cum dixisset, hoīem qdem uideo, humanitatē aūt non uideo. Vnde putabat humanitatem nihil rerum esse nisi cogitationis figmentum. ταῦτα ἐκεῖνος ἔλεγε, τῇ αἰσθήσει μόνῃ ζῶν. καὶ μὴ δυνάμενος ὑπὸ λόγῳ εἰς μείζονα εὑρεσιν ἑαυτὸν ἀνγκεῖν. Id est. Hæc ille dixit sensualitate sola uiuens & non potens ratione ad maiorem inuentionē se ipsum extollere. Ita Hermiades in Isagogis. Haud aliter tam sunt qdam obtuso ingenio, q acutius cotemplari nequeant, nisi quantū pupilla comprehendat, aut manus palpent, & q̄cunq̆ de uita cœlesti, de diis superis, aīabus in cœlo aut de cœlitibus audiunt, ea mox ad cœlum uisibile stellarūcq̆ sphæras, firmamentū mobile, & q̄s sensu pcipimus orbes referunt, ac si in tanta turbine motuū, & irrequieto mutationum tumultu, uita beata consistere posset, sequentes uero spiritalem sensum & subtilem mentis illuminationē, ipsi qdem intelligunt maiorem esse ueritatē in iis quæ non uidēt q̄ in iis q̄ uidentur. Ad hoc Pythagoreōtum propensa est uoluntas ut credant hunc mundū & q̄cunq̆ in eo locātur adumbratam esse imaginē eius q extra cœlum sit ueri mundi, comp̄hendentis solum intelligentias formas & animas a corpibus substātia uirtute & opatione separatas. Vnde animas hoīm ab omi sorde turpi defecatas abiecta corporali mole firmiter tenent & nullatenus dubitant extra hoc uisibile cœlū omne ac ultra qualēcunq̆ incōmoditatis aleam in ætheris nitatis olympo habitare, omni libertate donatas & nulli necessitati obstrictas. Sic em̄ Plotin9 ille insignis Pythagorista in libro de proprio cuiusc̆q̆ dæmone quarto Animas (inquit) extra sensibilē mundū profectas existimandum est naturā dæmonicam transcendisse, omnec̆q̆ gn̄ationis fatium, oēmq̆ huius mundi necessitatē q̄diu in mundo intelligibili habitant, huc usq̆ Plotinus. Quotiens igit de ueris diis, intelligētiis separatis, formis purioribus, spiritibus diuinis, superis, angelis & beatorum aīabus mentio fit, semp recordare ac animo tecum uersa mundum illū sup̄mum, intelligibilem, immaterialē, simplicem, abstractū, cœlum incorporeum, olympum inuisibilem, paradisum mentalem, supernaturalem æthera, nec sensu nec ratione pceptibilem. Eo nunc dimisso ad nostrū descendamus corporeū   X & sensibilem mundum cuius exemplar est in mundo incompabili deitatis & exemplū in mundo intelligibili formalitatis, & exemplariū αἰσθητικὸν in se ipso. Vtc̆q̆ unū origo est mentalis mundi, sic duo nobis exordiū erit mundi corpalis, q̄ non esset corpalis, nisi quatuor istis constaret, puncto, linea, supficie, crassitudine, ad exemplū cubicæ figuræ quam constituunt unum duo tria quatuor. Vnū em̄ positione fixum creat punctū. Linea de uno puncto ad alterum protracta e duobus fit. Supficies ex tribus oritur lineis. Crassitudo quattuor nascit̄, ante, retro, sursum, deorsum. Ideoq̆ sicut binarius per se multiplicatus numerando bis duo quaternionē producit, Ita binarius semetipsum in seipsum replicans atq̆ retorquens dicēdo, bis

Book Two

not to wander off course along with those unsophisticated thinkers who concern themselves only with what the eye can see. So wrote Ammonius the son of Hermias about Antisthenes when he said "Man I see, but humanity I do not," and because of this thought that "humanity" was nothing but a fiction of thought. Commenting on this in the *Isagoge,* Ammonius wrote: "So saying, he lived only by the senses, and was unable to achieve any greater discovery by reason." In much the same way there are those whose faculties are blunted and who are incapable of any more acute contemplation, unless it be what the eye takes in or the hands touch. Anything they hear of heavenly life, the gods above, souls in heaven or heavenly beings, they immediately relate to the visible heaven, the bands of stars, the moving firmament, and the circular paths that we perceive by the senses, as if blessed life could stand such turbulent movement, restless tumult and change. Those who strive for spiritual sense and the delicate light of the mind understand that greater truth lies in what is not seen than in what is.

In Pythagorean thought there is a tendency to hold that this world and everything in it is but the shadow-image of the real world beyond the heaven, a world which contains only intelligences, forms and souls separated from their bodies and from substance, force and activity. Thus they firmly believed and had no doubt that the souls of men, purified of all vile filth and free from the burden of the body, live in a place beyond this visible heaven, with every benefit in an Olympus of eternity, granted every freedom and unrestricted by need. The distinguished Pythagorean, Plotinus, says in his fourth book *On Our Allotted Spirits,* "in souls which have gone outside the sensible world, spiritual nature is held to have transcended the whole destiny of birth, and all the necessity of this world. They inhabit the intelligible world." Whenever reference is made to true gods, separate intelligences, purer forms, divine spirits, higher beings, angels and souls of the blessed, remember that highest world, and remind yourself of the intelligible, immaterial, simple, abstract world, an incorporeal heaven, an invisible Olympus, a paradise of the mind, supernatural aether, perceptible neither to sense nor reason.

Let us now take our leave there and come down to our own corporeal and sensible world, whose original is in the incomparable world of the deity and whose model is the intelligible world of forms. What is copied from the model is in the sensible world itself.

As "One" is the origin of the mental world, so "Two" is the beginning of the corporeal world. It would not be corporeal if it did not consist of these four things — point, line, area and volume. Take for example the cube that one, two, three and four make up. One, when put in a fixed spot, makes a point. A line drawn from one point to another is made of two. Areas comes from three lines. Volume is born with four: in front, behind, above, below. So, just as duality multiplying itself ("twice two") makes four, so duality folding back and twisting on itself "twice two twice" makes the first cube.

DE ARTE CABALISTICA

duo bis, primum cubum facit. Ergo post qnarium quę tetragonica est pyramis, quippe principium intelligibilis mundi, accedit sex laterum octonarii cubus, quem mundo sensibili architectum pficimus. Nam inter rerum principia, non habetur septenarii ulla memoria, qm uirgo est nihil pariēs, iccirco Pallas noīatur. Ad cubum ergo primū diuertimur, sane fœcundū numerū, multitudinis uarietatisq3 principem, ut q per duo sit & per quatuor cōstitutus. Vnde sicut Pythagorę pceptor Zaratas duo noīauit matrem, ita nos cubum inde progredietem appellamus materiam, omnium rerum naturalium fundum, & fundamentum sedemq3 substantialiū formarū. De q Timæus Locrēsis ille Pythagoreus in lib. de aīa mūdi scribit: ἐκ δὲ τοῦ τετραγώνο γινᾶθαι τὸν κύβον ἐφαπτότατον καὶ στεδαῖον πάντα σῶμα. ἓξ μὲν πλόυρας, ὀκτὼ δὲ γωνίας ἔχον. i. Ex tetragono nasci cubum solidissimum & stabile oīno corpus. sex qdem latera, octo aūt angulos habens. Huic sundo si qua forma demersa innitaī, huic solido receptaculo si fuerit illapsā & in hanc sedem materialem reposita, nō uage nec comuniter recipitur, sed stabiliter & singulariter sit indiuidua & incomunicabilis, tanq ascripticia glebæ, tempori & loco subiecta, & quasi de libertate in seruitutē materię proscripta. Igitur gemina profluere ab uno fonte rerū tpalium principia cernimus pyramidem & cubum.i.formā & materiam q ex eodem tetragono dephenduntī prodiisse, cuius Idea, ut ante ostēdimus, est Tetractys. Pythagoræ diuinum exemplar. Symbola igīt primordialia q̄to potui breuis explanaui, q̄ reuera nihil designant aliud q̄ materiā & formā. Cūq3 oportet tertium aliqd ponere q̄ uniantur, nec em sponte confluunt nec cōtingit fortuitus quarumlibet formarū cōcursus in materiā, necq3 unius rei materia contingentēr formam alterius recipit, non em ex corpore humano mox atq3 decesserit anima generatur æs aut ferrū, nec ex lapide sit lana, cū itaq3 oporteat ponere tertium aliqd quo uniant, erit, ut opinor, necesse prīcipium aliud q̄ priuatione Aristotelica adducere quo moueat materia ad formæ desyderiū, ita ut cessante hac & hac forma, introducat uicissim ista quædā & ista. Nam priuatio & potentia nihil substantiue agunt cum sint nullius actiuitatis realis ob idq3 minimę entitatis, q̄to magis certā formam alicui materię nequaq̄ iungere aut unire possunt. Vnde inuenti sunt q dicerent loco priuationis motum esse tertiū principiū, q cum sit accidēs quō erit principium substantiæ? aut qs eius motus erit motor? Quare sapientius contemplati Athenienses ambo, Socrates Sophronisci, & Plato Aristonis, pro motu seu priuatione agillimum actiuorū posuerunt deū dicentes, tria esse rerum principia. deū, Ideam & materiam, q̄d ante Pythagoras occulte symbolissauit arcanis his notis asserendo principia uniuersorum esse. Infinitū, unum & duo. Infinitudinis deum, unitatis formam, alteritatis materiam designans autores. Infinitum in mūdo supersupmo & incomparabili, unū seu identitatē in mūdo intellectuali, duo seu alteritatē

in mundo

On the Art of Kabbalah

After the "Four" which is the tetragonal pyramid, the beginning of the intelligible world, comes the six-sided cube with eight corners which we appoint the architect of the sensible world. We have no mention of a seven in these bases of nature, for seven is a virgin and does not give birth, and is called Pallas for that reason. So we turn to the first cube, clearly a fecund number, the basis of various abundance, as it is made up of two and four. In a similar way to Zaratas, the teacher of Pythagoras, who called two "mother," we call the cube that is derived from two "matter," the foundation of all in nature, and the ground and seat of substantial forms.

The Pythagorean Timaeus of Locri wrote in his book *On the Soul of the World*: "From the four-sided figure is born a solid cube, a completely stable body, with six sides and eight corners." If any impressed form leans on this, falls onto this solid refuge or rests on this seat of matter, its reception is not at all indefinite. It is made stable, particular, individual and specific; it is as if it had been tied to the soil, subjected to time and space, forbidden freedom and assigned to the slavery of matter. So we see that these twin foundations of temporality come from one source; the pyramid and the cube, that is, form and matter. They are derived from the same four-sided figure whose Idea is, as we have already shown, the Tectractys, Pythagoras' divine exemplar. I have explained the primordial symbols as briefly as I could. In reality they simply stand for matter and form.

But we should posit a third by which they are bonded together. They do not run together of their own accord, and the coming together of particular form and matter does not occur by chance. Neither does the matter of one thing take the form of another by accident. A soul on leaving the human body does not immediately produce bronze or iron, nor, on leaving stone, wool. It is best to posit a third thing to unite the two, and it will, I think, be necessary to bring in some principle other than Aristotle's "privation," whereby matter is made to "desire" form, and as this or that form is missing, so some other is introduced in turn. Privation and power do not act on substances. They have no real force of action because of their minimal entity. Thus, all the more, they cannot join or unite particular form and unspecified matter.

I have come across some who say that motion, not privation, is this third. But this is a property of accidents, and how can it be what substance is based on? Who will be motion's mover?

The Athenians, Socrates, son of Sophroniscus, and Plato, son of Ariston, whose thought went much deeper, both put in place of motion or privation the most active of active beings, namely God, and said that underlying the universe were three things: God, Idea, matter. Pythagoras had already proposed this symbolically, in signs encoding the bases of the universe, "infinity, one, and two," designating God the source of infinity, form the source of "one-ness," and matter the

LIBER SECVNDVS   XLIII

in mundo sensibili, est em materia qdem alterationis mater. Coniugit aut deus materia & formam per legē ipsi naturę impositā, Iccirco ante Pythagorae tpa uetustissimus ille Orpheus in libro hymnoru, post Iouem i. formam, qui ab eo noiatur ἀρχὰ πάντων. i. principiū uniuersorū. Et post Iunonem. i. materiam quam uocat Διὸς σύγκλιτον· παγγενέθλον. i. Iouis cōthoralē oīparentem. Iunonio enim cognomento materiam alloquitur his uerbis χωρὶς δ᾽ σέθεν οὐδὲν ὅλως ζώοις φύσιν ἔτευχε· κοινωνεῖς τ᾽ ἅπαντι κεκραμένη πλέα σεμνῶς. i. Absqꝫ em te nihil oīno uitae naturā agnouit, comunicas qdem uniuersis pmista supra q̄ pudice. Itaqꝫ post (inq̄) Iouem formā, & Iunonē materiā, addidit idem Orpheus legem id est distributionē ut esset tertium naturae principiū, cognoīauitqꝫ id φύσεως δ᾽ βέβαιον. i. naturę confirmatiuū. Nam lex dicitur nomos graece ut nosti a nemo νέμω ζω. i. partior & distribuo, perinde atqꝫ distribuens omibus qd suum est uel qd ad se pertinet. Hoc esse ait οὐράνιον νόμον σφραγίδα δικαίαν (Sic in hymnis suis concinuit) i. coelestē legē sigillum iustū, lex em naturę sigillat una forma multas materias, sicut tabellio una effigie annuli multas ceras. Iam uero quęlibet sigillate in materiam formæ non ultra uocant Ideę, hoc est species, sed ταυτὶ hoc est Ide scilicet formæ ὡς τὰ ἐν τοῖς κηροῖς ἐκτυπώματα ἀχώριστα τῆς ὕλης. i. Ceu illæ in ceris expressiones inseparabiles a materia, ut scripsit Ammonius. Proinde apta nobis iā extat sensibilis huius origo mundi, qué pyramidis & cubi cōiugiū lege naturę celebratū peperit. Earū figurarū tetragone bases cōtinuo uniteꝫ dodecaedron efficiunt pythagoricū quippe symbolū, q̄ designat ipsum uniuersum ex materia & forma compositū, illius recte meminit. Alcinous de dogmate Platonis sic dicens. τῳ δὲ δωδεκαέδρῳ ἐς δ᾽ πᾶνδ θεὸς κατεχρήσατο. i. Dodecaedro ad uniuersum deus utebatur, scilicet cum hunc mundū fabricaret. Octangulo nanqꝫ cubo si pyramidē ex quatuor triangulis æquicruribus eleuatā supposueris ędificiū dodecaedri artificiose construxeris ubi succumbit cubus seu talus uti mater, & īcumbit pyramis uti pater. Sic enim Timæus Locrus ille nobilis Pythagoreus in libro de anima mundi. ἀ μὲν ἐιδος λόγον ἔχει ἀρρενός τε καὶ πατρὸς· ἁ δ᾽ ὕλα, θηλέος τε καὶ ματέρος. ξίτα 3 τω τα τώτων ἔκγονα. i. Forma qdem inquit rationē habet maris & patris. Materia uero fœmine atqꝫ matris, tertia aut esse horū genimina. Ex his igitur oīa huius mundi quae sunt non pperam affirmamus certis seminibus & secreta facultate fieri, sane mira uarietate apparentiā propter uariā formarum ad suas materias commensuratione & infinitorū pene accidentiū q̄ συμπτώματα epicurus uocat admixtione, per abundantiā & defectū, litem & amiciciam, motum & quietem, impetum & tranqlllitatem, rarū & densum Vnde oriuntur orbes & stellæ, quatuor item elementa, ex quibus euaporant calidum & humidum, & frigidum & siccum, tum quęlibet etiam sen suum obiecta. Inde aliis aliud contingit, & efficit omnes res ut conuertant formas, mutentqꝫ colores, Lucretii testimonio. Sentis ne quantū nos iam

I

Book Two

source of "other-ness." Infinity lay in the supersupreme and incomparable world; "one," or "sameness" in the intellectual world; "two," or "other-ness," in the sensible world, for matter is the mother of "other-ness." By laws imposed on Nature God joined matter and form together.

Earlier still, before Pythagoras, Orpheus wrote in his book of hymns that, after Jupiter, that is, form, whom he calls "the beginning of all," and after Juno, that is, matter, whom he calls "Jupiter's bedfellow, mother of all,"—saying, as he calls matter "Juno" as well, "without you has nothing known what life is; you share in all, intermingled so chastely"—after Jupiter-form and Juno-matter, then, Orpheus added, as the third basis of nature, law, that is, distribution, and called it "what strengthens nature." In Greek, law is *nomos*, which comes from *nemo*, meaning "share and distribute"; so "law" is what distributes to each man what is his or what he has a right to. In his songs Orpheus says that this is "heavenly law, the seal of justice," for the law of nature with one form impresses its seal on matter many times, as a notary stamps many wax discs with the one seal. Particular sealed areas of matter are no longer called Ideas meaning "species," but Ideas meaning forms "impressed in the wax, as it were; inseparable from matter" (Ammonius).

The origin of the sensible world is now laid open to us, born of the marriage of pyramid and cube celebrated under nature's law. When four-sided bases of these figures are joined as one, they make a dodecahedron. This too is a Pythagorean symbol: it stands for the universe as it is, composed of matter and form, a fact accurately recorded by Alcinous when on the subject of Platonism he wrote: "God used the dodecahedron for the universe," that is, when he constructed the world. If you place a pyramid with four right-angle triangles constructed on its base onto an eight-cornered cube, you will have a dodecahedral figure. The cube, or die, lies underneath, as mother, and the pyramid on top, as father. Timaeus Locri, a distinguished Pythagorean, says in his book *On the World Soul*: "Form has the nature of a male and a father, matter that of a female and a mother. Tertiary things are the offspring of these."

We should not therefore be wrong to assert that all the things of this world are made from these seeds, this secret stock. Their appearance in amazing diversity springs without doubt from the diverse matches of form to matter, and from the near-infinity of attributes (what Epicurus calls *symptomata*); from surplus and shortage, strife and friendship, motion and rest, fury and calm, dispersion and concentration.

From these result the globes and stars, the four elements from which heat and damp, cold and dryness arise, and all the objects of the

DE ARTE CABALISTICA

cum plebe philosophorum ambulamus,& uulgariã terimus uiam quãdo
Y in hæc physica lapsi sumus,quare cum multi multa de natura scripserẽ mi
nus uirium nobis adhibendũ est ut quid de rebus naturalibus senserit Py
thagoras ostendamus,a nobilioribus & diuinioribus sumentes initiũ.Na
turales sunt dii,supernaturales uero dii deorum,illos mũdus inferior alit,
hos mundus superior fouet,unde & superi dicũtur,de quibus ante haud
parum multa disseruimʼ.Dii deorum simplicissimi & purissimi quia nusq̃
sunt ideo supercœlestes sunt,quia ubiq̃ sunt,ideo nobiscum sunt,istic in
digenæ,hic aduenæ.Nunq̃ enim in nostro mũdo sunt nisi missi,quare an
gelorum nomine gaudent cum ad hæc ima deuergunt, qm̃ regis regum
nuncii sunt, habitu tñ & facie nobis apparent quali uolunt iuxta liberta
tem arbitrii semp beneficiorum erga nos amantissimi.Sed inferiores dii
ad supercœlestia nuncq̃ migrant,ad nos uero & ad nostra qñcq̃ legationẽ
assumunt,unde & pari modo est qñ angeli nominant.Deus autem Opt.
Max. tam infima q̃ suprema & media singula penitissime inhabitat, ita ut
nihil sit entium sine deo.Præterea dii orbis nostri præstantiores sunt.In
feriores aũt in corpore humano animæ,quanq̃ illi apud corpora, hę i cor
Z poribus.In medio aũt horum sua loca tenent dæmones & heroes.Dæmo
nes prope deos heroes prope animas.Quorum Pythagoras in aureis car
minibus meminit,& singulis quibuscq̃ suum tribuit cultum. Nec illis tamẽ
aras sanguine fœdari nec animalia immolari permisit,nisi publicę utilita
tis causa,magis aũt thure atcq̃ hymnis quotidiana & priuata sacrificia fie
ri uoluit.Vnde illud extat,Thure deum placa,uitulum sine crescat aratro.
Cunque homo sit quędam mundi huius effigies unde Microcosmus hoc
est paruus mundus nuncupatur,in multis paria recepit mundana nomina
μεταφορικῶς & more tranlaticio.Mens enim in homine deus appellatur in
star mentis summæ ac primæ,aut per homonymian, aut per participatio
nem.Et anima rationalis quæ per mentem ad uirtutes & optima quæque
uoluntatem inclinat,dicitur dæmon bonus siue genius,quæ uero per fan
tasiam & prauas affectiones uoluntatem ad uitia & pessima quæque tra
hit,nominatur dęmon malus.Quamobrem Pythagoras deum orat ut ho
mines a malo liberet, & omnibus ostendat quo dæmone utantur. Exuto
demum corpore si fœdata uitiis manserit,fiet dæmon malus, & uita eius
δυσδαιμονία Id est infœlicitas uocatur.Sin uero abiecerit uitia nihilóque mi
nus impressus ei duret sollicitudinis character,nec penitus omnem erga
humanos & mortales etiam quantumuis uirtutis mores affectionem re
liquerit, aliquanto erit tempore bonus dæmon, & in huius mundi amœ
nitate fœliciter fortunatéque deget singulari semper cum lætitia, tan
quam quæ bene gesserit adhuc memori secum mente uolutans ad ea
dem recte gerenda nondum extinctam retineat uoluntatem, cuius uita

210

senses. Contact of one with another causes everything to alter its shape and change color, according to Lucretius. You see that now that we have lapsed into physics we are moving with the great mass of philosophers and treading a well-worn path, and although a good deal has already been written on the natural sciences, there seems no reason why we should not apply our energies to this. We shall show what Pythagoras thought in the natural sciences, and shall begin with the high and divine topics.

The gods are natural; the gods' gods are supernatural. The lower world nourishes the first group; the higher world sustains the latter, which are thus called "higher beings." These we have already discussed at some length. The gods' gods are quite without admixture or complication. Insofar as they are nowhere they are beyond the heavens, insofar as they are everywhere, they are with us; natives in the one place, aliens in the other. They are never found in our world unless they have been sent here, and so they rejoice in the name of angels on their descents to these lower regions, for they are the messengers of the king of kings. They appear to us in whatever garb or guise they will, following their free choice; they are always most desirous of our welfare. The lower gods never reach the region beyond the heavens, but they do sometimes carry messages to us and our world and so sometimes they too are called angels. The Great and High God dwells deep within every lowest and highest and middle thing to the extent that nothing is a being without God.

The gods of our world rank before souls in the human body: the latter are corporeal, the former not. Between these come spirits and demigods, spirits ranking after gods, and demigods next to souls. Pythagoras refers to all these in the *Golden Verses*, and grants each their proper worship, but did not allow them bloodstained altars and animal sacrifice, except where this was for reasons of public expediency. He preferred that daily private sacrifice be made with incense and chanting. Hence: "Placate the god with incense, and let the bullock grow up by his plough."

Let man be the image of this world—hence he is called the microcosm, that is, the small world. In many respects he has been named, analogically, in terms appropriate to the world. The god in man is called mind, like the first and greatest mind, perhaps because they are in fact homonymous, perhaps because it shares in it. The rational soul which through mind inclines the will to virtue and good, is called a good spirit or "genius," while the rational soul that through fancy and distorted emotions drags the will to vice and bad is called an evil spirit. So Pythagoras prayed to God to free men from evil, and show all men which spirit they should follow. If after leaving the body the soul remains vice-stained it will become an evil spirit, and its life will be called "unhappiness." However, if it shakes off vice, and yet the mark of duty is still stamped firmly on it, nor has it relinquished all feeling for human and mortal virtuous behavior, then it will in time be a good spirit. It will pass its time in the delights of this world, happily and blessedly and with remarkable joy; as if it turned over in its mind the memory of what was well done and retains the

LIBER SECVNDVS

græcis εὐδαιμονία, id est, fœlicitas dicitur. Vnde illud Virgilii Maronis ortum est. Quæ gratia curruum armorumq; fuit uiuis, quæ cura nitenteis pascere equos, eadem sequitur tellure repostos. Illam animam priscos lemurem nuncupasse accepi, cuius generis si quis sit qui beneuolentia erga nos ita ducatur, ut nostri & nostrorum curam sortitus, pacato & quieto numine domū possideat, lar dicĩt familiaris. Sin aũt propter aduersa uitæ merita nullis bonis sedibus, interuagatione ceu q̃dam exilio puniſ, terriculamentum bonis hoĩbus inane, at noxium malis, larua noĩatur. Cũ uero incertum est qua sortitione fruatur, lar ne sit an larua, nomine Manẽ deum nũcupant, cui honoris gratia dei uocabulum addidere, q̃m eos pronunciant etiam deos qui iuste ac prudẽter uitæ curriculo gubernato mortem sanctam obierunt. Cæterum promiscue deos, angelos & dæmonas etiam eos noĩamus ingenuos spiritus, q̃ singulis q̃busq; hoĩbus custodes addicti, minime conspicui, semp adsint non modo actorũ testes, uerũetiã cogitatorũ, q̃ nos q̃q; post mortem sequanſ usq; ad summi dæmonis potestatem iudicium atq; tribunal. Omnia hæc ad nos ex Pythagora fluxerunt, q̃ ipse partim ab ægyptiis, partim ab Hebreis atq; Chaldeis, & apud Persarum sapientissimos Magos didicit, posterisq; tradidit, q̃rum meminere pstantissimi autores. Mercurius Termaximus ægyptiorum illustris legislator & contemplantissimus scriptor in sermone perfecto ad Asclepium. Timæus Locrus in libro de aĩa mundi, Hesiodus in operibus & diebus. Plato per Diotimam in conuiuio. Per Socratem in Phædro. Itidemq; in Philebo. Per Atheniẽsem hospitem in legibus, & Epinomi, aliisq; librorum suorum locis. Porphyrius de abstinẽtia animatorum. Iamblichus de mysteriis. Proclus in Alcibiadem. Plotinus in libro de amore & in libro de proprio cuiusq; dæmone. Maximus Tyrius in binis disputationibus de dæmonio Socratis, multiq; græcorũ alii, q̃s e latinis Cicero in uoluminibus de natura deorum, de diuinatione, & in sexto de repub. & ille quoq; Madaurensis Apuleius in libro de deo Socratis, & reliqui post illos imitati sunt. Nec desunt ex peripateticis q̃ de motoribus orbiũ syderum atq; stellarum, & præsidibus elementorum tractauere, siue corporibus illis assistant, seu illorum cuiq; pro cuiusq; anima insint, mitto dicere. Iam solum quæ restant de mundo sensibili paucis enumerabimus. Mundũ igĩ hunc qui est æthernitatis imitator dixit Pythagoras, continentiã esse. olm totorum secundũ ordinationẽ quæ sit in eo, qui tametsi est corporeus tñ incorporea habuerit prima principia, cui stoici non sunt in hoc assensi, putauerunt eũ ea fuisse corporea quia spiritualia. Eundẽ ipse & genitũ & corruptibile asseruit sed prouidentia & indulgentia dei nunq̃ corrumpẽdum. Dixit q̃q; corpora elementorũ esse rotunda, p̃ter ignem q̃ coni figurã præferat, Colorem esse corpis apparẽtiam. Tempus, circulum, mũdi extimũ,

I ii

Book Two

will, still unextinguished, to do those same things well, its life is, in Greek, called "happiness." Hence the comment of Virgil that: "The pleasure in chariots and arms that the living have, their care in stabling gleaming horses, these things follow them when they lie in earth."

I understand that there was one soul that the ancients called a ghost, and one is of this kind which is guided by such goodwill towards us as to choose to care for us and ours. With its pacific and restful presence it keeps the house, and it is called the "household god." If however it does not merit a good resting place, because of its evil life, it is punished with a life of wandering, as if in exile. This frightful thing has nothing to do with good men; it harms the bad, and is called a hobgoblin. As for souls where there is doubt as to which is their lot—household god or hobgoblin—they are called "god-spirits of the dead." The word "god" is added in their honor; those who have driven the chariots of life with justice and good judgement and have died in purity are also called gods. Gods, angels and spirits we call "noble spirits" indiscriminately. They are dedicated to the guardianship of individual men. Invisible, but always present, witnesses of thought as well as action, they follow us after death too, right to the jurisdiction, the court of trial, the judgement seat of the highest spirit.

All this comes to us from Pythagoras, who himself got it partly from the Egyptians, partly from the Hebrews and Chaldees, partly from the deeply learned Persian Magians. Handed down to posterity by him, it has been recorded by some very distinguished authors: Hermes Trismegistus, the famous Egyptian lawgiver and a very perspicacious writer, in his *Address to Asclepius*; Timaeus of Locri in *On the World Soul*; Hesiod, in *Works and Days*; Plato, in the person of Diotima in the *Symposium*, in the voice of Socrates in the *Phaedrus* and in *Philebus*, as the Athenian guest in the *Laws*, in the *Epinomis*, and elsewhere in his writing; Porphyry in *On Vegetarianism*; Iamblichus in *On the Mysteries of the Egyptians*; Proclus in *Alcibiades*; Plotinus in *On Love* and *On Guardian Spirits*; Maximus of Tyre in his two discourses on the spirit of Socrates; many other Greek writers, and of the Latin writers, Cicero, in his books *On the Nature of the Gods*, *On Divination*, and part 6 of *The State*; Apuleius of Madaura in *On the God of Socrates*; and others after them. There are a good many Peripatetic writings dealing with the movers of the circles of the stars and constellations and the rulers of the elements, and whether these "rulers" stand beside these bodies or exist in each as a soul, but I won't go into that.

We will now go quickly through what there is left to say on the sensible world. Pythagoras said that this world copies eternity, and that everything it contains is ranked in accordance with its inherent order, for although corporeal, it is based on the incorporeal. The stoics differ on this, and think it corporeal because all things are spiritual. He asserted that this same world was created, and corruptible, though, through the providence and kindness of God, it would never in fact suffer corruption. He also said that the molecules of the elements were round, except for that of fire which tended to be cone-shaped. Color was the external appearance of a body. Time, orbit, the slightest movement of the world, any alteration or change in matter, these

DE ARTE CABALISTICA

motum, differentiã quãdam seu alteritatem in materia, generationi & corruptioni passibilem materiam subiici. Necessitatem incumbere mūdo, & quædam de necessitate fieri, quædā ex fato, quædā electione, quędā a fortuna, quædam casu, horũ causam esse humanæ rationi occultā, cui astipulatur & Anaxagoras. Mūdum itē cœpisse ab igne, arbitrabaī ipse noster. Dexterū eius in oriente, sinistrū esse in occidente. Tum sequutus Thaleta cœlũ in quincȝ zonas diuisit, deinde in æquinoctia & solstitia utracȝ bina & arctũ. Haud aliter etiã terrarũ orbē. Prēterea oīm primus repit obliquitate zodiaci iuxta solis meatũ. Lunā uideri aiebat solũ terrestre ignitũ, in se habēs cāpos mōtes & ualles. De aīa hoc modo pronũciauit q̃ sit numerus se mouens quā p uires ita distribuit. Vitale circa cor, rationale & mentale circa caput, Totã interire non posse, nā rationalē esse sempiterni dei opus, irrationalē uero corruptibilē. Eidē autori referenda uideī diuinatio uerior ad sacrificia. Humanũ semen utilissimi sanguinis spumã esse uoluit materię corporeæ, sed incorporea uirtute p̃ditam. Cęterũ fœminā pariter semen emittere. Deinde non solũ hoīem sed alia q̃cȝ animantia rōnem habere abscȝ tñ mente. Qz̃ aũt magna pars horũ nō rationaliter agere uideī certe corporũ dyscrasia culpaī, quia debitis non sint dotata instrumentis, Ideo uerba non hn̄t siue cicures seu ferę, sed symbola & notas certas pro uerbis tenent, ꝗbus signis inter se cogitatus suos exprimant. Sic igit bestię loquunī, nō dicunt, qd̃ græce significantius aiunt λαλοῦσι μὲν, οὐ φράζουσι δὲ oīm illorũ Plutarchi uolumina de placitis philosophorũ testes cito ualde bonos. De reliꝗs mũdi huius siue substātiis seu accidentibus scriptores extant penè innumerabiles in̄ oī philosophoꝝ secta, q̃rũ alii gn̄aliter sunt locuti de uniuersi natura, ut Aristoteles, Theophrast̃, & tui Arabes. Mauricȝ prope oēs, alii particulariter de singulis ꝗbuscȝ rebus, ueluti Iulius Pollux, Dioscorides, Plinius, & his similes. Capita cũctarũ tñ disciplinarũ q̃tusꝗcȝ posteriorũ a Pythagora philosophię thesauro tanq̃ hæres appꝛhendit, & eā hęreditatē literario studio excoluit, procȝ peculiari ꝗsꝗ bonitate ingenii q̃tũ ualuit maxīe adornauit & pro uirili extēdit. Sed qd cũcta uel scire uel opinari iuuat? si nō in hac nobis uita oēm adimant mœrorē & cruciatũ in altera post uacuitatē malorũ nō addāt cumulatissimā oīum bonorũ cōplexionē q̃ tā studiose didicimus. Quid iuuat deniqȝ q̃ bñ sciēdo malefacim̃, & malefaciēdo nō oīno metu uacare ac ita nullo animi trā q̃llo statu frui possum̃? Quid rursum q̃ monitis, p̄be obediētes instar iumētorũ sēmp iussa exeq̃mur, alioq̃ oīb̃ ī reb̃ stulti, stolidi, fatui, fungi, bardi, blenni, nihil a bruto distantes. Quare opportunũ uidebaī Pythagoræ oēm philosophiã ad beatitudīs exoptatę fastigiũ & expeditā ęterni gaudii securitatē destinare, quā ī cōtēplatiōe sūmarũ & diuinarũ reꝝ collocauit. Eũ fructũ ceu fœlicis arboris idefessa philosophādi studia nr̃a, p̃culdubio

he said, as changeable matter, are subjected to generation and decay. Necessity hangs over the world. Some things come into being of necessity, others from fate, choice, luck, or chance, and what causes these is hidden from human reason. (Anaxagoras agrees here.) Our master thought that the world started in fire; its right side lay to the east, its left side to the west. Then, following Thales, he divided the heavens into five zones, then into equinoxes, two solstices and the pole, and the earth the same. He was the first to find the elliptic path of the zodiac against the sun; and the moon, he said, seemed to be but a fiery version of the earth, with its plains, its mountains and its valleys.

On the subject of the soul he said that it was a self-moving number distributed in accordance with its powers, with the life-part in the region of the heart, the rational and mental in the region of the head. He said it could not perish completely, as the rational part was the work of the eternal God, though the irrational could suffer decay. To him also is attributed a more accurate system of divination from sacrifices, and he had it that human seed was the spume of the blood, the most beneficial part of the material body, but nevertheless provided with an incorporeal nature. He also said that woman too emitted seed.

He said that other animals besides men have reason, but not mind. That the great part of them do not seem to act rationally is blamed on the bad constitution of their bodies — they have not been given the required tools. Thus, from wild beasts to crickets they are wordless; instead of word they use marks or fixed signs and they communicate by means of these signals. So the beasts talk but don't speak. It has been put more tellingly in Greek: "They chatter, they do not discourse." The best source for all this is in one of Plutarch's books *The Opinions of the Philosophers*.

For the rest, on the substance and accidents of this world, there are nigh countless writers of every philosophical school. Some, as Aristotle, Theophrastus, your Arabs and almost all the Moors wrote general works on the nature of the universe, and others specialized on particular points such as Julius Pollux, Dioscorides, Pliny and the like. Philosophers following Pythagoras took the foundations of all their learning from him, like heirs taking from the treasure chest, and they cultivated this inheritance with literary application, they embellished it to the limits of ability, and took its development as far as man can.

What point is there in all this knowledge and this thinking, if all that we have so diligently learned does not take away all our pain and sorrow in this life, and if in the other life where we are emptied of our ills it does not add a whole garnering of good things? What is the point if despite our knowledge of good we do evil, and in so doing cannot be without fear, cannot enjoy peace of mind? Again, what is the good if heeding the warnings minutely, we carry out our orders like beasts of burden, and in all other ways are: "fools, blockheads, idiots, dolts, dullards and oafs," no different from brutes? How timely then seemed all Pythagoras' philosophy, aimed at heights of bliss, long desired, and the ready refuge of eternal joy which he set in meditation on the highest and divine. This, without doubt was the fruit, like the fruit of the noble tree, that he thought should be sought after in tireless devotion to

LIBER SECVNDVS   XLIIII

sequuturū putauit, si nos pri⁹ aīa purgata uehemēter declinem⁹ a uitiis, & colam⁹ uirtutes diligēter, q̄ plane nullius mali nobis ipis cōscii læta mente hilariucq̃ studio mathematicis speculationibus incubamus, q̄ nobis mediæ obuersant inter res naturales & diuinas, sunt ēm a materia partim insepa_ ratæ ut naturalia, partim separatæ ut diuina, circulus nancq̃ seu harmonia quanq̃ absq̃ materia non subsistit, tn̄ absq̃ materia esse intelligit, q̄nimo nullius materiæ agitur cura cum quælibet mathematica tractamus. Cum igitur difficile ne dicam impossibile fuerat intellectū nostrum subito a na_ turalibus ad supnaturalia & ab oīno materialibus ad penitus immateria_ lia transilire, iccirco uoluit Pythagoras discipulis suis quasdā res in mediū ponere quas & sensu aliq̃ modo possent & intellectu comp̄hendere, de_ monstrationesq̃ illarum ob hanc causam mathemata seu matheseis hoc est disciplinas noīauit, quem uero de iis librum cōposuerat Eruditionum siue Institutionum inscripsit, quasi iuuenibus ac pueris aptum, propter q̃s & id nominis elegit μαθήμασιν. in quo totum quicqd dici poterat de nume_ ris, de figuris, & de harmoniis explanauit. Inde tancq̃ ex uno illustri fonte quatuor lympidissimi riui emanauēre, quas nos quatuor liberales artium facultates appellamus, arithmetica, geometria, musica, sane astronomiam inter naturalia connumerans pro maxima parte in librū quem appellauit physicū coegit, ꝙ in motu corporū consisteret. At qm̄ de illis apud q̄plu_ rimos nostra ætate literarū peritissimos, tam lata est expeditio, ut q̄libet earum rerum singularē facultatem faciat, & quælibet facultas propriā das_ sem ducat, unaq̄quæq̃ suis p̄ceptoribus committa, & propter multā modo noctem cœnæcq̃ nostræ apparatus p̄sentes, fine loq̄di faciam q̄tot uer_ bis hactenus tolerantissimas auris tuas immodeste ausus sum obtundere. Tum Marranus. Iuro superos, inqt, tanta me dicēdo uoluptate oppleuisti ut nulla mihi sit musa gratior, & nunc cœnæ oblitus oēm pene famem ad doctrinæ tuæ cupiditatē retuli, quanq̃ uideo caupone circa magnificentiā & sumptus epularū esse curiosum, tu uelim tn̄ contētius reliquā Pythago_ ræ philosophiam explices eam q̄ ad uirtutes, mores & reipub. industriam p̄tineat, idq̃ utcunq̃ potes q̄breuissime, dum structores cœnaturis nobis tridinium sternant, & cætera parent. Igitur audi Marrane oēm (Philola⁹ inquit) hanc partē sub noīe urbanitatis, contineri Pythagoras uoluit, quo circa, unum inter reliqua uolumen composuit, qd πολιτικὸν noīauit i. ciuile seu ut fortasse haud satis proprie uerterunt latini, de repub. perinde atq̃ non solum explanet q̄ multitudinē concernant, uerūetiā singula cuiusq̃ sua q̄ morum sunt & uirtutis. Qui ēm ciuitati p̄ficitur nisi dignus sit etiā qui domum suam regat & seipsum quoq̃, is plane inauspicato eligitur. μέρος τι ἄρα ὡς ἔοικε καὶ ἀρχὴ ἥτοι τὰ ἤθη πραγματεία τῆς πολιτικῆς. i.Portio est igitur ut uidetur & principium circa mores tractatio, ipsius politicæ, ut

I iii

Book Two

philosophy. We have only first to purge our souls, to be active in the avoidance of vice and the cultivation of virtue, and then when it is clear that there is no evil left in us, in joy of mind, keen and happy we are to get down to mathematical enquiry, which seems to us to stand midway between things natural and things divine. A circle, or harmony, cannot exist without matter, but it can be understood without matter; so when we are dealing with a mathematical problem, matter is irrelevant to us.

It is difficult, not to say impossible, for our powers of comprehension to leap suddenly from the natural to the supernatural, from what is completely material to what is wholly immaterial. For this reason Pythagoras wanted to set his disciples something that lay between the two, which they could grasp by sense or intellect, either way. These proofs he called therefore *mathemata* or *matheseis*, that is, "exercises," "lessons." He wrote a book on them called *On Instruction* or *Education*; just as if meant for boys—hence the title he gave it: *Paedeuticon* ("Schoolbook"). In this book he set out all there was to say on the study of number, figures, and harmony. From this have sprung the four branches of what we call the liberal arts, like four limpid streams from one spring: arithmetic, geometry, music and astronomy, which he counted among the natural sciences, and included in this book on physics because it is about the movement of bodies.

But discussion of these matters by a great many distinguished scholars in our time has advanced so far on all fronts as to make separate disciplines of these branches, and each brings its own fleet along behind it, each one of them is committed to its own teachers. And the night is well on, and our dinner is all ready, so, having been so impudent as to batter your most tolerant ears with so many words till now, I shall stop talking.

MARRANUS: I swear by the gods above that all your talk has filled me with delight, to the point where no artistic pleasure could be more gratifying. I had forgotten all about dinner; I had almost converted my hunger into desire for your instruction. I see the innkeeper is busying himself with magnificent preparations for our feast, but I would rather you dealt with the rest of Pythagoras' philosophy and what he had to say on morality, law and the role of the state all as briefly as you can, while the waiters are setting out the chairs for us to dine and getting everything else ready.

PHILOLAUS: Well then Marranus, Pythagoras wanted to subsume all this section under the term "citizenship." One of his books is devoted to this. It is called *Politikon*—the rather unsatisfactory translation is *On the State*. He describes not only matters affecting the people as a whole, but deals too with morals and behavior as they affect individuals. A head of state is clearly badly chosen if he is not also fit to rule his household and himself. "Ethical discussion seems to be part of politics, and its basis," wrote Aristotle in *Nicomachean Ethics*. A state

DE ARTE CABALISTICA

in libro magnorū ethicorum ait Aristoteles. Quæ qdem ciuilitas ex omī uirtutū numero consistit, cuius ptes sunt uirtute pditi hoīes in unā consue tudinem admissi. Nam maloru conuersatio non iam ciuitas reputanda est sed coueticula ubi uitia sunt sicut inter bonos uirtus, ut Theognis ille Me garensis in libro ad Cyrnum. Disces recte qdem a rectis, at si sociere pra uis, tū perdes tecq animumcq tuū. Omissa itacq contēplatiua sapientia quā ad naturam retulit Pythagoras & in librum physicū redusit de principiis & causarum modis, cq ex Monade ideſinita dualitas, ex illis numeri, ex nu meris puncta, ex pūctis lineæ, ex lineis planæ figuræ, ex planis solidæ figu ræ, ex qbus solida corpa & sensibilis ille mundi globus cum suis orbibus, mistorumcq elementis, igni, aere, aqua & terra fiant oriāturcq, singula pe ne (ut ipse solet) p allegoriam obuoluta, tum denicq relictis pariter ma thematicis q per librum Pædeuticū, hoc est, de institutione, suis ostendit, recensendum arbitror strictim q de moribus docuit, de qbus in politico diffusius scripsit, & in carminibus aureis instar sūmæ cōtractius, Que cu ætate nostra legant publice, nunc sola prosequar eiuscemodi symbola sine scriptis tradita ut discipuli memoriæ uiribus freti consuescerent ad signa prolata bonis moribus uiuere professumcq philosophiæ ordinem qtidie inter se arcanis tesseris affirmare. Quorū e numero haud quaqq pauca illu stris ERASMVS patria ROTERODAMVS professiōe The ologus, eloquētissimorū nostro seculo facile princeps & dulcis siren cum ingenti sua laude quam de politiorū literarum studiosissimis qbuscq opti mo iure meretur, in libris suis uel posteritati admirandis Adagiorū lucu lenter expressit. In consequēdis sane uirtutibus Pythagoras haud parum consuetudini tribuebat, adeo in teneris cōsuescere multum est. Vnde mo res dicti sunt ἤθη quasi ἔθη, hoc est consuetudines, qd stagirita ille sæpe in ethicis approbat, & noster ipse, iussit optimā uitæ rōnem eligere, illā nācq iucundam (inqt) reddet consuetudo. Vniuersam itacq moralem philoso C phiam ordinabat in tris metas, principio in dei diuinorumcq cultu. Secū do in singulorum qrumcq hoīm ad se ipsos respectum. Postremo erga cę teros officium, nam qd ad diuina pstantius attinet In primis nihil esse gra tum superis docuit qd non sit sordibus uacuū & plane purgatū, quare id adagiōis tradidit crebro habēdū in ore μὴ ἀπότμῃν θεοῖς ἐξ ἀμπέλων ἀτμήτων .i. non esse libandū diis de uitibus non putatis. De purissimo qcq adore sta tuit sacrificia fieri. Vnde est suum illud. Ne sacrifices abscq farina. Sacrifi cium hoc Pythagoricum maxime uetustū est qd uino & pane fit. Quæ aut deo dicata sunt, ultra nō debent ad humanos usus transferri, admonebat igitur sæpe dicens, A gallo candido abstineas. Perseuerandū uero esse in humilitate ueris adoratoribus hoc symbolo pcepit καθῆσθαι προσκυνοῦντας .i. sedere adoraturos, nā cq in adoratione oporteat circūquacq prospicere

de quo

218

consists in a measure of all the virtues, because its constituent parts are men of morality, living in communication in one society. A community of the wicked should not be thought of as a state, but as an association of vices, like virtues among the good. As Theognis of Megara wrote in *To Cyrnus*: "You will learn what is right from the righteous, but if you associate with the wicked, you will lose yourself and your soul."

Let us leave on one side the mystical learning which Pythagoras applied to nature and included in his book on physics when discussing the origins and modes of causation. Nor let us consider the derivation of indefinite duality from the Monad, of numbers from that, points from numbers, lines from points, plane figures from lines, solid figures from plane figures, and from these solid bodies and this sensible world, a globe with all its orbits, its constituent elements: fire, air, water, earth. All these things are shrouded in metaphor, as was his way. Let us also leave aside mathematics, which he set out in his book *Paedeuticon*—"Instruction." We must, I think, confine our consideration to his teaching on morality.

This he set out at some length in the *Politics*, and more briefly in the *Golden Verses*, which are, as it were, abstracts. These are now general reading, so I shall just go through precepts of this kind which have been handed down by word of mouth, a practice pursued so that disciples should rely on their powers of memory, and should grow used to leading a life whose good conduct conformed to the indications he gave of it, and to daily affirming the philosophical order they professed by the secret tokens they shared.

One of these disciples is the theologian Erasmus of Rotterdam, distinguished in many fields and easily the finest writer of our time. A sweet siren indeed; he most justly deserves the praise lavished on him by every lover of classics. In *Adages*, one of his books which will be admired in many years to come, he has expressed these things most lucidly.

Pythagoras attributed much in morality to custom; there is much to which one must become accustomed in childhood. Thus, good conduct is termed in Greek *ethe*, with a long "e," which is like *ethe*, with a short "e," which means "customs." Aristotle, in the *Ethics*, often agrees with this. Our Pythagoras commands us to choose the best course in life; "custom," he says, "makes that course a pleasant one."

All moral philosophy he ranked in three bands: first, the worship of God and the divine; next, the respect that individual men owe themselves; lastly, a man's duty towards others, which he considered particularly close to the area of the divine.

On the first group he taught that those above delight only in things which are devoid of filth and completely cleansed. So he handed down this adage to be oft repeated. "One should not pour libations to the gods from the fruit of unpruned vines." He decreed that sacrifices should be made from the purest grain. Hence: "Do not make sacrifice without fine flour." This sacrifice of wine and bread is of especially long standing among the Pythagoreans. He often warned against converting to human use what had been dedicated to God, saying: "Abstain from a white cock." That true worshippers should continue steadfastly in humility he enjoined in the precept "Worshippers must sit;" that they should

LIBER SECVNDVS

de quo illud ortum est, Adora circūactus, prudentiam circa diuinas p̄ces indicat ne iure in nos ita retorqueri possit, nescitis qd petatis. Cęterū quo ad nos ipsos recte uiuendi norma consistit in hois decoro, q̄d extremorū est medium, inter abundantiam & defectum, utrolibet eīm uitiosus est & mācus & cētimanus. Inde symbolū hoc Staterā ne transilias, p̄cipit studiis & actis oībus moderamen adhiberi, apertius aūt q̄d ipse dixit. Salem ap‑ ponito, id ad affectiōes nr̄as q̄ passiones appellant recte p̄tinet. Est eīm sal nota modestię, qm̄ in cibatu hois admittū nec nimiꝰ nec minimus, utrūq́ȝ sane respuitur & q̄d insulsum est, & q̄d salsissimū. Igitur salem ne trās͞gre‑ diaris prouerbium q̄ cȝ fuit, Proinde affectiones in nobis passionesq̄ȝ uni‑ uersæ quadam mouent apparentia boni aut mali, bonis lętamur p̄sentibꝰ tristamur malis, rursum bona concupiscimus futura, mala timemus. Ergo gaudium & mœror elementa sunt passionū ex qbus oēs animorū nostro‑ rum motus oriuntur, q̄rum rectitudo uirtus dicitur, obliq̄tas uitium. Ap‑ parent tn̄ sæpe nobis bona q̄ mala sunt, & econtrario q̄ bona sunt, uident̄ non bona, multum eīm, ut ait Seneca, uerū & uerisimile inter se differunt, quare cōtingit error facile in imperito uulgo cuius magna copia est. Eum Pythagoras suis discipulis auertere studuit symbolice admonens Per uiā publicā ne ambules. i. ne uulgi sequaris errores. Nam cȝ usurpari etiā hoc uolebat Extra publicam uiā ne uadas, iam insinuauerat loquendū esse ut m̄lti, potiusq̄ cȝ q̄d apud oēs cōstat, tu ne impugnes. Vnde istud est, Aduer sus solem ne loquaris, ne uidelicet icidas in pericula, q̄d recte monet illud Acutum gladiū declines. Id sit si honesta uerecundia utaris in publico, cu‑ ius hæc nota est Aduersus solem ne meiito. Nunc igitur sublato circa bo‑ num & malum errore, temperandū esse statuit uoluptati & mœrori, cupi‑ ditati & timori, quare dixit, Risui ęque atq̄ȝ tristiciæ manus non dedendas. Nam gaudiis & uoluptate nos frui secundū harmoniā iussit, hoc est cum honesta quadā temperantia quam appellauit lyram. Vnde hoc symbolū ὡϛ χ῀ϑαι πϛ λύϱαν. i. cantibus utendū ad lyram, non prorsus inane my‑ sterium fuit, quo semp̄ ante initium soporis utebant, ne p̄turbatis molesta rentur insomniis, q̄ dum irruissent, surgētes iussit lecti stragula excutere ac conuoluere, hoc est insomnia glomerare in unū & reiicere, ne rememo rata grauarent. De mœrore sic loquebatur. Arctum anñulū ne gestato, p̄ q̄d exclusit cunctū animi dolorē, nisi sup̄ admisso peccato, quapropter in suis ita cecinit carminibus. Mala qdem si feceris dole. In cæteris Pythago ras Cor ne edēdū mādauit, id sic est, ne te excrucies, quin ubi efferbueris in iram Olle uestigiū in cinere confundito, q̄d designāt ab ira deseruescen dum & p̄teritorum malorȝ tollendam esse memoriam. De cupiditate hoc modo. Quæ uncis sunt unguibus ne nutrias, idq̄ȝ cōtra manus rapaces cō‑ stituitur, imo necȝ de q̄tidiano uictu sis abunde sollicitus, quare ait. Chœ

I iiii

Book Two

look all about them when praying by "Pray turned round"; he advises caution in our prayers to God lest deservedly we have flung back at us: "You do not know what you seek." As for what should be our norm for a righteous life, as befits a man, and what the mean between the extremes of excess and deficiency was, between he who has no hands and he who has a hundred, the precept runs: "Do not jump over the balance." He advises moderation in study and action, but himself says openly "Apply the salt," which relates to our emotions, called "passions." Salt is the mark of modesty. In human food it is sprinkled in neither too great nor too little quantity; either extreme, whether over- or under-salted, is spat out. There is another proverb, "Do not cross over salt." All our emotions and passions are moved by the presence of good or ill; we rejoice when there is good, we are saddened when there is bad, and again, we long for future good, and dread the bad. Joy and grief are the elements of the passion from which come all the movements of our minds. When straight, we call it virtue, when crooked, vice. But often good things seem bad to us, and contrariwise, good things are perceived as not good. "There is a great difference," says Seneca, "between truth and similarity to truth," which is why the great mass of ordinary and inexperienced people fall so easily into error.

It was error of this kind that Pythagoras was anxious to avoid for his disciples: he warned "Do not walk in the public way," meaning "do not follow the errors of the crowd." He also wanted this one to be followed: "Do not wander from the public way," implying that one should speak as do the mass of people, and not fight against what is generally agreed. And hence: "Do not speak into the sun, least you fall into danger," which is a similar admonishment to "Avoid the sharp sword." This comes about if you show a decent modesty in public behavior, for which we have "Do not urinate into the sun."

Once the mistake of good and bad has gone, delight and grief, desire and fear, must, he said, be regulated. To this end he said "Do not lend a hand to laughter or to sorrow." He bade us enjoy pleasure and delight in harmony, that is, with the noble temperament which he termed "the lyre." Hence this precept: "Sing with a lyre accompaniment." It was no vain rite that they would perform before going to sleep; to prevent disturbance by troubling dreams he ordered that when such dreams forced their way in, they should get up and shake and roll up their mattresses, thereby rolling their sleeplessness into a ball and throwing it out, so that they should not be oppressed by its memory.

On the subject of grief he said this: "Do not wear a tight ring." He thus shut out of the mind all sorrow, except sorrow for a particular sin that has been committed, and he wrote in the verses "grieve only if you have done evil." Elsewhere Pythagoras tells us that "the heart is not to be eaten," or, "do not torture yourself." And, when your anger boils over "The bottom of the pot should be spread with ash," meaning you should simmer down, and erase the memory of past ills.

On desire he writes "Do not nurse what has curved claws"; this is directed against grasping hands, that you should not be too worried about your daily bread. So he says: "Put not your trust in the Choenix." Choenix is a day's food,

DE ARTE CABALISTICA

nici ne insideas, est aūt choenix cibus diurnus, quam uocant p̄bendam, alii
sportulas appellant. Pariter uero ne ullum auariciæ in animo tuo recon-
ditæ argumentum ostentes, ita commonuit. Quæ decidérint (inquens) ne
tollito, per q̃d uetuit etiam suarū quæcq̃ rerum non decere ardentiorem
esse amatorem. De formidine ita. Ne reflectas ubi ad terminos pueneris,
q̃ symbolo nō tm̄ trepidare mortē prohibet, uerumetiā quicq̃d in satis est
q̃tumcuncq̃ terreat. Hi nancq̃ sunt termini definiti & determinati q̃s trans
ire non poteris. Frustra igitur times q̃d reflectere aut uitare nequeas, ab
eiuscemodi quippe casu nusq̃ resilire, fortitudinis qdem laudatæ ac egre-
giæ magnanimitatis est. Enumerauimus p̄functorie notas Pythagoricas.
Primum q̃ ad diuina p̄tinent, deinde q̃ ad hoīes singulos quosq̃. Nunc
alter erga alterum qbus moribus utatur, ausculta paucis; cuncq̃ nihil amicicia sit optabilius, incumbit summa post deos cura, uirtute amicos parare
ut est in carminibus aureis, tn̄ non transeunter quoslibet. Iccirco ipse dixit. Ne cuicq̃ inieceris dextram. Et dum penetralibus tuis dignū amicū in-
ueneris, oīm tuorum participem eum facias, Ob eam rem ipse Pythagoras hoc alios ante omneis usurpauit adagiū. Amicorum oīa comunia. Timæo & Cicerone attestantibus. Est em̄ amicus alter ipse, q̃ fit ut amicicia
sit ἰσότης. i. æqualitas & eadem aīa. Minime aūt admittendi sunt in amiciciā
hoīes alioquin interne albi, tn̄ nigram caudam foris gestantes (expto crede) qbus nihil fert terra pestilentius, picæ mendicæ Cyanoleucæ cauda inter scapulas nigticante, omīa simulantes & dissimulantes hypocritę. Dixit
itaq̃ Pythagoras μὴ γεύεσθαι τῶν μελανούρων. i. Ne gustes ex iis qbus est nigra
cauda, ii sunt falsi f̄res q̃s atratos uocāt, ϟ ᷉ Ἰουδεῖν ὅτι ἐχάρις μέτιον μελάνωτη
ut scripsit Tryphon grammaticus. i. Falsum em̄ in extremis nigrescit. Reli
quos leuioris amiciciæ parū utiles siue cognatos siue amicos supra modū
nec cōtemnas nec acceptes. Quod instituit allegoria hæc, Vnguium cri-
nīumcq̃ præsegmina nec cōmingito nec insistito. Necq̃ abest quin oēm in-
gratum conuictorē & singulos nobiscum susurrones hoīesq̃ garrulos cate uitare iubeamur, unde illud extat Cohabitantes nobiscū hirundines ne
habeamus, porro amicus consulto recipiendus est, at receptus non facile
abiiciendus. Frangere nempe amiciciā inhumanū est, quare dixit. Panē ne
frangito. Tu uero ita uelis amicus esse ut amici oīa perinde cures atq̃ tua
cui non blandis uerbis & sermonū fuco placeas, sed studio ueri. Sedes em̄
amiciciæ ueritas est, non adulatio, propter q̃d ipse dixit. Oleo sedem ne ab
stergas. Vtq̃ conciliandus est bonorū amor, sic nō est cōmoueda malorū
iracūdia, hoc ipsum admonet Ignem gladio ne fodito. Est p̄terea uiri boni
officium prodesse ōibus, nocere nemini. Nam si uel molestiæ autor, uel
oneri imponendo socius accesseris, non profuisse quidem, magis aūt gra
uasse diceris, ut ita uitio locum dedisse uidearis. Tunc autē uirtuti potius
tuæ gra

what some might call the daily dole, others perhaps the welfare ration. In the same way, to stop you displaying any signs of concealed avarice he issued the warning "do not pick up what has fallen." By this he forbade anyone to be too ardent a lover even of his own things.

On fear he says: "Do not turn back when you come to the limit." In this precept he will not have us tremble not just at death, but neither at whatever may come to pass, however frightening it may be. For these limits are precise and fixed, and you cannot cross them. Fear is wasted when you fear what you cannot avert or avoid; and not to shrink from such events is a mark of noble and admirable courage and greatness of spirit.

We have briefly run through the Pythagorean symbols, first those that relate to God, next those that relate to man as an individual. Here now is a little on how one man should treat another.

Nothing is more desirable than friendship, and after the gods, that we should devote ourselves to friendship. "Make friends in virtue," says the *Golden Verses*. But not with just anyone in passing: as Pythagoras himself said "do not give your right hand to anyone." When you have found a friend worthy of your deepest self make him a partner in all that is yours. Hence the adage that Pythagoras was the first to use, "All in common among friends," which Timaeus and Cicero also cite. A friend is another self; thus friendship is *equality*, the same soul. You should never admit to friendship men who are white within and who wear a black tail when out and about (I know, believe me). They are the worst plague on earth, scavenging magpies with a blackish tail dangling from their shoulders, hypocrites who simulate and dissimulate in everything. Pythagoras said "Do not taste what has a black tail." They are false brothers whom they call mourners; "falsehood grows black at the edges," wrote Tryphon the grammarian.[47]

As for the rest—those unsuitable for a lesser degree of friendship, whether relations or friends—you should neither condemn nor accept them beyond measure. This is laid down in the allusive "Do not defile or tread on nail- or hair-clippings." We are also told sharply to avoid having disagreeable people as our close companions, or rumor-mongers or chatterers. Hence: "Let us not have swallows living with us." You should be cautious about making friends, but once you are friends, friendship is not easily broken off. Breaking up a friendship is inhuman, and he said, "do not break bread." You should want to be the kind of friend who looks after a friend's affairs as you would look after your own, and you should please him not with smooth words and honeyed phrases, but with zeal for the truth. Truth, not flattery, is the seat of friendship, and thus he said "Do not sprinkle oil on a seat."

One should foster a love of good men, while not allowing one's anger for the bad to be stirred up, and he gave the warning: "Do not stab fire with a sword." It is the duty of a good man to help all and harm none. If you are the source of trouble or if you as an accessory assent to burdens being imposed, you will be seen not to have assisted, but rather to have oppressed, and to have given vice a foothold. You will earn more thanks when you run to help someone lay down a burden, so that he may be relieved more quickly. Pythagoras said: "Help to put

LIBER SECVNDVS

tuæ gratiam mereberis cum onus deponenti succurras ut leues pondere uelocius, hoc illud est q̃d dixit φορτίον συγκαθαίρειν μὴ δὲ συνεπιτιθέναι. i. Onus simul deponere, non aut simul imponere, haud secus atq̃ si dicat, ad id co adiuuato ut hões molestia leuentur, non grauent. Indignus uero & puer sis uir moribus sicut non est interimendus subito, ita tibi ueniat minimę fouendus. Quare interdixit Cibum in matellam ne immittas. Eam deniq̃ ferocitatē deponamus oportet ut prorsus nemo seuiat in queuis innocen tem. Pręcepit em̄ & illud Pythagoras Mitem arborē non uiolandā nec lę dēdam. Vnde illud extat in symbolis Pisces ne gustato. Est profecto piscis animal eiusmodi quod ipsa natura nullo pacto lædit hoīem. Nunc q̃tum ad rempub. attinet adhuc id restat citandū q̃d ipse dixit, Coronam ne car pseris, significans legē non uiolandā. Et illud itē ln uia ne seces ligna. Quo monemur publica & quæ sunt uniuersitatis non esse turbanda. Q̃ uero sapientem haud deceat fastus & maiestatis inflatio, publici ue honoris tu mor, arcanū hoc symbolū nos exhortat̄ A fabis abstinendum. Magistrat͛ em̄ fabis eligunt̄ priscorū more. Innumerabile aūt desyderat malū q̃sq̃s anxie occupat͛ est in capessenda republica. Quo magis ne populū dehor tando male offenderet, maluit discipulos recondito mysterio tanq̃ fidus magister ab omni ambitione auertere, ut memoria semper tenerent uide licet ὅτι οὐ δεῖ πολιτεύεσθαι. plura horum non dubiū est quin Hipparchus & lysis Pythagoræ auditores memoriter tenentes pcepta doctoris, q̃ illi cū cæteris conscholasticis ingenio suo pro libris seruarunt, in auditorio the barum prodiderunt. Ea tñ & non omnia uidi & ad finem properans non oīa pstringere uolui. Hoc unū uolui nescius ne esses & obliuioni haud cō mitteres oēm ferme Pythagoricā philosophiā esse notis uerborū & tegu mentis rerum plenam, euq̃ tradendi more ut ante dixi ab Hebreis credi & ægyptiis ipse ad græcos primus transtulisse. Solebant em̄ ægyptii qui busdā fictis iter sacerdotes literis sacra comunicare, ut essent plebi secre ta q̃ & diutius admirationi forent & attentius caperent. Vnde illi Colossi statuæ, aræ, arcus, & æra publice incisa literis ægyptiorū sacris, promine bant spectanda uniuersis, sed non nisi mystis & initiatis hieroglyphis intel lecta ut de iis Chæremon & Orus, ægyptiorūq̃ multi scripsere. Sic Pytha goras meus esse nõ putabat uiri sapientis asino lyrā exponere aut myste ria q̃ ita reciperet ut sus tubam, & fides graculus, & ungenta Scarabæus, Quare silentiū indixit discipulis, ne uulgo diuinorū arcana patefacerent, q̃ meditando facilius q̃ loquendo apprehendant. Tum Marranus. Ne, in quit, unus tibi possideas oro Pythagorā mi Philolae, sed nostrū esse patia ris, non solius tuum. Eqdem ipse mihi uideor de tuo sermone haud admo dum surdus neq̃ immemor Pythagorista euasisse, q̃ ut cuncta mysteria, metaphoras, ænigmata, sententias, apophthegmata, allegorias, symbola,

Book Two

a burden down and not to put one on," as if to say "Help to relieve men of their troubles, not to increase them."

A man whose behavior is base and depraved should not be straightway put to death, but similarly, you should not give him succor. On this he said "Do not put food in a pot." Lastly, we should put aside all savagery, and none will show cruelty to any innocent. Pythagoras' command was "Do not hurt or harm any fruitful tree," and from this comes the precept "Do not eat fish," for the fish is a creature which by its nature in no way harms man.

As far as the state is concerned, it remains to quote his words "Do not snatch the crown," meaning "do not flout the law." There is also "Do not cut wood in the road," which tells us that things held in common by all are not to be disturbed. That the flatulence of arrogance and grandeur, the swelling of public dignity, do not become the wise is indicated by the obscure precept "Abstain from beans," referring to the beans the ancients used in elections to civic office. He who busies himself in public administration is looking for countless trouble. Like a trusty leader, rather than offend the people with his dissuasion, he preferred a secret sign to turn his disciples away from all ambition and make them always remember that they should not go into politics.

No doubt there are many more of these precepts. Hipparchus and Lysis committed them to memory after hearing them from the learned man's lips—like many other scholars with them they relied on their minds rather than books—and expounded them in the lecture hall at Thebes. These I have seen are by no means all, and in drawing quickly to a close I have not wanted to run over them all.

One thing I have wanted, however, and that was that you should know and not forget that nearly all Pythagorean philosophy is full of signs for words and cloaks for things, a form of communication that he, so it is believed, was the first to take to the Greeks from the Hebrews, as I have already said, and the Egyptians. The Egyptian priests used a special alphabet to convey sacred information among themselves, so that the sacred would be kept secret from the common people; wonder would last longer and they would win greater attention. So we have the Colossi, the statues, the altars, the arches, the bronzes—all publicly inscribed with the secret Egyptian characters. They stand exposed to public gaze, comprehensible to none but priests and initiates in the hieroglyphs. All this comes from Chaeremon and Orus and many Egyptians writers.

In a similar way, my Pythagoras thought it was not the part of a man of learning to teach an ass the lyre, or a fool the mysteries, for they would receive them as a pig does the trumpet, the jackdaw the lute and the beetle the ointment. He therefore enjoined silence on his followers, lest the secrets of the divine be revealed to the mob, secrets grasped better in meditation than in speech.

MARRANUS: Don't keep Pythagoras all to yourself, Philolaus, I beg you. You must let him be our Pythagoras, not just yours. It seems to me that I have emerged from your talk—to which I was in no way deaf or inattentive—a Pythagorean.

Briefly, in passing, you have gone through the whole catalogue of mysteries, apophthegms, allegories, symbols, marks, signs and sacraments of this great man, the first philosopher of all. Now, to commit it

DE ARTE CABALISTICA

notas,signa,sacramenta,tanti uiri & oīm primi philosophi quæ tu obiter & pfunctorie catalogi specie recensuisti,cōmendarē memoriæ,locis Tullianis & arte rhetorū in te audiendo sum usus. Quin uis periculū faciā. Aſ seruisti em̄ si rite recordor Pythagoram tribus uoluminibus oēs philoso phiæ partes complexū fuisse physico,pædeutico & politico.i.naturali disci plinari & morali,q̄ moriens (ut alias audiui) filiæ testamento mandasse fertur,ne uel extra familiā ederet,immo nullatenꝰ publicaret.Ipse uero di gnis tm̄ & numero paucis,dum uiueret oīa q̄ illic continebant,maxīe aūt mathematica,uiua uoce nullo utens inuolucro plane demonstrauit. Cęte ris cætera in parabolis.Ergo aliter loquens,aliter sentiens (& si semp̄ idē sapiens) per quædam symbola ceu memoracula doctrinā suam suis imp̄ titus est,ita ut ad priscorū imitationē aliud dictū,aliud referret intellectū. Ab eo nanc̄ ut de primis exordiar pro deo ponit infinitū & unū,pro rebꝰ incorporeis numeri,pro corporeis figuræ,pro mistis harmonia,pro sor dibus & peccatis,uites non putatæ,pro eo q̄d est in uita purissimū, farina. Gallus cādidus nota est deo dedicati,Sedere designat humilitatē,Circūa ctio prudentiā,& hęc q̄ ad diuina.Istud ad rem priuatā & uirtutes spectat Statera symbolū iusticiæ,Sal notat moderamen, Via publica errores uul gi,Sol ponit loco manifesti & apti,Acutꝰ gladius significat picula, Lotiū inuerecūdiā,Cātus uoluptatem,Lyra harmoniā, Stragula lecti,insomnia, Annulꝰ strictꝰ dolorē, Esca cordis cruciatū, Olla ebullitionē iræ,Vngues recurui rapinā, Chœnix alimentum, Res decidētes fortunam, Termini fa tum,ista sunt hois quoad se ipsum,illud iam seq̄tur quod uersat erga ‘alte rū,Dextra notat amicitiā,Nigra cauda falsos fratres, Vngues et cries sym bola sunt propinq̄rū Hirundines garrulorū, & eorū qui excedūt ingra ti,Panis mysteriū est ueræ amiciæ, Oleū adulationis signū,Ignis iracun diæ,Gladiꝰ exacerbatiōis, Onꝰ molestiā insinuat, Matella figurat idignū, Arbor mitis hoīem utilem,Piscis hoīem innocētem. Hactenus de re pri uata. Nūc de republica.Corona signū est legis & regimis,Ligna uiæ res uniuersitatis,ambitionē Faba demōstrat, oīa symbolica,omnia figurata et allegorica.Qꜩ nisi plura in discipulis Pythagoræ putares inueniri posse, profecto hæc oīa reducerem ad eius uiri mathematicas proportiōes,qm̄ unum & duo prima progressiōe fiūt tria. Ecce rempublicā,& ter tria sunt nouem,ecce rem diuinā,& ter quatuor sunt duodecim. Ecce rem priuatā q̄ad alterum,& quater quatuor sunt sedecim.Ecce rem priuatam q̄ ad se. Est igit̄ respublica trigonus,& res priuata tetragonus,& sicut se habet se decim ad duodecim, ita se habet duodecim ad nouē,singula in proportio ne hemiolia,hoc est sesquialtera.Vide q̄ docilis te p̄ceptore sum,& q̄ egre gie pythagorisso.Tu uero quē meipsum facis? Tum Philolaus,Plane Py thagoreum,inqt,iam em̄ tibi p̄mitto rumpere silentium,satis disciplinarū

habes

On the Art of Kabbalah

all to memory I have made use of Ciceronian devices and rhetorical techniques. Would you like me to prove it?

You said, if I remember rightly, that Pythagoras had contained all his philosophy in three books, the *Physics*, the *Paedeuticon*, and the *Politics*—that is, natural science, education, and politics or morals. As he lay dying (this I have heard elsewhere), he is said to have instructed his daughter, in his will, not to promulgate these outside the family or to publish them in any form. He had himself in his lifetime shown orally to a small group of people worthy of them, all that was contained in his writing, and had done so in plain terms with no guarded language, in mathematics especially. The rest learned what remained in parables. Saying one thing while meaning another, yet remaining always the same wise man, it was through the Precepts—like mnemonics—that he imparted his teaching to his disciples, in such a way that each saying would refer to a different meaning, following the custom of the ancients.

To begin with the beginning: for God he put infinity, and One; for incorporeal things, number; for corporeal things, figures; for the composite, harmony; for foul sins, unpruned vines; for that which is purest in life, flour. A white cock denotes something dedicated to God; sitting marks humility; turning round means prudence. All this relates to the divine.

As for individual matters and morality, a scale is a symbol of justice, and salt is moderation; the public way denotes general errors; the sun stands for what is clear and open; a sharp sword means danger; urine immodesty; a mattress signifies sleeplessness; songs, pleasure; the lyre, harmony; bedclothes, insomnia; a tight ring, sorrow; eating the heart means pain; a boiling pot is anger; curved claws mean pillage; choenix is food; falling objects mean luck; limits mean fate. This has to do with man in regard to himself.

In man's relations to other men, the right hand denotes friendship; a black tail, false brothers; nails and hair symbolize those close to you; swallows stand for chatterers and extremely unpleasant people; bread means true friendship; oil, flattery; fire, anger; a word, provocation; a burden, trouble; a pot means the unworthy; a fruitful tree a useful man; a fish an innocent man. All of this deals with private matters.

As for the state, a crown is a sign of law and government; wood in a road indicates public affairs; a bean means ambition. All the precepts are allegorical and in code.

Unless you think there is more to be discovered in the disciples of Pythagras, I shall reduce all these things to his mathematical relationships. One and two, in the first progression, make three. Here is the state. Thrice three is nine. Here is the divine. Three fours are twelve, the private domain, with regard to others. Four fours are sixteen, the private domain as it regards the self. The state is a triangle, the private domain a quadrangle. As sixteen: twelve, so twelve: nine, and each thing in hemiolic proportion—that is, three: two.

See what a receptive pupil you have, and what a good Pythagorean I am! What do you make of me?

PHILOLAUS: I give you full permission to break the Pythagorean silence. You have learned enough, if you understand all this theory intellectually.

LIBER SECVNDVS

habes,si oīa formalia intellectualiter intelligas. Ad hæc Marranꝰ,Ego cer
te quid hoc sit ignoro. Dicam, ait ille, Si oīa quæ tibi apparent, a sensu ad
mentem transferas, hoc est, si corporeas passiones omneis reiicias & men
tis contemplatione pfruaris. Iam uerbi causa in latissimo campi spacio lon
ge distantem a te hoīem uidere te uelim, tu uero ignoras qd rerum sit exi
stimabis uel agri terminū, uel truncū esse, habet eṁ figuram rectā, & ma
teriam tua opinione immotā, propius cum aspexeris, cogitabiṫ in arbuscu
lam succreuisse. Reiecta igitur penes te cemetaria mole, uegetare id putas
uita plantæ, tum si motu progressiuo iuxta uos ambo accedatis, continuo
arboris forma euanescēte succurrit tibi aialis cuiusdā imago nescienti atcꝫ
dubitanti sit ne gryphes an ciconia, uel alia quęlibet ingens auis, bipes eṁ
est. Iamcꝫ factus propior cernis cꝫ caudam & alas non habet, & ambulat
erecto capite, mox relinquis oēs formas priores, & formam cogitas huma
nam. Ergo una cum obuia fueritis, salutem prior dicis, & respondet iste lo
quens rationaliter, tum necꝫ fauni necꝫ satyri aut alius tibi phasmatis ori
tur suspicio. Sed plane hoīem esse agnoscis uel uicinū uel amicum, quę ubi
de parentibus suis & propinquis ut fieri solet interrogas, ipse omni quæ
stioni tuę satis faciens recedit. Eocꝫ discedente, solus tecum meditaris hūc
hoīem & ex parentibus esse natum, & parentes rursum ex parentibus, &
illos ipsos pariter è semine humano, & semen illud ab hoīe q̄dam esse, tan
demcꝫ cum natura respuat infinitū, uidebit forte haud admodū impossi
bile unum aliquē assignare hoīem q̄ fuerit ortus sine semine humano. Ita
in xii. libro post naturalia scripsit Aristoteles, & eum appellat τὸ τέλιον.i.
pfectum. Cuncꝫ accepto feras dari a philosophis hoīem talem pfectū, cui
corpus non sit natū ut cęterorū hoīm, tunc discurres p ratione ad hois ani
mam, semp de pfecta ad pfectiorē & nobiliorē. Eadēcꝫ possibilitate arbi
traberis concedi q̄ꝫ aīam certam, non ita creatā ut cæteras aīas, sed forte
q̄ se ipsam cōcreauerit, et eam esse non solū pfectā aut aliis pfectiorē, uerꝫ
etiā cunctarū q̄ fuerūt, sunt, erūt aut fore possunt, pfectissimā, hanc in hois
mortalis corpe sita separabis a corpe, ac supra reliquas aīas separatas (q̄n
ipsa est nobilissima) locabis in nobilissimū nō locū sed habitaculū. Nobi
lissima uero mansio est proxima deo, q̄d Stagirita late prosequtur in lib. ad
Alexādrū de mūdo. Illā aūt nos in orizonte mūdi suꝑsuꝑmi q̄ diciṫ incom
parabilis habitare iudicamus, ubi est unio dei & creaturę. Sicut in orizōte
eternitatis ponimus motorē primi mobilis imobilē, in q̄ mūdus corporeꝰ
& incorporeus cōueniūt. Hac iam uia humanā formā, intellectualiter uer
tisti in formā separatā, & eandē mentaliter ad æthernitatis suꝑmā duxisti
mansionē. Vnde oībus angelis & aīabus gratiosis summa instillat beatitu
do, & oēs aīę salutiferę ad eandē aīam ceu ad regulā quandā regulantur.
Quod uticꝫ de corpe illo pfectissimo cuius ante meminimꝰ Pythagorice

Book Two

MARRANUS: I really don't know what that means.

PHILOLAUS: Let me tell you. It means that everything you observe you transfer from the senses to the mind, that is, that you reject all that the body feels; you enjoy the contemplation of the mind. For example, you are on a broad plain, looking at a man a long way away from you. You do not know what that thing is. You may think it is a boundary stone or a tree trunk, since it stands upright and does not seem to you to be moving. When you look more closely, it will seem to have grown into a small tree. So you reject the idea that it is something solid, you think it is organic plant life. Then, as you both move gradually towards each other, the idea that it is a tree vanishes and you picture some animal, though you cannot be sure whether it is a griffin or a stork or some other great big bird. It has two legs. And now you are closer still and can see that it has not tail or wings, and it walks with head erect, so you abandon the previous images and picture the human form. Then you meet. You greet him first; he replies in rational speech. You suspect no faun or satyr, nor that you witness some other apparition. You recognize a man, a friend or neighbor, you ask, as one does, after his parents and family and he gives satisfactory answers to your questions, and then he goes off.

When he has gone, you think things over for yourself: this is a man, born of his parents, and they of theirs, and their parents too, of human seed, seed which came from some man, and that at the end of the chain, since nature cannot take infinity, it will seem quite possible to suppose some man who was not born of human seed. So Aristotle wrote in Book 12 of the *Metaphysics*; he calls this man "perfect."

As you find it easy to accept that philosophers have posited such a "perfect man," whose body was not born in the same way as the rest of mankind, you arrive at the soul of man, by reason, always from the perfect to the more perfect and more noble. You will hold that by the same possiblity it must be granted that there is a soul created not as other souls are, but self-created, perhaps, this soul being not only "perfect," or "more perfect than other souls," but the most perfect of all that have been, are, will or could be. This soul is sited in the body of mortal man, but you will distinguish it from the body and place it above the other distinct souls (it being the most noble), in the place — rather the habitation — that is most noble. The noblest dwelling is next to God, as Aristotle often says in his book *On the World* addressed to Alexander. We judge that soul to dwell on the level of the supersupreme, or incomparable, world, where there is union of God and created. In a similar way we put the unmoving mover of the first movement on the level of eternity, where the corporeal and incorporeal worlds meet.

On this path you have now in intellect changed the human form into a distinct form, and in mind you have brought it to its supersupreme dwelling in eternity, the source of the great bliss poured out on all the angels and beloved souls, and the salvation-bearing souls are governed by that soul, on which they are modeled. I would not deny that this is the case too in Pythagorean teaching, as with the perfect body I have already mentioned.

DE ARTE CABALISTICA

nō negarē. Nā ipſe dixit hoīem poſſe fieri deū imortalē, p q̃d ſentētiā ſuā dare oſtēdit, cp una gloria parte hoīs utrāq; glorificare poſſit, & totū homīnē facere beatū, qñ maximus ipſe deus aut utrāq; inſorbit, ac ſua deitate ibibit, aut aīæ cōmittit ut corpori ſublimato claritudīne & glorificatiōne ſuā influat. ὡς ὁμοζύγῳ καὶ ὁμοπορεύτῳ, ᠪυαπογραφεί τί π καὶ ᠪυαθλίζωντι. i. Tanq̃ cōiugato & uiarū comiti, ſimulq; cēſito, & q̃d ſimul certauerit. Hoc Pythagorę dogma repullulauit ab Orpheo, q̃d in exitu hymni ad Mercuriū depḥendit. Iā tibi p̄ oculis pendentē cernis Homeri cathenā auream in Iliados octauo ab Ioue cœlitus fragilitati nr̄æ demiſſam in terras, p̄ quā temet ipſum ope diuina in ſublime leues cū agēdo tū contēplādo: Neceſſe nāq; fuerit prius ſecūdū mēnte uiuere, poſt tandē mēte cōtēplari & contēplātē ardēter aſcēdere, qm̄ uita eſt cōtēplatiōe prior, quarꝫ cū utrāq; deceat eſſe pura ad cōſequēdū id q̃ nihil eſt purius, certe purgāda prius uita eſt, dein de illumināda cōtēplatio. Quod igit in ea quā attulim⁹ rerū a rebus abſtractiōe uidiſti, tu id in te ipſo experire, ut p̄ rōnem ad mentē redeas, & exterrnis te oībus explices, q̃d M. Antoninus Impator impat ἄτλωσον σαυτόν. i. explicato te ipm. Oportet em ex hac uita migrātē in alterā, oīne indumentū exuiſſe ac nudū pficiſci, nō modo ab oī materia & corpeis appēdiciis, uerꝫ etiā ab uniuerſa pturbationū affectionū et paſſionū mole, pfugū atq; liberū, q̃d ſcite admodū Lucianus Samoſatēſis in dialogo Charonis & Mercurii oīm philoſophiſſimo docuit quē niſi legiſti lege & imitare. Quid aliud eſt obſecro q̃d Pythagoras in tria diuiſit q̃ nos in diuinæ uirtutis ueſtigia ponāt, niſi purgatio, illuminatio & pfectio. Sic em ait. ταῦτα πόνει ταῦτ' ἔκμελέτα τούτων χρὴ ἐρᾶν σε, ταῦτα σε τᾶς θίιας ἀρετῆς εἰς ἰχνία θήσει. i. Hęc labora, hæc meditare, hęc oportet te amare, hęc te diuinæ uirtutis in ueſtigia ponent, q̃d Hierocles de uiribus aīę nr̄æ rōnalis æque itelligi uoluit amori diuinorū applicatis, & hęc nos, inqt, deo ſiles faciēt. Verba Pythagorę cōſyderem⁹. Tria nāq; poſuit qb⁹ iūctis anagogice poſſum⁹ ad ſummā beatitudīnē puenire. Laborē uirtutisq̃ in actiōe cōſiſtit. Meditatiōnē q̃ multis diſcipliˊnarū ſtudiis nutriˊ, & Amorē q̃ nos ut neceſſariū uinculū deo connectit, primū moralis, ſecūdū naturalis cū mathematica, tertiū ſtudioſis theoloˊgia ubertim exhibet, nec unū ſine altero p̄ ſe ſatis eſt, ſed tria hęc cōuenire oportet. Id docte q̃dē ut oīa Porphyri⁹ maximus Pythagoricorū exploraˊtor in libro primo de abſtinētia aīatorū, tractat his uerbis q̃ ob graue teſtiˊmonii autoritatē afferre libuit. οὐκ ἔστιν inquit ἡ εὐδαιμονικὴ ἡμῖν θεωρία, λόγων ἄθροισις, κὴ μαθημάτων πλῆθος, ὡς ἄν τις οἰηθείη, οὐδὲ ζυιτέμενη κατὰ τὸ πῦρ, οὐδ' ἐν τῷ πως τῶν λόγων λαμβάνει τὴν ἐπίδοσιν. οὕτω γὰρ οὐδὲν ἐκώλυεν, τὸ πᾶν μάθημα βυζαντας, εἶν εὐδαίμονας. i. Nō eſt beata nobis contēplatio, uerborū accumulatio & diſciplinarū multitudo, queadmodū aliqs forte putauerit, neq; cōſtituˊta ſecūdū hoc, neq; pro q̃titate rationū ac ſermonū accipit incremētū. Sic em nihil prohiberet illos q omnem cōgregarēt diſciplinam fore beatos.

Et aliquan

On the Art of Kabbalah

Pythagoras himself said that man could become an immortal god; clearly this demonstrates his view that by one glory could either part of man be made glorious and the whole man happy: the great God either draws in both parts and absorbs them in His deity, or he entrusts to the soul the task of flooding the elevated body with his clarity and glorification.

"Yoked together, companions for the journey, assessed together, fellows in the struggle."

This doctrine of Pythagoras sprang from Orpheus, and it is found at the end of the hymn to Mercury.

Do you now see dangling before your eyes Homer's golden chain (*Iliad*, Book 8), sent down from Heaven to earth for our weakness by Jupiter? With it, you can with divine help, now in action, now in meditation, lift yourself on high. You must first live the life of the mind, then with mind must you meditate, and in passionate meditation you must rise up. Life is prior to meditation; thus, though each should be pure for the pursuit of that than which nothing is purer, surely life is the first to be purified; and only then is meditation to be enlightened. Attempt within yourself what you have seen of this abstraction of things from things which I have put forward. Retreat through reason to mind, extricate your self from all outward things, following the instruction of the emperor Marcus Aurelius: Extricate yourself. In the journey from this life to another every garment should be cast off, one is to set out naked, fleeing and free of not only all material and corporeal attachments, but all the burden of emotion, passion and feeling. Lucian of Samosata, the best of all philosophers, put this nicely in his dialogue of Charon and Mercury; if you have not already read it, you should do so and model yourself upon it.

What, I ask you, could those three things be that Pythagoras marked out, and which put us on the tracks of the divine, but purification, enlightenment, and perfection. He said: "Work at these, meditate on these, these you should love, and these will put you on the track of divine strength." As Hierocles, writing on the powers of our rational soul when applied to the love of the divine, said: "These will make us like unto God."

Let us consider these words of Pythagoras. He put forward three things by which, in a mystic sense, we are able to rise to the height of bliss: the work of virtue, which lies in action; meditation, nourished by much learning; love, which binds us to God with its inseparable chain. The moral man occasions the first; physics and mathematics the second; theology the third. No one is enough in itself without another; and these should be found in conjunction.

Here is what Porphyry, a great explorer of the Pythagorean system, said on this in Book 1 of *On Vegetarianism*. He speaks in these words, wanting to convey the weighty origin of what he says: "Meditation is no blessing to us when it is a heap of words and a great crowd of disciplines, despite what some may have thought. It is not like that, nor can it be increased by quantities of theory and discussion. If this were the case there would be nothing to stop those who swarm in every discipline becoming the blessed." And a little further on (for the sake of brevity I omit certain passages) he says:

LIBER SECVNDVS L.

Et aliquanto post, ut omittam reliqua breuitatis gratia sic ait. καὶ ἡμᾶς δε
ἴ ..... πρὸς τὰ ὄντως οἰκεῖα μέλλοιμέν τανιέναι ἃ μὴ ἐκ τῆς θνητῆς προσειλήφαμεν φύ
σεως, ἀποθέωαι πάντα, μετὰ τῆς πρὸς αὐτὰ προσπαθείας δι'ἧς ἡ κατάβασις γέγονεν ἀνα
μνηθῆναι δὲ τῆς μακαρίας καὶ αἰωνίου οὐσίας καὶ πρὸς τὸ ἀσώματον καὶ ἀπαθὲς ἀνιέναι
τὰς ἐπανελθεῖν, δύο μελέτας ποιεζομένους, μίαν μὲν καθ'ἣν πᾶν δ' ὑλικὸν καὶ θνητὸν
ἀποθησόμεθα, ἑτέραν δὲ, ὅπως ἐπανέλθωμεν καὶ ἀνελευσόμεθα ἐναντίως ἐφ'ἃ τὰ νῦν
ἐαίνοντες ἢ ἐνταῦθα καθήλωμεν .i. Et nos oportet hinc ſiqdē ad uere propria
uelimus redire quæ de mortali aſſumpſimus natura abiicere uniuerſa, cū
ipſa erga illa affectione per quā deſcenſus nobis contigit, reminiſci autē
beatę & æthernę eſſentię,& ad incorporeū ac impaſſibile ſtudętes aſcen
dere, duas meditationes facientes, una qdē ſecundū quā omne materiale et
mortale deponamus, alterā aūt quatenus reuertamur et redeamus,aliter
ad ea aſcendętes q̄ hic deſcędimus.Et iterū post ſermonē haud ualde mul
tum iubet nos illic Porphyrius a ſenſu & imaginatiōe oīcq̨ irrōnali quæ
ſequit inde conditione, paſſionibuſq̨ eiuſmodi, animū penitus ſegregare
quatenus p̱mittit naturę neceſſitas, rite uero diſponere articulatimq̨ cō
ponere q̄ ad mente p̱tinent,tranq̨llitate paeeq̨ ex bello q̄d aduerſum irra
tionalitate geſſimus pārates, ut nō ſolū de intellectu & intelligibilibus au
diamus,uerū etiā pro uirili ſimus fruętes eius contęplatione,tū in naturā
incorporeā trāſlati,tū uiuętes cū ueritate p̱ mente,nō ultra falſe cū corpo
rū cognatis.Soluere itaq̨ multa nobis indumēta debemus,tū uiſibile hoc
indumentū carneū,tū ea q̄bus interius ſumus induti pelliceis, p̱xima.Huc
uſq̨ Porphyrius q ea de re lōge plura diſſerēdo proſeq̨tur,oīa iſtuc ten
dentia ut p̱ ſenſibilia ueniamus ad ītelligibilis & mētalis boni fruitiōe,ho
neſte uiuędo, pure cōtemplādo, & diuine amādo, q̄ oīa de Pythagora no
ſtro tanq̄ e q̄dā ingēti cūctarū diſciplinarū flumine duxit. Ego uero, Mar
ranus aiebat,ab iis q̄ mihi ordine receſuiſti plane in eā moueor opinionē
ꝗ flumen illud ſuū, Pythagoras ex infinito Cabaliſtarū pelago cuius fœ
lice nobis Simon nauigationē pollicetur in agros grecorū limitauit, unde
noſtra tādē ſtudia irrigare queamus, Ita pares mihi uidēt eſſe inter ſe Si
monis de Cabaliſtis & tui de Pythagoricis tā ſermōes q̄ ſentētiæ. Nā qd
aliud intēdit uel Cabalęus uel Pythagoras,niſi aīos hoīm in deos referre,
hoc eſt ad p̱ſectā beatitudinem promouere.Quę aūt alia uia q̄ ſimilis utri
uſq̨ tradendi modus & ambobus æqua exercitatio per ſymbola & notas
adagia & parœmias, p̱ numeros & figuras, p̱ literas ſyllabas & uerba, Sic
hypſilon Pythagorę iuuętutis ſymbolū extat.Sic prima ſyllaba Iliados ſi
gnū eſt & nota oīm librorū Homeri q̄t ſint numero ī utroq̨ opę. Sic uer
bum cādidi ſignificat bonū,atri malū. Haud aliter & Simōnī primā Penta
teuchi literā, & pętagrāmati mediā ad alias res trāſtulit, & Raham, autore
Dauid Kimhi,allegorice pro Abrahā mutuat9 eſt, & cętera q̄ de ſermonę
ad nos habito ſatis meminim9.Sed audi q̄to clamore nos caupo ipſe ad cœ
naculū uocat,heus ad epulas.Et Philolas. Eq̄dē,inq̨t,cupięter edā,qn Imus

K

Book Two

If we intend to return to what really concerns us, we should discard all our assumptions about the nature of man and the fondness for those assumptions that led to our descent. We must call to mind the blessed and eternal Essence and so concentrating, rise up to the Incorporeal and Insentient with two thoughts in mind, one being how successfully to be rid of all things material and mortal, the other being how to undertake our reformation and so ascend to that Essence in a way different from the manner of our previous descent.

After a short passage Porphyry continues with instructions that insofar as is humanly possible, we should keep our minds apart from the senses and the imagination, apart from every irrational state that follows from them and all such emotion, instructing us to thrust them aside and piece by piece to build up the intellect, creating the peace of tranquillity out of the war we have waged against irrationality. Thus may we not only listen to discussion on the intellect and intelligibles, but also enjoy meditation on them as far as man can. Then, translated into incorporeality, and through the mind living with truth, we are no longer living false lives of things to do with the body. And so we ought to remove much of our clothing, both this visible garment of flesh and the layer within us, beneath the surface of the skin.

This lengthy and protracted account of Porphyry is leading to one conclusion, that we should come to delight in the good of the intellect and the mind through the world of the senses, by honest lives, undistracted meditation and divine love. All this he takes from our master Pythagoras, that great stream of all learning.

MARRANUS: Well, I am coming to the conclusion from your chain of argument that Pythagoras drew *his* stream of learning from the boundless sea of the Kabbalah whose successful navigation is promised us by Simon; and that Pythagoras has led his stream into Greek pastures from which we, last in the line, can irrigate our studies. What Simon says and thinks about the Kabbalists and what you say and think about the Pythagoreans seem to me to be exactly the same. What other intention has either Pythagoras or a Kabbalist, if not to bring men's minds to the gods, that is, to lead them to perfect blessedness? Another way in which they are similar lies in their means of passing on information, the equal interest they have in symbols, signs, adages and proverbs, numbers and figures, letters, syllables and words. Thus for Pythagoras the letter *upsilon* is a symbol of youth. Similarly the first syllables of the *Iliad* are considered significant and so is the number of all the books of Homer in each of his two works. A "white" word signifies good, while a "black" word signifies bad. In just the same way our friend Simon used the first letter of the *Pentateuch* and the middle letter of the *Pentagrammaton* for special purposes, and *Raham*, according to David Kimhi, is for allegorical reasons put in place of *Abraham*, and we can remember enough other instances from his discourse.

But listen! What a din the innkeeper is making calling us to table. Time for dinner.

PHILOLAUS: I'd love something to eat, let's go.

IOANNIS REVCHLIN PHORCENSIS LL.
Doc. De Arte Cabalistica, Liber Tertius.

POst ubi digreſſi lumẽcɋ obſcura uiciſſim Luna p̄mit ſuadẽtɋ cadẽtia ſydera ſonos, ambo ſoluũt i̅ ſopore̅, p̄miſſa adhortatio̅e alteri⁹ erga al terũ ne ultra primũ mane obdormiſceret, exp̱geſacie̅dos igi̅t fore curarũt Et poſtero die dũ de more i̅duũt, interea meminerũt ei⁹ diuerſorii Caupo nis uerba lõga & uaria qb⁹ ad heſternas epulas hoſpitib⁹ receſuerit fuiſſe q̅ſdã ſup̱iori die a romana curia Frãcofordiã miſſas, ꝑpoſitio̅es & co̅cluſi ones, co̅tra ihibitio̅e̅ ap̄licam ab Aſtaroto q̅dã fictas et co̅cinnatas aduer ſus Io. Reuchlin, propt̕ libros no̅ co̅bure̅dos iã plus qnqueñio crudeles p̱ ſecutio̅es inocēter ac ſip̄aio forti & i̅ſracto paſſum, p̱ forib⁹ ſapie̅tię act̕ pl orũ ueſtibulis Romę affixas, & mox i̅ lutũ ſterc˚ & coenũ ibi ˏpiectas & co̅culcatas iuſtis ex cauſis, tũ qa p̄ter Sũmi Po̅tificis uolu̅tate̅ & abſcɋ reue rēdiſſimoꝛ iudicũ noticia corã qb⁹ ea lis poſt Aſtaroti appellatio̅e hacte n⁹ trieñio i̅ Curia pẽderet tale facin⁹ fuiſſet attētatũ, tũ cɋ uniuerſis i̅noteſ ceret eã co̅ſcriptione aptiſſimis ſcatere mēdaciis. Principio nãcɋ polliceri Aſtarotũ i̅ p̄ſentia Papę co̅cluſio̅es eas fore diſputãdas, & Papã tñ nega/ uiſſe ac certe ˏphibuiſſe, qñ i̅ m̃itis ęſtate, p̱xia publicis Romę ſeſſio̅ib⁹ ha bitis ea cã plene fuiſſet diſputata & diſcuſſa corã doctiſſ. mũdi luminib⁹, eccleſię catholicę p̄latis, archepiſcopis, epiſcopis, gñalib⁹ ordinũ, et eoꝛ ꝑ curatorib⁹, poenite̅tiariis, doctorib⁹, magno numero theologię iuriſcɋ p̱i tiſſimis uiris, q̅ Capnio̅e̅ eſſe abſoluẽdũ decreuiſſent. Deinde cɋ ignomi nioſe appellauerit Oculare ſpeculũ ſcãdala & erroneas co̅tine̅tias, cũ tñ li ber iſte ſit p̱ apoſtolicã ſente̅tiã diffinitiue admiſſ⁹. Tũ etiã cɋ de eode̅ libro ita ſcripſerit, cɋ ſit a qnc̱ uniuerſitatib⁹ dudũ igni addict⁹, q̅ certe ſu̅t me rę nuge, clara et cãdida mēdacia, qa nulla in oḿi terrarũ orbe ſit aut fuerit uniuerſitas q̅ oculare ſpeculũ co̅dēnauerit, ſed tm̅ ſingularia q̅dã capitoſa capita, uertiginoſo cerebro heterodita, & ſupino errore decepta, co̅ueti cularit̕ & co̅ſpiratiue co̅tra iuris & iuſtitię formã i̅ oculare ſpeculũ liuo re tabuerint, & ſua, ut aiũt ſentimẽta conflauerint. Poſtremo eos aiũt q lu to & coeno corrollaría illa i̅uoluerint & reuoluerint affirmare ſolitos, i̅ eiſ dē co̅ſcriptio̅ib⁹ nihil co̅tineri ab alpha ad O, q̅d no̅ antea i̅ defenſio̅e pub lica Io. Reuchlin co̅tra calu̅niatores ſuos Colonie̅ſes iuſtificatũ ſolutũ & re ſolutũ fuiſſet, q̅d lectori cuicɋ lucidi⁹ ſtellis claruerit. Aſtarotũ itacɋ ſemp̕ eãdē cãtilenã ˏp turpi ſua lingua canere. Hos cauponi ſermo̅es fuiſſe cũ ho ſpitib⁹ & co̅uiuis ſuis dixerũt Philola⁹ iunior & Marran⁹, graue nimiũ pu tātes, i̅ re tã parua & puerili, tot annis tã ferociter digladiari, Et ſimul atcɋ ueſtiti erant, tũ Simonis domũ uti conſtituerãt uelociter ſeſe corripuerũt. Cũcɋ iter ſe ut ipſoꝝ uſ̕ ferebat amiciſſime co̅ſalutaſſent, Marran⁹ ſic i̅ci pit. Q̅nos delectauerit pridiana diſputatio tua uenerãde Simo̅ i̅credibile admodũ eſt & uix dici pot̕ ita ſum⁹ te nobis abſente i̅patie̅tes morę, q p̱ter ullã erubeſcētiã mox atcɋ p̄teriit ſabbathũ tuũ añlucani aduenimus. Et ille.

ON THE ART OF THE KABBALAH
by Johann Reuchlin of Pforzheim
BOOK III

Afterwards they left. The moon was dimming her beams in turn and the dipping stars were inviting slumber. Both fell asleep, promising each other that the first to wake up in the morning would not let the other sleep on, and arranging to be called as well.

The following day, as they got dressed as usual, they reflected on the long and complicated tale their host at the inn had told his guests at dinner the night before.

On the previous day there arrived in Frankfurt the judgement of the Roman curia that the trumped up ban imposed on Johann Reuchlin by Astarotus should be lifted. For writing books which were not now to be burned, Reuchlin had suffered cruel persecution for more than five years, innocent, silent, but uncowed. The ban itself had been posted on the doors of all public buildings and churches in Rome, and now lay torn and trampled in the mud and dung there, torn down in righteous anger, for there was evidence that it had been perpetrated without the Pontiff's blessing, and without waiting for the decision of the learned judges before whom the case had been pending for a period of three years now since Astarotus had brought his action. It was also well known to everyone that the charge sheet was dripping with obvious lies. Right at the beginning Astarotus had said in the presence of the Pope that he would dispute the verdict, and the Pope had quite definitely refused him permission since during the preceding summer in Rome, the matter had been fully argued and discussed in many open sessions before the most learned luminaries of the world: prelates of the Catholic church, archbishops, bishops, heads of the Orders and their procurators, confessors, scholars; an enormous number of distinguished theologians and jurists, who had declared that Reuchlin should be discharged. Astarotus then referred to the book *Mirror for the Eyes* as a public disgrace, said that it was a stumbling block and its contents misleading, even though the book had, in fact, received the apostolic imprimatur. He had also made other comments about the book to the effect that five universities had ordered its burning. He declared that it was clearly pure rubbish, all bare faced, blatant lies. He said that nowhere in the whole world was there a university that had not condemned the book nor would there ever be. Speculative philosophers were just a bunch of pigheaded woolly-minded perverts taken in by a fallacy born of idle thought. They had formed secret cells to study speculative philosophy which went against Law and justice and festered like sores, and they had, as they say, made conspiracies of their theories. Lastly it was said that those who had ripped down the notices of the ban and thrown them in the gutter constantly affirmed that the charges contained nothing, from beginning to end, that had not been already accounted for by Johann Reuchlin in his public defence against the accusations from those in Cologne. He had vindicated himself over and over again—vindication that was as clear as daylight to everyone who read it. And so Astarotus still had the same scurrilous song on his filthy lips.

LIBER TERTIVS

Veneritis prospe, iqt, amici optimi, an no & uos hodie ferię tenę́ quę dię́
Soli nūcupatis. Tū Philolaꝰ. Pythagorica sumꝰ turba, inqt, dies omneis fe
stos agimꝰ, qn̄ hilari mēte cōteplamur, nec sabbathū aliud q̄ppiā cēsemus
q̄ relictis negociis secularibꝰ dare opam ut adhęreat diuinitati. Sic em̄ no
bis Pythagoras iussit, autore Laertio, ϛωϗναι ωι ὂις θεςει. conuersari ŏpor
tet cū diis. Nisi ꝙ tu numerū ueneraris septimū, ocio aptissimū, q̄ etiā no
bis pythagoreis nihil rerū parit, & Minerua noı̄at. Tū Simō, Legi auscul
tādū est q̄ sua cuicꝗ distribuit & naturę ipsi pro aı̄a est, uoluit em̄ ea & uiri
bus corporū seruire, sine qbꝰ nec rō sana esse nec mētis lume cōseruari ua
lide possit, quapropter mediationē mēsis lunæ hoc est septimā uitę parte
q̄escere cōstituit, in qua nihil agere liceat, nisi ꝙd obmissum irreparabiliter
noceat. Eg̃ nōıantur si recte memini Romanis ferię statiuę uniuersi populi
cões & faciūdis rebus diuinis cōsecratę, itꝗ no sem̄p philosophari Neo
ptolemꝰ pmittet ille apud Enniū, ita nō sem̄p, nō oı̄bꝰ, nō oı̄a de deo medi
tari uel ex vris sunt q̄ p̄cipiāt, sed est & qn̄ & qbꝰ & q̄tū, Naziāzeno ad Eu
nomianos autore, quē aliqn̄ grece legi uirū & doctissimū et eloquētissimū
in Achaia cū degere. Ita nō uilescet ꝙd est optimū & īfinitū finite pro nr̄a
mēsura cōcipiet. Sex ergo diebꝰ opamur, at septimo qꝗ die & corpaliter
ociamur q̄tū pmittit uiuēdi necessitas, & mētaliter post uolūtatis purgati
onē diuinis ıtētı̄ sumꝰ, & festiuiꝭ cū oı̄ traq̄llitate res sacras laudamꝰ, soliꝗ
tuę deo seruimꝰ. Huc uergit ꝙd dicūt Cabalęi nr̄i שבת הוא סוד
אל חי .i. Sabbathū est mysteriū dei uiui, ut in Porta Lucis cap. ii. Extat
nācꝗ symbolū mundi supioris hoc est Iobelei ętnernitatis, ubi cessāt ōis la
bor, q̄re gemino dicēdi usu legibꝰ idicit qn̄to deuteronomii. Obserua dię
sabbathi, ꝙd uult ıtelligi actiōıbꝰ exteriorıbꝰ iuxta mūdū ıferiorē. Et Exo
di xx. Memora diē sabbathi ad sanctificādū illū, uidelicet aı̄æ uires cōıuge
do mēti ad cōteplatıōıs, pfectū iuxta mūdū supiorē. Agnoscitis iā ne ꝙ
sabbathū est nota diuini seruitutı q̄ sensꝰ & rō absoluūt ab occupatiōıbꝰ ma
terialibꝰ q̄tū pmittit humana ıbecillitas, & energia mētis alligat occupatio
nibꝰ formalibꝰ ad cōsyderādū q̄ sursū sunt. Istud lex uoluit p hęc duo v̄ba
inuere שמור זכור .i. obserua, memora, qbꝰ intelligūt ex magistris
nr̄is qdā p̄ceptū sabbati esse affirmatiuū & negatiuū dicētes, obserua .i.
caue, ꝙd semp eis uitare significat, quatenꝰ nos arceat ab oı̄ ꝙd sanctitati cō
trariū est. Alii obserua explanant custodi, ut nocti custodiā attribuāt, & re
cordationē diei, ac illud haud oblique ad Cabalistarū q̄drat fundamētū, q̄
hūc mūdū esse noctē & mūdū ueturū .i. supiorē ac ıtellectuālē esse diē pu
tāt, hic seruos degere, istic uiuere liberos, his dicēdū caue custodi obserua,
illis reminiscere recordare memēto, qm̄ hęc uox זכור .i. reminiscere cō
tinēs p̄ceptū affirmatiuū, p̄cedit ex amore, uerbū uero caue p̄ceptū nega
tiuū iplēt ex timore, liberorū aūt est amor, seruorū timor, ita oı̄m p̄cepto
rū reputamus alterū altero nobiliꝰ. Ferme in hāc sentētiā lōgiore tractatu

K ii

Book Three

Young Philolaus and Marranus talked over what their host had said to his customers and friends, but thought it was going too far to fight so hard and long over such a small and childish matter.

As soon as they were both dressed they rushed off to Simon's house with all haste, according to plan. They exchanged the usual greetings in a most friendly fashion, and Marranus began the conversation.

MARRANUS: Master Simon, the pleasure we had from yesterday's discussion is almost beyond belief, and it is hard to describe how time hangs heavy when you are not with us. That is why, despite our blushes, we have come as soon as your Sabbath is over and while it is scarce light.

SIMON: You have come at a good time, my dear friends — but surely you have a holiday today, the one called after the sun.

PHILOLAUS: We are a Pythagorean crew and keep every day holy for joyous mediation. We hold Sabbaths those days on which we put ordinary business aside to make time to be close to God. This is the command of Pythagoras who said, according to Laertius, "You should consort with the gods." Perhaps though it is the number seven you revere, one most suitable to leisure; to us Pythagoreans there is nothing in nature on a par with it, and it is called Minerva.

SIMON: We must heed the law of giving each its due; this law being the soul of nature. Its effect is of advantage both to soul and bodily strength. Without bodily strength the reason would be unsound, and the accompanying clarity of mind less dependable. That is why it is laid down that the mediation of a lunar month, that is a seventh part of life, should be a time of rest, in which nothing may be done except where not doing it would occasion irretrievable harm. If I remember rightly the Romans appointed statutory public holidays to be set aside for religious activities.

Neoptolemus (according to Ennius) does not permit philosophy to be practiced all and every day, and similarly, according to Gregory in his *Address to the Eunomians*, the contemplation of God should not be undertaken by everyone, nor should an individual do so continuously, nor on all aspects of God, nor beyond his particular capacity. Only certain people should attempt meditation, and they should plan in advance when, and what, and for how long they will do so. Gregory was a most learned and lucid writer, or so I read in the Greek while I was staying in Achaia. So we are not guilty of debasing something magnificent, treating the infinite in finite terms.

For six days we work and we rest the body on the seventh day allowing for the necessities of staying alive. Then we cleanse the will and in our minds concentrate on the divine. This is our holy day when, in peace of mind, we praise what is sacred and address ourselves to the service of God alone.

It is something close to this that our Kabbalists express when they say: "The Sabbath is a mystery of the living God." (*Gate of Light*, Chapter 2). The Sabbath stands out as a symbol of the world above,

DE ARTE CABALISTICA

Moyses Gerūdēsis i Exodo scripsit, qb̓ duo esse sabbatha recipim̓ ductī scripturę testimonio Ezechielis xx. Sabbatha mea dedi eis. Nā pluralis locutio duorū numero cōtēta est, qppe non solū ut gñaliter uno uocabulo singulas feriarū spēs i lege numeratas de᷃ exprobrare nobis uoluerit, quē admodū Dauid Kimhi & Thalmudici opinant̄, uerū etiā ut peculiari hoc noīe datū̃ optimū & donū pfectū a deo nobis cōcessum, q̃d Iobeleū supiap̓pellam᷃, memori sem̃p miente᷃ cōplectamur. De q̃ Porta lucis sic

D היא שביעית עליונה שנקראת יובל. i. hęc est hebdomada supra q̃ uocat̄ Iobele᷃. Vn ois remissio, ppiciatio & ifusio grę descedit quā satis nemo eloqualeat, cū nec ocul᷃ qdē uidit unq̃ o de᷃ pter te. Est em̃ שבת שבתון sabbathū qetis & sabbathū sabbathorū q̃ aię humanę oēs purę reiecta labe tādē redibūt libere ad hęreditatē patrū & mittēt i possessiōe uere nostrā atq̃ ppriā quā acq̃siuim᷃ & retinem᷃ p aīam Messihę de tribu Iuda septimi ab Abrahā pr̄iarchę, pcuratorio noīe in orizōte mūdi sup sup̃mi iuxta scripturā. Et supra Iubileū mittet radices suas. Ieremię xvii. Quę iterp̄tat Cabalista ille p̄stātissim᷃ Sopher Ama in libro חדרים i. recōditorū, psalmi undeuigesimi super uersu Dies diēi

רל איש אל משפחתו ואל נחלת אבותיו ישוב בלומך שיתעלו בבתות אל מקום אצילותו שהוא מלג אלחים מלא מים. i. Vult dicere unusq̃sq̃ ad familiā suā & ad hęreditatē patrū suorū reuertet̄, quasi diceret, q̃ ascēdēt p angelos ad locū destinatiōis suę qd est flumē dei repletū aq̃s. Hęc Rabi Ama, & sunt aquae q̃ supra coelos sūt in mūdo intelligibili שהרציא מרוח הקדוש ubi obseruātes sabbathū fruūt & ci bāt hęreditatē Iacob pr̄is eorū, ut dixit Isaias. Sane illud ip̄m qdē est sabbathū Cabalistarū oi tp̃e sanctificādū, i q̃ nō carnis sed aię seqmur uolūtatē & meditamur diuina, nihil cōtra deū intēdētes, qd pro lege oīb᷃ gētib᷃ extat, qm̃ ex ipsa natura pullulauit. Vos em̃ qb᷃ lex Moysi lata nō est, Iudeorū cerimonię haud astringūt ut numero seruiatis, qd & Iarchas quōdā recte Apollonio negauit. Nec a uobis numerū extorqbo, sed qetū & trāqlū aīum posco, soli deo diuinisq̃ deditū, q̃ maxīe in anagogica speculatiōe cōsistit, uti est ista iter nos disputatio a uobis tātop̃e desyderata. Tū Marran, Oīno pficēdū est, inq̃t, nā coepisti Cabalā uenuste admodū tractare q̃ iā nobis plusq̃ dare ostēderis nō tm̄ posse nos hodie uerū etiā debere de altissimis rebus dissertare. Id tu nōne mecū postulas Philolae? Acille.

E Certe qdē. Em̃uero nūc ei᷃ disciplinę itrauim᷃ nauim, & mox ī ipsa prora sentimus, Cabalā aliud nihil esse nisi (ut Pythagorice loquar) symbolicā theologiā, i qua nō mō lrę ac noīa sūt rerū signa, uerū res etiā rerū. Quo aīaduertim᷃ Pythagorę philosophiā fere ₊oēm esse a Cabaleis ortā, q̃ pari modo symbolicum tradendi morem ad graecos transtulit, qn egoip̃e q̃q̃

the eternal jubilee, where all work ceases. It is because of this that it is twice referred to in the Law; in Deuteronomy: "Keep the Sabbath day," which is to be understood as referring to outward actions in the world below; in Exodus, Chapter 20, it says: "Remember the Sabbath day, to keep it holy." This is to be interpreted as referring to the joining of the powers of the soul to the mind, to achieve direction of contemplation towards the world above. Do you understand now? The Sabbath is a mark of the service of God, for on that day sense and reason are free of everyday matters (given human weakness as a limiting factor), and the powers of the mind are engaged in formal thinking, in speculation on the above. This is the meaning of the two words we find in the Law—Keep and remember. Taking these two words, our sages have explained that the precepts of the Sabbath are both affirmative and negative. "Keep," that is, "be on your guard," to them means always "avoid." It keeps us at a distance from all that stands in opposition to holiness. Others explain, "keep" as meaning "stand watch," guard duty being something suitable for night time, while remembering is more appropriate to the day. This does not square at all badly with the Kabbalistic doctrine that this world is night and the world to come (the higher, intellectual world), is day. Here we are slaves, there we are free men, so, here we are told to be on guard, stand watch, keep, while there they are told to remember, recollect, and commit to memory; whence the argument that the word "remember" contains the positive command and is motivated by love, whereas "be on your guard" is the negative command, derived from fear. The one is the love of which free men are capable, the other the fear of slaves. Thus we consider one precept to be nobler than the other.

In a longer treatise on Exodus Moses Gerundensis has developed a theory that is clearly in this line of thinking. Here we have two Sabbaths, an idea derived from Chapter 20 of Ezechiel: "I have given you my Sabbaths." The use of the plural denotes the number two. Now God has not only in general tended to inicate individual festivals by having them listed in the Law in the singular, as is the view of David Kamhi and the Talmudists, but He has also granted us His best and most perfect gift with its special name, what we call the Higher Jubilee. We are always to remember it and hold it dear. On this, we find in *Gate of Light*: "This is the higher seventh day which is called the Jubilee." All pardon, propitiation and inpouring of grace descends from this; no human tongue can tell of it, for no eye has seen it, save you, O God. It is the 'Sabbath of Sabbaths,' the Sabbath of rest when all men's souls will at last be clean and free of all stain, when in freedom they will return to their father's inheritance, and will be possessed in truth of all that is ours, that which we acquired, and that which we retain through the soul of the Messiah, patriarch from the tribe of Judah, seventh

LIBER TERTIVS

cum sodali hoc meo te uehementer oro ut dicēdo ac potius docēdo pgas. Tum Simon. Non mihi tm iactantiæ usurpauerim, ut docere uos audeã, nec bene tutum fuerit in re tam perplexa, nondū extraneis cognita, p̄ser tim romane doctis, p̄ter admodum pauca quæ annis supioribus Ioannes Picus Mirandulæ Comes, & Paulus Ricius q̄ndam noster ediderunt, etiã uscp ad hodiernum latinis non satis intellecta. Vereor em si docerem tam peregrina dogmata, ne mihi haud secus atcp multis ante bonis contigit ui ris, inuidorum turba ignominiose obstrepat, qui omne q̄d nesciunt ipro bant, & facile malignandi studio uerba in alienum sensum detorquent cō tra loquentis uoluntatē, q̄s Cicero calumniatores uocat, ego si dici grāma tice liceat calumnienses appellauero, qm uos ipsi æque meos Theologi stas Pharisæenses noiare cōsueuistis. Sed palam testor utrūcp uestrum me nihil docere uelle, dicere aūt magis & recensere, si q̄d apud Cabalistas le gerim q̄d uobis haud displicere putem. Exequar igitur primum, q̄d illi ulti mum intēdunt, nam omne studiū suum & uniuersam opam uni huic pro posito impendere curāt, ut in hac uita fœlicitatē & futuri sui p̄ captu qcp suo ppetuam beatitudinē consequant. Quod maxime oīum hoc medio fieri posse confidunt, Si tandem aliqñ id q̄d sibi sentiūt pro utriuscp mun di statu esse optimū sedulo & gnauiter apphendant, cuius possessio ade ptis iucunda & pfecta sit quies, nimirum cum etiam quæcp alioquin aīalia q̄tumuis bruta fœlicitatē suam gestire tum uisa sint cum q̄ optima sibi exi stimant iis fruant, & ad ea ptingant quæ cupiditati suæ afferunt satietatē. Cernitis bouē depascere floridum aliq̄d & uiride pratum, non q̄dem totū sed deliberata electione nunc hanc inq̄rere herbam nunc illam. Subitocp aliam q̄dem facile relinquere, aliā aūt prorsus obmittere, donec ad consen taneum & uescum sibi alimentū pueniat q̄ cōsistat & requiescat. Hoc mo do Cabalistæ post campos scientiarū latissimos, & prata cōtemplationum oī amœnitate ornata multas & uarias qualitercūcp olētes herbas degu stant, ut demum toto gramine plustrato illud diuinū Moly reperiant, cui quanq̄ radix nigrescit, tn flos Homeri opinione albus enitet lacti similis, q̄ inuento cūctas repulisse miserias uident, appetitus sui finē in hoc mūdo consecuti fœlicem. Virtus uero Moly est, opa difficilia radix, flos animoru trãquillitas, hoc omne nisi p̄sentis seculi uera fœlicitas esse aliud nihil ne credi q̄dem possit. Futuri aūt beatitudo est apphensio summi boni, supra q̄d nullum bonū, & a q̄ est oīs bonitas, q̄d a nulla mera creatura comphē ditur. Sed tum apphendi asserit cum pro cuiuscp captu pxime accedit, ut si q̄s fimbriā uestimenti apphendat, hoīem indutū apphendisse dicat. Ad illud bonum q̄d deus noiatur non plane a nobis poterit ob nostræ cō ditionis fragilitatem nisi gradibus atcp scalis ascendi, q̄ q̄dem ut uos loqui cōsueuistis instar Homericæ catēnæ, ut uero Iudæi nos secūdū diuina elo quia dicim̄ certe ad speciē scalæ Iacob patris nostri de sup cœlestibus por

K iii

Book Three

since Abraham. He is called our agent on the level of the highest world, as it is written: "And above the Jubilee he sends his roots." (Jeremiah, 17) The distinguished Kabbalist Sopher Ama offers an interpretation of this in his book *On Mysteries*, commenting on the verse "Day unto day" in psalm 19: "This means that every man will return to his family and to the inheritance of his fathers, that is to say, they will ascend through the angels each to his appointed place, which is the river of God, filled with water." There are waters beyond the heavens which are in the intelligible world—"they issue forth from the holy spirit" in the place where those who keep the Sabbath enjoy and feed upon the inheritance of Jacob their father, as Isaiah said.

This then is the Sabbath of the Kabbalists, to be kept holy for all time. In it we follow the will not of the flesh but of the spirit, we contemplate the divine, giving no attention to what stands against God, for to all the nations he stands for Law, Law that springs from his very nature.

As for you, the law of Moses was not brought to you, and Jewish practices do not oblige you to revere this number—Iarchas once rightly forbade Apollonius to do so. I shall extort no number from you. I ask only calm and peace of mind, in surrender to God and the divine alone. Such a state is achieved above all in allegorical investigations of the kind we carried out in discussion between us as you so much wanted.

MARRANUS: And it must be taken to its final conclusion. You have begun a most beautiful exposition of the Kabbalah, and have shown all too clearly that today not only are we able to discuss the highest matters, but even that we ought to do so. Will you not join with me in this, Philolaus?

PHILOLAUS: Most certainly. Now that we have embarked on this study, I feel that soon we shall get to the bottom of it; that is, that Kabbalah is simply (to use the Pythagorean vocabulary) symbolic theology, where words and letters are code things, and such things are themselves code for other things. This drew our attention to the fact that almost all Pythagoras' system is derived from the Kabbalists, and that similarly he brought to Greece the use of symbols as a means of communication. With my friend here I too urgently beg you to go on talking or, rather, teaching.

SIMON: I should not be so presumptuous as to dare to teach you, nor would it be at all safe when the subject is so complicated and not understood by outsiders as yet, and scholars in the Latin world in particular know nothing at all about it, except the little work published

DE ARTE CABALISTICA

riguntur in terram, tanq̃ restis quædam aut funis aurea cœlitus ad nos directa, ueluti linea uisualis uarias penetrans naturas. Aspicitis nanq̃ solem cuius radius ad uisum nostrum proficiscit̃ p orbem Veneris, p orbẽ Mercurii, per orbem Lunæ, per orbem ignis, per orbem aeris, & tangit corp⁹ opacum speculi concaui, reflectitq̃ inde ad stupam aut lanam aridã quã splendore suo incendit uehementer usq̃ in cineres, eiusdem uero flammæ species ad oculos peruenit nostros, & a sensatione interiori suscipitur, suscepta iudicatur ab æstimatione, tandem discurrit̃ a ratione redeundo uiã qua p̃sens operatio ois est progressa, tum hæc prudenter nobis ostendit q̃ nam modo formæ interiores deferant̃ per spiritus animales ad imaginationem & æstimationis iudicium, q̃ etiam modo externæ ab intraneis recipiantur, q̃ item a flamma species in perspicuo usq̃ ad pupillã intendãtur, qua uia ex incedio speculi cõcaui orta sit flãma, & q̃modo radius incẽdere potuerit, q̃ deniq̃ modo p.multa media sibi non connaturalia continuet̃ splendor, qua rursus sit proportiõe compãdus aer ad ignẽ, ignis ad sphę̃ tã lunæ, & reliqui orbes ad reliq̃s. Singula hæc ratio nostra disputat per iter compositionis & resolutionis ultro citroq̃ susq̃ deq̃ gradiẽs, & modo hæc modo illa cogitans, necq̃ cessat ratiocinari usq̃ dum p phantasma effigiem, intentiones splendorẽ lumen lucem luminare scilicet ad ipsum de q̃ loq̃mur solem reuerterit. In primis imaginem lucidã agnoscit, deinde iudicat ipsam esse propriã illius flammę stupeę̃ quã pridẽ oculi uiderant, tum cp intentio eius a re uisa p diaphanon ad oculũ foris producta etiã intra fuerit recepta. cp item stupa sit terrestris, cp splendor sit aereus, cp flãma ignea, cp candor accidens diaphano inhærens, cp transeat p lucidum atq̃ pspicuum, siue aer illud sit seu ignis aut cœleste aliq̃d, secundũ formę substãtialis energiam & opationem peculiarẽ, deinde meditata sua nobiliori cuicq̃ semp accommodãs, relicta materia secũ de forma disputare incipit, non iam artificiali ut cuius scrutiniũ huc non attineat q̃ rectius figura nominetur q̃ forma, sed naturali tm aut supiore. Pergit itaq̃ ratio & formarum aliquas reperit esse particulares nunc & hic, reliquas uero uniuersales semp & ubiq̃, tum ex particularibus quasdam corpibus inexistentes q̃bus dent ut sint, alias aũt formas coassistẽtes q̃bus p̃stent ut sic sint, alias oĩno separatas a corporeis essentia uirtute ac opatiõe, q̃ tñ iccirco nomẽ q̃nq̃ formæ amittunt, atq̃ uel dii, uel angeli, uel intelligentiæ, uel animi beati, uel mentes, aut alio q̃libet uocantur noĩe. Quæcũq̃ aũt sunt uniuersales eæ non ultra formæ sed Ideæ siue species dicuntur a multis q̃ perq̃ proprie loqui didicerunt. Sic ratio sane tantisper ascendet dum poterit, cu aũt ita fuerit discurrendo extenuata ut formas q̃ corpibus nec insunt nec assunt tãq̃ naturæ nõ subiectas cõphedere negat, mox subsidiariũ accersit intellectũ q̃ plane ut hãc materiã abstrahit ab hac forma ceu asini cuiusdã

in agro

On the Art of Kabbalah

some time ago by Count Giovanni Pico della Mirandola and Paul Ricci, and even in the present day that little work is insufficiently understood. I am afraid that if I teach such foreign ideas, I shall suffer what many good men before me have suffered: there will be an ignominious outcry from the spiteful crowd who condemn everything they don't know about and with malignant intent readily twist words to read them in some sense other than that in which the writer intended. Cicero calls them slanderers. If the language will take it, I prefer "slanderees," for consonance with "Pharisees" which is what you usually call my religious writers.

I call you both to testify in public that I do not want to teach, and that I prefer to talk about and review whatever I have read in Kabbalah that I think would not displease you.

I will begin with the end for which they strive. All their drive, all their efforts, are carefully directed towards this single purpose: that they may attain happiness in this life, the perpetual bliss of the age (insofar as this can be understood) to come. Their belief is that this will come about in this particular way, that is, if they finally grasp, with great care and attention that which they feel to be the best thing for each world, given their circumstances. To possess this is a delight to those who achieve it and their rest is perfect. Even dumb animals seem in a state of elation when enjoying what they think best for them, having attained what satisfies their longings.

Look at a cow grazing in a green meadow full of flowers. It does not eat everything, it chooses with care, taking now this piece of grass, now that. Abruptly it leaves one piece of grass without hesitation, it passes over another further on, until it comes to the pasture that is the right food for it, where it stops and rests. In this fashion the Kabbalists crop the broad fields of knowledge, the meditative pastures studded with delights, tasting many and diverse scented grasses, till, having traversed the whole field at length, they discover divine Moly, the plant whose root is black but whose flower, according to Homer, shines white as milk. On this discovery all their sorrows seem to fall away; it is the happy end to their searches in this world. Moly is virtue. Hard work is the root, peace of mind is the flower. If in our age this is not true happiness, there is nothing else that can be.

In the future world, bliss is the apprehension of the highest good, beyond which there is no good and which is all goodness. No mere creature understands it. But a man is said to apprehend it when he comes as close as he can, as he who touches the hem of the garment is said to have touched the man who wears it. For our frailty we fall short of that good which is called God and cannot climb there except with steps and ladders. You customarily refer to the Homeric chain; we Jews look to Holy Scripture and talk about the ladder our father Jacob

LIBER TERTIVS LII

in agro sepulti, quam natura induit graminis forma ex cadauere illo florescente, ita rursus formam q̃q̃ simpliciter a materia conatur abstrahere, id uero experitur arduũ esse ac laboris plenũ, facile em̃ est abstrahere materiam a forma, sed forma abstrahere a materia difficile, quapropter intellectus ille purgatiorem se eleuat, ut menti occasionẽ in se influendi præbeat cuius claritate fretus formas agnoscit nonnullas esse penitus a corporeis essentia uirtute ac opatione absolutas, & ob id neq̃ loco neq̃ tp̃e condusas, quo uere oporteat eas arbitrari supra cœlos esse, ubi cessat motus & tempus. Hinc uolũtatem nostrã instruit ut esse quedã credat extra cœlos entia optimã uitam ducentia qua toto æuo fruantur, ibiq̃ illum secũdum inchoare mundũ, luminibus uiuis & metibus purissimis offertissimũ, quẽ possit intrare animus humanus fortiter conteplando, certe multo potius q̃ oculus corporeus transcedere orbem solis acute uidendo. Vtq̃ solem non aspicimus nisi sol nos respiciat, ita mundum supiorem uidere neqm̃ nisi & ille nos uideat, est em̃ totus oculus ipse q̃q̃ sole clarior, Solem aũt comphendimus per lumen solare, ita diuina comphendimus per lumẽ diuinum, & q̃ uisu corporeo possumus non solum orbẽ solis, uerum etiã superiores stellas & summũ cœli capere, cur non posset mens nostra q̃ uirtutem corpoream modo q̃dam infinite p̃cellit altius suspicere ac mundi archetypi cõtenta uidere, cum tanta propinquitate concauũ & conuexũ supmi cœli uniantur, a q̃ conuexo æthernitatis orizon nihil distare uideat. Intuemur itaq̃ (mihi credite) alterius mundi diuina mutuo, & illa nos uicissim intuentur, ueluti duo directe oppositi oculi p unicã lineam uisualem reciproce circũacti. Tum Philolaus. Oĩa, inquit, quæ doces Simon Pythagorica sunt & Italicæ philosophiæ propria quã inter nos heri discussimus parumper ego & Marranus mecũ. Ad hęc ille. Vos eqdem qd appellare duxeritis pythagoricũ ignoro, at hoc scio hæc esse Cabalistica q̃ hactens̃ proposui, a priscis Cabalæis tradita, & oĩa lege diuina Hebræorũ complexa. Hinc nascitur illa enumeratio quinquaginta portarum intelligentię circa quas tantop̃e Cabalistarũ studia desudãt, diuinitus a Moyse dei seruo receptarum, quarũ cognitionẽ ipse q̃q̃ posteris nobis tradidit uniuersitatis conditionẽ explicantium

וככה אמרו רבותינו החמשים
שערי בינה נבראו בעולם וכולן נמסרו למשה
חוץ מאחד שנא ותחסרחו מעט מאלהים.

i. Iamq̃ dixerunt Magistri nostri quinquaginta portæ intelligentiæ productæ sunt in mundo, & oẽs illæ traditę sunt Moysi p̃terq̃ una, quia dictũ est, minuisti eũ paulominus a diis. Sup isto Cabalistarũ sermõe dixit Ramban in Geneseos exordio, q̃ eiuscemodi omne Moysi traditũ per portas intelligentiæ, contentum est in lege diuina Iudęorum, uel sensu literali uel

K iiii

Book Three

saw, from the highest heaven stretching down to earth, like a cord or rope of gold thrown down to us from heaven, a line of sight penetrating deep within things. Picture the sun, whose ray we see crossing the sphere of Venus, of Mercury, of the Moon, of fire, of air, glancing off the solid body of a concave mirror and reflecting onto a piece of tow or a shred of dry wool which it burns to ash in its brightness. The image of that flame reaches our eyes and is taken up by the inner faculty of sense. We judge its value. Finally reason runs over it, making the return journey over the route of the present operation. Carefully it shows us how the inner images are carried through the animal spirit to the imagination and the seat of judgement, and how external images are received by the inner faculties, how the image is carried from the flame to the pupil across the atmosphere, how the flame arises from the glow of a concave mirror and the means by which the ray could set something on fire, and finally, how the brightness persists through several media which are not of the same nature, then what the relationships are between air and fire, fire and the sphere of the moon, and the rest of the spheres to each other.

Reason considers these matters one by one on its journey of comparison and explanation, passing this side and that, and up and down, thinking it over now here, now there, and the rational process does not cease until it transfers it attention through the inner image to the outer image, reaching out towards the bright light and the source of the light until it returns to the sun of which we spoke. To begin with there is recognition of a luminous image; next the decision is made that this is the image of the piece of burning tow which the eyes had already seen and that the attention the eyes have been paying it has led it through the atmosphere to the eye and there received it on entry, and that the tow is of the earth, the brightness belongs to the air, the flame is of fire, and the radiance is a property inherent in the atmosphere — how it is carried across and through the luminous transparency (whether that be of air or fire, or something belonging to heaven) depends on the substantial form and the particular way in which it works. Then, on reflection, reason adjusts itself to nobler things. It leaves matter on one side and begins an inner discourse on form — not "form" as discussed in art, better termed "shape," but natural, higher form. Reason proceeds. It discovers that some forms are particular, here and now, while others are universal, always and everywhere. Some forms exist with particular bodies and make them what they are. Others exist side by side, and so affect what they are. Others again are altogether distinct from bodies, in capacity and operation. They thus lose the name "forms" and are called gods, or angels, or intelligences, blessed spirits, minds, or anything else you like. Further, those that are universal are not called "forms" at all, but "ideas" or "species," by those who have learned to use the proper terms.

In this way reason climbs high while it can, but when it is exhausted by its perusal and cannot distinguish dwelling within bodies and dwelling beside them (not subject to nature) it soon summons intellect to its

DE ARTE CABALISTICA

allegorico, per dictiones, uel arithmeticas supputationes, uel geometricas literarum figuras siue descriptas seu transmutatas, uel harmonię consonātias ex formis characterū, coniunctionibus, separationibus, tortuositate, directione, defectu, supabundantia, minoritate, maioritate, coronatione, clausura, apertura & ordine resultātes. Et per illam q̃cɜ legem a diuino spiritu adeptus est Salomon rex sapiētissimus omne q̃d nouerat de q̃ scriptū est in libro Regum cɜ deus ei dederit sapientiā & prudentiā multam nimis quasi arenam in litore maris & creuerat sapiētia Salomonis sup sapientiā oīm orientaliū & ægyptiorū, & erat sapientior cunctis hoībus, & disputauit sup lignis a cedro q̃ est in libano uscɜ ad hyssopum q̃ egreditur de pariete, & disseruit de iumētis & uolucribus, & reptilibus, & piscibus. ultra hæc confirmat nostrā sentētiam Gerūdensis & concludit ita

וכל זה ידע בתורה והכל מצא בת בפירושיה ברקרוקיה באותיותיה ובקוצציה:

i. Oīa hęc cognouit per legem & oīa inuenit in ea per expositiones suas, per grammaticas subtilitates & per literas eius, & p calamistrationes illius. Contigit aūt ei hoc, postq̃ ad plenū fuisset duodeqnquaginta portarū intelligentiæ rationē consecutus, q̃ aperiunt oīm creaturarum cognitionē. Sunt em cunctæ res uniuersaliter in quinas conditiones distributæ. Nam aut elemēta sunt, aut elementata, aut anime, aut cœlestia corpa, aut supcœlestia incorporea. Horum fortasse q̃dlibet decem recipit consyderationes quarū capitula sunt q̃ sequunt̃. Genera generalissima, genera specialia, species generales, species specialissimæ, res indiuiduæ, q̃ ulterius cōstant materia & forma, uel q̃busdam utricɜ proportionalibus, contrahunturcɜ singulariter differentiis, proprietatibus & accidentiis. Decem hi tam essentiarū q̃ intelligentiarum modi per quincɜ multiplicati qnquaginta ianuas aperiunt per quas intramus in creaturarum penetralia illa eminentibus notis in opibus sex dierum designata, & a Cabalistis studiose dephensa receptacɜ. Iam isto artificio ænigmaticus scrupus a Comite Mirandulano inter noningētas cōdusiōes suas propositus, facile in enodem scirpū explanabitur. Aiebat em sic. Qui sciuerit q̃d sit denarius in arithmetica formali, & cognouerit naturam primi numeri sphærici sciet secretū quinquaginta portarū intelligentiæ, & magni Iobelei, & millesimę gñationis, & regnū oīm seculorum, hęc Mirandulanus. Ducatur itacɜ uelim sphæra plana siue circulus dece̅ figurarum numeraliū super cētrum q̃d sit quincɜ, est em mediū denarii & in eius circūferentia particulariter, denarię supputationis numeri singuli describantur, trāseatcɜ diameter a minimo ad maximū, hoc est ab uno ad nouem, cuius diuisio duos semicirculos efficiet, a parte siq̃dem dextra sphæræ, post unum & ante nouē superǐ commemorata ponātur duo tria quatuor quincɜ, a parte aūt sinistra post unum & ante nouem reponant̃ q̃ncɜ

sex septem

aid, which will abstract matter from form. An appropriate example is the form of a donkey buried in a field, which nature clothes in the form of grass rising as flowers from the corpse. So reason tries to abstract simple form from matter. But it finds it hard and laborious work. It is easy to abstract matter from form, but not form from matter. To this end intellect raises itself up in a purer form, affording the mind an opportunity to flow into it. Relying on the clarity of the mind, it recognizes some forms completely free from the corporeal essence, nature and mechanism, and as a result not bounded in time or space. They should be thought of as being beyond the heavens, where motion and time cease.

This brings us to the belief that there are certain beings outside the heavens leading lives that enjoy all eternity. There begins the second world, and with it, living luminaries and pure minds. By intense meditation the human soul can enter there, and can certainly do so more readily than the physical eye can get a clear picture scanning the sun's disc.

We cannot see the sun unless the sun can see us and, in the same way, we cannot perceive the upper world unless it perceives us. It is all eye, and more piercing than the sun. We comprehend "the sun" by means of the sun's light; similarly "the divine" by the light of the divine. Given that by physical sight we are able to see not only the face of the sun, but also the higher stars, and deep into heaven, why should mind, which infinitely exceeds out physical powers, not be able to see further and glimpse the contents of the archetypal world? Concave and convex in the upper heaven are very closely linked, and the eternity level seems not far away from this curve. Our inspection of the other, divine, world is equally returned; they in their turn inspect us. It is rather like two eyes placed directly opposite each other, returning one another's gaze along the same sight-line.

PHILOLAUS: Everything you are telling us, Simon, is Pythagoreanism and comes in the Italian philosophy we discusssed in detail yesterday, Marranus and I.

SIMON: I don't know this thing that you choose to call Pythagoreanism. But I do know that what I have put forward so far is Kabbalah, handed down from the earliest Kabbalists, and all included in Hebrew religious Law.

From this is derived the calculation of fifty gates of understanding on which so much Kabbalistic attention and effort has been focused. What Moses, the servant of God, received by divine inspiration was handed down to posterity in an interpretation by him of the nature of the universe.

"Our Masters said: Fifty gates of understanding were made in the world, and all were handed down to Moses save one, for it is said, 'You have made him a little less than the gods.'"

Commenting on this dictum of the Kabbalah, Ramban said in his introduction to Genesis that everything of the nature of that received by Moses through the gates of understanding is contained in the Jews' Law, whether in a literal or metaphorical sense, in oracular utterance,

LIBER TERTIVS LIII

sex septem octo, & trahantur lineæ per centrum a duobus ad octo, a tribꝰ ad septem, a quatuor ad sex, a quincꝫ ad quincꝫ. Tum si maximo cuicꝫ tm̄ subtraxeris q̄tum abundat supra quincꝫ, q̄d est sphærędenariędcentrum, atcꝫ idem suo minimo addideris qui a quincꝫ defecit, semp ex utriscꝫ op positis numeris quincꝫ & quincꝫ adæquata surgent, quare cōparatis inui cem linearū punctis quælibet lineæ descriptio numeralis, quincꝫ & qncꝫ obtinet. Quinarius igitur numerus in circulo denariæ reuolutionis dicit̄ sphæricus, quia, ut uidistis, ōes numeri sphæręad quincꝫ rediguntur, id aūt fit per quincꝫ lineas in sphæra ductas quarū singulæ decem continēt. Eo itacꝫ sphęrico numero per decem multiplicato nascēt quinquaginta siue portæ intelligentię seu anni Iobelei, cuius proportio dupla q̄ est arithme tica formalitas, in se multiplicata, millesimā gnationem procreabit, q̄d si ꝑpetuo sic facies, apparebit infinitudo, q̄ est regnum oīm seculorū a Ca balistis Ensoph noīatū, & est deitas ipsa sine indumiento. Reliqua em̄ de us produxit amictus lumine sicut uestimento ut esset lumen de lumine, ac inde cum uestimenti sui lumine creauit mundū intelligibilē spirituū sepa ratorum & inuisibiliū, q̄d Cabalistæ uocant coelum ut ex me sæpius acce, pistis. Ad hunc modū intelligo uerba sapientissimi & maximi Rabi Eliæ, zer, q cū istam proposuisset quæstionē, unde creatū sit coelū respōdit, מאור לבושו לקח .i. de lumine uestimēti sui sumpsit. Recitant hæc a Moyse Maimoni ostensore ꝑplexorum in xxvi. cap. libri secūdi, et a Rabi Ioseph iuniore Castiliensi, ciue Salemitano in Horti nucis uolumine secūdo, Vscꝫ huc ascēdit Moyses dei seruꝰ, ut cognosceret lume uestimēti eius, & sabbathū sabbatborū, & Iobeleum supius, & millesimā gnationē, q̄d totum nil aliud est q̄ mundus supior Idearum, angelorū, sœlicium ani morum. Igitur cum indumentū dei transcendere ac facie eius uidere nequ, uerit, recte dicetur ex quinquaginta portis intelligentię una caruisse, quā aliq̄ nostrum fuisse opinantur תחיית .i. uiuificatione, tn̄ iis haud assen tior, magis uero esse puto dei essentiā quam symbolū indicat tetragrāma, ton, & est mundus incōpabilis nulla cōphensibilis proportione. Dixit nancꝫ Moysi deus, Faciem meam uidere non poteris. Seu uerius sic. Et fa, cies męę non uidebuntur, sed uocabo nomē tetragrāma tō corā te xxxiii. Exodi, q̄d ex planāt Ca baliste השם שאקרא לפניך הגדול שלא תוכל לראותי .i. Vocabo coram te nomē illud magnum quod non poteris uidere, ita em̄ Ramban Nehmani scri bit. Quo plane apparet deum iuxta ipsum esse suum tetragrammaton, ⁊ Moyse non fuisse uisum. Hoc sane portarū est oīm principiū supra omnę creaturam ante creationis exordium, de q̄ legitur Creauit deus coelum & terram. Et chaldaica Onkeli translatio sonat ita, Creauit tetragrammatus coelum & terrā. Deus ergo tetragrāmatus creauit oīa, quem uos Tetra, ctyn nominare audiui. Dixit autem Rabi Eliezer ut in capitulis eius extat,

Book Three

through arithmetical computation, or through the geometry of the shapes of the letters (as they are written or by transposition), or the consonant harmonies in the shapes of the letters, conjunctions, divisions, through roundabout or straightforward expression, through missing or superfluous words, through decreasing or increasing, crowning, closing in and opening up, or setting in order.[48]

It was through that Law that King Solomon the wise learned from the holy spirit all that he knew. It is written in the Book of Kings that God gave him wisdom and understanding as bountiful as the sand on the sea shore, and that the wisdom of Solomon grew beyond the wisdom of all the peoples of the East and the Egyptians; he was wiser than all men, he would discourse on anything from the wood of the Cedar of Lebanon to the hyssop that grows in the cracks of the wall; he discussed animals and birds and reptiles and fishes. Gerundensis more than confirms my view, and concludes: "All these things he knew through the Law, and in it he found everything by his explanation, in the minutiae of grammar, in the letters and their ornaments." He arrived at this after he had comprehended fully forty-eight of the gates of understanding which open onto knowledge of all creatures.

Everything in the universe is classified in five groups, according to their state: the elements and things made of the elements, souls, celestial bodies, supercelestial bodies. Each of these subdivides under ten heads, as follows: main groups, sub-groups, main species, sub-species, individual things. Not included in these are matter and form, which each relate to each other in ways entailing attributes, properties and qualities. These ten modes of essence and understanding, multiplied by five, are the fifty open gates by which we enter creation's secret lairs, following the clues given in the work of the six days grasped fervently by the Kabbalists.

By these means it is easy to solve the ingenious difficult puzzle posed by Mirandola in his *Nine Hundred Conclusions*. He put it thus: "He who would know the denary number in formal arithmetic, and understand the first circular number, will know the secret of the fifty gates of intelligence, and of the great jubilee, and of the thousandth generation, and of the kingdom of all ages." I would have you think of a plane sphere, or circle, of ten numerical figures, on whose center is a five, which is the mean of ten, and written out separately on the circumference, the individual numbers from which the denary number is computed. A diameter crosses from the least to the greatest, that is, from one to nine, giving us two semicircles. On the right-hand side of the circle, between the one and the nine are placed the above-mentioned numbers two, three, four and five; on the left of the circle between the one and the nine are the six, seven and eight. Lines are drawn

DE ARTE CABALISTICA

עַד שֶׁלֹּא נִבְרָא הָעוֹלָם הָיָה הַקָּבָּ״ה וּשְׁמוֹ בִּלְבַד

.i. Vſcɋ quo non fuit creatus mundus, fuit deus & nomẽ eius ſolummodo. Alii q́ɋ Cabaliſtę aſſerũt teſtimonio Moyſi ęgyptii ca‑pite xxix. libri ſe‑
K cũdi pplexorũ ſic תְּחִלָּה שֶׁלֹּא הָיָה דָּבָר נִמְצָא בִּכְלָל אֶלָּא הַשֵּׁם וְחָכְמָתוֹ .i. Ab initio cum nõ eſſet ulla res erat penitus niſi nomen dei & ſapientia eius. Ergo anteq̃ eſſet creaturae quicq̃ iuxta Cabalæ doctrinam, nihil erat niſi deus, & nomen eius tetra‑grammaton, & ſapientia eius. Sola certe tria hæc receptio noſtra continet quæ prima creationis porta magiſtro noſtro Moyſi nequaq̃ fuit aperta. Quare dicitur lege diuina pueſtigaſſe tm̃modo per nouem & quadragin‑ta portas. Ioſue aũt denuo una minus ſcilicet per octo & quadraginta. Sic em in libro explanationũ alphabeti, a Rabi Akiba rece‑pimus

וְאַחַר מִיתָתוֹ שֶׁל מֹשֶׁה נִתְעַלֵּם מִיְהוֹשֻׁעַ שַׁעַר אֶחָד וְנִשְׁתָּאֲרוּ מ״ח שְׁעָרִים וּשְׁלֹמֹה נִתְקַשָּׁה עַל אוֹתוֹ שַׁעַר לְהַחֲזִירוֹ וְלֹא הָיָה יָכוֹל

.i. Et poſt mor‑tem Moyſi abſcondita fuit de Ioſue porta una & relictæ fuerunt quadra‑ginta octo portæ, & Salomon laborauit ſup illa porta ad reducendũ eam ſed non erat potens. Hoc ita receperunt Cabaliſtæ qm̃ de Moyſe ſcriptũ eſt xxxiiii. Deuteronomii. Non ſurrexit propheta ultra in Iſrael ſicut Moy‑ſes. Non igitur Ioſue ualuit tm̃ aſcendere quantũ Moyſes aſcẽderat, iccir‑co haud ab re affirmatur uno fuiſſe gradu inferior. De Salomone aũt Ec‑cleſiaſtis xii. legitur cp̃ quæſiuerit ut inueniret res beneplaciti, ſed addunt Cabaliſtę deũ ei pcepiſſe ſic. Scribas recte uerba ueritatis, ea eſſe dicimus tradita & recepta p uiam Cabalæ, quatenus aliud cõſcribere non auderet niſi quod recepiſſet, idq̃ fuit duobus gradibus inferius q̃ Moyſi receptio. Poſt deum porta ſecunda eſt mundus archetypus, & dicitur Cœlũ a deo tetragramato in ſapientia creatũ iuxta Thargũ Hieroſolymitanũ qd̃ loco בְּרֵאשִׁית .i. in principio poſuit בְּחָכְמָתָא .i. in ſapiẽtia, quippe confirmans q̃ diximus, cp̃ in ſapientia creauit deus Tetragrammatus cœ‑lum, cõ daue angelorũ, de q̃ plane nihil a Moyſe fuit expoſitum, ne rudi et agreſti populo uel non intellecta uileſcerent, uel idololatriæ p̃berẽt occa‑ſionem. At uiſibilis iſte mũdus terra intelligitur, quẽ inter portas tertiam eſſe affirmamus. Per inane aũt ſymbolice notari materiã putabimus, por‑tam intelligentiæ quartã. Per uacuũ hoc eſt priuationẽ, quintã. Eſt & ſexta horum appetitus naturalis abyſſus. Deinceps pro qbuſuis ſex dierũ opib9 reliquæ portæ ſequuntur. Iam em quatuor elementorũ ſignacula portas quatuor indicant, purum nãcɋ elementũ ignis ſecundũ Moyſen egyptiũ libri Perplexorũ ſecundi capite xxvi. tenebræ nuncupat, ſpiritus aer, aqua humor elementaris, lux forma ſubſtantialis, dies, accidentia q̃ maxime no‑bis conferunt ad cognoſcendũ cp̃ qd eſt. Nox ſunt proprietates occultæ,

through the center: two to eight, three to seven, four to six, five to five. If you subtract from the greater number the amount by which it exceeds five, the center of the denary circle, and add to the lesser number, that amount by which it is less than five, the pairs of opposite numbers always yield the equalized five and five. If you compare the points of the lines in turn, the numerical value of any line is always five and five. The number five, in the ten-circle, is therefore said to be "circular," because, as you see, all the numbers on the circle reduce to five, and further there are five lines drawn within the circle which each make up ten. When this circular number is multiplied by ten it makes fifty—gates of understanding or years of the jubilee. Double this number (a formality of arithmetic), multiply it by itself, and comes the thousandth generation. If its surface were perpetual, infinity would result, the kingdom of all generations, called *Ensoph* by the Kabbalists, the naked deity. God produced all the rest while cloaked in light as a garment, that there might be light of light, and then, with the light of his garment he created the intelligible world of distinct and invisible spirits, which the Kabbalists call "heaven," as you have often heard me say. This is how I understand the words of the great and wise Rabbi Eliezer. He posed the question, "from what was heaven created?" and replied "from the light of his garment he took it."

It is recorded by Moses Maimonides, in Book 2, Chapter 26 of *Guide to the Perplexed*, and by Rabbi Joseph the Younger of Castile, from Salema, in Book 2 of *The Nut Garden*, that Moses the servant of God rose high enough to discern the light of his garment, the Sabbath of Sabbaths, the higher jubilee, the thousandth generation, which were all none other than the higher world of ideas, angels, happy spirits. Since he scanned God's garment and yet was unable to see his face, it is right to say that he was missing one of the fifty gates of understanding. That gate was, our scholars believe, "The Making of Life," but I do not agree and think rather that it is the essence of God, indicated by the Tetragrammaton symbol, and that it is the incomparable world that cannot be made comprehensible by any analogy. For God said to Moses: "My face you will not be able to see." Or better, "My faces shall not be seen, but I shall proclaim before you the Name of the four letters." (Exodus 33) The Kabbalists interpret this as: "I will proclaim before you that great name which you will not be able to see" (Ramban). This shows clearly that, according to God Himself, he is his own Tetragrammaton unseen by Moses. This is the origin of all the gates, above all creatures, before the beginning of creation—as it is written, "God created the heaven and the earth;" the Chaldaean translation of Onkelos reads "The Tetragrammaton created heaven and the earth." God, then, the Tetragrammaton, created all things, he whom I have heard you call the "Tetractys."

Rabbi Eliezer said, as it says in his book: "While the world was uncreated, there was God and his Name alone." Other Kabbalists, accor-

LIBER TERTIVS

Vesper corruptionis uia, Mane gñationis, Dies unus, qui certa ratiõe nõ dies primus noiatur, sed dies unus, significat compositũ in lucem editum. Die secundo, aquæ supra firmamentũ sunt species rerũ uniuersales. Firmamentũ orizon æthernitatis & tpis. Aquę sub firmamento influętię cœlestium corporũ naturales. Die tertio sequr aliud cœlum uisibile ac materiale, porta scilicet undeuigesima. inde terra quã terimus; deinde maria q̃ nauigam⁹, sic herbæ, semina, ligna, fructus. Quarto aũt luminaria, signa tempora, dies, anni, splendor, sol, luna, qbus planetis cæteri cõicatione caloris & frigoris, siccitatis & humoris cõphendunt. Calet & siccat Saturnus Mars ac Iupiter cũ suo Sole, humectat & infrigidat Mercuri⁹ ac Venus cum sua Luna etiã si septẽ hæ sphæræ distinguant specifice. Designãt p̃terea portam reliquæ stellæ nonã & trigesimã, tum die quinti prodeũt animæ uiuentes q̃ est uita mortaliũ, & in aquis reptilia & cete & pisces, & generatim uolatilia, & particulariter aues. Sexto aĩal progressiuũ in terra, & reptile terrestre, & iumẽta, & bestiæ. Tandẽ porta qnquagesima q̃ est homo. Hi sunt quadraginta nouem creaturarum cognoscẽdarum modi שערי בינה & suprema porta unus creator omniũ a nullo hoĩe nisi a Messiha plane cognitus, qm ipse est lux dei & lux gẽtiũ, ideoq̃ & cognõscit deũ & deus cognoscit p̃ eũ. Regius em̃ propheta Dauid ad deum sic exclamat. Mitte lucẽ tuã, q̃d interp̃tat Rabi Salomon Gallus המשיח שצרמה לאור שג ערבתי גר למשיחי i. Messiha q compatur luci, qa scriptum est. Paraui lucernã christo meo. Et Isaias ait Dedi te in fœdus populi in lucem gentiũ. Et rursus. Ambulabunt gẽtes in lumine tuo. Scripsit aũt Aristoteles id q̃d esse uerũ arbitror uisionẽ fieri non posse, nisi cũ lumine, ut legit in lib. de aĩa οὐχ ὁρατὸν ἄνευ φωτός. i. nil uisibile sine luce. Quapropter ambulãtibus nobis ad rerũ oim̃ inspectionẽ conducit admodum itineri adhibere lumẽ, ut uiam qua possimus absq̃ pedum læsione proficisci matura cum prouidentia eligamus. Ad q̃d receperunt Cabalistæ tramites q̃sdam luminosos & illustria experimenta q̃ nominarunt לב נתיבות החכמה i. triginta duas semitas sapiẽtiæ quarum meminit Abraham in libro de creatione quem sic incipit, בשלשים ושתים נתיבות פלאות חכמה הקק יה יהוה צבאות שמו i. Triginta & duabus semitis mirabilibus sapientiæ excussit seu exculpsit deus Tetragrammatõ Zabaoth nomen suum. Sup q̃ scripsit Rabi Iacob Cohen, q dicit mirabilibus eo significat has semitas esse arcanas reconditas & occultas, hanc suã interp̃tatio nem confirmando p Thargum. Et cõmentator Rab Ishac in eundẽ librũ צירה testatur, q̃ prisci sapiẽtes uiri cordati mites & recti p fundamẽta legis in Cabala plurimũ exercitati docuerunt nos q̃ maiores nostri & patres ambulauerunt p uias multas ut tandem starent in semitis istis quę

Book Three

ding to the Egyptian Moses in Book 2, Chapter 29 of *Guide to the Perplexed*, say: "From the beginning, when nothing was, there was nothing besides the Name of God, and his wisdom." So, according to Kabbalist teaching, there was nothing besides God, and his Name, the Tetragrammaton, and his wisdom. Our tradition alone contains these three things, the first gate of creation that was not open to Moses our teacher. It is said that he sought out the Law through forty-nine gates, and Joshua one less, through forty-eight. So we have from Rabbi Akiva, in the book explaining the alphabet: "After the death of Moses one of the gates was hidden away from Joshua, and forty-eight were left. And Solomon made great efforts to get that gate back, but he had not the strength." This is the Kabbalist doctrine on the verse in Deuteronomy 33: "There will never arise in Israel a prophet like Moses."

Joshua could not climb as high as Moses had, and so to say that he was one step below is of some significance. It is written in chapter 12 of Ecclesiastes that Solomon tried to discover pleasing things; the Kabbalists add that God ruled he should accurately write the words of truth. Handed on in the chain, I tell you, in the way of Kabbalah, none being so bold as to write down something he had not received, was this: he was two steps below Moses' receiving.

The second gate, after God, is the archetypal world, and, according to the Jerusalem Targum, it is called "Heaven created in wisdom by God the Tetragrammaton." For "in the beginning," is substituted "in wisdom," surely confirming what we have said, that in wisdom God the Tetragrammaton created the heaven, the hall of the angels. Moses offers no clear account of this, in case it should be misunderstood and abused by a wild and backward people, or so as not to afford an opportunity for idolatry.

The third of these gates is, we say, understood to be this visible earth. The fourth gate of understanding is, we understand from symbolic indications, matter, and the void that is deprivation is the fifth. The sixth is the abyss of natural appetite. After these follow the rest of the gates corresponding with the six day's labor. Four gates exhibit the insignia of the four elements: fire, the pure element is signed, according to Maimonides in chapter 26 of *Guide to the Perplexed*, by darkness; spirit by air, water the humid element, and light the substantial form of day, properties which greatly assist in our understanding of what is.

DE ARTE CABALISTICA

dicuntur admiranda sapientiæ, tradita p Zadkiel Abrahę patri nostro in traditione foederis, hęc ille. Recensebo itacǫ uobis auditores optimi si modo dignū aliqd existimatione uestra iudicabitis. Et Philolaus. Perge obsecro, & Marranus imo cōfestim exorsa ptexe obtestor ambo inquiūt. Tu ille triginta duæ ait semitę a sum‚mo culmi‚ne ad ima basis tēdūt, hoc modo notandę quarū prima est שבל מופלא i. intelligentia miraculosa, sic a qbusdam dicta, sed rectius multo noīabitur Intelligentia occulta. Nam Rabi Salomō Gallus in libro Deuteronomii cap. xxx. probat hoc uerbum מופלא significare מכוסה in uersu, qm mandatū hoc qd ego pcipio tibi hodie non supra te est, ubi docet legendum esse non occultatum a te est, idcǫ per chaldaicas translationes illic citatas. Est aūt lumen dans intelligere pcedentia sine principio, noīaturcǫ gloria prima, qm nulla creaturarum mera essentię ac ueritati eius ualet appropinquare. Secūda שבל מקדש i. Intelligentia sanctificans, est fundamentū sapiētię ætherne, q uocat fides, & no minat parens fidei, eo cǫ de ei uirtute fides infunditur. Tertia שבל שלם i. Intelligentia absoluta, est intētio principiorum q nō radicauit ad reducēdum sibi aliqua in penetralia maiestatis suę que infundant ab anteriore. Quarta שבל טהור i. Intelligentia munda purificat numeratiōes Cabalisticas & figuratione earū emēdat, disponitcǫ terminos & extremita‚tes suas ut sint abscǫ detruncatione aut dispersione. Quinta שבל מזהיר i. Intelli‚gentia fulgida dicitur a Cabalistis gloria secunda. Sexta שבל מתנוצץ i. Intelligentia resplendens, sedet super throno splēdoris, & illustrat fulgorem luminariū, & infundit influxum suum pfecto supficierū & eminentiarū. Septima שבל מנהיג i. Intelligētia inductiua, est ipe thro‚ni glo‚riæ, perficitcǫ ueritatem comunicationum spiritualium. Octaua שבל שרש i. Intelligentia radicata, q conueniens unio dicitur, & est proprium ipsius prudentiæ q infunditur a sapiētia superiore. Nona שבל צצחי i. Intelligentia triūphalis uel æther‚na, uocat paradisus uoluptatis paratus sanctis. Decima שבל חהרגש i. Intelligētia dispositiua, aptat sanctis in fide apparatum ut induāt spiritu sancto, & est illud qd uocatūr Thiphereth i statu supnorum, Vndecima שבל בחיר i. Intelligentia claritatis, est species ipsa magnificētię dicta חוזנית qm ex ea orit uisio uatibus uisione uidentibus. Duodecima שבל קבוץ i. Intelligētia notata, insignis raptus, a qua defluunt uirtutes spirituales instar infusiōis unius ab altera secundum primi influētis etergiā. Tredecima שבל נסתר i. Intelligentia recondita, illustrat solum potentias taliū intelle‚ctuū q per cogitationem fidei creditę uidēt. Quartadecima שבל מאיר i. Intelligentia illuminans, quę est ipse Hasmal angelus Ezechielis, quasi species electri, institutor arcanorū, aialium sanctuarii, &

intentionum

On the Art of Kabbalah

Secret attributes are night, evening is the way of corruption, morning of generation. Day one (there is a particular reason why it is "day one" and not "the first day") signifies the production of what was wrought in light. On the second day, the waters above the firmament are nature's universal types; the firmament is where time borders on eternity. The waters beneath the firmament are the natural influences of heavenly bodies. On the third day, there comes another, visible and material heaven, at gate nineteen. Here is the earth we stand on, the seas we sail, grass, seeds, trees, fruit. On the fourth day are the luminaries, the constellations, the seasons, hours, days, years; brilliant light, sun and moon—these heavenly bodies in communication with which other things are made hot and cold, dry and wet. Saturn, Mars and Jupiter with the sun are heat and dry; Mercury and Venus, with the moon, make wet and cold, even if these seven spheres are differentiated by particular type. The rest of the stars mark out the thirty-ninth gate. On day five come forth living things, which is mortal life; in the water, creeping things, whales and fish; and flying things after their kinds, and birds in particular. On the sixth day come animals that go upon the dry land: land reptiles and creeping things, domestic and wild animals. And at last comes the fiftieth gate: man.

These are the forty-nine means of understanding creation, "the gates of understanding." And at the highest gate is the one creator of all, unknown to man, save the Messiah, for he is the light of God and the light of the nations; he knows God and through him is God known.

David, the royal prophet, addressed God in the words, "Send your light." Rabbi Solomon Gallus interprets: "The Messiah is compared to light, because it is written: 'I have prepared a candle for my anointed one.'" And Isaiah says: "I have given you for a pledge to the people, to be the light of the nations," and again, "The nations will walk in your light." Aristotle wrote that what I think is true vision cannot be so unless it is with light: it says in *On the Soul*, "Nothing is visible without light." He advised us whose walk is directed towards the examination of all things to take a light for our journey, that we may choose the path where we can walk without stumbling.

To this end the Kabbalists have a tradition of paths of enlightenment and luminous experiences which they call "the thirty-two paths of wisdom." Abraham speaks of these in the *Creation*. He writes: "In thirty-two miraculous paths did God, the Tetragrammaton, carve or engrave his name Zebaoth." On which Rabbi Jacob Cohen writes that he says "miraculously," and means by this that these paths are secret, hidden and concealed, and backs up this interpretation by reference to Targum. Rabbi Isaac, commenting on the same book (*Yetzira*), is authority that the wise men of old—prudent, mild and upright men, expert in Kabbalah on a firm basis of Law—taught us that our forebears and our fathers walked down many roads to arrive at last on these paths of wisdom that are, they say, fit for marvel. These paths were handed down to Abraham at the time of the giving of the covenant, by Zadkiel (according to Rabbi Isaac).

LIBER TERTIVS   LV.

intentionum eorum. Quintadecima שבל מצוחצח id est Intelligentia subtiliata, disponit ordinē, quo conceditur accessus per gradus ascensionis. Sextadecima שבל נאמן id est Intelligentia fidelis, qua augent uirtutes gratificatæ iuxta uitas eorum in quibus habitant. Septimadecima שבל נסיון id est Intelligentia probatoria, est tētatio & probatio antecedens in qua consistit donū dei benedicti erga omnes sanctos eius. Octauadecima שבל קיום id est Intelligentia confirmans est uirtus restaurans in numeratiōibus Cabalisticis, si quid illis desit, uestiendo eas de spiritu sanctitatis suæ. Nonadecima שבל הרצון id est Intelligentia uoluntatis prouidet omnibus creatis, & per eam cognoscūt Cabalistę ueritatē sapiētiæ supioris. Vigesima שבל מעמיד id est Intelligentia constituens, facit stare ipsaṁ creationē in caligine imūda. Et magistri Cabalæ dicūt ꝙ sit caligo, iuxta illud caligo in circuitu eius Vigesima prima שבל מחודש id est Intelligentia irinouans, per quā reparantur et innouantur omnia creata in hoc mundo. Vigesima secunda שבל בית השפע id est Intelligētia domus largitatis, de medio infusionis illius trahiuntur arcanum & absconditum, quæ habitāt in umbra eius & adhæret eduĉtionis stuḋio atꝗ diligentię promouentis ad alta. Vigesima tertia שבל הפעולות id est Intelligētia actiuitatum, est collectio & uniuersitas operationum spiritualiū, sic dicta propter influxum qui congregat in ea de fonte pelagi superioris & glorię excelsę. Vigesima quarta שבל נבדל id est Intelligentia medians, qua colligitur influentia gratiarum & ipsa infundit largitatē in oīa stagna seu piscinas benedictionum a se appropriatarum. Vigesima quinta שבל כללי id est Intelligentia collectiua, qua colligunt astrologi iūdicio stellarum fatales euētus & notitiam eorum perficiūt sphæris & orbibus suis. Vigesima sexta שבל נעבר id est Intelligentia adminiculáris, concurrit in subsidium ad omes operatiōnes planetarum & alios influxus cœlestes. Vigesima septima שבל תמידי i. Intelligētia ꝑpetua, qtidie cōtinuat ꝑ meatū solis & lunæ secundum conditiones eorū. Vigesima octaua שבל מוגשם id est intelligentia corporalis informat omne corpus qd corporatur sub orbibus, itęꝗ magnitudinem illorum. Vigesima nona שבל החפץ המבוקש id est Intelligentia complacentiæ quæsiti, recipit diuinam infusionē ut participet de irrigatione eius super omnia creata. Trigesima שבל מורגש id est intelligentia concitatiua sensuum, qua fiūt entia sub orbe supremo & omnia genera mistorum. Trigesima prima שבל המיוני id est Intelligentia imaginaria qua uariantur & alterantur omnes figurę ac imagines creatæ iuxta superficies rerū & naturas earum. Trigesima secūda שבל מוטבע id est Intelligentia naturalis, qua consummatur na

L

Book Three

I will go over these paths for you, excellent audience as you are, if you think they merit your attention.

PHILOLAUS: Please, do go on.

MARRANUS: I protest that you must finish what you have begun.

SIMON: There are thirty-two paths which run from the very top to the very bottom. They are designated as follows:

The first is called "miraculous understanding" by some, but is more correctly named "hidden understanding." Rabbi Solomon Gallus, writing on chapter 30 of the book of Deuteronomy, shows that in the verse "the command that I give you this day is not beyond you," the Hebrew word *mufla* means *mekusah*, and he says that the verse should be read "has not been hidden from you," quoting the Aramaic translation on this. Further, there is a light, giving understanding of things which have no beginning called "the first glory;" no created thing can approach the purity of its essence and truth.

The second is called "understanding that sanctifies." It is on this that eternal wisdom, called faith, is founded; it is named "faith's parent," because it is from the strength of this that faith is diffused.

The third is "understanding," that is, one's application to first principles, which has not taken root and reduced itself into its inward parts within its own majesty, where infusion has already taken place.

The fourth is "clear understanding." It renders pure the Kabbalistic sefiroth and corrects faults in their form; it lays out their limits and scope in such a way that they are neither truncated nor thrown too far apart.

The fifth is the "shining understanding," and the Kabbalists call it "the second glory."

The sixth is "resplendent understanding." It is seated on the throne of splendor, lighting up the glow of the heavenly bodies and pouring out its inflowing all over the surfaces and peaks.

The seventh is "inductive understanding;" the throne of glory itself, it completes the truth of spiritual communion.

The eighth is "rooted understanding," called "concordant union," and belonging to the judgement that is an outpouring from the higher wisdom.

The ninth is the "triumphal understanding," or eternity, called the paradise of delight made ready for the holy.

The tenth is "ordered understanding," it adapts the magnificent preparations to the holy in faith, involving them in the holy spirit, and it is this that is called Tiphereth, in the higher order of things.

The eleventh is "understanding of clarity," itself a manifestation of magnificence, and call *Hazhazit*, because from it is derived the vision of prophets who see visions.

The twelfth is "marked understanding" which is concerned with signs. From it flow the spiritual virtues like the inflow of one thing to another with the force of the first influx.

The thirteenth is "secret understanding." It lights up only the powers of those intellects that "see" through the consideration of faith and belief.

The fourteenth is "enlightening intelligence," *Hasmal*, the angel of Ezekiel with his face of amber, the originator of the teacher of the mysteries, of the living things, of the sanctuary, and director of their purposes.

DE ARTE CABALISTICA

tura rerum materialium sub sphæra lunæ ad perfectionem suam. Cōplexus sum breui catalogo uiri externorum dogmatum cupidissimi quæ nostri maiores & de quinquaginta prudentiæ portis, & de duabus atcȝ triginta itineribus sapientiæ multis in libris difficiliore studio tractant, & est res profecto meliore digna magistro ac multi sudoris sane q̄ maximam uim habeat ad cohortandum nos ut fermè semper cum angelis uersemur in cōtemplatiōe summarum & diuinarum rerum, quibus si familiares esse cœperimus, nihil nobis erit aut dictu aut factu difficile. Familiaritatem eam literæ conciliant, quæ illorum munus sunt. Eas si adhibuerimus decem numerationibus Cabalisticis, statim consurgit duorum & triginta numerus Quod scriptū in libro Ietzira legitur עשר ספירות בלימה ועשרים ושתים אותיות .i. Decem numeratiōes Belima, & uiginti duæ literæ. Quapropter non pauci scriptores & decem istis proprietatibus silentio dignis, & uiginti duabus literis hanc semitarum cōstā summam pro meo quidem more in eum ordinem digestarum, quem tamen alii haud pariter obseruāt. At uero illud literarum collegium si quinquaginta portis diligēter applicuerimus, inde septuagiuta duorum angelorum fœlicem seriem comperiemus quibus Semhamaphores id est nomen expositorium illud magnum summi dei constare perhibetur. Nā ad quinquaginta uiginti duo addita lxxii. procreabunt. Hi sunt angeli fortes uniuersæ terrę, per quos putatur Moyses ille miraculorum operator manu sua mare usqȝ ad siccum diuisisse, quoniam ipsi sunt angeli diuisionis. Et diuisit deꝰ terram iuxta numerum angelorum eius. Sic enim in libro Portarū iusticiæ quē Rabi Ioseph Ben Carnitol celebris in Cabala magister cōscripsit inter alia legimus ונשארו כל אומות מסורות ביד ע שרים . Id est. Et relictæ sunt omnes gētes traditæ in potestatem septuaginta præfectorum, hoc est principum angelorum, quibus Racanat peritissimus Cabalista Genesis xlviii. septuaginta palmas applicat illas circa duodecim fontes quos nostis. Quinetiam certum est, duas ibidē fuisse columnas nubis & ignis, quibus duo præpositi erant angeli. Quare non inaniter existimabimus in eiuscemodi sectione maris & liberatione filiorum Israel accessisse Moysi septuaginta orbis terrarum angelos & duos illos columnares in ministerium salutis quæ nobis plane contingit ex nomine Tatragrammato ineffabili, per septuaginta duo nomina quæ de sacra scriptura colligūt explanato Exodi quartodecimo a uersu. Tollēscȝ se angelꝰ usqȝ in finē, ubi legit diuisacȝ est aqua. Sūt nimirū ea nobis sacrata signacula hodierna ętate memori mēte reposita, qb̄ symbolis angeli uocati ferunt opē hoīb, ad laudē & gloriā ineffabilis dei, de quo scripsit Rabi Salomon in expositione Thalmud testimonio Gerūdēsis in Geneseos exordio. Symbolorū itacȝ characteres hi sunt, quos digito uobis pingo.

On the Art of Kabbalah

The fifteenth path is "understanding made acute," which sets out the regularity which makes possible approach by the steps of ascent.

The sixteenth is "faithful understanding." It increases the virtues that are pleasurable in the lives of those in whom they are found.

The seventeenth path is "recommending understanding," the attestation and the antecedent examination, in which consists the gift of the blessed God to all his holy ones.

The eighteenth path is "strengthening understanding" or restorative strength, and if any of the Kabbalistic numerations is lacking, it clothes them in the spirit of its sanctity.

The nineteenth path is "understanding of the will," which cares for all it creates, and it is through it that Kabbalists come to know the truth of the higher wisdom.

The twentieth is the "constituting intelligence" which makes creation itself stand in decent darkness. The masters of Kabbalah say that it is darkness, citing "darkness is in its compass."

The twenty-first is "renewing understanding." By it are all created things in this world repaired and renewed.

The twenty-second is "understanding of the house of abundance." From the very core of its flow are drawn the hidden and secret things which live in its shadow, clinging to the desire to go forwards, to move stealthily toward the heights.

The twenty-third is "understanding of the power of action," the gathering together in their entirety of spiritual activities, so called because of the downpouring into it from the fountain of the higher sea and the lofty glory.

The twenty-fourth is the "dividing understanding" in which the inpouring of the graces is collected, and which itself pours out the mass of blessings belonging to it into all the pools and ponds.

The twenty-fifth is the "collecting understanding." By it the astrologers collect together the stars that influence fate, in their orbits and circuits, bringing about what happens.

The twenty-sixth is "supporting understanding," which goes to the aid of the planetary movements and other changes in the heavens.

The twenty-seventh is "perpetual understanding." Day by day it is given uninterrupted succession in the movements of sun and moon appropriate to each.

The twenty-eighth is "bodily understanding." It gives shape to everybody under the heavens, and gives them their concordant size.

The twenty-ninth is the "understanding of a favor requested"; it receives the divine infusion, and more than any other creature is watered by it.

The thirtieth is "impulsive understanding of the senses," by which are the beings beneath the highest heavenly body and all mixed kinds made.

The thirty-first path is the "imaginary understanding" by which are varied and altered all forms and creature-appearances, in accordance with the external and internal characteristics of things.

The thirty-second path is "natural understanding," by which all matter in the sublunary sphere is brought to completion.

וְהוּ יְלִי סִיט עָלָם מֶהָשׁ לְלָה אָכָא כָּהַת הָזִי
אֶלַד לָאו הֶהַע יְזַל מְבָה הֲרִי הֲקָם לָאו כְּלִי
לְוַו פְּהָל נְלָד יְיִי מָלָה הֶחֹו בָּתָה הָאָא יְרָת
שָׂאָה רְיִי אוּם לְכָב וּשָׁר יְחָו לְהָת כּוּק מְנָד
אָנִי חָעָם רָהָע יְיָז הָחָה מִיָּךְ וָול דָלָה סָאָל עָרִי
עָשָׁל מִיָּה וְקוּ רְצִי הָחָשׁ עָמָם נְנָא צִית מָבָה
פּוּי נְמָם יָיל הֶרָח מִצָר וּמָב יְהָה עָנוּ מָחִי
דָמָב מְנָק אִיעַ חָבוּ רָאָה יְבָם הָיִי מוּם Oïa hæc
nomina manāt de proprietate clementiæ, ut asserunt Cabalistæ, illa uero
una extat ex decēnnumerationibus, quaru uobis arbore demōstrabo sī ui
nuerint superi & uos si me audire parati eritis. Quin paratissimi, ambo in
quiunt, qui ob id tanta itinerū pericula obiuimus, tot & tantis sumptibus
erogatis. Sed perge aiunt ut de istis angelis aliqd discamus, qrum nomina
Marrano mihi nunq audita fuere, credo & tibi qq Philolao pariter. Cer
te, ait ille, ut ne uisi sunt unq isti mihi angeli qdē, ita ne ipōru cognita mihi
sunt noia, sed amabimus te uir optime, indesinenter pge. Tum Simon, Fu
isse angelos, inquit, multos qui ad tantū & tam admirandū Moysi op'eō
curreret cum aquas maris ita diuideret ut Israelitæ siccis pedibus trāsiret,
id ex ipsa possum° sacra scriptura dephēdere, ne quis me ueteratore pu
tet. Verba nāq diuina i eo loci hęc sūt וַיִּסַּע מַלְאַךְ הָאֱלֹהִים
.i. & migrauit angelus angeloru. Non ut uos pronunciatis latine, Tolleq
se angelus domini. Non ēm Adonai positum est hic qd interptamur dñm
Sed Elohim qd uos pariter angeli tranlatū qtidie legitis, Minuisti eū pau
lo minus ab angelis. Et In conspectu angeloru psallā tibi. At nequaq etia
hic scribitur, ut alias crebro angelus Elohim. Sed memorabiliter sic ange
lus ha elohim intercedente articulo demonstrante, perinde atq dicere sa
cra historia uellet. Per hunc nubis angelum castra pcedētem, cognoscite
hic plurimos qq alios adesse angelos orbis terrarū principes. Astipulat
nobis Thalmud in Mechilta, ubi Rabi Nathan a Magistro nostro Sime
one Ben Iochai cognato meo huius quæstiōnis petit solutioném. Quæro
inquit, quare ubiq scribitur angelus Adonai, hic aūt angelus ha elohim
cui respondet אֵין אֱלֹהִים בְּכָל מָקוֹם אֶלָּא רָיִן Non
deus in omni loco scilicet significat nisi pses siue pfectus. Igit angelus ille
simul cū septuaginta psidibus prouinciaru intelligit affuisse, ob idq ita di
ctus Mallach ha elohim, angelus illoru psidum seu pfectoru, & alter item
angelus ignis eorundē psidu socius, ut iure optimo septuaginta duo nume
rentur, qru signa uidistis iam pride a me descripta, qs si uultis uel potius q
uultis (noui ēm uos uelle) docebo qua namuia e sacris literis educant. Ia

L ii

Book Three

For people who long so for foreign creeds, I have briefly catalogued our forebears' beliefs concerning the fifty gates of knowledge and the thirty-two paths of wisdom. They dealt with these matters in many books. It is a difficult subject and deserves a better teacher and much hard work. For it has great power to rouse us to near uninterrupted converse with the angels, in meditation on the highest and the divine; if we become closely associated with them, we shall find nothing — in word or deed — difficult.

Such close association is achieved by the alphabet, which is its function. If we join the letters of the alphabet to the ten Kabbalistic numerations, straightaway we get the number thirty-two. In the book *Yetzira* it says "There are ten *sephiroth*, *Belima*, and twenty-two letters." Following this a good many writers using both these ten properties that deserve silence and the twenty-two letters arrive at this highest of paths.

If we pay attention and add this alphabet to the fifty gates, we find the happy ranks of the seventy-two angels, by whom is said to stand Semhamaphores — that is, the great interpretive name of the high God; for fifty and twenty-two make seventy-two. These are the angels strong over the whole earth. Through them, it is thought, did Moses the miracle-worker divide the sea with his hand down to the sea-bed, for these are the angels of division, and God divided the earth in accordance with the number of angels. In the book *Gates of Justice*, the famous master of Kabbalah, Rabbi Joseph ben Carnitol wrote: "And all the nations were left, given into the power of the seventy rulers," that is, the dominion of the angels to whom the distinguished Kabbalist Racanat assigns (writing on Genesis, chapter 48) the seventy palms that are round the twelve fountains which you know. It is clear that there were two pillars, of cloud and of fire, on which were set two angels; so it is not an empty belief that in Moses' dividing the sea and setting free the children of Israel, the seventy angels of the world and the two angels of the pillars undertook the work of salvation, something which clearly comes to us from the ineffable Tetragrammaton name through the seventy-two names which, once this verse from chapter 14 of Exodus has been explained, are culled from Holy Scripture. "And the angel raised himself and went to the end," in the passage "and the water was divided."

These hallowed signs are in the present day stored in memories, and by these symbols the angels are summoned and bring help to men, to the praise and glory of the ineffable God. According to Gerundensis in his introduction to Genesis, Rabbi Solomon wrote in his exposition of the Talmud that: "These are the shapes of the symbols; I am tracing them with my finger:

DE ARTE CABALISTICA

hos ipsos assumite treis uersus ויסע ויבא ויט ac in modū erectę columnæ singulos more Cabalistico a dextra ad sinistrā ita conscribite ut uniuscuiusq; uersus literæ a summo ad imū continuo, altera sequat alterā tunc primi uersus characterem primū ponite qui vau nomiatur. Deinde secundi uersus characterem ultimū usu retrogrado accipite, q est he, tum postremo recurrite ad tertii uersus initium, qd rursus inuenietis vau esse. Cunq; treis characteras ordine isto conjunxeritis, nascetur primi angeli memoriale vau.he.vau. Et secūdi Iod lamed iod. Et tertii Samech iod teth Sic qq; de reliquis semper ternis atq; ternis, psenti aūt modo tribus columnis rite ut fieri debet erectis, qdlibet signaculū Tetragrāmati expositorium constabitur. Eia uidete consyderate contēplamini bene, num hoc ipm summa lętitia est, omne huius seculi gaudium excellens, recordari sanctos nutus dei & diuinos uultus qs hebręi Mallachim, gręci angelus, latini de os roiant, tractare aio & manibus tam puras, tā pias, tam cōsecratas res cō uersari studiose cū illis candidissimis speciebus quarū splendor non nisi p spicacib9 generosarŭ mētiū oculis illucescit. Interesse cōuiuijs atq; collogijs spirituū beatorū q nos supra q oim mortaliū mos est fraterne diligūt nec diligūt modo sed amāt. Gestire mihi parietes uident & hoibus nobis gratulari cp dei bonitate factū sit ut p qdam humanæ imbecillitatis sigilla & artificiosa charagmata in hilares coetus admittamur angelorū, pro uirium nostrarum capacitate, cum quibus tranquillo corde gaudeamus & lætemur, quos colamus & ueneremur, quib9 honore tali & tā sublimi naturę debitū impēdamus, a qb9 uicissim & amemur & instituamur & custodiamur. Tum Marran9, characteres quidē uideo insqt sed noim sonos nō audio, qua igitur pronūciatione inuocentur angeli nescio. Ad hæc Simon, ut oculis uidentur, sic auribus audiūtur, & ut nos uident, ita uocantes audiunt. Id qui modo fieri possit duobus uerbis dicam. In spiritu & ueritate, ut quales habent linguas nostræ mentes, tales habeant aures angeli. Et sicut spiritus diuini linguis angelorum loquuntur, ita spiritus humani auribus mētium auscultēt. Non igitur ea necessitate sibi noia imponunt; cp uelint palam nominari & clamari, sed signacula memoratiua tradūt cp cupiant a nobis recordari, ne omnem putetis uim diuinam in uoce latere. Symbola igitur hæc frequentem angelorum memoriā poscunt, qrū sedula reminiscentia nos in amore dei mutuo traducit, & uicissim amor in rememoratione. Que em fortiter amam9, eius frequēter meminim9, ut est in puerbio. Meminerūt oīa amātes. Icirco nomē tetragrāmatō nobis de9 cōdonauit, nō ut illo se uocem9 qd est ineffabile, recteq; a uobis Anekphoniton appellatur id est non uocabile. Quid enim respondit creator quærenti Moysi quod est nomen tuum, certe hoc aiebat, i. h. v. h. hoc est nomen meum in æthernum, & hoc memoriale meū in generatione & generatione.

On the Art of Kabbalah

VHV	YLY	SYT	'LM	MHSh	L'LH	AKA	KHTh	HZY
ALR	LAV	HH'	YZL	MBH	HRY	HQM	LAV	KLY
LVV	PHL	NLK	YYY	MLH	HHV	NGH	HAA	YRT
ShAH	RYY	AVM	LKB	VShR	YHV	LHH	KVQ	MNR
ANY	H'M	RH'	YYZ	HHH	MYK	VVL	YLH	SAL
'RY	'ShL	MYH	VHV	RNY	HHSh	'MM	NNA	NYT
MBH	PVY	NMS	YYL	HRH	MSR	VMB	YHH	'NV
MHY	RMB	MNQ	AY'	HBV	RAH	YBM	HYY	MVM

All these names spring from the quality of forbearance, say the Kabbalists. This forbearance comes from the ten numerations. I will outline the tree of the numerations, please God, if you are ready to listen.

PHILOLAUS AND MARRANUS: Of course we are ready. It was for this that we risked all the perils of the journey and incurred such vast and recurrent expense. Proceed—let us learn something of these angels.

MARRANUS: I have never heard their names, and I believe it is the same with you, Philolaus.

PHILOLAUS: That's right. Never have I seen these angels or known their names. Excellent sir, we shall be extremely grateful if you go on and never stop.

SIMON: We can learn from the Holy Scriptures that there were many angels assisting in Moses' great and wonderful work when he divided the waters of the sea that the Israelites might cross dryshod. I do not want to be thought too clever.

These are the divine words from scripture: "and the angel of angels went," and not as the Latin translation runs, "and the angel of the Lord raising himself." Here there is no *Adonai* for which you can write "Lord." It says *Elohim*, for which you usually read "angels," as in "You have made him a little less than the angels," and "In the sight of the angels will I hymn thee." But here "angel" is not written as it is elsewhere *Elohim*. It should be borne in mind that *elohim* here has the definite article *ha-* prefixed as if the meaning of the sacred verse is "understand by this angel of the cloud preceding the camp that there were many other angels also present, the rulers of this world."

Talmud concurs. In *Mechilta* Rabbi Nathan seeks an answer to this question from Simon ben Yochai, a member of my family: "Why, I ask, is it that everywhere else 'angel of Adonai' is written while here it is 'angel of ha-elohim'?" The reply is: "The term *elohim* is only used to indicate a judge or ruler." Thus the angel of the smoke is understood to have been present together with the seventy governors of their areas, and he is called therefore *Malach ha-elohim*, angel of the governors. Thus one would be right in counting seventy-two—you have just seen me write out their signs. If you want—rather, because you want (for I know that you want), I shall show you how they are derived from these sacred letters.

LIBER TERTIVS   LVII

Est igitur Tetragrammaton, æthernitati nomen, generationi aut memoriale tm̄, quia nequit ulla uoce humana componi nomen q̄d diuinitatis natura æquare possit. Ab opibus angelos cognoscimus, quare pro eisdē uirtutum opibus noīa pariter pronunciamus, ut a medicina Raphael, a uirilitate Gabriel, a stupore ac admiratione Michael, q̄d iterp̄tamur quis tam fortis, propria uero noīa qm̄ essentiam ignoramus, nostræ mortalitatis infirmitas inuenire non ualet, nec inuenta imponere, nisi q̄tum nobis diuina est reuelatione cōcessum. Ex numeris itaq̄ ac figuris diuinitus traditis cō templantissimi quiq̄ secundū uoluntates angelorū noīa sibi formare instituunt sicut pueri ex literis uoces cōponere docent, uel hebraicis uel græcis uel romanis, uel arabicis, uel ægyptiis, non cp uox enuncianda egeat literis eiuscemodi, sed propter nostræ imbecillitatis memoriā, ut sint noīa quasi notamina quæ sensus nostros incitent uel figura uel uoce, rursumq̄ sensus moueat phantasiam, phantasia memoriam, memoria rationem, ratio intellectum, intellectus mentem, mens angelum. Scripsit huius generis aliq̄d perq̄ elegāter ex uestris q̄dam insigni noīe philosophus Tyris Maximus in libro τῶν ἐν ρώμη διαλέξεων τῆς πρώτης ἐπιδημίας disputatiōe octaua. Vnde id uobis coniectura innotescit, satis esse, si tres uersus, per me ante resolutos in angelorum septuaginta duotū reuerentiā & ueneratiōe, legeritis ea serie qua spiritus sanctus dictauit, prorsusq̄ p eorum dilectiōnem in noīs dei summi ardentissimū amorē & extaticā adorationem incubueritis, pensiculatim cōmemorando cp sicut ex numero tetragrammati arithmetica proportione progreditur numerus septuaginta duorū, ita septuaginta duo angeli ex signaculo creatoris q̄dā effluxu diuino producūt. Cum em̄ quælibet litera hebraica numerum peculiarē designet, oriunt ex iod.he.vau.he. duo & septuagita, hoc modo. Iod notat decem, he quinq̄, vau sex, he iterum quinq̄. Totum hoc ex arte arithmetica sic colligat Iod decem, Iod he quindecim, Iod he vau unū & uiginti. Iod he vau he uiginti sex. Comp̄hendite nunc singula, Decem, quindecim, uiginti unū & uigintisex, & oriunt septuaginta duo. Hæc reputantes uobiscū aperte intelligetis ad inuocandos spiritus uoce spirituali opus esse, non aūt clamore, ceu sacerdotū Baal qb9 ab Helia propheta dicit tertio Reg. xviii. Clamate uoce maiore forsitan deus in diuersorio est aut in itinere aut certe dormit ut excitet. At si qua orōne in supplicatiōibus utimur non ideo fit ut deū uel angelos syllabis aut dictionibus tanq̄ erga mortales usi cōmoueamus, sed ut uires nostras in ardorem illorū incitemus & fiduciā in eos quasi ancorā figamus, ueluti appellendo nauim in portū solent nautæ resti eiecta uel fune prolato terrā attrahere, quanq̄ immobilē, q̄ conatu ad terrā se ipsos trahunt. Pari ratione per sensibilia nos signa q̄cunq̄ instituto composita uidemur inuisibilē diuinitatē attrahere, cum tm̄ reuera nos ipsos mobiles ad immobilē diuinitatē attrahamus. Hoc arcano fundamento sacramenta

L iii

Book Three

Take the three verses beginning *vayisa*, *vayabo*, and *vayet*, and write them out one by one in a vertical column in the Kabbalistic manner from right to left such that the letters of each word follow on one from another from top to bottom without a break. Then take the first letter of the first verse, which is called *Vav* (*V*); next working the other way take the last letter of the second verse, *hay* (*H*) and lastly go to the beginning of the third verse, which you will find is *Vav* again. When you link up these three letters in this order the first angel's mnemonic *V-H-V* is obtained, the second angel is *Y-H-Y*, and the third is *S-Y-T*. So too with the rest, whenever they are set out three by three, with the three columns kept properly straight and tidy, some sort of sign that explains the Tetragrammaton will be produced.

Well look, consider and contemplate this well, for this is the greatest happiness, the highest joy, surpassing all joy in this age: to remember God's holy commands, the divine features, called *Malachim* in Hebrew, *angels* in Greek, and *gods* in Latin; and to occupy hand and brain in things so faultless, good, and hallowed; to keep close company with those shining white shapes whose splendor gleams only for the sharp-sighted eyes of noble minds; to be among the guests and confidants of the blessed spirits which care for us more than mortals, as brothers — and not just care, but even love. Even the walls seem to exult and rejoice with us that God's goodness has given us these alphabetical constructions, these signs of human weakness through which we are admitted to the happy bands of angels (given the limits of human ability). With the angels we rejoice and delight, our hearts at rest, worshipping and reverencing them. We pay them the honor due to such sublimity, those by whom we are loved, taught and guarded.

MARRANUS: I see the letters but do not know what they sound like, and so do not know how to utter these words and invoke the angels.

SIMON: As the eyes see them, so do ears hear them, and as they see us, so do they hear us calling. I will tell you in two words how this comes about: in spirit and in truth. As our minds have tongues, so angels have ears, and just as divine spirits speak with the tongues of angels, so do human spirits listen with the ears of the mind. They do not give themselves names through any wish for acknowledgement or acclaim therefore. They are jogging the memory, wanting us to bear them in mind. Do not think that all the strength of the divine is found in speech. These symbols urge that we continually remember the angels; making a practice of doing so brings us into the love of God, and in turn love brings remembrance. We often remember what we greatly love — as it says in the proverb, "Lovers remember everything."

God has not given us this name of the Tetragrammaton that we should call out what is unutterable: you are right to call it *anekphoniton*, that is, "unpronounceable." To Moses' question, "What is your name?", the Creator replied "*YHVH* is my name to eternity, and this is my memorial from generation to generation." The

DE ARTE CABALISTICA

uniuerſa & cerimoniarum ritus pſtant. Hinc ſignis, characteribus, et uoce utimur, hinc hymnis & canticis, hinc tympano & coro, hinc chordis, cymbalis & organo, aliiſcp id genus muſicis, non ut deū quaſi fœminā emollimus, nec ut noſtris blandimentis & adulationibus angeli capiant. Sed ut deum ac diuina exaltando, noſtrę conditionis exiguitatē agnoſcamus, ſubiectionē & obedientiā humillime profiteamur, & oēm uoluptatē humanā in res diuinas cōferamus. Ad ſummū aūt, hoc pacto amorem inteſum & ardentem erga diuinitatē concipiamus, qui unus pter cætera id efficit magis, ut oīm gratiarū capaces ſimus, propterea palmas tendimus, brachia expandimus, genua flectimus, ſtantes oramus, iuſſi quocp uacā triennem capram triniam, turturē, columbā, per medium diuidimus, ariete in uepribus hærentē cornibus gladio occidentes, igne cremamus, Thau ſup poſtes ædium ſanguine notamus, Serpētē æneum aſpicimus, Cherubim & alias imagines figuramus. Verba cōpoſita loqmur atcp uouemus, Sanctuarium ſtruimus, Pontificē tam uario & admirando indutū ornatu attoniti reſpicimus. Vniuerſa hęc & ſimilia propter nos ipſos fiunt, ut nos moueant, nos incitent, nos auertant, nos conuertant, a uiſibilibus ſcilicet ad inuiſibilia, fidem augeant, ſpem cōfirment, & uerā inter nos charitatē deo gratiſſimam diligenti Anacephalęoſi in diuinorū amore transſerant. Dogmata hæc oīa Cabaliſtarū ſunt, q ut liber tertius pplexorum Moyſi ægyptii atteſtat ſic dicūt שבונת העבורות החם וברון השם תמיד ויראתו ואהבתו ושמירת המצות כולן ושיאמין בשם ית מך שהוא הברחי לבל

i. cp intentio cerimoniarū eiuſmodi eſt, memoria dei frequens & timor eius, & amor eius, & obſeruantia mandatorū oīm, & cp credatur in deum altiſſimū, id qd neceſſariū eſt unicuicp. Nimirū graui nos mole corpis oppreſſi ualde qdem egemus ad ſomnolēti animi excitationē cōmouentibr rebus, ut generoſus equus itinere iam longo fatigatus cum claſſicū pſonu it in robur erigitur, ſtare loco neſcit, micat auribus, & elephantus ſegnicie torpeſcens, igne oſtenſo reſurgit in audaciā, ita rebus ſecularibus enerua/ ta uirtus noſtra, externis & corpalibus incitabulis ſiue uocū ſeu figurarum indiget, ut animi noſtri uigor ſpirituali operi robuſtius inſtet, & contēpla tio noſtra tanto acrius in ſublime prouehat, qto magis attoniti antea obſtupuerimus. In hanc utilitatē dementes angeli ſæpe figuras characteras formas & uocęs inuenerunt, propoſueruntcp nobis mortalibus & ignotas & ſtupendas, nullius rei iuxta conſuetū linguæ uſum ſignificatiuas, ſed per rationis noſtræ ſummā admirationē in aſſiduā intelligibiliū pueſtigationem, deinde in illorū ipſorū uenerationē & amorē inductiuas, non em ſecūdū inſtitutū aut placitū hois ſignificāt ſed ad placitū dei. Vnde ad uos illud a nobis tranſtulit doctiſſimus ueſtra ætate atcp ſecta Mirandulanus

On the Art of Kabbalah

Tetragrammaton then is a name for eternity. But for a generation it is only a memorial, as no human word can encompass the name which equals the divine nature.

We know the angels from their works and we have names for them from their individual works: Raphael from medicine, Gabriel from manliness, Michael from wonder and awe—we interpret *Michael* as "who is so strong." Being mortals, we are too weak to discover their proper names as we do not know their real nature, nor could we use the names if we discovered them, except if it were by concession of divine revelation. And so a few scholars of insight set themselves to form the names of the angels from the numbers and figures handed down of the divine. They were like boys taught to derive sounds from letter, whether Greek, Roman, Arabic or Egyptian, not because the sound to be voiced lacked letters, but because of our imperfections. So there are names and signs that either by their shape or their sound arouse our senses. The senses stimulate the imagination, imagination memory, memory reason, reason understanding, understanding rouses mind, and mind the angel.

Your distinguished philosopher Maximus of Tyre wrote something on these lines very neatly in section 8 of *Discourse on my First Visit to Rome*.

Thus this conjectural inference becomes clear to you. It is enough that you read the three words that I have just resolved into the seventy-two names of the angels with reverence and veneration, in the order the holy spirit laid down, and that you press on directly through love of them in the names of God most high, in burning ardor and fearful adoration, taking great care to bear in mind that just as the number seventy-two is derived arithmetically from the numerical value of the Tetragrammaton, so the seventy-two angels are produced from the sign of the creator, as if by divine issue.

Any Hebrew letter you take stands for a particular number. Thus, in this way, *YHVH* equals seventy-two; *Y* means ten, *H* five, *V* six, *H* five again. Put together arithmetically, *Y* is ten, *YH* fifteen, *YHV* is twenty-one, *YHVH* twenty-six. Now add ten, fifteen, twenty-one and twenty-six, and the answer is seventy-two.

Consider these and you will understand clearly the need for the voice of the spirit to invoke spirits, not shouting, as the priests of Baal thought, to whom the prophet Elijah says in *3 Kings 18*: "Shout louder. Perhaps your god is hiding or traveling or asleep and you must wake him." If we use speech for prayer, let us not try to move God and the angels with syllables and sentences as we would with mortals. Rather let us summon our powers of desire for them and trust in them as in an anchor, as sailors bringing a ship into port throwing out cable or rope and pulling land toward them such that though the land does not budge, their own efforts drag them to land. We in the same way seem by sensible signs ordered by some kind of preordained rule to drag ourselves towards the invisible divinity.

LIBER TERTIVS LVIII.

Comes q̃d in nongentis conclusionibus ait, Non significatiuæ uoces plus possunt in magia q̃ significatiuæ, quælibet em̃ uox uirtute habet in magia in q̃tum dei uoce format̃, quia illud in q̃ primũ magicã exercet natura, uox est dei, hęc Picus. Tum Philolaus. Soporatos & stertentes, inq̃t, nos hoies maiori mouerẽt excitatiõe huiuscemodi noĩa, si plures sensus & non unũ solũ mouerent ut non modo nostris obtutibus per figuras & characteres appareret, uerum etiã articulata uoce aures simul nostras pulsarent. Quare plurimum opto si fieri possit ista non solũ picta uidere, sed dicta q̃q̃ audire. Tum Simon. Valde segnes, inquit, putandi sunt mea sentẽtia, ac si cũ tua uenia dici liceat ualde q̃dem hebetes q̃ extraneo motu egent, quanq̃ ita sumus nati ut semp aliud magis aliũ afficiat, & non idem om̃es pariter. Ad hæc assentior tibi Simon doctissime uera dicẽti Marranus ait, hoc em̃ & nostri affirmant, angelos hoĩbus apparere aliter atq̃ aliter pro conditione ac natura uidentis. De q̃ Chrysostomus sup Matthæũ late ut om̃ia tandem his uerbis de Ioseph scribit, κατ' ὄναρ φαίν(εται) ὁ ἄγγελος. ἡ γὰρ ἡμέρα πρὸς καθὼς τοῖς παιδίοις καὶ ἐπὶ ζαχαρίᾳ καὶ τῇ παρθένῳ. σφόδρα πιστὸς ἦν ὁ ἀνὴρ. καὶ οὐκ ἐδεῖτο τῆς ὄψεως ταύτης. i. Per somnium apparet angelus & quare nõ manifeste, quemadmodũ pastoribus & Zachariæ & uirgini. Vehementer credulus erat ille uir, & non egebat uisione ista. Cui Simon rursus. Et id tu recte q̃dem, ac haud aliter Cabalistæ sentiunt dicentes, q̃ uirtus uisiua in Abrahã fortior erat q̃ in Lot, iccirco Abrahæ apparuerunt uiri, & Lot angeli. Sed de his alio forte loco. Nunc q̃d ad nostram attinet causam, magna ut pnostis est hoĩm diuersitas. Quidã satis grati & ea sorte cõtẽti sunt angelos in forma humana uidisse, alii in forma ignis, alii in forma uenti ac aeris, alii in forma fluuii & aquæ, alii in forma uolucrũ, alii in forma gem̃marum aut mineræ, aut pciosorum lapidũ, alii in energia prophetię, alii ĩ spiritu q̃dam habitante intra se, alii in literarũ & characterũ figura, alii in sonitu uocis, & sic de pluribus uisionũ speciebus, in sacra scriptura depħe sis, uobis aũt dum hi characteres septuaginta noĩm nequaq̃ satisfacere uĩdebuntur, demonstrabo recta uia, non tm̃ in characteribus cõmemoratis, uerum etiã post ea cõmemorandis, q̃nam modo ex effigie literarũ dictio fiat q̃ possit articulate pronunciari. Eius artis deũ ipsum habemus autorẽ. Legimus nanq̃ in xxiiii. Exodi. Ecce ego mitto angelũ meum ante te ad custodiendum te in uia, & ad ducendũ te in locũ quẽ destinaui, Sis cautus a conspectu eius, & audi uocẽ eius ne exacerbaueris eũ, qa non ignoscet sceleribus uestris, q̃m nomen meum est in illo. Per q̃d cognoscimus nomen angeli optimo ritu comphendere nomẽ dei q̃nq̃ debere. Ideoq̃ Cabalei cum angeli cuiusuis nomen significatiue pronunciare nequerint, subsidio alicuius noĩs dei q̃d illi adiungũt, totũ simul proferre consueuerunt. Sicut em̃ tris hos characteres מיך aut גברי uel רפא ad significãdũ an geli nomẽ improprie uidẽr usurpari, nisi addatur nomẽ dei El, ut Michael

K iiii

Q

Book Three

On this hidden foundation rest all the sacred rites and ceremonies. It is because of this that we employ signs, letters and phrases, the hymns and canticles, drums and choirs, stringed instruments, cymbals, organs and other musical instruments: not so that we may soften up God as we would a woman, and not so as to catch the angels with our sweet words and terms of endearment. We do it so that in the exaltation of God and the divine we may acknowledge the poverty of our own condition, humbly confess our subordinate and obedient state, and so unite all human desires in matters divine. In this way we conceive for the Highest an intense and burning love, one which renders us able to give thanks more than anything else. So we stand with outstretched hands and arms; so we bend the knee, standing to pray; so we have been commanded to cut open a three-year-old cow and three-year-old goat, a turtle dove and a dove, to burn on the fire a ram caught in the thicket after killing it with a sword between the horns. So we put the letters "Th" over the doors of our houses, so we look with respect on the brazen serpent and make the cherubim and other such images. We use set forms for speech and oath-swearing. We build sanctuaries and gaze in awe on the priest clothed in various and wonderful garments.

All these things, and all things like them, are made for us, intended to move us and excite us, to turn us away from the visible and towards the invisible. They are designed to increase our faith and strengthen our hope, to transform true love of each other, which is most pleasing to God, by diligent recapitulation into love of the divine. This teaching is wholly Kabbalistic, as, in Book 3 of the *Guide to the Perplexed*, Maimonides says: "It is intended that the ceremonies serve to remind us frequently of the fear and love of God and of obedience to his commands, and to make us believe in God most high, which all men need."

We are weighed down under the burden of the great mass of the body. We are much in need of means by which to arouse our sleepy minds. It is like a noble horse exhausted by a long journey that stands strong and upright when the trumpet sounds. It forgets how to stand still and pricks up its ears — or like a slow and stolid elephant whose courage is roused at the sight of fire. Our strength is worn away in secular matters, and we need the external physical stimuli of sound and sight to fortify our minds before they can apply themselves to spiritual work, and carry our contemplation to the sublime with energy equal to our previous dumbstruck lethargy.

The angels have been good to us in such a use of images and have often found and introduced to us mortals figures, letters, forms and phrases which before were unknown and incomprehensible to us and which in no way conform to the normal use of language. They were designed to lead us from the admiration of reason to continual investigation, and thence to the worship and lore of the intelligible. They have significance not in man's rules or whims but in accordance with the will of God.

Count Mirandola, an outstanding contemporary and religionist of

DE ARTE CABALISTICA

Gabriel Raphael. Ita ipsi q̃cɜ in aliis angelicis noibus sacram scripturā cōnātes imitari dicunt Raziel. Iophiel. Zadkiel. Peliel. Malthiel. Vriel, & similí more caetera. Quin uero ut Romani deum suū capitolinum noiant Optimū Maximū, propter beneficia optimum, propter uim maximū. Ciceronis testimonio in orōne ad pontifices pro domo sua. Sic Iudaeorū natio deum suū propter beneficia uocat Iah, & propter uim ac uirtutem appellat El. Ita em̄ Cabalistae sup̄ Dauid regis sermo, ne cū ait Si iniq̄tates obseruaueris, Iah, domine q̃s sustinebit dicunt יה שהוא עולם הרחמים ארני שהוא עולם חדין. i. Iah, q̄ sit seculū clementiae, Adonai q̄ sit seculum seueritatis, ut in Portae lucis cap. viii. De El aūt ita legitis Numeri xvi. Fortissime El deus spirituum ois carnis, num uno peccante contra oēs ira tua desaeuiet? Optimus igĩ nobis deus est, q̄a clemētissimus, & maximus q̄a fortissimus, q̄d duo haec noīa diuina repsentant Iah & El, q̄rum alterum si q̄tocuicɜ septuaginta duorū noīm coniunxeritis, nimirū insigne uocabulū oxytonon efficietis. Hoc certe modo sem per pronunciando, ut dictiones fiant trissyllabicae ac aspirationes p̄ singularem hanc notā scriptae .h. flatu forti tanq̃ duplici spiritu latinae literae .h. ex imo pectore prodeant, & ubicɜ Iah unice p̄ i consonante pronunciet. Similiter & El. nam utracɜ harū dictio etiam in cōpositione noīm monosyllabice profert, & in eandem accetus cadit. Sunt itacɜ lxxii. noīa sacra, q̄d unum Semhamaphores. i. sanctissimi Tetragramati nome expositoriū d̄ p̄ inuocatiōes angelorū ab hoībus deo deditis, deuotiscɜ cū timore ac tremore sic enuncianda. Vehuiah. Ieliel. Sitael. Elemiah. Mahasiah. Ielahel. Achaiah. Cahethel. Haziel. Aladiah. Lauiah. Hahaiah. Iezalel. Mebahel. Hariel. Hakamiah. Louiah. Caliel. Leuuiah. Pahaliah. Nelchael. Ieiaiel. Melahel. ḥaiuiah. Nithhaiah. Haaiah. Ierathel. Seehiah. Reiaiel. Omael. Lecabel. Vasariah. Iehuiah. Lehahiah. Chauakiah. Manadel. Aniel. ḥaamiah. Rehael. Ieiazel. Hahahel. Michael. Veualiah. Ielahiah. Sealiah. Ariel. Asaliah. Mihael. Vehuel. Daniel. Habasiah. Imamiah. Nanael. Nithael. Mebahiah. Poiel. Nemamiah. Ieialel. Harahel. Mizrael. Vmabel. Iahhael. Anauel. Mehiel. Damabiah. Mauakel. Eiael. ḥabuiah. Roehel. Iabamiah. Haiaiel. Mumiah. Praesto iam sunt ad manū uiri optimi cum q̄bus nō modo ab imi pectoris penetralibus cladestina colloquia mussare, uerumetiā expressas quocɜ uoces miscere & quemlibet symbolico suo nomie inuocare queatis, quaq̄uā singularū regionum praesides tn̄ nihil non comunicatum habentes. Taetsi enim in mundo supercoelesti habitāt, at ista nihilominus inferiora curāt. Si enim hoc influentiis naturalibus contingit ut in coelis commorentur, & simul terrena gubernent, multomagis uirtutibus nobilioribus, tenuioribus & simplicioribus mūdi superioris, eiuscemodi magistratus pariter sunt concessi, ut penetrent nostra, & a nostris uicissim penetrētur, Ad id utar Plotini uestri assertione i libro de Intellectu & Ideis

yours, has transmitted all this to you from us. In his *Nine Hundred Conclusions* he says, "Meaningless sounds have more magical power than meaningful ones. Any sound is good for magic in so far as it is formed from the word of God, because its nature works magic primarily through the word of God."

PHILOLAUS: We men are fast asleep, and utterances of this kind would awake us more if they affected several senses and not just the one. Then not only would their shapes and letters be apparent to the sight, but they would also strike our ears at the same time with distinct and separate sounds. So, if possible, I very much hope not just to see the names drawn but also to hear them aloud.

SIMON: Only idiots need a push from without. If you will excuse my saying so, such people are pretty dim. We are, though, born unequal, and different things always affect different people in different ways.

MARRANUS: I agree, learned Simon. You speak the truth. Our teachers assert this too: that angels appear to men in different ways, depending on the state and nature of the person seeing. Chrysostom in his commentary on Matthew, writing in his usual verbose style, has these words to say on this subject about Joseph: "The angel appears in a dream. Why not openly, as to the shepherds and Zachariah and the Virgin? Because that man was a strong believer and had no need of a vision."

SIMON: You are right. The Kabbalists feel just the same and say that Abraham's strength of seeing was stronger than Lot's. Therefore Abraham had an apparition of men only, but angels came to Lot. But I will perhaps say more of this elsewhere.

Now for a subject of importance to our case. There is, as you know, great diversity among men. Some men have been quite happy and content just to have seen angels in human form. Others have seen them in the form of fire, or wind and air, at streams and waters, in birds, gems, minerals and precious stones, in prophetic frenzy, through a spirit living inside them, in the shape of letters, or the sound of a voice, and so on. Holy Scripture contains many kinds of vision. But since these letters of the seventy names do not seem to satisfy you, I will show you, not only in the characters already mentioned but also in some to be mentioned shortly, how one may pronounce whatever is pronounceable from the shapes of the letters. We have it that God himself was the inventor of this skill, for we read in Exodus 23, "Behold, I send my angel before you to guard you on the way and to lead you to the place that I have appointed. Be careful in his sight and heed his voice lest you annoy him: he will not pardon your crimes, for My Name is in him." By this we understand that properly the name of an angel ought sometimes to include the name of God. So when the masters of Kabbalah could not derive meaning from the name of any angel, they used the whole of a name of God and formed the angel's name from it. They saw that it was an improper use of the letters *MICH* or *GABRI* or *RAPHI* to signify by them the name of an angel without the addition of the name of God, i.e. *EL*, resulting in Michael, Gabriel and

LIBER TERTIVS

& ente q̃ ait. Mũdus iste sensibilis uno tm̃ loco determinat. Mũdus aũt intelligibilis est ubicɋ, pinde ac si dicatɋ ille huc nostrũ & ambiat & ordiet & coeruet & penetret. Aiaduertite aũt q̃d admiratiõe dignũ cabalistarũ sapientes huc afferãt ingentes ita אין לך כל עשב ועשב מלמטה שאין לו מזל ברקיע שמכה, אותו ואומר לו גדל. i. Non est tibi ulla herba aut planta inferius, cui non sit stella in firmamento q̃ percutiat eam & dicat ei. Cresce. In eã iuerũt ipsi sententiã sacris literis muniti ut legit in Iob cap. xxxviii. Num nosti leges coelorũ si posueris p̃fectũ seu p̃side uel executore eius in terra. Nõ itaqɋ uos retrahãt orbis terrarũ tante sollicitudines acrerũ inferiorũ cure qb9 suptanoiati angeli dispe̅satiõe creatoris sunt destinati, q̃min9 illos etiã in nouem choros supcoelestium hierarchiarũ referatis. Cum em̃ angelus sit alteritas, sicut deus identitas, prima uero alteritas sit binarius, recte opinabimur qɋ ex binarii multiplicatione numerus angelorũ oriatur. Multiplicatio autẽ binarii cubica sic fit, bis bini bis, & erunt octo primus cubus, Octonos uero q̃scɋ angelos in nouem choros si distribueritis, erunt septuaginta duo, tot em̃ sunt nouies octo. Redite nunc si uultis per choros ad cubum, p̃ cubum ad Tetractyn uestrã, quã nos tetragrammato, Romani quaternitudinẽ appellant ab ea ad binariũ, angelicã naturã significantem, & idẽ ad unitatẽ Deũ Opt. Max. & experiemini certe si nostrũ studiũ ad angelos applicuerimus, qɋ etiam p̃ angelos deo iungamur Tetragrammato ineffabili lod. he. yau. he in q̃ primum resplendet angelorũ istorũ nobilissima natura. Nam si ex quatuor illis literis יהוה quater lod posueritis sicɋ descendendo ter he, bis yau, semel he, mox uobis surget septuaginta duorũ suma, expositoria nois dei inenarrabilis & incomprehe̅sibilis ad q̃d oĩa sacra noĩa referũt, q̃rɋ ingens copia est, singula tm̃ appellatiua sunt, hoc solum dei propriũ est & appropriatũ quare מיוחד cognoĩatur. Haec aũt septuaginta duo dicũt unũ nomen symbolicũ, eo qɋ intentio illorũ sit unum Deum Opt. Max. significare licet p̃ multas & uarias rõnes angelorum, quomodo notam9 principẽ p̃ aulicos & imp̃atorẽ p̃ exercitum. Et ea sane uenerant atqɋ colunt Magistri Cabalae plurimũ qbus deuoti hoĩes miranda op̃antur & mirabiliora q̃ eloqui mihi phas sit, ego tm̃ uirum doctissimũ in hac causa testem citabo Racanat in cõmentariis Exodi xiii. q̃ hos characteras & has literas affirmat esse אותיות פורחות למעלה בעיקר המרכבה והם ממונים לעשות כל דבר בהם ומעלותיהם ידועים למקובלים. i. Characteres uolantes sup̃rẽ in fundamento sapientiae spiritualis & su̅t administratorii spiritus seu p̃fecti ad faciendũ oem̃ rem p̃ eos, & op̃atiões eorum sunt notae Cabalistis, hucusɋ Rabi Mnahem Racanat. Et secundũ

Book Three

Raphiel. When it came to the other angelic names, they tried to imitate Sacred Scripture and say Raziel, Iophiel, Zadkiel, Peliel, Malthiel, Uriel and others like that.

The Romans call their god on the Capitol "Best" and "Greatest," being "Best" because of his kindnesses and "Greatest" because of his strength. (Cicero bears this out, in his speech to the priests *On behalf of his own home*). In the same way, the Jewish nation call their god *Yah* because of his kindnesses and *El* because of his strength and virtue. The Kabbalists comment on the words of King David, when he says: "if you have seen our iniquities, Yah, O Lord who will sustain us?": " 'Yah' shows that he is the world of mercy, 'Adonai' ('O Lord') that he is the world of harshness," as it says in *Gate of Light*, Chapter 8.

On *El*, you read in Numbers 16, "O Strongest 'El,' God of the spirits of all flesh, will your anger strike against all for the sin of one?" So to us, God is best because he is merciful, and greatest because he is strong, and this is represented by these two divine names, *Yah* and *El*. And if you join one of these to any of the seventy two names you will make an impressive and striking word. You must always pronounce it with three syllables and the aspirate, written in Latin with the designation "h." It must come out from the bottom of the chest as if there were a double breathing of the Latin letter "h". In all cases *Yah* will be pronounced just by the consonantal "y." *El* is the same. Both are pronounced as monosyllables even when in a name composed of parts, and in both cases the accent falls in the same place.

So there are seventy-two sacred names. They are (in one word) the Semhamaphores that explains the holy Tetragrammaton. They are to be spoken only by men dedicated and devoted to God and must be pronounced thus in fear and trembling through invocations of the angels: Vehuiah, Ieliel, Sitael, Elemiah, Mahasiah, Ielahel, Achaiah, Cahethel, Haziel, Aladiah, Laviah, Hahaiah, Iezalel, Mebahel, Hariel, Hakamiah, Loviah, Caliel, Levuiah, Pahaliah, Nelchael, Ieiaiel, Melahel, Haiviah, Nithhaiah, Haaiah, Ierathel, Saeehiah, Reiaiel, Omael, Lecabel, Vasariah, Iehuiah, Lehahiah, Chavakiah, Manadel, Aniel, Haamiah, Rehael, Ieiazel, Hahahel, Michael, Veualiah, Ielahiah, Sealiah, Ariel, Asaliah, Mihael, Vehuel, Daniel, Hahasiah, Imamiah, Nanael, Nithael, Mebahiah, Poiel, Nemamiah, Ieialel, Harahel, Mizrael, Vmabel, Iahhael, Anavel, Mehiel, Damabiah, Mavakel, Eiael, Habuiah, Roehel, Iabamiah, Haiaiel, Mumiah.

Gentlemen, you now have access to words with which you can do more than mutter secretly to yourselves in the depths of your hearts, for now you can express sounds aloud and in conjunction. You can summon whatever angel you like by his own symbolic name, for, although each rules over his own separate area, there is nothing they do not share. Though they live in the world above the heavens, none the less they care that they remain in the heavens and at the same time govern the earth—so much nobler, finer and clearer are the virtues of

DE ARTE CABALISTICA

Rabi Akiba procedūt de throno gloriæ dei, Sed ne quis uana fupſtitioē ductus putet ab angelis omnia humanę mortalitati cœlitus conferri ac nō potiꝰ per angelos ab ipſa dei maieſtate. וְכָמְצִבְיֵהּ עָבַד בְּחֵיל oīa fieri etiam in angelis, ut in Daniele Nabuchadnezer chaldaice teſtaꞇ שְׁמַיָּא וְדָאֲרֵי אַרְעָא .i. Et ſecundū uoluntatē ſuam facit in exercitu cœli & habitatoribus terræ. Ideo recepeꝛūt Cabalæi de libro pſalmorum pias orōnes ad deum ſeptuaginta duobus uerſibus habendas, q̄rum unuſquiſqꝫ nomen Tetragrammaton cū nōīe angeli ex lxxii. cōtinet, uno haud ab re excepto q̄ principium Geneſeos indicaꞇ, eleuant aūt q̄tum fieri poteſt aīos ſuos iſtis uerſibus ad deum, fortiter aſcendendo de angelo ad angelum. Et ſemp inter laudes dei toꞇ & tantas ab altera ad alterā in ſublime tēdendo. Ad illud eos iuuāꞇ angeli, ut relicta ſeculari ſollicitudine pro captu ſuo uehant in deū, ceu leuiſſima pluma tenuiſſimi ſpiritus adiumēto ad ſublimia cœleſtiacꝫ ſuſtolliꞇ. Videte & audite orōnem uerſuum cū tetragrammato & angelis, utrūqꝫ em̄ uobis tā digito q̄ uoce monſtrabo ſic.

וְאַתָּה יְהֹוָה מָגֵן בַּעֲדִי כְּבוֹדִי וּמֵרִים רֹאשִׁי
וְאַתָּה יְהֹוָה אַל תִּרְחָק אֱיָלוּתִי לְעֶזְרָתִי חוּשָׁה
אוֹמַר לַיהֹוָה מַחְסִי וּמְצוּדָתִי אֱלֹהַי אֶבְטַח בּוֹ
שׁוּבָה יְהֹוָה חַלְּצָה נַפְשִׁי הוֹשִׁיעֵנִי לְמַעַן חַסְדֶּךָ
דְּרַשְׁתִּי אֶת יְהֹוָה עָנָנִי וּמִכָּל מְגוּרוֹתַי הִצִּילָנִי
זַמְּרוּ לַיהֹוָה יֹשֵׁב צִיּוֹן הַגִּידוּ בָעַמִּים עֲלִילוֹתָיו
רַחוּם וְחַנּוּן יְהוָה אֶרֶךְ אַפַּיִם וְרַב חָסֶד
בֹּאוּ נִשְׁתַּחֲוֶה וְנִכְרָעָה נִבְרְכָה לִפְנֵי יְהֹוָה עֹשֵׂנוּ
זְכוֹר רַחֲמֶיךָ יְהֹוָה וַחֲסָדֶיךָ כִּי מֵעוֹלָם הֵמָּה
יְהִי חַסְדְּךָ יְהֹוָה עָלֵינוּ כַּאֲשֶׁר יִחַלְנוּ לָךְ
חַי יְהֹוָה צוּרִי וְיָרוּם אֱלֹהֵי יִשְׁעִי
לָמָה יְהֹוָה תַּעֲמֹד בְּרָחוֹק תַּעְלִים לְעִתּוֹת בַּצָּרָה
הָרִיעוּ לַיהֹוָה כָּל הָאָרֶץ פִּצְחוּ וְרַנְּנוּ וְזַמֵּרוּ
וִיהִי יְהוָה מִשְׂגָּב לַדָּךְ מִשְׂגָּב לְעִתּוֹת בַּצָּרָה
וִיהִי יְהוָה לִי לְמִשְׂגָּב וֵאלֹהַי לְצוּר מַחְסִי
יְהֹוָה אֱלֹהַי יִשְׁוַּעְתִּי בְיוֹם צָעַקְתִּי בַלַּיְלָה נֶגְדֶּךָ
יְהֹוָה אֲדֹנֵינוּ מָה אַדִּיר שִׁמְךָ בְּכָל הָאָרֶץ
שָׁפְטֵנִי בְצִדְקָתְךָ יְהֹוָה אֱלֹהָי וְאַל יִשְׂמְחוּ לִי
קַוֵּה קִוִּיתִי יְהֹוָה וַיֵּט אֵלַי וַיִּשְׁמַע שַׁוְעָתִי
וּבְשֵׁם יְהֹוָה אֶקְרָא אָנָּא יְהֹוָה מַלְּטָה נַפְשִׁי

On the Art of Kabbalah

the higher world! As rulers they have been given two equal tasks: to penetrate our world and themselves to be penetrated by our world. On this subject, let me make use of the comment of your Plotinus in his book on *Understanding and the Ideas and Being*. He says: "This sensible world is located in one place only, but the intelligible world is everywhere," which is as if he were saying that the intelligible world walks in and orders and preserves and penetrates this world of ours.

Now see what admirable words the Kabbalist sages have to say on this subject: "There is no grass or plant below that does not have a star in the firmament that strikes it and says, 'Grow.' They have reached this opinion strengthened by sacred scripture, as it is written in Job Chapter 38: "Do you know the Laws of heaven if you have put a guardian or ruler or his agent on the earth."

So do not be distressed by troubles on this earth or by the cares of the lower world, for the above named angels have been appointed to deal with them by the dispensation of the Creator. You should not think that they too belong to the nine choirs of the hierarchy above heaven.

For since the angel is otherness, as God is identity, and since the first otherness is "being two," so we will be right to think that the number of the angels comes from a multiplication of twoness. The cube of two, (two times two times two), is eight, the first cube. If you distribute eight angels into each of the nine bands there will be nine times eight, which is seventy-two.

Return now if you will through the bands to the cube, and through the cube to your Tetractys that we call Tetragrammaton, and the Romans call Quaternity. Go from that to twoness, which indicates the angelic nature, and then to the Unity, God, the Good and Great. You will find that, if we apply our study to the angels, we find that it is even through the angels that we are joined to God, the ineffable Tetragrammaton *YHVH* in whom the first thing to shine is the noble nature of these angels.

If from the four letters *YHVH*, you posit four *yods*, and going down, three *hays*, two *vavs*, one *hay*, you will soon get the sum of seventy-two, which explains the ineffable and incomparable name of God to which all sacred names lead. There are a great number of such sacred names, but each of them is derivative except for the name of God—which is of its own kind and self-possessed—hence it is called *Meyuhad*. They say that these seventy-two are really one symbolic name, because their intention is to indicate the good, great God, though by many varied angelic methods, just as we mark out a prince by his courtiers and a general by his army.

The masters of Kabbalah greatly worship and venerate these names. By being faithful to them, men work unutterably wonderful miracles. But I will cite in this matter the very'learned Recanat, who in his com-

LIBER TERTIVS LX.

וַאֲנִי עָלֶיךָ בָטַחְתִּי יְהוָה אָמַרְתִּי אֱלֹהַי אָתָּה
יְהוָה שָׁמְרְךָ יְהוָה צִלְּךָ עַל יַד יְמִינֶךָ
יְהוָה יִשְׁמָר צֵאתְךָ וּבוֹאֶךָ מֵעַתָּה וְעַד עוֹלָם
רָצָה יְהוָה אֶת יְרֵאָיו וְאֶת הַמְיַחֲלִים לְחַסְדּוֹ
אוֹדֶה יְהוָה בְּכָל לִבִּי אֲסַפְּרָה כָּל נִפְלְאוֹתֶיךָ
קָרָאתִי בְכָל לֵב עֲנֵנִי יְהוָה חֻקֶּיךָ אֶצֹּרָה
חָלְצֵי יְהוָה מֵאָדָם רָע מֵאִישׁ חֲמָסִים תִּנְצְרֵנִי
אֱלֹהִים אַל תִּרְחַק מִמֶּנִּי אֱלֹהַי לְעֶזְרָתִי חוּשָׁה
הִנֵּה אֱלֹהִים עֹזֵר לִי יְהוָה בְּסֹמְכֵי נַפְשִׁי
כִּי אַתָּה תִקְוָתִי יְהוָה אֲדֹנָי מִבְטַחִי מִנְּעוּרָי
אָבוֹא בִּגְבֻרוֹת יְהוָה אֱלֹהִים אַזְכִּיר צִדְקָתְךָ לְבַדֶּךָ
כִּי יָשָׁר דְּבַר יְהוָה וְכָל מַעֲשֵׂהוּ בֶּאֱמוּנָה
יְהוָה יֹדֵעַ מַחְשְׁבוֹת אָדָם כִּי הֵמָּה הָבֶל
יַחֵל יִשְׂרָאֵל אֶל יְהוָה מֵעַתָּה וְעַד עוֹלָם
אָהַבְתִּי כִּי יִשְׁמַע יְהוָה אֶת קוֹלִי תַּחֲנוּנָי
יְהוָה אָהַבְתִּי מְעוֹן בֵּיתֶךָ וּמְקוֹם מִשְׁכַּן כְּבוֹדֶךָ
יְהוָה אֱלֹהִים צְבָאוֹת הֲשִׁיבֵנוּ הָאֵר פָּנֶיךָ וְנִוָּשֵׁעָה
כִּי אַתָּה יְהוָה מַחְסִי עֶלְיוֹן שַׂמְתָּ מְעוֹנֶךָ
שְׁמַע יְהוָה וְחָנֵּנִי יְהוָה הֱיֵה עֹזֵר לִי
לָמָה יְהוָה תִּזְנַח נַפְשִׁי תַּסְתִּיר פָּנֶיךָ מִמֶּנִּי
יְהוָה הַצִּילָה נַפְשִׁי מִשְּׂפַת שֶׁקֶר מִלָּשׁוֹן רְמִיָּה
יְהוָה יִשְׁמָרְךָ מִכָּל רָע יִשְׁמֹר אֶת נַפְשֶׁךָ
וַאֲנִי אֵלֶיךָ יְהוָה שִׁוַּעְתִּי וּבַבֹּקֶר תְּפִלָּתִי תְקַדְּמֶךָּ
צָרְכוֹת פִּי רְצֵה נָא יְהוָה מִשְׁפָּטֶיךָ לַמְּדֵנִי
אִם אָמַרְתִּי מָטָה רַגְלִי חַסְדְּךָ יְהוָה יִסְעָדֵנִי
טוֹב יְהוָה לַכֹּל וְרַחֲמָיו עַל כָּל מַעֲשָׂיו
מָה גָּדְלוּ מַעֲשֶׂיךָ יְהוָה מְאֹד עָמְקוּ מַחְשְׁבֹתֶיךָ
הוֹרִיעַ יְהוָה יְשׁוּעָתוֹ לְעֵינֵי הַגּוֹיִם גִּלָּה צִדְקָתוֹ
גָּדוֹל יְהוָה וּמְהֻלָּל מְאֹד וְלִגְדֻלָּתוֹ אֵין חֵקֶר
חַנּוּן וְרַחוּם יְהוָה אֶרֶךְ אַפַּיִם וּגְדָל חָסֶד
יְהִי כְּבוֹד יְהוָה לְעוֹלָם יִשְׂמַח יְהוָה בְּמַעֲשָׂיו

Book Three

mentary on Exodus 14, asserts that these characters and letters are: "Characters flying above on the level of spiritual wisdom. They are the spirits that control or rule the doing of every thing by their means, and their works are known to the Kabbalists." According to Rabbi Akiba, they came down from the throne of the glory of God. One must not be led astray by the empty superstition that all things are brought from heaven to mortals from the angels; one should rather believe that *everything*, even in the angels themselves, comes from the Majesty of God through the angels. Nebuchadnezzar bears witness in the Book of Daniel when he says in Chaldaic: "And in accordance with his own will he acts upon the Host of Heaven and the inhabitants of the earth."

Therefore, the Kabbalists have excerpted from the Book of Psalms pious prayers addressed to God that necessarily consist of seventy-two verses. Each of these verses contains the Tetragrammaton with the name of one of the seventy-two angels (except for one relevant verse that comes at the beginning of Genesis). By these verses they lift their minds as high as they can go towards God and, surrounded by such great praise, courageously ascend from angel to angel, always reaching from one to the next into the sublime. The angels help them in their task so that they leave secular care behind and are carried as far as they are able to God, like light feathers wafted up by the lightest of breaths to the sublime regions of heaven.

Watch and listen! Here is the prayer that is formed from the verses that include both Tetragrammaton and angels. I will indicate them both to you both with my finger and with my tone of voice, like this:

[Translator's note: Reuchlin gives the Hebrew and then translates into Latin. It is the Latin that is followed here. The capital letters by the side of each verse indicate the angel's name included in that verse in the order in which they appear in the Hebrew. Reuchlin marks them by .·. above the Hebrew letter.]

> "And You, Lord, are my protector and my glory, and You lift up my head.   VHV
>
> And you, Lord, do not take your help from me but look to my defence.   YLY
>
> I will say to the Lord, "You are my guardian and my refuge." My God, I will hope in him.   SYT
>
> Turn, Lord, and save my soul. Make me safe because of your mercy.   'LM
>
> I asked the Lord and he heard me, and he snatched me away from all my tribulations.   ShMH
>
> Sing psalms to the Lord who lives in Zion. Announce his great deeds among the peoples.   HLL
>
> Pitying and merciful Lord, far from anger and great in loving kindness.   AKA

DE ARTE CABALISTICA

אודה יהוה בצדקו ואזמרה שם יהוה עליון
ידעתי יהוה כי־צדק משפטיך ואמונה עניתני
יהוה בשמים הכין כסאו ומלכותו בכל משלה
ועתה יהוה לעולם תשב כסאך לדור ודור
סומך יהוה לכל הנופלים וזוקף לכל הכפופים
יראי יהוה בטחו ביהוה עזרם ומגינם הוא
ונפשה נבהלה מאד ואתה יהוה עד־מתי
מזורח שמש עד מבאו מהלל שם יהוה
צדיק יהוה בכל דרכיו וחסיד בכל מעשיו
יהי שם יהוה מבורך מעתה ועד עולם
ראה כי פקודיך אהבתי יהוה כחסדך חייני
עברו את יהוה בשמחה בואו לפניו ברננה
הנה עין יהוה אל יראיו למיחלים לחסדו
שובה יהוה עד מתי והנחם על עבדיך
אל תעזבני יהוה אלהי אל תרחק ממני
והתענג על יהוה ויתן לך משאלות לבך
הודו ליהוה כי טוב כי לעולם חסדו
יהוה מנת חלקי וכוסי אתה תומך גורלי
בראשית ברא אלהים את השמים ואת הארץ
אודה יהוה מאד בפי ובתוך רבים אהללנו
שובי נפשי למנוחיכי כי יהוה גמל עליכי

Ostendi iam uobis optimi uiri qualibet in linea nomen esse Tetragrāma
ton, & tris literas angeli uel recto uel transuerso ut fieri solet positas ordi
ne de tribus uersibus Exodi xiiii. ריסע ובא וט qs tamen Roma
ni hactenus non sunt integre interpretati. Psalmodian autem latini sicle
gūt ut ante forsitan uel i Capnione de Verbo Mirifico uidere poquistis.
Et tu domine susceptor meus es gloria mea & exaltans caput meum.
Et tu dñe ne elōgaueris auxiliū tuūm a me ad defensionem mea cōspice
Dicam dño susceptor meus es tu, & refugiū meū dˀ meus sperabo in eū
Conuertere dñe & eripe aīam meā saluū me fac ppter misericordiā quā
Exqsiui dñm & exaudiuit me, & ex oībus tribulatiōibus meis eripuit me
Psallite domino qui habitat in sion adnunciate inter gentes studia eius
Miserator & misericors dominus longanimis & multum misericors
Venite adoremus & procidamus & benedicamus ante dñm qui fecit nos

On the Art of Kabbalah

Come, let us adore him, fall down and worship before the Lord who made us. ThKH

Remember your mercy, O Lord, and your loving kindness which exist from eternity. ZYH

Let your mercy be above us, O Lord, as we have hope in you. DLA

The Lord lives and my God is blessed. May the God of my salvation be raised up! VAL

Why, O Lord, have you gone far off, why do you shun us in times of trouble? H'H

Sing praises to the Lord all the earth, sing, dance and play the lyre. YLZ

And the Lord has become a refuge for the poor man, a helper in times of trouble. MBH

And the Lord has become my refuge, and my God is the refuge of my hopes. HRY

O Lord, God of my salvation, I have called on your name day and night in your presence. MQH

O Lord, Our Lord, how wonderful is your name in all the earth. VAL

Judge me in accordance with your justice, O Lord, my God, and let them not rejoice over me. YKL

I have waited, waited for the Lord, and he has turned to me and listened. VVL

And I will call on the name of the Lord: "O Lord, free my soul." LHP

But I have hoped in you.I have said: "You are my God." NLK

The Lord guards you, the Lord is your protection over your right hand. YYY

The Lord will guard your going out and your coming in from now and for ever. MHL

The Lord is pleased with those who fear him and in those who have hope in his mercy. VHH

I will confess to you, Lord, in all my heart. I will tell all your wonderful works. HNTh

I cried in all my heart: "Hear me, Lord. I shall search after your justifications." AAH

Snatch me, O Lord, from an evil man, from a man of violence snatch me away. ThRY

God, do not go far from me. My God, look down to help me. AShH

Behold God helps me and the Lord is the protector of my soul. RYY

Since you are my forbearance, Lord, O Lord, my hope from my youth. AVM

LIBER TERTIVS

Reminiscere miserationu tuaru dne, et misericordiaru tuaru, q a seculo sūt
Fiat misericordia tua domine sup nos, quemadmodum sperauimus in te.
Viuit dominus & benedictus deus meus, & exaltetur deus salutis meæ
Vt quid dñe recessisti longe despicis in opportunitatibus in tribulatione.
Iubilate domino omnis terra, cantate & exultate & psallite.
Et factus est dñs refugiū paupi, adiutor in opportunitatibʹ ī tribulatione.
Et factus est mihi dñs in refugium & deus meus in adiutorium spei meæ.
Domine deus salutis meæ, in die clamaui & nocte coram te.
Dñe dominus noster qadmirabile est nomen tuum in uniuersa terra.
Iudica me secundū iusticiā tuā dñe deus meus & non supergaudeāt mihi.
Expectans expectaui dominum & intendit mihi.
Et nomen domini inuocabo, o domine libera animam meam.
Ego autem in te speraui, dixi deus meus es tu.
Dñs custodit te, dominus protectio tua, super manum dexteram tuam
Dñs custodiet introitum tuum & exitū tuum ex nunc & usq; in seculum.
Bñplacitū est dño sup timentes eū, & in eis q sperāt sup misericordia eius.
Confitebor tibi domine in toto corde meo, narrabo oia mirabilia tua.
Clamaui in toto corde, exaudi me domine, iustificationes tuas requiram.
Eripe me domine ab homine malo, a uiro iniquo eripe me.
Deus ne elongeris a me, deus meus in auxilium meum respice.
Ecce deus adiuuat me, & dominus susceptor est animæ meæ.
Quoniam tu es patientia mea domine, dñe spes mea a iuuentute mea.
Introibo in potentias domini, deus memorabor iusticiæ tuæ solius.
Quia rectum est uerbum domini, & omnia opera eius in fide.
Dominus scit cogitationes hominum quoniam uanæ sunt.
Speret Israel in domino ex hoc nunc & usq; in seculum.
Dilexi quoniam exaudiet dominus uocem orationis meæ.
Domine dilexi decorem domus tuæ, & locum habitationis tuæ.
Dñe deus uirtutum conuerte nos, & ostende faciem tuam & salui erim̃.
Quoniam tu es domine spes mea, altissimum posuisti refugium tuum.
Audiuit dominus & misertus est mei, dominus factus est adiutor meus.
Vt quid domine repellis animam meam auertis faciem tuam a me.
Domine libera animam meam a labiis iniquis & a lingua dolosa.
Dominus custodiet te ab omni malo & custodiet animam tuam.
Et ego ad te domine clamaui & mane oratio mea præueniet te.
Voluntaria oris mei beneplacita fac domine & iudicia tua doce me.
Si dicebam motus est pes meus, misericordia tua domine adiuuabit me.
Suauis dominus uniuersis & miserationes eius super omnia opera eius.
Q̃ magnificata sunt opa tua dñe nimis profundę sunt cogitationes tuæ.
Notum fecit dñs salutare tuū, in conspectu gentium reuelauit iusticiā suā.

M

Book Three

I will enter into the power of the Lord. God, I will remember only your justice. BKL

Because the word of the Lord is straight, and all his works are in faith. RShV

The Lord knows the thoughts of men, since they are vanity. YVH

Let Israel hope in the Lord from now and for ever. HLH

I have loved him, for the Lord will hear the sound of my speech. KQV

O Lord, I have loved the splendor of your house and the place of your habitation. NMD

O Lord, God of virtues, turn to us, show your face and we will be saved. AYN

Since you are my hope, O Lord, you have placed your refuge very high. MH'

The Lord has listened and taken pity on me. The Lord has become my helper. H'R

Why, O Lord, do you thrust away my soul and avert your face from me? ZYY

O Lord, free my soul from unjust lips and a deceitful tongue. HHH

The Lord will keep you from all evil and will guard your soul. YMK

And I have cried to you, O Lord, and in the morning my speech will come before you. VLV

Make the gifts of my mouth pleasing, O Lord, and teach me your judgements. YHL

Whenever I say "My foot has moved," your mercy, O Lord, will help me. ALS

The Lord is good to all, and his mercy is in all his works. R'Y

How your works, O Lord, are magnificent; your thoughts are very deep. L'Sh

The Lord has made known your salvation, in the sight of the nations He has revealed his justice. YHM

The Lord is great and much to be praised, and there is no end to his greatness. VHV

Pitying and merciful is the Lord, far from anger and great in loving kindness. NYD

May the glory of the Lord be for ever. The Lord will rejoice in his works. HShH

I will confess to the Lord according to his justice and I will sing psalms to the name of the high Lord. MM'

I know, O Lord, that your judgements are fair and it is in your truth that you have afflicted me. ANN

DE ARTE CABALISTICA

Magnus dominus & laudabilis nimis & magnitudinis eius non est finis.
Miserator & misericors dominus patiens & multum misericors.
Sit gloria domini in seculum, laetabitur dominus in operibus suis.
Confitebor domino secundum iusticiam eius, & psallam noī dñi altissimi.
Cognoui dñe quia aequitas iudicia tua, & in ueritate tua humiliasti me.
Dñs in coelo parauit sedem suam, & regnum suum omnibus dominabit.
Tu aūt dñe in eternū pmanes, & memoriale tuū in gñatione & gñationē.
Alleuat dominus omnes qui corruunt, & erigit omnes elisos.
Qui timent dñm sperauerunt in dño, adiutor eorū & protector eorū est
Et anima mea turbata est ualde, sed tu domine usque quo.
Ab ortu solis usq ad occasum, laudabile nomen domini.
Iustus dominus in omnibus uiis suis, & sanctus in omnibus operibus suis
Sit nomen domini benedictum, ex hoc nunc & usq in seculum.
Vide qm mandata tua dilexi dñe, secundū misericordiā tuā uiuifica me.
Seruite domino in laeticia, introite in conspectu eius in exultatione.
Eece oculi dñi sup metuentes eum, & in eis q sperāt sup misericordia eius
Conuertere domine uscq quo, & deprecabilis esto super seruos tuos.
Ne derelinquas me domine deus meus, ne discesseris a me.
Delectare in domino & dabit tibi petitiones cordis tui.
Confitemini dño quoniam bonus, qm in aethernum misericordia eius.
dñs ps hereditatis meg et calicis mei, tu es q restitues hereditatē meā mihi
In principio creauit deus coelum & terram.
Confitebor dño nimis in ore meo, & in medio multorum laudabo eum.
Conuertere anima mea in requiem tuam, qm dominus benefecit tibi.

¶ Tum Marranus. Adeo ne inquit te una in re tantopere laborantē pa
timur expaciari, q ad artē ipsam si qua est Cabalae toto desyderio prope
T ramus. Et Philolaus. Non est arbitror una res de qua Simon disseruit, sed
tercq quatercq plures ac multoplurime. Sabbathū em sabbathorū qd est
requies aetherna & finis Cabalae, post aūt qbus gradibus ad eā ascedam
tā portarū prudētiq sapiētiq semitarū, & de noīs Tetragrāmati exposito
ribus angelis & Semhamaphores clara nos uoce instituit. Ad hec Simon.
Reliqua si bñ recordamini, eqdē nōnihil de illa digna religiōe decē nume
rationū Cabalisticarū pmisi & fortasse promisi dicturū me, faciācq p cata
logum si me attēte audiatis. Tū audimꝰ cupide ambo dixere, quapropter
V pge incūctanter. Mox Simon ait. Decē numerationes a Cabalaeis עשׂר
ספירות appellatas multi ex nobis multipharia tractāt, qdā i arboris
modu, alii ad forma hois, ut saepe mētio fiat de radice, truco, ramis & corti
cibꝰ. Sepe uero etiā de capite, humeris, cruribꝰ, pedibꝰ, latere dextro & sini
stro. Eae sūt decē diuina noīa q nos mortales de deo cōcipimꝰ, uel essentia
lia, uel psonalia, uel notionalia, uel cōia, & noīantur sic כתר .i. corona,

On the Art of Kabbalah

The Lord has made ready his seat in heaven and his kingdom will rule over all. YKTh
But you, O Lord, remain to eternity and you are remembered from generation to generation. HMB
The Lord lifts up all who have fallen and sets upright those who have slipped. PVY
Those who fear the Lord will have hope in the Lord, for he is their helper and protector. MNM
And my soul is very troubled; but you, O Lord until, when? YLY
The name of the Lord is to be praised from the rising of the sun to its going down. ZHH
The Lord is just in all his ways, and holy in all his works. SRM
May the name of the Lord be blessed, from now and forever. BMV
See how I have loved your commands, O Lord! In your mercy, give me life. HHY
Serve the Lord in joy, enter in his sight in exultation. 'VN
Behold, the eyes of the Lord are on those who fear him and on those who hope in his mercy. MHY
When will you turn, O Lord, and hearken to the prayers of your servants? DMB
Do not leave me, Lord, my God; do not go from me. QMN
Delight in the Lord, and he will give you the desires of your heart. 'ThA
Confess to the Lord for he is good; for his mercy exists to eternity. VBH
The Lord is part of my inheritance and my cup; You are he who will restore my inheritance to me. AHR
In the beginning God created the heaven and the earth. YBM
I will confess to the Lord very much in my mouth, in the midst of many will I praise him. YYH
Turn, O my soul, to your rest, for the Lord will do good to you. NMN

LIBER TERTIVS LXII

חָכְמָה i. sapiētia בִּינָה i. prudētia siue itelligētia חֶסֶד i. dementia
seu bonitas גְּבוּרָה i. grauitas ul'seueritas נֵצַח i. or. nat9 תִּפְאֶרֶת i. triūph. הוֹד i. cōfeſſio laudis יְסוֹד i. fūdamētu מַלְכוּת i. regnū
Supra coronā uero ponit אֵין סוֹף i. infinitudo, & est abyſſ. Eloquar
an ſileā, Res est nimirū profundę ſpeculatiōis & ǫdā pelagus imēſum, in
ǫd ois nr̄a cōtēplatio demergit & demerſa ǫdā hiatu abſorbet. An nō me
mineritis ǫtū nouicii ia fermę oīm nationū theodidaſcali dies atǭ noctes
deſudant fere ſolum in conceptibus attributalibus, quas eorū alii pſeſtio
nes in diuinis nominant, alii attributa tum negatiua tum affirmatiua tum
abſoluta, tum relatiua ſeu connotatiua, ǭ facile nunc ut arbitror de libro
Cabaliſtico compendiū Portę lucis, quē Paulus Ricius uir egregie doct9
quondā ex noſtris unus, nunc chriſtianus ex Rabi ǭdam Caſtilienſi colle
git, & de Iſagogis quas ſcripſit in Cabalā diſcere poteſtis. Ea pariter de rę
magnę ille Magiſter Cabalę Rabi Ioſeph filius Carnitolis librū שַׁעֲרֵי
צֶדֶק i. Portarū iuſticię conſcripſit, & ſcripſere cōmentatores circa ar
borem decē numerationū multi multa, q cauſam hanc intolūtā euoluūt,
& tota fere ſacrā ſcripturā uetere in has decē numerationes, & per eas in
decem ipſa dei noīa, & p ea in unū Tetragrammati nomen, redigunt atǭ
reducunt, affirmantes ǫ Enſoph ſit Alpha & O, qui dixit, Ego primus &
ego nouiſſim9. Et ǫ כֶּתֶר i. Corona regni oīm ſeculorū ſit fons ſine fun
do & אַב הָרַחֲמִים i. miſericordiarū pater, cuius myſterium illud
eſt ǫ Ehieh ſigillat per Emeth, hoc eſt eſſentiā p ueritatem. Sicut nobilis
ille dictator ait Eliezer Haklir אֱמֶת חוֹתָמוֹ i. Emeth eſt ſigillum
eius. Probat hoc ratio arithmetica quam imitantes ſi multiplicauerimus
Ehieh p Ehieh ſurgent quadringenta qua draginta & unū, ǭ ſimul ſunt
אֱמֶת hoc eſt uerū ſeu ueritas, ſicut אַרְצִי שָׁלוֹם i. Dn̄i pax. Plu
ra huc reducunt, ut Aleph magnū, timorē dn̄i, lucem inacceſſibilem, dies
ęthernitatis, ut eſt illud, Egreſſus eius ab anterioribus a diebus ſeculi. Sic
ſcribit iſignis Cabaliſta Tedacus Leui in lib. de decē numerationibus. Ad
ſecundā aūt numerationē ǭ eſt ſapiētię referūt hęc, ex attributis aut pprie
tatib9, priogenitura. Ies. i. ens. Lex primitiua. Iod litera prima tetragrāmati
terra uiuentiū, triginta duę ſemitę, ſeptuaginta legis ſpecies, bellum, iudi
cium, Amen, liber, ſanctū, uoluntas, principium, & alia id genus. Et forte
mirū eſt ǫ ſecunda numeratio dicatur principiū, legit nanǭ in Racanat
excellē ti Cabalę Magiſtro circa Geneſeos initium hoc modo וְאוּלַי
תִּשְׁאַל שֶׁהַחָכְמָה הִיא סְפִירָה הַשְּׁנִיָּה לָמָּה
קָרָאת רֵאשִׁית i. Et forte quęres, cu ſapientia ſit numeratio ſecū
da, quare dicat principiū. Scriptū eſt em ī libro Bahir אֵין רֵאשִׁית
חָכְמָה אֶלָּא חָכְמָה i. Nihil eſt principiū niſi ſapiētia. Cui eqdem recte
mihi uidear reſpondere, ǫ infinitudo ipſa trium ſummarū Cabaliſticę ar

M ii

Book Three

Now I have shown you, gentlemen, that there is in every line the Tetragrammaton and the three letters of the angel, placed either straight or in reverse order as normal. They come from the three phrases of Exodus 14, "And he came, and he went, and he turned," although the Romans have not yet interpreted this rightly. The Latins read the hymn as follows, as perhaps you have been able to see before in Capnion's book *On the Wonderful Word*.

MARRANUS: Should we let you go on with this one subject and work at it so hard, when what we really want to get on to is the actual skill in Kabbalah?

PHILOLAUS: It is more than one subject that Simon has discussed, I reckon. He has spoken of three or four or more. He has talked about the Sabbath of Sabbaths which is eternal rest and the goal of Kabbalah, and then about the steps of the gates of understanding and the paths of wisdom by which we rise to it; next he has taught us clearly about the angels who explain the Tetragrammaton and the Semhamaphores.

SIMON: If you can recall all the rest quite well, I made a few comments earlier on about the fine and sacred study of the ten kabbalistic numerations, and I did perhaps promise then that I would talk about them at a later time. If you listen attentively, I shall list them down.

PHILOLAUS AND MARRANUS: We are eager to hear you. Please do not hesitate to go on.

SIMON: Many of our people deal with the ten numerations (called *Sephirot* by the Kabbalists) in a number of different ways. Sometimes the image used is that of a tree and sometimes it is that of a man, so they often mention not only root, trunk, branch, and bark, but also head, shoulders, legs, feet, and right side and left side in their images.

These are the ten divine Names that form the mortal conception of God, whether they be part of his essence or attached to him specifically, and whether they be conceptual or actual. The names are: "Crown," "Wisdom," "Understanding" or "Intelligence," "Loving Kindness" or "Goodness," "Seriousness" or "Gravity," "Beauty," "Victory," "Praise," "Foundation," and "Kingdom." Above the Crown is placed *En Sof*—"Infinity," which is the Abyss.

Am I to talk or to keep silent? The matter is one for speculation too deep for us. It is an immense sea into which all our contemplation is sunk, and once sunk is sucked away down a sort of cleft.

You remember how much the novice theology students of nearly all nationalities sweat away days and nights on more or less nothing but the concepts of attributes? Some of them call these concepts "perfections in the divine" while others call them "negative" and "affirmative" and "absolute" and "relative" or "connotative." I think that you can

DE ARTE CABALISTICA

boris numerationū quas uos treis in diuinis psonas appellare cōsueuistis
absolutissima essentia quum sit in abysso tenebrarū retracta, & immanēs
ociosaq; uel ut aiunt ad nihil respiciēs, iccirco dicitur אֵין .i. nihil siue nō
ens ac non finis, hoc est אֵין סוֹף quia nos tam tenui erga res diuinas
ingenii paupertate mulctati de iis q̄ nō apparent haud secus atq; de iis quæ
non sunt iudicamus. At ubi se ita ostenderit ut sit aliqd & reuera subsistat
tum Aleph tenebrosum in Aleph lucidū cōuertitur, scriptū est ēm, Sicut
tenebræ eius ita et lux eius, & appellatur tunc qdem Aleph magnū, qñ exi
re cupit, & apparere oīm rerū causa per Beth proxime sequentē lite ram
De qua sic scribit Mnahem Racanat עלכן תמצא האות
הזאת פעלה הדברים כלם .i. Sic repies literā hanc sci
licet Beth facientē res oēs, quapropter Aleph eandē uti propinqssimā &
& foecūdiorē literā sibi recipit, noīaturq; אֲב pater ois gñationis & pro
ductiōis. Deinde assumptum Beth, rursus ablegat in uniuersitatē entium,
ex infinito אֵין finem suum consequi desyderās, quare finalē literā Nun
coniungendo Beth generat בֵּן .i. filium quæ prima est productio in dei
tate, ac principiū alteritatis, unde cognoīatur רֵאשִׁית .i. Principiū, tā
&si est secūda emanatio ex infinitudine, hoc est secūda Cabalistica nume
ratio, p quā oīa facta sunt. Scriptū est ēm. Oīa in sapiētia fecisti, hoc modo
primus efflux⁰ fit secunda numeratio, qa terminus gñationis est filius. Re
stat tertio mediū inter Aleph & Nun qd est Iod, nota sancti nois יוּד cuis
ambos characteras si alternis uiciḃ⁰ noī בֵּן intertexueritis erit בִּינָה
intelligentia prudentia seu prouidentia, scilicet emanatio in diuinis tertia,
cui attribuit Adonai, spiritus, aīa, uotū, mysteriū fidei, mater filiorū, rex se
dens in throno miserationū. Iobeleus magnus, Sabbathum magnū, funda
mētū spirituū, lume mirificū, dies suprma, qnquaginta portę, dies propici
atiōis, uox iterior, fluui⁹ egrediēs de paradiso. Lra secūda Tetragrāmati,
poenitētia, aquæ profundæ, soror mea, filia patris mei, & alia. Hucusq; no
tauimus tres numerationes q̄ dicitur a Cabalistis teste Rabi Ishac in cō
mentariis libri Ietzira סְפִירוֹת הָעֶלְיוֹנוֹת בְּסוֹד אֶחָד .i.
Tres numerationes summę atq; suprmæ sedes una, in qua sedet Sanctus
Sanctus Sanctus dñs deus Sabaoth. Bonitati siue clementię q̄ est quarta
numeratio, cū diuino noīe El appropriātur etiā hęc, gra, misericordia, bra
chiū dexterū, ino cēs, dies terti⁹, ignis cādid⁰, facies leonis, pes prim⁰, Abra
hā senex. Oriēs, aquæ supiores, argētū dei, Michael, sacerdos, angel⁰ in spe
cie electri Hasmal, uestes albę, auster, & alia. In qnta numeratione seuerita
tis diuinū nomē est Elohim & applicāt ei timor, pprietas rigoris seu gra
uitatis, pcepta legis negatiua, brachiū sinistrū, ignis egrediēs ab aqs, ut i li
bro de creatiōe. Itē dies quart⁹, occidēs, gabriel, Ishac senex, nox, fortitudo.
altare aureū, pes secundus, sanctificatio. caligo. Metattrō, aglo. spēs fusca.

On the Art of Kabbalah

now gain easy understanding of these from both the summary of the Kabbalistic book *The Gate of Light*, which Paul Ricci, a most learned man who was once one of us but is now a Christian, collected from some Rabbi in Castile, and from the *Isagoge* that he has written on the Kabbalah. On this subject too that great master of Kabbalah, Rabbi Joseph, the son of Carnitol, wrote his book *The Gates of Justice*, and many commentators have written a great deal on the tree of the ten *Sephirot*, unwrapping this involved subject, and reducing and leading nearly all the ancient sacred Scripture to these ten *Sephirot*, through them to the ten Names of God, and through them to the one Name of the Tetragrammaton.

They assert that *En Sof* is alpha and omega, for he said: "I am the first and the last." They say too that the "Crown" of the kingdom is the bottomless fount of all the ages and the Father of mercies, whose mystery is that he seals up Essence through Truth. As our noble teacher Eliezer haKalir says: "Truth is his seal." This can be proved by arithmetical calculation. If we multiply *Ehieh* (meaning "essence") by *Ehieh* we will get 441, which is the same as *Emeth*, the word for "true" or "truth," and the same as *Adonai Shalom*, which means "Lord of Peace."[49] There is more too that comes down to this same source, such as the great *Aleph*, the Fear of the Lord, the inaccessible light and the days of eternity. As it is written in the book on the ten *Sephirot* by that great Kabbalist Tedacus Levi, "His goings forth have been from of old, from the days of eternity."

As for the second *Sephira*, which is wisdom, these are among the properties or attributes referred to it: primogeniture, *Yesh* or "being," primitive law, *Yod* the first letter of the Tetragrammaton, the land of the living, the thirty-two paths, the seventy kinds of Law, war, judgement, Amen, book, holy, will, beginning, and so on. Perhaps it is surprising that the second *Sephira* are called "the beginning." It is said by Recanat, a fine master of Kabbalah, on the beginning of Genesis: "And perhaps you will ask, why, when Wisdom is the second Sephira, is it called the beginning?" It is written in the book of Bahir: "There is no beginning without wisdom."

I think I am right in replying that infinity itself exists in the three summits of the Kabbalists' tree of ten *Sephirot* (which you usually call the three divine Persons). Infinity is the most absolute Essence, drawn back in the depths of shadows, and, lying or, as they say, reliant upon nothing, is hence called "Nothing" or "Not being," and "Not end" (*En Sof*) because we are so damned by our feeble understanding of divine matters that we judge things that are not apparent in the same way as we judge things that do not exist.

But when it shows itself and becomes something and actually subsists, the dark *Aleph* is changed into the bright *Aleph*. For it is written: "As is its darkness so is its light." It is then called the great *Aleph*, because it desires to come out and be seen as the cause of all things, through *Beth*, the letter that follows next. Menahem Recanat writes on

LIBER TERTIVS LXIII

Sextæ applicāt Eloha, speculatio illuminans, lignū uitæ, uoluptas, linea media, lex scripta, sacerdos magn⁹, ortus solis, species purpurea. Et scribit Tedacus Leui cp de hoc loco explanant septuaginta nationes in terra, & sigillum eius est Emeth Adonai, & uocatur pax, & forma eius figurat in luna, & mysteriū eius est tertia litera Tetragrammati, & mysteriū hoc Pater noster qui est in cœlis, homo supern⁹ seu Adam cœlestis, iudicium, sententia. Michael. Israel senex. Deus Iacob. Ad septimā referunt, Adonai Sabaoth, crus, pes, colūna dextera, rota magna, uisio prophetiæ, Moyses &c. Octauæ conueniunt Elohe Sabaoth. Mysteriū columnæ ac pedis sinistri & Booz, & inde trahitur serpens antiquus, disciplina dñi, ramus, Aharō Cherub, filii regis, molæ molentes & alia. Nonę appropriat Sadai, fundamentum mūdi, sion, fons piscinarū, iustus, deus uiuus. Sabbathū integrum Medium inter custodi & memento. Dies quinquagesima de Leuiathan, Aries. Ioseph iustus. Salomon. iusticia. robur. lignum scientię boni & mali, Fœdus dñi, arcus testimonii, gloria dñi, fundamentum prophetię Dauid, Redemptio. Seculum aīarum. Reducunt & ad decimam numerationem. Adonai, regnum, uita, cherub secundus. Speculatio non illuminās. Posteriora. Finis. Ecclesia Israelis, Sponsa in canticis canticorū. Regina cœli. Virgo Israel. Mysterium legis ab ore datæ. Aquila., Litera quarta. Tetragrāmati. Regnū domus Dauid. Templū regis, dei ianua, arca fœderis, & duę tabulæ in ea. Dominus uniuersæ terræ. Audistis breue rationariū decem proprieta, tū siue notionū aut attri butorū in diuinis, q̄ dicūt a Cabalistis בלימה quod intelligunt alii בלי .i. absq̄ uel p̄ter, & מה .i.qd ut si diceret dece p̄ter qd, scilicet excepta dei qdditate. Vnde inter p̄tari solet Be limah hoc esse, p̄ter id qd est ineffabile, alii ab ipso בלום פיך ולשונך מלדבר .i. coartando seu costringendo linguā tuam ne loquaris, tanq̄ uerba sacra q̄ non sint uulgo prodenda. Dicēdum nunc esset de angelicis principibus & dæmoniacis p̄fectis q̄s ad latera dementiæ & seueritatis ponunt Cabalistæ, rem profecto indigentē multilóquio, si non meridiem transgressi ueheremur in uesperū. Quis eñ paruo in tp̄e tam magna exponere? Quis triginta quinq̄ principes puritatis, ac septuaginta principes Ismaelis in latere numerationis quartæ tam cito absoluere? Quis item in numeratione quinta grauitatis atq̄ timoris pariter triginta quinq̄ principes reatus, & septuaginta prīcipes Esau tam obiter & tam p̄functorie posset satis explanare? quæ propria qdem uolumina poscunt, & certe admodum lata, quare his in p̄sentia intermissis procedamus ad artem. Beatitudo inq̄ cōtemplantissimorū hoīm pro electiōre modo a meditatione legis hoc est uiginti quatuor librorū q̄s Essrim Varba noīamus diurna & nocturna pendere sacris ex literis dep̄henditur. Scriptū est eñ, beatus uir inter cætera q̄ in lege eius meditabit die ac nocte, nō

X

M iii

Book Three

this: "So you will find this letter Beth doing all things." So *Aleph* accepts this letter as the closest letter to itself and as the most productive, and it is called *AB*, meaning "father of all generating and producing."

Once *Aleph* has taken up *Beth*, it sends it off again into the universe of beings, wanting to attain its end from the infinite "Not" (*AYN*). So by joining on to the final letter *Nun*, *Beth* produces *Ben*, meaning "son." This is the first production in the deity and the beginning of otherness; hence it is called "beginning," although it is the second emanation from infinity, the second Kabbalistic *Sephira*, through which all things have been made. It is written: "You have made all things in wisdom." In this way the first influx becomes the second *Sephira*, because the end of generation is the Son.

There remains the third letter which lies in the middle (of *en*), between *Aleph* and *Nun*, which is *Yod*. This is a mark of the holy name *Yah*. If you weave both letters of *Yah* between the letters of *Ben*, with the letters of each word alternating, you will get *Binah*, meaning "understanding" or "foresight," which is the third emanation in the divine. To this is attributed: Lord, spirit, soul, prayer, the mystery of faith, mother of sons, the King sitting on the throne of mercy, the great Jubilee, the great Sabbath, spiritual foundation, miraculous light, the lightest day, the fifty gates, the Day of Atonement, the inner voice, the river issuing forth from paradise, the second letter of the Tetragrammaton, repentance, the deep waters, my sister, the daughter of my father, and other things.

We have now noted the three *Sephirot* which, according to Rabbi Isaac in his commentary on the book on the Creation, are called by the Kabbalists: "The lightest and the supreme" and which are the one seat, on which sits the Holy, Holy, Holy Lord, God of hosts.

The following belong to the fourth *Sephirah*, that of loving kindness, along with the divine name: kindness, mercy, right arm, innocent, the third day, bright fire, the face of a lion, the first foot, the old man Abraham, East, higher waters, the silver of God, Michael, priest, angel in the appearance of the electrum Hasmal, white clothes, south wind, and others.

In the fifth *Sephira*, that of seriousness, is the divine name *Elohim* coming forth from water (as is stated in the book on Creation). It is also the fourth day, west, Gabriel, the old man Isaac, night, bravery, the golden altar, the second food, sanctification, darkness, Metattron, Aquilon, the dark appearance.

Attached to the sixth *Sephira* is *Eloha*, enlightening speculation, the wood of life, pleasure, the Line of the Mean, the written Law, the High Priest, the rising of the sun and the color purple. Tedacus Levi writes that it is from this place that the seventy nations are spread out over the earth and that its sign is the Truth of the Lord, and that it is called Peace and has its shape pictured in the moon. Its mystery is the third letter of the Tetragrammaton and this mystery is "Our father who is in heaven," the man above or the heavenly Adam, judgement, opinion, Michael, the old man Israel, the God of Jacob.

DE ARTE CABALISTICA

qui legat, non q̃ scribat, nõ qui loquatur. Sed qui meditetur, ne forte scri
ptio legis aut lectio qñcɜ terminata & desinens, etiam beatitudinem cessa
re ac desinere compellat. Sed is tandẽ q̃ cogitationes in corde suo illuc co
git, ut dimissis carnalibus, spiritualia legis meditetur, is inq̃ is beatꝰ est, cũ
corde mundo deum uidebit. Non ẽm tanta erat meo arbitratu diligẽtia
opus ad sacræ scripturæ historias q̃ tã patẽt hebræis, q̃ Titꝰ Liuiꝰ latinis.
Itẽ ad mãdata & p̃cepta q̃ numerũ habent, tũ ad religiones & cerimonias
q̃ rudi ac indocto etiã uulgo uel sepe nõ sine uitio ac peccato pagũt, unde
nõ mereãt tantã beatitudinẽ q̃ corporeis sensibus cõstãt, ut ad illa reqrãt
tã assidua, tã cõtinua, & tã diligẽs meditatio diei atcɜ noctis. Sed longe ma
ior beatitudo in theoriæ gradibꝰ sublimioribus inueniri posse demõstrat
q̃ ad legis Cabalisticam intelligentiam uscɜ adeo tendat ut spirituali medi
tatiõe mẽtes nr̃as imbuat, & quasi in similitudinẽ sui formet. Hanc esse cõ

Y   iicimꝰ legis meditationem q̃ Moysi post datam in igne lege & fractis iam
reparatiscɜ lapideis tabulis tãdem ab ore dei tradita est. Primo nãcɜ, ut
asserunt Cabalæi, deus legem suã in globum igneum conscripsit p̃ ignem
fuscum super ignem candidum, ait enim Ramban Gerundensis שׁבָּא
לָנוּ בְקַבָּלָה שֶׁהִיתָה בִּכְתוּבָה בְּאֵשׁ שְׁחוֹרָה
עַל גַבֵּי אֵשׁ לְבָנָה׃ i. Q₂ apparet nobis p̃ Cabalã, q̃ fuerit scri
ptura in igne fusco sup dorsum ignis candidi. Vnde illud extat deuteronõ
mii xxxiii. De dextera eius ignea lex eis. Erantcɜ tũ literæ ut aiunt confusę
ac inglomeratæ, quas studiosissimi quicɜ speculatiue intuẽtes ac diligẽter
consyderantes spiritu sancto ducti facile possent hinc & inde suscɜ decɜ ul
tro citro prorsus rursus eligere legere colligere ac in uerba quælibet for
mare sententiã in bonis bonam in malis malã significantia. Deo aũt Moy
ses edoctus in ordinẽ cunctas redigebat populo edendas, ut q̃ legis essent
uniuersi scirent & obseruarent, & inde lex in libros distincta & in arca re
posita est, sicut ipse recepit a dñ̃o. Artem tñ ordinandi & uariandi literas
& sacram scripturã ad mentis eleuationẽ dulcissime interp̃tandi a diuina
tunc maiestate receptam, ut rem diuinissimã a rudibus inp̃ceptibilẽ, uulgo
non patefecit. Sed electis tñ Iosue & septuaginta ore ad os tradidit, a q̃
bus postea semp electiores quicɜ receperunt, & ea receptio, ut ante audi
uistis, noĩata est Cabala. Nõnihil astipulant etiã sapientissimi christiano
rum doctores q̃rum plurimos ego quanq̃ Iudæus tñ libenter in aliena ca
stra tancɜ explorator irrepens legi. De nostro enim Moyse Gregoriꝰ Na
zianzenus ille græcus cognomento magnus theologus in libro de statu
episcoporũ sic ait. δέχεται νόμον, τοῖσ δ μὲν πολλοῖσ, τὸν τῦ γράμματοσ· τοῖσ δ ὑπὲρ
τοὺσ πολλοὺσ, τὸν τῦ πνεύματοσ. i. Accipit legem, ipsis qdem multis eam q̃ est
literæ, ipsis aũt sup multos, eam q̃ est spiritus. Et in libro primo theologię
βουλὴ δ οὕτω πλαξὶ στερραῖσ καὶ λιθίναισ ἐγγράφεσθαι, κὴ ταύταισ ἀμφοτέρωθεν λάπε δ φα

On the Art of Kabbalah

To the seventh *Sephira* apply the Lord of hosts, the leg, the foot, the right column, the great wheel, the prophets' vision, Moses and so on.

In the eighth are gathered God of hosts, the mystery of the column and the left foot and Booz, and from here comes the ancient snake, the Learning of the Lord, the branch, Aaron, the Cherub, the sons of the king, the grinding millstones and other things.

To the ninth *Sephira* are attached *Sadai*, the base of the world, Zion, the source of the fish ponds, the just, the living God, the complete Sabbath, the mean between "Keep" and "Remember," the fiftieth day from Leviathan, the Ram, Joseph the Just, Solomon, justice, strength, the Tree of Knowledge of good and evil, the treaty of the Lord, the bow of the Covenant, the glory of the Lord, the foundation of the prophecy of David, redemption, the age of souls.

To the tenth *Sephira* come the Lord, the kingdom, life, the second cherub, unilluminating speculation, later things, the end, the church of Israel, the bride in the Song of Songs, the Queen of heaven, the virgin Israel, the mystery of Law as transmitted by word of mouth, the eagle, the fourth letter of the Tetragrammaton, the kingdom of the house of David, the Temple of the king, the doors of God, the Ark of the Covenant and the two tablets in it, the Lord of all the earth.

You have heard a brief account of the ten properties or notions or attributes in the divine. They are called *Belimah*, by the Kabbalists, which some understand as *Beli*, meaning "without" or "beyond" and *Ma*, meaning "which," as if it said "ten beyond which," that is "with the essence of God left out." These people, then, usually interpret *Belimah* as "Beyond what is ineffable." Others understand it to come from *Belom* meaning "bridle" in the phrase "Bridle your tongue and do not speak," because sacred words must not be uttered profanely.

My next topic ought to be the princes of the angels and rulers of the demons that the Kabbalists place next to Mercy and Harshness. It is a matter that deserves a lengthy exposition, but we have passed midday and evening draws on. It would be impossible to explain matters of such importance in any concise fashion. Who could deal so quickly with the thirty-five princes of purity and the seventy princes of Ishmael by the side of the fourth *Sephira*? Or who could sufficiently explain the thirty-five princes of guilt in the fourth *Sephira* of Gravity and Fear, and the seventy princes of Esau when only a perfunctory survey is possible? These things need a volume each, and a large one at that. So, for the present, let us miss them out and go on to deal with the Art.

The blessed state of contemplative men comes, I would say, from a superior method of meditation. Day and night they study the Law (the twenty-four books that we call *Esrim ve Arba*, which means "twenty-four") and their happiness is derived from the sacred text. It is written, "Happy is the man who, among other things, will meditate on his Law

LIBER TERTIVS

νόμ(ου) τ̄.ρόμου. καὶ τὸ κρυπ̃όμβον. ὅ μὲν τοῖς πολλοῖς καὶ κατὰ μέρ{η}, τὸ δ̀ τοῖς ἀλ
ᠵοις καὶ ἄνω φαίνεται .i. Vult ita tabulis folidis & lapideis cōfcribi & iis altrin
fecus propter manifeftum legis & occultū,illud qdem multis & inferius
manentibus, hoc aūt paucis & furfum puenientibus. Quibus è uerbis apparet qbufdam ualde doctis etiam ueftris hoîbus cp Moyfes legis textū
plebi tradiderit, at myfteria parabolas & fymbola ipfi fibi ac pftantiorib.
referuarit. Eam Cabalæ artem in tris uias diuifam fuiffe accepimus, Salo
monis teftimonio q xxii. prouerbiorū ait. Certe fcripfi tibi tripliciter con
fulto & è fententia ut notificarē tibi rectitudinem eloqorum ueritatis. Sic
em gens nr̄a loqui cōfueuit cū habēda eft Cabalę mentio ut appellēt eā
על דרך האמת .i.eloqa ỹitatis fcripta fcilicet
.i. Secundū uiam ueritatis qd eft Cabalæ. Hic mos fuit ægyptio & Gerun
defi cæterifcp creber. Alii uero quincp Cabalæ partes exhibuerūt ut Rab
Hamai i libro. תיקון וציחות Speculatiōis quas ita nominat
ומאמר ומכל וחשבון .i. Rectitudo & cōbinatio & oratio
& fententia & fupputatio. Vefter Mirandularius in nongentis conclufio
nibus fcripfit his uerbis. Quicqd dicant cæteri Cabaliftæ, ego prima diui
fione fcientiam Cabalæ in fcientiā Sephiroth & Semoth.i.numerorum &
noîm tanq̄ in practicam & fpeculatiuā diftinguerē. Sed Rabi Iofeph Bar
Abraham Salemitanus & Cabaliftarū multo maxima pars fequunt̄ Salo
monem regē, in eo cp tripliciter illam poffe artem non tm̄ fpeculari, uerū
etiam practicari plane credunt, iuxta triplicē rerum oîm conditionem,nu
merum figurā & pondus, quippe illa quincp in hæc tria reducentes. Cum
em totū negociū fit allegoricū, & aliud pro alio p aliud intelligat, ut ipfa
fentētia fit alia pro alia Dicemus palā, cp aut dictio pro dictiōe ponit̄ aut
lr̄a p dictiōe, aut lr̄a pro lr̄a. Principio nēpe dictio fumit̄ pro dictiōe, uel p
trāfpofitionē q̄ metathefis nūcupat̄, uel p numerū æqualem dictiōibus in
clufum. Litera ponitur pro dictione uel in capite uel in fine uel ubilibet p
fuppofitam notam. Litera ponitur pro litera p alphabeticariā reuolutio
nem, plane totum, ut oîs tandem proportio compleat̄ arithmetica geome
trica & mufica. Verbi caufa, illud pfalmi xxi. Dn̄e in uirtute tua lętabit̄ rex,
intelligimus Cabaliftice de Meffiha dicentes. Dn̄e tetragrammate in uir
tute tua Meffiha rex, fubaudiatis uenit uel opatur. Eft em̄ Meffiha uirtus
dei & opatur in uirtute tegrāmati ad id, me ducit hęc dictio ישמח cui
fi literę tranfponant̄ erit משיח .i. Meffiha. Alio item in loco dominus
dixit ad Moyfen, qm̄ pcedet te angelus meus. Exodi xxiii. Ecquis eft ille an
gelus iuxta Cabaliftas, dicūt alii cp Michael, transponendo em̄ literas
מלאכי fit Michael, alii accipiētes illum fecundū artis Cabalifticę mo
dum, affirmant cp fit Metattron, eo cp deus aiebat qm̄ eft nomen meum
in illo. In Metattron aūt eft nomen Sadai p numerū æqualē utrifcp dictio

M iiii

Book Three

by day and night." It is not a case of reading, writing or talking, but of meditation. Otherwise, an end or cessation of writing or reading of the Law would require an end to the blessed state also. But the man who controls the thoughts in his heart to such an extent that he can expel affairs of the flesh and meditate on spiritual matters enshrined in the Law, that man, I say, is blessed, for he will see God with a pure heart.

There was no need for so much diligence in understanding the stories of Sacred Scripture, I think, for they are as clear in Hebrew as Livy is in Latin. Similarly straightforward were both the commands and the enumerated precepts and the rites and ceremonies, for they were carried out by rough, uneducated people who were often not untainted by vice and sin. So it is that those who live by their physical senses do not merit as great a blessedness as that achieved by such assiduous, continuous and diligent, day- and night-long meditation. It is proven that a far greater state of blessedness can be found on the higher steps of speculation: speculation leads to a Kabbalistic sort of understanding of the Law that imbues our minds with spiritual meditation and shapes them as if into its own likeness. This, we reckon, is the meditation on the Law that was handed down to Moses from the mouth of God after the Law had been given to Moses in the fire and the stone tablets had been broken and repaired.

"At first," the Kabbalists assert, "God wrote his Law onto a fiery globe, applying dark fire to white fire." As Ramban says: "It appears to us through Kabbalah, that Scripture came into being in black fire on white fire." Hence in Deuteronomy 33: "From his right hand is a Law of fire for them."

The letters, so they say, were confused and jumbled up at that stage, though studious men could look at them and speculate with careful consideration until, under the influence of the Holy Spirit, they had no difficulty in picking and choosing letters from every place possible after thorough scrutiny, and then collecting and forming them into particular words, to show good for the virtuous and bad for the sinner.

So Moses, under God's instruction, reduced all the letters to order for telling to the people. Everyone then knew what the Laws were and could keep them, and the Law was divided up into books and put into the ark in the same form as Moses had received it from the Lord. Moses did not explain to the vulgar the art either of ordering and varying the order of the letters or of sweetly interpreting Sacred Scripture to elevate the mind, even though he had by then received that art from the divine Majesty. This art was too divine a matter and was imperceptible to the unsophisticated, so he handed it on to the elect alone—Joshua and the seventy—by word of mouth. It is from them that the chosen of all ages have received this art, and this receiving, as you have already been told, is called Kabbalah.

The most learned of the Christian scholars also agree with some of this. Like a spy in an alien camp, I, though a Jew, have read with pleasure much of their work. Gregory of Nazianzus, the Greek theologian called "the Great," says of our Moses in his book *On the State of the Bishops*: "He receives the Law—for the many, the law of the letter, but for those above the many, the law of the spirit." And in his first book on *Theology* he writes: "He wanted the Law to be written on both sides of solid tablets of stone, because the Law

DE ARTE CABALISTICA

nibus indusum, q̃d mirifice amplectitur Gerundensis in loco ante citato. Cernitis iam duas Cabalę symbolicas uias? Quin uultis q̃ tertio literam uidere pro dictiõe reponi? Legite Isaiam capite lxv. Bene dicetur in deo Amen. Ecqs est iste deus? Cabalistæ respõdebũt q̃ est ארצי מלך נאמן .i. Dominus rex fidelis, tris em̃ has dictiones per capita, tres lr̃æ אמן notabũt, ut scripsit Racanat Exodi xv. Quarta species & tertia Cabalæ pars est commutatio literaria, ut dictio certis literis scripta symbolice designet aliam dictiõe p alias literas compositã, & fit per alphabeticariam reuolutiõe iuxta librum creationis Abrahæ uariationibus uiginti duabus, secũdũ q̃ ibi tot alphabeta legunt. Exemplũ p̃bet nobis Mazpaz nomen dei q̃d literis his quatuor conscribit מצפץ de q̃ Mirandulanus uester sic ait. Nomen dei quatuor literarũ q̃d est ex mem. zade. pe & zade regno Dauidis debet appropriari, cunq̃ illud in sacræ scripturę textu plane non legatur, cuius nam rogo esse symbolũ p̃hibebitur? Respondet Cabalistæ, q̃ sit symbolũ atq̃ signaculum Tetragrammati ineffabilis & procedit ex alphabeto ultimo q̃d est uigesimum secundũ libri q̃ noĩat Sepher Ietzira, diciturq̃ Ath bas, illic em̃ commutant iod pro mem, & he pro tzade, & vau pro pe, ut sit Mazpaz Adonai Iod he vau he. Dixi mõ ad artem p̃tinentia q̃ fit uel transuersis uel transpositis uel commutatis dictionibus, syllabis aut literis, secundũ quatuor rõnes q̃bus scripturarũ sensa ingeniose ac artificiose allegorizatur. Nam de iis quæ sine arte constãt & sola traditione fiunt Atechna, satis supq̃ uos feci certiores, quanq̃ ante ipsi ambo q̃ uestra professio est haud parum multã de illis cognitionem proprio studio adepti estis q̃ scilicet modo simplicia de compositis & superiora de inferioribus abstrahãtur, ac fere oĩa in mũdũ intelligibilẽ aut supsup̃mum & incompabilem referãtur. Possunt & pietatis argumenta non nulla sæpe nobis legendo sanctas literas in mente uenire q̃ ad diuinorum admiratiõe primũ, ac etiã tũ in amore eorũ nos alliciat, nec tñ certa quauis arte tradi queant, ut q̃ Gabriel fortiore sit uirtute q̃ Michael, q̃m de eo legitur in Daniele duplex uirtus uolando uolans. De Michael aũt solũ q̃ uenit in adiutoriũ, quare inter intelligentias Gabriel philosophice uirtus reputatur intellectus agentis, & Michael uirtus intellectus passibilis. Ita scribit Rabi Leui Ben Gersom q̃ a latinis noĩatur Magister Leo de Banolis. Plurimũ cõferre mihi uidetur, Philolaus inquit, ad artem Cabalisticam optime Simon id q̃d tu Atechnon appellas, nisi em̃ habeant in manibus reuelata maiorũ q̃ recte q̃dem sub artem cadere non putas, esset ois q̃tumcunq̃ temeraria oĩbus concessa exponendi licẽtia & uertendi sacrã scripturã q̃rsum q̃sq̃ uellet, queadmodũ accepimus uulgarios q̃sdam sophistas agere ut hac ętate uideantur suis syllogismis illa sanctissima diuini spiritus oracula prope in publicũ contemptũ adduxisse. Nunc aũt q̃n ad

reuelata

has both manifest and hidden parts, one for the many who remain below and the other for the few who arrive above." These words make it clear that your most learned sages, like ours, believe that Moses gave the text of the Law to the people but kept the mysteries, parables and symbols for himself and the elite.

We are taught that this art of Kabbalah has been divided into three paths. Solomon says in Proverbs 22: "Have I not written to you threefold words so as to show to you the rightness of the words of truth?" This is the way our people normally refer to Kabbalah, calling it *Words of Truth*," that is, written "according to the way of truth," which is Kabbalah. This was the custom of the Egyptian Maimonides, Moses of Gerona and many others.

Others reckon that Kabbalah has five parts. For instance, Rabbi Hamai in his book *On Speculation* calls them "rightness, combination, speech, opinion and reckoning." Your friend Mirandola wrote in his *Nine Hundred Conclusions*: "Whatever the other Kabbalists may say, I would make a primary division in Kabbalah between knowledge of *sephiroth* and knowledge of *Shemoth* (that is, names and numbers), which corresponds to the distinction between practical and speculative science." But Rabbi Joseph bar Abraham of Salema and most other Kabbalists follow Solomon the king and believe that the art can be divided into three, both in the speculative and the practical aspects, since there are three states of all — number, shape and weight. So they reduce the five parts to these three.

What is at issue is allegory. One understands one thing for another by using a third thing, thereby changing the whole sense of a phrase. So we say quite frankly that a word may be substituted for a word, or a letter for a word, or a letter for a letter. So, to begin, a word may be taken for another word either through transposition (called *metathesis*) or through the numerical equivalence of the letters in the two words. A letter may be posited to stand for a word, whether it lies at the beginning or end, or anywhere else, by a mark placed above it. A letter may be posited to stand for another letter through the alphabetical circle, the whole process assuring that, in the end, every arithmetical, geometrical and musical proportion is achieved.

Take an example. Psalm 21: "O Lord, in your strength the king will rejoice," is understood by Kabbalists as referring to the Messiah: "O Lord, Tetragrammaton, in your strength the king Messiah. . ." (understand 'comes' or 'operates'). The Messiah is the strength of God and works in the strength of the Tetragrammaton. I understand this from the word *YShMH*, meaning "will rejoice," whose letters transposed make *MShYH*, meaning "Messiah."

Similarly in another passage the Lord said to Moses: "Since my angel will go before you" (Exodus 23). Who is that angel according to the Kabbalists? Some say that it is Michael because *MLAKY*, "my angel," with the letters transposed makes Michael. Others, interpreting the name in similarly Kabbalistic fashion, assert that he is Metattron because God said: "Since my name is in him;" and the name

LIBER TERTIVS

reuelata sunt (ut arbitror) applicanda uniuersa, ducitur quędā linea, quā ultra citraq̃ nequit cōsistere rectum, ut q̃ artis sint, opa pessimorū hoim non uergant ad inertiā. Tum Simon. Aperte ucra p̃dicas inquit, fere nāq̃ est aliud nihil q̃d plus erranter ad sensa cuiusq̃ retorqueatur q̃ oracula, tametsi non id semp malicia sit, sed plus sæpe ignorantia, quis em̄ dedita opera piaculum ī sacra cōmitteret? Ita Saul q̃ndam uerbi ambiguitate deceptus errauit ab oraculo, cum promisisset deus Exodi xvii. אמחה את זכר עמלק .i. Delebo memoriā Amalek, credens si mares abstulisset satisfieri p̃cepto, qm̄ זכר masculū significaret. Deus aūt magis deleri memoriā Amalek per hoc uocabulum זכר uoluit q̃d memoriam q̃q̃ designat. Nondum em̄ erat scripturæ distinctio p puncta & accentus q̃ ab annis Ezrę primū coepit. Ergo זכר sine punctis & memoriā & masculum enuncians Sauli occasionē dedit ruinæ. Ad hęc Marranus. Contigit & Italis & græcis simile de uerbo φως q̃d & hoīem significat & lumen Vnde q̃ndam saturnaliorū cultores amphibologia decepti hoīem aliquē q̃tannis Saturno immolarunt, cum æque sacrificiū illud iuxta oraculū accensis luminibus fieri potuisset ut placaret Saturnus. Sic em̄ gens illa tam stulta postremum Hercule magistro resipuit. Et miserandū est etiā ætate nostra q̃tum stolidi hoīes & suṗbi quidam sophistæ imperitia linguarum errent, q̃d esset tn̄ ferendum, nisi se non errasse contenderent, & mōstrantibus uiam nō etiam usq̃ ad internecionē inuiderent. Sed o noster dux artem Cabalisticā cui⁹ exordiū inchoasti prosequere plenius. Tum Simon. Artem hanc rebus cōstare tribus inquit, peritiorū ut diximus opinio est. Primū numerorū supputatione q̃ גימטריא .i. Geometria noīatur, quasi terrestriū characterū inuicem numeralis dimensio, q̃ tn̄ pendeat ab arithmetica illa ob abstractam sui simplicitatē nullis sensibus tractabili; & ideo ne nouiciorū q̃dem artificio rudi subiecta. Potius igit̃ nuncupata est prima pars Geometria q̃ arithmetica q̃uis utrunq̃ reuera unū & idem in hac arte ualeat. Deinde transmutant qnq̃ syllabæ ut sit & transmutata dictio aut conuertitur uerbū simpliciter. Secundo q̃ litera ponitur pro dictione & appellatur Notariacū ab apicibus notariorū, qm̄ ibi quęlibet litera in culmine notatur, ut sit alicuius integri uocabuli signum. Tertio cōsistit hæc ars in literarū mutuatione, cum altera pro altera ingeniose locatur, & appellatur commutatio, q̃ factū est ut Rabi Ioseph Minor Salemitanus libros de hac arte a se conscriptos Hortū noīauerit, id est גנת propter ternas huius dictionis literas, quarū singulæ singulas portiones artis Cabalisticę designāt. Nā gimel significat נוטריקון Nun גימטריא i. Arithmetica Thau תמורה Vt sint partes toti⁹ artificii hæ גמטריא נוטריקון i. Notariacū quasi notatoriū, & תמורה i. Cōmutatio elementorū. Huic titulo allegat autor uersum Salomonis capite

Book Three

Shaddai is enshrined in the name Metattron because their numerical equivalents are the same,[50] a subject excellently discussed by Ramban in the passage cited above.

So now you see the two symbolical paths of Kabbalah. Would you like to see also the third method in which a letter is taken as meaning a word? Read Isaiah chapter 65: "He will be blessed in God. Amen." Who is this God? Kabbalists reply that he is the "Lord, King, Faithful," for the three letters of Amen (*AMN*) denote the first letters of these three words (*ADNY, MLK, NAMN*) as Recanat writes on Exodus 15.

The fourth kind, which is the third part of Kabbalah, is exchange of letters: one word written with one set of letters symbolically designates another word composed of different letters. This occurs, according to the book *On the Creation* by Abraham, in twenty-two variations through the revolutions of the twenty-two alphabets.

For example, the Name of God, Mazpaz, is written with the four letters *MSPS*. On this your friend Mirandola says: "The Name of God of four letters *MSPS*, should be taken as referring to the kingdom of David." This word is not in the text of Sacred Scripture, so of what will it be said to be a symbol? The Kabbalists reply that it is a symbol and a sign of the ineffable Tetragrammaton and that it comes from the last alphabet, the twenty-second of the book called the *Sepher Yesirah*. This alphabet is called *Athbas*, and in it "Y" is exchanged for "M," "H" for "S," and "V" for "P," so that *Mazpaz* is *Adonai*, that is, YHVH.

I have spoken only of the elements of the art of alternating, transposing or exchanging words, syllables or letters in accordance with the four methods of subtle allegory in Scripture. I have already sufficiently explained those skills that work without the aid of this art, the *Atechna* that rely on tradition alone, though I am sure that you have both also acquired much knowledge about them from your own studies since this is your area of expertise. I refer to methods for abstracting simple from complex and higher from lower and of referring nearly everything to the intelligible, supremest, incomparable world.

Quite a few proofs of piety can be found in reading the holy letters. As they enter our thoughts they bring us to admiration of divine matters and then bind us fast to them in love. However, there is not always a specified skill involved in doing this. For instance, Gabriel is said to be stronger in power than Michael, for it is written in Daniel about Gabriel that he had a double ration of power because he was "flying in flight," whereas it says about Michael only that he "came to help." So also among the intelligences, Gabriel is philosophically thought to be the power of the active intellect and Michael the power of the passive intellect. So writes Rabbi Levi ben Gershom, called in Latin Rabbi Leo de Banolis.

PHILOLAUS: Good Simon, this thing that you call *Atechnon* seems to me to be of the first importance for the art of Kabbalah. For if we did not hold in our hands the revelations of the elders, which you are right to think are not themselves part of the art, a license to expound, however rashly, would be granted to absolutely anyone, and anyone could manipulate the Sacred

DE ARTE CABALISTICA

sexto Canticorum. Descendi in hortū nucis. Pro prima itaq; parte exordiar ab eo q̃d est principium. Et scribitur in Zacharia cp̃ dn̄s Tetragrammatus erit אחד .i. unus, & nomen eius אחד .i. unum, forte multo uerius dominus deus erit Aleph. i. principiū, ut uos grçce dicitis Alpha & O, & חד .unum, ut q̃ sit principiū unius. Ipse nanq; supra oēm unitatē & ois unitatis sempiterna origo est. Et forte non dicitur unum sicut non dicitur ens, qm̃ est supra omne ens a q̃ emanat quicqd est. Vnde a contēplantissimis nominatur אין id est non ens, ut legitur Exodi xvii. היש יהוה בקרבנו אם אין .i. Num est ens Adonai inter nos an non ens? Legit aūt in libro de Via fidei & expiationis, cp̃ sit utruncp̃ היש ואין .i. Ens & non ens, qm̃ ea q̃ sunt, et ea q̃ non sunt, ex ipso sunt, & post ipsum sūt. Ita q̃ç; nō unum est, qm̃ ois unitatis causa est, & unitas post ipsum est, & nihil eorum est tam quç post ipsum sunt cp̃ q̃ nō sunt, ut in libro Speculatiōis. Rabi Himai qui post multa sic ait שכלם נאצלים מאחדותו והוא אינו רומה לאחד .i. Q; ōia ea deriuantur ab unitate sua & ipse nō est similis ipsi uni. Nec; id solū nostri sa tentut uerū etiā asseuerant Marrane uestri pariter q̃s esse sapientissimos probatis. Dionysius em̃ Areopagita in libro de Mystica theologia eidem sententiç de deo subscripsit his uerbis οὔτε ἀριθμός οὐδε τάξις, οὔτε ἐνότης. i. Deus necp̃ numerus est, necp̃ ordo, necp̃ unū, necp̃ unitas. Quid tandē est? Respondit Hieroni Simonides, q̃to magis cogito tanto minus intelligo. Et mihi accidit simile, cum exactis oībus creatis ascendero supra omne ens, nō inuenio aliud q̃ infinitū pelagus nihilitudinis, & fontē omnis entitatis ex abysso tenebrarū manantē perenniter. O altitudo, O profunditas, O nostra infirmitas. At satis uideri debet id nos de illo nosse q̃d ipse nobis de se reuelauit, quia sit principiū hoc est Aleph, & Tetragrāmaton q̃d p̃ aleph significatur, notatecp̃ essentiā diuinā, nihil uticp̃ aliud q̃ חויה uidelicet, est. q̃d certe propemodū erit idem cum essentia יהוה. Nā propter çqualem ualorē scriptura utruncp̃ coniunxit tarq̃ eius q̃ est primus & ultim9. Exodi ix. הנה יד יהוה הויה .i. Ecce manus Tetragrāmati hoiah, quasi est, scilicet finis opum & miraculorū dei, ut patet in decē plagis çgypti. Nam alibi ea dictio sic non inuenitur. Indicat aūt Salomōis Trecēsis testimonio instantē essentiā. Q; uero Tetragrāmaton a Iod coepit, plane nostri causa factū est, ut agnoscamus ipsum esse punctū infinitū & ois numeri hoc est rei cuiuscuncp̃ complementū. Iod em̃ decē significat. Et in resolutiōe nois tetragrāmati est litera decia sic יהוה יהו יה Vbi post Tetragrāmaton repitur יהו q̃d est symbolū ipsius Ehieh, hoc est entis p̃ çqualitatem numeri. Et nihilo q; minus significat essentiam creatoris, ut Exodi iii. Ehieh misit me ad uos, non illa q̃ immanet sed quç fluit extra. Est em̃ sigillū dei יה q̃ Ehieh sigillauit mudū, & dr̃ אמת .i.

uerum

On the Art of Kabbalah

Scriptures to any purpose they desired. Indeed, that is what we understand some sophists have been doing in the present time through their syllogisms, almost bringing the sacred oracles of the divine spirit to public contempt. But all things of Kabbalah refer to revealed truths, and those truths define what is the right stance. Thus it is not possible for bad men to subvert what genuinely belongs to the art.

SIMON: What you say is obviously true. Nothing gets more twisted to the predispositions of the individual than oracles, not always through ill will but more often through ignorance. Who would sin in sacred matters on purpose?

Saul once erred from the true meaning of an oracle because of verbal ambiguity. God had promised in Exodus 17: "I will wipe out the memory (*ZKR*) of Amalek." Saul thought that if he removed the males he would fulfill the command, because *ZKR* signifies "masculine." But God meant for the memory of Amalek to be blotted out when he used the word *ZKR*, for this word also means "memory." There were not yet the distinguishing points and accents in writing that first began in Ezra's time. *ZKR*, without pointing, denoted both "memory" and "male," and so caused Saul's destruction.

MARRANUS: A similar thing happened to the Italians and Greeks in the word *Phos*, which means both "man" and "light." Worshippers in the Saturnalia were deceived by the ambiguity and sacrificed a man every year to Saturn, although the oracle could equally well have been obeyed, and Saturn placated, by the burning of lamps. The fools became wise in the end through the teaching of Hercules.

It is a pity that even in our own time some stupid and proud sophists go wrong through lack of linguistic knowledge. It would be bearable if only they did not insist that they have not gone wrong at all and if only they were not so mortally jealous of those who do show them the way.

But please, sir, continue our guidance in the art of Kabbalah.

SIMON: The opinion of the experts is, as I have said, that this art consists of three parts.

First there is equivalence of numerical calculation. This is called *Gematria* or "geometry." Geometry is the numerical measurement of shapes on earth but relies on a sort of arithmetic which, because of its abstract simplicity, cannot be worked on by any of the senses and so is not subjected to the crude efforts of novices. Thus the first part is called geometry rather than arithmetic, although both of them in fact have equal importance in this art. Thereafter one can transfer syllables and thereby create either a transformed expression or a completely altered word.

Second is the placing of a letter in the place of an expression. This is called Notariacon from the marks or *notaria* on the top of each letter. Any letter may be marked on top to be a sign of another whole world.

The third part of the art is exchange of letters, when one letter is cleverly put in the place of another. This is called Commutation.

This is how Rabbi Joseph the Younger of Salem came to call the books that he wrote about this art *The Garden*, in Hebrew, *GNTh*. The three letters of this word each denote a separate part of the art of Kabbalah. *G* denotes *Gematria*, *N* denotes *Notariacon*, *Th* denotes *Themura*. These, then, are the

LIBER TERTIVS

uerum,quippe qd in se ipsum arithmetice multiplicãdo nascit̃. Tum seqͭ ר'ה nomen essentiæ meriti ac retributionis,ut in psalmis. Si iniquitates obseruaueris Iah. Tria igit̃ noĩa essentialia in Tetragrammato cernitis. Ineffabile notat essentiã primã.Ehieh essentiam in rebus,& Iah essentiam in meritis,& p̃dicant in eo qd quid est,Idcͣ appellatur מה.i.quid.Nam Tetragrammaton יוד הא ואו הא per æqualitate numeri signi- ficat מה utrunc em continet xlv. Cuncͥ dixisset Moyses.Quid nomen eius,qd dicã,̔respõdebat̃ ei.Ehieh. Deinde cõsydera diligeter̃ sp̃us sancti uerba q̃ haud frustra ponunt̃ in eodẽ Exodi iii. לי מה שמי מה .i.Mihi qd nomẽ eius qd. Et uidete lr̃as terminales eoru,habebitisͣ quã triliterum ineffabile יהוה cuius principiũ est Ehieh.Mediũ Iah,Finis in- finitudo.Partes em̃ eius sunt י יה יהי quas diuidemus in tria inter- ualla.Primum est יה Secundũ ריה Tertiũ יהי Oia ad esse ac essen- tiam deseruientia.De Iah legitur Exodi xv.Fortitudo mea & laus Iah.De יהי eodem in loco.Et factus est mihi in salute.De יהי Genesis primo Fiat lux.Hec ambo uerba nouissima plurimũ ad mundi opificiũ & rerum existentiã contulerunt,ut יהי אור ויהי אור Fiat lux,& facta est lux.Et erat uesper,& erat mane. Fiat firmamentũ,& sit distinctio,& factũ est ita.Congregent̃ aquæ,& factum est ita.Germinet terra,& factum est ita.Producat terra,& factum est ita.Fiant luminaria,& factũ est ita.Semp̃ addito eo,& factum est uesper & factũ est mane.His omnibus(ut reuera sint) dep̃hendimus inesse seminaliter & occulte nomen ineffabile. Solũ uero Elohim.i.deus,in illis sex diebus exp̃ssum cernimus.Sed cum iã mun- dus appareret esse p̃fectus,postcͣ uaria & admiranda diuinissimaru uir- tutum op̃a consummata,tandẽ pro merito triũphus esset celebrandus,& festus dies indicendus,ecce cum Elohim Tetragrãmatus rex regũ & dñs dominantiũ incessit,& dictum est tum primũ.Iste sunt g̃nationes cœli & terræ qñ creatæ sunt in die q̃ fecit Tetragrãmatus Elohim cœlũ & terrã. Hic Tetragrãmaton publice auribus oĩm creaturarũ primo intonuit,q̃ intelligimus clementiam dei cũ iusticia,nam in q̃cuncͣ loco sacræ script̃u- ræ Tetragrammaton sibi iungit Elohim,ibi proprietatẽ animaduertimus: clemẽtiæ simul & iusticiæ.Componit̃ qñcͣ cum אן ברי ut in oratione Habakuk.Tetragrãmatus Adonai fortitudo mea,& nos sic legendo, uir- tutem Tetragrammati descẽdere intelligimus ad ipsum Adonai p̃olatũ Sin ordine conuerso rep̃itur Adonai Tetragrammatus,ut Geneseos xv. Adonai Tetragrãmate qd dabis mihi,̔tum mente cõcipimus cͣ numera- tiones hoc est diuinæ proprietates ab inferiore ad sup̃iʲs ascendent̃es,sup̃- mam lucem app̃hendant.Fit & qñcͣ ut repiatur̃ iunctum nomen El.Psal- mo Cxviii.El tetragrãmatus & illuxit nobis,& significat̃ clementiã. Haud absimiliter cum additur Elohim,& dicitur sic.El Elohim Tetragrãmatus

Book Three

parts that make up the art: *Gematria* (or Arithmetic), *Notariacon* (manipulation of letters), and *Themura* (commutation of letters). The author gets support for this title from the verse of Solomon in *Song of Songs*, chapter 6: "I went down into the garden of nuts."

Well, then, for the first part, let me begin at the beginning. It is written in Zechariah that the Lord the Tetragrammaton will be One (*Ehad*, i.e. *AHD*) and his name One. Or perhaps, more accurately, that the Lord God will be aleph, meaning "the beginning" like your Greek alpha and omega, and *had* or "one" because that is in the beginning of One. For he is above all unity and the eternal origin of all unity. Perhaps he is not called "one," just as he is not called "Being," because he is above all being and from him all being emanates. So the contemplative name him *AYN* or "Not-being," as is written in Exodus 17: "Is the Lord a Being among us or a Not-being?" But it is written in the *Book On the Way of Faith and Atonement* that he is "both Being and Not-being" because both things that are and things that are not exist from him and after him. In the same way he is not One because he is the cause of all unity and unity exists after him and he himself is neither the same as the things that come after him nor as those that do not come into being at all. As Rabbi Hamai says, after much else, in this book *On Speculation*: "All these things are derived from his unity and he is not like to the one."

It is not our teachers alone who admit this, for the men you Greeks profess most wise assert this too. Dionysius the Areopagite, in his book on *Mystic Theology*, subscribes to the same opinion about God with these words: "God is neither number nor order nor one nor unity." So what is He? Simonides replies to Hiero: "The more I ponder, the less I understand." The same happens to me. When I pass through all creation and climb above all being I do not find anything except an infinite sea of Nothingness and the spring of all being eternally gushing forth from the depths of darkness. O deep, deep depths! O how weak we are!

It must suffice us to know about him what he has revealed about himself. He is the Beginning or "aleph," and he is the Tetragrammaton, which is denoted by aleph and refers to the divine Essence (*HVYH*) which is nearly the same as the essence *YHVH*. Both words add up to the same number, so Scripture has joined them just as they both belong to him who is the first and the last: "Behold, the hand of *YHVH* exists (*HVYH*)." (Exodus, chapter 9) This refers to the purpose of God's works and miracles as made clear in the ten plagues of Egypt since this word is not found elsewhere. Solomon of Troyes attests that it indicates the present Essence.

The fact that the Tetragrammaton begins with *Y* was clearly intended to help us realize that he is both a boundless point and the sum total of all number, that is, of all things. *Yod* means ten and in the unravelling of the Tetragrammaton it is the tenth letter: *YHVH YHV YH Y*. After the Tetragrammaton we get *YHV*, which is a symbol of *Ehieh* or "Being" because they add up to the same number.[51] It also signifies the essence of the Creator, as in Exodus 3: "Ehieh sent me to you," not essence that is immanent but essence that flows out. *YHV* is a sign of God, by which *Ehieh* put his seal upon the world, and it is called *Emeth*, or Truth, because it is created by multiplying itself by itself arithmetically.[49]

DE ARTE CABALISTICA

locutus est & uocauit terrā. Psalmo quinquagesimo, tum denotat nomen ineffabile gratia & seueritate uestitū. Aliqñ legitur idcp tm in propheticis & Hagiographis. Tetragrammatus Sabaoth psalmo xlvi. Tetragramatꝰ Sabaoth nobiscū, susceptor noster deus Iacob. Insinuatcp hoc modo proprietatem iudicii. Atcp ideo prophetæ isto more increpādo ad seueritatē utuntur. De huiuscemodi explanationibus pquirere latius poteritis in libro Portæ lucis, & multo latissime in libro Portarū iusticiæ Rabi Ioseph Carnitolis. Adhuc & de tredecim eiusdem tetragrāmati proprietatibꝰ q̄s legislator Moyses inuocauit Exodi xxxiiii. in hanc sententiā. Tetragrammate dñe deus misericors & gratiose, longanimis, multæ clementiæ, & uerus, custodiens misericordiā in millia, tollens iniqtatem, ptransiens scelus, atcp peccatum, & innocens non innocentabit, uisitans iniqtatem patrum sup filios & sup filiorum filios in tertiā & quartā progeniē. Vos hic appello uos optimi uiri, hoc em dicere libet certe sine falso, qm multis & studiis & uerbis esset opus ei q cūcta nois tetragrammati mysteria publicare uellet, cuius ne finis qdē ullus reperitur unq̄, sicut nec substātiæ dei. Omisso itacp noīe proprio essentiæ diuinę, ostendam deriuata numero pauca. Sic em fieri cōsueuit ut pro grāmaticorū decreto appellatiua de propriis formemus. Sūt aūt hæc אל אלהים אלוה q̄rum unumq̄dcp originem suam ex ineffabili tetragrāmato sortitum est qd literas cōtinet quatuor, ecce quatuor, & designat xxvi. ecce uiginti & sex, q̄ oīa sunt unū dei symbolum, ecce unū. Iunge singula uidelicet quatuor, uiginti sex, & unū, & fit אל cui si addideritis terminationē tetragrāmati וה nascet Eloha. Nunc de Elohim sic dicit cp eius Mem nō est rei significatio, sed grammatica inflexio, qd inde apparet. Nam si p affixum aut regimen consequētię legendū illud fuerit, haud dubium quin Mem litera carebit, ergo si principio tetragrammati Iah ordine conuerso El addideritis, mox fit Elohi, & assumendo declinationē grammaticā q̄ est Mem in fine pronunciabit̄ Elohim, qd & sæpe per literas ineffabilis scribit̄, & Elohim nihilominus punctatur. Est aūt in Cabala frequēs ordinis conuersi usus, & magna eius uirtus uirtutiscp laus, cum q̄quomodo syllabæ transponant̄ cp abscp diminutione tñ eædem manent literæ, licet sæpe non eædem significationes, cuius rei Abraham in libro Ietzira meminit cum ait זכר ונקבה זכר באמש ונקבה באשם .i. Marem & fœminā, mare in Emes, & fœminā in Esem, ubi trāsp positio literarū, rei q̄cp mutationem indicat.

Verbi causa לא & אל .i. deus, & nō, Quod cū alias frequēti sit ī more, ēñ hoc est uehementer admirabile in hoc nōīe ineffabili, cp eius literæ q̄tumcuncp hac illacqp puertant, semp unam & eandē rem significāt. suidelicet esse ac essentiam dei q̄ dixit. Ego tetragrammatus & non mutor. Quod isto uobis usu erit manifestius. Resoluat tetragrāmaton nomen in

On the Art of Kabbalah

Next comes *YH*, the name of the essence of merit and retribution, as in the Psalms: "If you have heeded iniquities, Yah."

So you see three names of essences in the Tetragrammaton. The ineffable name denotes the first essence. Ehieh denotes essence in things. Yah denotes essence in merit. They are predicated in the word "what," called in Hebrew *Mah*. The Tetragrammaton, written out to give the full names of the Hebrew letters, signifies *Mah* through numerical equivalence, since both add up to 45.[52] When Moses said, "What is his name? What shall I say?" the reply was "Ehieh." Then consider carefully the words of the Holy Spirit given, for good reason, in the same passage of Exodus chapter 3: "[They say] to me, "What is his name?" What [am I to say?]." Look at the last letters of the Hebrew words and you will find the ineffable four letters *YHVH*, whose beginning is Ehieh, middle is Yah and end is infinity. Its parts are *YHV*, *YH* and *Y*, which we divide into three separate sections. First is *YH*, second is *VYH* and third is *YHY*, all of them being in the service of Being and Essence.

On Yah we get in Exodus 15: "My strength and praise, Yah." On *VYHY* in the same place: "And he was made [*VYHY*] for my salvation." On *YHY*, there is the first chapter of Genesis: "Let there be [*YHY*] light." Both these last words refer in particular to the making of the world and the existence of things. Hence: "Let there be [*YHY*] light, and there was [*VYHY*] light." And it was evening and it was morning. Let there be a firmament and a distinction, and so it was done. Let the waters be gathered together, and so it was done. Let the earth sprout forth, and so it was done. Let the earth bring forth, and so it was done. Let there be light, and so it was done. Always added is: And it was evening and it was morning. In all of these we gather that to ensure geniune existence there is, basic but hidden, the ineffable Name.

For in those six days the only Name of God expressed was Elohim. But when the world seemed finished, and the varied and wonderful works of the divine powers complete, the deserved triumph had finally to be celebrated and a festive day decreed. Then comes the God of the Tetragrammaton, the King of Kings and Lord of Lords and then is his Name first spoken. These are the generations of the heaven and the earth when they were created, in the day that God the Tetragram made heaven and earth.

Then, for the first time, the Tetragram was sounded in public for all creatures to hear, and for us to understand God's clemency combined with his justice. For in every passage of Sacred Scripture where the Tetragrammaton is joined to Elohim, there we see the property of clemency combined with justice.

Sometimes the Name is written with Adonai, as in Habbakuk's words: "*YHVH* Adonai is my strength," and then, as we read it, we understand that the power of the Tetragram goes right down to the Adonai mentioned. But if the order is reversed and we get Adonai *YHVY*, as in Genesis 15: "Adonai *YHVH*, what will you give to me?", then we mentally conceive that the numerations (that is, divine properties) go up from lower to higher and finally apprehend the highest light.

Sometimes we may find the Name joined to *El*, as in Psalm 118: "El, the Tetragram, has given us light." This signifies clemency. Similarly, when

LIBER TERTIVS

duodecim uariationes (nec em̄ poterimus ultra proficisci) tunc quicq̄d inuentum fuerit nulli alii nisi essentiæ deseruiet, cuius symbola sunt hæc.

יִמְוָת יְהַוָּה יָהְוִה הֻוִהֵי הִיוָה וְהָיָה וִיהָיֵה
וְהֵיהֵי הָיָה הִיהָן הִיוְיִ הֵהִוִי Duodecim igit̄ ista noīa, unū nomē apud Cabalistas censentur, tanq̄ unius rei significatiuū, quanq̄ sunt duodecim expositoria, q̄rum singulis applicant de sacra scriptura unā clausulam q̄ illud apte p notariacū referat, non expositionis sed memoraculi tm̄ loco ne subeat eius obliuio, ut si dicerem. Attēde et audi Israel hodie, q̄d legitur Deuteron. xxvii. hebraice sic הַסְכֵּת וּשְׁמַע יִשְׂרָאֵל הַיּוֹם horū quatuor uerborū capita notabitis, & facient הָיָה q̄d nomen est essentiæ atq̄ resolutio Tetragrāmati, pariter de cæteris fiant cætera. Sed maneamus tantisper in prima Cabalæ specie, dum adhuc quædā cognitu necessaria uiderimus. Iā em̄ q̄d dixi, de secunda parte sumendū fuit, aggrediamur aūt hanc arte si uultis mēbratim cæsimq̄, modo ne diu in unoq̄q̄ immoremur ut diurna opa cū die transeat. Quin id q̄d prius tetigi nūc iterum breuiuscule citabo ut firmius hæreat, q̄ deus ante creationē ineffabilis, in creatione noīatus est Elohim, & post creationē habitans in mundō tanq̄ in templo suo dicitur אֲדֹנָי Adonai. Vnde illud legit Psalmo xi. Tetragrammatus in templo sancto suo tetragrāmatus in cœlis thron⁹ ei⁹ ut qui dn̄atur in opib⁹ suis. Nam ipse est ut scriptura dicit Deuteronomī x. Dii deorū & dn̄i dn̄orum El magnus, quare templum Cabalistice nota est Adonai & cōuer̄sa uice p æqualitatē numeri. Perinde atq̄ in Adonai אֲדֹנָי tanq̄ in suo הֵיכָל i. teplo adorandus sit ineffabilis tetragrāmatus, & deus in deo amandus, iuxta triplicē mundū. Ieremiæ vii. Templum dn̄i, templū dn̄i, templū dn̄i. Restat aliud nomen appellatiuū שַׁדַּי i. Sadai. Exodi vi. Ego tetragrāmatus, & apparui Abrahā Isaac & Iacob p El Sadai, & nomen meū tetragrāmaton non feci sciri eis, ubi solū hoc appellatur nomē suū q̄d est ineffabile, q̄a hoc tm̄ est summo deo propriū quatenus ipse est ut nihil eorū q̄ sunt, sed supra oīa est, non habens respectū extra se. Cætera sunt etiā aliarū proprietatū & relationū appellatiua, ut Sadai, q̄d latini uerterūt dicentes oīpotens, sed aptius hebraice significatur Sibi sufficiens, se contentus, & nullius indigens, q̄d græci rectius αὐτάρκως iter̄pretantur. Nam שׁ id est q̄, & דַּי sufficit uel satis est, grāmatice dicimus Cæterū si audieritis solitarie in sacris uocari שֵׁם i. nomen, confestim Tetragrammati uobis in mente ueniat, q̄d κατ' ἐξοχήν & hyperbolice nomē dicitur super omne nomen q̄tumuis in sermone quotidiano rei oīs sit q̄ habeat existentiam. Sadai aūt qm̄ non est ei opus alterius adiutorio, ideo patribus in El Sadai hoc est in forti qui se ipso contentus sit Tetragrammat⁹ apparuit ut qui per se sufficiat miracula & prodigia facere, non aūt fecit illos scire q̄ nomen Tetragrammaton sit illud nomen in quo possit homo

N

Book Three

Elohim is added and it says: "El Elohim, the Tetragram, has spoken and called on the earth" (Psalm 50). In this case it denotes the ineffable Name clothed in grace and severity.

Elsewhere, though only in the Prophets and the Hagiographa, it is written: "Tetragram of Sabaoth," as in Psalm 46: "The Tetragram of Sabaoth is with us, our protector is the God of Jacob." He indicated in this way the property of Judgement and so when the prophets rebuke, they use this phrase to indicate greater severity.

You can look more widely into explanations of this kind in the book *The Gates of Justice* by Rabbi Joseph Carnitol.

Similarly with the thirteen attributes of the same tetragram that the lawgiver Moses invoked in Exodus 34 in this way: "O Lord, Tetragram, God, merciful and gracious, long-suffering, abundant in clemency and truth, keeping mercy to thousands, removing iniquity, passing by wickedness and sin, and not pardoning the guilty,[53] for he will visit the sin of the fathers onto the sons and the sons' sons to the third and the fourth generation." Gentlemen, I appeal to you. It would not be misleading for me to say that anyone intending to make public all the mysteries of the Tetragram would need much study and many words since there is no more an end to the Tetragram than to the substance of God. So, leaving aside the real name of the divine essence, I shall instead show a few of the things derived from it.

Our usual practice is to form descriptive names from proper names like grammarians. In this case these are El, Elohim and Eloha. Each of these originates from the ineffable tetragram: the tetragram contains four letters (so four) which make 26 (so twenty-six) which are altogether one symbol of God (so one), which when joined together (4, 26 and 1) produce EL (*AL*).[54] When the last part of the tetragrammaton, *VH*, is added to this it gives Eloha (*ALVH*). As for Elohim, it is said that the letter "M" does not signify anything, but is just a grammatical inflexion. This is clearly so, since when the word is read with a connection or regulator after it, it consistently lacks the letter mem. So if you take the first part of the Tetragrammaton *YH* and turn it round and then add to it El, you will get Elohi (*ALHY*) and by attaching the grammatical inflection "M" on the end it will be pronounced Elohim. This is often written with the ineffable letters but the vowel dots of Elohim.

In Kabbalah another method frequently used is reversed order. The best and most praiseworthy aspect of this method is the fact that, however the syllables may be transposed, the same letters still remain without loss even when the meaning changes. It is to this that Abraham refers in his book on the *Creation* when he says: "Male and female, Male in *AMSh*, female in *AShM*," where the transposition of letters indicates a corresponding change of matter. Take as another example, *LA* ("Not"), and *AL* ("God").

A particularly remarkable disposition in the ineffable name (despite similar occurrences in many other cases) is the fact that its letters, however much they may be twisted this way and that, always mean one and the same thing, namely the being and essence of God who said: "I, *YHVH*, verily do not change."

DE ARTE CABALISTICA

tanquam cooperator & delegatus a deo efficere miracula, de hoc apertiᵉ in Capnione de Verbo Mirifico. Est præterea ipsius Sadai ministratoriᵉ spiritus Metattron per æqualitatem numeri sic nominatus, qui dux & mõstrator uiarum esse perhibetur, quod postea si me commonueritis tractabimus apertius, Accedit aliud nomen Sabaoth quod hebraice sic legitur צבאות & ita dicuntur exercitus, quorum primus est intelligẽtiarum omnino separatarum & angelorum. Secundus motorum orbium & assistentium uirtutum. Tertius animarum corpora informantium, & non inuenitur nisi post nomen dei. Vnde tripliciter quoq; legitur Sanctus Sanctus Sanctus Tetragrammatus Sabaoth. Isaiæ sexto ac aliis in locis similiter. Omnis igitur primæ partis Cabalæ status qua procedat institutiõe au diuistis. Nam cum totus in sacrorum uerborum commutatione consistat & quælibet uerba bifariam alterentur, necessario fatebimur ei parti duas subesse species, alteram quæ sit syllabarum aut dictionum transpositio, alteram numerorũ æqualitas. Vt si uerbi causa legero Isaiæ quadragesimo מי אלה ברא Id est. Quis hęc creauit? & Cabalistice trãsponam duo hęc, couertãq; i אלהים tũ, actu redibit exordium Geneseos מי אלה ברא pro אלהים ברא ut stet sententia, qs hæc creauit? Deus creauit. Et Ezechiel sedit ad fluuium Chobar. i. ad influentia cherub, transponat em בכור & sit ברוב Et Nohe inuenit gratiam. Gen. vi. conuertendo em חנ sit נח Similia cũcta eueniunt p metathesim propter literarũ primariã confusionẽ q̃ in igneo globo apparuerat ut licuerit quasi de chao literas educere atq; eas hinc & inde legere, prorsus rursus, ita primæ partis species prima consummatur. Nunc ipse mecũ cõstitui accessu mẽbri alterius de parte prima nõnihil exẽpli gratia mõstrare, ut pnoscatis rem liquidius & firmius q̃q; memoria teneatis. Legitur de Ishac & Rebecca xxv. Geneseos ותהר רבקה אשתו i. & cõcepit Rebecca uxor sua. Ex quo diuinare cõmodũ nobis concedit qdnã Rebecca cõceperit? Quin certe ut uerba indicãt cõcepit Rebecca אשת Vos aũt consyderate uiri doctissimi ec qd sit אשת In hac primæ partis secunda specie per גימטריא i. numerorũ cõmensurationem, reperietis iuxta æqualitatem numeri significare אש וקש id est Ignem & stipulam, utrunq; enim in se continet septingenta & septem, concepit ergo Rebecca ignem & stipulam quod sacra comprobant eloquia teste Abdia qui ait. Et erit domus Iacob ignis & domus Esau stipula. Similiter quando audimus legem fuisse latam in sapientia חכמה Videamus quæ sit illa sapientia quæ ad legem ferendam congruat. Et certe sunt edicta & interdicta, iussiones & prohibitiones. Symbolum autem est חכמה Id est. Sapientia omnium mandatorum dei, cum enim quatuor illius uocabuli elementa de propriis scripturis pronunciaueritis,

On the Art of Kabbalah

For better clarification of this usage, let the Tetragrammaton be resolved into twelve variations, the most that we can possibly extract. Anything we find will be bound to designate the essence. These are the symbols: *YHVH*, *YHHV*, *YVHH*, *HVHY*, *HVYH*, *HHYV*, *VHYH*, *VYHH*, *VHHY*, *HYHV*, *HYVH*, *HHVY*. The Kabbalists consider these twelve names to be only one name because they signify only the one thing despite the twelve methods of exposition. To each of these they apply a particular clause from Sacred Scripture that fits aptly through Notariacon, not for exposition, but as a mnemonic intended to remind. If I were to say: "Give heed, O Israel, and hear this day," which is written in Hebrew in Deuteronomy 27, you should note the first letter of the four Hebrew words in this passage. They make *HVYH*, which is the name of the essence and a resolution of the tetragrammaton. There are other phrases of the same kind for the other names.

Let us stay a while with this first kind of Kabbalah, since there is still more there that is worth knowing that we should examine. What I have just said was taken from the second part. Let us attack this art, if you will, limb by limb and bit by bit, and in that way we shall get a day's work done in a day.

I will now quote again what I touched on before, just briefly to fix it more firmly in the memory. God was ineffable before the creation. In the creation he was named Elohim. After the creation, living in the world as if in his Temple, he was called Adonai. Hence it is written in Psalm 11: "Tetragrammaton in his sacred temple. Tetragrammaton who has his throne in the heavens, who is the Lord in his works." He is, as Scripture says (Deuteronomy 10): "God of gods and Lord of lords, great El." Thus the temple is denoted in Kabbalah by Adonai and vice versa through their equal numerical value.[56] Just as the ineffable Tetragrammaton is to be worshipped in Adonai (*ADNY*) as if in his own *HYKL* (Temple), so God is to be loved in God in accordance with the three-fold world (Jeremiah 7): "Temple of the Lord, Temple of the Lord, Temple of the Lord."

There remains another appellative name, Sadai, as in Exodus 6: "I am *YHVH* and I appeared to Abraham, Isaac and Jacob through El Sadai, and I did not make my name, the Tetragrammaton, known to them." Here, the only name called his own is the ineffable one, because this is the only one intrinsic to the great God. In so far as he is himself, he is nothing of those that are but is above all things and has no regard for things outside himself. In contrast, the other names are appellatives of distinct properties and relations. Such is Sadai, which is translated by Latin speakers as "all-powerful" but means in the Hebrew something more like "self-sufficient," "self-content" or "complete in himself." The Greek work *autarkes* gets it right. The *Sh* means "what," and *DY* means "enough" or "sufficient" grammatically.

If you hear the word *Shem*, meaning "name," pronounced by itself in a sacred context, immediately let the Tetragrammaton come to mind. The Name is spoken of par excellence as being above any normal name of anything that has existence, no matter how great it may be. As for Sadai it is because Sadai does not need any external help that the Tetragrammaton appeared to our ancestors in El Sadai, that is, in the "mighty, self-sufficient one," for the Tetragrammaton is sufficient in himself to perform miracles

חית בת מם הי cōflabitur ex eis numerus sescentorū & tredecim mandatorū dei q̄ doctores uostri תרי״ג appellant. Ad summum in hoc genere speculationis primo legis characteres elementa & literas in cōsulso fuisse repositas, & hac atq̨ illac legibiles, memoratu dignū erit. Secūdo nullis accentibus aut punctis distinctas. Tertio singulas alphabeti literas primordiales certū significare numerū, etiā qnq̨ terminales, quas longe post ille prudens Ezra simul cū pūctis adinuenit. Nam primitiuæ sunt duæ ac uiginti qbus solis ab initio scriptura ois depicta extitit, quas usq̨ adhæc tpa Cabalistæ locant & dislocant pro cuiusuis iucūdæ contēplationis amœnitate. Vltimo est nobis intentanda uniuersalis hæc meta q̄ tametsi Cabalistæ sit officiū, aliud legere ac aliud intelligere, tn inuiolabiliter istū q̄sq̨ obseruet canonē, in bonis bona, in malis mala, ne albo nigrū applicet aut diem nocti. Tum Marranius. Id genus artis, inqt, haud secus cogitauero q̄ si q̄s Dorotheū aliquē appellauerit pro Theodoro, aut pro Nicodemo Demonicū, siue pro Demophilo Philodemum. Sicut græci dicere solent σωματόφιλον καὶ φιλοσώματω. Ad hæc Simon ait. Certe id q̄d dicis nonnihil quadrat, sed exēpla enumerādo admodū breui fatigaberis propter aliarū linguarū inopiā q̄ ad hebræam tanq̨ oīm linguarū fonte compate paupes sunt & egestatis suæ impatientes ut q̄ & reliquarū nationū ascīscant idiomata. Nec em plenū numerū accipiunt, nec cōpositionē utile admittunt. Quapropter ars ista in alterius gētis sermone traduci minime potest. Q̄ nisi uos pariter hebraice peritos nossem, frustra hæc de Cabala qtuliber paucula uobiscū egissem, aut iam acturus essem. Sed propere accedamus ad secundā huius institutionis parte q̄ נוטריקון dictur. i. notaria cūm q̄d est conuentū q̄ddā dam receptū inter Cabalistas ut literæ singulariæ sine coagmentis syllabarū certa uerba designent, quē admodū notariis & actuariis est in more, & quondā belli ducū furtiua scripta literis unicis incondite repositis arcana mentis protulerūt. Est adeo Probi grāmatici cōmentarius, ut scribit Aul. Gellius, satis curiose factus de occulta literarum significatione, haud aliter forte in huius artificii prosecutione sit q̄ si q̄ pacīscantur inter se Iod literā, propter indiuisibilis puncti figurā ineffabile tetragrāmatō q̄d uul. go dn̄m interp̄tamur notare. Sicut & illud ipsum propter tres עליונות i. summitates i decē numerationibus q̄ sunt una & eade עטרה i. unū diadema tribus punctis signare solet. Aiunt em Cabalistæ כי לסוד זה כותבין השם ג יודי״ן בזה. i. Q̄ ad mysteriū hoc scribunt nomen tribus Iod, uti hoc ׃׃׃ Vbi unicum quatriliterū tribus unicis lr̄is cōscribit, q̄d usu q̄tidiano approbat. Fuit & quondā in diebus Antiochi Eupatoris Iudas Matthathiæ filius. Bellator nobilis & dux belli pro legib̄s, tēplo, ciuitate, patria & ciuibus Iudæorū acer

N ii

Book Three

and prodigies. But the Tetragrammaton did not inform them that the name Tetragrammaton is the name through which a man can effect miracles, by acting as a fellow-worker and as a delegate from God. A clearer account of this is given in Capnion's book *On the Wonder-working Word*.

Next is the ministering spirit of Sadai, Metattron, so called because of the numerical equivalence of the two words.[57] He is said to be a leader and guide on the way. If you so request, I shall give a clearer account of this topic later on.

There follows another name, Sabaoth, in Hebrew *SBAVTh*, which refers to military hosts. The first is the host of completely separate intelligences and angels, the second is the host of orbs that cause motion and the powers that assist by them, and the third is the host of souls that give form to bodies. The word is only found after the Name of God. From this comes the triple statement: "Holy, Holy, Holy *YHVH* of Sabaoth," in Isaiah 6 and other places.

Now you have heard the rules by which the first part of Kabbalah is regulated. It consists totally in the changing round of sacred words, and, since any word may be changed in two ways, we have to admit that there are two separate methods in this part, one of which is the transposition of syllables or words while the other is numerical equality. For example, if I read Isaiah 40: "Who has created these?" and in Kabbalistic fashion transpose the first two words, I will turn them into Elohim (*ALHYM*) and so produce the beginning of Genesis: "God created," in place of "Who has created these?" The sentence would now read: "Who has created these? God has created them."

Similarly, "Ezechiel sat by the river Chobar," could be "Ezechiel dwelt under the influence of a cherub," by transposing the letters of *KVBR* to make *KRVB*. Noah found grace, in Genesis 6, because *NH*, Noah's name, becomes *HN*, which means "grace." All such discoveries occur through transposition because of the primordial confusion of letters in the fiery globe, so that one can take out the letters as if from chaos, pick them from different places and read them forward and backwards. So the first section of the first part is now completed.

Now I have decided, as we begin the second section of the first part, to show you an example of the first part to help you to understand the matter more clearly and to retain it the more firmly in your memory. It is said of Isaac and Rebecca in Genesis 25: "And conceived Rebecca his wife." In this phrase we are helped to divine what it was that Rebecca conceived. The text says: "Rebecca conceived *AShThV*." Consider, learned gentlemen, what this *AShThV* is. By the second method of the first part of Kabbalah, through *Gematria* or numerical measurement, you will find that *AShThV* signifies, through numerical equivalence, *AshVQSh*, which means "fire and straw." Each phrase has letters that add up to 707.[58] So "Rebecca conceived fire and straw," thereby proving the sacred words that Obadiah bears out when he says: "And the house of Jacob will be fire and the house of Esau straw."

It is similar when we hear that a law has been passed in wisdom (*HKMH*). Let us see what is that wisdom which is relevant to the passing of law. There are edicts, interdicts, orders and prohibitions. But the symbol is *HKMH*, which is wisdom in all the commands of God, for when you pronounce the

DE ARTE CABALISTICA

rimus, contra q̃s cū iam Antiochus & illius ois exercitus irruẽrẽt, dedit Iu
das angelo monitus cōmilitonibus suis ceu belli tesserā hoc nobile signũ
מכבי ut se quatuor his literis fortiter in pugna exhortarẽt, promittẽs
cp futurũ esset signũ uictoriẹ dei, q̃d Iudęorũ milites aio lęto i uim magnę
cōsolatiōis acceperũt, & sub eo signaculo ualide pugnãtes interfecerũt in
castris Antiochi uirorũ quatuordecim millia & ingentẽ numerũ elephan
torũ cũ iis q̃ suppositi fuerãt. Quo factũ est ut priceps belli Iudas sic antea
dictus, deinceps ab oĩbus Machabai cognoiarẽt, eo cp hi quatuor chara
cteres syllabice ita sonarẽt. Cũcp tãta eius signi uirtute tot se crederẽt p̃lio
rũ uictores fuisse, admirati sunt tribuni militũ & sapiẽtes in Israel rogãtes
Iudã q̃nã modo tot triũphi sub hoc eis dato signo cõtigissent. & respõdit
Iudas Machabę⁹ in isto signo p̃sentiã esse dei oĩpo-tẽtis ineffabilis. Ostẽ
ditcp illa ỹba Moysi Exod.xv.dicẽtis מי כמוך באלים יהוה
.i. Quis sic ut tu in fortib⁹ tetragrãmate. Hi nãcp quatuor characteres hæc
uerba designãt tanq̃ eorũ initia, ubi Iod significare nome tetragrãmatori
plane dephẽdit, ac esse reuera מכבי diuini nois lxxii.literarũ p æqua
litatẽ numeri memorabile symbolũ. Eo cōmoti q̃ erãt de Iudę exercitu ite
rũ pugnãtes prostrauierũt nō min⁹ triginta q̃ncp millia ut scripta indicãt,
p̃sentia dei mirifice delectati & patria uoce oĩpotẽtẽ dñm tetragrãmato
bñdicẽtes. Hinc ergo itelligitis uerbũ q̃dã totũ, p unã posse literã signifi
cari uel si ea demũ stet singulariter, uel uerbũ q̃dlibet aliud collectiue p̃si
ciat. Sicut tota dictio ferẽ integrã pariter orõnem notare, ut Danielis v.
מנא תקל פרסין .i. Numerauit, põderatũ est, diuisum est. Quæ
q̃dẽ hoc illi Nabũchadnezer rep̃sentarũt. Numerauit deus regnũ tuũ &
cõsummauit illud. Põderatũ est i statera & inuentũ est deficies. Diuisũ est
regnũ tuũ & datũ est Medis & Persis. Aut igit una dictio p lr̃as dispersa
plures efficit, aut multę dictiões p certas earꝫ lr̃as retract̃ę una colligit, hic
ex multis unũ & ex uno multa. Quod ne utiq̃ mirũ esse ostẽdit duorũ mo
nosyllaborũ frequẽs usus ut aiũt Maronẽ scripsisse i carminib⁹. Est & nõ
cũcti monosyllaba nota frequẽtãt, iis dẽptis nihil est hoĩm q̃d sermo uolu
tet, ergo tota ferme oĩm hoĩm colloq̃a, est & nõ, significãt. Q̃obrẽ in hac
arte q̃s dubitare uelit una litera dictionẽ itegrã, & una dictiõe orõnem ex
tẽlam, atcp uersa uice sib̃ter una orõne dictionẽ aliquã electã & intẽtatã no
tari posse. Vnde oritur occulta quædã & admirabilis epistolarũ techno
logia, quam sæpe imitatus ego, in grauibus periculis & summo rerum dis
crimine lingua germanica, per epistolam scripsi quæ a latino uiro in Thu
scia uel Ethruria cognosci desyderabã, & cõuerso more scripsi latine q̃d
alemanũ hoĩem latinitatis imperitũ scire uolui. Accipiatis hoc uelim qcq̃d
tñ illud est grato aĩo & sensibus imis res est nõ parua diligẽter reponatis.

On the Art of Kabbalah

four letters of that word, with the letters all written out in full — Heth, Kaph, Mem, He — you get from them the number 613, which is the number of the commands of God, which our sages call *Tharyag*.[59]

To sum up this first kind of speculation. Firstly it is worth remembering that the characters, elements and letters had been in confusion and were capable of several different readings. Secondly, that they were not distinguished by any accents or points. Thirdly, that each of the basic letters of the alphabet signifies a certain number, even the five final letters which were invented by Ezra the sage long afterwards, at the same time as the vowel points. The primitive alphabet had only 22 letters, and in the beginning all Scripture was written in these letters alone. These are the letters that the Kabbalists, up to the present day, position and displace in accordance with each Kabbalist's favored contemplation. Finally, we must emphasize this universally applicable limit: although it is the work of a Kabbalist precisely to read one thing but understand it in a different way, nevertheless he will keep to the inviolable rule that good must be understood as good and bad as bad, lest he apply black to white or day to night.

MARRANUS: This kind of art, I reckon, is just like calling someone "Dorotheus" instead of "Theodorus" or "Demonicus" instead of "Nicodemus" or "Philodemus" instead of "Demophilus." As the Greeks often say: "body-loving and loving-body."

SIMON: Certainly some of what you say squares. But you will soon run out of examples to enumerate because of the poverty of other languages. Compared to Hebrew, the fount of all languages, they are poor, and so impatient of their shortcomings that they even adopt the idioms of other nations. They do not have a full complement, nor do they allow the useful composition of new words. Hence this art can only with great difficulty be translated into the speech of other nations. If I did not know you to be equally skilled in Hebrew, I would have gone over these little hints on Kabbalah with you to no avail. I shall now continue my discussion of them.

Let us hurry on to the second part of this instruction, the part called Notariacon. This is the convention, passed on in secret from one Kabbalist to another, by which single letters not combined into syllables designate certain words. Notaries and actuaries do the same, and at one time leaders in war used to write secret coded messages with single letters positioned at random. The grammarian Probus, so Aulus Gellius writes, wrote a carefully composed work on the hidden significance of the letters. The method perhaps involves nothing very different from individuals stipulating that among them the letter yod, because of its shape as an indivisible dot, should denote the ineffable tetragram that we commonly interpret as "Lord."

Similarly, because of the three *Summits* in the ten numerations which are one and the same *Diadem*, one usually indicates the Name itself by three dots. For Kabbalists say that "for this mystery they write the Name with three yods, as you see." Here the unique four letter word is written with three single letters, a practice established in everyday use.

In the days of Antiochus Eupator, there was once a man called Judas, son of Mattathias. He was a noble warrior and leader in war who fought fiercely

LIBER TERTIVS

Vsu aut nobis ueniunt si rite operemur huiusce generis literæ quatrifariã aut em̃ sumũtur ab initio uerbi ad aliquid aliud significandũ, ut in exorsu Geneseos יוֹם הַשִּׁשִּׁי וַיְכֻלּוּ הַשָּׁמַיִם .i. Dies sextus & p̃fecti sunt cœli, ecce Tetragrammaton, aut a fine cuiuscunq̃, ut psalmo primo אָמֵן לֹא כֵן הָרְשָׁעִים q̃ transpositæ faciunt אָמֵן .i. Amen. Hoc nãq̃ intelligi uoluit. Non sic impii, qm̃ non dicent amen, iccirco in Gehennam mittentur, aut sunt q̃ se offerant singillatim quælibet p̃ integrã dictionem una comp̃hensæ, ut psalmo tertio Multi insurgũt aduersum me. Qui sunt isti multi? Respondent Cabalistæ רַבִּים sũt Romani. Babyloniũ. Iones. Medi, aut postremũ non relatiue ad aliorũ uerborũ constitutionẽ destinã tur, sed earũ quælibet secundũ suæ proprietatis significationẽ sumitur, ut q̃n duorũ seculorum mentio fit, futurũ seculũ Iod litera significat, & l̃ra he seculum p̃sens, uidelicet istum mundum Genesis ii. Istæ sunt g̃nationes cœli & terrẹ בְּהִבָּרְאָם .i. in he creauit ea. Nimirũ extrema scilicet hęc de literis consyderatio ad substantiã characteris attinet q̃ad se, at nequaq̃ ad accidẽtalẽ relationem uti supiores tres, q̃tum ad aliud. Sic em̃ iam hac destinatione significant uel iuxta grammaticã institutionẽ res ipsas, positi one prima oblatas, uel numeros arithmetica disciplina ordinatos, uel non nullas rationes uerbis magistrorũ nostrorũ applicatas, uel deniq̃ omnẽ creaturã a prima causa profectã, & rursus in prima causam reducibilẽ. De primitiua positione literarũ ita monstrant, q̃ Aleph sit uia seu institutio, Vnde dicit Iob xxxiiii. Docebo. i. instituã te sapientiã. Beth domus. Psalmo xxiii. Habitabo in domo d̃ni. Gimel retributio. Psalmo cxvi. Quia d̃ns retri buit tibi. Daleth ostium, fores uel ianua. Gen̄. xix. Et prope erant ut fr̃ge rent ostium. He ecce. Gen̄. xlvii. Ecce uobis semina. Vau uñcñus retortus. Exodi xxvi. Quarũ erunt capita aurea. Sdain arma. iii. Regũ xxii. Et arma lauerunt iuxta uerbum d̃ni. Heth terror. Iob vii. Terrebis me p̃ somnia. Teth declinatio, per metathesim thet. Prouerb. iiii. Ne declines ad dexterã & ad sinistram. Iod confessio laudis, Genesis xlix. Laudabunt te fratres tui. Caph uola, Ecclesiastis iiii. Melius uola plena requie. Lamed doctrina. Psal mo cxliii. Doce me facere uoluntatẽ tuã. Mem aquæ, Isaiæ lv. Ões sitiẽtes uenite ad aquas. Nun filiatio, Isaiæ xiiii. Filiũ & nepotẽ. Samech apposito, Deuteronomii xxxiiii. Quia imposuit, hoc est apposuit, Moyses manũ suas sup̃ eum. Ain oculus, Exodi xxi. Oculũ pro oculo. Pe os, Exodi iiii. Quis po suit os homini, Tzade latera, Exodi xxv. Sex calami egredietur de lateribꝰ eius. Kuph reuolutio uel circuitus, Exodi xxxiiii. Redeũte anni t̃pe. I. circui tũ anni. Res egestas, Prouerb. x. Pauor pauperũ egestas eorũ, alii tñ hære ditatem iterpretãtur. Sin dens. Iob quarto. Et dentes catulorũ cõtriti sunt. Thau signũ, Ezechielis nono. Signa Thau sup̃ frõtes uirorum. Ista est lite

N iii

Book Three

for the laws, the temple, the state and nation and the citizens of the Jews. Against the Jews came Antiochus and all his army. Judas, on the advice of an angel, gave his fellow soldiers as watchword for the war the fine sign *MKBY*. By these four letters they were to make themselves brave in battle. He promised it would be a sign of the victory of God. The soldiers of the Jews took it with joyful heart for it had great power of consolation, and fighting bravely under that banner, killed fourteen thousand men and a huge number of elephants with their riders in the camps of Antiochus. So the general, whose name had been Judas, was henceforth called Maccabeus by all, that being the sound made by these four characters when pronounced in syllabic form.

The military tribunes and sages of Israel believed that they had been victorious in many battles through the great power of that sign, and in amazement asked Judas how such a triumph had come about under the sign he had given them. And Judas the Maccabee replied that in that sign is the presence of the omnipotent, ineffable God. He pointed them to the words of Moses in Exodus 15, where he says: "Who is like you among the mighty, *YHVH*?" These four letters indicate these words like initials. Here yod clearly signifies openly the Name of the Tetragrammaton, while *MKBY* is in fact a memorable symbol of the divine name of 72 letters, because of their numerical equivalence.[60] Excited by this information, the men of Judas' army fought again and slew not fewer than thirty-five-thousand, as Scripture shows. They were wonderfully pleased that the presence of God was with them and blessed the omnipotent Lord of the Tetragram with their ancestral words.

From this you understand that the whole of a word may be signified by a single letter, either by the letter standing on its own, or by the letter in conjunction with other letters forming a new word.

In the same way, a complete word is said to denote a whole speech. So, in Daniel 5: "He has numbered; it has been weighted; it has been divided." This meant for Nebuchadnezzar: "God has numbered your kingdom and brought it to an end; it has been weighed in the balance and found wanting; your kingdom has been divided and given to the Medes and Persians."

So one word with the letters dispersed makes many words or many words with certain letters picked out make one complete word. Hence one is produced from many and many from one.

Our frequent use of two monosyllables shows that this is not so remarkable; they say that Virgil wrote this in his verse. "Yes" and "no" are monosyllabic words common to everyone. With these removed, human conversation could not keep going; therefore almost all human discourse is encapsulated in "yes" and "no." So no one should doubt that a complete word may be contained in one letter or a sentence in one word or that, conversely, a particular word may be stretched out and denoted by a sentence.

From this comes the wonderful secret science of letters that I have often used when in grave danger and extreme difficulties. I wrote a letter in German words that I wanted to be understood by a Latin man in Etruria, and in the opposite fashion I have written in Latin something that I wanted a German who did not speak Latin to know.

DE ARTE CABALISTICA

rarum grammatica expositio, quomodo solet rebus qbuslibet noia imponere uel primitiua uel deriuata. Nihil ut arbitror ab altiore speculatioē alienum si quis figuratæ locutionis studiosus extiterit. Tum Philolaus. Nos inquit oportet (ut coniicio) senes elementarios fore, qbus denuo ferula sit opus. Nam interim multo studio ad alphabetū redacti sumus. Et Marranus. Certe repuerascimus, hæc est Philolae palingenesia tua illa Pythagorica. Quibus Simon. Nolite, inquit, respuere, magna profecto res est et digna philosophis, si Platoni uestro creditis, minimeq ridicula, ut in Cratylo Socrati uisum erat, cognoscere literas, non ēm habemus quicq inqt illo melius, q̄ de ueritate primorum noim iudicemus. ἐπειδὴ συλλαβοῦστε καὶ γράμμασιν ἡμιμοῦσης τῶν χεῦ οὐ(α τ οὐσίας, ὀρθότατόν ἔςι διελόθη τα σοιχεία πρῶτον. q̄n quidem syllabis & literis imitatio sit essentiæ rectissimū est discernere elementa primū. Vnde puto dicta sunt elementa quasi hylementa hoc est materialia ex qbus minimis maxima fiunt, ut est illud Hesiodi. Si paruum paruo supaddas & simul omne cōponas. magnus fors tandē fiet aceruus. Prouehere Simō, Phil. laus ait, oia ēm uere dicis, nos hoc sermōe cū tua uenia iocati simus. Tum ille. Ad disciplinæ arithmeticæ numeros trāsibo

K q literis hebraicis designant. Nec ēm est ulla in orbis terrarū spacio alia lingua cuius literæ q̄slibet numeros tam p̄secte ostendant. Conati sunt tñ nouicii græcorū Iudæos imitari ut & similiter alphabeto suo numeros exponerēt. Sed erat necesse duas sibi figuras intercalare, tam sexti q̄ nonagesimi, q̄ quidem figuræ literaliter ex ordine alphabeti non sunt. Schemata ēm duo hæc. ϛ. ϟ. figmenta sunt hoim nouorum imitādi studio ductorū cui rei testes Homericos libros citamus. Sane Romani paucos numeros literis explicant, de qua re Priscianū Cæsariēsem legistis olim ad Symmachū de numeris, ponderibus & mensuris scribentē. Faciamus itaq numerorum quatuor gradus, q̄rum primus est digitorū, secundus denariorū, tertius cētenariorū, quartus millenariorū. Primus gradus alphabeti figuris notatur ab Aleph ad Teth. Suntq signacula nouem, singillatim numeros nouem referentia, ut אב גד הו זחט i. unum. duo. tria. quatuor. quinq. sex. septem. octo. nouem. Secudus denariorū ordo, nouē ēq continet alphabeti figuras יכ לם נס עפצ i. Decē. uiginti. triginta. quadraginta. quinquaginta. sexaginta. septuaginta. octoginta. nonaginta. Tertius gradus centenariorum habet similiter nouem characteres. קרשתתרסםןץ i. Centum ducenta, trecenta, quadringenta, quingenta, sexingenta. Septingenta. octingenta. noningenta. Quartus gradus est millenariorum, in quo reuertendū est ad priorum numerorū figuras; quanq esse debent statura grandiores ita ut dicatur magnū Aleph, quasi aleph latum & pronunciatur p patha secundū a Italicū. Sic beth magnum q̄d duo millia significat. Inde usq ad nouem millia, demum Iod magnum decē millia, quo in ordine q̄dam pro statura solent figuras apicibus notare

Deinceps

314

On the Art of Kabbalah

Please accept this, whatever its value, and appreciate it, for it is not to be considered a small matter. Store it away carefully in the inner recesses of your thoughts.

Letters of this kind become useful to us in four ways if we use them in the right fashion. They may be taken from the beginning of each word to mean something else, as in the beginning of Genesis: "The sixth day, and the heavens were finished." Here you find the Tetragrammaton.[61] Or they may be taken from the end of each word, as in Psalm 1: "Not thus the wicked," in which the final letters transposed make *AMN*, meaning Amen. This means that the wicked will be sent to Hell for refusing to say "Amen." Or there are the letters presented singly, but forming a complete word when put together, as in Psalm 3: "Many rise up against me." Who are these many? The Kabbalists reply that the *RBYM*, meaning "many," are the Romans, the Babylonians, the Ionians and the Medes. Or, finally, there are letters not considered significant relative to the construction of other words but only in so far as they designate a property of their own. So, when two ages are mentioned, the letter *Y* signifies the future age and the letter *H* signifies the present age, that is, this world. So, in Genesis 2: "These are the generations of the heavens and of the earth. In *H* he created them."

This last speculation from letters concerns the substance of the letter with regard to itself and not its accidental relations to another letter as in the three former methods. Thus, in this method they signify either the things exhibited in their original positions in accordance with grammatical rules, or their numbers set in order by arithmetical rules, or other reasonings applied to the words of our teachers, or lastly all creation that began from the first cause and is reducible again to the first cause.

So, on the original position of the letters, they show that aleph is the Way or Rule (Job 33: "I will teach," i.e. "I shall instruct you in wisdom"); beth is the house (Psalm 23: "I shall live in the house of the Lord"); gimel is retribution (Psalm 116: "Because the Lord has given you retribution"); daled is a door or entrance (Genesis 19: "And they were near to break the door"); he is Behold (Genesis 47: "Behold, your seed"); vav is a bent hook (Exodus 26: "Their hooks will be golden"); zain is weapons (3 Kings 22: "And they washed their weapons in accordance with the word of the Lord"); heth is terror (Job 7: "You will frighten me through dreams"); teth is a slipping down, by transposition with thet (Proverbs 4: "Do not slip down to right or left"); yod is a confession of praise (Genesis 49: "Your brothers will praise you"); kaph is the palm of a hand (Ecclesiastes: "Better is a handful of quietude"); lamed is teaching (Psalm 143: "Teach me to do your will"); mem is water (Isaiah 55: "All you who are thirsty come to the waters"); nun is sonship (Isaiah 14: "Son and posterity"); samakh is placing (Deuteronomy 34: "Because Moses placed his hands on, sc. to him"); ain is eye (Exodus 21: "Eye for eye"); pe is mouth (Exodus 4: "Who gave man a mouth"); sade is sides (Exodus 25: "Six reeds will come out of its sides"); quph is a turning or circuit (Exodus 34: "With the time of the year returning," i.e. "with the circuit of the year"); resh is neediness (Proverbs 10: "The fear of the poor is their neediness," or, according to others, "their inheritance"); shin is tooth (Job 4: "And the teeth of dogs are worn down"); thau is a sign (Ezechiel 9: "The signs of thau on the foreheads of men").

LIBER TERTIVS

Deinceps non figuris utuntur, sed uerbis רִבּוֹ רְבָבוֹתִים i. mille mil
lia, bis mille millia, & reliqua. Viam istā alphabeti numerorū, maximoꝑe
sunt amplexi Cabalistæ, q̃ dicūt annorū duo millia, initiū p̃cessisse, anteq̃
hic mūdus fieret. Eo q̃ ante רֵאשִׁית i. initiū scriptura ponit Beth ma
gnum dicens בְּרֵאשִׁית. Ita sapientes nostri exponunt eum locū Pro
uerbiorum viii. Dn̄s possedit me initio uiarum suarū anteq̃ quicq̃ faceret
ex tunc. Quicquid uero millia transgreditur, infiniti loco habet. Nam finis
numerorū in sacris millia sunt, ut cum uellet Dauid infinitatem p̃dii osten
dere psalmo Cxix. dixit Bonum mihi lex oris tui sup̃ millia auri & argenti
hoc est sine numero. Tertiam nunc speciē substantiæ literarū breuissimē
recenseamus, quæ ad aliquas magistrorum nostrorum intentiones referūt, ut
aleph beth illis significat prudētia, et gimel daleth remuneratione paupū,
et mem. i. Meamar uidelicet sermonē aptum & sermonē occultū, & sic de
aliis, q̃ paulo inferius recitabimus Thalmudicis tn̄ usu frequētiora. Quar
ta earum literarū species consistit in rebus conditis atq̃ creatis oībus, ma
xime qdem utilis Cabalæ studiosis, q̃ facilius creaturas reuocare in creato.
rem possint, id quippe qd illius disciplinæ maximū est & singulare studiū.
Literas igitur in suum quasq̃ ordinē locabo ut elementa singula singulari
ter cognoscatis, atq̃ sic incipiam. Ab aleph usq̃ ad Iod ordines siue cho
ri angelorū significant q̃s intelligentias separatas & formas liberales īcor
poreas & insensibiles philosophi appellant, progressas & deriuatas a uir
tute dei q̃ formam non habet neq̃ imaginē neq̃ similitudinē. Dixit enim
Isaiæ xl. Cui assimilauistis me & adæquabor. Et paulo ante. Cui ergo simi
lem fecistis deum:̃ aut quā imagine disponetis ei:̃ Cęterū maī o istā no
minatur עוֹלָם הַמַּלְאָכִים i. seculum angelorū siue mūdus an
gelicus. Deinde a litera Caph ad literā zade cœlorū ordines designantur
q̃ dei creatoris uirtute donati ab angelorū influxu dispensant̃, & uocatur
עוֹלָם הַגַּלְגַּלִים i. seculum orbiū seu sphærarū. Porro a zade ad
thau interueniunt quatuor elemēta cum suis formis & simul oīa mista tā
uiuentia q̃ non uiuentia q̃ a dei uirtute pendēt q̃bus influit esse & uiuere,
ut est in Isaia. Creans cœlos & extendens eos, firmans terrā & q̃ germināt
ex ea, dans flatum populo q̃ est sup eam, & spiritū calcantibus eam seu am
bulantibus in ea. Dirigunt aūt ab in̄ fluentiis angelorū & sphærarū atq̃
totum id uocatur עוֹלָם הַיְסוֹדוֹת i. seculū elemētorū, & in eo est
homo q̃ appellatur עוֹלָם קָטָן i. seculum paruū, qd græci dicunt
μικρόκοσμος hoc est minor mundus, seu rectius paruus mundus. Nam in ho
mine ipso relucent oīm creatuẓarū proprietates summarū & infimarum,
Hæc forte utilius memoria repetemus si q̃rum nam literæ singulæ phibe
antur esse symbola demonstrabimus, rem sane iucundā, & antiq̃ssimis au
toribus celebratā, ne sint futuri aliq̃n qui hāc artem ut tenuem ac ieiunā

N iiii

316

Book Three

This is the grammatical exposition of the letters by which they give names, whether primary or derived, to things of all kinds. Nothing, in my view, cannot become the subject of the higher speculation, so long as there is someone around who is keen on questions of figurative speech!

PHILOLAUS: I reckon we shall have to become schoolchildren under the rule again in our old age. For our efforts have brought us back to the alphabet!

MARRANUS: We have returned to our boyhood. Philolaus, this is your Pythagorean rebirth!

SIMON: Do not scorn it. It really is an important matter and worthy of philosophers, if you believe your Plato. For he, like Socrates in the *Cratylus*, thought it not at all foolish to understand the letters, saying: "We have no better means than that for judging the truth of the primal names. Whenever we imitate essence with syllables and letters, it is right first to pick out the basic elements." It is from this, I think, that the elements are so named, being the *hylementa* in Greek, or the materials from which, despite their small size, big things come. As Hesiod says: "If you add small to small and put it all together, it may in the end become a big heap."

PHILOLAUS: Go on, Simon. You are quite right. Please excuse our flippancy.

SIMON: I shall pass on to the arithmetical numbers, which in Hebrew are designated by the letters.

There is no other language in the world whose letters so perfectly show any number. Novices among the Greeks tried to imitate the Jews and get numbers from the alphabet in the same way, but they had to intercalate two figures, for 6, and for 90, even though these figures were not literally derived from the alphabet. These two characters were made up by newcomers in their eagerness to imitate. We cite the Homeric books as proof of this. As for the Romans, they denote few numbers by means of letters. On this matter you will have read Priscian of Caesarea when he wrote to Symmachus about numbers, weights and measures.

Let us divide the numbers into four grades. The first is the single digit, the second is the tens, the third the hundreds and the fourth the thousands.

The first grade is denoted by the figures of the alphabet from aleph to teth. There are nine signs, referring to nine numbers. *A, B, G, D, H, V, Z, H, T* making one, two, three, four, five, six, seven, eight, nine.

The second order is that of tens. It contains also nine figures of the alphabet. *Y, K, L, M, N, S, ', P, S* are ten, twenty, thirty, forty, fifty, sixty, seventy, eighty and ninety.

The third grade, that of hundreds, also has nine characters: *Q, R, Sh, Th,* Final *Kh,* Final *M,* Final *N,* Final *P,* Final *S*. They are one-hundred, two-hundred, three-hundred, four-hundred, five-hundred, six-hundred, seven-hundred, eight-hundred and nine-hundred.

The fourth grade is the thousands. In this we must revert to the figures of the former numbers, although they should be written bigger. Thus it is called "big aleph" (like a wide aleph, it is pronounced with the *patakh*[62] like the Italian "a"). Similarly, "big beth" signifies two-thousand. And so on to nine

DE ARTE CABALISTICA

cauillentur. Est igitur Aleph nota summarū & altissimarū rerū, q̃ primo effluxu diuinæ bonitatis subsistunt, ut puta angeli qui dicuntur חיות הקדש haioth.i.animalia sanctuarii, uel potius uitę absq̃ medio subter deum. Hi angeli uirtute dei, proxime inferiores purgant illuminant & pficiunt, q̃ comuni uocabulo, illorū dicit̃ influentia. Beth secunda litera secundum significat ab ipso deo gradum angelorum, qui dicuntur אופנים Ophanim.i.formę seu rotæ, ac secundo loco deriuant a dei uirtute p intelligentiam priorem, & ipsi a deo quoq̃ inferioribus influunt. Dixere simul etiam sapientes q̃ Beth sit nota sapiētiæ. Gimel repsentat ex essentiis superioribus angelos q̃ dicuntur אראלים Aralim.i.angeli magni fortes & robusti, q̃ descendunt ordine tertio a diuinæ maiestatis bonitate, illuminanturq̃ uirtute dei p intelligentiam secundā, & ipsi pariter inferioribus influunt. Daleth symbolum est emanationis quartæ apud superos eorum q̃ dicuntur חשמלים Hasmallim, & in uirtute dei p medium intelligentiæ tertiæ influuntur, & illa uirtute inferioribus influnt. He l'ra designat entia supiora, quintæ ab ipso deo emanatiõis q̃ sunt שרפים .i. Seraphim, & influuntur de uirtute dei p medium intelligentię quartæ, ac eadem uirtute inferiorib9 influ ūt. Vau notat essentiā supnorum emanationis sextæ, q̃ dicuntur מלאכים Mallachim.i.angeli, & influuntur de uirtute dei p medium intelligentiæ quintæ, ac eadē uirtute inferiorib9 influūt. Zain signacu lū est spirituū beatorū supiorum emanatiõis septimæ q̃ noiantur אלהים Elohim.i.dii, & influunt de dei uirtute p sexti ordinis angelos, ac eadē uirtute inferioribus influunt. Heth signū est superorum emanationis octauę, & sunt angeli q̃ uocatur בני אלהים Bne Elohim.i.filii deorū, de uirtute El p angelos septimi ordinis infussi, ac eadem dei uirtute inferioribus influentes. Teth nota est angelorū emanationis nonæ, q̃ uocantur כרובים Cherubim, & influūt de uirtute dei p mediū intelligentiæ octaui ordinis, & eadē uirtute inferioribus influūt. Iod litera decima significat essentiā intelligentiarū emanatiõis decimę, appellantur autē אישים Issim nobiles & patricii, suntq̃ oībus hierarchiis inferiores, & dei uirtute illustrātur p nonum chorū, eadēq̃ uirtute influūt filiis hoīm cognitionē & scientia rerū mirificāq̃ industriā. Vnde dicītur q̃ tali sunt p̃diti facultate filii איש .i. hoīes nobilis intelligentiæ, de qb9 Psalmo xlix. Quicq̃ terrigenæ & filii hoīm, q̃d proprie sic legitur, tam filii plebei q̃ filii patricii, quasi diceretur, tam agrestes q̃ nobiles. Eam denoīationem ab hoc intelligentiarū ordine sumimus nos ipsi. Est eni in nobis intellectus agens summa pars aīæ quā Aristoteles νοῦν hoc est mente appellat, q̃ nobis sola deforis aduenit. Inde proceꝑ dūt uisiões, pphetice ac oīa magna & sancta, uocatur autē שכל הפעל q̃ finit mundus angelicus. Sequur Caph, ea litera designat primū mobile ab ipso El Sadai tanq̃

a causa

thousand, and finally "big yod," which is ten-thousand. Once in this grade some people, instead of changing the size, mark the tops of the letter. After this they do not use letters but words. "A multitude of multitudes" meaning a "thousand thousands," "two-thousand thousands" and so on.

The Kabbalists have wholly embraced this alphabetical numerical mode. They say that two-thousand years preceded the beginning when this world was created. This is because before the word *RAShYTh*, meaning "beginning," Scripture places a "big beth," reading *BRAShYTh*. In a similar fashion our sages expound the place in Proverbs 8: "The Lord possessed me in the beginning of his ways before the most ancient of his works."

Anything more than thousands is considered infinity. The highest number in scripture is in thousands. When David wanted to indicate infinite preciousness in Psalm 119, he said: "The Law of your mouth is better for me than thousands of gold and silver," meaning "without number."

Let us now briefly consider the third aspect of the substance of letters, when they are put to our teachers' particular uses. According to this, *AB* signifies prudence, *GD* signifies the reward of the poor, and *M*, meaning "saying," signifies open and secret speech. Similarly with the other examples that we will go over soon below, although these are more commonly used by Talmudists.

The fourth type of letters exists in created things and in all creation. It is very useful to those who study Kabbalah, for they are enabled by it the more easily to bring creatures to the Creator, which is the most important, and the particular aim of their discipline.

I will put the letters into order for you to understand the separate elements one by one. I begin:

From aleph to yod the ranks or bands of angels are signified, which philosophers call separate intelligences and incorporeal and insensible, free forms. They proceed from and are derived from the power of God who has neither form nor image nor likeness. He said in Isaiah 40: "To whom will you compare me and to what shall I be like?" and a little earlier: "To whom, then, have you likened God? Or what image will you attribute to him?" This abode is called the "world of the angels" or the "angelic world."

Then the letters from kaph to sade are designated the ranks of the heavens. They have been given the powers of God the Creator, and are regulated by the angels' influence. This place is called the "world of wheels" or "spheres."

From sade to thau come the four elements with their forms and all the things mixed from those elements, both living and not-living. They rely on the power of God. He has influenced their being and their living. As it says in Isaiah: "Creating the heavens and stretching them out, making firm the earth and whatever springs from it, giving breath to the people who are on it and spirit to those who walk or trample upon it." They are directed by the influence of the angels and the spheres. The whole of this is called the "world of the elements." In it is man, who is called the "small world" or, in Greek, the *Mikrokosmos*, meaning "lesser" or "small world." For in man all the properties of all the creatures, both high and low, shine forth.

Perhaps we should remember these better if we showed what each letter is said to symbolize. It is a pleasant task, frequently undertaken by the ancient authors, and worth doing to forestall those who would cavil at this art as feeble and jejune.

LIBER TERTIVS LXXI.

a causa prima imediate licet per rationalis uitæ spiritū comunicatiue modum q est angelus Metattron, & dicitur intellectus agens mundi sensibilis p penetrationē formarū inferioribus oībus uiā pbens, quare influit uirtute diuina in omne qd est mobile. Chaph finalis significat girum stellarū fixarū, q sphęra octaua noiatur quantū ad nos, sed qad supiora est orbis secundus in duodecim zodiaci signa diuisus, q̄ nos מזלות appellamus, influiturq̄ de uirtute dei p mediū intelligentiæ ipsius caph, similiterq̄ inferiorib⁹ influit. Lamed est signū primę sphærę planetarū & dicuntur לכת quasi ambulones q̄s latini errones appellant instar gręcorum q ob id eos asserunt esse πλανῆτες. Diciturq̄ orbis septimus Saturno attribut quę שבתאי nūcupamus, influit & influitur. Mem aptum notat sphæram Iouis q a nobis צדק noiatur, & a uirtute dei p mediū intelligentię supioris influitur, eadēq̄ uirtute inferiorib⁹ influit. Mem clausum est symbolū sphærę Martis quę appellamus מאדים orbis quinti, & uirtute dei creatoris influitur p angelū proxime supiorę, & eadē uirtute inferioribus influit. Nun significat luminare maius, qd uocatur שמש i. Sol, & eius sphæra dicitur orbis חמה influiturq̄ a deo p mediū intelligētię sextę, qua & influit in inferiora. Nun finale sphærā indicat Veneris, q̄ a nobis uocat נוגה Noga, & dei uirtute constat, influitq̄ mediāte intelligentia septima. Samech est symbolū cancellarii q dicit כוכב Cochab & latine Mercurius, influitur aūt uirtute dei a supioribus, eadēq̄ uirtute inferiorib⁹ influit. Ain est nota sphęrę Lunę q a nobis dicit ירח lareah & apparet quasi oculus sinister mundi. Estq̄ inter astrifera ultim⁹ orbiū & propter albedinem qnq̄ noiatur לבנה Cūcta hæc facultati astrologicę cōmittim⁹. Pe significat aīam intellectualę, singularę & ūniuersalę, & dirigitur ab intelligentiis separatis qbus infunditur a deo tā in sphæris q̄ in stellis & in oībus aīatis supioribus & inferioribus sphærarū & elementorum. Phe finale denotat spiritus aīales q̄ diriguntur ab intelligentiis supioribus de uirtute atq̄ mandato dei. Zade symbolizat materia tam cœlorū q̄ est intelligibilis q̄ elementorū q̄ est sensibilis oīumq̄ mistorū. Diriguntur aūt uirtute diuina p intelligentias separatas, & p formas proprias. Zade finale monstrat elementorū formas q̄ sunt ignis aer aqua terra. Et regitur diuina uirtute p angelos q dicunt אישים Issim, & uirtute cœlorū, & uirtute materię primę q̄ est fons & origo cūctorū elementorū. Kuph est symbolū inaīatorum & mineraliū & eorū q̄ dicuntur elementata & mista Diriguntur aūt uirtute diuina p sphæras cœlestes & intelligētias sepātas q̄ uocant אישים issim. Et influunt inferioribus in regione quatuor elementorū. Res significat oīa uegetātia fructus & fruges ac terręnascentia influunturq̄ uirtute dei a corpibus cœlestibus & intelligentiis sepatis nomine אישים iteq̄ complexionibus elementorū. Sin designat oīa sensitiua tam reptilia terrę ac progressiua q̄ aquarum pisces & aeris uolucreī

320

Book Three

Aleph is a sign of the highest things, which exist under the emanation of the divine goodness. Such are the angels who are called *Hayoth hakodesh*, meaning "living beings of the sanctuary," or, rather, "lives directly under God." By God's power these angels purify, illumine and complete those next below them—this is, in common parlance, their influence.

Beth, the second letter, signifies the grade of angels second from God. They are called *Ophanim*, that is, "forms" or "wheels." They lie in the second place and are derived from the power of God through the earlier intelligence. They also have an influence derived from God on the lower grades. The sages have also said that beth is the mark of wisdom.

Gimel represents angels out of the higher essences. They are called *Aralim*, meaning "great, strong angels." They lie further down in the third rank from the goodness of the divine majesty and are illuminated by the power of God through the second intelligence. They similiarly influence the lower grades.

Daled is a symbol of the fourth emanation among the higher beings, those called *Hasmalim*. They are influenced in the power of God through the medium of the third intelligence and they influence the lower grades by that power.

The letter "he" designates the higher beings of the fifth emanation from God. They are the *Seraphim*, which, influenced by the power of God through the medium of the fourth intelligence, influence the lower grades, through that same power.

Vav denotes the essence of the higher beings of the sixth emanation. They are called *Malakhim* or "angels" and, influenced by the power of God through the medium of the fifth intelligence, they influence the lower grades, by that same power. Zain is a symbol of the blessed higher spirits of the seventh emanation. They are called *Elohim* or "gods." They are influenced by the power of God through the angels of the sixth rank and they influence the lower grades by the same power.

Heth is a sign of the higher beings of the eighth emanation. They are the angels called *Ben Elohim* or "Sons of gods." They are full of the power of *El* through the angels of the seventh order, and they influence the lower grades by the same power of God.

Teth is a mark of the angels of the ninth emanation. They are called *Cherubim* and are influenced by the power of God through the medium of the intelligence of the eighth rank, and they influence the lower grades by the same power.

Yod, the tenth letter, signifies the essence of the intelligences of the tenth emanation. They are called *Ishim*, or "Nobles," and are the lowest of all the hierarchies. They are illuminated by the power of God through the ninth band, and, by the same power, influence understanding, knowledge and miraculous powers among the sons of man. Those endowed with such an ability are called sons of *AYSh* or "Men of noble intelligence," as it says in Psalm 49: "Those born on earth and the sons of men," which is properly read as: "Both the sons of the people and the sons of the nobles," i.e. "both the common men and the nobles." We have ourselves taken the name from this rank of the intelligences, for we have in us active understanding, which is the highest part of the soul, called by Aristotle "mind," and which is the only part

DE ARTE CABALISTICA

simul & q̃cūcq̃ irrationalia uitalem motū habentia q̃ uirtute dei regunt̄ a
corpibus cœlestibus & intelligentiis quas uocam̃ אישים & cõplexio
nibus elemētorū. Thau est symbolū hois & naturę humanę q̃ est pfectio
& finis oim creaturarū, dirigiturq̃ a deo cõplexionibus ac qualitatibus
elemẽtorū iuxta influentias cœlorū & p officia peculiaria intelligentiarz
separatarū אישים lissim, qui sunt angelicę cõditionis, & sicut sunt finis
ac consummatio in mundo angelorū. ita est homo finis & pfectio creatura
rū in mundo elemētorū q̃n potius in mūdo uniuersorū, cõstitutus est eni
ex duobus mundis, sicut scriptū est. Formauit dñs deus hoiem de limo ter
ræ, & spirauit in facie eius spiraculū uitę. Tractant hæc uberius a nostris
maioribus q̃rū posteris nobis clare apparet erga sacras literas ardẽtissm̃ꝰ
amor q̃ de oibus etiã minutissimis rõnem reddere studuerūt. Verbi causa
De aleph scriptū est in lib. הבהיר .i. de Cādore, ubi sedit Rabi Amo
rai & disputauit, quare aleph ponatur in capite alphabetiꝯ & respõdet, q̃a
fuit ante oia q̃netia ante legē, q̃d de Rabi Rahumai eius libri autore cõme
morat Mnahem Racanat in distinctiõe geneseos prima. Iterū aūt q̃obrem
proxime sequatur Beth, certe q̃a fuit le gis initiū. Et qua re Gimel nõ sit
noiatū gidel, cū i sacris lr̃is, p̃po nat גדל & seq̃tur גמל Gen.xxi.
ubi scribitur ויגדל הילד ויגמל Talia & his paria scrutari cer
te nõ sunt dedignati sapiētes uiri. Quanq̃ sunt etiã aliq̃ numero q̃ breuita
tis causa, reddere aliq̃rū rõnes ptergressi, tn̄ scripserẽ q̃ simpliciter ad rē
attinēt, q̃m sem̃p ad sublimiora oi diligētia & studio conati sunt propera
re, ut rabi Iacob Cohen i lib. cui titulꝰ est פירוש השם הקדוש
.i. expositio nois sancti. Nã, de alphabeto strictim sic dicit, Aleph אויר
Beth חיים Gimel שלום Daleth חכמה He האיה Vau
שמיעה Zain ריחה Heth שיחה Teth לעיטה Iod
כשב Caph עושר Lamed מלאכה Mem מים Nun
הלוך samech רוח Ain שחוק Pe זרע zade הרהור Kuph
שינה Res חן Sin אש Thau משלה ac si ea enumerasset iis
uerbis, Aura, uita, pax, sapientia, uisus, auditus, odoratus, locutio, infusio,
cubatio, opes, negocium, aquæ, meatus, spiritus, risus, semen, suspicio, so
por, gratia, ignis, potestas. Hæc & eiuscemodi reliqua quæ audistis ex pa
trū monumētis q̃to potui breuissime decerpsi, ut uobis uel aliquã degusta
tione literarię professionis exhiberē. Scripsit em̃ de iis nõ negligē ter insi
gnis autor Rabi Akiba, quē imitati sunt cõplures ex nostris hoies litera
tissimi q̃s multo dignamur honore. Dixerunt em̃ q̃ in expositione alpha
beti latent multi sensus. Et Rabi Abrahã Aben Esra de hoc in libro q̃ pscri
bit סוד התורה .i. de Mysterio legis ita inq̃t והאמת כי טוב
הוא למשכיל שילמד מזאת החכמה .i. Et uerum
est q̃ bonū sit hoc, ut intelligatur, q̃a discitur ex eis sapientia, Non ut oi tū
uitæ nostræ tpe in literatoria laboremus arte (ait ipse) ut dies ac noctes

On the Art of Kabbalah

of us to venture outside us. From it derive prophetic visions and everything great and holy. It is called *Sekel haPoel* and with it the angelic world is complete.

Next comes kaph. This letter designates the first moveable after *El Sadai* himself and acts as if directly affected by the first cause, although it is in fact moved through the spirit of rational life which is the angel Metattron. This is called the active intellect of the sensible world which opens the way to all lower beings by means of penetration of the forms. Thus it flows by the divine power into everything that is moveable.

Final kaph signifies the ring of the final stars. It is called the eighth sphere in its relation to us, but in relation to the higher beings it is the second orb, divided into the twelve signs of the zodiac, which we call *Mazaloth*. It is influenced by the power of God through the medium of the intelligence of the ordinary Kaph and similarly influences the lower grades.

Lamed is the symbol of the first sphere of the planets. They are called *Leketh*, "walkers," in Latin *errones* like the Greek word *planetai*. It is called the seventh orb and is attributed to Saturn, whom we call *Shabatai*. It both receives and transmits influence.

Mem when open denotes the sphere of Jupiter, called by us *Sedeq*. It is influenced by the power of God through the medium of the higher intelligence, and by the same power it has influence over lower beings.

Mem when closed is a symbol of Mars, whom we call *Madim*, the fifth orb. Through the power of God the Creator it receives influence from the angel that is next most high, and by the same power itself, influences lower beings.

Nun signifies the great luminary called *Shemesh*, or "Sun." Its sphere is called the orb of *Hamah*. It receives influence from God through the medium of the sixth intelligence and by the same intelligence it has influence on lower things.

Final nun indicates the sphere of Venus, which is called by us *Noga*. It exists by the virtue of God and has influence with the help of the seventh intelligence.

Samekh is a symbol of the "doorkeeper," who is called *Kokhab*, in Latin, *Mercury*. It is influenced by the power of God from on high, and by the same power it influences things below.

Ain is a mark of the sphere of the moon, called by us *Yareah*. It appears like the left eye of the world. It is the last of the orbs among the stars and, because of its whiteness, it is sometimes called *Lebana*. All this we entrust to astrology.

Pe signifies the intellectual soul, particular and universal. It is directed by the separate intelligences into which it is poured by God as much in the spheres as in the stars and in all the upper and lower animated beings of the spheres and the elements.

Final pe denotes the animal spirits which are ruled by the higher intelligences through the power and command of God.

Sade symbolizes the material both of the heavens (which is intelligible matter) and of the elements (which is sensible matter) and of all that is mixed of the two. They are controlled by the divine power through the separate intelligences and their own forms.

Final sade indicates the forms of the elements, which are fire, air, water and

LIBER TERTIVS

in uoluminibus Rabi Iuda torqueamur, q̃ primus fert hebrẹis grãmaticus esse, uel in illis uiginti libris̃ q̃s de institutione literaria Marinus cõposuit, uel q̃s Samuel Nagid eadẽ de re duos & uiginti edidit. Hucusq̃ Abrahã Aben ezra, nec frustra sensit ita hõ prudentissimus & literarũ peritissim⁹ ad maiora eṁ & altiora nati sumus. Dixi modo q̃ ad substantiã literæ ptĩ nent cõsyderationes quatuor, nũc mea opinione terminandũ est id q̃d de accidẽtali relatione literarũ agere dudũ cœpimus, & בוטריקון i. no tariacon appellat, qua in parte id cõsyderamus q̃ litera q̃uã dictione signi ficet. Habet aũt tres q̃q̃ species. Cũ eṁ signaculũ aliq̃d ab initio dictionis accipit, & ut fieri solet apicibus in sublimi notatur, ia ראש התיבה i. caput dictionis notatur atq̃ de more ita scribit ר״ת Qñ itẽ sumit a ter mino & fine uerbi alicuius propositi tũc סוף התיבה i. finis dictio nis cognotatur q̃d cõsueuerũt figurare hoc modo ס״ת Sin aũt a singulis uerbi cuiuslibet literis notæ singulæ deducũtur, id tũc generali uocabulo notariacon appellam⁹. Ad hæc Philolaus ait. O noster Simon q̃ sunt hæc externis hoĩbus arcana & recõdita. Tũ ille. Multo forte occultiora inquit ostendã uobis in hac tertia cabalẹ parte q̃ תמורה notatur, ubi mutua sit literæ pro l̃ra positio, & totiens fit q̃tiens alphabeta p̃mutãtur. Permutã tur aũt iuxta numerũ literarũ bis & uigesies, q̃a uiginti duas legimˀ Iudẹo rũ literas, semp̃q̃ binis q̃busq̃ literis cõiugatis licebit alterã sumere, p al tera, et ea cõbinatio dicitur צירוף ut si ex istis sex literis alphabeti latini ab cd ef cõtinuo binas & binas cõiugauero quaten⁹ sub iugo primo sint a b, sub secũdo cd, sub tertio ef, uelimq̃ p epistolã, huiˀ artis peritũ aliquẽ hortari ut supplicaturus principi, cadat ante pedes eiˀ. Sic scribo, dbcf. q̃d ille intelliget Cade, ita & de aliis. Totũ hoc opificiũ euenit ex alphabetica ria reuolutione ut succedat mutuo litera pro litera proprio sibi iugo cõbĩ nata, scilicet uicissim a pro b, & b pro a, similiter c pro d, & d pro c, itemq̃ e pro f, & f pro e. Quod facilius in hebraicis nullo q̃dẽ obstante procedit, q̃a uoces quas latini uocales noiãt nõ sunt in ordine alphabeti Iudæorũ repositẹ. Prisca igit ẽtate motus inde pater noster Abrahã dixit, ut in libri Ietzira cap. ii. legit. Aleph cum omnibus & oĩa cum aleph, haud secus atq̃ Beth cum omnibus & omnia cum Beth, & ita de singulis. Quare ut exem plo id fiat manifestius uiginti duo alphabeta producam in mediũ quæ in eodẽ creationis uolumine Abraham scite admodũ & utiliter ordina uit.

אל בת גש דר הק וצ זפ הע טס י"צ כ"ם
אב גת דש ה"ר וק זצ ח"ף ט"ע י"ס כ"נ ל"ם
אג דת הש ור ז"ק ח"צ ט"פ י"ע כ"ס ל"נ ב"מ
אד בג הת וש ז"ר ח"ק ט"צ י"פ כ"ע ל"ס מ"צ
אה בד ו"ת ז"ש ח"ר ט"ק י"צ כ"פ ל"ע מ"ס נ"ג

Book Three

earth. They are controlled by the divine power through the angels called *Ishim*, by the power of the heavens and by the power of the primary matter which is the original fount of all the elements.

Kuph is the symbol of inanimate things and minerals, and of those things that are called "made of the elements" and "mixed." They are impelled by the divine power, through the spheres of heaven and the separate intelligences called *Ishim*, and they influence things below them in the fourth region of the elements.

Resh signifies all vegetation, fruit, crops, and things born on the earth. They are influenced by the power of God through the heavenly bodies and the separate intelligences called *Ishim* and also by the combinations of the elements.

Shin designates everything that can feel, things that crawl and move on the earth, and the fish of the sea, and birds of the air, and all irrational beings that possess the movements of life. These are controlled by the power of God through the heavenly bodies and the intelligences that we call *Ishim* and by the combinations of the elements.

Thau is a symbol of man and human nature which is the most perfect of all created things. It is controlled by God through the combinations and qualities of the elements in accordance with the influence of the heavens, and through the particular work of the separate intelligences called *Ishim*, which are angelic by nature. As *Ishim* are the final completion of the world of the angels, so is man the final perfection in the world of the elements, or rather in the world of all things, since he is constituted of the two worlds. It is written, "The Lord God formed man from mud and breathed into his face the breath of life."

These matters were fully discussed by our forebears and their burning love for the sacred letters is clear to us, their posterity. They were eager to give an explanation for everything, however small.

For example, on the letter aleph there is a passage in the book on *Brightness* where Rabbi Amorai sits and discusses why aleph is put at the head of the alphabet. The answer given is that aleph was before everything, including the Law, an explanation that Menahem Recanat records in his first section on Genesis in the name of Rabbi Rahumai, the author of that book.

Again, beth comes next for the obvious reason that it was the beginning of the Law. And as to why Gimel is not called *Gidel*, it is because in Scripture, *GDL* is followed by *GML* in Genesis 21 where it is written: *Vayigdal hayeled vayigmal*. The sages have not scorned to investigate such things and their equivalents and, even though there are some other matters where explanation has been omitted for brevity's sake, they have, nevertheless, written simply what is relevant. They always try to hurry on to the sublime, with thoroughness and enthusiasm, as Rabbi Jacob Cohen writes in his book called *Explanation of the Holy Name.*.

He takes the alphabet bit by bit and says that aleph is *Avir*, beth is *Hayim*, gimel *Shalom*, daled *Hokhmah*, he *Reyah*, vav *Shemiyah*, zain *Reyhah*, heth *Sihah*, teth *Laytah*, yod *Miskab*, kaph *Osher*, lamed *Melakhah*, mem *Mayim*, nun *Halokh*, samekh *Ruah*, ain *Sehoq*, pe *Zera*, sade *Hirehur*, kuph *Shinah*, resh *Hen*, sin *Esh*, Thau *Memshalah*, as if ascribing to those letters air, life, peace, wisdom, sight, hearing, smell, speech, confusion, lying down, wealth, work, water, walking, spirit, laughter, seed, suspicion, sleep, grace, fire, power.

DE ARTE CABALISTICA

או בה גר זת חש טריק כצ לפ מע נס
אז בר גה חת טש יך בק לץ מפ נע רס
אח בו גו דה טת יש בר לק מץ צפ סע
אט בה גז דוית בש לר צ מק נצ סף הע
אי בט גח דו הו כת ל ש מר נק סץ עפ
אכ בי גט דט רח הז לת מש נר סק עצ זפ
אל בכ בג רט חח וז מת נש סר עק פצ
אמ בל גכ רי חט ות נת סש ער פק וצ
אנ בם גל דכ הי וט זח סת עש פר צק
אס בנ גמ דל הכ ר׳ הב זי עת פש צר חק
אע בס גצרמ הל ופ זי חט פת צש קר
אפ בע גס דנ המ ול זכ חי טת קש צר
אצ בפ גע רס חג ומ ול חב טי קת רש
אק בצ גפ רע חס ונ זמ הל טרהת יש
אר בק גצ דפ הע וס זנ חמ טל יב שת
אש בר גק דצ הפ וע זס חנ טמ יל כת
את בש גר דק הצ ופ וע חס טנימ כל

Elementorum hæc uiginti duorū cōmistio nequaq; erit rustice ac indocte
intelligenda, oia em spiritus sunt. Sic in libro Ietzira scribitur, & sculpsit cū
illo spiritu deus uiginti duas literas, tres matres, septē duplices, & xii. simplices, & quęlibet illarū est spiritus, ad cōtēplandū itaq; spiritualiter inge-
tī cū gaudio, nobis tradita hæc sunt, nō ad obloquendū, nō ad irridendū.
Sed pia fide mysteria scripturarū amplexādū. Credētes em literis, facilius
altiora speculamur, et abscōdita cōfidimus in literis repire posse, quasi dei
Q sermonē in medio caliginis q dixit ad Moysen. Ecce ego uenio ad te in dē
sa nube ut audiat populus cū loquiar tecū, gn etiā בך .i. uiginti duab' cre-
dent in ppetuū. Oportet nāq; Cabalista nō aniliter sed fortiter credere et
q̃ sunt patrū mādata literis, singulari amore ac animo iucundo lęto q; red-
pere cū gaudio & fiducia, ut Psal. lxx. Exultēt & lętent בך .i. uiginti duab'
q quærūt te. Nā duas & uiginti lęas, scitote fundamēta esse mūdi & legis
ut copiose in libro tractaf Horti nucis secūdo, quē uel legistis uel legetis.
Tū Philolaus. Certe ait tales libros nec legi nec uidi unq̃ q etiā nō parua
usq; hucopa ubi nā laterēt scrutatus sum. Et Marranus. Nescio inqt q̃ pacto illiusmodi librorū tāta Iudæis parsimonia sit ut ne amico qde eos liberaliter edāt, aut q̃cūq; tn ære uēdāt. Tūc Simō. Statutū nobis est i quit
arcana legis nō dari pegrinis sed ליועץ חכם .i. Cōsiliario sapienti

On the Art of Kabbalah

These and the rest that you have heard I have culled as briefly as I could from the memorials of our fathers, to give you a taste of the business with the letters.

That great author Rabbi Akiva wrote some thoughtful things on this subject and many of those of our scholars whom we hold in great honor have imitated him. They have claimed that many senses lie hidden in the exposition of the alphabet. On this, Rabbi Abraham ibn Ezra says in the book entitled *On the Mystery of the Law*: "And the truth is that it is good to understand that wisdom is learnt from these." However, he says that we are not to work on the interpretation of the letters all our life and struggle for days and nights, either with the books that Rabbi Judah, said to be the first Hebrew grammarian wrote, or with the twenty books that Marinus composed on the rules of the letters, or with the twenty-two that Samuel Nagid published on the same subject. Hear what Abraham ibn Ezra had to say. He was a sensible man, most learned, and his judgement is not to be taken lightly. We have indeed been born for a greater and higher purpose.

I have spoken only of the four considerations relating to the substance of the letters. Now I think we should finish off the subject of the accidental relations of the letters with which we began dealing some time ago. It is called *Notariacon*. We shall now consider the method in which a letter is taken to signify a word.

This part also itself has three sections. When a sign is taken from the beginning of a word, and, as is usual, has a mark on the top of the letter, it is called *Rosh haTeibah*, the "Head of the Word," normally written *RT*. If it is taken from the very end of a proposed word, then it is called *Soph haTeibah*, the "End of the Word," indicated usually by *ST*. But if single marks are taken from each of the letters of any word, then we use the general term *Notariacon*.

PHILOLAUS: My dear Simon, this is all very mysterious and difficult for foreigners to understand.

SIMON: I shall be telling you far more recondite information in discussing the third part of Kabbalah, called *Themurah*, in which letters change place with other letters for as many permutations as the alphabet can provide. These permutations occur in accordance with the number of the letters, which is twenty-two letters. Since these letters are always joined in pairs, any one can be exchanged for any other. This sort of combination is called *Siruf*.

The process is like joining in pairs the six letters in the Latin alphabet "a," "b," "c," "d," "e" and "f," without gaps, so that the first pair is "ab," the second "cd" and the third "ef." So if I wanted to urge someone who understood this art to appeal to a prince and fall before his feet, I should write "dbcf," which he would understand as "cade"[63] and so on. The whole practice is achieved by moving letters round so that each letter can take the place of another letter particularly associated with it. Thus "a" takes the place of "b" and "b" the place of "a," and similarly with "c" and "d," and with "e" and "f."

This occurs more easily in Hebrew and with fewer problems, for the sounds called in Latin "vowels" do not exist in the Jewish alphabet. Encouraged by this at an early date, our father Abraham said, according to the book of *Creation* chapter 2: "aleph with everything and everything with aleph," and similarly, "beth with everything and everything with beth," and so on with each letter.

LIBER TERTIVS LXXIII.

Non domestico etiā consiliario tm̄, nec sapienti modo, sed simul cōsiliario sapienti, q̄ nō sit extraneus, & non sit indoctus. Nec id ægre feratis uos obsecro. Sæpe nācp iminentis periculi causa in tā diuturna dispersione cōstitutis nobis cōuentus, patrū sollicitus prouide statuit ברת שחוא ברת ממה שנפל בו באחרונה .i. Ea lege ut ipse fugeret ab eo, in q̄d cecidit posterius. Moyse nostro ægyptio autore, q̄ causas enumerat & recitat eueta ī capite lxxi. libri primi p̄plexorū. Sed spero uos hæc & alia nostræ gētis boni cōsulere, quare ista disputatiōe dimissa parte artis Cabalisticæ tertiā prosequar. Accepistis de cōbinationibus literarū ducentis & quadraginta duabus p̄mutationes cōiugationum ducetas triginta unā, p̄ter alphabetū uulgo cōsuetū cuius tn̄ binas quascp suo ordine lras pariter etiā cōnectere ad mutuas uicissitudines solet. Rē uulgō exilem ac forte prima specie im̄pitis cōteptā, sed q̄ tn̄ ue‿ niat plurimū exaltādā hoībus. Vt legit psalmo xii. ברם זלות לבני אדם .i. Exaltando despectiones filiis hoīm. Ad q̄d ibi citat Rabi Salomō id q̄d dicit a Psalmista Lapidē quē reprobauerūt ædificantes, factus est in caput anguli. Vos eq̄dē oro haud negligēter cōsyderate q̄d nō frustra scriptū est ברם nā de גמטריא Cabalistice significat duceta & quadraginta duo, tot em̄ sunt cūctæ supi⁹ descriptæ cōbinatiōes, & ex illis unā & triginta ducetascp uariatiōes deceti honore ueneremini. Oīa em̄ ex illis oriunt q̄ sunt & q̄ dicunt, de iis nācp lanuis quas appel‿ lāt, pater nr̄ Abra‿ hā ut est in libro Ietzira dixit ונמצא כל חבור וכל חצור יצא מהן .i. Et existit om̄e dictū & om̄e creatū progrediēs ex illis, q̄ q̄dē nobis illorū adminiculo facile possumus in nostrā ordinare salutē, q̄m reducēdi sumus p̄ oīm rerū creatarū cōsyderatiōe in unius creatoris pro humana uirili cognitiōe q̄ est salus nr̄a & uita ætherna, hoc sit a deo p nomē suū rursus in deū. Ipse est ipsemet nomē suū quatriliterū in secula seculorp semp bn̄dictū, q̄d ostēderat Psaltes cū aiebat. Et cognoscēt cp tu es nomen tuū tetragramatō solū tibi supmū sup oēm terrā. Iccirco solū hoc nome di‿ cit Sehamaphores. i. nome expositoriū essentiæ dei. Cuiᵉ expimētū sumit de prima huius artificii parte. Aliud est dei nome in isti⸱ locū succedēs q̄d xii. lris scribit, eiuscp ratio de secūda parte recipiet. Aliud p̄terea nome est q̄d in hac Cabalæ tertia parte cōmodissime tractat. Nomē xlii. characterū. Nō cp uni⸱ nois una ͵platio q̄draginta duabus literis cōstet. Notū em̄ est apud quælibet ītelligētē, ut docet Moyses Maimoni, cp unū nome iueniri nequeat uscp tot literis scriptū. Sed plura sunt noīa iter se & in se ipsa cōplexa, ex multis literis aggregata, q̄ ducāt Cabalista p quasdā rōnes occultas ad ueritatē cognitionis dei Tetragrammati יוֹד הֵא וָו הֵא q̄d similiter arithmetice xlii. significat. Huiusmodi xlii. characteres p talia noīa sic coniuncti dicūtur unū nome eo cp finaliter solū unā rē significāt queadmodū

Book Three

So, as a clearer example, I will lay out openly the 22 letters of the alphabet that Abraham very cleverly and usefully put in order in that same book on the Creation:

AL BTh GSh DR HQ VS ZP H' TS YN KM AB GTh RSh HR VQ ZS HP T'
YS KN LM AG DTh HSh VR ZQ HS TP Y' KS LN KM AR BG HTh VSh ZR
HQ TS YP K' LS MN AH BD VTh ZSh HR TQ YS KP L' MS GN AV BH GD
ZTh HSh TR YQ KS LP M' NS AZ BV GH HTh TSh YR KQ LS MP N' DS
AH BZ GV DH TTh YSh KR LQ MS NP S' AT BH GZ DV YTh KSh LR MQ
NS SP H' AY BT GH RZ HV KTh LSh MR NQ SS 'P AK BY GT DH HZ LTh
MSh NR SQ 'S VP AL BK GY RT HH VZ MTh NSh SR 'Q PS AM BL GK
DY HT VH NTh SSh 'R PQ ZS AN BM GL RK HY VT ZH STh 'Sh PR SQ
AS BN GM DL HK VT ZT 'Th PSh SR HQ A' BS GN DM HL VK ZY HT
PTh SSh QR AP B' GS DN HM VL ZK HY TTh QSh SR AS BP G' RS HN
VM ZL HK TY QTh RSh AQ BS GP R' HS VN ZM HL TD RTh YSh AR BQ
GS DP H' VS ZN HM TL YB ShTh ASh BR GQ RS HP V' ZS HN TM YL
KTh ATh BSh GR DQ HS VP Z' HS TN YM KL

These combinations of the twenty-two should not be understood in any boorish or uneducated way, for every one of them is the Spirit, as is written in the book of *the Creation*: "And God formed with that spirit twenty-two letters—three mothers, seven doubles and twelve simples, and each of them is the Spirit." We must contemplate them spiritually with great joy for they have not been handed down to us for denigration or mockery but for us to embrace the mysteries of Scripture with pious faith. By trusting in the letters we shall find it easier to speculate on higher things. We have confidence that we can find secrets hidden in the letters, like the word of God given to Moses in the midst of the cloud: "Behold, I come to you in dense cloud so that the people may hear when I speak with you," that is, "in *BK*, i.e. in the twenty-two, let them believe for ever and ever."

A kabbalist should not hold his beliefs as does an old woman, but should be strong in his convictions. He should, with great love and cheerful mind, accept the instructions of his fathers regarding the letters with joy and faith. As it says in Psalm 70: "Let them exult and rejoice *BK*, that is, in the twenty-two, when they seek you." You must realize that the twenty-two letters are the basis of the world and of the Law, as is fully explained in Book 2 of the *Garden of Nuts*. And if you have not already read that book, you will.

PHILOLAUS: Certainly I have not read any such books. I have never even seen them despite great efforts investigating their hiding place.

MARRANUS: In one way and another the Jews are so frugal with books of that kind that they do not produce them freely even to a friend, or sell them at any price.

SIMON: There is a rule among us that the secrets of the Law must not be given to outsiders but only to a "Wise Counsellor." Such a man

DE ARTE CABALISTICA

econtrario alia noïa cõposita & collectiua sæpe cõpluria sunt unice signifi
cantia. Potuit igitur in p̃sentiaru contingere ǫ ratio illa qua intellect⁹ no
ster duceret in deũ nequerit nisi multis & literis & uerbis explicari. Nec
id mirũ, qm̃ p multos & diuersos riuulos solet ĩgeniosi opifices scaturigi-
nem inuestigare. Ita de fontis sui abysso emanare fecit deus cunctas res
& ad infinitam uoraginem refluere. להוציא דבר במאמר
ומאמר בדבר עד להעמיד כל הדברים
במעין הזהב והשלהבת במאמר כמעין
אין חקר ואין מצר לאורה המתעלמת
בתוכיות החשך והשתרה בכלל ארבעים
ושתים אותיות Hæc sunt uerba cõtẽplatissimi doctoris Hamaï
in libro ספר מעין i. Speculationis, ad q̃ utiliter allegat ip̃e
החכמה i. librũ Fontis sapientię, quanq̃ uir tã integer testimonio nõ
eguisset. Iam tẽtabo si ea latine interp̃tari ualeam, ita salte ne quid sentẽtia
detrimenti patiatur. Vt produceret inquit rem in uerbo & uerbũ in re, q̃
usqꝫ restitueret omnes res in fontem respl̃edentię, & resplendentiã in uerbum, tanq̃ fonte cuius nec terminus sit, nec numerus, ad lucẽ inaccessibilẽ
agmento tenebrarũ recondita in uniuerso quadraginta duarũ literarum,
hucusqꝫ Hamaï. Appellant aũt hoc tam uenerandũ & colendum nomen
duabus & quadraginta literis designatũ p̃stantissimi sapientũ, q̃rũ memo
ria in benedictione est קדוש ומקודש i. sanctũ & sanctificatum.
Ideoqꝫ p alphabeticę reuolutiõis cõmistione rudib⁹ & indignis occultatũ
atqꝫ tm̃ sanctis cõtẽplatiuã uitã agẽtib⁹ ex alphabeticaria cõbinatiõe p Ie-
remiã est reuelatũ, q̃ sępe legere solebat in lib. Ietzira, ut repitur scriptum
בספר בטחון i. in libro de Spe, cuius autor est Rabi Iuda q̃ cõpo
suit illũ. Cũqꝫ Ieremias librũ Ietzira multũ & sępe nocturna uersaret ma
nu atqꝫ diurna, uenisse ad eũ בת קול i. filia uocis dicit q̃ iuberet illum
tribus annis uolumini eidẽ insudare. Post itaqꝫ annorũ triũ finẽ qñ iam ei
placuit characterum coniugatio & tractatus, ut operaretur in eis, mox
sibi atqꝫ sodalibus creatur homo nouus & in ipsius fronte scriptum erat
יהוה אלהים אמת Id est. Tetragrammatus deus uerus, tum
sentiens ille homo nuper creatus scripturam in fronte, haud ultra remo-
T   ratus est quin subito citata manu primam dimoueret ac adimeret literam in אמת quę est Aleph. Ita manebat reliquum his uerbis יהוה
אלהים מת id est. Tetragrammatus deus mortuus. Ob quam
rem Ieremias indignatione perculsus scidit uestimenta sua & dixit ei. Qua
re tu deponis Aleph ab Emeth, qui respondit, quoniam defecerunt ubiqꝫ
a fidelitate creatoris qui uos creauit ad imaginem & similitudinem suam.
Dixit Ieremias. Quomodo igitur apprehendamus eum. Respondit ille.

On the Art of Kabbalah

must be not just a native and not just wise, but both a counsellor and wise and neither foreign nor unlearned. Please do not take this badly. Considering the dangers that threaten us so often in so long a dispersion, this is really quite a sensible decree for the assembly of the fathers to have issued "by the rule of running away from the danger into which he might later fall," as Maimonides says in enumerating causes and reciting events in chapter 71 of Book 1 of *The Guide to the Perplexed*. I hope you interpret all this and other matters affecting our people in a favorable way. I shall leave that topic and go on to talk about the third part of the art of Kabbalah.

You have now learnt about the 242 combinations of letters, comprised of 231 permutations of pairs plus the ordinary alphabet, whose letters are combined in pairs in their ordinary order to facilitate mutual exchange. The practice seems shallow in normal terms and is perhaps likely to be despised at first sight by the inexpert, but it deserves great exaltation by men, as it says in Psalm 12: "In exalting the base for the sons of men." On this, Rabbi Solomon cites the Psalmist: "The stone that the builders rejected has become the corner stone." Consider carefully, please, the fact that *BRM* is written here for specific reason. By *Gematria* in kabbalistic terms it signifies 242,[64] and these are the total combinations written down above, from which come the 231 variations that we venerate with fitting honor.

All existence and all speech arises from these combinations, for of those that are specially termed Gates our father Abraham said in the book of Creation: "And every spoken thing and every created thing exists by its progress from them." By reliance on them we can with ease employ them to the aid of our salvation. Consideration of all created things leads back, within the bounds of human capability, to understanding of the one Creator. That understanding is our salvation and eternal life. Thus we pass from God, through his Name, back to God. He himself is his own Name of the four letters, which is blessed always to eternity, as the Psalmist showed when he said: "And they will understand that you are your Name, the Tetragrammaton, alone, supreme for you above all the earth." So this name alone is called *Semhamaphores* meaning "Name that explains the essence of God." Proof of this comes from the first part of this art. A second Name of God that can take the place of the first and is written with twelve letters will be understood from the second part. Finally, there is yet another name, dealt with in the third part of Kabbalah, and that is the name of 42 letters. Not that a single utterance of a single name consists of 42 letters, for any intelligent person would realize, as Maimonides teaches, that no single name can be found written with so many letters. But a number of names entwined closely together and pieced together from many letters lead the Kabbalist through hidden reasonings to the true understanding of God the Tetragrammaton, *Yod H Vav H*, which also signify arithmetically 42.[65] Forty-two letters of this sort, joined in such a way through such separate names, are referred to as one name

LIBER TERTIVS

כתבו האלפאביתות למפרש באותנו העפר
הנזרק בבינות לבבכם

Scribite alphabeta ad spacium in hunc puluerem dispersum, iuxta intelligentias cordiũ uestrorũ. Et fecerũt ita. Est factus est ille homo in horũ conspectu puluis & cinis atq; sic dispa-ruit. Quare Ieremias se tunc ab ipso deo uirtutes & potestates alphabeto-rum & elementariarum commutationum recepisse asserebat, nam dispo-sitionem coniugationis de libro creationis ante nouerat. Inde ad posteros alphabeticaria hęc Cabala id est receptio transmigrauit per quam arcana diuinorum maxima pandũtur. Cum enim p̃ ões literarum combinatiões nomen illud magnum & pro uiribus maximis extollendum ab ultimo ad primum circũduxerimus, tum se nobis diuina eius noticia liberaliter ostẽ-det ac uoluntati nostræ suas facultates offeret, demēterq; subiiciet, si nos inuenerit dignos atq; animi puritate, fidei synceritate, spei firmitudine amoris ardore p̃ditos & munitos. Noluerunt em̃ patres nostri (ut Rabi Tarphon, Rabi Moyses ægyptius, & Rabi Hamai, cæteriq; scripserunt se-cundum p̃cepta Magistrorũ nostrorũ illud nomẽ cuiq; mortali ostẽdere nisi admodũ digno. Sic em̃ dixerunt cp̃ non tradatur nisi humili, & ei qui stat in dimidio dierũ suorũ, non iracundo, nec ebrioso, nec prauis moribꝰ foedato, sed uiro pacifico & q̃ suauiter loquatur cum creaturis, & q̃ custo-diat illud cum mundicia, talis em̃ dilectus est sursum & circa nos desydera-tus deorsum, & timor eius cadit sup creaturas. Vt uero nomen illud uobis patefaciã more Cabalistarũ, primo partiar xlii. literas in septẽ uerba, dein-de q̃dlibet uerbum in duas dictiunculas, quarũ singulæ contineant iuxta idioma linguæ hebraicę ternas literas. Facta igit̃ multiplicatione arithme-tica dicendo sexies septẽ, erunt quadraginta duo scilicet literarũ eius nois collectio uniuersa quã inspectioni oculorũ uestrorũ hoc charagmate sub-iicio sic

שגת במא שגתהבצ מיתאצב ימיפתא
צתגגהפץ תגהצמא צצפמשט

Equidem hoc in uersu dũ q̃tasqualq; literas comp̃hendero, confestim mihi altera pars dictionis unius è septẽ quæuis disyllaba nascitur. Vna em̃ quæq; huius tam p̃ciosi nois dictio sex constare characteribus dignoscitur, tñ hebraicis tm̃, nõ aũt alterius linguę. Nam latine pluribꝰ erit opus, ut Sagathbama, Sagaththe-chaz, Miathazab, Iemibatha, Zethaghaphaz, Thegazama, Zaazpapas, q̃ in antiquorum uoluminibus inueniũtur usq; hodiernũ in diem Roma-no sermoni pegrina & incognita, sed non iccirco despicienda cp̃ dura sunt & barbara. Nemo em̃ tam lippis oculis in aspectu sacrorũ utatur ut reco-dita cõtemnat, nemo auribus in audiẽdo diuina tãtas delitias indulgeat ut solũ ea uenereĩ, ea laudet, ea sequaĩ q̃ sensibus sint iũcũda, oculis amoena, tactu mollia, & uoculatione blãda. Sed spiritalia capessat magis q̃ corpo-ralia & constantia magis q̃ leuia, ueraq; magis q̃ sucata. Em̃uero sepe asp̃a

O ii

Book Three

because in the end they signify only one thing, just as in the opposite case, other names may be made up of a number of elements collected together to signify many separate things through a single word.

So what has happened in this case is that the reasoning by which our understanding is led to God could not be deployed except through many letters and words. Nor is this surprising since clever engineers usually trace the source of a spring by its many different streams. So God made everything emanate from the depths of the fountain for it to flow back again to the infinite chasm, *"lehosi dabar bemaamar ve maamar bedabar ad leha'amid kol hadebarim bema'ayan hashalhebeth vehashalhebeth bemaamar kema'yan ein heqer ve ein mispar leorah hamitallemeth be thosefeth hahoshekh hamesuthereth biklal arba'im veshtaim otioth."* These are the words of that excellent contemplative scholar Hamai in his book *On Speculation*, to which he usefully attaches the book on the *Fountain of Wisdom,* though so fine and clear a man has no need of such a testimonial. Now I shall try to translate this passage into Latin without, if I can, affecting the quality of his thought: "To produce matter in word and word in matter until he may restore all things to the fountain of the splendor and restore the splendor to the word like a fountain with neither end nor number, rendered inaccessible to light by the increase of shadows and hidden in the total of the 42 letters." This name that deserves such worship and veneration and is designated by the forty-two letters is termed by the best of the sages (may their memory be blessed!) as the "Holy and Sanctified."

So the confusion of letters produced by exchanges within the alphabet has hidden information from the uncouth and the unworthy that has been revealed, by the combining of letters, to holy men who lead a contemplative life. The revelation came through the agency of Jeremiah, for he used often to read the book of *Creation*, according to a passage in the *Book on Hope* written by the author Rabbi Judah. Jeremiah used to immerse himself in the book of *Creation* a great deal and would often spend all night and all day with it in his hands. It is said that this was because there once came to him a *Bath Qol*, or voice from heaven, which ordered him to spend three years sweating over the one volume. At the end of the three years, when he was sufficiently interested in the combining of letters and other such methods to be able to employ them, he soon managed to create for himself and his fellows a new man. On the forehead of this newly created man was written *YHVH ALHYM AMTh*, i.e. "God the Tetragrammaton is true." The man felt the writing on his forehead and without hesitation moved his hand and removed and destroyed the first letter in *AMTh,* which is aleph. There remained then these words: *YHVH ALHYM MTh,* meaning "God the Tetragrammaton is dead." Jeremiah was struck with indignation, tore his clothes and asked him: "Why do you take the aleph from Emeth?" He replied: "Because everywhere men have failed in faithfulness to the Creator who created you in his own image and likeness." Jeremiah asked: "So how are we to lay hold on Him?"

DE ARTE CABALISTICA

& horrida p̄cedunt dei p̄sentiam.Recordamini q̄ contigerunt Eliæ prophetæ cum in monte dei Horeb intra cauernas & in specu lateret, nonne dictū erat ei sic.Ecce Tetragrāmatus incedit & flatus grandis atq̄ fortis subuertens montes & discindens ac cōterens petras ante Tetragrāmatō, non in flatu Tetragrāmatus,sed post flatū cōmotio,& non in cōmotione Tetragrammatus,sed post commotionē ignis,Non in igne Tetragrāmatus sed post ignē uox submissa tenuis,& in illa uoce locuta est ad eum gloria Tetragrāmati q̄ noīatur בבה. Ita uos post desertū horridū & senticosum,post montē & petras,post flatū & terræ motū,post ignē,post uocem in ipso cauernarū & specuū uestibulo dimissa occupationū secularius multitudine audietis gloriā dei ad uos loquentē Quid uobis hic? Pergite ultra,ut extat enarratū iiii.Regū xix.Igitur non hic standū est,sed reuertēdum nobis cum Elia propheta in uiam nostrā per desertum,hoc est per has hispidas barbaricarū connexionū reuolutiones & perplexas uepres in uiam sacræ atq̄ canonicæ scripturę,uiam uere nostrā q̄ est ueritas eloqorum dei ut ungamus regē in Syria qui ab unctione dicitur Messiha. Tantisper nanq̄ p̄ coniugationes duorū & uiginti alphabetorū ambulabimꝰ dum ad supmum atq̄ primum alphabetū uigilanti sollicitudine ac indefessa diligentia uentum fuerit.Oportet eñ nos artificiose per singulas cō binationes tam diu discurrere quousq̄ uox dei pateat,& apertus se nobis offerat sacratissimarū scripturarū textus.Illa nēpe uox dei, omnibus alphabetis a primo ad ultimū uidelicet uigesimū secundum,uirtutem suā & ualorem largiter impluit, ut combinationes aliquanto maiorem efficaciam quæ reputantur non significatiuę q̄ nomina primario significatu præ stent,ueluti radius solis fortius quidem urit q̄ sol ipse unde manauit. Hinc illud extat Mirandulani Comitis in Conclusionibus,ubi sic ait. Quælibet uox uirtutem habet in Magia inquantum dei uoce formatur. Præsentis ergo nominis quadraginta duarum literarum uirtus operatio uigor efficacia complementum & perfectio a dei uoce pendet,quam intendimus p omnes omnium alphabetorum connexiones & retia uenari, donec septē nomina quadraginta duabus literis comprehensa usquam in scriptura sa cra comperire queamus. Verbi causa.Si quæratur ex primo & uigesimo alphabeto similiter septem uerba quæ possint uel ullius diuinæ scripturę uersus esse symbola,reponantur mihi s.Jua ut sunt memorata superius. Itidem ex ī pso & uigesimo,adhuc autem & decimo nono & eodem modo deinceps oīa p̄ currēdo,usq̄ ad primū q̄d a suo exordio ceu reliqua nomē accepit ut diceret בת אל .i.Albath, cuiꝰ ex cōbinatione hoc mutuemur exēplū תרל לאק גנב גבל בקג כנב צלב קלד רצק לרו קנג קבץ צצת quod simul etiam est nomen diuinum quadraginta duarum literarum ex primo alphabeto libri

On the Art of Kabbalah

To which he replied: "Write the alphabets in the space cleared in this dust in accordance with the understanding of your hearts." They did so, and the man became dust and ashes in their sight and disappeared. That is why Jeremiah used to say that he then received from God himself the virtues and powers of the alphabets and exchanges of their elements. For the purpose of the combinations of letters he had already known from the book of Creation. From that time on this alphabetical Kabbalah or Receiving has travelled to posterity and through it are laid open the greatest mysteries of the divine.

When we have led that Name, so great and worthy of all the praise of which men are capable, through all the combinations of letters from the first to the last, then its divine knowledge will show itself to us freely. Then, so long as it finds us worthy and endowed with pure hearts, sincere faith, firm hope and ardent love, it will offer its riches to our wishes and will in mercy put them into our power.

Our fathers, Rabbi Tarphon, Maimonides, Rabbi Hamai and other writers, refused, in accordance with the precepts of our teachers, to show that Name to any mortal unless he was worthy of it. They said that it should not be handed down to anyone unless he be humble and middle-aged, a man not prone to anger or drunkenness or befouled by perverted habits, but rather a man of peace who addresses himself pleasantly to his fellow creatures and keeps that Name in purity. Such a man is beloved above and desired among us below, and the fear of him falls upon every creature.

I will reveal to you that Name in the fashion of the Kabbalists. First let me separate the forty-two letters into seven words, then each word into two distinct parts in each of which will be three letters in accordance with Hebrew idiom. If you multiply six by seven, you will get 42, which is the sum total of the letters of that Name, which I entrust to your personal inspection with this drawing: *SGThBMA ShGThThKS MYThASB YMYPThA SThGHPS ThGHSMA SASPPSH*. Having put so many letters into this verse, I can immediately derive from these seven words any other disyllabic portion of any single word. Each single utterance of this precious Name consists of six letters, as you see, but only in Hebrew, not in any other language. In Latin one needs more letters, producing *Sagathbama*, *Sagaththechaz*, *Miathazab*, *Iemibatha*, *Zethaghaphaz*, *Thegazama* and *Zaazpapas*, which are names found in the books of the ancients but remaining to this day foreign and obscure in Roman speech. Do not, however, despise these names because they are rough and outlandish, for no one should be so bleary-eyed in his examination of sacred matters as to despise the recondite, nor so indulgent to aural delights in hearing about the divine as to venerate, praise and follow only those things that are pleasant to the senses, pretty to the eyes, soft to touch and seductive in their intonation. Man should grasp the spiritual rather than the physical, the constant rather than the fickle and the real rather than the counterfeit.

LIBER TERTIVS   LXXV.

Ietzira permutato receptum. Sola nanq permutata & trãspoſita pater nõ
ſter Abraham in eo creationis libro poſuit, cũ nõ dubitaret alioqn uulga
rii alphabeti rectũ ordinẽ cũctis eſſe notũ. Solet aut & hunc pari modo cõ
binare dicetes אבג ut Rab Hamai docuit ĩ libro illo de Speculatiõe
nomeq deſcribit quadraginta duarũ literarũ etiã ex eadẽ ſua cõbinatione
pductũ ſic אקבתטש אקבבכו טנבשות נטצהבש
ורקפחן בקפוטש וֹשוהחא qd ſimiliter ut cætera, deũ be
nedictũ iuxta ſuã proprietatẽ ſymbolice ſignificat. Sicut em quatriliterum
ieſſabile notat deũ ut eſt ſup omẽ eſſe, & Ehich repſentat deũ ut eſt in oĩ
eſſe, & Adonai deũ ut eſt oĩm dñator, & Sadai ut nullius eget, ita pari mo
do xlii. literarum ſiue recipiatur ex trãſpoſitis ſeu rectis combinationibus
quodlibet deſignat deum quatenus eſt creator cœli & terræ, uiſibilium
oĩm et iuiſibiliũ. Qʒ obrẽ iſta uiginti tria noia diuina qrũ qduis quadragin
ta duabus figuris pingit, ſingula ſecũdũ uiginti triũ alphabetorũ ordines
ducunt e duobus ſacrę ſcripturę primis uerſibus, In principio creauit deꝰ
cœlũ & terrã, terra aũt erat inanis & uacua. Incipiẽdo a prima lra Beth, &
in ultima Beth litera terminãdo, q̃ cũ ſic hebraice legunt ut ſunt a ſpiritu
ſancto dictatę, quadraginta duas figuras abſoluũt, ſemp ponẽtibꝰ nobis li
terã pro lra ſub uno & eode cõbinatiõis iugo. Inueniunt & alii Cabaliſtæ
ſublimius ſpeculãtes, q trãſcẽdũt creationẽ & creaturas, & in ſola deitatis
emanatiõe pſiſtunt, quam ſancte per nomen ſanctum xii. characterum &
per nomen xlii. literarum digniſſimis & deo deuotis hoĩbus ſub fido ſilen
tio largiunt receptunt & ſcriptũ בספר אגרת הסודות .i. iñ
libro epiſtolę ſecretorũ, ubi ad quæſtionẽ Antonini Romani de ſacroſan
ctis noĩbus rñdit Rab Hakados cp ex tetragrãmato fluit nomẽ xii literarꝭ
אב בן ורוח הקדש .i. pater filius & ſpũs ſanctꝰ. Ex q̃ deriuat
nomẽ quadragita duarũ litera rũ qd ita pnũciat אב אלהים בן
אלהים רוח הקדש אלהים שלשית באחד
אחד בשלשת .i. Pater deus, filius deus, ſpiritꝰ ſanctus deus, tres
in uno & unus in tribus. O q̃ta eſt hęc altitudo, q̃ta profunditas, q̃ ſola fide
apphendit. Tũ Philolaus. Quãtę uero Simon inqt tibi agedę ſunt gratię
q oĩa nobis tã dilucide atq clare oſtendis, ſi modo quicq in hac arte clarũ
eſſe pot, ac nõ potius maxia pars horũ inuolucris recluſa, & fugere ad ſali
ces uiſa. Et Marranus. Tace obſecro Philolæ, inqt, Sine huc progredi, an
nõ uides? ueſper ingruit, & hic quaſi diurnũ pactus eſt. Porro tu ppetuo
loquere Simõ qcqd rerũ erit. Tũ ille. Cõpleui artẽ totã & edocui, niſi ſint
q̃ particulatim reſtare putetis de qbuſdã noĩbus dei, & angelorũ & uirtu
tũ, & cõſecratis ſigillis, quorum ui ac poteſtate facturos ſe multi multa pro
miſerunt q̃ uulgo admiranda uideant. Et Marranus. Obliuio forte te cœ

O iii

Book Three

What goes before the presence of God is often rough and unsightly. You remember what happened to the prophet Elijah when he was lying hidden in caverns and caves on Horeb, the mountain of God. This is how he was spoken to: "Behold the Tetragram came, and a great strong wind uprooting the mountains and tearing apart and trampling the rocks before *YHVH*, and *YHVH* was not in the fire; but after the fire was a still, small voice, and in that voice the glory of *YHVH*, which is called *Kavod*, spoke to him." So will you, after the rough, thorny desert, after the mountain and the rocks and the wind and the earthquake, after the fire and after the voice in the very entrance of the caverns and the caves, so you will hear, once you have shed the mass of your secular occupations, the glory of God saying to you: "What is this place to you? Go on your way." As the narrative goes in 3 Kings 19.

So we must not stand still but must turn back with the prophet Elijah to our road through the desert, that is, through these prickly circles of barbaric tangles and confused thorns that lie on the road of sacred canonical Scripture. That way is truly ours. It is the truth of the declarations of God, uttered so that we might anoint a King of Syria, to be called Messiah because he is anointed.

We shall proceed through the combinations of the twenty-two alphabets until with careful, prudent and unflagging diligence we reach the highest and first alphabet. We need to run through each combination carefully until the voice of God becomes clear and the text of Sacred Scripture is opened up and offered to us.

The voice of God rains power and strength in abundance on all the alphabets, from the first to the last, the twenty-second, so that sometimes combinations that are thought insignificant display greater efficacy than names with primary significance, just as a ray of the sun burns more strongly than the very sun from which it emanates. On this, Count Mirandola comments in his *Conclusions*: "Any sound has power for magic in so far as it is formed from the sound of God." It is this that we strain to catch in our nets when we scour through all the possible combinations in all the alphabets to find eventually in Scripture the seven names enclosed in forty-two letters.

For example, one seeks seven words in the twenty-first alphabet which may in the same way be symbolic of a verse of divine Scripture. I have laid them out clearly in the passage where I discussed them above. Similarly with the twentieth alphabet, and the nineteenth, and so on with all of them until we reach the first alphabet, and the nineteenth, and so on with all of them until we reach the first alphabet, which from its first pair of combinations is given the name of *Albath*. By using the combinations of this alphabet we get this new example: *ThDL GNB ThRL LAQ GKL BQG KNK SLB QLK VSQ LRV QNN QBQ SSTh*. This is also the divine name of forty-two letters given as the first alphabetical permutation in the book of Creation.

DE ARTE CABALISTICA

C pit, inquit, cp de nomine duodecim literarum q̄cp dicturus eras, quamuis secundæ partis materiam esse affirmares quæ iam præteriit. Tum Simō. Parum est quod de illo exponam nisi cp postquam crebro & frequēti prauorum hominum usu passim uilescebat nomen Tetragrāmaton antea cū tanta cura & sollicitudine, cum tanta reuerentia & tam prudenti moderamine idoneis & electis tm̄ sacerdotibus septimo quocp anno traditum ut discerent per illud populo benedicere in sanctuario, tunc ad maiestatē huius nominis conseruandam prohibitum fuit sacerdotibus eo imprecari, solis cp summis pontificibus q̄tannis permissa erat eius pronunciatio in diebus ieiuniorum & propiciationis. Quare illius loco cæteris substituerunt nomen duodecim literarum, cp esset aliquanto sacratius q̄ nomen Adonai, & tamen ineffabili Tetragrammato longe minus diuinum quo sacerdotes in benedictionibus uterentur. Consueuit autem quatuor his literis

הקבה cum apicibus in capite cuiuslibet notariace signatis conscribi
& ita pronunciari הקדוש ברוך הוא .i. Sanctus bn̄dictus ipse
Per quod benedictionem a deo Numeri sexto mandatam posterius super populum pro Tetragrammato ita proferebant. Benedicat te sanctus benedictus ipse, & custodiat te, Ostendat sanctus benedictus ipse faciem suam tibi & misereatur tui. Leuet sanctus benedictus ipse faciem suam ad te, & ponat tibi pacem. Quo in loco Salomon Trecensis commētator sacræ scripturæ ordinarius sic scribit לבד הבהנים פורסים
בפיהם לום הקבה עמד אחריבו שנ הנה
זה עומד אחר בהלינו משגיה מן החלובות
מביך אצבעות של בהנים .i. Itacp sacerdotes distendunt manus suas dicendo, sanctus benedictus ipse stat post nos, sicut scriptū est. En ipse stat post parietem nostrum, animaduertens de fenestris inter digitos sacerdotum. Sic in uetusti codicis membrana scriptum teneo quamuis impressa quędam uolumina chartacea uerbis istis careant. Firmissime uero credunt nostri & nullatenus dubitant hac forma expressam benedictionem tantæ prosperitatis esse causam quantæ fuisset si nomen Tetragrammaton quod nunc Adonai pronūciant in istis imprecationibus permaneret. Mutatio enim hæc facta est ad honorem Tetragrammati, ne totiens iteratum, neglectui tandem subiaceret, quod Deus Optimus Maximus omnium maxime auertat. Habetis omnem hortum Cabalisticum id est גנת tribus areolis distinctū quæ sunt Geometria, Notariacō, thmura, & radicibus, herbis, florib9 infinitis excrescēte cū oī ornatu suo ad unū hortulanū respiciētē, q̄ rigat, plātat, & īcremētū dat de9 Opt.Max.incōprehensibilis, ineffabilis, innoīabilis, cui est q̄cp nome incōp̄hēsibile, ieffabile innominabile tetragrāmaton, ex q̄ fluit & deriuat oē q̄d est ī sacris sacrū.

On the Art of Kabbalah

For our father Abraham only put down the permutations and transpositions in this book of Creation because he assumed that the correct order of the ordinary alphabet was known to everyone.

Some people are accustomed to combine the normal alphabet also in parallel fashion, writing *ABGD*, as Rabbi Hamai taught in that book of his on *Speculation*. He writes the name of 42 letters produced from this same combination like this: *AQBThTSh AQBBKV TNBShVTh NTNHBSh VBQPHV BQPVTSh VShVHHA*. This, like the others, symbolically signifies the blessed God in accordance with his properties.

The ineffable four letters denote God as he is above all being. *Ehieh* represents God as he is in all being, *Adonia* shows God as he is the Lord of all, and *Sadai* shows him as he is lacking nought. Similarly, the name of the 42 letters, whether it be received from transposed or straightforward combination, designates God the Creator of heaven and earth and of all that is visible and invisible.

So these twenty three names, each of which has forty-two letters taken in accordance with the order of the twenty-three alphabets, are all derived from the first verses of Sacred Scripture: "In the beginning God created the heaven and the earth. And the earth was empty and void." Starting with beth as the first letter and ending with beth as the last letter in the Hebrew text as spoken by the Holy Spirit, the Kabbalists produce the 42 letters by always putting one letter for each letter under one and the same combinatory yoke.

There are other Kabbalists who have indulged in higher speculation and transcend creation and the creatures, who stand in the sole emanation of the Deity. In holy manner they bestow that emanation, under a vow of silence and through the holy name of twelve letters and the name of 42 letters, upon those worthy men who are devoted to God. This traditional name is written in the *Book of Secret Letters*, where, in answer to the question of the Roman Antoninus about the holy names, Rabbi Hakados says that from the Tetragrammaton comes the names of 12 letters: *Av Ben veRuakh haKadosh*, meaning, "Father, Son and Holy Spirit." And from this is derived the name of 42 letters: *Av Elohim, Ben Elohim, Ruah hakadosh Elohim. Shalosha beehad, ehad besheloshah*, which means: "God the Father, God the Son, God the Holy Spirit, Three in One and One in Three."

What heights and what depths in matters understood by faith alone!
PHILOLAUS: We must thank you, Simon. Your explanation has been excellently clear and lucid—if anything in this art can be clear when most of it is veiled and seems to "flee behind the willow trees."
MARRANUS: Please be quiet, Philolaus, and let him go on. Do you not see that evening is coming on and Simon has only, so to speak, contracted for the day? Go on without interruption, Simon, speak on whatever topic comes up.

Reliqua em si qua iueniunt rerū diuinarū symbola, notę, sacrameta, signa
pfecto, ex hoc ipso ducūt originē. Verbi causa בוזו significat יהוה D
אחד deus unus, per primā huius artis parte גימטריא opando
arithmetice ut supra explanatū est, illud idē tn nomē בוזו symbolice rep̄
sentat itegrū ipm nomē tetragramato p secūdā Cabalę parte, ut scribit Io
seph Bar Abrahā ciuis p̄fecturę Salemitanę in secūdo uolumie Hortinu
cis his uerbis י תמורתו כ ובנ ה תמורתו ו ובו ו
ו תמורתו .i. Iod cōmutatio ei⁹ caph, & sic he cōmutatio eius vau, &
sic vau cōmutatio eius Sdain, q̄ aiaduertimus deū in essentia sua unū esse
unissimū q̄ nihil est unius, quanq̄ multa secudū alias relatiōes dicūt de ipo E
ppter q̄ uocatus est Elohim Kadosim. i. Dii sancti. Iosue ultio, & Elohim
Haiim. i. dii uiui Deuteronomii v. Et Mallachię primo de se ipso loq̄t sic.
ואם ארונים אני איה מוראי .i. Et si dn̄i, ego, ubi est timor
meus, q̄ in loco se deus pluratiue appellat dn̄os. Iuxta immanentiam ergo
unus est, iuxta egressiones aūt plures, q̄ dixit. Faciamus hoīem ad imaginē
& similitudinē nostrā. Nō q̄ linguę sanctę mos fuerit ut in summa cōstitu
ti maiestate de se ipsis pluratiue loquerent, ut Rab Saadia scribit in libro.
אמונות .i. credulitatū. Hoc em tenue argumentū est, qm subito post
ipse singulariter loq̄tur ita. Faciā ei adiutoriū simile sibi. Hāc unitatē & hāc
pluralitatē in diuinis nō inuiti admittūt Cabalistę diuersis rōnibus, unde
asserūt tres primas numeratiōes cabalisticas כתר חכמה בינה
unā esse summi regis coronā, ut scribit Rab Asse in lib. יחיד singulari
unionū seu collectorū. Cernitis hoc exēplo q̄ oību Cabalę ptibus ultro ci
tro promiscue utimur uidelicet uniuersa literarū syllabarū & dictionum
metathesi, deinde numerali supputatiōe, notatiōe capitali, & cōmutatione
literali cū singulis speciebus quas priori sermone patefeci. Sic em trāspo
nim⁹ nomē tetragramato ut sit Va & Ia, oriaicq̄ הריה .i. essentia q̄ oim
rerū prima est, a qua sunt oīa entia uera & bona. Vnde Ehieh Adonai si
gnificat arithmetice tatundē q̄d Elohim cui⁹ summa lxxxvi. Sicut & מה
nota est ipsius Elohim si sic extēdat האה מם hoc est פ .lxxxvi. Et
nome tetragramato, qa sit xxvi. q̄d si extēdat בת וה facit cxii. & designat F
tetragramato Elohim, hoc est dn̄s deus. De q̄ primū scribit. Istę sūt gnatio
nes coeli & terrę qn creata sunt in die q̄ fecit tetragramatus Elohim terrā
& coelū. Est aūt noīs tetragramati principiū Iah. Et ipsius Elohim medium
Iah, & finis Ehieh Iah. Quod totū est p̄fectio ipsius הריה .i. essentię, q̄d
significat יה .i. ipm, et י esse diuinū. Vnde q̄tidiano tritu est usu ut ipm
esse dicat aliqd diuinū necessariū & incorruptibile. Ome q̄ppe q̄d est qā
est huius gratia necesse est esse, nec tūc cōtingit nō esse. Virtus itaq̄ illius
essentię ducebat in opatiōe q̄ uerbū dei q̄ dixit יחי .i. sit, q̄ dicto creatę G
sunt in una summa. Ideq̄ uniuersę ac uirtutes intellectuales absolutissime p̄

O iiii

Book Three

SIMON: I have finished teaching you this art. I have covered all of it, unless there are particular details that you think are still left to discuss, such as, for instance, some of the Names of God and the angels, and the powers and the sacred signs by whose force and power many have promised to achieve feats that to the vulgar seem astonishing.

MARRANUS: Perhaps you have forgotten that you were intending to speak of the name of twelve letters as well, although you asserted that it belonged to the second part which we have now finished.

SIMON: There is little to say on the subject except that, because the wicked used to use the Name of the Tetragrammaton, which had before that only been handed down on every seventh year to suitable, selected priests, with the most careful precautions and with reverent prudent moderation, in order that they might learn to bless with it the people in the sanctuary. So, to preserve the majesty of the Name, it was forbidden to the priests to use it in prayer and only the high priests were allowed to pronounce it each year in the days of fasting and atonement.

As a substitute they used the name of twelve letters. This was somewhat more sacred than the name *Adonai* but was still far less divine than the ineffable Tetragrammaton which the priests used in their blessings. This name used to be written with the four letters *HQBH*, marked on top of each letter in notariacon fashion. It is pronounced *HaQadosh Barukh Hu*, meaning, "The Holy one, blessed be he." Through this name, they used to pronounce the blessing laid down at a later date by God, in Numbers chapter 6, to be said over the people in place of the Tetragrammaton: "May the Holy one, blessed be he, bless you and may he keep you. May the Holy one, blessed be he, show his face to you and be merciful to you. May the Holy one, blessed be he, lift up his face towards you and give you peace." On this passage Solomon of Troyes, the main commentator on Sacred Scripture, writes: "The priests extend their hands as they say: 'The Holy one, blessed be he, stands behind us,' as is written: 'Behold he stands behind our wall, looking through the windows between the fingers of the priests.'" I have seen this written on the parchment of an old codex, though some printed versions lack these words.

Our people hold to the firm and unwavering belief that the blessing expressed in this form is as felicitous as the Tetragrammaton which they now pronounce *Adonai* would have been if it had remained in their prayers. The exchange has been made in honor of the Tetragrammaton, lest it be repeated so many times that it finally suffer neglect (may the great and good God prevent this of all things!).

Here, then, is the total garden, *GNTh*, of Kabbalah, with its three flower beds marked out — *Gematria, Notariacon* and *Themurah*. Its growth is full of roots and plants and an infinite number of flowers, but with all its ornament it looks to one Gardener, who waters, plants and gives growth. He is the great and good God, incomprehensible, ineffable, unnameable Tetragrammaton, from whom flows the stream of everything sacred in all that is sacred.

DE ARTE CABALISTICA

hoc q̃d ipſe mãdauit ſic. Fiat lux, & mox facta eſt lux. Quã uniuerſitatẽ ſecuta eſt angeloru ad miniſteria deputatorũ natura qñ dixit וְיְהִי כֵן .i. & factũ eſt ita, q̃d principẽ & ſacerdotẽ magnũ deſignat q noiatur Michael, lucidũ argumẽtũ angelicę cõditionis, q̃d ex unitate & numero centenario cõſtituit. Vnde putant primo die Ideas extra cauſam primã eſſe ꝓductas & formas abſolutiſſimas q̃ ad eſſe & opari. Die aũt ſecũdo hinc angelos eſſe creatos. Nõ em̃ in primo die aiebat וְיְהִי כֵן .i. factũ eſt ita, ſed ĩ die ſecũdo, cũ firmamẽtũ fieret cœli iuxta Rabi Eliezer de luce ueſtimẽti eius creati. Dece em̃ ueſtibus ĩdutus erat deus qñ mũdũ creauit ut dicũt cabaliſtę, ac de ultimi ueſtimẽti ſui luce ſumpſit & creauit cœlos, nõ q̃dẽ ſenſibiles, ſed illos inuiſibiles & ĩtellectuales חֲוֹת רוּחֲנִיּוֹת .i. entitates

H ſpirituales, de qbus Pſaltes ait Cœli enarrãt gloriam dei, ubi nõ ſcribitur שָׁמַיִם .i. Cœli q ſunt orbiculares, q̃d memorabiliter notauit Rabi Ama in lib. Recõditoru, pſalmi xix. Sed הַשָּׁמַיִם qbus addit articulus ha, ut ĩ ſummario argumẽto Geneſeos legit. In prĩcipio creauit deus Haſamaim .i. cœlos illos eximios, illos famigeratos, illos admirabiles, nunq̃ uiſos nec mortalibus oculis uidẽdos. Alii nãq̃ cœli q nõſcribunt p ha articulũ ſunt q̃dẽ firmamẽtũ, ſed tñ uocãt noĩe cœli, quare ſcriptũ eſt, & uocauit deus firmamẽtũ cœlos, & dr̃ ipſius cœli firmamẽtũ inuiſibilis, in q̃p, q̃d appellat Cœli cœlorũ, unde ſeq̃tur ita. Fiãt luminaria in firmamento cœli, Nimirũ illa extẽſio in modũ pellis tanq̃ literis inſcripta luminaribus & ſtellis propter localẽ expãſionẽ dicitur Rakia q̃d nos a firmitudine firmamẽtũ appellamus. Nã cœlũ inuiſibile nõ egebat luminaribus, qm̃ p ſe ſpiritualiter eſt illuſtrẽ ac mẽtaliter a prima cauſa illuminatur. Ideo noĩantur ĩtelligentię ſepatę, de qbus ait autor cauſaru. Oĩs intelligẽtia plena eſt formis, q̃ dũ intelligit dicitur audire & loq, quare Moyſes ait, Audite cœli q̃ loquar. Et Dauid Cœli enarrãt gloriam dei. Et deus apud Oſeã. Exau ̃diã cœlos & iſti exaudiẽt terrã. Vñ lumẽ ꝓpheticũ deſcẽdit q̃d dr̃ אַסְפַּקְלַרְיָא הַמְּאִירָה .i. uiſio illuminãs, q̃ fuit Moyſi, nã aliorũ ꝓphetarũ uiſio erat אַסְפַּקְלַרְיָא שֶׁאֵינָהּ מְאִירָה .i. nõ illuminãs, & ea dr̃ terra, nõ nihil mẽtionis in primo ſermõe de iis habitũ eſt. Eq̃dẽ mihi recte uideor credere ob id ſapientes nr̃os dixiſſe, Aſpectus Moyſi ſicut aſpectˢ ſolis, & aſpectus Ioſue ſicut aſpectˢ lunę. In creatiõe igit ſenſibiliũ utit̃ deˢ hoc ſymbolo ĩtelligibiliũ וְיְהִי כֵן ut deſignetur miniſteriũ angelorũ rebus naturalibus cõcreatũ ſub noĩe comuni Michael tanq̃ ſpeciei angelicę appellatiuo, q̃ p eã orõnem וְיְהִי כֵן in ſequẽtibus q̃ncq̃ dieru opibˢ re

I citatã iuxta primã Cabaliſticę artis parte ęqualitate numeri ſymbolicę ſignificatur, p q̃d inſtituimur q̃ oẽs angeli ſunt eiuſdẽ ſpeciei, ſingula porro corpa ſiue cœleſtia ſeu terrena ꝓprios habẽt rectores uirtutũ ac pſectos ꝓuationũ, tã ea q̃ ſũt rationalia, ut cœli, ſtellę, hoĩes, q̃q̃ irrõnalia ut beſtię ac elemẽta. Philoſophis nẽpe tũ primũ peripateticis id probatur q̃d cœli

On the Art of Kabbalah

If there are any remaining symbols of divine things, whether they be marks, sacral objects or signs, then they take their origin from this.

For example, *KVZV* signifies *YHVH AHD*, meaning One God. This is discovered by working through the first part of this art, *Gematria*, using arithmetic as explained above.[66] The same name *KVZV* symbolically represents the whole Tetragrammaton through the second part of Kabbalah, as Joseph bar Abraham, a citizen of the prefecture of Salem, writes in volume 2 of the *Garden of Nuts*: "Yod is exchanged with kaph and he is exchanged with vav, and vav is exchanged with zain." From this we see that God in his essence is the most one-like One than whom nothing is more one-like, despite the many names given to him to signify his other aspects. Such is the name *Elohim Kedoshim*, meaning, "holy gods" (last chapter of Joshua) and *Elohim Hayim*, meaning "living gods" (Deuteronomy 5). And in the beginning of *Malachi* he speaks of himself thus: "And if I am Lords, where is my fear?", in which passage God is referring to himself in the plural as Lords.

In relation to his immanence he is one, but in relation to his goings forth he is many, as he said: "Let us make man in our image and likeness." This is not because it was the custom in a holy language for those in the greatest mystery to speak about themselves in the plural, as Rabbi Saadia writes in his book on *Items of Faith*. This is a weak argument, for immediately after this passage God talks in the singular when he says: "Let me make a helper for him like unto him." The Kabbalists are not unwilling to admit this unity and plurality in the divinity for diverse reasons. So they assert that the three first Kabbalistic numerations — Crown, Wisdom and Understanding — are the single crown of the highest king, as Rabbi Asse writes in his book on *Singularity* (i.e., of collectivities).

You see from this example that we use all the parts of Kabbalah promiscuously, that is, the general transposition of letters, syllables and words, then numerical calculation, notation in capitals and exchange of letters, with each of the kinds that I have explained in my earlier discussion. For we transpose the Tetragrammaton to get *Va* and *Ya*, and thus *HVYH*, the essence which is the first of all and from which all beings are true and good. In the same way, *Ehieh Adonai* signifies arithmetically the same as *Elohim* since they both make 86.[67] So, too, *MH* is a mark of *Elohim* if it is written out as *MM HA*, which is *PV* or 86. And *KV* signifies the Tetragrammaton because it is 26; and if it is written out as *KPh VV* it makes 112 and designates Tetragrammaton *Elohim*, that is, the Lord God[68] on whom it is first written: "These are the generations of the heaven and the earth when they were created, in the day when the Tetragrammaton *Elohim* made the earth and the heaven."

The beginning of the Tetragrammaton is *Yah*, the middle of *Elohim* is *Yah*, and the end of *Ehieh* is *Yah*. The whole is the perfection of *HVYH*, essence, which signifies *HV*, meaning "He," and *YH*, meaning "is divine." Hence it is a trite statement to say that he is something divine, necessary and incorruptible. Everything that exists necessarily exists so long as it does exist by his grace, and cannot then not exist. So too, the power of that essence was brought into operation through the word of God, who said *YHY*, Let it be. By this word all the Ideas and absolute, intellectual powers were created in one completion through this command of his: "Let there be light, and straightway there was light made."

LIBER TERTIVS

quodlibet sphæricũ p̄ter formā suā essentialē habeat assistentē ītelligētia orbis sui motricē, q̃ uocatur angel⁹, eo cp̃ ad hoc officiũ missa, intelligēs & uolēs cōplet iussa creatoris, tanq̃ inter deũ & naturā uirtus media à qua sī unt opationes in rebus quas natura earũ uel nō faceret, uel nō sic faceret, quas alii prouenire dicũt a proprietate occulta & alii q̃a tale. Mot͡ em̄ cœloru & stellarũ quãq̃ naturaliter est circularis, tn̄ ab oriēte moueri ad occi dentē uel ecōuerso nō naturę est sed uolūtatis, At habet liberā uoluntatē angelus, natura uero ad certũ solũmodo instinctũ coartatur, unde semper agit eodē modo, Angeli aũt nō mouēt orbes semp eodē modo. Quo sit ut nō semp eodē modo fīat mutatiōes horũ inferiorũ. Maximā nãcp̃ uim ac potestatē angelica exercet conditio in res corporeas, quapropter intelle ctus agēs a q̃ influ͡ ut formę noīat angel⁹ teste Rabi Moyse Maimoni & appellat שַׂר שֶׁל עוֹלָם .i. p̄fectus uniuersitati, ut dixerũt sapiētes n̄ri, uocātcp̃ Metattron, a q̃ qdē gubernātur oēs uirtutes singulares humanę aīales & naturales q̃ pariter angeli dicũtur, eorũ est multitudo q̃ ad nos īsinita, sed q̃ ad creatorē certa terminata & finita. Cuius rei Bresith Raba meminit ubi legit cp̃ creator q̃tidie creat cœtũ angelorũ, q̃s alii uocāt formas, cp̃ sint substātię formales qbus tota sphęra generābiliũ & corruptibilū absq̃ numero plena est. Haud secus atq̃ uester q̃cp̃ recepit Hesiodus, in opibus em̄ & dieb⁹ sic ait. τρίς γὰρ μύριοί εἰσιν ἐπὶ χθονὶ πουλυβοτείρῃ ἀθάνατοι Ζηνός, φύλακες θνητῶν ἀνθρώπων οἵτε φυλάσσουσίν τε δίκας καὶ σχέτλια ἔργα, ἠέρα ἑσσάμενοι πάντη φοιτῶντες ἐπ' αἶαν .i. Ter em̄ decē mille sunt sup terra multos pascēte imortales Iouis, custodes mortaliũ hoīm, q̃ uticp̃ obseruāt & iusticias & miserãda facta, aerē ī duti ubicp̃ euntes sup terrā, Quorũ instar in hoīe du as uolūtatis potētias noīant duos angelos יֵצֶר טוֹב וְיֵצֶר הָרָע autorē boni & autorē mali, ut in מִדְרָשׁ תַּנְחוּמָא legit que citat rabi Asse in sua collectura. Eiuscemodi autem Hesiodios custodes corpi coassistētes latini spiritus nũcupāt, eorũ q̃sq̃s sollicitudini negociorũ inferiorũ destinatus fuerit Mamona seu Mamon dicit, quē grece dęmona seu dæmon uocāt, nō uticp̃ in malā parte. Sane aliud qdē est dęmō aliud dęmoniũ, q̃d a nobis putat̄ diuinitatis extenuatiuũ esse, quapropter diminutiue a diuinis excluditur, q̃q̃ plane fateor Homero & uetustissimis scriptorib⁹ aliũ eius uocabuli usum fuisse, q̃rũ multi de Socratis dæmonio laudāda & ueneranda p̄dicarũt, q̃d Apuleius de deo Socratis iterp̄tatus est. Q̃ aũt latini uocarũt sp̄us instar uētorx̃, a nobis originē sumpsit q̃ eosdē רוּחוֹת appellamus. De qb⁹ Rabi Tedacus Leui in lib. de decē numeratiōib⁹ post explanatos q̃tuor uētos a gloriae, meridionalē, orientalē & occi˙ dē˙ tali˙, tandē sic scribit וְאֵלּוּ אַרְבַּע רוּחוֹת בָּרָא אַרְבַּע מַלְאָכִים דִּמְמוּנִּין עֲלֵיהֶן בְּיוֹמָא וּבְלֵילְיָא .i. Et ilis quatuor uētis creauit quatuor angelos q̃ p̄fecti sũt sup eos ī die & ī nocte. Deinde seq̃tur eodē autore cp̃ Michael q̃ est de parte clemētię ac mise

O v

Book Three

After this totality came the nature of the angels deputed to minister, for he said: *"VYHY KN"*—"And it was so"—which designates the prince and high priest called Michael—clear evidence of the state of the angels, which consists of one added to a hundred.[69] So they think that on the first day all ideas, apart from the first cause, were produced, along with the forms that are most absolute with regard to being and operating. On the second day, the angels were created, for he did not say *VYHY KN*—"and it was so"—on the first day, but on the second day, when the firmament of the heaven was created; made, according to Rabbi Eliezer, out of the light of his garment.

For God was clothed with ten garments when he created the world, so the Kabbalists say, and from the light of his last garment he took and created the heavens, not the physical ones but the invisible, intellectual spiritual entities, about which the Psalmist says: "The heavens tell of the glory of God." The word written here is not *Shamayim*, which are the heavens of the orbs, as Rabbi Ama memorably pointed out in his book on Mysteries in Psalm 19, but *HaShamayim*, with the article *Ha-* added, as in the summary in the preface of Genesis: "In the beginning God created *HaShamayim*." These are the most high, most celebrated and most wonderful heavens, that have never been seen and never will be seen by mortal eyes. The other heavens, those written without the article *Ha*, are really only the firmament, and "Heavens" is only its name, for it is written: "And God called the firmament heavens." The firmament is called the firmament of the invisible heavens and has, I claim, the name of Heavens of the heavens because of the following passage: "Let there be lights in the firmament of heaven." Surely it is because of its extension in space that that extended sheet, inscribed like a parchment with the luminaries and stars for its letters, is called *Rakia*, while we, because of its solidity, call it the firmament. In contrast, the invisible sky has no need of luminaries, for it is lit by its own spirit and illuminated by the first cause as by a mind.

Thus the heavens are also called separate intelligences, as the author of *Causes* says: "All intelligence is full of forms," and so long as it understands is said to hear and speak—hence Moses said: "Hear O heavens, what I say," and David said: "The heavens tell of the glory of God;" and God says in Hosea: "I will listen to the heavens and they will listen to the earth."

From this comes down the prophetic light which is called "Illuminating Vision" and was given to Moses, for the vision of the other prophets is "Non-illuminating Vision," and is called "Earth." We said a little on this in our first discussion.

I think I am right in believing that it was because of this that our sages said: "The appearance of Moses was like the appearance of the sun and the appearance of Joshua was like the appearance of the moon."

So in the creation of sensible things, God uses this symbol of the intelligibles, *VYHY KN*, to designate the angels created to attend on natural things, all signified together by the one name Michael, which is like a descriptive name for the angelic species. Michael is signified by this phrase *VYHY KN* which is recited in the account of the following five days' work, and which is a symbol for Michael according to the first part of the Kabbalistic art of numerical equality.[70] By this we are informed that all the angels are of the same species and, besides, that every body, whether in heaven or earth, has its own guide of its powers to control its activities, whether it be a rational body like the heavens, the stars, and men, or irrational like the beasts and the elements.

DE ARTE CABALISTICA

rationū cōstituitur Mamona.i.pfectus sup uentū oriētalē usq; ad dimidiū diei,& usq; ad noctē.Regitq; uentū occidētalē Raphael q; similiter est de parte clemētię. Tū Gabriel in uirtute iudicii et seueritatis pfectus est cū uē to boreali sup dimidiū noctis & duas mensuras mūdi.Noriel uero psidet austro.Hucusq; Tedacus Leui.Cęterę plures illi sub se species habet quas liber סורות .i.arcanorū continet,& in Porta lucis ita legitur כי מן
האךץ ועד הרקיע אין שם מקום פנוי אלא
הבל מלא המוצנים מהם· טהורים מהם בעלי
חסד ורחמים ויש למטה במך בריאות
טמאות מזיקות ומקטרגות ובלם עומדים
ופורחים באויר· ואין מן הארץ ועד הרקיע
מקום פנוי אלא הבל המונים מהם לשלום
מהם למלחמה מקם לטובך מהם לרעה
מהם לחיים מהם למות· וכל זה במדור
התחתון שאנו בו׃ .i.Q a terra usq; ad firmamētū nō ibi loc⁹
uacuus,sed omē plenū formis.ex illis purę,ex illis capaces gratię ac misera
tionū,& sunt iferi⁹ multę effigies foedę,noxię,tetatrices,& oēs cōmorātes
& uolātes in aere.Et nō a terra usq; ad firmamētū locus uacuus,qn totum
sint spēs,ex iis ad pacē,ex iis ad bellū,ex iis ad bonū,ex iis ad malū,ex iis ad
uitā,ex iis ad mortē.Et oē id in habitatiōe inferiori in qua nos sumus,haec
Ioseph Castiliēsis. Sed absit a sancto proposito nostro ut multa de squalē

K tibus & turpissimis dęmonibus illis humani gñis hostibus q̄ dicitur cōtra
rię fortitudines disputare pgamus,uel q̄ supiorē regionē puagari putant,
ignei,uel q̄ propinquo nobis aere oberrāt,uel q̄ terreni terrestria territāt,
uel q̄ lacus & fluuios habitant,ac sępe ipsum mare quatiūt,uel q̄ sub terra
illos qnq; iuadūt,q̄ puteos effodiūt & metalla,itē hiatus terrae prouocāt,
flammiuomos uētos agitāt,& fundamēta cōcutiūt,extremū, q oīa lucis ac
splēdoris fugiūt inpscrutabiles & penitus tenebricosi,q nō modo gen-hu

L manū uerū etiā bruta uexāt,sermones suos absq; sonitu igerētes. Aduers
q̄rū machinatiōes sunt ex nostris q̄ multa se arbitrātur exptos,ac nō dubi
tāt & bonos spiritus mulcēdo attrahere,& malignos oppositis passiōibus
ppulsare,sacris & diuinis rite noībus ac characterib-suffulti.Iubet hoīem
futuris piculis exponēdū recipę mēbranā tenuissimam q̄ dicitur uirginea
tanq̄ syncera mūda & imaculata,ut psagiat actoris puritatē,tū deinde hos
characteras inscribere sic צמרכה at extra in hispidiore folii parte si
gna q q̄ hęc בוור qua ligatura firmissime sperante in deū uniuersitatis
creatorē pącipiūt nullas formidare puersorū hoīm machinatiōes. Id ita pā
dunt mysteriū,sunt eīm symbola primorū qnq; uersuū Geneseos,tā capita

On the Art of Kabbalah

The philosophers, and first among them the peripatetics, proved this, since every celestial sphere has besides its own essential form, an intelligence next to it that moves it in orbit. That intelligence is called an angel because it has been sent for this duty.[71] It has will and understanding, and in them fulfills the order of the Creator, like a power median between God and nature. By it work is done on things that their own nature either would not do at all or would not do in this way. Hence such work is often accredited either to a hidden property or to the process outlined above.

The movement of the heavens and the stars is by nature circular, but whether this be a movement from East to West or in the opposite direction is a function not of nature but of will. An angel has free will, while nature is confined to fixed instinct alone. So nature always works in the same way but the angels do not always move the orbs in the same way, and so it is that change in these lower regions does not always occur in the same way. The angelic state wields the greatest force and power on physical things, which is why the active intellect from which the forms flow is called an angel, as Maimonides testifies. It is called *Ruler of the Universe*, so our sages say, and is pronounced "Metattron." By it all the particular human, animal and natural powers are governed. They are equally called angels and there is a multitude of them, in our perspective infinite, though to the creator fixed and finite.

There is a mention of this in a passage of *Bereshith Rabbah* where it is written that every day the Creator creates the company of angels, whom some call Forms because they are the formal substances of which the whole sphere of creatable and corruptible things is full beyond number.

Your friend Hesiod knew of a similar tradition, for he says in the *Works and Days*: "There are thirty thousand immortals of Zeus above the many-feeding earth, custodians of immortal men who are on watch for justice and wicked deeds, clothed in air and flitting over all the earth."

In similar fashion, the two powers of will in man are referred to as two angels, the *Author of Good and the Author of Bad*, according to the *Midrash Tanhuma* cited by Rabbi Assi in his collection. Similarly, the Latins refer to Hesiod's guardians that attend the body as spirits.

Of these, those that are appointed to care for affairs of the lower regions are called *mamona* or *mamon*—*daimona* or *daimon* in Greek. This does not imply wickedness. A *daimon* is not the same as a *daimonium*. This latter, is, I believe, simply a weaker sort of divinity and therefore only slightly separate from the divine—though I have to admit that Homer and the ancient writers had another use of the word and that many of them made laudable and fine remarks about the daimonium of Socrates which Apuleius translated as Socrates' god.

As for the phenomenon that the Latins call Spirit, such as the winds, this custom originated with us, for we call them *ruhoth*. Rabbi Tedacus Levi writes on this subject in his book on the *Ten Sephiroth* after explaining the four winds, north, south, east and west: "And for these four winds he created four angels that rule over them day and night."

LIBER TERTIVS

q̃ termini iuxta secũdā cabalisticę artis partē. Scripsit q̃ndā de physicis liga
turis Costa Ben Luca res nō physicas tñ expientia ut opinanť, p̃batas, qui
ait, Auricularis digitus abortiui si mulieris collo suspēdať, nō cōcipiet dũ
collo hærebit, at nũc uerba qb' creator oĩpotens fecit cœlũ & terrā alliga
ta, nũ putauerit inqunt aliqs nihil posse: Sane multũ p̃fecto credũt meę
sectæ hoīes magno magistro Rabi Asse, q scripsit in סֶפֶר הַיָּתִיר
uolēs petere ac ĩpetrare optata cōuertat se ad clemētiā & mīserationēs dei
utedo iis characterib' אַגְקְתָם פְּסְתָם פְּסְפְּסִים דְּיּוּגְסִים
q̃ inueniunť esse digna sacrę scripturę memoracula, cuiusmodi habent &
alia cōpluria qbus ferme oēs Cabalistarũ libri sunt referti. Studeť qq̃ alii
e diuinis literis sigilla illustria fabricare, q̃ cōtra hoīm aduersas ualetudīes
& reliquas molestias ualeāt diuturno usu probata, Veluti est illud uerbi
causa, qd Rab Hama in lib. Speculatiōis ex quatuor nō magicis sed solēni
bus & cōibus sacris noībus composuit qn potius cōpositũ a patribus rece
pit יְהוָה אֱלֹהֵי יִרְאֵי אֲתָיָה Est auť יִרְאָא cabalistice idē qd. El.
Accipiũt igiť eius scientię artifices primũ charactere primi noīs, & primũ
secũdi, & primũ tertii, & primũ quarti, sitq̃ sigillũ primũ יִרְאָא Deinde
opanť pari modo circa secũdas quatuor noīum sacratissimorũ lr̃as & oriť
הַרִיה Tertium sigillum ita cōficiunt, tertias quasq̃ lr̃as coniũgunt &
nascit רְגָא Postremũ eodē more copulāt ultia & exurgit quartũ sigil
lũ qd est הַרִיה Horũ quatuor sigillorũ intētio est יְהוָה אֱלֹהֵי צְבָאוֹת
יְהוָה אֶחָד .i. Dñs deus noster dñs un', & hęc inqunt esto quatuor
simul iũctorũ sigillorũ supscriptio. Demũ in membranę tergo depingunt
אֶחָד רֹאשׁ אַחְדוּתוֹ רֹאשׁ אַרְאָרִיתָא qd iterp̃tať sic
יִיחוּדוֹ תְּמוּרָתוֹ אֶחָד .id est. Vnum, principium unitatis suę,
principium singularitatis suæ, uicissitudo sua, unum. Et intelligitur uicissi
tudo hæc literaria secundum tertiam Cabalę partem. Stant itaq̃ cum sigil
lis & inscriptiōibus corā altissimo mēte deo deuota, & q̃libet bñdictionē
de illis decē octo bñdictiōibus, aut in aliis iustis p̃ǐbus cōtentā postulaue
rint, infallibiliter se ipetrare sperāt, oēmq̃ uel cœlit' imminētē sæpe sorte
fragere, uel Adrastiā. i. diuinarũ legũ ineuitabilē potestatē orōnib' sacroȝ
uerborũ mitigare posse cōfidũt. Nā haud modo characteribus & figuris,
uerũ etiā uerbis & carminibus bene initiatũ Cabalistā putāt quęuis tũ q̃
sint admirāda efficere, qd & uestri qdā posse fieri cōfitenť. Plotinus em̃ de
dubiis aīę libri secũdi cap. xxxv. enumerat quatuor qb' mirabilis insit uirt
scilicet, qualitates specierũ occultas, & figuras, & cōcētus, & uota. Porphy
rius etiā & Iāblichus aiũt p̃ deū p̃prie, p̃q̃ bonos angelos aduersus infi
mos spiritus ĩperiũ nos habere, nec iuenit ullũ in orbis terrarũ ambitu ge
nus hoĩm qd in hāc sentētiā facilius eať q̃ ut fama est diuiniores christiani,
q noībus & figuris dęmonia eiiciũt, & manus supra ęgros ĩponũt, & bene
habēt, & mortifera sanāt; & miracula consimilia opanť. Sed (ut asserētib'

Book Three

Later in the same book he writes that Michael, who is on the side of Clemency and Pity, is *Mamona*, that is, the ruler over the east wind up to the middle of the day, and up to the night. Raphael controls the west wind and is similarly on the side of Clemency. Gabriel, in the power of Judgement and Severity, rules with the north wind over the middle of the night and two measures of the world. Noriel presides over the south wind. (This is all Tedacus Levi).

The angels then have many sorts of things under them as listed in the book of Mysteries. So one reads in the *Gate of Light*: "Because from the earth to the firmament there is no empty place. All is full of forms. Some of them are pure and some are capable of clemency and mercy, but there are below them many foul, noxious, tempting images, all drifting about, flying in the air. And there is not an empty place from the earth to the firmament. All is full of beings, some peaceful, some war-like, some good, some bad, some for life and some for death. And all this is in the lower habitation in which we live." These are the words of Joseph of Castile.

But it is not part of our holy design to discuss at length those lewd and shameful demons, the enemies of the human race, that are called Contrary Powers, whether they be reckoned to wander round the upper regions of fire, or to flit close by us in the air, or to be terrestrial beings causing terror on earth, or to inhabit lakes and rivers and often shake the very sea, or to attack on occasions under the earth and, digging wells and mines and provoking earthquakes and exciting flame-belching winds, to shake the fundaments or, finally, to avoid everything of light and brightness and, in inscrutable shadows, to vex not only the human race but also the brutes, pouring out their speech without sound.

Against the machinations of these powers, many among us believe themselves expert, and have no doubt that they can both attract good spirits by sweet words and draw off malignant spirits by the opposite, relying on sacred and divine names and letters.

They bid a man who is to be exposed to future danger to take a very thin parchment, called "virgin" by virtue of its uncorrupted, pure and undefiled nature which presages the purity of the man himself. Then they bid him write these letters: *SMRKH*, but on the outside, rougher part of the leaf to write as well these signs: *BVVVV*. They believe that anyone with this amulet whose hope is firmly in God, the Creator of the universe, will fear no machinations of wicked men.

They explain this mystery by saying that these are the symbols of the first five verses of Genesis, taking both the first and the last letter in accordance with the second part of the art of Kabbalah.[72]

Costa ben Luca once wrote that natural amulets are not naturally efficacious but are proved only by experience, as a man believes: "If the small ear-lobe of an abortion be hung from a woman's neck, she will not conceive so long as it remains on the neck." But when the words with which the omnipotent Creator made the heaven and earth are used as amulets, could anyone possibly think that they too have no power? Men of my religion have much confidence in the great teacher Rabbi Asse, who wrote in the *Sepher haYahid* that whoever wants successfully to seek or beg for something he

DE ARTE CABALISTICA

illis uera loquar) oīa ea fidei potius tribuūt, q̃ tanq̃ & orōnibus nōnullā eſſe inſitā poteſtatē opinant. Dicūt em atq̃ credūt cp oro fidei ſaluabit infirmū, necp aliter idonei Cabaliſtę ſentiūt, q pariter affirmāt opatiōes miraculoſas ex ſolo deo, & ab hois fide pēdere. Mēdaces igit & ſtultos eſſe ī **M** los, pnūciāt q ſoli figurę, ſoli ſcripturę, ſolis lineamentis, ſolis uocabus aere fracto natis, tātā miraculorū uim & poteſtatē cōcedāt, ut teſtat̃ Rabi Moyſes ægyptius in libri pplexorū primi capite lxxij. Ad hæc nō ſolū, inqt Philolaus, Hebręorū Cabaliſtę ſed etiā Gręcorū pſtātiſſimi multū ſignaculis & ſigillis fidei tribuerūt. Antiochus em cognomēto Soter cū eſſet in expeditiōe cōtra Galatas uiros fortes & militū innumerabili cōcurſu munitos, pliū difficilimū cōmiſſurus, qn iā ut de eo Lucianus ſcribit τῶν πονηρὰς ἐχέλας ἐλπίδας. noctu uidit p ſomniū aſſiſtere ſibi Alexādrū, iuberecp, ut militib9 ſuis ante pugnā pro bellica teſſera ſignaculū q̃ddā ſanitatis ediceret, p q̃d ſibi cōtingere uictoriā pollicebat̃. Id erat eiuſmodi q̃ in ueſtibus inſignirent, ut idē Samoſatēſis de cōpellationis errore notauit ϛιγαλοῦν ϟίγνυον Διαβάλλων τὸ πεντάγραμμον. i. Triplex triāgulus inter ſe qnquilinęaris. Antiochus aūt ſigno eo leuato mirabilē aduerſum Galatas nactus eſt uictoriam. Ego ipſe, pfecto illud pētagoni ſymbolū ſępe in Antiochi argētea moneta pcuſſum uidi, q̃d reſolutū in lineas oſtēdit uocabulū ὑγίεα. i. ſanitas. Annō in rē erit, Marranus inqt, id q̃d Magno Cōſtātino q̃ndā dei ſignū (ut tūc appellabāt crucē) in ipſa meridiei hora corā oi exercitu ſupne apparuit latinis lris inſcriptū ſic. In hoc uince. Et uicit q̃de Cōſtātinus eodē ſignaculo, atcp tūc plauſu populi Romanorū Impator lectus ac ſalutatus, oiumcp impatorū inuictiſſimus fuit cognoſcatus. Quātū igit ualuerūt ſigilla & ſigna **N** cula teſtes erūt ſummi uiri, Iudęis Machabęus, Gręcis Antioch9, Romanis Cōſtātinus. Nec te fallit, Simō q̃d de Chriſtianis paulo ante loquutus es. Nā ea gente nihil ſub hoc ſeculo eſt in opificio ſignorū, characterū & uocū admirabilius, q figura crucis & noīe Ieſu ſiſtūt maria, uētos mitigāt, fulmina repellūt. Eſt pterea charactere illo & effigie crucis nihil etiā fortius, & in piaculis nihil magis ſalutiferū, quāq̃ non alia (ut libere fatear) ob rē niſi cp ueri Saluatoris ſymbolū extāt, ſicut uobis dei ſymbolū eſt nomē illud Tetragrāmaton. Quodcp Cabaliſtę poſſunt in noīe ineffabili cū nupa te mōſtratis ſigillis & charagmatis, id multo ualidiore modo poſſunt fideles Chriſtiani p nomē IESV effabile cū pprio ſignaculo crucis, cū ſe arbitrēt nome tetragrāmatō lōge recti9 pnūciare in noīe יֵשׁוּהַ ueri Meſſihę, ad hoc citāt̃ id q̃d in Midras Thillim ueſtri ſcripſerūt אָמַר

אָמַר רַבִּי יְהוֹשֻׁעַ בֶּן לֵוִי בְּשֵׁם רַבִּי פִּנְחָס בֶּן יָאִיר
מִפְּנֵי מָה מִתְפַּלְלִין יִשְׂרָאֵל בָּעוֹלָם הַזֶּה וְאֵינָן
נַעֲנִין עַל יְדֵי שֶׁאֵינוֹ יוֹדְעִין בְּשֵׁם הַמְּפוֹרָשׁ

i. Dixit Rabi Ioſue fili9 Leui allegādo magiſtrū Pinhes filiū Iair. Propter

On the Art of Kabbalah

wants, should turn himself to the Clemency and Pity of God by using these letters: *ANQThM PSThM PSPSYM DYVNSYM*. These are worthy reminders of Sacred Scripture. There are many others also available, for nearly all the books of the Kabbalists are full of them.

Other Kabbalists enthusiastically put together excellent amulets that use the divine letters and prove efficacious in continuous use in the combating of ill health and other problems. Here is an example. Rabbi Hama in his *Book on Speculation* composed it from the four, not magic but solemn and sacred words—or, rather, he had them already composed in the tradition from his predecessors: *YHVH ADNY YYAY AHYH*. *YYAY* is the kabbalistic equivalent of *El*.[73] So the experts in this art take the first letter of the first name, the first of the second, the first of the third and the first of the fourth and thus make the first seal: *YAYA*. Then they do the same with the second letters of the four sacred names and get *HDYH*. They make the third seal by joining every third letter and produce *VNAY*. And finally they join the last letters in the same way and get the fourth seal, which is *HYYH*. The meaning of these four signs is "The Lord our God is One Lord," and such, they say, is the superscription of the four signs joined together. Lastly, they draw on the back of the parchment *ARARYThA*, which is interpreted: "One, the Beginning of his Unity, the beginning of his Oneness, his Exchange is One." This exchange of letters is understood in accordance with the third part of Kabbalah.

The Kabbalists, then, stand with their signs and inscriptions in devotion to the highest God and, in every demand for a blessing, whether in the special eighteen blessings or in any other of their just prayers, they hope for infallible success. They have confidence that they can either break every mischance that is threatening them from heaven or soften the Adrastia, the ineluctable power of divine Law, by speaking the sacred words. For they believe that any well initiated Kabbalist can do miracles not only with letters and figures but also with words and songs.

Your people also admit the possiblity of this. Plotinus in *On the Doubts of the Soul*, Book 2, chapter 35, enumerates four things in which there is the power to work miracles: hidden qualities of species, figures, harmonies and prayers. Porphyry, too, and Iamblichus say that we have power against the lower spirits, especially through God, but also through the good angels.

Nor is there any race of men in the whole world more cheerfully conversant with this opinion, so it is said, than the Christian divines. For they use words and figures in expelling demons, in laying hands on the sick, in achieving prosperity, in healing fatal diseases and in working other miracles of this sort.

However—and it is reasonable for me to speak the truth, since my audience agrees with me—they are inclined to attribute all this to faith even though they do admit that some little power is contained in the words they say. For they say in firm belief that a prayer of faith will save the weak. Good Kabbalists agree with them entirely, equally asserting that miraculous works rely on God and faith alone. So they denounce as stupid liars those who attribute such miraculous strength and power to the figures, the writing, the lines and the sounds produced by cracking the air alone in themselves, as

LIBER TERTIVS

qd orāt Israel in mundo isto & nō exaudiunt. Propterea cp nō nouerunt Sehamaphores.i.nome tetragrāmato,hec ibi. Tū Simō. Fortasse tu, sed qd uerbis: certe hāc figurā crucis sapiētiores Cabaliste ad lignū aenei serpētis in deserto erectum referre uolunt, licet ualde silenter, & occulte, idcp per גימטריא .i. p equalitatē numeri. Horū nācp צלם .i. crucis & עץ .i.ligni, characteres, utrincp cētū & qnquaginta symbolissant, quare facilis de altero ad alterū fit trāsitus de cruce ad lignū,& de ligno ad cruce. Sed digito cōpesco labellū. T'pis angustia coartat optimi amici ut minus q̃ uo lui dixerim, & me frustror tn aegre meo gaudio illo excrescēti de ornamē to & dignitate orōnis uestre cū in tā desa nocte qn cubādū est defecero, q nō tanq̃ sophiste uulgari nugatorio & exili sermōe, necp gladiatorio cer tamine uerborū aut cōtētione opinionū hactenus mecū disputatis, sed ac curata & acuta dicendi rōne, sentētiis rei de q̃ agit aptis & accomodatis, ut optarē maiora nobis dierū spacia cōcedi. Nemo.n.de arte cabalistica puo mometo satis dicere pōt, tāte sunt res, tā alte, tā inumerae, tā discriminosae, ut oporteat sūmis īgenii uirib9 niti quelibet ei9 causae auidū & studiosum. Et circūspicere nō modo qua iudustria sit addiscēda sed etiā q̃ sit piculo mo derāda & exercēda. Nā cū ea sciētia sit & rerū spiritualiū & spiritualis, nec possit hō facile de spiritibus afferre iudiciū is etiā cui est iter angelos & de mones iudicādi cōcessa potestas qualibet discreta pēsiculatiōe uel uscp ad equatā regulā, p̃fecto nō sine multa uticp formidine ac nisi purgatis ante morib9 isti facultati & isti exercitio recte incūbit ne Balaā pphete sorte pa tiamur, ne uiuētiū matrē imitemur, ne sub figura lucis tenebras sequamur Metuite uobis ab istis fulmine deiectis spiritib9 & sc̃uissimis hostib9 ñris, atcp credite mihi, serūt iter nos mortales ut angeli sic diaboli uexilla quicp sua. In exercitu dei q̃tuor ānsignani מיכאל גבריאל אוריאל רפאל .i.Michael. Gabriel. Vriel. Raphael, istar elemētorū quatuor, se cūdum quatuor situs, aut iuxta quatuor numerationes spirituales, ut quō dam filii Israel quatuor uexillis proficiscebantur Numeri secūdo. Ad ori entē Iudas, ad meridiē Ruben, ad occidētē Ephraim, & Dan ad aglonē.In exercitu pariter Satanae latissima gerunt signiferi ultores uela סמאל עזאזל עזאל מחזאל .i.Samael. Azazel. Azael. Mahazael, de qb9 Mnabem Racanat Leuitici xvi.& ī lib. primo Pētateuchi sermōe tra ctat, q̃ in loco & Thargū Ionathā ipse sup Genesim allegat. Deinde adhuc magne crebrescūt turme demoniorū & legiōes tartari, pfuge ac fugitiuae oēs portionē suā habētes in capro emissario, q̃ ppter eorū foeditatē & hor rorē hic recēsere omittā, quāq̃ multa pars ī sacra scriptu ra comphēdunt Sed cū puerbio cabalistarū dicēdi fine nūc facio .i. המשביל יבין prudēs intelliget, si etiā hoc addidero cp sicut Michael הוא הכהן הגדול .i.lle sacerdos magn9 sacrificās in mūdo supiori, aias hoim im

Book Three

Maimonides attests in his *Guide to the Perplexed*, Book 1, chapter 72.

PHILOLAUS: It is not only the Hebrew Kabbalists who deal with such matters, for the most understanding of the Greeks also attributed much to signs and seals of faith.

Antiochus, surnamed Soter, once went on an expedition agains the Galatians, a strong nation protected by a huge military force. He was about to engage in a very difficult battle of which, so Lucian writes, "he had very poor hopes," when in the night he saw in a dream Alexander standing by him, ordering him to issue his soldiers before battle with a particular sign of health as their watchword in the fight. Through this sign he was promised victory. The sign that was marked on their clothes was, as the same author from Samosata remarks in his *On a Mistake in Accounting*, "a triple triangle which forms a pentagram." Uplifted by this sign Antiochus won a miraculous victory against the Galatians. I have myself often seen that symbol of the pentagon struck on the silver coins of Antiochus. When the lines are laid out straight they reveal the Greek word *hygeia* meaning "health."

MARRANUS: It is surely relevant to mention the "Sign of God," as they used to call the Cross at that time, which appeared to Constantine the Great at the very hour of midday and in the presence of his whole army. It appeared on high, inscribed in Latin letters, with the words: "In this conquer." And Constantine did conquer with this sign, and was then chosen as Emperor and saluted to the applause of the Roman people, and was named the most invincible of all emperors.

So the witnesses to the power of signs and symbols are important men — Maccabeus for the Jews, Antiochus for the Greeks and Constantine for the Romans. Nor were you far wrong, Simon, in what you said a little while ago about the Christians. There is no one in this generation more marvelous in the working of signs, letters and sounds than those people. With the sign of the Cross and the name of Jesus they still the seas, abate the winds and repel thunderbolts.

Besides, nothing is stronger or more conducive to safety in danger than the character and effigy of the Cross, though the only reason, as I freely confess, is the fact that they stand as a symbol of the true Savior, just as for you the symbol of God is the Name of the Tetragrammaton. All that the Kabbalists can do through the ineffable Name with the signs and characters you have just shown us, can be done in a much stronger way by faithful Christians through the effable name *IESV* with the sign of the Cross that belongs to it. They believe that they have much the best pronunciation of the Name of the Tetragrammaton in the name of *YHSVH*, the true Messiah, and to this end they cite what your people have written in Midrash Tehillim: "Rabbi Joshua ben Levi said in the name of Rabbi Pinhas ben Yair: Why do Israel pray in this world and are not heard? Because they do not know the Semhamaphores, that is, the Tetragrammaton." That is what it says in that passage.

SIMON: Perhaps you are right, but why should you have to use words? At any rate, the better Kabbalist sages tried to liken this figure of the Cross to the tree of the bronze serpent set up in the desert, though they did so silently and secretly. This they did through *Gematria*, that is, numerical equality, for

maculatas deo bñdicto p̃sentat, imũdas aũt & uitiis oneratas ad diabolum mittit, ita p̄otifex ī mũdo īferiori ut ſcriptũ eſt in leuitico iubet aīalia mũda & īsontia offerre deo, criminibus aũt & noxarũ mole onerata, tradere Satange, q̃d & Cabaliſtę ſedulo approbãt dicētes כִּי כָל הָעֶלְיוֹנִים
הַתַּחְתּוֹנִים הֵם מִנְגָּרִים לָעֶלְיוֹנִים וּבְפִי
הָעֲשׂוֹת לְמַטָּה בַּד נַעֲשֶׂה לְמַעְלָה. i. Q: oēs res inferiores ſunt repſentatiuę ſupiorũ, & uti ſit inferius ſic agit ſupius. Portedũt hæc aliqd & uirtutibus debitũ & uitiis, ut cauēdũ cuicq̧ ſit q̃ uiuat & q̃ moriat modo. Tota nancq̧ philoſophia noſtra hæc eſt, ut bñ uiuēdo, bñ moriamur, ne forte ſua portio futuri ſimᵒ tartaro & ultricibus furiis omī fruſtrata ſpe, atcq̧ tũ eueniat malo male. Nũc qd ualde diſcruciat puto diſcedēdũ nobis eſſe qñ a mane ad noctē ſupra q̃ decuit multiloquᵒ uobiſcũ fabulor. Nã ut de me humaniter cõiecturã facio, ita nō indigne de uobis iudico cp̃ dormitũ ſopor abire ſollicitat. Tũ illi. Diuellimur adeo moleſte inqunt abſte Simō, optãtes p̃petuo te audire, q̃obrē de multilogo ne uerbũ qdē. At cp̃ ita iubes more tibi gerimus & abimus, redituri ad te in craſti nũ, niſi tibi incõmodũ eſt. Ad hæc Simõ ait. Nequeo cælare amicos uos qd mecũ cōſtituerim. Cras ad lōginqua migrabo uocatus nuptiarũ cauſa qm patruus uxorē Ratiſponte duxit, q̃ res bñ uortat. Tũ Philolaus, Vrgerē īnqt totis uiribus ut maneres niſi non æquũ eſſet, qn haud modo nobis (fateor) nati ſumus, parte noſtri, amicis ſuo iure locamus. Igit gratias tibi agētes fauſta p̃camur itineri tuo tuiſcq̧. Hic Marranus una mœrore tacto Vade inquit ſiniſtris auibus proſpere fœlitercq̧ amiciſſime Simon atcq̧ uirorũ optime. Interea finem nundinarum Frãcofordienſium expectare cogimur, ut cum mercatoribus noſtratibus ab hoc emporio in patriam quiſcq̧ ſuam tutius remeare queamus. Tum Simon de more gentilicio inquit, Pax uobis. Ad quod ambo iſti. Vale aiunt, I decus, I noſtrum.

Habes ſanctiſſime LEO DECIME a Capnione humili ſeruo tuo, breui compendio recitatas in ſymbolica Pythagoræ philoſophia, & Cabalæ ſapientia ueterum opīniones atcq̧ ſententias, exigui licet numeri, tamen quæ ſtudioſis multo amplius cogitãdi ac inueſtigandi anſam p̃beant. De quibus ego mediocris ingenii & minutæ prudentiæ homo nihil iudicare auſim, nec ſane iudicauero. Sed totum hunc librum tuæ ſubiicio autoritati, cuius in arbitrium collata eſt totius mundi cenſura, ut quæ diſpliceant reiicias, & tum lætabor cætera placuiſſe. Conatum hunc certe meum quem & noſtri & Reipublicæ cauſa ſuſcepiſſe me potes exiſtimare, uideri tibi nō plane improbum cōfido, tum cp̃ aliena meo labore noſtris pateant, tū cp̃ hoc Semeſtri legēdis illis id quinquenne bellũ quod aduerſum me hoſtes mei te ſciente gerũt, ſi omnino nequibat uitari at leuare ſtuduerim, tũ deniq̧ ut & meorũ eſſet apud te aliquid quo ſit beneuolētior memoria noſtri tua, quoties paternũ erga me animũ tuũ frangere ac auertere inimici moliunt. Non em̄ intermittut (ſcio) quotidie ſuſurris attentare pias aures tuas, modo per proxenetas cōducticios, modo per epiſtolas, ut quas ad te proxime xiiii. Kal. Octobres ex Agrippina Colonia datas nuper legi, quarũ ſimul cũ falſa delatione titulᵒ etiã mentit autorē. Non em̄ tā colēda Colonia tā eius ueneranda Vniuerſitas, ſed particulæ ritas & q̃dã inimicorũ ſingularia colluuio minimacq̧ pars ciuitatis & ea inſanior, hoc facinus fecit ut tuæ ſanctitati affirmarent quæ uera non ſunt, idcq̧ contra Inhibitiones

On the Art of Kabbalah

SLM, meaning "Cross," and *'S*, meaning "Tree," both have letters symbolizing one-hundred-and-fifty.[74] So passing from one to another, from cross to tree and tree to cross, is easy.

But I put a finger to my lips. Time is brief, my good friends, and I am restricted from saying all I might wish. It is with regret that I deprive myself of the joy that comes from the distinction and dignity of your conversation. The night has become dark and fit for sleep, and I am tired out. Your discussion with me has been neither a sophistic vulgar trifle or feeble chat, nor a gladiatorial combat of clashing opinions. You have, instead, used an accurate and sharp method of speaking and opinions suitably accommodated to the matter under discussion. I wish more days were allowed us.

No one could say enough about the art of Kabbalah in so short a time. The matters are so wide, so deep, so innumerable and so dangerous that anyone keen and eager for this study must strive with all the might of his intellect. He must consider carefully not only the effort required to learn this art but also the danger involved in its controlled exercise. This is a spiritual science, dealing with spiritual things, and no man can find it easy to be discriminating when spirits are concerned, even if he has been granted the ability to discriminate, after infinitely careful scrutiny, between angels and demons. Even such a man should not devote himself to this without great fear and purged morals. Otherwise we might suffer the fate of the prophet Balaam or imitate the Mother of the living, and pursue the darkness that appears to be light.

You should fear for yourselves the cruel enmity of the spirits who were flung down by the thunderbolt. Believe me, the devils parade their squadrons among us mortals just as much as the angels. In the army of God there are four leaders before the standards, Michael, Gabriel, Uriel, and Raphael, as there are four elements, in accordance with the four regions or the four spiritual numerations, as the Children of Israel once set off in four squadrons (Numbers 2) with Judas to the East, Reuben to the South, Ephraim to the West and Dan to the North.

Similarly in the army of Satan the standard-bearing avengers hoist their great sails: *Samael, Azazel, Azael* and *Mahazael*. Menahem Recanat discusses them in the context of Leviticus 16 and the first book of the Pentateuch, where he actually cites Targum Jonathan on Genesis. Then there are the great hordes of demons and the legions of Tartarus in their crowds, deserters and fugitives, every one with its portion in the Scapegoat. I shall not tell of them here, for they are too foul and horrible, though many of them are mentioned in Sacred Scripture.

I shall now end with the Kabbalists' proverb: "The wise man will understand." But let me add just one more thing. Just as Michael "is the High Priest" sacrificing in the world above, presenting the unspotted souls of men to the blessed God, while sending the foul and vicious souls to the Devil, so is the priest on earth, as is written in Leviticus, bidden to offer pure, guiltless animals to God, and to hand over to Satan those that are burdened with crimes or heavy faults. Of this the Kabbalists heartily approve, with the assertion that: "All things below are representations of the things above, and, as the lower is, so is the higher."

apostolicas,& contra mandata Cæsaris pace. Vides etiã quanta in eisdē literis audacia tanq̃ Solonianas tibi leges p̃scribere,fonteq̃ iuris docere p̃sumāt qua oporteat uia in iudicio ad nutū & uoluntatē eorū procedere,ut facilius me sordibus uincāt,quasi non iā certa toti ferme orbi habeat̃ innocētia mea. Vn̄ adduci non possum ut suspicer istis te fidē habere q̃ despecta Inhibitiōe apostolica,& cōtemptis cēsuris tuis q̃ minimē ob seruato iuris tramite libellū meũ lite p̃edēte cōbusserūt.Credes uero potiᵘ grauioribᵘ uiris Alemaniæ supioris om̄i exceptione maioribᵘ,q̃ nullū scādalũ posui,nullā ruinæ occasionē paraui corã ulla plebe Germanorū qui mihi eiusdē linguæ societate iunc̄ti sunt,in qua lingua istis Belgis ignota Consiliũ meũ illud Camerariũ cum plana eius declaratione uno contextu certe ut decebat edidi,ac secure quidē credere potes, eoq̃ firmius quo de mea innocētia,pietate,fide,integritateq̃ a pluribus illustrissimis latissi marū terrarū nostræ natiōis regnatoribus. Magistratibus,populisq̃ Germanorum, & sanctissimis Diocesium nostrarū Episcopis oppidis & ciuitatibus ferme triennio ante per literas obsignatas,& fide dignas factus es certior. Extant penes te ab inuictissimo Romanorū electo Imp.Maximiliano Maximoleoni tibi, & a reuerēdissimo Cardina li dn̄o meo Gurcensi pro mea innocentia terq̃ quaterq̃ oblata testimonia.Dederunt & post Episcopos illustrissimi prouinciarū p̃æsides atq̃ duces nobilissimo sanguine prognati. Electores Imperii Fridericus Saxoniæ,& Ludouicᵘ Bauariæ Interrex,& dux Virtembergensis,& Marchio Badensis princeps,& strenuissimᵘ Magister ōrdinis Teu tonicorū.Et e regiōe horū Reuerēdi ac deo amabiles Germaniæ pōtifices. Episcopus Vormaciensis,Episcopus Argētinēsis.Episcopus Constantiensis q̃ me ouem suã pastor agnoscit.et Episcopus Spirensis ille a tua sanctitate huic liti datus iudex,qui autoritate tua functus,de cōsilio peritorū pro mea & scriptorū meorū innocētia diffinitiuā tulit sententiā.Cum illis dederūt pariter quinquagita tria Sueuæ oppida,oēs officiosissimi fortissimi,& integerrimi uiri,cōmendaticias epistolas & literas recte fidei,probitasq̃ meæ indemnitatisq̃ testes.Addūt illorū testificationi robur & pondᵘ insigni doctrina & grauitate p̃ælati ecclesiæ, quos Reuerēdissimis causæ nostræ iudicibᵘ Grimano & Anconitano Cardinalibᵘ,orthodoxę fidei columnis tāq̃ peristylia iunxisti senatorios assessores,mūdi lumina.Archiepiscopi,Episcopi,Ordinū generales,& eorū Procurato res.Sapiētiæ Romanæ magistrat̄ᵘ.Pœnitētiarii, & alii theologiæ atq̃ iuris lectissimi Doctores,p̃ suis singulorū dignitatibᵘ in historia de t̃pibus meis nominādi, q̃ tot sessi onibus publicis in tuæ Maiestatis domestico sacrario quā Capellam Pontificiā uocāt habitis.semp agēte rem meā ut oīa solet fideliter oratore iurispitissimo Ioanne Van derbico tā equestris ordinis nobili uiro q̃ in causarū patrociniis disputatore acerrimo & eodē Procuratore meo,tandē in ultima sessione causa plene cognita per sentētias scriptis editas decreuerūt me ab hac p̃sequutiōe iniuriosa liberādū esse ac absolutēdũ, Nec ulli dubiū qn̄ diffinitiua q̃q̃ paris oraculi sentētia reuerēdiss.Iudicū ut debuerat secuta fuisset,nisi tūc mādatū de sup̃sedēdo abste ut dicebāt accusatores impetrassent. Eorū oīm quos iā citauimus undequaq̃ testimonia & uota si recordaberis,& acta iudi ciorū si corā te legi curabis, plane inuenies me ab omni delātorū insimulatione pror sus alienū.Assilit huic meæ puritati tota ferme urbs Romana, & cūctarū nationū oēs doctissimi,quorū ego decretales quotidie lr̃as accipio, etiā a finibus orbis ,cōfirmātes me nullis hoibᵘ scādalo fuisse unq̃ scriptis meis,qn̄ me potius ædificare in dies, planta req̃ uariis linguis ecclesiā spiritui sancto,q̃ per diuersitatē linguarū cunctarū gentes in unitate.fidei cōgregauit,Animaduertūt nimirū q̃ ego primᵘ oīm græca in Germaniā reduxi,& primᵘ oīm ecclesiæ uniuersali arte & studia sermōis Hebraici cōdonaui atq̃ tradidi,q̃re spero me nō frustra sperare posteritatē ecclesiasticā meritis meis futurā nō ingratā, teq̃ p̃sentē Beatiss. LEO Pont.Maxime rerū magis q̃ uerborū æstimatorē p̃ tot & tā duris laboribᵘ meis in orthodoxā fidē bn̄ficii loco collatis,pacē mihi & ani mi trāquillitatē iuste redditurū.Sin me uero cupias in hac uita malorū p̃secutiōi p̃pe tuo subiacere,uehemēter gaudebo uideri dignᵘ q̃ tātas p̃ Christo nr̃o iniurias patiar.

Hagenau apud Thomam Anshelmum Mense Martio.M. D. XVII.

On the Art of Kabbalah

These things portend that virtue and vice are rewarded and that each man should take care how he lives and how he dies. This is our total philosophy, that, in living well, we die well, and thereby avoid a future existence in Tartarus with the avenging furies and every hope dashed, and that to the evil man comes evil.

Now, though it grieves me, I think we must part. I have been too garrulous, babbling on from morning to night. I imagine that, as is only human, you are in the same state as I am and that sleep urges you two to bed.

PHILOLAUS AND MARRANUS: We are saddened to tear ourselves away from you, Simon, and would be happy to hear you go on for ever — so no talk about garrulity. As you bid, we shall call a halt and go away. But we shall return to you tomorrow, unless you find it inconvenient.

SIMON: You are my friends and I cannot conceal from you my decision. Tomorrow I shall set off on a long journey, for I have been invited to the wedding of my uncle in Ratisbon (may it turn out well!).

PHILOLAUS: I should urge you with all my strength to stay if it were not an unfair thing to do. Since, as I believe, we are not born for ourselves alone, it is right that we should give some of ourselves to our friends. Very many thanks. May all go well with the journey and all that is yours.

MARRANUS (in similarly sad vein): Go with all good omens, prosperously and happily, Simon, dear friend and best of men. We, meanwhile, shall have to wait for the end of the Frankfurt fair when each of us can make his way safely back from the market with our compatriots among the merchants.

SIMON (in the manner of his people): Peace be with you.

PHILOLAUS AND MARRANUS: Farewell and good journey, noble friend.

Your reverence Leo X, here you have the opinions and beliefs of the ancients with regard to the symbolic philosophy of Pythagoras and the wisdom of the Kabbalah, written in summarized and abridged form, by your humble servant Capnio. What I have said here is but meager, though it may afford an opportunity to the studious for further thought and investigation. On these matters, I, a man of only ordinary intelligence and little wisdom, would not dare to judge, nor shall I judge. Instead, I submit all this book to your authority, in whose judgement the opinion of all the world is enshrined. Throw out what displeases you and then I shall be happy that what is left has pleased.

I have confidence that this attempt of mine, which you may rightly imagine has been undertaken for the sake of our cause and the State, will not any any rate seem to you completely wrong. Firstly, the learning of other peoples is now revealed to our people through my work. Secondly, in the six months I have spent reading these works I have striven to assuage the five year war which, as you know, my enemies have been waging against me, even if I could not avoid it altogether. Finally, I have written this for you in order to give you something of mine to ensure that your memory of me be benevolent whenever my enemies strive to break or avert your paternal attitude towards me.

I know they never stop whispering every day in your pious ears, using paid agents, or letters like the one I have just read that was sent to you from Cologne on last September 18th and whose title lies even about its author, let alone the false tale-bearing of its contents. It is not the town of Cologne nor its respectable university but a specific, unpleasant clique of enemies, a very small and foolish section of the populace, that has done this crime, asserting

On the Art of Kabbalah

falsehoods to your Holiness, contrary to apostolic prohibition and the Emperor's command for peace.

You see too the degree of their boldness in those same letters. They have the audacity to write down instructions for you like Solonian laws and presume to teach the fount of justice how to proceed in trial in accordance with their whims in order to facilitate their final obscene victory over me.

As if my innocence was not now considered certain by nearly all the world! I cannot bring myself to believe that you have any faith in men who have despised the apostolic prohibition and your censure and, disregarding the path of the law, burnt my books while the law suit was still in progress. You will be more inclined to believe the important men of Upper Germany, for every great man there affirms that I have made no scandal nor engineered any opportunity for destruction for any of the peoples of Germany who are joined to me by our common language, a language of which those Belgians are ignorant and in which I published my *Counsel of the Chamber*, with its clear and fitting declaration in one context.

You may safely have all the more confidence in me since you have been informed of my innocence, piety, faith and integrity by many illustrious rulers of the vast territories of our nation, by the magistrates and peoples of Germany, by the very reverend bishops of our dioceses and by towns and states in signed and reliable letters for nearly the three years past.

You have with you the testimony as to my innocence proffered three or four times by the invincible elected Emperor of the Romans, Maximilian, and by my Lord the most reverend Cardinal of Gurk. After the bishops, the illustrious rulers of the provinces have also given evidence, and Dukes born of the most noble blood, Electors of the Empire, Frederick of Saxony, Louis Interrex of Bavaria, the Duke of Wurtemburg and the Marquis, prince of Baden, and the most martial Master of the Order of the Teutons. And from their side the reverend priests of Germany, beloved of God: the Bishop of Worms, the Bishop of Strasbourg, the Bishop of Constance, who has fostered me like a shepherd, and the Bishop of Speyer, who was appointed as judge in this suit by your Holiness and who, with your authority, gave the definitive opinion of the council of experts on the side of my innocence and the innocence of my writings.

Along with these the fifty-three towns of Swabia, all of whose citizens are dutiful and brave men of integrity, have sent commendatory epistles and letters as witnesses of my upright faith, honesty and innocence. Strength and weight is added to their evidence by the learned and grave prelates of the Church whom you have joined, like a peristyle to the pillars of orthodox faith, to the most reverend judges of my case, Cardinals Grimani and Anconitan, to act as senatorial assessors. They are the light of the world: archbishops, bishops, heads of orders and their deputies, magistrates of the Wisdom of Rome, penitentiaries, and other doctors learned in theology and law. Each of them must be named in the history of my affairs in accordance with his dignity, for it was they who decided, after many public sittings in your Majesty's private chapel that they call the Pope's Chapel and, with my agent John Vanderbic, a noble knight and acute counsel in legal defence work, conducting my case always with his usual fidelity, eloquence and skill in law, it was they who finally decided, in a written decision in the last session with the whole case fully heard, that I should be free and absolved from this most damaging charge.

There is no doubt that a definitive judgement of similar substance would have followed from the reverend judges, as it ought, if the accusers had not then started demanding from you, as they said, an order to set it aside. If you bear in mind the evidence and prayers of all those I have cited here, and if you will take the trouble to have the correct record read to you, you will find me completely innocent of all the charges that my accusers have brought.

On the Art of Kabbalah

Nearly all Rome leaps to attest my innocence. All the learned of every nation are on my side. Every day I receive their testimonials even from the end of the earth, confirming that I have never caused scandal to any man by my writings but that, on the contrary, I constantly build and plant the Church in various languages for the Holy Spirit, which, across the diversity of many tongues, has gathered together the peoples in one faith. They observe that I was the first to translate Greek into German and the first to donate and hand down to the universal Church the art and study of the Hebrew language.

I hope, and I trust not in vain, that the Church in years to come will be not ungrateful for my merits, and that in the present time you, most blessed Pope Leo, will judge by deeds rather than words, and will in justice give me the peace and tranquility of mind that I deserve in recompense for the many sufferings I have endured in place of thanks for my services to the orthodox faith.

But if you would rather that I spend this life under perpetual persecution by evil men, then I shall rejoice greatly that I should seem worthy to suffer such injustice for our Christ.

* * * * * * * * * * * * * * * *

[Printed] At Hagenau at the press of Thomas Anshelm, March 1517

PROPER NAMES APPEARING IN THE TRANSLATION

(excluding references to biblical characters and the tannaitic (q.v.) rabbis listed on page 136f. For the rest, only sufficient information to clarify the text is given)

ABENRUST	Ibn Roshd or Averroes. 12th cent. Arab philosopher.
ABENSINA	Ibn Sina or Avicenna. 10th-11th cent. Arab philosopher and physician.
ABRAHAM	The Patriarch, to whom the *Sepher Yetzirah*, 3rd-6th cent. A.D., is ascribed.
ABRAHAM IBN EZRA	12th cent. poet, grammarian, philosopher, astronomer and physician in Spain. Wrote biblical commentaries with Neoplatonic and Platonic elements.
ABUBACHER	Abu Bakr or Avempace. 12th cent. Arab philosopher.
ABULAPHIA, Abraham	13th cent. Kabbalist from Saragossa, working in Italy. Wrote a mystical commentary on Maimonides' (q.v.) *Guide*.
ABULAPHIA, Todros ben Joseph ha Levi	13th cent. Spanish Kabbalist in Castile.
AKIVA	2nd cent. tanna (q.v.) and martyr.
ALBO, Joseph	15th cent. Spanish philosopher and preacher. Used Islamic and Christian scholastic philosophy to give a reasoned presentation of Judaism.
ALCINOUS	Platonic philosopher, probably 1st cent. A.D.
ALCMAEON	Natural scientist 5th cent. B.C. in Southern Italy.
ALEXANDER OF APHRODISIAS	Early 3rd cent. B.C. peripatetic (q.v.) philosopher in Athens. Commentator on Aristotle.

Proper Names in Translation

ALEXANDER POLYHISTOR	1st cent. B.C. literary scholar from Miletus. Taught in Rome. Studied Greek, Roman and Jewish literature.
ALGAZEL	Abu Mohammed al-Ghazali. 11th cent. Arab philosopher.
ALPHARABIUS	Alfarabi. Arab philosopher and encyclopaedic writer.
AMA, Sopher	s.v. Todros ben Joseph ha Levi Abulaphia.
AMMONIUS SACCAS	Platonist philosopher 3rd cent. A.D.
ANACHARSIS	6th cent. B.C. Scythian prince said to have traveled in search of knowledge.
ANAXAGORAS	Greek philosopher in Athens 5th cent. B.C.
ANAXIMANDER	Greek philosopher 6th cent. B.C.
ANSHELM, Thomas	Printer in Pforzheim from c. 1495. Moved to Tubingen, then Hagenau. Published Reuchlin, Brant and Filelfo.
ANTIOCHUS SOTER	Antiochus I, ruler of Seleucid empire in Syria 3rd cent. B.C.
ANTIPHON	Greek scholar probably 3rd cent. B.C., quoted by Diogenes Laertius (q.v.).
ANTISTHENES	Athenian cynic philosopher, 5th-4th cent. B.C.
APOLLODORUS	2nd cent. B.C. scholar in Athens. Wrote on the philosophical schools.
APOLLONIUS of Tyana	1st cent. A.D. Neopythagorean ascetic sage.
APULEIUS	2nd cent. A.D. African poet, rhetorician and novelist.
ARCHYTAS	4th cent. B.C. Pythagorean mathematician from Tarentum in S. Italy.
ARETINO, Leonardo Bruni	1369-1444. Translated Greek into Latin.
ARISTOBULUS	Alexandrian Jew of 2nd cent. B.C. Asserted dependence of some Hellenistic Greek writers on the septuagint translation of the Pentateuch.
ARISTOPHANES	Athenian 5th cent. B.C. comic dramatist.
ARISTOPHON	Athenian politician of 4th cent. B.C.
ARISTOTLE	Greek philosopher 4th cent. B.C.
ARISTOXENUS	4th cent. B.C. Greek philosopher and numerical theorist from Tarentum in Italy.
ASSE	Unidentified author of book *Ha Yahid* quoted by Abraham ibn Ezra (q.v.).

Proper Names in Translation

ASTAROTUS	Name used to refer to a demon, here a pseudonym for Reuchlin's enemy Hochstraten.
ATHANASIUS	Christian theologian 4th cent. A.D. Bishop of Alexandria.
ATHENAGORAS	2nd cent. A.D. Christian apologist from Athens.
ATHENAEUS	2nd cent. A.D. eclectic scholar and literary antiquarian.
ATHENODORUS	Greek philosopher 1st cent. B.C. Stoic.
AZARIEL BEN SOLOMON of Gerona	13th cent. Spanish Kabbalist.
BOETHIUS	Latin Neoplatonist scholar and theologian 6th cent. A.D. Italy.
CAPNION	Reuchlin's adopted Latin name.
CHAEREMON	1st cent. A.D. Egyptian priest. Stoic philosopher, historian and grammarian.
CHRYSIPPUS	Stoic philosopher 3rd cent. B.C. in Athens.
CHRYSOSTOM, John	4th cent. A.D. bishop of Constantinople. Preacher and theologian.
CICERO	Roman politician and scholar, 1st cent. B.C.
CONSTANTINE	4th cent. emperor. First Christian ruler of the Roman empire.
CORNUTUS	1st cent. A.D. philosopher and rhetorician in Rome. Wrote on Aristotle and Stoicism.
COSIMO de' Medici	First of the great Medici in Florence 1389-1464.
CRATINUS	5th cent. B.C. Athenian comic playwright.
CURTIUS	Mythical hero mentioned by Livy in the history of early Rome.
DAMASUS	4th cent. Roman pope.
DECIUS, Mus Publius	Son and father said to have devoted themselves to save Rome in 4th and 3rd cent. B.C.
DEMETRIUS CHALCONDYLAS	Athenian who came to Florence and taught Greek 1428-1511. Published grammars and edited Homer, Isocrates and the Suda. Taught Reuchlin.
DEMOCRITUS	Greek philosopher 5th cent. B.C.
DEMOSTHENES	4th cent. B.C. Athenian politician and orator.
DIOGENES LAERTIUS	Compiler of lives and doctrines of earlier philosophers 3rd cent. A.D.

Proper Names in Translation

DIONYSIUS THE AREOPAGITE	Athenian mentioned in the Acts of the Apostles. Works of c. 500 A.D. combining Christianity with Neoplatonism were attributed to him.
DIOSCORIDES PEDANIUS	Roman physician and writer on medicine. 1st cent. A.D.
EBERHARD PROBUS	Duke of Swabia, 1445-1496. Visited Italy in 1469.
EGYPTIAN MOSES	s.v. Maimonides
ELEAZAR	Eleazar ben Judah of Worms, c. 1165-c. 1230. Hasid, halakhist and biblical exegesist.
ELIEZER	Eliezer ben Hyrcanus, 1st-2nd cent. A.D. tannaitic (q.v.) rabbi.
EMPEDOCLES	Greek philosopher from Sicily 5th cent. B.C.
ENNIUS	2nd cent. B.C. Latin poet.
ERASMUS	Scholar from Rotterdam 1466-1536. Expert at Greek. Taught in England and France.
EURIPIDES	Athenian tragic dramatist 5th cent. B.C.
EUSEBIUS	Bishop and church historian 4th cent. A.D.
EUSTATHIUS	Metropolitan of Thessalonica and classical scholar as well as spiritual leader, fl. 1150-94.
FABER OF ETAPLES	Jacques Lefèvre d'Étaples c. 1455-1536. French classicist and biblical scholar. Studied Greek classics, Neoplatonist mysticism and a little Hebrew.
FICINO, Marsilio	Florentine Platonist 1433-1499.
GALEN	Philosopher and medical writer 2nd cent. A.D.
GERUNDENSIS	s.v. Nachmanides, of Gerona.
GREGORY OF NAZIANZUS	4th cent. Christian theologian with classical education from Cappadocia.
HAKADOS	s.v. Judah ha Nasi, portrayed in conversation with Roman emperor Antoninus.
HALI	Abu Hali Miskawayh, early 11th cent. Minor Arab philosopher, reconciling Aristotle with Neoplatonism.
HAMA	s.v. Hamai ben Hanina.
HAMAI BEN HANINA	The *Book of Rab Hamai* is a non-extant work first mentioned in 12th cent. Provence; *Sefer Ha-Iyyun* is an anonymous, probably slightly earlier text.
HAMAI	s.v. Hamai ben Hanina.

Proper Names in Translation

HERACLIDES PONTICUS	Athenian philosopher in Academic tradition, 4th cent. B.C.
HERMES TRISMEGISTUS	Greek name for the Egyptian god *Thoth*. Reputed author of philosophico-religious treatises called *Hermetica*, from 3rd cent. A.D. and after.
HERMIPPUS	5th cent. B.C. Athenian writer of comedies.
HERODOTUS	5th cent. B.C. Greek historian.
HESIOD	Greek poet 8th-7th cent. B.C.
HIERO	5th cent. B.C. ruler of Syracuse in Sicily.
HIEROCLES	2nd cent. A.D. Stoic philosopher.
HIPPARCHUS	Pupil of Pythagoras (q.v.).
HIPPOLYTUS, Pope	Bishop of Rome c. 170-c. 236 A.D. Bishop of Rome in rivalry with Callistus.
HOMER	Author of the Iliad and Odyssey, c. 8th cent. B.C.
IAMBLICHUS	Neoplatonist philosopher, 3rd-4th cent. A.D. from Syria.
ISAAC	Isaac ben Jacob, Spanish Kabbalist fl. mid-13th cent.
JACOB BEN JACOB HA KOHEN	Spanish Kabbalist fl. mid-13th cent.
JEROME	Church father and theologian 4th cent. A.D.
JOCHANAN	Yohanan ben Zakkai, 1st cent. A.D. tanna (q.v.).
JONATHAN CHALDAEUS BEN UZZIEL	Pseudo-Jonathan, to whom the translation of the Prophets into Aramaic in the early centuries A.D. is attributed (the Targumim).
JOSEPH BEN ABRAHAM GIKATILLA	Influential Spanish Kabbalist, 1248-c. 1325.
JOSEPH BEN CARNITOL	Joseph ben Abraham Gikatilla (q.v.).
JOSEPH OF SALEM	Joseph ben Abraham Gikatilla (q.v.).
JUDAH HA LEVI	12th cent. Hebrew poet and philosopher from Spain.
JUDAH HA NASI	Tannaitic (q.v.) rabbi. Compiler of the Mishnah c. A.D. 200.
JULIAN	4th cent. Roman pagan emperor and apostate from Christianity.
JULIUS POLLUX	2nd cent. A.D. scholar and rhetorician.
JUSTINUS	2nd cent. A.D. Christian apologist and martyr.

Proper Names in Translation

KIMHI, David	Grammarian and exegete of Hebrew from Provence c. 1160-c. 1235.
LANDINO, Cristoforo	Florentine scholar under Medici patronage 1428-98.
LEO X	Giovanni de' Medici, 1475-1521. Pope 1513-21.
LEVI, Tedacus	s.v. Todros ben Joseph ha Levi Abulaphia.
LEVI BEN GERSHOM	Mathematician, astronomer, philosopher and biblical commentator from France. 1288-1344.
LONGINUS	Athenian rhetorician and philosopher 3rd cent. A.D.
LORENZO	Lorenzo de' Medici the Magnificent, father of Leo X (q.v.) 1448-92, ruler of Florence 1469-1492.
LUCIAN	Rhetorician and satirist from Samosata, 2nd cent. A.D.
LUCRETIUS	Epicurean Latin poet 1st cent. B.C.
LYCON OF IASSUS	Peripatetic philosopher 3rd cent. B.C.
LYSIS	Pythagorean philosopher from S. Italy, 4th cent. B.C.
MACROBIUS	Neoplatonist philosopher and scholar 4th-5th cent. A.D.
MAIMONIDES	Moses ben Maimon, or Rambam 1135-1204. Spanish philosopher, rabbi, spiritual leader and doctor working in Egypt. Put medieval Jewish philosophy on an Aristotelian base.
MARCUS AURELIUS	Roman emperor and Stoic philosopher 2nd cent. A.D.
MARTIN	Bishop of Tours 4th cent. A.D.
MAXIMILIAN I	Emperor of Germany 1459-1519.
MAXIMUS OF TYRE	Moralizing Platonist philosopher 2nd cent. A.D.
MENAHEM BEN BENJAMIN RECANATI	Italian Kabbalist and expert in Jewish law, fl. c. 1400.
MEIR	Tannaitic (q.v.) rabbi, 2nd cent. A.D.
MENIPPUS	Cynic philosopher who wrote serious philosophy in humorous style, 3rd cent. B.C.
MERCURIUS TERMAXIMUS	Hermes Trismegistus (q.v.).
MIRANDOLA	s.v. Pico della Mirandola.
NACHMANIDES	13th cent. Spanish rabbi from Gerona. Talmudist, philosopher, Kabbalist, poet and physician.
NATHAN	Tannaitic (q.v.) rabbi 2nd cent. A.D.

Proper Names in Translation

NEOPTOLEMUS	Probably Greek poet and scholar 3rd cent. B.C.
NICHOLAS OF CUSA	Cardinal, mathematician, scientist and mystical Platonist philosopher, 1401-1464.
NUMENIUS	Pythagorean philosopher and historian of philosophy. 2nd cent. A.D. Influenced by oriental, especially Gnostic ideas.
ONKELOS	Proselyte to whom was ascribed the translation of the Pentateuch into Aramaic dating from early centuries A.D.
ORPHEUS	Mythical singer to whom were ascribed mystical poems of the 6th cent. B.C. and after.
ORUS	Horus, Egyptian god identified by Romans with the child Harpocrates.
OVID	Elegiac Latin poet 1st cent. B.C.
PARMENIDES	Greek philosopher 5th cent. B.C.
PERIPATETICS	Aristotelian school of philosophy in Athens after 4th cent. B.C.
PETRARCH	Italian poet and humanist 1304-1374.
PHILELPH	Francesco Filelfo 1398-1481 Renaissance author.
PHILINUS	Sicilian historian of the 1st Punic War from the Carthaginian side.
PHILOPONUS	John Philoponus, 6th cent. A.D. Christian grammarian and commentator on Aristotle.
PHILOSTRATUS	Greek philosopher and historian of philosophy c. 170-c. 244 A.D.
PICO DELLA MIRANDOLA	Provocative aristocratic scholar 1463-94.
PINDAR	Greek lyric poet 5th cent. B.C.
PLATO	Athenian philosopher 4th cent. B.C.
PLAUTUS	Roman comic playwright 3rd-2nd cent. B.C.
PLINY	Polymath, historian and encyclopaedist 1st cent. A.D. Uncle of Pliny the Younger (q.v.).
PLINY THE YOUNGER	Roman politician and man of letters 1st-2nd cent. A.D.
PLOTINUS	Platonizing philosopher in Rome 3rd cent. A.D.
PLUTARCH	Greek philosopher and moralizing biographer 1st-2nd cent. A.D.
POLITIAN, Angelo	Angelo Ambrogini Poliziano 1454-1494. Florentine author and scholar of Greek.

Proper Names in Translation

PORPHYRY	Polymath, philosopher and student of religion. Influenced by Pythagoras and later a pupil of Plotinus (q.v.). Anti-Christian polemicist 3rd cent. A.D.
PRISCIAN	Latin grammarian early 6th cent. A.D.
PROCLUS	Pagan Neoplatonist philosopher in Athens, 5th cent. A.D.
PSEUDO-JONATHAN	s.v. Jonathan Chaldaeus ben Uzziel.
PTOLEMY SOTER	General of Alexander the Great and Macedonian king of Egypt. Lived c. 367-283 B.C.
PYTHAGORAS	Greek philosopher and mathematician from Samos 6th cent. B.C. Taught in Italy. Details of life and beliefs are obscured by later legend.
RAMBAM	s.v. Maimonides.
RAMBAN OF GERONA	s.v. Nachmanides.
RASHI	Rabbi Solomon ben Isaac. French rabbi and leading commentator on the Bible and Talmud 1040-1105.
RECANAT	s.v. Menaham ben Benjamin Recanati.
RICCI, Paul	Humanist, translator from Hebrew and apostate from Judaism. Probably from Germany but taught philosophy and medicine in Italy. Fl. 1504-1541. Translated Gikatilla's *Gates of Light*, published 1515.
SAADIA	Saadia Gaon 882-942. Geonic rabbi. Wrote philosophy in Arabic influenced by Aristotle, Plato and Stoicism.
SAMUEL NAGID	Statesman, poet and scholar in Spain, 993-c.1055.
SENECA	Stoic philosopher and playwright in Rome 1st cent. A.D.
SIMEON BAR YOHAI	Tannaitic (q.v.) rabbi, 2nd cent. A.D.
SIMONIDES	Greek lyric and elegiac poet, 6th-5th cent. B.C.
SIMPLICIUS	Commentator on Aristotle, 6th cent. A.D.
SOCRATES	Athenian philosopher 5th cent. B.C.
SOLOMON OF TROYES	s.v. Rashi.
SOLOMON THE COMMENTATOR	s.v. Rashi.
SOLOMON GALLUS	s.v. Rashi.
SOPHER AMA	s.v. Todros ben Joseph ha Levi Abulaphia.
SYMMACHUS	Roman aristocrat, consul A.D. 485. Descendant of the 4th cent. A.D. letter writer whose work is extant.

Proper Names in Translation

TANNA	Term denoting the rabbis of the first and second centuries A.D. whose sayings make up the Mishnah, compiled c. A.D. 200.
TERENCE	Roman comic dramatist 2nd cent. B.C.
THALES	Early Greek sage, 7th-6th cent. B.C.
THEMISTIUS	Pagan Greek philosopher in Constantinople 4th cent. A.D. Paraphrased Aristotle and disapproved of Christianity.
THEOGNIS	Greek elegiac poet 6th cent. B.C.
THEOPHRASTUS	Peripatetic philosopher in Athens 4th cent. B.C. Pupil and successor of Aristotle.
TIMAEUS	Pythagorean philosopher from Italy known only from Plato's dialogue of the same name, written in 4th cent. B.C. A paraphrase of Plato called *De Natura Mundi et Animi* was attributed to him in 1st cent. A.D.
TIMON	Sceptic Greek philosopher. 2nd cent. B.C.
TODROS BEN JOSEPH HA LEVI	s.v. Abulaphia, Todros.
TRYPHON	Greek grammarian working in Rome in late 1st cent. B.C.
VALORI, Filippo	Florentine scholar, friend of Ficino (q.v.). 15th cent.
VARRO	Roman polymath 1st cent. B.C.
VIRGIL	Roman epic poet, late 1st cent. B.C.
VESPUCCIO, Giorgio	Florentine scholar and teacher. Dominican. 15th cent.
XENOPHILUS	Pythagorean philosopher in Athens 4th cent. B.C.
XENOPHANES	Greek philosopher in Sicily, 6th cent. B.C. Possibly influenced by Pythagoras.
XENOPHON	Athenian philosopher, soldier and historian 4th cent. B.C.
ZAMOLXIS	Zalmoxis, Scythian deity to whose followers Plato (q.v.) attributed certain metaphysical doctrines.
ZENO of Elea	Greek philosopher early 5th cent. B.C. Not to be confused with the 3rd cent. founder of the Stoic school of philosophy.

NOTES

1. Nomadic people found in the Caucasus in late Medieval times and only partly Christianized.

2. The supposed family of Simeon bar Yohai (q.v.) to whom the Zohar was ascribed.

3. The expulsion of the Jews from Spain was in 1492. Reuchlin was writing in 1517, in fact 25 years later.

4. This is a description of the Kabbalistic tree in which man is put at the center, the tree also serving the purpose of placing in relation the qualities or "numerations" (sephiroth) on which some forms of Kabbalah concentrate speculation. The sephiroth are the primordial numbers from which the world is created along with the twenty two letters of the alphabet. Each has its own quality; together they form the separate sphere that surrounds the divine.

5. These are the three highest of the sephiroth surrounding God.

6. The leading angels in the speculative system centered round the Throne-Chariot (see below, note 7, on Merkavah).

7. The central element in a kabbalistic system first evolved by at least the second century A.D. The Merkavah is the Chariot or Throne of God described in detail in Ezekiel chapter 1 and to be reached only through travel through a series of Halls (hekhaloth). The relation between this form of speculation and the sephiroth (see note 4) is at times tenuous.

8. In Psalm 89.

9. These terms are not consistently applied by Reuchlin and have no Hebrew parallel. They seem to be fabricated in parallel with *theology* and *theologisten*, the similarity of *theologist* to *sophist* rendering it a rude term.

10. Reuchlin was himself attacked on this ground by Hochstraten and successfully defended on it by Paul Ricci.

Notes

11. The numerical equivalent of the letter *Shin* is 300 and the equivalent of the letters of the Hebrew words for "in mercy" (*BRHMYM*) is also 300 ($B=2$, $R=200$, $H=8$, $M=30$, $Y=10$, $M=40$). The two are therefore interchangeable according to the principle of *Gematria*.

12. The system of numerical equivalence described above in note 11.

13. The principle by which any letter can be taken to stand for a complete word of which it usually forms either the first or, occasionally, some other part. Therefore, *M* stands for *Metokh*, meaning "in the middle of."

14. This insertion of *Sh* in the middle of the Tetragram is to be the main revelation of the book, at the end of Book III.

15. A reference to the Kabbalistic tree.

16. *Sh* is the first letter of *Shemen*. Another reference to the revelation to be made at the end of Book III.

17. $Sh=300$, $L=30$, $H=8$, $N=50$, $Y=10=398$, though $M=40$, $Sh=300$, $Y=10$, $H=8$ comes to only 358.

18. This list of the traditors of the oral Law is found in the *Mishnah*, tractate *Aboth*. The list is continuous from Moses down to the middle of the 2nd cent. A.D. when the *Mishnah* was redacted, but it is far more detailed in relation to the rabbis of the late first and second centuries A.D. (the tannaim).

19. Zadok and Boethus are postulated in the later (5th cent.) Talmudic texts in order to explain the origin of the Zadokite and Boethusian sects which flourished in the centuries before A.D. 70.

20. These allusions are to the Dominican monks led by Hochstraten who were at the forefront of the opposition to Reuchlin and his books.

21. Another reference to Reuchlin's struggle against the Dominicans. The burning of many Jewish books and some of Reuchlin's own works was the point at issue.

22. These titles are culled from mentions of non-extant works in the extant Old Testament books.

23. The Zohar, perhaps the most influential of the Kabbalistic works, purports to be the product of Simeon bar Yohai in mid 2nd cent. Palestine but is first attested in Spain in the late thirteenth century and is most likely to have been composed there.

Notes

24. The book *Ha Bahir* was probably composed in France at the end of the 12th cent., although it may have been imported from the East. In Spain it was assigned to rabbis of the first centuries A.D.

25. Bereshith speculation involved close study of the first chapters of Genesis. it began at least in the first centuries A.D. (cf. the *Sepher Yetzirah* ascribed to the patriarch Abraham (q.v.), and developed separately from Merkavah mysticism (see note 7).

26. This conventional number of 613 precepts is the number signified by the arithmetical connotations of the letters in *Tharyag* ($Th=400$, $R=200$, $Y=10$, $G=3$).

27. "B" begins the word *Bereshith*, meaning "in the beginning," the first word of Genesis.

28. *Et* signifies that the word following is the direct object of the verb. *Ha* means "The."

29. A reference to the fabled land mentioned in Genesis 2:11.

30. This is a particularly ungainly translation of the Hebrew into Latin.

31. See note 11.

32. Mercy = RHM ($R=200$, $H=8$, $M=40$) = 248, like Abraham ($A=1$, $B=2$, $R=200$, $H=5$, $M=40$) = 248.

33. Nicholas of Cusa, 1401-1464, cardinal, mathematician, scholar, and mysticizing Platonist philosopher. He was the first great humanist of German origin and had much influence on Reuchlin.

34. This list comprises those foreign peoples believed by the Greeks to possess hidden wisdom.

35. The Eleatic method of rational argument involved drawing contradictory conclusions from the premises of opponents in order to clarify concepts.

36. The Council of Nicaea of A.D. 325 was called by the emperor Constantine to resolve the Arian crisis over the relation between Father and Son in the Trinity.

37. The Tetractys is a central element in Pythagorean thought. It represents the number Ten as the sum of the first four integers, portrayed as a pyramid with a base of Four and apex of One.

Notes

38. This is a rather poor translation into Latin of the original Greek.

39. The Old Testament books.

40. General council of the Catholic Church, originally called in 1431 to deal with the Hussite heresy but eventually resolving into a struggle between the bishops of the Council and Pope Eugenius I who had transferred a rival council to Ferrara.

41. Also known as 'symbols' or 'Precepts.' The collection of gnomic sayings originating as taboos among the earliest Pythagorean communities and later augmented after the 4th century B.C. with symbolic interpretation and explicitly ethical principles.

42. The earliest law code of Repucblican Rome, dating to the mid 5th century B.C.

43. See note 41.

44. On the left side will be 9876, on the right will be 1234, with 5 in the middle.

45. This is a rather lengthy pun on the Greek word meaning 'to see.'

46. This is a reference to the Pythagorean doctrine that the four elements (fire, water, earth and air) can be represented by geometric figures.

47. This is another reference to the Dominicans who opposed Reuchlin.

48. This principle that nothing in the Written Law is superfluous includes the way that the individual letters are formed on the written page, including the crowns, i.e. flourishes at the top of the letters, and the size, etc., of each of them.

49. All these words add up to 441. Ehieh = $AHYH$ ($A=1$, $H=5$, $Y=10$, $H=5$) = $21 \times 21 = 441$; Emeth = $AMTh$ ($A=1$, $M=40$, $Th=400$) = 441; Adonai Shalom = $ADNY\ ShLVM$ ($A=1$, $D=4$, $N=50$, $Y=10$, $Sh=300$, $L=30$, $V=6$, $M=40$) = 441. So too (page 299) YHV ($Y=10$, $H=5$, $V=6$) = $21 \times 21 = 441$.

50. Shaddai ($Sh=300$, $D=4$, $Y=10$) = 314; Metattron ($M=40$, $T=9$, $T=9$, $R=200$, $V=6$, $N=50$) = 314.

51. YHV ($Y=10$, $H=5$, $V=6$) = 21; Ehieh = $AHYH$ ($A=1$, $H=5$, $Y=10$, $H=5$) = 21.

52. Yod = YVD ($Y=10$, $V=6$, $D=4$) = 20; He = HA ($H=5$, $A=1$) = 6; Vav = VAV ($V=6$, $A=1$, $V=6$) = 13; He = HA ($H=5$, $A=1$) = 6; $Yod\ He\ Vav\ He$ = 45; Mah = MH ($M=40$, $H=5$) = 45.

Notes

53. Reuchlin actually writes: "The 'innocent' he will not pardon."

54. Tetragram makes 26 ($Y=10$, $H=5$, $V=6$, $H=5$); AL ($A=1$, $L=30$) = 31.

55. AMSh means "yesterday"; $AShM$ means "guilt."

56. Temple = $HYKL$ ($H=5$, $Y=10$, $K=20$, $L=30$) = 65; Adonai = $ADNY$ ($A=1$, $D=4$, $N=50$, $Y=10$) = 65.

57. Sadai = $ShDY$ ($Sh=300$, $D=4$, $Y=10$) = 314; Metattron = $MTTRVN$ ($M=40$, $T=9$, $T=9$, $R=200$, $V=6$, $N=50$) = 314.

58. AShThV ($A=1$, $Sh=300$, $Th=400$, $V=6$) = 707; $AShVQSh$ ($A=1$, $Sh=300$, $V=6$, $Q=100$, $Sh=300$) = 707. $AShThV$ means "his wife."

59. Heth = $HYTh$ ($H=8$, $Y=10$, $Th=400$) = 418; Kaph = KPh ($K=20$, $Ph=80$) = 100; Mem = MM ($M=40$, $M=40$) = 80; He = HY ($H=5$, $Y=10$) = 15; $418 + 100 + 80 + 15 = 613$; Tharyag = $TRYG$ ($Th=400$, $R=200$, $Y=10$, $G=3$) = 613.

60. Maccabee = $MKBY$ ($M=40$, $K=20$, $B=2$, $Y=10$) = 72.

61. [In Reuchlin's text, the Hebrew letters are each marked by three superscribed dots.]

62. Hebrew vowel like the "a" in "father."

63. The imperative of the Latin word meaning "to fall."

64. BRM = "In exalting" = 242 ($B=2$, $R=200$, $M=40$).

65. Yod = YVD ($Y=10$, $V=6$, $D=4$) = 20; $H=5$; Vav = VV ($V=6$) = 12; $H=5$.

66. **Page 263.** *Gematria .... as explained above.* KVZV ($K=20$, $V=6$, $Z=7$, $V=6$) = 39; YHVH AHD ($Y=10$, $H=5$, $V=6$, $H=5$, $A=1$, $H=8$, $D=4$) = 39.

67. **Page 263.** *Elohim since they both make 86.* Ehieh = $AHYH$ ($A=1$, $H=5$, $Y=10$, $H=5$) = 21; Adonai = $ADNY$ ($A=1$, $D=4$, $N=50$, $Y=10$) = 65; $21 + 65 = 86$; Elohim = $ALHYM$ ($A=1$, $L=30$, $H=5$, $Y=10$, $M=40$) = 86.

68. $K=20$, $Ph=80$, $V=6$, $V=6 = 112$; Tetragrammaton = $YHVH$ ($Y=10$, $H=5$, $V=6$, $H=5$) = 26; Elohim = $ALHYM$ ($A=1$, $L=30$, $H=5$, $Y=10$, $M=40$) = 86; $26 + 86 = 112$.

69. VYHY KN ($V=6$, $Y=10$, $H=5$, $Y=10$, $K=20$, $N=50$) = 101.

Notes

70. Michael = $MYKAL$ ($M=40$, $Y=10$, $K=20$, $A=1$, $L=30$) = 101.

71. A pun on the Greek word *angelos* which means "messenger."

72. Verse 5 of Genesis chapter 1 is taken to end with the word $LYLH$, night.

73. $YYAY$ ($Y=10$, $Y=10$, $A=1$, $Y=10$) = 31, EL = AL ($A=1$, $L=30$) = 31.

74. Actually, 160. SLM ($S=90$, $L=30$, $M=40$) = 160; 's ('=70, $S=90$) = 160.